PRINCIPLES OF COUNSELING AND PSYCHOTHERAPY

Researchers have shown that the most effective way to prepare students for practice with real clients is for them to learn how to think in a new way, rather than simply learning and using a set of steps. Although there is much to be learned from what master practitioners do in their sessions, there is even more knowledge to gain from learning how they think. The second edition of *Principles of Counseling and Psychotherapy* offers students and practitioners a way to understand the processes behind effective outcomes with a wide variety of clients.

The second edition is infused with real-world clinical case examples and opportunities for readers to apply the material to the cases being presented. New "thought-exercise" sections are specifically designed to engage the reader's natural nonlinear thinking, and transcript material both from cases and from master therapists themselves are interwoven in the text. Accompanying videos, available through Alexander Street Press, bring the text to life, and instructors will find testbanks, transition notes, and narrated PowerPoints available for free download from the book's website at www.routledge.com/cw/Mozdzierz/

Gerald J. Mozdzierz, PhD, is a professor in the department of psychiatry and behavioral neurosciences at Loyola University and also maintains a private practice.

Paul R. Peluso, PhD, is an associate professor and chair of the department of counselor education at Florida Atlantic University. He is the coauthor of five books and author of numerous articles and book chapters.

Joseph Lisiecki, LCSW, has 32 years of clinical experience at Hines VA hospital in Illinois.

D0025436

PRINCIPLES OF COUNSELING AND PSYCHOTHERAPY

Learning the Essential Domains and Nonlinear Thinking of Master Practitioners

SECOND EDITION

GERALD J. MOZDZIERZ, PAUL R. PELUSO, AND JOSEPH LISIECKI

Routledge
Taylor & Francis Group

NEW YORK AND LONDON

Second edition published 2014
by Routledge
711 Third Avenue, New York, NY 10017

and by Routledge
27 Church Road, Hove, East Sussex BN3 2FA

*Routledge is an imprint of the Taylor & Francis Group,
an informa business*

First edition published by Routledge 2009

Library of Congress Cataloging-in-Publication Data
Mozdzierz, Gerald J., 1940–
Principles of counseling and psychotherapy : learning the essential
    domains and nonlinear thinking of master practitioners / Gerald J.
    Mozdzierz, Paul R. Peluso, and Joseph Lisiecki. — Second edition.
        pages cm
    Includes bibliographical references and index.
  1. Psychotherapy.   2. Counseling.   3. Nonlinear theories.
I. Peluso, Paul R.   II. Lisiecki, Joseph.   III. Title.
    RC480.5.M69 2014
    616.89′14—dc23
    2013029443

ISBN: 978-0-415-70460-1 (hbk)
ISBN: 978-0-415-70461-8 (pbk)
ISBN: 978-0-203-76192-2 (ebk)

Typeset in Minion
by Apex CoVantage, LLC

Contents

Foreword

In 1960, in his preface to his collection of essays on personality titled *Personality and Social Encounter* (Allport, 1960), Gordon W. Allport, one of the wisest men ever to come to grips with the issue of personality, asked, "What is human personality?" He found he could offer no definitive answer. Instead, he gave voice and recognition to the truth that lay in all those positions that honestly sought the answer to that question, even though they provided responses to it that he termed *paradoxical*. He wrote,

> Some would say that it [personality] is an ineffable mystery—a shaft of creation, an incarnation. Since no man can transcend his own humanity, he cannot hold the full design of personality under a lens. The radical secret will ever elude us.
>
> Others would say that personality is a product of nature. It is a nervous-mental organization, which changes and grows, while at the same time remaining relatively steadfast and consistent. The task of science is to explain both the stability and the change.
>
> Those who would hold either of those views—or both—are right. . . .
>
> Some say that personality is a self-enclosed totality, a solitary system, a span pressed between two oblivions. It is not only separated in space from other living systems, but also marked by internal urges, hopes, fears, and beliefs. Each person has its own pattern, his own unique conflicts, he runs his own course, and dies alone. This point of view is correct.
>
> But others say that personality is social in nature, wide open to the surrounding world. It owes its existence to the love of two mortals for each other and is maintained through love and nurture freely given by others. Personality is affiliative, symbiotic, sociable. Culture cooperates with family in molding its course. 'No man is an island.' This view, too, is right. (p. v)

And, of course, Allport recognized that other frames also merited consideration.

Instead of quailing at the metaphysical paradoxes posed by these seemingly veridical yet competing views of what it is to be a person—either by retreating to the ideological security provided by one of the part views of human existence generated by a great man's theory, and in so doing blind himself to that which is also true, or by restricting his descriptions of human nature exclusively to "facts" gleaned by an army of social insects following well-marked, approved trails, and thereby miss the larger picture or leave the field in abject surrender—Allport (1960) chose to bravely soldier on, much, I believe, to his advantage and ours. His approach, he wrote,

> is naturalistic, but open-ended. Naturalism, as I see it, is too often a closed system of thought that utters premature and trivial pronouncements on the nature of man. But it can and should be a mode of approach that deliberately leaves unsolved the ultimate metaphysical questions

concerning the nature of man, without prejudging the solution. My essays are all psychological and therefore naturalistic, but they have one feature in common—a refusal to place premature limits upon our conception of man and his capacities for growth and development. (Allport, 1960, pp. v–vi)

Given that, explicitly or implicitly, therapeutic interventions are based wholly or in part (sometimes one just repeats that which one perceives to have worked, with no other reason for doing so) upon one's conceptualization of personality, one would expect, if Allport's analysis of the state of personality theory were correct, that a proliferation of psychotherapies would ensue, a goodly number containing a kernel of actuality in addition to their other constituents. This is indeed the case, I believe.

Today we stand not 10 years past the midpoint of the previous century, but 10 years into a new century. Although I have little doubt that our understanding of the human condition has improved somewhat in these 50 intervening years, I believe it has done so in detail. The larger picture, that divined by Allport, remains basically unchanged. And although there seems to be increased agreement that the efficacy of a subset of the panoply of interventions labeled psychotherapeutic has been reasonably established, and that these work effectively to reduce human misery and some specific miseries more so than others, how and why they do so are still moot in spite of, I believe, sectarian claims to the contrary.

That you are reading this foreword at all, I take as evidence that you, as well as Allport and the authors of this excellent book, have not yielded to the seductive enticements of nihilism, be it represented by a retreat to ideology, *factism,* or *burnout.* What, then, to do? What other course provides a good-faith alternative, one that, again to quote Allport (1960), can "open doors and clear windows so that our chance of glimpsing ultimate philosophical and religious truth may not be blocked?" (p. v). To my mind, the authors of this work, Gerald Mozdzierz, Paul Peluso, and Joseph Lisiecki, provide one. The overarching aim of psychological treatment, as they envision it, is to foster clients' *disengagement* from preoccupation with symptoms, pathology, dysfunctional frames, and defective action patterns so that engagement with healthier beliefs and behaviors can occur. The tack they employ is to teach how master therapists think across the essential domains of competence that are necessary if a therapist—whether a beginning, advanced, or established therapist—is to be effective with patients. These are (1) connecting with and engaging clients; (2) assessing the clients' readiness for change and their strengths and goals; (3) building and maintaining a therapeutic alliance; (4) understanding, empathizing into, and working respectfully with the clients' cognitive schemata; (5) addressing the clients' emotional states and traits; (6) understanding and working with clients' ambivalences about change; and (7) using insight-generating nonlinear thinking and interventions to communicate more effectively with clients and to help clients communicate more effectively with themselves. The authors emphasize and demonstrate cogently, clearly, and to good effect that master practitioners do not think exclusively in conventional, linear ways, but at crucial times in the process of intervening in the lives of their clients distinguish themselves by a recourse to nonlinear thinking and communications in the service of engendering positive changes in their clients.

Befitting a text that takes such pains to distinguish degrees of therapeutic sophistication, the authors give considerable attention to the "stages of development" that would-be therapists traverse on their path to mastering the science and art of intervening for the better in the lives of those who come to them for help. The model the authors adopt to schematize that journey is that proffered by Stoltenberg (1997). Using this flexible, three-level, integrated, developmental schematization of counselor development, the authors define and describe the personal preoccupations of therapists at each level that may interfere with their growth as therapists and offer workable suggestions as to how they might get back on track should they be detoured.

Just as I have, I trust that you, regardless of where you place yourself on the ladder of psycho-therapist development, will find this book useful and enlightening, for its authors have done an excellent job of summarizing and synthesizing the relevant literature, empirical and theoretical, on how psychotherapy, when it is psychotherapy, proceeds and works. Their presentation on training and developing psychotherapists is also state of the art. Their prose is lucid, straightforward, and nuanced. Just as I have, you will, I trust, appreciate the breadth and depth of knowledge that they express so clearly. Although that is all well and good and cannot be gainsaid, the exceptional worth of this book inheres in the insights it conveys into how master therapists function with their clients. And, make no mistake about it, the authors give every indication that they are indeed master therapists. Their clinical illustrations are apt, pithy, and illuminating. They write of their clients with warmth, respect, and empathetic and insightful understanding. Their examples of nonlinear intervention are well-chosen, witty, enlivening, and perspicacious.

To sum up, to my mind, little has changed since Allport (1960) fully 50 years ago concluded that no one veridical, comprehensive view of personality had yet emerged. Instead, he believed that the human sciences created numerous descriptions of human nature and action, many of which represented an aspect of truth, but none the total picture. Although one could hope to build an accurate whole out of analyzing and synthesizing these part pictures, Allport (1960) surmised that it was impossible to harmonize their fundamentally conflicting elements. His response to this state of affairs was not to leave the field or proceed to study it in bad faith. His alternative: to continue on, while refusing to prematurely limit the conception of what it is to be human, and to work toward a valid naturalistic approach to human nature that, as he put it, "must have open doors and clear windows, so that our chances of glimpsing ultimate philosophical and religious truth may not be blocked" (Allport, 1960, p. v).

Because our understanding of psychotherapy and counseling is inherently linked to our understanding of human personality, those who wish to rightly alter for the better the state of those who present themselves as clients are faced with the same choice that Allport confronted. The authors of the text before you, Mozdzierz, Peluso, and Lisiecki, have provided, I believe, an appropriate response to that challenge. Train oneself and train others in the strategies and thinking that master therapists employ to engage and assist their clients in living better. Mozdzierz, Peluso, and Lisiecki's text is admirably designed to assist in that task. It is up-to-date and factual. Its principles of intervention are applicable to a diverse clientele experiencing diverse difficulties. It enables therapists of differing theoretical orientations to employ the frameworks provided by the theories they adhere to while applying the schemas that master therapists use in treating their clients. And, it teaches them admirably well, for not only are its authors master therapists, but they are also master teachers.

Herbert H. Krauss, PhD
Pace University
September 29, 2008

Preface to the Second Edition

A second chance. We are told that life is full of them. We tell our clients that they deserve them. But what about books? Do they deserve a second chance? It is a funny thing to revisit a book and write a second edition, but it is also a wonderful opportunity. From an aesthetic point of view, it is a chance to correct flaws that were in the original. It is a chance to say things even better than you did the first time around. If it is a textbook, like this, you can improve on things that may have worked wonderfully in your head while you were writing, but fail miserably in front of a room full of students! In the sciences, it is a chance to incorporate new research findings, or new approaches, that were not available or en vogue the first time around.

In the first edition of this book, we were much more acutely aware that the field of counseling and psychotherapy was in flux, and that the methods that were being used to teach new clinicians how to be therapists were neither keeping pace with the changes in the science, nor were they upholding the best traditions of the past. Instead, there was a mad scramble to find the best "evidence-based" approach that would have the greatest potency to combat the most difficult-to-treat clients and conditions. However, in the second decade of the 21st century, there are indications that the practice of psychotherapy may be on pace to flourish anew, and that scholars and practitioners are interested in seriously understanding the mechanisms of change and the way that the *practitioner* interacts with the client in order to work together and bring about change. Now, more than ever, the stigma of seeking mental health treatment is dissipating, as more people are finding success with their problems by turning to a counselor. Another area of development is taking the field beyond the idea that mental and physical illness are intertwined, but that psychological and medical *treatments* are intertwined.

So with all of these developments and possibilities, we have another chance to make this book live up to the promise we had for it when it was being written almost ten years ago: to provide a substantial contribution to the training of new clinicians in methods that are proven to be effective. In the first edition, we introduced the nonlinear thinking of master practitioners and the seven domains of competence. We infused the text with real-world clinical case examples and provided opportunities for readers to apply the material to the cases being presented. In this edition, we have added new "thought exercise" sections specifically designed to engage the reader's natural nonlinear thinking. We have added to each of the domains corresponding clinician attitudes or dispositions that we feel that master practitioners exhibit with clients. We have realigned several of the domains to incorporate new research findings on the therapeutic relationship, schema dynamics, methods for working with client emotions, as well as client ambivalence. We have also included transcript material from two separate cases interwoven in the text, and we have included transcripts from master therapists working with real clients that illustrate elements of each of the domains, regardless of their theoretical orientation. In addition, we have created an accompanying video section, in conjunction with

Alexander Street Press that is available for streaming through university libraries, as well as through Routledge Press.

So we invite the reader to enjoy this upgraded text. We hope that it will encourage you to explore the domains of competence and discover your own natural nonlinear thinking.

Acknowledgments

A project like this requires dedication and support in order for it to get through the process to publication. There have been many people who have helped us keep our dedication and have supported us throughout. One person in particular who was instrumental in making this work was the indefatigable Anna Moore and everyone from Routledge. We would be remiss if we did not also acknowledge those friends and colleagues who have encouraged us along the way, most especially John Gottman, Paul Ekman, Jon Carlson, Jeffrey Kottler, Jim Bitter, Richard Watts, and Bernard Shulman. In addition, those individuals who made many of the unique features of this book possible, including "the Avengers" from the Alliance Lab at Florida Atlantic University, especially Ashley Luedke, Mike Norman, and Rob Freund. Finally, we are indebted to Elizabeth Robey at Alexander Street Press who helped make the fantasy of including video from master practitioners come true and make this edition really come alive.

We are also grateful to the countless clients and families with whom we have worked who sparked our imaginations, stimulated our thinking, and, in the end, promoted our development as better clinicians. These nameless individuals were the inspiration for the clinical case examples contained in the book.

Last, and most heartfelt, we could not have devoted the time, energy, and effort that a work such as this requires without the love and support of our families, especially our spouses, Charlene Mozdzierz, Jennifer Peluso, and Mary Ann Lisiecki. We also extend a specific loving acknowledgment to our children (Kimberly, Krista, Pamela, and Andrea Mozdzierz; Helen and Lucy Peluso; and Ann Marie, Joseph, Teresa, and Paul Lisiecki).

Introduction

Learning to Think Like a Therapist: Characteristics of Expert Therapist Thinking and Why It Is Important to Learn How to Think Like a Therapist

The Problem of the Sorcerer's Apprentice

In the Disney movie *Fantasia*, Mickey Mouse takes the role of the sorcerer's apprentice. It is a story that dates back 2,000 years to a Middle Eastern tale of a powerful sorcerer and his apprentice who watches the master's great feats and wants to learn the secrets of the magic. The apprentice (Mickey Mouse) is consigned to perform menial tasks, including getting water from a well. But the apprentice aspires to be a great sorcerer himself (of course), and one night he borrows the sorcerer's magic hat. He tries to cast a spell in order to animate a broom and get it to fetch water for the household. At first he's successful, and soon he begins to dream of becoming a great sorcerer and commanding the stars, the clouds, and the waves. The problem is, he can't make the broom stop fetching water, and it begins to flood the house! In a panic, Mickey tries to hack the broom to pieces with an ax. But each fragment becomes a whole broom, and the army of brooms brings a deluge of water that floods the entire house. Just when it seems that there is no hope of controlling the spreading deluge, the sorcerer appears as a *deus ex machina*, takes his hat back from the apprentice, magically dries up the flood, and restores order. The sorcerer then chastises Mickey for mistaking technique for mastery and overestimating his powers.

In many ways, beginning a career and developing expertise as a psychotherapist resembles the story of the sorcerer's apprentice. In our training, we watch videos of legendary masters of the craft, or perhaps witness a live demonstration at a workshop or conference. These masters seem to resolve the most complex of problems with penetrating insight or exacting skill. Often, it is our first clinical supervisors who seem so skilled and so knowledgeable at a time when we are stumbling to find our way through the maze of all that there is to learn about clinical practice.

All of these individuals have one thing in common: They all seem to be sorcerer-like in their ability to illuminate cases and develop treatment strategies, especially as compared with our own abilities as beginners. When new therapists begin to work with their first clients, there is generally very little therapeutic movement or success. Anyone who remembers treating their first personality-disordered client, unrepentant perpetrator, or entrenched substance abuser can recall having an overwhelming feeling of utter futility or failure. Sometimes, we may even try to mimic a master or supervisor, and (just like Mickey Mouse) unintentionally overreach ourselves, creating more havoc than help.

Often the beginning therapist becomes frustrated with a complicated case or difficult client, and either acts out or emotionally withdraws from the client, which makes a complex situation still more complex. Later, the supervisor easily brings the client's issue into its proper therapeutic context. The supervisor demonstrates that what was needed was something simple and well within the beginner's reach. Just like the sorcerer, the master practitioner brings order from chaos and reinstalls normalcy. And are we beginners happy? Rarely! Such skilled supervision more often than not leaves the novice feeling foolish, inept, and in awe of the supervisor's expertise.

As a result, the beginning therapist will go through the motions and use the same techniques as his or her supervisor, but not necessarily with the same results. In fact, successfully mastering the craft is about something beyond going through the motions or using techniques that have worked with another therapist. We believe that these initial disastrous results occur because novices do not know the thought processes behind the craft. They do not understand or know how and why certain therapist behaviors are effective and others are not effective.

It seems that novices' misguided therapeutic activities, in which they mimic their supervisors, is virtually universal and that most developing therapists experience them with mixed results. But, depending on the complexity of the client's problems, novice therapists may not easily recover from early failures. Instead of learning from these early experiences, they risk lapsing into a career of uneventful routine sessions, that is, endlessly doing the same therapy with every client. Ronnestad and Skovholt (1993) discussed the consequences for students of improper training and early clinical failures. Specifically, these students become increasingly anxious for quick fixes and look to supervisors to teach them "how to." Inexperienced supervisors often make the mistake of responding too quickly to these students, and "may easily and quickly resort to giving suggestions as to how to act, instead of engaging in the more difficult task of dwelling on understanding and unraveling the complexity that is being expressed" (Ronnestad & Skovholt, 1993, p. 398). This only compounds the problem because students develop a limited therapeutic flexibility, fail to fully appreciate complex clinical situations, eventually stagnate—and perhaps burn out—rather than evolve into competent therapists. As a result, treatment outcomes for clients in therapy are often inconsistent and call into question for the therapist (and others) the effectiveness of counseling and psychotherapy as a whole (Miller, 2004).

As a result, the problem of the sorcerer's apprentice or learning to be a competent therapist is summarized like this: *What* apprentices are learning in schools (e.g., applying techniques, learning skills, using one therapeutic orientation for every problem, or person), or attempting to mimic masters, is not the way that great therapy is done and taught. Unfortunately, too often, it is taught to beginning therapists this way. The reality is that this is simply not adequate enough to prepare new clinicians for becoming an effective master therapist!

Learning from Experts—Those Who Demonstrate Their Effectiveness

Learning to become a master practitioner is essentially learning what is involved in developing *expertise*. Expertise is itself a subject matter that has been studied for over 100 years. It is only in the last 10 years, however, that some of the most groundbreaking studies of expertise, and what makes a person an expert have taken place. K. Anders Ericsson (2006), a leader in this area of research, referred to expertise as, "The characteristics, skills, and knowledge that distinguishes experts from novices and less experienced people" (p. 3). As it turns out, however, actually delineating those "characteristics, skills, and knowledge" is far from a linear pursuit. That is, in some fields, there are objective criteria for demonstrating expertise, whereas for other fields it is far more difficult. Psychotherapy is one of those fields in which it is far more difficult to develop the objective "characteristics, skills, and knowledge" that distinguishes novices from experts.

Another expert on expertise, Chi (2006) described a number of characteristics that distinguish experts from nonexperts, which may help to define these characteristics in the therapeutic field.

First, they are able to generate the best solution for a given situation, and they can do this better than nonexperts. Second, they can detect and recognize features of a given situation that novices cannot such as deeper concerns or structures in a given situation or problem. Third, experts seem to spend a lot of time analyzing a problem qualitatively, thus bringing in knowledge from both within and outside their given field to apply to a problem. Fourth, experts are also able to engage in self-monitoring, thereby evaluating their progress more accurately. Fifth, experts are *opportunistic*: They make use of whatever information sources or resources are at their disposal and are able to choose more effective strategies in problem solving while using minimal cognitive effort, compared with novices. Put simply, experts are able to achieve better results because they bring together and use many seemingly intangible resources when they work, and they appear to do it effortlessly.

We conclude that the same is true for therapists: Some clinicians (i.e., experts) are more effective than others with different clients (Lambert & Barley, 2002). Thus, they get different results. For example, Wampold and Brown (2005) found that for clinicians who achieved the poorest results in a "predictor" set of cases (i.e., were in the bottom 25% of the entire sample), their clients had only a 20% chance of achieving reliable change in their level of functioning. On the other hand, the clients who were seen by master clinicians (in the top 25%) *exceeded* the expected level of improvement. Similarly, Hubble, Duncan, Miller, and Wampold (2010) found that clients of the most effective therapists have *half* the rates of client dropout (i.e., clients leaving therapy before achieving meaningful change) as less effective therapists. At the same time, the clients of the most effective therapists achieve 50% more improvement than those seen by average clinicians.

How Do Master Clinicians Achieve Mastery?

What, then, makes for an expert practitioner? Do such therapists become masterful as a function of time spent doing therapy? Does each have innate abilities that are unique to that individual, or are there some common traits that each of these therapists share that make them experts? Researchers have studied the problem-solving methods of novices and compared them with those of experts. Lambert and Barley (2002) found that clinicians with more than six years of experience seemed to get better results, but Hubble et al. (2010) found that age or number of years as a clinician *did not correlate* with outcome. Neither of these studies quantified expertise, however. Skovholt and Jennings (2004) reported that, when novices in the physical sciences are given complex problems and asked to solve them, they tended to apply a particular formula and solve backward from the formula. Experts, on the other hand, tended to reason forward from the problem, "as if cues or signposts for potential problems are embedded in the problem itself" (Skovholt & Jennings, 2004, p. 4). Feltovich, Prietula, and Ericsson (2006), in their study of expertise, also found similar tendencies in experts across multiple fields. In other words, experts tend to find a solution embedded within a problem itself, which allows them to "see deeper, faster, further, and better than the novice" (Skovholt & Jennings, 2004, p. 4). The only legitimate conclusion to draw from such studies of expertise is that experts think differently.

In psychotherapy, novice practitioners don't seem to get as good results as experts because they may tend to rely on a particular theory or technique of counseling without fully accounting for the uniqueness of a client's perspective or circumstances. According to Skovholt and Jennings (2004), this is primarily due to the difficulty that novices have in dealing with the ambiguous nature of client problems and the therapeutic process itself. As a result, novices tend to move quickly toward "premature closure," or the "tendency to latch on to one simplistic solution, theory, or frame of reference with which to view clients in order to avoid being cognitively or emotionally overwhelmed" (Skovholt & Jennings, 2004, p. 20). Novices are vulnerable to feeling overwhelmed, uncertain and, hence, less than adequate to deal with the complex and ambiguous task at hand. As a result, they may very well gravitate toward using more simplistic solutions. This cognitive belief or emotional feeling of inadequacy is what frequently leads to problems such as premature termination and other manifestations of client resistance. Such developments can leave the beginning therapist feeling lost, confused, frustrated, and ill-prepared in addition to feeling inadequate to help clients. In fact, when novices are confronted with the complex and demanding problems of their clients, they can become subject to cognitive and emotional overload, discouragement, and burn out (Jennings, Skovholt, Goh, & Lian, 2013).

By contrast, experts' performance "requires . . . vast amounts of knowledge and a pattern-based memory system acquired over many years of experience" (Skovholt & Jennings, 2004, p. 3). In other words, experts think differently, in part, because they have a broad perspective that derives from having considerable experience that helps them to recognize familiar patterns that they have built on over many years. Goldberg (2005) has called this the "wisdom paradox," namely, a demonstration that in later life (i.e., as experience has been accumulated), we develop a mental strength or an integration of thought and analysis. This does not mean that novice practitioners cannot learn to be alert for and recognize essential elements and patterns that can help them achieve better results.

Experts have a vast database of both client experiences and psychotherapeutic practice in general to call upon when faced with the inherent ambiguities of client issues or responses (Martin, Slemon, Hiebart, Hallberg, & Cummings, 1989, as cited in Skovholt & Jennings, 2004). They are able to "draw upon this knowledge efficiently and parsimoniously to determine the best course of action regarding specific client problems" (Skovholt & Jennings, 2004, p. 25). Experts recognize that while clients' complaints may be similar (e.g., complaints of anxiety or depression), they don't focus on that solely; they are readily alert and attentive to the uniqueness, subtleties, ambiguities, and nuances that each client offers that distinguishes them from another client with similar complaints (Jennings et al., 2013). Furthermore, experts' experience, knowledge base, and sense of comfort with the processes of psychotherapy can have a cumulative result: reducing the potential hazardous human effects (e.g., feeling inadequate as a practitioner, frustrated, lost, etc.) that dealing with client ambiguities can have on them.

They do not have to prematurely foreclose on a single solution, but rather understand that therapy is a process of exploring multiple solutions that can be generated by the therapist, the client, or jointly. In contrast, as we noted earlier, novices seek closure too soon, before a client is ready, falling back on techniques or formulas they have learned or mimicking something they saw an experienced therapist do in the hopes of "making something happen" with the client without knowing whether it will happen or, if it does, why. Experts, on the other hand, know, understand, and trust the processes underlying therapeutic effectiveness. In other words, they *think differently!*

Learning to Think Like a Therapist: The Characteristics of Expert Therapist Thinking and Why It Is Important

All professions share a certain common rule in training and educating new professionals. Whether it is medicine, law, journalism, nursing, physical therapy, or financial investing, students of any discipline we can call to mind are taught to think in a particular way, that is, how to go about achieving the stated goals of their particular profession. This kind of thinking customarily consists of appraising a particular problem, deciding what not to do, and choosing the best way of professionally dealing with the particular unique set of circumstances that are the current focus of attention from within their given discipline. For example, from the beginning of their training, physicians are taught to think in a certain way beginning with the first rule of medicine, namely, "Do no harm." Doctors are taught in many instances that not doing something can be as important as—if not more important than—doing the wrong thing or doing something too quickly and needlessly aggravating a condition. Although few people might guess this, the first rule of dentistry is not to find and fix dental cavities.

The first rule of dentistry is *prevention*. As a result, dentists are taught to instruct their patients on how to maintain good oral hygiene and prevent the decline of their teeth.

Successful stockbrokers and stock analysts also demonstrate a way of thinking that is distinct from that of the uninitiated. John Q. Public will not want to buy stocks when they are depressed in price or out of favor. Professional stockbrokers and mutual fund managers, however, see such circumstances as potential opportunities to buy underappreciated and undervalued stock assets (i.e., when "blood is running in the streets"). More recently, billionaire investor Warren Buffet has coined a simple phrase that captures his investment strategy: "When everyone gets scared, I get greedy. When everyone gets greedy, I get scared." The meaning behind each of these orientations is that unknowledgeable people are selling in panic at the bottom of stock market cycles in order not to lose everything and are buying at the peak in order not to miss out (i.e., greed) on making a fortune like everyone else. They are caught buying high and selling low—an impossible way to make money. Among other things, professional stockbrokers and traders don't get trapped by focusing only on what a stock has done in the past; they care where it is going. They think differently.

Likewise, law students are taught a process of thinking. That process not only involves how to construct the side of an issue they are defending, but also how to construct their opponent's side of the issue. They learn that knowing the other side of the issue will help them to see the arguments that they will encounter and thus how to derive counterarguments.

The same principle of learning how to think ought to hold true for psychotherapists and counselors. Unfortunately, training today does not appear to emphasize an awareness of thinking processes of experts, or to help therapists explicitly learn how to think like therapists. Instead, training programs continue to teach antiquated methods designed to train students how to mimic experts, but not how to *think* like them. A major consideration of this text is that master practitioners have learned to apply what we call *nonlinear thinking* to their professional work. Although many of these experts have developed their nonlinear thinking skills over the course of many years of study and practice, we do not believe that one must necessarily wait for 5, 10, or 20 years of practice experience (i.e., trial, error, and clinical failure) in order to begin cultivating this way of working effectively with clients. In fact, this text develops, in depth, not only what those nonlinear thinking processes are, but also how they can be applied from the beginning of one's career. We define nonlinear processes as being at the heart of a master practitioner's work and learning how to think like a therapist.

Linear versus Nonlinear Thinking

Linear thinking is essentially defined graphically by a straight line from a simple problem to a simple solution. (A simple case example is illustrated in the clinical case example below.) Common sense is an example of the usefulness of linear thinking. Most people can agree on what constitutes a commonsense approach across typical human experiences: It is best not to smoke because tobacco has proven to cause cancer. Eat healthy food, drink alcohol moderately, don't use illicit drugs, and get a moderate amount of exercise.

However, life is often not that simple, and many people violate all of these commonsense principles everyday. The simple reason for this is that we are actually one step removed from reality and must make decisions based on our *perceptions* of reality. In turn, our perceptions are influenced by a highly engrained schematic representation (i.e., ideas, beliefs, convictions, etc.) of ourselves, others, and the world around us. For example, many people believe that they can consume a high-fat diet and drink lots of alcohol without any ill effects. They believe that the negative effects of such behavior is what happens to *other* people but not them.

Another example of the violation of common sense can be seen in clients who are anorexic or bulimic and may know that their eating disorder and weight loss are potentially killing them and that they should just eat (linear thinking, simple solution), but they often continue to restrict their dietary intake to dangerous levels because they fear getting fat (distorted perception of themselves). So it is clear that problems are often created by client's violations of common sense. As a result, merely using a commonsense approach to correct the problem will not work!

Nonlinear Thinking

The term nonlinear appears to be the best poetic metaphor that we can conjure to describe the sort of thinking in which we envision that master practitioners often engage in to deal with such violations of common sense. It is frequently defined as being disproportional to its inputs (like an equation), or, to put it in more generic terms, "The sum is greater than the whole of its parts." A nonlinear way of thinking does not resemble a straightforward, characteristic, one-dimensional, *logical* approach to human problem solving (i.e., "You are overweight, have high blood pressure, lead a sedentary life, and are smoking cigarettes all of which can lead to a premature death. Therefore, you need to lose weight, get more exercise, and stop smoking."). Rather nonlinear thinking is the sort of thinking that turns things upside down and inside out—it departs from the linear way of thinking about things. In other words, it is a reorientation in the way behaviors, emotions, feelings, attitudes, and so forth are viewed. De Bono (1994) discussed what he calls "lateral thinking," which is similar to nonlinear thinking, as follows:

> Lateral thinking is both *an attitude of mind* and also a number of defined methods. The attitude of mind involves the willingness to try to look at things in different ways. It involves an appreciation that any way of looking at things is only one among many possible ways. It involves an understanding of how the mind uses patterns and the need to escape from an established pattern in order to switch into a better one. (pp. 59–60; emphasis added)

Lateral thinking "involves escaping from a pattern that has been satisfactory in the past" (de Bono, 1994, p. 70) but that may not be effective in a particular set of circumstances. When such an escape from traditional thinking occurs, de Bono indicates, "We switch to a new pattern and suddenly see that something is reasonable and obvious" (de Bono, 1994, p. 57). Linear thinking is the process of looking at a problem along one dimension, a familiar, unconscious, habitual, automatic, unreflective, and perhaps previously successful way of approaching a problem or even life itself. At its core, linear thinking represents the characteristic and traditional way in which a particular personality approaches life and problem solving. By contrast, nonlinear (or lateral) thinking is "out-of-the-box" thinking. It requires therapists to see and understand the client's characteristic, old, personally linear pattern; envision a new, alternative way (or pattern) of seeing and behaving; and communicate that new way to the client. Thus, it may appear to be mysterious, seemingly askew, perhaps risky, and not logically following from what the client presents. However, when nonlinear interventions are presented to the client, the thinking is revealed to be dynamic, energizing, and deeply understanding of the client's concerns on a profound level.

Clinical Case Example: A Broken Heart and Obsessing

A man entered counseling complaining of being unable to stop thinking about his ex-wife. To stay preoccupied and obsessed with his ex-wife would appear to be, for all practical purposes, nonproductive and certainly disruptive to his daily functioning. She is gone, and the prospects of repairing the relationship is dismal. A client may *know* that but can't accept it. For the therapist to tell the client to stop thinking about his ex-wife (i.e., linear thinking, which is direct and straightforward and common sense) is futile because if he could heed such counsel, he would have stopped doing so and not needed counseling in the first place. Hence, when confronted with the rigid pattern of the client's maladaptive behaviors (i.e., obsessing about one's ex-wife), the master practitioner considers ways of understanding the client's pattern of thinking and suggests a new, larger pattern that the client's obsessing behavior may be a part of.

This is demonstrated when the therapist suggests how useful and helpful it may be for a man to keep thinking about his ex-wife. What frequently follows such an unexpected intervention from the therapist is an unconventional response (i.e., quite different from the characteristic manner in which a person has been thinking); a changed and enriched reality follows, as the client understands how the new or enlarged pattern encompasses his old behavior. At this point, the client must make a choice about what to do next. Thinking about one's ex-wife may very well serve a protective function—an individual obsessed with what happened in the past, by definition, can't be thinking about what he needs to do to get on with his life. He simply may not be ready to begin thinking about life and making decisions about what to do without his former wife. In fact, thinking about his ex-wife may even be presented to him as a useful barometer of how prepared or unprepared he is at that particular moment to actually think about much more frightening matters such as the seriousness of his cardiac condition. As such, letting the man know that it may very well be useful to him to *not* get his ex-wife out of his mind right now would simultaneously have an unexpected as well as a distinct emotional impact. It has become axiomatic in the therapy literature that shifts in an individual's thinking are more likely to occur when there are elevated levels of affect or arousal. An unexpected (i.e., nonlinear) response from a therapist triggers just such an unexpected response and elevated affect or arousal from a client.

So is this what you thought of? Would your first instinct be the *linear* intervention to "Just stop it!" (It's okay if it is!) Did the nonlinear suggestion make sense to you? Can you see where it has the chance to be *more* effective than the linear one? If so, you may be a natural nonlinear thinker!

As de Bono (1994) has suggested, nonlinear, or lateral, thinking is in part an "attitude of mind" that involves a willingness to look at things in different ways (i.e., thinking nonlinearly). In our clinical case example, the patient just can't stop thinking about his ex-wife. His thinking is automatic, unreflective, and effortless. Part of the process of therapy for the man in the case example involves facilitating his engagement in a different way of thinking about his problem (i.e., thinking more slowly, deliberately, in previously unexplored ways, etc. and seeing how paradoxically *useful* his seemingly uncontrollable thinking is).

But thinking in new and previously unexplored ways can not only be hard work, it can be quite risky to do so! As such, for maximum efficacy, a nonlinear way of thinking must be incorporated with—and integrated into—client's circumstances and philosophy along with other salient aspects of psychotherapy (e.g., assessing the client's readiness for change; assessing and accessing the client's strengths; aligning properly with the client's motivations, goals, and strengths; creating a strong therapeutic relationship; showing respect for the client; appropriately confronting inconsistency; understanding his or her schematic representations of the world; and handling emotional content). Now, before you misinterpret what it is that we are advocating, we wish to make it very clear that practitioners need to use *both* linear and nonlinear thinking. Linear thinking is essential in understanding the factual nature of a client's personal narrative, namely, what led up to their current problematic circumstances, what is happening at the present time, and what they would like to happen. The facts can typically be understood in terms of such things as times, dates, names, events, circumstances, and history. After all, it would be a very linear thing for us to do to advocate using only one type of thinking!

Am I a Nonlinear Thinker?

When confronted with a concept such as nonlinear thinking, students may experience varying degrees of apprehension or confusion. This uneasiness can be characterized by unexpressed thoughts such as "I don't understand what a nonlinear thinking counselor or therapist really is . . . will I be able to think in nonlinear ways . . . how come everyone else seems to understand what nonlinear thinking is and I don't?"

Perhaps the first thing to consider is that *something* drew you to this field, and not to law, medicine, business, or some other career path. And although many people will say, "I just want to help people" (and this may be true), many readers will probably say: "All my life, people have just always found it easy to talk to me and tell me about their problems." This is often the beginning of some natural tendency toward a career in one of the helping professions. Sometimes, people are drawn to this field because they themselves have been helped by counseling and have experienced relief from the pain in their own lives thanks to a skilled practitioner. And although these two elements—natural empathy and an understanding of the power of the therapist-client relationship—are key, there is one more element that, we believe, draws people to this field: They are inherently curious and familiar with nonlinear thinking in a vague sort of way.

This vague familiarity with nonlinear thinking is reflected in clinicians' everyday lives (and perhaps yours, also). Most clinicians (especially those who stay in the field and continue toward mastery) enjoy people, how mysteries unravel, dramatic involvements, solving puzzles, and forth. Each of these activities requires the application of nonlinear thinking. The point is that you may already be quite familiar with nonlinear thinking, but simultaneously not familiar with it from the perspective of being a practitioner. Human beings are nonlinear thinkers; otherwise, we could not read (i.e., understand the meaning of) nonverbal gestures, facial expressions, and so on, or understand jokes, expressions of irony, sarcasm, and puns. (Humor and its relationship/use in psychotherapy is discussed more fully in our advanced text.) One of the main purposes of this book is to learn about the nonlinear thinking of practitioners and provide clinical examples to become more familiar with it, as well as opportunities to practice it.

Exercising Your Nonlinear Thinking

Periodically in this book (and the advanced text), we present exercises that are designed to get the reader to think in nonlinear ways. Most interesting, many of these puzzles are ancient, and some are more modern. This one comes from ancient Greece.

Heraclitus was a Greek philosopher who lived in 500 BCE. He believed that life was constantly changing and evolving. One of his most famous sayings was "You cannot step into the same river twice." Now the nonlinear question to ask yourself is: Is Heraclitus correct? Let's consider this.

On the one hand, you can step into the same river over and over again. Suppose you take a car ride as a child across the country to Los Angeles, and you stop off at the Grand Canyon and you decide to take a swim in the Colorado River. Then, after a week, you go back the way you came and upon getting to the Colorado River, you take another swim in the river in the exact same spot. Therefore, you do swim in the same river twice. So this proves Heraclitus was wrong, right?

Well, not so fast! Did Heraclitus mean the physical *place* of the river, or did he mean the *water* in the river? In that case, then you cannot step into the same river twice. Because it is always flowing, the river (the water molecules, the fish that were swimming in that spot, etc.) that you walked in when you went to Los Angeles is long gone by the time you make the return trip and take the second swim. In fact, even if you got out and immediately walked back in, it would not be the same river! So this proves that Heraclitus was right, right?

So what is the right answer?

The bottom line (and the nonlinear truth) is that neither are completely wrong and both are right! This has implications for counseling. Often what is true or valid in one context or circumstance is not necessarily true in another. Many times clinicians have to help clients to see this. As a result, nonlinear thinking is critical, and if you are able to reason this out and understand the implications of this, then you have taken your first step toward being a master practitioner, and you are probably a natural nonlinear thinker!

Expertise and Learning How to Think Like a Practitioner

How does someone learn about nonlinear thinking and how to use it in therapy? Generally, therapists learn the thinking exemplified in the clinical case example only slowly and gradually through a sometimes painful trial-and-error process, or if they are referred to certain literature, if at all. Again, we do not believe that this *has* to be the case! In fact, we believe that individuals should learn these nonlinear thinking processes from the earliest points of their training. Some of the basic findings from research into expertise, that generalizes to all experts, may be particularly useful here. According to Feltovich et al. (2006), expertise does require knowledge of content matter in the discipline. In fact, expertise requires large and integrated cognitive units that are abstracted and can be applied to new situations. Therefore, studying theory, seeing a wide variety of clients, case conceptualization, diagnosis, and research in the field of counseling and psychotherapy is important. The experience component is especially important. This is the case because the knowledge and experience gained in working with previous clients can be used quickly to be able to understand a new client and know how to proceed with them. Expertise involves automated *basics*—meaning that most expert therapists seem to use essential and fundamental clinical processes without looking as though they are doing them in an effortless and natural way. This explains why many master therapists often seem to be having a pleasant chat with clients, whereas many novice therapists look like they are interrogating a suspect. Expertise requires reflection and selectively attending to relevant information. For master clinicians, this is the process of focusing on the most important information in a client's story and not becoming sidetracked.

How We Will Do It: Development of Mastery and Deliberate Practice

Although this process of mastery does take time, we don't believe that it must necessarily be a painful or mysterious journey. Coexistent with the educational purpose of this text, we also hope to demystify the seemingly unfathomable. We do not believe that the lengthy process of mastery should be an excuse for providing substandard therapy to clients. According to Ericsson (2006) and others, mastery does not come from mindless practice (i.e., putting in hundreds or thousands of hours), without any structure or guidance. Mastery is achieved by *deliberate practice*. This type of practice is "focused, programmatic, carried out over extended periods of time, guided by conscious performance monitoring, evaluated by analyses of level of expertise reached, identification of errors, and procedure directed at eliminating errors" (Horn & Masanuga, 2006, p. 601). Specific goals are set at each successive stage of development and involves objective feedback about performance that help the learner to internalize how to identify and correct errors, to set new goals, to focus on overcoming weaknesses and to monitor progress (i.e., thinking like a master).

One of the more important elements in designing any program to achieve mastery is to have a method for the practice to happen, for new changes to be made in a conscious manner, that are incremental and easily measured to give feedback. According to Ericsson (2006):

Deliberate practice is therefore designed to improve specific aspects of performance in a manner that assures that attained changes can be successfully measured and integrated into representative performance. Research on deliberate practice in music and sports show that continued attempts for mastery require that the performer always try, by stretching performance beyond its current capabilities, to correct some specific weakness, while preserving other successful aspects of function. This type of deliberate practice requires full attention and concentration, but even with that extreme effort, some kind of failure is likely to arise and gradual improvements with corrections and repetitions are necessary. With increased skill in monitoring, skilled performers . . . focus on mastering new challenges by goal-directed deliberate practice involving problem solving and specialized training techniques. (p. 698)

Generally speaking, during the first phase of learning (Level 1), beginners try to understand the requirements of the activity or discipline and focus on performing the tasks (basic listening and understanding, assessment, developing a therapeutic relationship) while avoiding gross mistakes. In the second phase, when people have had more experience, noticeable mistakes become increasingly rare, performance appears smoother, and learners no longer need to focus as intensely on their performance to maintain an acceptable level. After a limited period of training and experience— frequently less than 50 hours (their first practicum experience), they develop an acceptable level of performance and can automatically, and with minimal effort, perform these skills. But as their actions become automatic, practitioners cannot actively control and modify these behaviors. Some clinicians will at some point in their career give up their commitment to improvement and stop their deliberate practice to further improve performance. This leads to a plateauing, which results in premature automation of their performance.

However, expert performers who seek mastery consciously counteract this automaticity. It is our contention that if a person masters the linear and nonlinear thinking aspects of each of the domains (which we describe in the next chapter) for a particular level of development, the end result will be a more effective and personally satisfied clinician, compared with trainees who do not undertake this. Furthermore, as a therapist progresses from level to level and masters the domains of each successive level, he or she will be able to be more effective with a greater versatility in the same way that master therapists are.

So How Will We Do This?

Skovholt and Jennings (2004) recommended training that focuses on providing corrective feedback to trainees about how they conceived the problem and derived their intervention(s). This feedback would increase the trainees' flexibility and increase their tolerance for complexity. In other words, they recommended training that gives attention to the thought process behind interventions and techniques in order for trainees to achieve mastery. Taken altogether, this kind of training would decrease the likelihood of "premature foreclosure," instead "setting the stage where one can continuously strive toward mastery of the highly ambiguous, difficult to understand phenomena" (Skovholt & Jennings, 2004, p. 21). These are the strategies that will increase effectiveness and solve the problem of the sorcerer's apprentice.

Of course, one of the first things is to learn from masters. According to Ericsson (2006), "more-accomplished individuals in the domain, such as professional coaches and teachers, will always play an essential role in guiding the sequencing of practice activities for future experts in a safe and effective manner" (pp. 698–99). For this edition, we have created an accompanying video component that shows master clinicians working with real clients and displaying the domain-specific skills. In addition, transcripts from these master clinicians' sessions will be embedded in the text for the reader to further illustrate the specific element of the domain, as well as the universal nature of the domain (i.e., used regardless of their theoretical orientation). Next, we provide thought exercises that will demonstrate aspects of nonlinear thinking to the reader. Finally, we have clinical case exercises, derived from actual cases, to work through specific domain elements that we are presenting.

New knowledge, like the kind that has been generated by the last two decades of research presented above, requires new approaches to training beginning therapists. Without these new approaches to training, the field of psychotherapy runs the risk of repeating the same errors (i.e., focusing exclusively on learning formulaic techniques, micro skills, and theories of therapy) that will perpetuate the problems outlined above. That simply prolongs the problem of the sorcerer's apprentice.

Unfortunately, training methods do not appear to have kept pace with advances in understanding how to be more effective in treating our clients. In fact, one of the main reasons why there are so few training environments that target mastery is that they don't emphasize the type of deliberate practice that is necessary. The amount of support that is required to have students practice and receive feedback on a regular basis that focuses on extended performance is extensive. It is not simply a matter of talent. In fact, even child prodigies with innate gifts need to have their skills honed by practice over a number of years in order to attain mastery (Ericsson, 2006). Again, the recent trend in the instruction of beginning therapists is to teach them how to *act* like therapists—that is, to follow one's particular interpretation of a theory of therapy, utilize a technique-based practice, or perhaps implement a somewhat formulaic evidence-based practice. There are several reasons for this, including reduced time for training, increased training demands, expanded requirements for credentialing (accreditation and licensure), demands for increased productivity, diminishing resources and pressures from third-party payers. As a result, in their training programs today, beginning practitioners often do not explicitly learn how to think like therapists.

The disparity between coursework knowledge and competent application in clinical settings creates a significant theory–practice gap. Students who have the most difficulty and the most to overcome are also those who experience the widest gulf between what they have learned and what they are called upon to do in the field (Ronnestad & Skovholt, 1993). Hence, if the necessary processes aren't properly instilled during formal training, the beginning therapist has few opportunities to effectively correct them. If they are fortunate, they slowly pick it up through trial and error or through good prelicensure supervision. The sad part, however, is that the majority of practitioners never get exposed to the thought processes that belie clinical expertise and mastery, and thus never reach their full potential (Jennings et al., 2013). Like birds born in captivity, if they don't learn the songs of their species at the critical moments, they are permanently impaired and often do not survive burnout in the wilds of clinical practice.

The Purpose of This Book

The easy and obvious solution to this dilemma is to institute a system of training that is effective, focuses on therapist development, emphasizes effective common (i.e., convergence) factors, assesses outcomes in practice, fosters strong therapeutic relationships, and teaches students how to tailor treatment for each individual client, while placing less emphasis on fad treatment approaches, outdated modalities, or formulaic protocols (Duncan, Miller, Wampold, & Hubble, 2010; Miller, Mee-Lee, Plum, & Hubble, 2005; Norcross, 2011; Ogles, Anderson, & Lunnen, 1999). Instead, Gordon Paul (1967) proposed a seemingly logical challenge to the profession, namely, to find what treatment and by whom is most effective for a particular individual, with what specific problem, and under what specific set of circumstances. More recently, Orlinsky (2010) defined the problem even more specifically in this way:

> There are individual differences among clients in relationship skills and in their ability to be moved by cognitive, affective, imaginal, or enactive aspects of experience. There are also individual differences among therapists in these respects. Some clients are more receptive and ready, with some therapists, using some procedures to engage in and benefit from an effectively therapeutic relationship. Some therapists are more proficient, with some clients, and with some types of problems in creating and cultivating an effective therapeutic relationship. Some procedures are more efficient with some clients, in some circumstances, and in the hands

of some therapists in producing and maintaining an effective therapeutic relationship. These are all variables in the therapeutic equation, but the constant in psychotherapy is a relationship, cocreated and sustained by client and therapist, that is applied by clients effectively as a source of corrective influence in their lives. (p. xxii)

The problem as defined by Paul (1967) and refined by Orlinsky (2010) is not merely the question ("What treatment, by whom works for which clients?"), however, but rather how the field has tried to answer it. The field has searched for an answer that seeks to fill in all of the blanks of the type of client, the type of problem, the types of treatment, and the types of circumstances. Clearly, it is an impossible task to research each of these variables, and every possible combination of them. Frankly, we think that this is the wrong way to address Paul's question.

As Miller et al. (2005) have cautioned, and as we mentioned earlier, decades of research have shown "that 'who' the therapist is accounts for six to nine times as much variance in outcome as 'what' treatment approach is employed" (p. 50). Hence, the only way to properly answer the question is to focus on the therapist and how he or she is trained. It is our assertion that if they are taught that the primary factor in any treatment is the establishment of a therapeutic relationship, they will get a better result. It is also our contention that if they are taught the ways that therapists think along with the domains of competence that are couched in a model that facilitates proper development, then they should be able to work more effectively within their own theoretical orientation, with a fairly wide range of clients, using empirically/scientifically based methods under a fairly wide variety of clinical circumstances and settings. As Hubble et al. (1999) concluded, "The survival of the mental health professions, in other words, will be better ensured by identifying empirically valid *treaters* rather than empirically validated *treatments*" (p. 439, emphasis added). The aim of this book is to help the development of such practitioners.

This book has been written with both novices and more seasoned practitioners in mind. We hope to make more sense of our profession by helping to develop a way of thinking about the work necessary to be effective. In addition, we earnestly hope that practicing professionals who believe that they are missing some training, skill, or awareness of how to practice effective therapy will find our work helpful in reenergizing them and bringing seemingly disparate elements of counseling/psychotherapy together. It is very possible that even the most well-intended practitioner may be working too hard at the wrong things. Our text is designed to provide understandings to help developing therapists, both novice and experienced, to learn about the processes that underlie effective outcomes with a wide variety of clients.

This goal is guided and supported by several recurring themes that represent the major thrust of our work:

1. **LEARNING TO THINK LIKE A THERAPIST:** Highly effective (i.e., expert) therapists think in a different way, namely, nonlinearly, from novices that allows them to connect and intervene with clients successfully and efficiently. Readers are introduced to the thinking processes of those practitioners (i.e., therapists with consistently good therapeutic outcomes) as they pertain to clinical assessment and intervention, which we believe will increase their knowledge and skill as therapists as well as reduce feelings of loss, confusion, frustration, inadequacy, and burnout.

2. **ATTENDING TO THE MOST IMPORTANT VARIABLES:** Empirical research has revealed a *convergence of understanding* about a common set of factors that very effective master practitioners attend to and utilize in treatment that are repeatedly associated with good outcomes. Convergence of these factors, or domains of competence, does not force a therapist to adopt a certain theoretical orientation, but rather allows a therapist to operate within her or his own

unique philosophical framework. By exposing the reader to the seven domains of competence, which must be attended to in addressing individual patient concerns, therapists can target their strengths or weaknesses, and begin to increase their effectiveness. We describe these in the next chapter.

3. **DEVELOPMENTAL PROGRESS TOWARD MASTERY:** Therapists' abilities seem to mature according to a progressive model of development. As a certain set of domains are mastered, therapists are able to advance to levels of greater complexity and ambiguity, which allow them to be able to work with clients who present multifaceted psychological problems. By placing the aforementioned domains of competence within a model of therapist development, readers can understand the logical progression toward mastery that will decrease feelings of being lost, confused, and stuck. These are also detailed in Chapter 1.

Given these guiding philosophies, it becomes clear that this is not just another basic counseling skills textbook. Rather, it represents the first major attempt to help beginning therapists and established practitioners learn about the essential domains of competence and thinking processes that are required in order to be effective with a broad spectrum of clients, rather than having to rely on a series of disconnected techniques or theories of personality. We address each of these themes in the next chapter.

1
Overview of the State of Psychotherapy and the Domains of Competence

The Current State of Psychotherapy

In the introduction, we described the universal feature of all master practitioners: nonlinear thinking. Before going further, there are other elements that structure our discussion of master practitioners. In addition, we wish to present some relevant findings regarding the current status of research on the effectiveness of psychotherapy and how the field has tried to explain and quantify it. Last, we discuss how we present an overview of the best methods for training new practitioners (as well as other practitioners) who wish to learn how to become more effective.

Therapy Is Effective in Helping People with Mental Disorders, Adjustment Problems, and Relational Difficulties in Life

The first and most important fact to keep in mind is that therapy *is* effective in helping people with mental illnesses, *period*. This fact has been established and reaffirmed over years (and decades) of research (See Cummings, 1999; Cummings & Follette, 1968; Mumford, Schlesinger, Glass, & Patrick, 1998; Smith, Glass, & Miller, 1980; Wampold, 2001, 2010). Miller et al. (2005) summed up the findings of over five decades of significant research on the effectiveness of psychotherapy:

> Research leaves little doubt about the overall effectiveness of therapy, once it is obtained. Regardless of the type of treatment, the measures of success included, the duration of the study or follow up period, study after study, and studies of studies, document improvements in physical, mental, family, and social functioning. (pp. 42–43)

Indeed, as we detail below, many aspects of therapy and the therapeutic process have been put to the test and found to be scientifically valid over a number of studies. More recently, advanced statistical methods (i.e., meta-analyses) have been used to evaluate groups of studies together. Their results are robust and replicable (Asay & Lambert, 1999; Duncan et al., 2010; Horvath, Del Re, Flückiger, & Symonds, 2011; Miller et al., 2005; Norcross & Lambert, 2011; Norcross & Wampold, 2011). Recently, Hubble et al. (2010) noted that studies of psychotherapy continue to substantiate its effectiveness by consistently producing what is statistically called effect sizes (i.e., a measure of how strong an observed effect really is) of 0.8 standard deviations. That may not mean much to those allergic to all things statistical, but put another way, it means that the average client in therapy is better off than 80% of the people who have not received treatment (Hubble et al., 2010). Any way such a research outcome is viewed, it is *remarkable*.

The benefits of therapy described above are not confined to the laboratory. Several researchers (Minami et al., 2008; Stiles, Barkham, Mellor-Clark, & Connell, 2008) found that clinicians in out-patient settings got similar effect sizes as clinicians in randomized control trials for depression, and across several schools of therapy (psychodynamic therapy, cognitive-behavioral therapy, and person-centered therapy). Furthermore, according to Wampold (2010), "Psychotherapy typically is as effective as drug treatments for emotional problems and is more enduring and creates less resistance to multiple administrations than drugs" (p. 55). As DiAngelis (2008) noted, "Research shows fairly consistent results: For most nonpsychotic disorders, behavioral interventions (i.e., psychotherapy) are just as effective as medications and they hold up better over time" (p. 49).

Some skeptics may claim that psychotherapy is not as effective as medical treatments are. Well, Hubble et al. (2010) point out that, by comparison, medical research often labels *breakthroughs* with a far lower statistical effect size. For example, the effect size of aspirin for heart disease was .03 (compared with the average effect size of .80 for psychotherapy), and was seen as powerful enough to stop the research for fear that denying the placebo group (who got no aspirin) was *unethical* (Wampold, 2010). So next time you are at a family reunion and someone says, "So all you do is listen to people's problems?" you may want to ask them, "Do you take an aspirin to prevent a heart attack?" If they answer "Yes," you may want to tell them that psychotherapy has over 25 times *more* benefit for its recipients than aspirin has for those who take it to avoid a heart attack!

The real take-home point of all the above discussion is to reinforce *the fact* that what you have chosen to do as a profession is *effective* in helping individuals to combat the miseries of everyday living!

Therapy Can Be Effective Quickly and Is a Cost-Effective Treatment

The second contextual fact that is important to know before embarking upon a career as a practitioner is that about 75% of clients improve during the first 6 months of therapy and about one half of all clients show improvement in as few as 8 to 10 sessions (Asay & Lambert, 1999). This is particularly important when viewed in light of the high personal, financial, and societal costs of mental and behavioral health troubles. According to Prochaska (1999), "Mental health and behavioral health problems, such as depression and the addictions, are among the most costly of contemporary conditions—costly to the individuals afflicted, their families and friends, their employers, their communities, and their health care systems" (p. 233). Mental health issues are responsible for over 50% of missed days at work or performing other life tasks (Merikangas et al., 2007). In other words, the economic impact in terms of lost productivity and time (for both clients and their loved ones) for those with disordered neurobiology or trouble adjusting to life circumstances can be substantial (U.S. Department of Health and Human Services, 2000). More important, helping those people function more effectively has a significant economic benefit. These facts led John C. Norcross, a nationally recognized leading researcher and writer on psychotherapy effectiveness, to conclude: "In a climate of accountability, psychotherapy stands up to empirical scrutiny with the best of health care interventions" (2002, p. 4).

Some critics of mental health treatments point out that mental and behavioral health problems are chronic. Well, *some* mental health problems *are* chronic, but even those with severe mental health diagnoses get better and function more effectively, and, by extension, society benefits. In fact, individuals who have a diagnosable mental illness can expect to lose approximately $16,000 in salary annually, which translates to almost $194 billion dollars in lost salary each year (Kazdin & Rabbitt, 2013; Kessler et al., 2009). In addition, for a single episode of depressive disorder, it can cost about 5 weeks of productivity. This is conservatively translated into a loss of $36 billion dollars to businesses annually (Kazdin & Rabbitt, 2013). We also point out that high blood pressure, diabetes, arthritis, obesity, asthma, and so on are also chronic problems. The chronicity of mental health problems is not an argument that holds much water in a debate about whether or not therapy is cost-effective. We also note that many individuals who avail themselves of psychological treatment for painful specific life circumstances feel better, are more functional, and no longer need treatment.

The take-home point from our brief discussion above is that not only is therapy effective but it can achieve its results quickly and in a cost-effective manner.

Despite These Potential Benefits, Therapy Is Ineffective and Underutilized

The third essential piece of background information has to do with the utilization of therapy. According to some estimates, less than one fourth of individuals with a diagnosable DSM-5[1] (*Diagnostic and Statistical Manual of the American Psychiatric Association*; American Psychiatric Association, 2013) disorder will ever seek therapy. Furthermore, of those who do seek treatment, roughly one half drop out of treatment before there is significant improvement (Norcross & Lambert, 2011; Prochaska, 1999), even though research shows that treated patients are far better off than untreated patients (Asay & Lambert, 1999). In previous generations, the stigma of therapy might have been blamed for this situation. Over the last 30 years, however, therapy has become more and more acceptable. In one survey, 91% of the people surveyed said that either they would consult a mental health professional, or would recommend that a friend or family member should do so if they needed it. Why, then, do patients either not seek treatment when it is needed or leave it prematurely?

The answer may lie in the results of a Harris Poll of those who needed help but did not pursue it. The two most prevalent reasons that survey participants cited for not pursing treatment were its cost and that they had doubts about the effectiveness of therapy. In 1998, the American Psychological Association (hereafter, APA) conducted another survey of potential consumers of psychotherapy. Seventy-six percent of participants reported that the main reason they were not seeking treatment was that they did not have confidence in the outcome of therapy (American Psychological Association, 1998), and when the APA repeated this survey in 2004, the results were not any better! Almost 8 out of 10 people (78%) said that they lacked confidence in the effectiveness of therapy as the reason for not pursuing it. In fact, the percentage of individuals who lacked confidence in the outcome of therapy was far greater than that of individuals who reported that therapy had a stigma attached (53%).

Another disturbing finding comes from a recent analysis of the 1998 and 2007 Medical Expenditure Panel Surveys. These surveys are representative of the general population, sponsored by the Agency for Healthcare Research and Quality (a division of the U.S. Department of Health and Human Services). In an analysis of these surveys, Olfson and Marcus (2010) found that over the last 10 years, the rates of individuals using *only* outpatient psychotherapy to treat mental illness *declined* from 15.9% to 10.5%, and individuals using a combination of psychotherapy and psychopharmacology *together* declined from 40% to 32.1%. However, in the same time period, the percentage of people who used only psychotropic medication *increased* from 44.1% to 57.4%. In terms of expenditures, the amount of money spent on mental health care overall increased from 1998 to 2007 from $15.4 billion dollars to $16.03 billion dollars, but at the same time, the amount spent for *psychotherapy* decreased from $10.94 billion dollars to $7.17 billion dollars. This constitutes a serious lack of confidence in psychotherapy itself despite its demonstrated benefits (Miller et al., 2005).

The Painful Truth: Effective Therapy Is Not Being Provided on a Consistent Basis

The fourth and final fact has to do with the wide variability in the skill of practitioners. Although it might be difficult to admit, therapists vary in their consistency. According to Hubble et al. (2010), this should not be a surprise. Lambert and Barley (2002) point out that, just as in other fields, some clinicians are more effective than others with different clients, and as a result, they get different results. However, "The disturbing news is that the poorest performing therapists consistently deliver a quality of service that would be classified as second rate . . . This may also explain why many clients who begin therapy drop out before experiencing significant benefit" (Lambert & Barley, 2002, p. 32). In one study, Wampold and Brown (2005) found that for clinicians who were in the bottom 25% of effectiveness outcomes, their clients had only a 20% chance of achieving reliable change in their level of functioning. Thus, it is not simply because there are naturally gifted therapists and (conversely) naturally dreadful therapists. If it were so, then the therapists with poor outcomes would do poorly all the time. But, they did not do poorly all of the time. In fact, they were able to have a positive impact with *some* clients.

This is a serious problem. As Brown, Dreis, and Nace (1999) reported, if clients do not begin to improve by the third visit, they are not likely to improve at all *and* are twice as likely to terminate therapy as those who are improving. Thus, the people who need therapy the most are the ones who are not being helped. Why is this the case?

According to Ogles et al. (1999), new professionals are being trained in ways that primarily emphasize specific techniques and treatment approaches, and, although these are useful, "With few exceptions, existing research evidence on both training and treatment suggests that individual therapist techniques contribute very little to client outcome" (p. 216). However, according to Wampold (2005), the therapist is one of the most potent factors: "[t]he variance of outcomes due to therapists (8%–9%) is larger than the variability among therapists (0%–1%), the alliance (5%), and the superiority of an empirically supported treatment to a placebo (0%–4%)" (p. 204). In other words, techniques bring a very small return on investment, explaining only 15% of the accounted variance attributable to positive therapeutic outcomes (Lambert & Ogles, 2002; Norcross & Lambert, 2011). We conclude that although it might be difficult to objectively quantify expertise in psychotherapy as Chi (2006) and Hubble et al. (2010) have noted, expertise *does* matter.

Improving the Process of Learning How to Become an Effective Therapist: Proposed Solutions and Their Limitations

How has the field responded to these dilemmas? We suggest that there are two major answers. First, active research has been ongoing to develop evidence-based treatments (i.e., evidence-based, psychological, practices) that are applied to a given problem and have expected results (much like the physician and the prescription). These are sometimes referred to as manualized treatments. Second, there has also been a search for a unified approach to therapy that all practitioners can use to be effective, called *integration* (much like a medical protocol that advocates a best practices approach to treating a specific condition such as an infection). Both of these movements are guided by the best of intentions, namely, to improve the practice of psychotherapy, and the results obtained from it as well reduce consistently escalating health care costs. Although both have made contributions to the field, neither approach has been sufficient to answer the challenge of how to help developing therapists become more proficient or how to have a better understanding of the therapeutic processes. As national concern over burgeoning health care costs has continued to escalate, the impetus behind these movements has received momentum from other sources, as Kazdin (2008) noted:

> State legislators and third-party payers . . . are drawing on research to decide what is appropriate to do in practice, what is reimbursed, and what the rates of reimbursement will be . . . the merits of this or that treatment or set of studies and the generalizability of findings now have a larger audience. (p. 156)

We discuss these two important contemporary trends and their implications for treatment, below.

The Movement toward Manualization or Evidence-Based Psychological Practices

Practitioners and theorists in the 1950s and 1960s who were frustrated by the apparent (and, in some respects, actual) lack of rigor in the field were inspired by Gordon Paul's (1967) call to find "what treatment by whom is most effective for this individual with that specific problem, and under what specific set of circumstances" (p. 111). As a result, a line of research was built on the belief that effective therapies must have similar steps that—if identified, quantified, and replicated—would reliably produce the same effective results, regardless of who the client or the therapist was. These researchers felt that the way to accomplish this was to break down a particular therapeutic approach into its constituent parts, so that any practitioner could learn it and faithfully reproduce the treatment with a client (Orlinsky, 2010). And so we saw the birth of treatment manuals, providing a how-to method for clinicians to follow and establishing guidelines for treating specific conditions with specific treatments and techniques, and their implementation. These manuals are typically derived from studies that carefully select patients who meet rigid criteria for the establishment of the particular diagnosis from the DSM-5 for the treatment that is under study. Patients are evaluated periodically, and if there is sufficient (i.e., statistically significant) improvement with a majority of the clients, then the treatment is considered *empirically supported* (i.e., evidence-based). This represents the basic foundation for the development of what is today called by a variety of names such as, *evidence-based treatment,* or empirically supported treatment (EST; also called *empirically validated treatment,* EVT, or evidence-based psychological practices, EBPP).[2]

How did such efforts fare? As could be anticipated, researchers found evidence (as mentioned above) that psychotherapy in general was beneficial and effective. Hubble, Duncan, and Miller (1999); Orlinsky (2010); Wampold (2010); and others all seem to agree on that. However, as Hubble et al. (1999) put it, there was no support for the "head-to-head horserace" between various approaches: "As it turned out, the underlying premise of the comparative studies, that one therapy (or more) would prove superior to others, received virtually no support" (p. 6). Furthermore, any previous research that had once demonstrated that there were some therapeutic approaches that seemed to work better with certain diagnoses (e.g., behavior therapy with phobias, and cognitive therapy with depression) were found to be fraught with problems (Norcross & Wampold, 2011; Wampold, 2010). And although they were cautious not to be critical of the attempt to establish an evidence base (via clinical trials, seen as the "gold standard") for treatment, Norcross and Wampold cautioned: "These studies are often plagued by confounds, such as researcher allegiance, cannot be blinded and often contain bogus comparisons" (Norcross & Wampold, 2011, p. 426).

To a larger extent, Wampold (2001), following a review of EVT research, also warned that "adherence to a protocol is misguided" (p. 201), and Whipple et al. (2003) pointed out that overreliance on EVT research is risky because it is based on small treatment effects. In fact, other researchers (e.g., Castonguay, Goldfried, Wiser, Raue, & Hayes, 1996; Henry, Strupp, Butler, Schacht, & Binder, 1993) suggested that over adherence to a *manualized* approach to treatment can actually produce *negative* effects (e.g., client dissatisfaction with therapy or premature termination) and be harmful to clients (Ogles et al., 1999). Finally, Kazdin (2008) noted that "an EBT may have support for its effects, but within individual studies and among multiple studies, the results often are mixed (i.e., show different effects or no effects)" (p. 148).

Where do these attempts to create manualized treatment go awry? One problem is that people do not fit neatly into diagnostic categories, as Kazdin (2008) noted:

> [P]atients in controlled trials have been characterized as having less severe disorders and fewer comorbid disorders than patients who routinely come to treatment . . . recruiting, selecting, and enrolling cases for research (e.g., soliciting and obtaining informed consent, conveying

that the treatment provided will be determined randomly) differ considerably from the processes leading individuals to come . . . for their treatment. (pp. 147–148)

Last, and perhaps most important, the biggest flaw is that researchers appear to take the person of the therapist out of the equation. In some studies, researchers were so preoccupied with training the therapists to adhere to the treatment manual that they did not pay attention to *basic, effective counseling skills.* In other cases, therapist skill level was more likely to predict the positive treatment effects than the treatment itself—a result that is tantamount to the empirical validation of quality therapists, rather than techniques or theories (Brown et al., 1999; Hubble et al., 1999; Norcross, 2002; Wampold, 2001). Norcross and Lambert (2011) agreed with this sentiment taking into account the science behind EBPPs, practitioner experience in using them and the limitations of such treatments:

Recent years have witnessed the controversial compilation of practice guidelines and evidence-based treatments in mental health . . . All of the efforts to promulgate evidence-based psychotherapies have been noble in intent and timely in distribution. . . . At the same time, many practitioners and researchers have found these recent efforts to codify evidence-based treatments seriously incomplete. While scientifically laudable in their intent, these efforts have largely ignored the therapy relationship and the person of the therapist. If one were to read previous efforts literally, disembodied therapists apply manualized interventions to discrete DSM disorders. Not only is the language offensive on clinical grounds to some practitioners, but the research evidence is weak for validating treatment methods in isolation from the therapy relationship and the individual patient. (pp. 6–7)

Miller and Rollnick (2002) noted that treatment outcomes, even at six-month follow-up interviews, can be attributed to the therapist's style: high empathy and low confrontation in the first few sessions. This style is associated with retention of clients in treatment and positive outcomes. This finding suggests that therapists demonstrating such behaviors are crucial elements of the change process; hence, it is beneficial, and even essential, to begin to understand these therapist factors (Brown et al., 1999). At the same time, Miller, Hubble, Duncan, and Wampold (2010) note: "How little we know about successful therapists; it is somewhat distressing how little research has been devoted to this subject" (p. 425).

EBPPs are an important development in the ongoing evolution of providing effective treatments for mental health and adjustment problems. Nevertheless, controversy remains. Practitioners new to the field are *certain* to encounter increasing attention being paid to and call for the use of the best EBPP method of treating certain conditions. But, it will be incumbent upon the practitioner as the responsible health care provider to make certain that clinical judgment prevails in assessing what a client is looking for, what a client needs, what best serves their needs, and how to accomplish specific treatment goals. When a therapist is considering a manualized treatment for a particular client, it is always important to assume a sense of balance and context in applying such an approach because treatments cannot be applied in a strictly linear way, as research from wide-ranging treatments for a variety of human problems informs us. Norcross and Lambert (2011) have provided a very sage and balanced perspective on what they call the "culture wars" described above that pose the treatment method (i.e., EBPs) against the therapy relationship as the key element in treatment effectiveness:

Do treatments cure disorders or do relationships heal people? Which is the most accurate vision for researching, teaching, and practicing psychotherapy? Like most dichotomies, this one is misleading and unproductive on multiple counts. For starters, the patient's contribution to psychotherapy outcome is vastly greater than that of either the particular treatment method or the therapy relationship (Lambert, 1992; Wampold, 2001). The empirical evidence should keep us mindful and a bit humble about our collective tendency toward therapist-centricity (Bohart & Tallman, 1999). For another, decades of psychotherapy research consistently attest that the patient, the therapist, their relationship, the treatment method, and the context all contribute to treatment success (and failure). We should be looking at all of these determinants and their optimal combinations. (p. 4)

The Search for an Integrated Approach to Therapy

Long before the results of EVT studies demonstrated it, there were those practitioners and researchers who maintained that the therapist was the *chief catalyst* for change in the therapeutic process. They noted that when investigators observed research findings on effectiveness across vastly different settings and with vastly different populations, they found that clients seemed to improve at roughly the same rate (Miller, 2004; Prochaska, 1999). This ran counter to conventional wisdom, because the approaches were so widely varied, ranging from psychodynamic, to behavioral, to systems theory. Furthermore, they concluded that the way to best achieve (and later train others to achieve) effectiveness in providing therapy was to see what factors composed effective therapeutic responses and to integrate them into a single coherent approach. The hope was that this work would equip clinicians with everything that they needed in order to be more effective with a broad variety of clients, using the best from all theories of counseling.

Although they did not do so specifically in response to the EVT–EVB research, several practitioners and theorists turned from a focus on external behaviors or procedures toward a focus on the internal features of the therapist and on the elements that make up effective therapy. This quest created three levels or types of integration (or eclecticism): technical, theoretical, and common factors (Messer & Warren, 1995).

Technical eclecticism (or *technical integration*) refers to the pulling together of techniques or interventions that come from two or more different systems or schools of therapy, but that are used with a given client because of their perceived usefulness in helping with a specific client problem (Hansen, 2002). For example, a client may seek help to stop smoking. The therapist might not be a behaviorist, but he or she may choose to use principles of reinforcement or perhaps implosion techniques to break the smoker's habit. Unfortunately, this form of integration is a "hit-or-miss" approach that focuses on specific techniques to instill change—and a technique-driven approach is a fundamentally unsound strategy on which to base client treatment (Asay & Lambert, 1999; Miller et al., 2005).

The *theoretical integration* movement in psychotherapy sought to find commonalities among approaches to psychotherapy from a transtheoretical (one-theory-fits-all) approach. Hence, the promise of integration was to translate valuable concepts from one "language" to another and to enhance prospects of learning what is effective. How did the theoretical integrationists do? Norcross (1997) put it bluntly, stating that "psychotherapy integration has stalled. . . . [T]he meaning . . . remains diffuse, its commitment typically philosophical rather than empirical, and its training idiosyncratic and unreliable" (p. 86, as cited in Miller et al., 2005, p. 2).

At the turn of the 21st century, some 500 different theoretical approaches to psychotherapy could be identified, with the majority representing attempts at some kind of integration (Miller et al., 2005; Norcross, 2002). Different models of psychotherapy have been derived from a synthesis of theories, techniques, and formats, all in the name of simplicity of theory. Clearly, creating this mind-boggling number of theories was *not* what the proponents of the integrated approach wanted.

The attempt to create a single unified or integrated theoretical approach to psychotherapy, like the attempt to create a manual of specific treatment strategies, fails to take into account the therapist's personal talents, personality traits, personal styles, and theoretical-philosophical preferences (Norcross & Lambert, 2011). Although the "one-size-fits-all" approach of integration may tantalize developing practitioners with the idea that a grand unified theory can be adopted and easily implemented, the result is that the clinician then has very little freedom to adopt a perspective that is in harmony with his or her view of the world. Instead, with theoretical integration, every therapist must adhere to an a priori way of looking at the world of psychotherapy.

The *common factors* or *convergence* approach (Messer & Warren, 1995; Miller et al., 2010; Orlinsky, 2010) also begins with the idea that there is considerable overlap among the various theories and systems of psychotherapy. But rather than seeking to combine theories, those who subscribe to the convergence movement seek to identify the universal elements of the change process that are common to all effective systems of psychotherapy regardless of the different languages they use to describe what they do.

Actually, the *common factors* model has been around quite a bit longer than most seasoned practitioners might want to admit. Miller et al. (2010) point to the work of Saul Rosenweig (1936), whereas Watson (1940), reporting on the conclusions of a panel of experts about the commonalities of different theoretical orientations to psychotherapy deduced that:

> If we were to apply to our colleagues the distinction . . . between what they tell us and what they do, we might find that agreement is greater in practice than in theory . . . we have agreed further . . . that our techniques cannot be uniform and rigid, but vary with the age, problems and potentialities of the individual client and with the unique personality of the therapist . . . *a therapist has nothing to offer but himself.* (p. 29, *italics added*)

Orlinsky (2010) put it more bluntly:

> Despite the field's love affair with technique, nearly a half-century of empirical investigation has revealed that the effectiveness of psychotherapy resides not in the many variables that ostensibly distinguish one approach from another. Instead, the success of treatment is principally found in the factors that all approaches share in common. (p. xxvii)

Frank and Frank (1991) described these common or convergence factors with the metaphor of shared *therapeutically active* ingredients. These ingredients are contained in all therapeutic approaches and can be thought of like the ingredients of painkillers, which compose a variety of products under different names. There may be subtle and unique differences that make each one ideally suited for different conditions (e.g., migraine headaches versus muscle pain versus arthritis), but all have common core elements. Research by Lambert and Barley (2002), which is perhaps the most widely known analysis of common factors, identified four elements that account for the explained variance in all effective psychotherapy and the relative contribution of each to overall client improvement:

1. Extra therapeutic factors (client factors) were the most important, accounting for 40% of the total change.
2. Expectancy, or the placebo effect, accounted for 15% of the improvement.
3. Therapeutic techniques accounted for an additional 15%.
4. Common factors (i.e., the variables that contribute to the therapeutic relationship that can be considered common to most therapies) accounted for 30% of the overall improvement.

The common factors that Lambert and Barley (2002) identified comprise a variety of variables including therapist warmth, empathy, acceptance, and encouragement of risk taking (Lambert, 1992).

These effects are seen regardless of theoretical orientation, and no particular school of psychotherapy seems to be more effective than another (aspects of Lambert and Barley's common factors are discussed in greater detail in Chapters 4 and 5, whereas a larger discussion of the explained and unexplained variance in psychotherapy outcome is discussed in Chapters 5 and 6).

Are these four factors (i.e., warmth, empathy, acceptance, and encouragement of risk taking) all that any clinician needs to be successful? The reality is that, although these factors make up the core elements (and 30% of the effectiveness) of any successful therapeutic endeavor, they are not finally sufficient in guiding a clinician in *how* to conduct therapy. In fact, researchers have shown that training that emphasizes the therapeutic alliance is *not* sufficient to produce client change (Horvath, 2001). According to Miller et al. (2004), "[L]ogically, there is and can never be a 'common factors' model of therapy because all models by definition already include the factors. Even the usefulness of the factors as general organizing principles for clinical practice is uncertain" (p. 3).

It would, nevertheless, appear that "establishing these common content factors of counseling approaches would be a significant step," but "speculations about common content factors of counseling approaches are seldom mentioned in the counseling literature" (Hansen, 2002, p. 315). This makes it difficult to create a clinically useful approach to training or conducting therapy without becoming merely a technical eclectic or theoretical integrationist. We think understanding common factors of the treatment process that all practitioners must face is critical to becoming an expert therapist. The rest of this chapter—and this book—will suggest what we hope is an understanding of the common content factors of effective psychotherapy approaches. The common factors we suggest are based upon a foundation of solid empirically derived research that is clinically useful enough to enhance overall effectiveness, while preserving the poetic individualism and integrity of each individual therapist's approach. What practitioners say they do may be quite different from each other, and what they say they do may be quite different from what they are actually doing. And yet what they all do in common may be simultaneously, paradoxically, and basically the same; they simply describe it differently. Although we earnestly wish that we could take credit for such an observation, Fiedler (1950) can be credited with having empirically come to that conclusion in a small sample size study that was nevertheless prescient of what is being learned with today's mega studies using meta-analysis:

> (1.) Expert psychotherapists[3] . . . create a relationship more closely approximating the Ideal Therapeutic Relationship than . . . nonexperts. (2.) The therapeutic relationship created by experts of one school resembles . . . that created by experts of other schools than it resembles relationships created by nonexperts within the same school. (3.) The most important dimension (of those measured) which differentiates experts from nonexperts is . . . the therapist's ability to understand, to communicate with, and to maintain rapport with the patient . . . less obvious . . . seems to be . . . experts' greater ability to maintain an "appropriate" emotional distance. (p. 444)

The literature from expert clinicians, theoreticians, and researchers has repeatedly reinforced the development, importance, use, and efficacy of the common or convergence factors (see below). In their essence, they represent commonalities between and among all theoretical orientations. According to Hubble et al. (2010),

> Bluntly put, the existence of specific psychological treatments for specific disorders is a myth. By contrast, the empirical case for the common factors is compelling . . . common factors refers to ingredients or elements that exist in all forms of therapy. The body of research amassed on the subject . . . affirms that a core group of factors shared by all treatment

approaches is responsible for change. It also calls for a major reconceptualization of psychotherapy, with particular emphasis on what constitutes the pantheoretical (universal) ingredients, how they are structured, and the way in which they interact to foster positive outcomes. (pp. 28–29)

As such, a convergence factor represents an aspect of the therapy process that is recognized as salient and critical in understanding and facilitating the process of change across a broad spectrum of theoretical diversity. In fact, we believe that there are a number of convergence factors (i.e., universal ingredients or *therapeutic factors*) in psychotherapy that have emerged to provide greater clarity regarding the process of learning how to help others to make changes in their lives. Although we do not claim that the previous edition of our text (Mozdzierz et al., 2009) shaped the authors' thinking, Orlinsky (2010) states that Miller et al. (2010),

abandoned the traditional distinction between common factors and specific factors as an organizing framework . . . and have replaced that with a simpler, more inclusive emphasis on *therapeutic factors* . . . a comprehensive view of all psychotherapy based on research that demonstrates the factors that contribute to effective change for clients. When described in terms of effectiveness . . . there is really only one psychotherapy—defined by what works—and what works derives from elements that are combined more or less effectively in all forms of therapy. (p. xxii)

We argue in this text that there are therapeutic factors that represent a *convergence of understanding* that can be found at the heart of all successful therapy and represent what master practitioners pay attention to. We call these "Domains of Competence," and they are as follows:

1. Connecting with and engaging the client.
2. Assessing and accessing the client's motivations, goals, and strengths.
3. Building and maintaining the therapeutic relationship—an alliance with the client.
4. Understanding a client's cognitive schemas.
5. Addressing and managing the client's emotional states.
6. Understanding and addressing client ambivalence about change.
7. Understanding and using nonlinear-paradoxical understandings, thought processes, and interventions in treatment.

Research and the Convergence of Understanding: Learning and Understanding the Seven Domains of Competence

The second defining characteristic of this book is drawn from the research on *common therapeutic factors* (or what we term *domains of convergence*). Wampold (2010) put it thus: "A model that emphasizes the common factors predicts that, with some qualifications all cogent treatments, embraced by therapists and client competently delivered to a client motivated to engage in the process are equally effective" (p. 56). These factors are the basic ingredients that consistently appear to be identified in the literature as vital to all effective therapy, regardless of a practitioner's theoretical orientation. Several authors have tried to identify and quantify these factors. As mentioned earlier, Lambert and Barley (2002) cited and summarized numerous studies over the last 40 years that have provided interesting, consistent clues regarding therapists' contributions to successful therapeutic outcomes. In particular, they concluded not surprisingly those therapists who exhibit more positive behaviors—warmth, understanding, and affirmation—and fewer negative behaviors—belittling, neglecting, ignoring, and attacking—were consistent predictors of positive outcome. Furthermore, they emphasized the *vital* importance of having a strong therapeutic alliance, focusing on the therapeutic relationship and making discussions about it a regular part of dialogue in therapy, and being willing to spend time on complicated issues with a sense of optimism, which are all positive characteristics of successful therapies. According to Hubble et al. (2010):

> In reality, the common factors are not invariant, proportionally fixed, or neatly additive. Far from it, they are interdependent, fluid, and dynamic. Unlike a manufacturing operation, with linear inputs and predictable outputs, therapy is a reciprocal [non-linear] process, in which the inputs are changed in and by the participants' interaction. In short, their role and degree of the influence of any one factor are dependent on the context: who is involved; what takes place between therapist and client; when and where the therapeutic interaction occurs . . . Much like raw materials in nature, the common factors exist in an unprocessed or minimally processed state and must be used or acted on to create a product or structures. The eventual form a treatment assumes is thus entirely dependent on the materials available; the skills of the artisan; and most important, the desires and preferences of the end user. (p. 34)

The critical, technically complex, and universally agreed upon important areas of focus for all therapies are assessing readiness for change, successful problem solving, and goal alignment; fostering a solid therapeutic relationship; dealing *appropriately* with client defensiveness; understanding complex cognitive schemas, a willingness to focus on the therapeutic relationship; navigating with clients through their emotional landscape; and developing *experiences* of healing. As a result, these factors can be more challenging to learn than techniques. The word *techniques* implies a linear application of simple and easily replicated steps from one instance to another without variation or consideration of context (see Mozdzierz & Greenblatt, 1994). Learning the constellation of factors noted above is demanding and requires learning how to think like a therapist. So if the common factors are the "raw materials" of psychotherapy (as Hubble et al. date so eloquently state), then the nonlinear thinking of master practitioners is the process by which these raw materials are refined into their most potent and useful state. Hence, once one learns how to think like a therapist, the process of providing treatment flows becomes professionally challenging but thoroughly rewarding and enjoyable. Nevertheless, for present purposes, these factors are all integrally related to the crucial domains for which beginning therapists need training.

What Are Domains?

A *domain* can be defined as the scope of a particular subject or a broad area or field of knowledge (Skovholt & Rivers, 2004). In other words, it encompasses all aspects (the breadth and depth) of a particular topic. Regardless of the field of knowledge, mastery of essential domains is what accounts for the differences between the abilities and results of novices *and* experts. Novices can learn the basics of the domain (the breadth) and, over time, develop a richer understanding of the subtleties of it (the depth). As a result, it is worth stressing that domains are not the same as skills or techniques—skills are applied within the context of a domain of knowledge (or field). As such, they represent a refinement of one's thinking within a certain area rather than an application of mechanical skills. The refinement of one's thinking within particular domains includes the thought processes behind skills, explanations, and theories regarding the topic, and research about the subject area. It represents an *understanding and discernment.* The skilled surgeon knows how to operate, whereas the wise surgeon knows not only *how* to operate but also *whether or not to operate* in a given instance.

To further illustrate the difference between being trained to do something and knowing how and when to use it in therapy, consider the use of hypnosis or systematic desensitization. Learning the techniques of hypnosis or systematic desensitization is significantly different from understanding the circumstances of when and *how* it is (or is not) appropriate to use them. *That* is an example of being competent within a particular domain (i.e., fostering a therapeutic alliance). A practitioner may be gifted in the ability to induce a hypnotic trance or construct an anxiety hierarchy for systematic desensitization (skill competence). But if he or she tries to use them in the initial session or with every client (domain incompetence), the result is likely to be more therapeutic failures and discouragement for both the client and the therapist than successes. In fact, this is indicative of linear thinking within a given domain (i.e., "This technique has worked in the past, so it will or should work now"), whereas knowing when *not* to use the particular skill is a type of nonlinear approach to the domain.

When researchers looked at different practitioners' use of these domain-specific concepts compared with procedural concepts (i.e., skills), they found that "experienced counselors displayed greater consistency in the concepts they used than novices" (Skovholt & Rivers, 2004, p. 25). In other words, these experts seemed to be more familiar with the multifaceted and multidimensional aspects of the client's problem behavior (social, interpersonal, etc.) without having to rely on technical aspects of therapy (i.e., techniques) as the novices did. According to Skovholt and Rivers, 2004, this familiarity with domain-specific concepts (e.g., client readiness, treatment goals, the therapeutic alliance, cognitive schemas, and emotional underpinnings) gave them a greater sense of optimism and encouragement about making progress with the client. By contrast, novices tended to focus more on the procedural aspects of a given client problem (i.e., "How do I work with a . . .") rather than focus on the client's concerns. Therefore, it is important to be thoroughly familiar with a domain in order to work within it efficiently (i.e., apply the skill, use the concepts, maximize the result, etc.) and be able to apply nonlinear thinking within the domain to work with a client effectively. In this text, we draw distinctions between linear and nonlinear thinking within each of the domains.

One way or another, one description or another, we contend that all therapies must deal with the issues described in the seven domains. The domains can be called something different, and most often they are known by different names. Different theories may describe the content areas of the different domains in different ways, but the final result is that the domains represent what it is that master practitioners pay attention to.

What Domains Are Not

We do not recapitulate domains into a therapeutic system that forces a therapist to adopt a certain theoretical orientation. Rather, domains of competence enable the therapist to operate within his or her own, unique philosophical framework (Horvath, 2001; Miller & Moyers, 2004). As a result, the domains of competence are the common active ingredients that are a part of all successful therapy, but that offer multiple perspectives within them for counselors to explore and develop lifelong understanding and appreciation (Frank & Frank, 1991). Further, the reader is cautioned *not* to look at these domains as rigid constructs that run parallel to one another and never intersect. Rather, they merge seamlessly within the therapeutic endeavor so that almost every interaction between therapist and client encompasses many (if not all) of the domains together.

Although a therapist could learn all of the basic (and even advanced) skills of psychotherapy, without an understanding of the broader picture of how the seven domains of competence converge and interact with their nonlinear thought processes, many developing and practicing therapists wind up wandering from client to client, becoming frustrated that an intervention or given skill set works with one client, but fails to work with another. However, with sound training and opportunities to develop these elements (i.e., nonlinear thought processes within the seven domains of competence), beginning and more advanced practitioners can develop deeper, more meaningful conceptualizations of their clients' presenting concerns. *That* is what allows for a clearer understanding of *how* to proceed in an efficient and effective manner (Skovholt & Rivers, 2004).

Introducing the Seven Domains of Competence

1. *The domain of connecting with and engaging the client—Part 1: listening and Part 2: responding.* This domain includes both linear and nonlinear listening and responding to clients as primary vehicles for connecting with and engaging the client in the work of therapy. By understanding linear and nonlinear aspects of connecting with and engaging clients—especially in the initial interview—clinicians will be able to increase the probability of clients becoming invested in the therapeutic process in the crucial first sessions.

2. *The domain of assessment—Part 1: clients' symptoms, stages of change, needs, strengths, and resources and Part 2: the theme behind a client's narrative, therapeutic goals, and client input about goal achievement.* This domain describes the linear and nonlinear methods of assessing clients' presenting problems and concerns at multiple levels. That includes attending to clients' readiness for change and their symptom patterns, diagnoses, strengths, and (untapped) resources that can be used in overcoming problems. The domain of assessment also includes actively eliciting client cooperation in the treatment-planning process and developing appropriate preliminary goals for treatment, which are especially important in the early stages of therapy and represent another dimension of connecting with and engaging the client in the treatment process.

3. *The domain of establishing and maintaining the therapeutic relationship and the therapeutic alliance—Part 1: relationship building and Part 2: the care and feeding of the therapeutic alliance.* This domain encompasses perhaps the central aspect of psychotherapy: developing a therapeutic alliance. An integral part of this domain concerns developing an understanding of what factors contribute toward building a trusting therapeutic relationship with a client in the service of establishing and maintaining the therapeutic alliance. It includes such elements as listening empathically, demonstrating respect, and providing hope and ongoing goal alignment. In addition, clinicians must learn to be constantly alert to possible ruptures in the therapeutic alliance and how to repair them.

4. *The domain of understanding clients' cognitive schemas—Part 1: foundations and Part 2: assessment and clinical conceptualization.* This domain requires a clinician to have both linear and nonlinear understandings of clients' schematized view of self, view of others, and view of the world around them. This domain deals with global concepts such as clients' internal response sets and belief systems that guide attitudes, thoughts, and behavior that can impact treatment. As such, it is important for clinicians to understand the nonlinear components of clients' schematized belief systems. It includes becoming proficient in working with the effects of clients' developmental (family-of-origin) dynamics on their perceptions. In addition, utilizing this domain includes skills for helping clients challenge and alter distorted perceptions of the world around them.

5. *The domain of addressing and managing clients' emotional states—Part 1: basic understandings and Part 2: managing common negative emotions in therapy.* This domain defines the nature of emotions in all of their complexity. In addition, it requires the clinician to have an understanding of the relationship between affective expressions, internal feelings, and emotional states, and their role in treatment progress (or lack thereof). Clinicians must learn the art of managing overwhelming emotions (e.g., grief and anger) that clients may express, allowing them to feel emotion in appropriate and productive ways. Likewise, in this domain, clinicians must learn how to access clients' affective states—especially when no emotion appears to be expressed and there ought to be.

6. *The domain of addressing and resolving ambivalence—Part 1: understanding and identifying client ambivalence and Part 2: working with and resolving client ambivalence.* This domain deals with understanding the process of client *ambivalence* in its multiple dimensions as well as developing effective strategies for dealing with it, appropriately holding clients accountable, and successfully helping clients maintain therapeutic focus.

7. *The domain of understanding nonlinear thought processes and utilizing paradoxical interventions.* This domain is the pinnacle of the therapeutic endeavor. It is not a trick or technique, but

a sophisticated method of nonlinear thinking that can be learned and used to quickly and efficiently help to facilitate some relief for clients' suffering and progress toward their therapeutic goals by neutralizing, energizing, tranquilizing, or challenging dysfunctional thought and behavioral patterns. It crystallizes the direct relationship between nonlinear thinking and the previous six domains. Nonlinear interventions are elegant, complex, and yet simple reflections of how human perception contends with reality on an everyday basis. Such interventions reflect a mature understanding of human communication, motivation, and positive influences in encouraging change.

Nonlinear Clinician Attitudes or Dispositions

So imagine a future where scientists will be able to build the perfect clinician. Sounds crazy, right? Some mad, brilliant scientist creating a "Franken-therapist" in a laboratory? But just imagine it for a moment. If you ever saw any of the *Matrix* films, then you saw that the characters had the ability to upload vast information or skills (from flying a helicopter to being a martial arts master) into their brain before going into the matrix (an alternate world) that would make them experts. They would *seem* to be like masters in that world. As it turns out, perhaps the most powerful predictor of a successful therapeutic outcome is the *client's appraisal* of the therapist's qualities. In other words, they *seem* masterly. Lambert and Barley (2002) put it this way:

> In their comprehensive review of more than 2,000 process-outcome studies since 1950, Orlinsky, Grave, and Parks (1994) identified several therapist variables that have consistently been shown to have a positive impact on treatment outcome. "Therapist credibility, skill, empathic understanding, and affirmation of the patient, along with the ability to engage with the patient, to focus on the patient's problems, and to direct the patient's attention to the patient's affective experience, were highly related to successful treatment." (p. 22)

And perhaps one day, neuroscience will make that science fiction into science fact. But until then, you will still have to read and employ deliberate practice. But it did get us wondering, what would such a being need in order to be an ideal therapist? Super caring powers? Deep knowledge or vast intellect? Of course, we would naturally want him or her to have these things, as well as be nonlinear thinkers! But what if we asked the question like this: If such a technology existed, what would you want to have uploaded into your skill set? Well, just as we believe that there are universal domains that all master practitioners use—to some degree or another—we think that there are corresponding attitudes or dispositions that go with each of the domains, which if you watch master practitioners at work, you will see elements of all of these dispositions. So alongside each of the seven domains (in both this text and the advanced volume), we also describe each of these attitudes or dispositions in turn. Briefly, they are:

Domain	Corresponding Clinician Attitudes or Dispositions
1. Connecting and Engaging	1. Curiosity
2. Assessment	2. Collaboration
3. Therapeutic Relationship	3. Optimism and Hope
4. Schema Dynamics	4. Pattern Recognition
5. Emotional System	5. Self-Soothing
6. Ambivalence	6. Mindfulness
7. Paradoxical Intervention	7. Irony

Although these are, by no means, the *only* thing that practitioners should consider, we do feel that each one is paired appropriately with the domain that fits it best. As Orlinsky and Howard (1977) stated, "The inescapable fact of the matter is that the therapist is a person, however much he may strive to make himself an instrument of his patient's treatment" (p. 567). It is the person-hood of the therapist that the client experiences, evaluates, and reacts to in treatment, seemingly no matter what sort of treatment, theory, or technique the therapist espouses to practice.

We also think that, just like with domains, each of these are *additive*. For example, although connecting and engaging requires curiosity as the main nonlinear strategy for clinicians, assessment requires both curiosity *and* collaboration (just like it requires connecting and engaging). Focusing on the therapeutic relationship involves optimism and hope, as well as the capacity to be curious and collaborative. We feel that each of these seven attitudes adds together to make a good picture of what a nonlinear thinking therapist considers when approaching a client, and we present them as a guide for what an aspiring nonlinear thinker considers. In each of the domains, we include how each corresponding nonlinear strategy helps the clinician work more successfully with clients, and we present opportunities for readers to deliberately practice each of the strategies with case studies, transcripts of interactions with masters, and exercises that make these strategies more concrete and applicable. So if you take all seven of these attitudes or dispositions, and incorporate them into *your* thinking and *your* work with the seven domains, we feel that you will go a long way toward becoming a master practitioner.

There is one last piece of the puzzle to complete a therapist's journey from novice to master. That puzzle piece is a roadmap that helps to guide a practitioner to his or her own professional growth and development.

A Developmental Model of Therapist Growth: Guiding the Reader through the Learning Process to Help Speed Understanding of the Seven Domains of Competence and Nonlinear Thinking

It is not enough to simply know about the content areas of the domains (linear thinking); one must also apply them and appreciate the richness, depth, and utility of each (nonlinear thinking). That is the essence of competence, or the ability to do something well. George Leonard, former president of the Esalen Institute in California, eloquently defined mastery as "the mysterious processes during which what is at first difficult becomes progressively easier and more pleasurable through practice" (1992, p. xi). Therapists who can operate within each of the domains competently and have an appreciation for all the factors mentioned above characterize masters in the field (e.g., appreciation of complexity, personal growth, and valuing depth and breadth). It is not something that happens overnight; it is a process of development. We do not want to imply in this text that mastery happens quickly just because a practitioner thinks nonlinearly and can utilize the seven domains. We believe that these are the elements that—when competently employed—make clinicians more effective. However, according to Skovholt and Jennings (2004), in order to achieve mastery, certain things have to take place. In particular,

It is important for developing practitioners to work within a structure that provides opportunities for innovation and support when facing complexities and challenges. In addition, the structures most conducive to growth offer the developing therapist or counselor balanced opportunities for, to use Piaget's terms, assimilating and accommodating new knowledge.

Ultimately, this is all part of the "support/challenge balance," where counselors are not only provided experiences that stretch and even exceed the confines of what they know, but are supported while navigating through what they do not know. (Skovholt & Jennings, 2004, p. 22)

In other words, the keys to successful growth for clinicians are: good learning atmospheres that allow for divergent (i.e., nonlinear) thinking to occur, and supportive experiences that provide the developing therapist opportunities to explore the essential elements that compose successful therapy (i.e., the seven domains). Ideally, this should all take place within a predictable arc of development. Other fields, like medicine, have predictable arcs of development for beginners. There are milestones and benchmarks that trainees hit along the way to mark their progression toward mastery. Until recently, however, models that tracked counselor development throughout their career did not exist (Jennings et al., 2013; Skovholt & Rivers, 2004). Indeed, this lack of a roadmap has often contributed to the problem of therapists feeling lost, confused, frustrated, and ill-prepared to help clients in the real world. The real problem was that many practitioners felt that it might never get better, which typically leads to burnout, or worse (Miller, 2004).

No matter how diverse a community of skilled practitioners may *appear* in their work—what they do, and what processes they attend to and emphasize in working with clients—their practices represent a *convergence* of what is effective! This convergence reflects the thinking of Lave (1988) and Lave and Wenger (1991) and what they have called *situated learning*—the idea that novices gradually acquire expertise from their association and collaboration with a community of experts. Lave assumed the position that a case can be made for learning being social and stemming in large measure from experiences of actually participating in the community of daily activities of what is being learned.

A community of practice involves much more than the technical knowledge or skill associated with undertaking some task. Members are involved in a set of relationships over time . . . communities develop around things that matter to people. . . . For a community of practice to function it needs to generate and appropriate a shared repertoire of ideas, commitments and memories. It also needs to develop various resources such as tools, documents, routines, vocabulary, and symbols that in some way carry the accumulated knowledge of the community . . . it involves practice . . . ways of doing and approaching things that are shared to some significant extent among members. (Situated Learning, n.d., emphasis added)

Lave and Wenger (1991) indicated that novices begin as peripheral participants in a community, but as they improve in their skill level, they move toward "learn(ing) from talk as a substitute for legitimate peripheral participation . . . to learn(ing) to talk as a key to legitimate peripheral participation" (pp. 108–109). Receiving and providing feedback from a community of practice is also an important part of developing mastery through deliberate practice (Ericsson, 2006).

Stoltenberg's Developmental Model

Stoltenberg (1997; Stoltenberg & Delworth, 1987), in recognizing this deficit, proposed a three-level integrated-developmental model of counselor development. These three levels are meant to facilitate a sense of the *typical* personal and professional issues confronted by clinicians at various stages of growth and development. As therapists are able to locate and gauge their sense of progress, they can determine which professional areas (domains) need improvement. Development and growth in professional skill and judgment are not rigid concepts.

According to Stoltenberg, 1997, Level I counselors are characterized by focusing primarily on themselves, feeling highly anxious, and requiring structure. They may not be particularly insightful, and often look for specific techniques (i.e., "How do you . . .?") to utilize with clients. Level II counselors tend to have more confidence in their own ability and seem ready to concentrate on the cognitive and emotional experience of the client. There are, however, some shortcomings in therapists at this stage of development, as they may become overconfident in their abilities, oversimplify issues, or become emotionally overinvolved with their clients and lose professional objectivity. Last, Level III counselors demonstrate an awareness of the cognitive, emotional, and relational aspects of the interaction between the client and themselves. These therapists can listen reflectively with the "third ear", calculate the impact of particular interventions on a client, and see the client completely within his or her context without losing sight of the empathic, therapeutic alliance that is necessary to be effective.

Integrating Stoltenberg's Developmental Model with the Seven Domains

Within each of these levels of development, we insert the corresponding domains of competence that every therapist needs to acquire in order to be effective. Figure 1.1 graphically illustrates this. It is in the shape of a cone in which each level represents a greater refinement and appreciation of

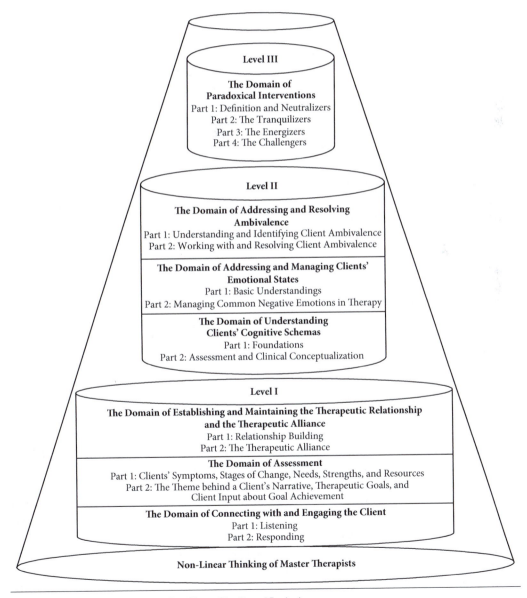

Level III

**The Domain of
Paradoxical Interventions**
Part 1: Definition and Neutralizers
Part 2: The Tranquilizers
Part 3: The Energizers
Part 4: The Challengers

Level II

**The Domain of Addressing and Resolving
Ambivalence**
Part 1: Understanding and Identifying Client Ambivalence
Part 2: Working with and Resolving Client Ambivalence

**The Domain of Addressing and Managing Clients'
Emotional States**
Part 1: Basic Understandings
Part 2: Managing Common Negative Emotions in Therapy

**The Domain of Understanding
Clients' Cognitive Schemas**
Part 1: Foundations
Part 2: Assessment and Clinical Conceptualization

Level I

**The Domain of Establishing and Maintaining the Therapeutic Relationship
and the Therapeutic Alliance**
Part 1: Relationship Building
Part 2: The Therapeutic Alliance

The Domain of Assessment
Part 1: Clients' Symptoms, Stages of Change, Needs, Strengths, and Resources
Part 2: The Theme behind a Client's Narrative, Therapeutic Goals, and
Client Input about Goal Achievement

The Domain of Connecting with and Engaging the Client
Part 1: Listening
Part 2: Responding

Non-Linear Thinking of Master Therapists

Figure 1.1 The Seven Domains that Master Practitioners Attend to and Emphasize

increased complexity, on the way toward mastery. Because Level I counselors are new and focused on more concrete, performance-based aspects of the therapeutic process, the domains of competence that must be mastered at this stage of development include effectively connecting with and engaging the client, performing an accurate assessment, determining the client's readiness for change, setting achievable treatment goals, and building a strong therapeutic alliance.

As therapists mature and develop some mastery in these domains, they begin to realize that there is more to doing therapy effectively than these particular skill sets. It is at this plateau point (between Level I and Level II) that most beginning practitioners are likely to feel lost if they do not know about the normal developmental arc of therapists' abilities. Quite paradoxically (i.e., nonlinearly), such a plateau does not necessarily signify a frustrating conclusion to the learning process, but rather can be a sign of a period of consolidating what has been learned. Those therapists who work through the frustrations of such a period of consolidation (usually through effective supervision) begin to develop mastery of the Level II domains of competence.

At Level II, therapists are better able to focus on more complex client issues and are not as preoccupied with their own performance. These issues include understanding the client's underlying schemas or personality dynamics, managing and working with the client's emotional states, understanding client ambivalence, and being able to comfortably confront client resistance in a nonthreatening manner. These clinicians often feel a sense of pride in their development as they master the various domains. However, just as with the transition from Level I to Level II, if clinicians are not aware of or able to move to the next level, they are likely to eventually become discouraged and impatient with the pace and results of treatment. Likewise, Level II counselors can become impatient with the process of supervision and demonstrate their own sense of autonomy by challenging their supervisors directly or acting out (e.g., displaying inappropriate behavior with clients), all of which can lead to burnout.

If therapists are able to move past this transitional frustration, however, they proceed to the third level of development and begin to synthesize all the domains of competence and development. There is a flexibility and a seamlessness between the cognitive, emotional, and relational elements of the therapeutic process, as well as an ability to be able to be fully present with the client, while at the same time be able to critically reflect on the content and process levels of the session. In effect, there is a maturity in their *thinking*. All of these processes are part of the advanced, nonlinear thought processes of the master therapist. The ultimate demonstration of such nonlinear thought processes is the ability to use appropriate paradoxical interventions to strengthen the therapeutic alliance, increase rapport, orchestrate symptom disengagement (by neutralizing, tranquilizing, energizing, or challenging the client), and facilitate personal growth more quickly and efficiently.

Conclusion

Although this process of mastery does take time, we don't believe that it must necessarily be a painful or mysterious journey. Coexistent with the educational purpose of this text, we also hope to demystify the seemingly unfathomable. We do not believe that the lengthy process of mastery should be an excuse for providing substandard therapy to clients. It is our contention that if one masters the linear and nonlinear thinking aspects of each of the domains for a particular level of development, the end result will be a more effective and personally satisfied clinician compared with those who do not undertake this. Furthermore, as a therapist progresses from level to level and masters the domains of each successive level, he or she will be able to be more effective with a greater versatility in the same way that master therapists are.

In order to accomplish this, this book does the following:

- Targets the training and development of a therapist's thinking ultimately and specifically converging on the use of nonlinear thinking.

- Helps students to learn the essential factors (the seven domains of competence) necessary for any and all effective therapists regardless of their theoretical orientation or individual personality characteristics based on empirical and clinical research as well as clinical experience.
- Places each of the seven domains of competence within the context of Stoltenberg's three-level model of therapist development.
- Places not only the tools but also the thinking behind the use of these tools solidly in the hands of readers, so they can begin incorporating and utilizing them in practice settings or field placements.
- Discusses how current neuroscience research findings relate to the psychotherapy process.
- Discusses how issues of diversity, culture, and context relate to the psychotherapy process.

In addition, we feel that this text is highly innovative in what it does *not* purport to do, such as the following:

- Claim that you will be a miracle-working therapist in seven easy steps! Becoming a therapist takes training, experience, supervision, and time. What this book *does* hope to do is accelerate the natural development of many individuals by introducing the seven domains of competence in a way that is demystified.
- Propose any of the seven domains of competence (especially paradoxical interventions) as a trick, gimmick, or technique that is used to put something over on clients. Rather, we take a relational approach that a therapist must collaborate with clients and be able to gain their cooperation in order to be effective.
- Indoctrinate readers into any particular theoretical orientation or rigid way of conducting therapy. Rather, we help the student to learn the thought processes underlying successful therapy that can be utilized as a part of any school of psychotherapy.

Last, in this second edition of the book, we have added several new features to make it easier to understand the concepts that are presented. First, in the text, there are transcripts with master practitioners working within the domains that we are describing. These sections we have entitled "Don't take OUR word for it!" Here readers can read (and then view, where available) each master working with a client in the specific domain. Also, we have included some transcript material from two full-length cases (The Case of Ashley and The Case of Mike). The videos of these are posted online and can be accessed by going to (ctiv3.alexanderstreet.com). This will allow the reader to be able to watch various elements of each domain to be demonstrated. Last, there is produced introductory material for each domain that can be accessed by going to (ctiv3.alexanderstreet.com). This may be subject to university subscriptions, check with your local library for full access.

In closing, Miller et al. (2005) have cautioned that decades of research have shown "that 'who' the therapist is accounts for six to nine times as much variance in outcome as 'what' treatment approach is employed" (p. 50). This book is written for you and your development as a practitioner with that very idea in mind.

Notes

1. We will discuss the DSM-5 (American Psychiatric Association, 2013) further in Chapter 3.
2. In August 2005, the American Psychological Association's Council of Representatives passed a proposal entitled "Evidence-Based Practice in Psychology" (EBPP), as reported by Gill (2005): "The proposal presented to Council stated that the goals of evidence-based practice initiatives are aimed at improving quality and cost-effectiveness and to enhance accountability. Just as importantly, however, it speaks with one voice about what APA stands for to legislators and third-party entities" (p. 4). For a thorough discussion of the multitude of issues that arise regarding evidenced-based treatments, see Norcross, Beutler, and Levant (2005); Hunsley (2007a); and Kazdin (2008).
3. Psychoanalytic, Rogerian and Adlerian.

The Level I Practitioner Profile

This section introduces the reader to the Level I Practitioner Profile.

Each of the three levels of clinician development that we address (two in this text, the third in our advanced text) represents milestones of accomplishments with certain domains of competence that realistically and typically require understanding and mastery before the practitioner is able to undertake more complex domains. As Stoltenberg (1993; Stoltenberg & Delworth, 1987; Stoltenberg, McNeill, & Delworth, 1998) suggested, Level I practitioners are obviously new to the treatment setting. Although they may have experiences in other helping professions, they most likely are new to the experience of specifically being a therapist or counselor. Having acquired the theoretical academic exposure that is a prerequisite for becoming a practitioner, Level I therapists must now begin to translate what it is that they have learned in the classroom into the practical realm of relating to *real* people with *real* problems; classroom exercises are no longer the focus of attention. Clearly, the transition from the academic to the clinical world is a daunting task for the Level I clinician. Although Level I practitioners may vary considerably in age and life experience (from the new baccalaureate graduate to the midlife career changer), one of their most prominent characteristics is their skewed understanding (or lack of it) of what it is to be a novice practitioner. Both in the literature on training, and in our experiences teaching in courses, conferences, seminars, and workshops throughout the United States, Canada, and Europe, we have observed students at Level I demonstrate many of the same preoccupations and concerns.

Self-versus-Other Focus

One of the signature psychological features of Level I therapists is an understandable but excessive preoccupation with their performance and ability, rather than focusing on the task or client. The self-focus has four different basic elements or components: anxiety, the quest for perfection, insecurity, and an underdeveloped sense of clinical judgment. We outline these briefly here.

Anxiety

The first manifestation of self-focus is the feeling of anxiety about being inadequate to fulfill the role of a therapist. The difference between the level of self-expectation and perceived level of performance can be viewed as the approximate degree of anxiety experienced by the Level I practitioner. If counselors' personal expectations are unreasonably high (and they generally are in the beginning) while they simultaneously doubt their ability, then the anxiety level can be *high* to the point of near immobilization. For some beginning therapists with more realistic appraisals of their abilities, the feeling is more muted. Thus, the more personally mature and life experienced the Level I person is, the more attenuated the feeling of inadequacy may be than in those individuals who have yet to establish a mature personal identity.

The Quest for Perfection

The second manifestation of self-focus found in the Level I practitioner is the muted and implicit search for *performance perfection* in one form or another. This search for perfection is most typically demonstrated in questions such as "How do you . . . ?" "What do you say when the client . . . ?" or "What does it mean when a client . . . ?" The motivation for performance perfection is generally a genuine desire to do good work, help clients, develop expertise, and enhance self-esteem through one's work. However, the sort of questions above represent a reflection of underlying anxiety about being inadequate, doing harm, doing something wrong, being good at what one does, and not doing the right thing. As mentioned above, in this stage of development, such blocks are most likely precipitated by an implied striving to be the ideal or perfect therapist rather than oneself. Such therapists seek comfort in trying to do the right thing and learn techniques as solutions to addressing clients' concerns and problems. Those techniques serve as substitutes for relating to clients in an authentic way. Again, such preoccupations are indicative of focusing on the counselor's ability, rather than on the client's issues and experiences. These preoccupations can cause the counselor to feel blocked or at a loss as to how to help the client, which amplifies the feelings of inadequacy.

Insecurity

The third manifestation of self-preoccupation is a feeling of uncertainty, insecurity, and lack of confidence. Experiencing a lack of confidence prompts Level I therapists to engage in invidious comparison of their own performance with what they perceive the performance of others to be. This has been aptly expressed by a noted master clinician and psychotherapy researcher, Scott Miller:

> [T]he first major crisis in my career was at the outset! Others seemed much more certain of their ability and skills than I did. I'd watch my supervisors or fellow students work and was surprised, and secretly envious, of the confidence with which they stated their diagnostic opinions and offered their technical expertise. I, on the other hand, was plagued by doubt. (quoted in Walt, 2005, p. 1)

Again, this is a common experience for new therapists. Because of the general lack of confidence and uncertainty in a new role, perhaps the biggest manifestation of this is an implied concern with one's performance (i.e., "How well am I doing?"). Obviously, such concern reflects self-preoccupation about one's performance and not a focus on how the client is doing.

Underdeveloped Sense of Clinical Judgment

The fourth manifestation of self-focus in Level I counselors is the underdeveloped sense of *clinical judgment.* At Level I functioning, because of a lack of clinical experience and of clinical judgment due to inexperience, the counselor-in-training can be prone to developing an overidentification with the client. Identification with the client should be in the service of developing empathy with the plight and feelings of the person and not the person himself or herself. There is a substantial difference between these two positions of identification. The former expresses, "It's just awful to feel taken advantage of!" The latter expresses, "I feel just like Suzy, who *is* being taken advantage of." In such instances, clients' difficulties become compounded by the practitioner's failure to keep her or his personal issues from interfering with clients getting the benefits for which they came to therapy. The Level I practitioner is vulnerable to such misjudgments, which can lead to practitioner burnout.

Where to Begin?

Given these basic Level I challenges, cautions, and concerns, where does one begin? This is a question with several different meanings. First, where do we begin in presenting the entirety of the field of psychotherapy? The truth is that although, in this text, the Level I domains are presented serially— (1) connecting with and engaging the client; (2) assessing the client, accessing strengths, and goal setting; and (3) establishing a therapeutic relationship and the therapeutic alliance—they are interwoven during the therapeutic encounter. The reader is cautioned about thinking, "Okay, I have to master all of domain 1, then all of domain 2 . . ." In fact, that would be a perfect example of linear thinking.

So how does one do this? We believe that to effectively work with these contradictory elements, the initial therapy session requires the development of nonlinear thinking as a means of accomplishing multiple tasks such as:

- Connecting with and engaging the client in the therapeutic process.
- Assessing clients' needs and symptoms, as well as their strengths and resources.
- Empathically understanding the client *and* her or his unique situation through their stage of change or story of their problem.
- Establishing rapport and instilling hope in a client that he or she can experience relief from symptoms that are disruptive and emotionally painful though the therapeutic relationship.

The clinician must do all of this without alienating the client. Although this may appear to be a very tall order, we believe that even the Level I therapist, with the proper training, can accomplish these beginning tasks. This represents the beginning of effective psychotherapy and can offer much-needed help to clients, even if they come to therapy with complex and difficult issues. The first very important task for Level I practitioners to understand and become familiar with is connecting with and engaging the client for treatment—it is the first domain of competence to which we turn our attention.

2

The Domain of Connecting with and Engaging the Client

Listening

Introduction: The Mob Boss Is Your Client

The first session with a new client can be daunting. But imagine how much more intimidating it would be if the client was a mafia boss. This is the premise of the movie *Analyze This* with Robert DeNiro and Billy Crystal. In their first session, DeNiro (as mob boss Paul Viti) says that he is there to get help for a "friend" who has been having panic attacks. He is resistant when Crystal (as psychiatrist Bernie Sobel) tries to get DeNiro to focus on himself. Finally, Crystal, employing some nonlinear thinking, realizes that something is not quite right, and says: "I'm gonna go out on a limb here, and say that your 'friend' is really you." At which point DeNiro looks at him, smiles knowingly, and points his finger saying: "You . . . you got a gift. You saw right through me. You're good. You, my friend, gotta gift!"

Now although this might not be the most clinically amazing depiction of the psychotherapeutic art at work, it does say something about the first domain—connecting and engaging with the client. In the first session, clients may not tell you exactly what their problem is, or—as in the case with DeNiro—*who* the client is, until they feel a sense of connection and engagement in therapy. This is the therapist's first, and possibly most important job. To do this successfully requires linear and nonlinear listening and responding, and this is what we feature in these next two chapters.

Truly understanding what someone's verbalizations mean is vital for a therapist. That's the task set for the therapist, and as such, the first session is an adventure in listening and understanding while simultaneously connecting and engaging with a client. That can be daunting for Level I counselors. Entire books have been devoted to the topic of how to conduct this crucial, initial meeting. There are multiple tasks that must be accomplished: informed consent, orientation to the therapeutic process, the collection of essential demographics, mandated intake forms, issues of payment, cancellation policies, satisfaction surveys, privacy policy, and more. Unfortunately, with so many different tasks requiring attention, the client and his reason for coming for therapy are almost afterthoughts. In recognizing the many demands impinging on the Level I counselor, it is relatively easy to understand why it is tempting for such a beginning practitioner to take a default position that is linear in its emphasis.

One of the characteristics of linear thinking/processes is its expediency—after all, the fastest way to get from one place to another is in a straight line. The initial interview guided by linear thinking then becomes a series of checklists and a sprint to find the correct answer for the question "Does this client fit the criteria for this particular DSM-5 diagnostic category?" The answer to such a linear question (i.e., simple question, easy answer) accomplishes many purposes simultaneously. It helps to focus a practitioner's attention by looking for symptoms that cluster logically (e.g., depressed mood, weight loss, insomnia, lack of pleasure in most things, suicidal thoughts, etc., all diagnostic signs of depression). It also decreases a Level I practitioner's level of anxiety about what to do (e.g., things required by a clinical supervisor, clinic procedures, quality assurance, insurance companies, laws, and government regulations) and how to do it (e.g., ask the questions that get the "facts" to fill out the required forms). Each of these boosts feelings of confidence (e.g., "I got all the right information and the diagnosis!"). Thus, a linear approach can facilitate rapport building simply by decreasing the therapist's anxiety. (More on the assessment of symptoms is covered in Chapter 4, and rapport building is covered in Chapter 6.)

However, such linear thinking alone does not necessarily guarantee doing the client much good either in the short term or in the long term. As Dr. Katherine Nordal, the American Psychological Association's executive director for professional practice, has said, "Psychotherapy is not a linear practice where 'patient plus effective treatment always equals good outcomes,'" (DiAngelis, 2010, p. 42). For example, the majority of clients don't necessarily derive much benefit from knowing their DSM-5 (American Psychiatric Association, 2013) diagnosis, unless, that is, they have come for treatment wanting to know, "What's wrong with me?" Most times, clients *know* what is wrong with them (e.g., they're anxious, depressed, traumatized, can't sleep, conflicted over an important decision, facing some sort of failure, etc.) and really just want the clinician to help them get better (Miller et al., 2005). The first step toward helping a client is by making a positive *connection* with the client. When a therapist successfully *connects* with a client and *engages* a client, the therapist can also simultaneously accomplish the task of collecting the necessary linear information required for diagnosis, billing purposes, and so on, as well as begin to address the client's question (i.e., "Can I be helped?"). Decades of psychotherapy research overwhelmingly reveal that the best way of making such a therapeutic connection is by listening and responding to a client in very particular ways.

Connecting with a client means that there is a felt mutual understanding between client and clinician as to what a client is feeling and thinking. As Novotney (2013) notes,

> Research suggests that effective therapists have a sophisticated set of interpersonal skills, including verbal fluency, warmth, acceptance, empathy and an ability to identify how a patient is feeling. They also can form strong therapeutic alliances with a range of patients. (p. 50)

In our discussion below, we discuss listening attentively and acutely in both a linear and nonlinear manner as ways of connecting. It is incumbent upon clinicians to make themselves available to their clients. That is, to allow themselves to resonate in harmony to what a client is feeling and thinking. It is simultaneously demanding, potentially draining, but very rewarding work.

Clinician Attitude and Disposition: Curiosity

"The important thing is not to stop questioning. Curiosity has its own reason for existing."
—Albert Einstein

"The cure for boredom is curiosity. There is no cure for curiosity."
—Dorothy Parker

Curiosity. It may be the most important—or basic—attitude or disposition that a clinician may have. And it is not just because it inspires creative problem solving, deep probing, or being nosy (all of which are synonymous with curiosity). It is important because of an older, deeper meaning. Curiosity comes from the Latin root word *cura,* which means "to care for, to cure." Therefore, to be curious about something, or someone, really means to care about them and to seek a cure. This is the *best* place to start for a clinician: to care about the plight of the client and to want to learn more in order to help them. Curiosity is defined as "A desire to know or learn . . . A desire to know about people or things that do not concern one . . . An object that arouses interest, as by being novel or extraordinary."

Kashdan and Steger (2007) define curiosity as "intentionally seeking novel and challenging events, people with greater curiosity stretch or expand their knowledge, skills, and goal-directed efforts" (pp. 160–161). People who are more naturally curious tend to report better well-being and tend to derive more meaning out of life. These individuals tend to approach (rather than avoid) novel situations or complex activities. This is an ideal description of most master clinicians. Remember the discussion in the Introduction chapter ("Am I a Nonlinear Thinker?"), if you found yourself nodding yes to the description of liking puzzles or mysteries, then you may be more naturally (i.e., trait) curious.

So when master clinicians are meeting with a client for the first time, they are connecting and engaging with them through their curiosity. They are deeply concerned for the individual, and they pay attention to things that arouse their natural curiosity. As you watch the videos of these masters at work, see how they follow this curiosity and how it develops in session. Look for how it helps to connect with and engage the client in therapy. Also see if these instances of curiosity also have elements of nonlinear thinking in them?

Finally, consider your own curiosity. What makes you curious? Do you remember times in your life when your curiosity led to some discovery that you would have never found out if you were not curious? And how does one develop curiosity? Think about how curiosity helps you to listen better (i.e., nonlinearly) to what a client is saying. (Variation: Discuss the above questions in class and develop a list of examples of, or activities to develop curiosity.)

Listening

Listening. At the heart of all counseling and psychotherapy, listening is the one common activity required by all therapists in every session. After all, listening ultimately has a significant effect on what and how a practitioner responds to a client. But, *how* individual therapists listen and *what* they listen for are important to distinguish. Master practitioners use listening effectively to identify those client statements that are more clinically significant. This allows the therapist to respond more effectively, as well as help the client to feel validated, affirmed, and significant. Knowing how to listen nonlinearly is especially important because it helps to shape what to listen for, which in turn helps to shape the questions therapists will want to ask as well as the comments they make. Such listening also helps clients move along the change process. Listening in both linear and nonlinear ways facilitates the identification, clarification, and development of strategic goals that a client would like to accomplish. Yet this is often overlooked or given short shrift in training programs. We distinguish between linear and nonlinear listening, provide guidance on how to effectively listen both ways, and delineate how both are essential to the domain of connecting with, engaging, and assessing.

How Do You Listen in a Linear Way?

Listening effectively in psychotherapy as well as in other areas of life requires both linear and non-linear awareness. In fact, it is the true master practitioner who realizes that he or she is listening both linearly and nonlinearly at the same time. No matter how disjointed, evasive, quirky, exaggerated, or hesitant a story may appear, what a client has to say gives therapists their first glimpse into a client's world. It is a mistake to gloss over and dismiss what a client says and how the client says it on the surface. As a result, we touch on what it is to listen in a linear manner and how to listen linearly. That is the starting point of all psychotherapy. The two basic elements of linear listening are listening for content or information, and listening for feelings.

Listening for Content or Information

Listening for content or information is the most basic aspect of communication. It represents one person simply transmitting information to another person. It is the *what* that is being said (Carkhuff, 2009). To use the cliché from the old television show *Dragnet,* when you listen for content or information, you are listening for "Just the facts, ma'am." Content is factual or observational in nature, and can be about the past, present, or future. Content represents the *what* we are talking about. For example: "I had pancakes for breakfast this morning." The content is factual (pancakes for breakfast) and about the past (this morning). Being factual means that there was little or no interpretation necessary (i.e., there is not that much to interpret when it comes to pancakes). Observational comments, however, may contain ambiguity and require some interpretation. For example, consider the statement "I think my husband is cheating on me." It is a statement about the present and about what a client has been thinking, and the content is observational because the person believes this is happening, but is not sure. Hence, it is open to interpretation and is ambiguous. That is, does cheating mean a torrid sexual affair, an emotional entanglement, or innocent flirtation? In addition, because it is observational, there is no proof but rather only suspicion of cheating. In Clinical Exercise: Listening for Content or Information, we present an exercise regarding various patient comments that are made that require judgments about the nature of listening for content or information.

Clinical Exercise: Listening for Content or Information

Directions: Read each statement and determine if the information or content is factual or observational, and if it is about the past, present, or future.

1. "I wish that I hadn't rushed into the marriage. I wish I had gotten to know my husband better, first!"
2. "I developed migraine headaches in my third year of medical school."
3. "I've seen lots of therapists in the past, so I'm familiar with therapy. I need a neutral resource and some tools to get through a crisis."
4. "When I'm made partner in my firm, my finances will improve."
5. "I have three children, ages 10, 6, and 4."

Variation: Each person writes a statement and shares with others. Make sure it is either factual or observational, and that it is either past, present, or future focused.

Why is content important? Listening for content provides basic information about what the client reports to be his or her problem, where it stems from, potential goals for treatment, and client assets that may be used to address the problem. Content also reveals what area of a client's life needs to be the focus of attention. For the Level I therapist, consciously paying attention to content is a way of slowing down the pace of one's thinking, focusing more and not getting too far ahead of the client. This determination to slow down on the therapist's part decreases the likelihood that the therapist will foreclose (or decide) on a strategy or conclusion before a client has told the full story. In addition, listening for content and information can also help a therapist know how to respond in a way that solidly engages the client and facilitates an assessment of the situation (Carkhuff, 2009).

When we describe listening for content as being validating to a client, it is more than an exercise in collecting facts. From a humanistic point of view, it is reasonable to conclude that every human being has a story to tell—it is *their* story and it is a personal, sensitive, sometimes sad, and even tragic account, often times with many twists and turns, triumphs, and failures. Allowing a client to tell their story is important from the client's point of view. At the same time, listening to the client's story and its pathos (arousing pity or sorrow in a listener or reader) as a practitioner can be frustrating at times. Clients are not necessarily accomplished in reporting their history. They often ramble, don't remember dates, jump from one topic to another, don't complete their thoughts, leave out information, are confused, distraught, become lost in laborious details, assume that the clinician knows more about them than is the case, and report that they must sound like they are not making any sense (a very frequent comment from clients). Contrast that with the clinician who is in need of collecting information for administrative, professional/clinical, legal, and bureaucratic purposes. However, the investment of time to hear the client's story can often create a more powerful bond with the client (see Chapters 6 and 7) and may yield some important diagnostic information (see Chapters 4 and 5).

Listening for Feelings

If listening for content and information provides the facts in black and white, then listening for feelings gives therapists all of the colors, thus enriching a client's story and making it their very personal narrative. Clients universally have multiple wide-ranging feelings of varied intensity about the content that they are relating. The type and intensity of feelings provide crucial additional information about the importance of the statements that they are making or the stories that they are telling (Carkhuff, 2009; Skovholt & Rivers, 2004). But clients sometimes report having no feelings. Because of our increasing understanding about the psychological impact of all sorts of trauma, we understand that such reports are really a manifestation of *psychological numbness*. The irony is that numbness is actually a feeling state. That said, what is it about given facts and circumstances that a client is relating that gives rise to such intensity of feelings (including a client's numbness) that, in turn, often become a focal point for the work of therapy? There are three basic methods for determining what a client is feeling: by what the client says, by the client's demeanor, and by the counselor's own feelings in reaction to the client's story or verbalizations about some particular circumstance (see list below).

Methods of Listening for Feelings

Listening for feelings based on what the client says
Listening for feelings based on the client's demeanor (i.e., behavior or what the client is doing)
Listening for feelings based on the counselor's feelings in reaction to the client (cognitive tier)
Listening for feelings based on the counselor's feelings in reaction to the client (emotional tier)

Consider this example:

Mike:	"Yeah, I dunno . . . I just don't want to look weak in front of people."
Therapist:	"I know what looking weak means to me, but I'm not sure how you mean it."
Mike:	"Well, you know . . . I don't want people to think they can walk all over me."
Therapist:	"What's your thinking? What would it mean to you if people could 'walk all over' you and take advantage of you?"
Mike:	"Because if people can walk all over me then I'd feel . . . you know . . . weak, powerless, pathetic . . . and not much of a man. I'd be a nobody, a failure. I don't matter."
Therapist:	"Weak, powerless, pathetic . . . and not much of a man . . . that really sounds like an ugly way to go through life."
Mike:	"You got that right!"

The first method, listening for feelings based on what a client says, is the most linear and straight-forward. When Mike says, "I don't want to look weak" the *stated* feeling that is associated with the statement is fear. Of course, listening for feelings isn't as simple as that (as we discuss below). There are elements of uncertainty to the expression of feelings (e.g., what does it feel like to be "weak, powerless, pathetic?"). But generally speaking, when feelings are expressed, it is a fairly accurate place for counselors to begin understanding their client.

The second method for determining, assessing, and understanding a client's feelings is listening for feelings based on a client's demeanor. This type of listening involves detecting what emotion a client is conveying with his or her comments and behavior. For example, if a client is talking about someone or some event and begins to cry, his *demeanor* suggests that he is sad. Likewise, if a client is describing an accomplishment that she is proud of and is smiling broadly, it suggests that she is feeling happy. Or if a client's eyes begin to well up with tears even slightly while discussing something, it suggests very sad and strong feelings that require follow-up. Such behaviors are a genuine expression of feeling, particularly because clients are usually unaware of them until they are pointed out. Novice practitioners all too often will tend to ignore such behavioral expression of feelings for a variety of reasons including: not knowing what to say, not wanting to upset a client any further than they already are, not knowing what such behaviors mean, and so forth.

Listening for feelings based on a client's demeanor requires observation or reading of the client—what a client looks like when speaking? What is it that can be seen on a client's face?[1] What are the qualities of the client's speech? Is it loud, soft, subdued, or the like? What is the tone of voice? Calm? Excited? Agitated? Monotone? Does this appear to be the client's characteristic way of communicating or specific to the circumstances for which they are coming for treatment? All of these, if accurately read, yield clues for astute clinicians to gather. Equally valid observations can be made when therapists are confused by what they are reading in a client's voice and demeanor, and simply ask the client for clarification of what they have observed. That's correct: It is perfectly legitimate for a clinician to report being confused. That's especially the case when the practitioner observes a notable difference between stated feelings and behavioral expressions. Many of these same elements are a part of sound assessment, which is discussed in Chapters 4 and 5.

Sometimes a therapist can determine what a client is feeling by using her or his own feelings as an emotional barometer. But when a counselor uses her or his own feelings in order to listen for client feelings, this is a less straightforward (i.e., nonlinear) process. Thus, there is a greater possibility for error (i.e., misreading a client). Such nonlinear listening, which we discuss later in this chapter, requires some degree of intuiting or guessing (Carkhuff, 2009; Egan, 2009).

There are two tiers to listening for feelings: the *cognitive tier* and the *emotional tier*. Only one, the cognitive tier, is linear and better suited for Level I counselors. Becoming at ease with using this type of listening, however, allows a person to deal with the emotional tier more easily (these topics are discussed in the chapters related to the therapeutic alliance and client emotions).

In listening for feelings using a counselor's own feeling-cognitive tier, a counselor listens to a client's story and asks, "If I were in this person's shoes, how might I feel?" Think about the vignette with "Mike" above, what does it mean to be "weak" or "pathetic"? Another way of putting this is to ask, "What would it be like to be in this person's shoes?" This approach is particularly helpful when a client may have a more constricted emotional range and is unable or unwilling (for whatever reason such as lack of trust, resistance, stage of change, or personal emotional disposition) to share much information with the counselor. For example, a client may come for treatment and describe in a dispassionate tone of voice how he got into an automobile accident in which his car was hit and spun into oncoming traffic, and faced a tractor-trailer truck barreling down on him. But if neither the client's words nor demeanor shows the slightest hint of feeling, something is amiss. Thus, a counselor must ask, "If I were in this situation, how might I feel—what would that experience be like?" The answer would probably be some variation of "That would be terrifying!" Having this information can help a counselor to decide how to best respond to the client, and can also provide important clues as to a client's problems, state of mind, and readiness for change, which are all crucial to the process of connecting with, engaging, and assessing the client. Listening for feelings is also important because it is the window to what is important to an individual. How often do you have feelings about something that isn't important to you? Not very often. What is important to a client is something that the client values; that's what they have feelings and emotions about: What is valued.

We present Clinical Exercise: Listening for Feelings to illustrate this further.

Clinical Exercise: Listening for Feelings

Directions: Find a classmate or partner, and practice listening for feelings. Have each person in the dyad recall and record a recent event that evoked particular feelings (positive or negative). After writing down what was felt without sharing it with your partner, take turns listening to each other's story. When the person verbally sharing his or her story has finished, the listener should record what the storyteller was feeling and what method of listening for feeling (e.g., what was said, demeanor, or feeling reaction in the counselor) was used to draw that conclusion. Switch roles and have the first listener share his or her story while the partner listens. Repeat the step of writing down the storyteller's feeling(s) and what listening for feeling method was used. Once both partners have taken turns, compare the original feeling(s) written down by the storyteller with the feeling(s) recorded by the listener and method used for identifying the feeling(s). How accurate were the written responses? What methods did you use? You may you want to pay particular attention to the actual vocabulary words that signify feelings and emotions.

Variation: In a public place (e.g., a store, restaurant, or mall food court), do some people watching. Pick out individuals who are engaging in conversations and try to determine what they are feeling and what emotions they are expressing. Positive or negative? Which method of listening for feeling did you use to determine it?

How to Listen in a Nonlinear Way

Listening in a linear manner is an important but limited basic tool for all therapists. The therapeutic information that is derived by training oneself to listen for content and information as well as listen for feelings is important. But it does not necessarily provide important details about clients' lives such as information that a client is unprepared to disclose to a clinician. Thus, for a fuller picture of a client, it is important to learn to listen in nonlinear ways. Clinical Exercise: Beginning the Use of Nonlinear Thinking may help to begin to demonstrate this.

Clinical Exercise: Beginning the Use of Nonlinear Thinking

Because human beings have become more and more civilized, they have become increasingly reliant upon formal language as a means of communicating with one another. At the same time, it soon becomes obvious that important aspects of communication have very little to do with verbal language. It has long been known that the manner in which someone says something is as important as, if not more important than, the particular words that are said. Lederer and Jackson (1968) elaborated on this in a more elemental way:

> Every message has at least three aspects—the report aspect, the command aspect, and the context aspect. The report aspect consists of what is said or written, the actual meaning of the words, the content of the message—what is literally asked for, reported. The command aspect helps define the nature and meaning of the message, indicating how it is supposed to be heard, how the sender is attempting to influence the nature of his or her relationship with the receiver.... When "Go to hell" is said with a snarl and a menacing glance, the report and command aspects reinforce each other. A very different message is conveyed by "Go to hell" said with a smile.... The context aspect is determined by the cultural implications of the situation of the communicants.... There are many instances when the message received is not the message sent. (pp. 100–101)

As a brief example of this, consider the following identical sentences. But as you read them to yourself, accent the particular words that are italicized and ask yourself how the meaning of the sentence is changed slightly by emphasis on a different word. A different version of this same exercise would be to say these six sentences out loud with your voice inflection emphasizing the italicized words in each sentence:

I don't want to go with you.
I *don't* want to go with you.
I don't *want* to go with you.
I don't want to *go* with you.
I don't want to go *with* you.
I don't want to go with *you*.

- What were the linear aspects of these sentences (information and feelings)?
- When speaking the sentences (or hearing them spoken), what differences in meaning did you detect when emphasis changed to a different word?
- How did the sentences differ when you heard the different inflections?
- Do some of the sentences with different inflections signify potentially more noteworthy meanings?
- What noteworthy meanings can you detect that would most likely be conveyed to someone?

This enjoyable little exercise illustrates the fact that we are influenced not by words alone (i.e., all six sentences are identical in the words used) but by the various ways in which human beings can qualify the meaning of the words they use to express themselves through tonal inflection. Now imagine, as Lederer and Jackson (1968) noted above, how the interpretation changes if the person says this with a wry, playful smile—or an angry scowl. Does the meaning change substantially? This is but one example of the complex phenomenon of human communication and the need to listen nonlinearly. (See the end of the chapter for suggested possible meanings when the emphasis is placed on different words in each of the identical sentences.)

As the above exercise demonstrates, there is more to listening than just the information contained in what a person is saying (i.e., "I don't want to go with you") and the emotion. In fact, nonlinear listening requires that a therapist does several things when hearing a client's story, including the following:

1. *Listening* not only with one's ears but also with one's eyes, feelings, and intuitions, and a generally open mind.
2. *Hearing* things that aren't spoken or are conspicuous by their absence.
3. *Identifying* certain things that clients may spend too much time discussing (i.e., red herrings).
4. *Understanding* the subtleties of language, and what the words, expressions, images, behaviors, and feelings a client expresses really signify.

In order to demonstrate this kind of listening more clearly, we have organized the typical examples of nonlinear listening into the following categories:

1. Listening for congruence (i.e., correspondence—or lack of correspondence—between what is said and what is meant)
2. Listening for absence (i.e., what is not said—either by silence or information overload)
3. Listening for presence (i.e., nonverbal behaviors that add meaning)
4. Listening for inference (i.e., the purpose behind "I don't want . . ." statements)
5. Listening for resistance (i.e., the desire not to change)

In order to remember this, we conveniently use the acronym, CAPIR (like "caper"). We describe each of these categories below.

Congruence (i.e., Correspondence—or Lack of Correspondence—between What Is Said and What Is Meant)
Listening for correspondence between what someone says and how it is said is called *congruence,* and it is an important part of nonlinear listening. At its most fundamental level, incongruence (or the dissimilarity between what someone says and how he or she says it) represents a discontinuity between processes: When a client's story or messages are incongruent, what he or she is experiencing inside and what he or she is expressing outside simply do not match. A discussion of congruence and its importance in therapy must make several distinctions.

Although it may not come as a surprise, most human beings do distort, exaggerate, withhold information, and even lie. Some people may do such things better than others. There are any number of reasons why a client might do this, but one of the most prominent is because he or she is not prepared to accept the consequences of telling the truth (e.g., out of embarrassment, shame, guilt, or fear of loss of prestige). Another prominent reason that someone might lie is because it can provide him or her with some benefit (e.g., rewards, putting others at a disadvantage, and getting off the hook). How do you know if a client's narrative is truthful?[2] Sometimes it is impossible to tell, and sometimes not. What a therapist is more interested in determining is whether or not there is correspondence between the conscious story and the unconscious story being told in therapy. The way that human beings commonly sense if someone is being congruent is by determining whether what a person says matches with what they do (their behavior) or how they appear (demeanor). When therapists listen for congruence, they are listening in a nonlinear way to determine if two stories (i.e., conscious and unconscious) match. It is essential for integrity to rule the psychotherapeutic process.

Part of that integrity depends on an honest exchange taking place between client and therapist and between the client and him- or herself. For example, if a woman describes a bad marriage at considerable length, but then states half-heartedly (with a heavy sigh), "I guess I should get a divorce," it obviously lacks conviction. The words don't necessarily match the deep sigh or any conviction. It is at that moment in time that the therapist can state, "It doesn't sound as though you are terribly convinced of your own conclusion." When the therapist notes the discrepancy, it can help the client to become familiar with his or her ambivalence (see Chapters 12 and 13) as represented between the conscious story (i.e., "I guess I should get a divorce") and the unconscious story (i.e., the deep sigh and lowered tone of voice). Detecting such a disconnect can potentially be the gateway to understanding the core of such a client's dilemma: "I want to get a divorce, but I can't do so without feeling like a failure, facing great uncertainty, losing face, and becoming just another divorcée!"

Sometimes, the discrepancies detected are a matter of therapist interpretation or a matter of miscommunication between the therapist and the client. At times, however, inconsistencies are a matter of deception (i.e., either self-deception or deceiving the therapist). Whatever the underlying reason, inconsistency provides information for a therapist that may not be present on the surface, but that is crucial to being effective. When these inconsistencies happen, therapists can respond in ways that foster a client's engagement. Pointing out inconsistencies should never be conducted in an aggressive or accusatory manner, but rather in a friendly way as if the therapist is confused or looking for clarification, as described below (and in Chapter 3).

Nonlinear listening for congruence involves using all of one's senses, including a sense of curiosity and empathy. Taking a client's words only at face value is a linear approach to therapy that can be counterproductive. As mentioned earlier in this chapter, one thing that is integral to the process of nonlinear listening is a counselor's sense of curiosity. The curiosity of nonlinear listening must always be finely tuned and begins with sensitizing oneself to the words that a client uses. Words expressing emotions and feelings such as *hate, hurt, fear, love, sad,* and *lost* have vastly different meanings from one person to another and must be elaborated upon for their specific meaning to a particular client. If they are not, a therapist runs the risk of proceeding with a client from a faulty set of assumptions. Consider the following example. Because of his adult son's long history of disappointments, arguments, incidents of drug abuse, and hospitalizations for mental illness, a client stated, "I think I hate my son! I'm ashamed to say that!" In actuality, despite the overt power of the statement, the man's expression of feeling hatred for his son is somewhat ambiguous, as is the way in which he said it. Exactly what does the word *hate* mean to him? It may pass through his lips in one way, but what passes through his lips, what we hear, and what he actually means upon closer scrutiny may have entirely different meanings. Does he mean he hates (i.e., detests) his son? Or, does he perhaps mean that he hates his son's behavior? Hating his son and hating his son's behavior contain two vastly different meanings. Separating the son's behaviors from the personhood of the son is an important distinction to make. The first step in nonlinear listening is to make sure that you listen for such distinctions. They can have vastly different implications for the direction of therapy. Or take this example:

Ashley: "Well, I'm here because I feel that I have recently hit my limit. I am at my wits end."
Therapist: "That sounds serious, can you tell me a bit about what's going on?"
Ashley: "I don't know where to begin. I have been married for almost 8 years. I have two children, aged six and three, and I work for a local hospital here in town as a medical billing supervisor, which is very stressful in this economy."

Therapist: "Wow! That is a lot to manage. How do you do it?"

Ashley: "Well, that's the thing. We've won awards for our efficiency and productivity 10 out of the last 12 months this year. So the expectations on our department are huge. I have to be on top of everything. And if I'm not, it all comes crashing down."

Therapist: "Can you give me a recent example of when you were not 'on top of things' and they 'all came crashing down?'"

Ashley: "Sure, that's kind of the reason that I came to see you. The other day I was home with my kids because school and daycare were closed due to the holiday. The person who comes and cleans weekly couldn't come, and the house was especially messy (which I can't stand). I had to do some work via telecommuting . . . even though I had taken the day off. It was the end of the month, and if I didn't get a particular report done, there would've been thousands of dollars lost for the hospital. So I got the kids situated with a movie, then started to straighten out the house, but I kept feeling like I had to answer e-mails from work. I felt guilty that the kids were plopped in front of the TV, but I needed to get some work done. But before I could even get to that, I really had to clear the clutter (I can't work if there is clutter around!). Before I knew it, the morning had gone, it was lunchtime, and I was still in my pajamas. So as I got the kids' lunch together, I got a call from my assistant saying that the CEO was looking for me and needed to speak with me right away. I had an awful feeling that it was not good. At that very moment, my three-year old spilled his entire lunch of Spaghetti-Os all over our new sofa (light beige, so it stained it nicely!), and I lost it. I started crying and shrieking. I called my husband to come home, and I went to bed. I couldn't get out of bed the whole next day I had such a splitting headache. Thank God it was a Saturday, and I didn't have to be at work."

By listening carefully to Ashley and what she meant by her comment of "all came crashing down," the therapist is able to draw out more detail and get into Ashley's world as she describes her perspective on what happened.

When a lack of congruence is due to some deception on the client's part, it is important to understand the circumstance surrounding it (e.g., is the client trying to save face versus trying to evade being caught doing something wrong?). For example, you see Bob drop a bowling ball on his foot, yell out in pain, grimace, and start hopping around on one foot. You would use your powers of observation and (correctly) conclude that he was in pain. However, when you go over to help him, Bob dismisses you and says, "I'm okay! I'm okay!" while he is still wincing. This is not consistent (or congruent) because you know it isn't true! Bob is deceiving himself, when it is obvious that he is in pain. Inconsistencies in what and how clients express something reveal that they are unsettled about something. Pursuing such unsettled discrepancies between conscious and unconscious processes is one of the major avenues through which therapeutic movement occurs. Returning to poor Bob, why would he want to deny what is obvious? Maybe he feels embarrassed at his carelessness, or perhaps he feels that to acknowledge pain is a personal failing (i.e., weakness). In that case, he is clearly unsettled about it and chooses to deny physical pain to avoid emotional embarrassment.

There are certain psychological processes, however, that by their nature are incongruent. One of those processes is psychological *numbing*. This refers to the general lack of emotional responsiveness that an individual can demonstrate subsequent to being exposed to very traumatic circumstances that are not part of typical human experience. A *flattened affect* is also one of the conditions that demonstrates a disconnect between unconscious and conscious processes. In and of themselves, such signs are symptoms and can be indicative of a particular underlying psychological condition.

Specific Behaviors to Watch for in Evaluating Congruence

- A change in tone of voice that doesn't match with what is said.
- A shift in body posture while saying something that may indicate discomfort.
- A facial expression that does not match with the literal content of what a person is saying.
- Inability to look the therapist in the eye when saying something of importance.

If clients are congruent in their statements, the process of therapy (most notably, connecting with the client) becomes much more straightforward. When they are not congruent, the process of therapy (especially engagement) becomes more complex. But there are ways to understand and work with incongruence that can actually foster rapport and encourage a client to engage in treatment. It is the nonlinear-listening and nonlinear-thinking therapist who is attuned to the potential meaning of such behaviors and pursues them when they are in evidence. We discuss how to respond to these below.

Listening for Absence (i.e., What Is Not Said—by Silence, Avoidance, or Information Overload)
Absence can take two forms: what is not said or when too much is said! Although they may seem to be on opposite ends of the spectrum, the underlying thread binding such communications is the lack of information provided to the therapist. We address both below.

What Clients Do Not Discuss: Omissions
At times, what clients do not discuss can be as important as what it is that they are discussing, if not more so. Sometimes a client not discussing an issue simply may be because he or she does not believe or experience it to be problematic. Although that may be true at times, at other times such omissions may not be the case. On the other hand, particularly painful experiences, events, circumstances, failures, and issues for which a client does not want to be held responsible, for fear of being found lacking at times, are conspicuous by the client's avoidance of them. Nonlinear listening requires patience and the development of the ability to be attuned for such things. For example, if a person with two children enters therapy but talks about only her older child as problematic and never mentions the younger child, a therapist may become curious. A therapist wondering and asking why something is not being discussed may very well be a clue that something is amiss and conspicuous by its absence. It will be important to explore this curiosity, even if there really is nothing wrong with the younger child.

When Clients Talk Too Much: Land Mines, Rabbit Holes, and Other Red Herrings
At times, a client may wish to bring up material that one might discuss for a lifetime without any hope of resolution. This type of material can be classified as *land mines, rabbit holes,* or *red herrings*. A landmine is just that: A topic that is so emotionally explosive that a therapist will never want to step on it twice! For example, a client came for treatment because his stepdaughter had called the police and accused him of fondling her. Every time she came up in session, the client would become enraged, call her a "bitch" and a "whore," and make other unpleasant comments. Even though she was central to the presenting concern that brought the client for treatment, it was almost impossible to approach the subject without enduring an abusive tirade. As a result, many beginning (and even experienced) therapists might want to avoid such a topic so as not to incur the client's anger. In doing so, however, the relationship with the stepdaughter can't be explored. The conversation gets directed to safe, emotionally neutral topics. This is precisely what the client wants, although it spells certain doom for any therapeutic progress to be made.

Some clients will want to *war story*—repeatedly talk about what they did or what happened without forward movement or resolution. This is an example of a therapeutic *Alice in Wonderland* rabbit hole,[3] material that has the potential to lead treatment in an unfruitful direction. Clients in substance abuse treatment or some victims of abuse may repetitively review details of their experiences over and over, but are unable to utilize the discussion to make any progress. As therapists engage such clients in these stories (either as part of an intake session or in later sessions in the hope of gaining some useful information), the stories become more powerful for the client and dominate the therapy, to the exclusion of anything else. As a result, other aspects of the client's story (e.g., his or her strengths, potential, hopes, and alternatives) can't be explored.

Red herrings are the scrumptious tidbits that clients throw out. They seem like real issues, but don't necessarily have anything to do with a client's needs (much like rabbit holes). However, although rabbit holes may have some therapeutic benefit, red herrings usually do not. At times, clients will talk about sensational issues (e.g., past overindulgences or fantastic insights about themselves) or want to explore hidden dimensions of themselves (via hypnosis or dream work). These can be *false leads* used to deflect a therapist from focusing on the client. As an example, a client entered therapy complaining about symptoms of depression that were interfering with her work. During the initial interview, however, she went into extreme detail about episodes of past sexual abuse. In subsequent sessions, the topic of the past abuse dominated the conversation, and any discussion about present-day concerns was avoided. When listening for absence, it is essential for a therapist to remember that he or she is listening to a client's story: "What is it that I am not hearing in this client's story that may be very important?"

Listening for Presence (Nonverbal Behaviors That Add Meaning)
Nonlinear listening necessitates developing a capacity for understanding the potential implied meaning of messages. These messages may be conveyed through a client's tone of voice or bodily expressions (e.g., facial expressions, body posture, blushing, nervous giggles, a rolling of the eyes, changing posture, and deep sighing). The nonlinear-thinking therapist will follow up with a client on these subtle body messages (i.e., body language) in order to clarify what is being said. Such body messages are qualifiers of what a client is saying verbally. To put it another way:

> It is first of all necessary to remember that the scope of "communication" is by no means limited to verbal productions. Communications are exchanged through many channels and combinations of these channels, and certainly also through the *context* [emphasis added] in which an interaction takes place. Indeed, it can be summarily stated that *all* behavior, not only the use of words, is communication (which is not the same as saying that behavior is *only* communication), and since there is no such thing as non-behavior, it is impossible *not* to communicate. (Watzlawick & Beavin, 1977, p. 58)

In other words, even if a client is defiantly refusing to speak, or is limiting responses to one-word answers, he or she is still communicating messages through nonverbal behavior.

Pioneers in family therapy can be credited with recognizing the importance of all behavior in communicating meaning. Specifically, classical communication theorists such as Haley (1963), Lederer and Jackson (1968), Satir (1964), and Watzlawick and Beavin (1977) all highlighted the importance of nonverbal communication. Classic powerful research by Mehrabian and Ferris (1967) provides empirical support for the assertion that in human communication, the transmission of meaning tends to come from three important sources. Actual words spoken may account for as little as 7% of meaning expressed. Most interesting, the tonal characteristics of the speaker's voice may account for as much as 38% of meaning conveyed. Significantly, Mehrabian and Ferris (1967) found that facial expression accounts for up to 55% of the messages communicated. Some practitioners prefer the term *body communication,* rather than *body language,* to convey the fact that there are important messages contained in this nonverbal behavior: "Body communication . . . is the communication made through bodily movements and changes. It's the communication given by a person's physical bearing, facial expressions and physiology" (Emerick, 1997, p. 89).

It is essential to grasp the importance of nonverbal messages that are conveyed by clients. What a client does during a therapy session (i.e., behaviors demonstrated) is as important as what he or she is saying. Gottman (1995) has reported epic research and powerful conclusions on the communication between spouses in troubled marriages:

> *Body Language.* In its most subtle form, contempt is communicated with a few swift changes of the facial muscles. Signs of contempt or disgust include sneering, rolling your eyes, and curling your upper lip. At times in our research, facial expressions offered the clearest clue that something was amiss between a couple. For example, a wife may sit quietly and offer her husband an occasional "go on, I'm listening" while he airs his grievances. But at the same time, she is picking lint off her skirt and rolling her eyes. Her true feelings—contempt—are written in body language. (Gottman, 1995, p. 81)

Listening for the presence of nonverbal behaviors means that a therapist takes into consideration not just words spoken but also voice tone and body language (Hill, 2004). Such nonlinear listening is a fundamental part of nonlinear thinking. In the example provided by Gottman (1995) above, if the husband irately proclaims, "Hey! You're not listening to me!" The wife may retort, "What do you mean—I *told* you I was listening." Linear thinking ignores anything beyond spoken words (and agrees with the wife). Nonlinear thinking, however, makes note of the presence of the behavior that the wife is demonstrating in rolling her eyes with a dismissive and contemptuous attitude. Consider this example:

Therapist: "And that's why you have to work harder than everybody else? Because you don't want to be cast aside, cast away?"

Ashley: [Slowly] "Yeah . . ."

Therapist: "I'm noticing that you seem to have an unusual expression on your face. Your body posture also seems more subdued. Can you tell me what you are feeling right now?"

Ashley: "Sad . . . (sighs) . . . I feel sad."

Therapist: "You try and try as hard as you can. You work so hard to do your best, and it still doesn't completely work out."

Ashley: "That's why I got so fed up the other day with the kids. I just felt like it didn't matter what I did . . . nothing was going right. I felt like the house was collapsing on me, and I was trapped underneath."

Learning to be sensitive to behaviors that qualify words being articulated (e.g., tone of voice, facial expression, body posture, rolling of the eyes, clucking of the tongue, and finger drumming) is without a doubt a vital part of therapist development that is best addressed early and often by a Level I practitioner.

Listening for Inference (The Purpose behind "I Don't Want . . ." Statements)
As incredible as it may seem, clients typically enter therapy with vague ideas about what they want to accomplish—indeed, many times they actually have poorly formulated specific goals for treatment. Instead, what clients almost universally do come to therapy with is a formulation of what they don't want. In other words, they infer what their goals are, without making them explicit.

Common examples of how clients vaguely describe their goals are "I don't want to lose control of myself," "I don't want to fight with my wife anymore," "I don't want to be depressed," "I don't want to be anxious," "I don't want to smoke," "I don't want to drink anymore," "I don't want to be fat," and "I don't want to be a loser." When clients frame their problem by telling you what they don't want, in most instances they are acknowledging that actually they do have a problem. They do not know what would be occurring if they weren't fighting with a spouse, drinking excessively, or being depressed. This is an important consideration because disengaging from symptomatic behavior is required before one can embrace more constructive pursuits. But a client must have specific goals and objectives if he or she is to disengage from what he or she doesn't want.

Other clients claim that someone else is the problem. They frame their problems in similar negative terms: "I don't want my husband (or wife, boss, parents, children, etc., as the case may be) to treat me that way!" Such expressions only serve to prompt and promote a client's grappling with the problematic or symptomatic behavior and remaining stuck with it. That is, the client struggles with it, tries to overcome it, and generally fails. The linear-thinking client's focus of attention typically is the struggle to stop or get rid of something. But the more that a person wrestles with getting rid of something, the more he or she is actually engaged with that something, much like "trying hard not to think of alligators." The more someone repeats, "I'm not going to think of alligators," the more he or she is actually thinking of alligators. It is important for clinicians to remember this because clients so preoccupied with what they don't want most often have no specific idea of what they do want. It is the clinician who must first listen for these implicit or inferred goals and then present them to the client.

It is also important to remember that clients generally seek treatment only after they have repeatedly struggled with a problem or symptom without success. Thus, a client may have built up a problem-centric view of him- or herself and can't see alternative views. The clinical case example below may help to illustrate this point.

Clinical Case Example: Nervous in Cars

A successful businesswoman in her 30s sought help after many years of suffering from anxiety. When asked why she was seeking help for her anxiety at this particular point in time, she indicated, "It's particularly noticeable when I'm in cars and someone else is driving. I realized that this wasn't normal. I want this fixed. It would be nice to not have to worry about what could happen. It would be nice to not be so nervous in the car." The reader will notice that this young woman has expressed what she doesn't want—to be nervous when riding in a car. But an expression of what she doesn't want gives no indication of what she does want. What would she be doing, and how would she be acting if she wasn't fretting while riding in a car as a passenger? Does her anxious fretting represent a trait anxiety? Or might her anxiety be related to something traumatic that occurred while she was a passenger in a car accident?

This phenomenon of inference spans the entire scope of clinical practice. A couple that complains of marital strife may have no clear idea of how they should or would interact with each other if they were not arguing and distant from one another. Substance abusers, particularly problem drinkers, have no clear idea what they would be doing if they were sober during the multiple hours previously spent drinking daily. How would the chronic marijuana user or abuser relax if not using cannabis to do so? Most obese people have no clear idea of what they would do in their lives, and how their lives would change substantially (e.g., the broad implications of normal weight) if, indeed, they were to adopt sensible eating habits, modest regular exercise, and increased general activity, and lose their excess weight—perhaps that is why so many individuals with major weight loss (an estimated 95%) gain back the lost weight and then some.

In part, therapy uncovers inferred goals and translates them back to a client so treatment can move toward addressing problems, meeting client needs, and achieving more clearly defined and reasonable goals.

Listening for Resistance: The Desire Not to Change

Clients may come to therapy but, for many reasons, are not ready to make the essential and substantial changes necessary to resolve their problems. Many times, they may express good intentions but soon fail to show the commitment that is necessary for change to take place. In such instances, it is the therapist's role to help clients to not only remain in therapy but also benefit from it. At other times, clients may enter therapy stating that someone else is the problem or someone else made them come, and that they are not happy to be there! Chapter 4 presents a method for classifying a client's readiness for change, which is crucial for the initial assessment of the client.

However, the first warnings about a client's level of readiness for a commitment to change come from clients' verbal expressions. Therapists must be attuned to these overt or covert signals and be able to react in a manner that helps clients to overcome their resistance and engage in the therapy. Although a more thorough discussion of the concept of client resistance is presented in Chapters 3 and 5, there are some basic verbalizations clients frequently use that can betray signs of resistance. Several common verbalizations that clients use, especially in the initial stages of counseling, to express resistance are "I'll try . . . ," "I know that I should . . . ," "Yes, but . . . ," "I've already done that, and it didn't work. . . . ," and "I can't because . . ."

On the other hand, clients may complain that they are incapable of doing something routine (e.g., paying bills on time or cleaning the house) but claim that they are able to do other extraordinary things (e.g., play music professionally or program computers) that most other people can't do easily. The question then becomes, is this something that the person is unwilling to do, unprepared to do, or unable to do? If they are unwilling to do something, then that is not congruent with the statement that they cannot do something. If they are unprepared to do something, they are likely to face failure if they attempt it. The important thing is to listen for additional instances of this behavior that would indicate a pattern, which would be suggestive of an area to work on. Consider this example:

Ashley: "Okay, if we had more time ourselves, we'd go out to eat, and maybe see a play or a movie."
Therapist: "That sounds nice. So what stops you from doing that?"
Ashley: "Nothing I guess, maybe finding a babysitter."
Therapist: "So do you have someone that you can use as a babysitter?"
Ashley: "Yeah, there is a teacher at the kids' daycare center that we've used before."
Therapist: "Okay, so what's the real obstacle?"
Ashley: "I don't know, I guess the planning. But I don't want to be the person to plan everything."
Therapist: "Ah! So you want to be asked out on a date?"
Ashley: "Yes! Yes I do!" (Smiles.)

Perhaps the most common of all statements that clients use to express little expectation for change is some variation of the statement "I'll try." Expressing good intentions, or trying, may also express some lingering doubt about their ability to change or an underlying ambivalence about making a change. For example, a client may say, "I've tried everything else, and nothing has worked, so I thought I'd give therapy a try." Embedded in that statement is the unspoken sentiment "but I am pretty sure it will not work." This statement acts as a covert expression that the client has little or no expectation of success.

A close linguistic and psychological relative of the statement I'll try is "I should . . ." This expression suggests that a client knows what it is he or she is supposed to do, but not what it is that he or she wants or intends to do (hence, resistance; see Chapter 7). The client may describe the unacceptable problem behavior as a habit or use the phrase "I can't help myself." This can also reflect a self-image of being a victim who can't change these strong habits (Mosak & Gushurst, 1971). For example, a client who complains of a compulsive gambling habit, saying, "I've destroyed my finances because of gambling. I should stop; it shouldn't be that hard, but it is" already has the seeds of doubt as to his ability to stop gambling, with failure the most likely result.

Finally, practitioners like Berne (1964), Gottman (1995), as well as others (e.g., Adler, 1956) have observed one of the most potent verbalizations of resistance, called the "Yes, but . . ." statement. Simply put, the initial *yes* that the client says in response to a therapeutic comment or suggestion is instantly negated by a *but* asserted after it. Superficially, a client appears to be agreeing with what the therapist is saying. On closer inspection, however, it reveals a socially polite way of saying, "I disagree with everything you just said and don't propose to do anything different!" In a similar vein, a parent may lecture a teenage child about the need to call when he is out late to tell the parent that he is safe. Often, children know that this makes sense and agree with their parents: "Yes, I know that it is important to call you, but what if I can't get a cell (or it is too late, or . . .)?" The simple fact that the person is conceiving of an instance in which he might not be able to comply with what was agreed to (via the yes part) suggests that there is some resistance (i.e., disagreement) to it in the first place. Such expressions bear taking note of because therapists can fall into the trap of thinking that the client is on board, when he or she is not. Clinical Exercise: Clinical Nonlinear Listening is meant to enhance sensitivity to nonlinear listening.

Clinical Exercise: Clinical Nonlinear Listening

Directions: Read each vignette and answer the questions at the bottom. (Answers are provided at the end of the chapter.)

A. A client states that she wants help for her son, whose grades are poor. She further complains that he doesn't do any studying at home. When asked what his grades are, she replies, "B's, but he should be getting A's with all the money I am paying for his private school!" The client goes on to add, "I just don't want him ending up like his father!"

B. A 40-year-old gentleman comes to an initial session of therapy stating that he wants counseling for issues related to life management. He reports that he has seen counselors on and off for the last 15 years, but never stays long. Presently, he lives with his mother, is still in college, and complains that he cannot seem to finish things in his life. When pressed for details, he is vague and evasive.

C. An in-patient being treated for substance abuse comes for an individual session stating that the staff is abusive to her: "They were abusive to me first, so I slapped at one of them. Now they won't let me go to outside AA meetings! I need them for my recovery." The client then states, "I'm not sure why I am even here; I don't have a problem." A few minutes later, she adds, "I slapped at the staff, so that they would discharge me!"

D. A client reports being in an abusive relationship with her husband. She relates an incident about her husband getting angry, yelling at her, and pushing her into a crowd while they were in public. She coolly states that she really doesn't believe that he will do her harm, although she noticeably fidgets and has a tremble in her voice whenever she talks about her husband.

E. A busy executive comes into an initial session stating that he wants to make more time for his family. As you start to make some suggestions about how he might strive to achieve his goals, he begins to discuss his work obligations and how he must work around them. Finally, he says, "All right, I will give some of these suggestions a try."

1. Listening for content or information. What are the facts that the client is reporting?
2. Listening for feelings. What is the client feeling?
3. What type of nonlinear listening is required by the client's story?
4. What do you hear from the client based on these nonlinear approaches to listening?
5. How does the nonlinear approach to listening change your understanding of the client based on the linear approaches (Questions 1 and 2)?

Listening in a nonlinear way requires sensitizing oneself to a variety of possible meanings implied in client verbalizations and behavior. It is implied meanings that provide opportunities for clarification, the development of understanding, and interventions that foster engagement (Carkhuff, 2009; Hill, 2004). In fact, nonlinear listening becomes an avenue to all of the nonlinear interventions in the subsequent portions of this text. It is to the other half of the domain of connecting with and engaging the client, namely, responding, that we now turn our attention.

Our Nonlinear Brain: Mirror Neurons and Connecting with a Client

Recent discoveries into brain functioning have presented some tantalizing clues about how the process of connecting with another person may work at the neuronal level. Through the use of animal research and imaging technology, researchers have discovered brain cells called mirror neurons that seem to work to accomplish this. But what are mirror neurons? If a neuron in your brain performs in the very same manner when someone else is doing something as it does when you are actually doing the same thing, it is called a mirror neuron.

Researchers have recently described the discovery of mirror neurons and the results of their research efforts that shed light on how it is that we human beings understand how others feel— it is because others' feelings are being reproduced in us (Iacoboni, 2009; Keysers & Gazzola, 2010; Rizzolatti & Sinigaglia, 2008). In very practical everyday terms, Goleman (2006) relates a poignant incident from his childhood that describes what mirror neurons do in interactions between individuals:

"I must have been just two or three years old, the memory remains vivid in my mind. As I wandered down the aisle of the local grocery store at my mother's side, a lady spotted me—a cute little toddler—and gave me a warm smile. My own mouth, I still recall, startled me by involuntarily moving into a smile in return. It felt as though somehow my face had become puppetlike, drawn by mysterious strings that widened the muscles around my mouth and puffed out my cheeks. I distinctly felt that my smile had come unbidden—directed not from within but from outside myself . . ." Mirror neurons do just that . . . reflect back an action or have the impulse to do so. These do-as-she-does neurons offer a brain mechanism that explains the old lyric, "When you're smiling, the whole world smiles with you." (pp. 40–41)

In discussing contemporary work regarding the subject, *The Economist* (2006) defines a mirror neuron as,

one that is active both during the execution of a particular action or the production of a feeling by the individual concerned, and also when that individual observes the same action or feeling in another individual. In other words, it mirrors the actions and thoughts of others. (p. 10)

In fact, mirror neurons may be an important link in understanding the development of autism. Hirstein, Iversen, and Ramachandran (2001) point out that the mirror neuron system in autistic children does not work the way it does in normal children. It is precisely in empathy, emotional attachment, and understanding the rules of social interaction that autistic children experience the most deficits. Further work by Carr, Iacoboni, Dubeau, Maziotta, and Lenzi (2003) suggests that mirror neurons are active in determining the intentions of others. Mirror neurons have also been projected as being responsible for empathizing with the feelings that great musical artists demonstrate when performing, actors performing in soul-stirring roles, as well as understanding what other people are doing, feeling, or expressing.

The implications of the role of mirror neurons in psychotherapy and autism are not the only understandings to emerge regarding these fascinating specialty neurons. Rossi and Rossi (2007) recently have explored the neurobiology and genetic underpinnings of mirror neurons to shed light on an understanding of the age-old mysteries of hypnosis:

> Neuroscience documents the activity of "mirror neurons" in the human brain as a mechanism whereby we experience empathy and recognize the intentions of others by observing their behavior and automatically matching their brain activity. This neural basis of empathy finds support in research on dysfunctions in the mirror systems of humans with autism and fMRI research on normal subjects designed to assess intentionality, emotions, and complex cognition. Such empathy research now appears to be consistent with the historical and research literature on hypnotic induction, rapport, and many of the classical phenomena of suggestion. (p. 263)

New and exciting discoveries about mirror neurons as underpinnings for understanding therapeutic rapport, empathy, and suggestion are being discovered literally on a daily basis. Quite remarkably, according to research work of Jackson, Brunet, Meltzoff, and Decety (2006) the same brain (via its mirror neurons) that allows a therapist to genuinely experience the empathic pain and suffering of a client also differentiates such pain from one's own pain. Hence, although it is possible to identify and experience empathy for another's pain and suffering, the brain is wired in such a way as to also be able to maintain objectivity at the same time and differentiate someone else's pain and suffering from one's own. Keysers and Gazzola (2010) also found evidence of *anti-mirror* neurons that also seem to fire at the same time as mirror neurons in order to allow a person to observe another person's behavior, but not repeat the behavior. Obviously, maintaining objectivity and simultaneously being genuinely empathic are extremely important abilities that master practitioners demonstrate. Such abilities are integrally related to the necessity of maintaining appropriate boundaries at all times regardless of the emotional environment that is a therapist's office.

Possible Meanings Associated with Statements in Clinical Exercise:
Beginning the Use of Nonlinear Thinking

1. "*I* don't want to go with you."

   - Possible meaning: "You may want me to go, but I just don't want to go!"

2. "I *don't* want to go with you."

   • Possible meaning: "You may want me to go with you, but I don't wish to go with you."

3. "I don't *want* to go with you."

   • Possible meaning: "*You* want me to go, but *I* don't want to."

4. "I don't want to *go* with *you*."

   • Possible meaning: "I don't mind going, but I don't want to go with you."

5. "I don't want to go *with* you."

   • Possible meaning: "I might not mind going and getting there after you do, but I don't want to go with you at the same time that you do."

6. "I don't want to go with *you*."

   • Possible meaning: "You may want me to accompany you, but I want to go alone or with someone else."

Can you come up with still other possible meanings for the statements with the emphasis placed on different words?

Answers to Clinical Exercise: Clinical Nonlinear Listening
(A) Inference; (B) Absence; (C) Congruence; (D) Presence; and (E) Resistance.

Notes

1. A major development in reading others comes from the "recognition of facial affect" and pioneering research done in this area by Ekman (1992, 1995) and Ekman, Levenson, and Friesen (1983). Research on the recognition of facial affect involves identifying specific facial muscles that human beings cross-culturally use in expressing different basic emotions.
2. For an elaborate discussion of research about human beings being able to detect when someone is not telling the truth, we recommend the work of Ekman (1995) and Gladwell (2005).
3. *Rabbit hole* is a reference to Lewis Carroll's *Alice in Wonderland*, in which Alice followed the rabbit down into a wonderland of the bizarre.

3

The Domain of Connecting with and Engaging the Client

Responding

Introduction

Second only to listening, responding is perhaps the most important thing that a therapist does. It is wise for Level I therapists to be aware of the subtleties and implications of language and the influences—intended or not—that responses can have on their clients. Words from a person in a position of power and influence (e.g., a psychiatrist, psychologist, counselor, or social worker) must be chosen carefully, because clients are vulnerable and suggestible (see Peluso, 2006).

Just as there are differences between linear and nonlinear listening, there are also differences in responding linearly and nonlinearly. These logically follow from the categories of linear and nonlinear listening described in Chapter 3. This chapter focuses on responding linearly and nonlinearly to a wide variety of client statements. In subsequent chapters, we expand on how to respond to clients in effective ways that address increasingly complex aspects of therapy.

Linear Responding

Linear responding follows from linear listening—from the statements a client makes. If done well, linear responding facilitates the engagement process, signaling to a client that someone understands his or her story at a basic level without judgment or blame. In turn, linear responding encourages a client to reveal more of the story because it is safe to do so. The two types of linear responding we discuss are responding to content or information, and responding to feeling.

Responding to Content or Information

Carkhuff (2009) has detailed the importance of responding to content. It provides the conversational space for a client to know that he or she is being heard and understood by the therapist, and can continue with the story. Just as listening to content is about the facts of a client's statement, responding to content is a therapist's reflection of the facts of the client's statement. This type of responding represents the lowest level of intensity or threat that a therapist can utilize. Carkhuff recommended starting sentences with "You're saying . . ." and then reflecting back to the client a summary of what he or she has been saying. Others recommend posing a question like "So what I hear you saying is . . . ?" The main purpose of such linear responding is twofold: gaining clarification and the therapist conveying an understanding of what a client is saying. Such clarification invites a client to proceed further with the story or the theme of what is being discussed. But clients aren't always direct in what they are saying or implying—their meanings can be obscure and unclear.

As a clinical example, after much debate a client may state that she has resolved to quit her job. A response to the content or information may take the form of "So you've made a decision to resign." When therapists respond to content or information, they should do so in a way that conveys a neutral stance (i.e., neither agreeing nor disagreeing) and that they are genuinely interested in hearing more factual information about a client's story. Typically, other avenues for discussion begin to follow. In the example above, a client may decide to talk about future plans (e.g., "I'm going to open my own business!") or discuss her concerns (e.g., "Yeah, it was hard to do, and I'm nervous about what is going to happen."). Responding in a linear manner is ultimately limited, and responding at a deeper level is necessary to gain greater depth of understanding and rapport with a client. It is important to note that the more robotic and mechanical that therapists are (i.e., like a parrot) in feeding back what a client is expressing, the less effective they will be in connecting with and engaging a client.

A brief summary of different ways in which a practitioner can express that they understand what a client is saying includes statements such as:

- "You're saying . . ."
- "You seem to be saying . . ."
- "If I understand you correctly, you seem to be saying that you are going to . . ."
- "So what I hear you saying is . . ."

Responding to Feelings

A therapist's verbal statements of empathy and understanding that are congruent (i.e., in harmony) with the way in which such statements are made play an important role in a client feeling valued, validated, understood, and accepted (Carkhuff, 2009). In turn, such harmonious expressions of empathy are an essential component of building a strong therapeutic alliance—the foundation for all work that is accomplished in therapy. Responding to clients' feelings communicates that you understand and can connect with them on a deeper, more intimate level—beyond understanding the linear facts they present. Again, following listening for feeling, these responses usually take the simple form of "You feel . . . (insert a feeling word here or another word, phrase, metaphor, etc.)." For example, suppose a client says, "I just wish that my mother would stop treating me like a child! It infuriates me when she tells me what to do with my life. It's like she doesn't think that I can take care of myself!" As a therapist listens to the client, it is important to listen for the feelings being expressed by (1) what the client says ("infuriates me"), (2) the client's demeanor (e.g., face contorted in an angry expression), or (3) reference to a therapist's own feeling (i.e., recall the distinctions between these categories described in Chapter 2).

The next step, before responding, is to simply ask oneself, "What is it that this client is feeling?" The answer to that question becomes the basis for a response. So in the previous example, the answer to what a client may be feeling could be angry, upset, distressed, or frustrated (amongst others). The response could be "So—you really feel upset with your mother for treating you like you were 5 years old." This communicates an understanding of the emotional impact of the client's story. This is especially true and very important when a therapist's response matches the level of a client's feeling. As a result, a further question that therapists need to ask themselves before they respond is "To what degree does the client feel this way? A mild, medium, or large degree?" The therapist must match her or his response in proportion to the client's expression in order to be effective in fostering a sense of understanding, engagement, and connectedness. Again, utilizing the example above, if a therapist used feeling words that were too severe and didn't match the clients' feelings (e.g., "You feel enraged at your mother") or not strong enough (e.g., "You feel uneasy about your mother"), a client may feel emotionally misunderstood or perhaps that the clinician did not care about him. Consider this excerpt from "The Case of Mike":

Mike:	"Yeah, I dunno, I just don't want to look weak in front of people. I don't want people to think they can walk all over me."
Therapist:	"Because?"
Mike:	"Because then I'm a nobody. I don't matter."
Therapist:	"And you'd feel?"
Mike:	"Weak, powerless, pathetic."
Therapist:	"And that makes you feel . . . mad, sad, scared . . ."
Mike:	"Sad."
Therapist:	"Sad . . ."

Another pitfall for clinicians when responding to a client's feeling is using the client's exact phrasing (commonly referred to as *parroting*). Just like inaccurately responding to feelings, parroting makes the processes of connecting with and engaging a client more difficult, if not impossible. Thus, it is important to understand a client's particular feeling and the level of the feeling, and then summarize it accurately, but not just spit back clients' words to them. The clinical exercise below provides some information on increasing your feeling vocabulary.

Clinical Exercise: Increasing Your Feeling Vocabulary

Accurately responding to feelings or getting a *recognition reflex* requires a therapist to have a wide vocabulary of feeling words. As human beings, we have a rich and wide-ranging palette of feelings (much like an elaborate color palette with all the shades of various colors). As children grow and develop, they begin experiencing the full range of these feelings and must look to their parents and other adults to help them interpret and label what they are feeling (Gottman & DeClair, 1997). Many times, adults do not have a rich vocabulary to guide children in identifying their feelings. As a result, they are taught basic feelings of *happy, sad, mad,* and *scared.* When these limited words are applied to the broad and subtle variations of feelings that human beings experience, confusion can result, and many people report that they do not feel many things at all. In addition, they may use nonfeeling words like *good, bad, fine,* and I *don't know.* It is as if parents brought their child to the ocean, gazed upon a crystal aquamarine sea framed by an icy azure sky, and called them both blue. Although this is true, it does not accurately convey the breadth and impact of the encounter, and, as a result, something of the experience is lost. It is the same with feelings. For example, a person may have ended a long-term relationship and is feeling devastated. Meanwhile, another person could have ended a weeklong relationship and feel mildly upset. If both of these people describe themselves simply as sad, would it tell the whole story? What would be missing? Clearly, it is technically accurate, but it does not tell the entire story. Instead, good, useful information comes with the subtle shading. As a result, therapists must have a repertoire of feeling words for each of the major feelings (happy, sad, angry, afraid, and hurt). They also need words of low intensity, medium intensity, and high intensity in order to help clients label their own feeling state. The more feeling words at your disposal, the more likely you will hit a client's *emotional solar plexus.*

Primary Feeling	Low Intensity	Medium Intensity	High Intensity
Happy			
Sad			
Angry			
Afraid			
Hurt			

Instructions: Develop a repertoire of feeling expressions by filling in low-, medium-, and high-intensity words for each of the basic emotions. Share your words with class members to develop a larger list of feeling words for each.

Variation: Form small groups and pick one of the basic feelings. Then, create case scenarios that match each of the categories (low, medium, and high). Present the case scenarios to the other groups and ask them to assign a feeling word that best matches the case scenario.

Accurately responding to feeling fosters greater engagement, whereas inaccurately responding to feeling can create a rupture (i.e., break) in the therapeutic relationship (this is covered in more detail in Chapter 7). How do you know if you have responded to a client's feelings accurately? Again, sometimes therapists will know that they have correctly responded to what a client is feeling when they hear a client say, "That's it!," "That's exactly how I feel!," or "You hit the nail on the head!" In some instances, a client will actually tell the therapist if he or she is correct or not.

Many times, however, clients will not necessarily tell therapists verbally that they are correct. But there is an automatic response that people have when they hear what they are feeling reflected back to them. Called a *recognition reflex*, it usually takes the form of a smile, eyes brightening, or some form of head nodding (Dreikurs, Grunwald, & Pepper, 1982). It can also take the form of tears welling in a client's eyes. In fact, it is almost impossible to not have a recognition reflex if a therapist accurately reflects back the exact emotion that a client is feeling. It is as if a client says, "How did you know that?" Some people indicate that they feel warmth radiating from their stomach (sometimes called hitting the emotional solar plexus).[1] Hence, accurately listening for and responding to feelings afford clinicians another opportunity to connect with clients on a deeper, more intimate level and facilitate their engaging in the therapeutic process.

Advanced Linear Responding

In addition, combining a response to content or information with a response to feelings can foster a very deep level of exploration and engagement. Carkhuff (2009) referred to this as a "response to meaning," which takes the general form of "You feel . . . (fill in the feeling word) because (fill in the content) . . ." Using the earlier example, a therapist may respond to the client who was in conflict with his mother by saying, "You really feel upset with your mother because she treats you like a baby and doesn't respect you." These linear responses are limited, however, since they often do not go to the core of a client's concerns. Researchers have shown that clients who don't feel that their problems are understood by a therapist in the early sessions do not stay in therapy very long and do not get the help they need (e.g., Brogan, Prochaska, & Prochaska, 1999; Hubble et al., 2010; Orlinsky, 2010).

A final note about the strategic use of linear responses, particularly when a client is overemotional: At such times, a therapist may choose to respond to content (i.e., information) as a way of helping clients to disengage from unproductive ruminating about feelings and have them concentrate on more rational elements (thinking, logic, problem solving, etc.). Likewise, there are times when responding to feelings can be used to help clients to evaluate their own emotional states (i.e., being too emotionally rigid or robotic) when they are unable. By strategically using these linear responses, therapists help such clients to focus on internal processes that they are not accessing.

To summarize linear listening and responding, in essence, it is the therapist's job to (1) detect as closely and exactly as possible what core meanings, sentiments, emotions, and feelings a client is expressing by her or his verbal and nonverbal expressions and (2) succinctly reflect those core meanings, sentiments, emotions, and feelings back to the client in an empathetic way so as to elicit the client saying the equivalent of "Yes! That's it exactly!" Although at first this may seem like a daunting task, mastery of it requires less technical skill than a way of thinking. Once a novice gets the notion, the rest is practice that ultimately morphs into a natural way of attending to clients. As a result, although reflecting accurate empathy back to a client and congruence on the part of the therapist have been called *facilitative conditions to therapy,* they are not enough (Lambert & Barley, 2002). Instead, clients require a level of response that gets to the heart of their problem or concern. This necessitates responses that are nonlinear in their approach.

Exercising Your Nonlinear Thinking:
The Quirks of Language and the Importance of (Mis)perception

Winston Churchill once said that the United States and Britain were "Two great countries separated by a common language." This ironic statement sums up the importance of this domain, and the purpose of this nonlinear thinking exercise. It is all about the quirks of language and the importance of (mis)perception. We present two types of these for you to exercise your nonlinear thinking: spoonerisms and reading misspelled words.

Spoonerisms

These are words or phrases with sounds that are swapped. Usually this happens accidentally, particularly if a person is speaking fast. There are potentially millions of possible spoonerisms, but the most interesting ones are where the spoonerism makes just as much sense as well as the original phrase, but are more amusing (e.g., "bottle in front of me" versus "frontal lobotomy"). Because spoonerisms are phonetic transpositions, it is not the letters that are swapped, but it is the sounds themselves. Spoonerisms can be either a transposition of whole words or just the transposition of sounds. Here are some examples:

Original	Spoonerism
Blow your nose	Know your blows
Go and take a shower	Go and shake a tower
Picking your nose	Ticking your pose
You have very bad manners	You have very mad banners
A pack of lies	A lack of pies
So help me God	Go help me sod
Flipping the channel on TV	Chipping the flannel on TV

Here are a few spoonerisms, see if you can figure out the original word or phrase (answers at the end of the chapter):

1. Wave the sails
2. I hit my bunny phone

3. Plaster Man
4. Chewing the Doors
5. Birthington's Washday

Variation: Now try to come up with your own spoonerisms.

Reading Misspelled Words

An e-mail has circulated on the Internet over the last decade that cited some research that stated:

Aoccdrnig to a rscheearch at an Elingsh uinervtisy, it deosn't mttaer in waht oredr the ltteers in a wrod are, the olny iprmoetnt tihng is taht frist and lsat ltteer is at the rghit pclae. The rset can be a toatl mses and you can sitll raed it wouthit porbelm. Tihs is bcuseae we do not raed ervey lteter by it slef but the wrod as a wlohe.

Were you able to read the above paragraph? Chances were that by the end you were. Now, the reality was that the science behind this was only partially true. The origins of this can be traced to a dissertation published in 1976 and a paper published in 2003 (Shilcock & Monighan). In fact, Matt Davis, a Cambridge linguist (http://www.mrc-cbu.cam.ac.uk/people/matt.davis/Cmabrigde/) provides a thorough explanation of the phenomenon and what parts of it may be backed up by science and which parts are not.

The bottom line for both exercises is that language (both the listening to it and the responding to it) can be nonlinear, and at times, taking what is presented by the client, and subtly rearranging it can provide a whole new meaning for the client. This is what we explore in this domain.

But, if rdeanig this is esay for you, eevn tuhgoh tehir are msipleled wrods, you mhigt be a nrtual nloinenar tikehnr! (Now, isn't that a "Hick in the Ked?")

Nonlinear Responding

Responding nonlinearly is clearly different from responding in a linear manner. Remember that by nonlinear, we mean things that are askew, that may not logically follow from what has been presented, but that ultimately do begin to shed new light on a given issue for a client. Therapists' nonlinear responses are motivated by several factors, including client ambivalence about making changes and therapist curiosity about elements of the client's story that may be vague. Nonlinear responses often break the linear flow of a client's story and can alienate a client if done poorly. On the other hand, if nonlinear responding is done well, it can foster quicker rapport as well as facilitate therapeutic progress. We offer a clinical case example to illustrate.

Clinical Case Example: Impulsivity, Panic, and a Need to Know Why

A 60-year-old attractive divorced woman sought treatment for being depressed and anxious. Her major preoccupations were several. Initially, she began describing her concern over the fact that her adult divorced daughter and a young adult grandchild who had been living with her had recently moved on their own, a circumstance that the woman felt badly about but realized was ultimately in everyone's best interests. She realized that it was time for her daughter to be more independent and move on with her life without depending upon her mother. More to the point, however, the woman described that she was now living all alone in her beautiful home that she had decorated tastefully and with great care over the course of a 20 plus year marriage that ended in divorce a few years before. She described the home and its partially wooded lot in a prestigious suburb in loving, serene, artistic, and nostalgic terms.

Being well-educated beyond a bachelor's degree, she explained that after her divorce she found herself having to reenter the work force in her mid-50s after many years of being a traditional-role housewife and mother who pursued leisurely but sophisticated activities such as decorating and caring for her home, pursuing an advanced professional degree, and so forth. She had always maintained an active and productive style of living. But while the job she found paid well, it was also exceptionally demanding, competitive, and fast-paced, and required frequent domestic travel and at times international travel. She described coming home after her travels as resulting in very emotionally ambivalent terms. On the one hand, it was wonderful to be returning to the safety, security, familiarity, and comfort of her beautiful home that she clearly enjoyed and took pride in. On the other hand, she was profoundly aware of the fact that she was all alone in a five-bedroom home with no date life, no phone calls, and literally no social life: "It's been 7 years since I've been with a man, and there are absolutely no prospects on the horizon. In fact, I work with all women, so I don't even have an opportunity to meet anyone on the job." Her life had become a scenario of diminishing prospects across many different dimensions: She was alone; there were no visible prospects for her to meet someone; her adult children were busy with their lives and had little time for her and diminishing interest/time in carrying on with family traditions that she loved and idealized; her divorce had left her with a beautiful but unpaid-for house that was increasingly expensive to maintain and in fact was becoming unaffordable; she had little money in retirement savings; and she was now 60 years old.

After several sessions of discussing the above developments, the therapist urged that becoming active could perhaps help her to feel less helpless and hopeless and more efficacious and in charge of her life. She responded well to that suggestion and spontaneously indicated that there was a real estate development with a model that she was totally infatuated with that she had initially seen several years ago on a lark. After the therapist's suggestion, she returned to that model home development several times, and each time she indicated that in walking through one particular model, she felt elated, and when she would return home, she would feel palpably depressed. Finally, she made a somewhat impulsive offer to the developers to buy that model, but they refused it as too low; she explained that she didn't know why but that she ultimately countered their offer for essentially their asking price and they accepted it. Within a few days of having made the offer on the model home, she came to therapy in a literal shaking panic not knowing but needing to know what had prompted her to make that offer when she hadn't sold her home. She described the new home was *new,* airy, bright, beautifully decorated, but at the same time, it was not convenient to any transportation, shopping, her job, or her family members—and in addition to those considerations, it was in a much, much lesser prestigious suburb. She had to know *why* she had made such an impulsive decision when she was hardly prepared to sell her house and move into a beautiful but downsized place with no room for a garden, located in the middle of nowhere, in a suburb far down the socioeconomic scale from where she was used to living. She was desperate to know how to relieve the panicky feeling she described in great detail.

The therapist suggested that, "Perhaps you made the offer because the new home was like a drug to you! You've been suffering under the oppressive and depressing weight of being overworked, having no social life, experiencing profound loneliness with family members not around, and your mother having passed away, among other things such as being physically exhausted and financially stressed. No wonder a new, airy, bright, tastefully decorated model home was so appealing to you and made you *feel* good, just like a drug might make you feel good—for a time!"

The woman's face showed astonishment: Her eyes widened, her mouth opened, and her jaw dropped while she straightened her back and replied, "That is absolutely it! You are so right. With everything going so poorly in my life, no wonder I kept going back to that place so many times and *felt* good about being there every time I went. It *is* like a drug! That's perfect! The effect of going to see that model would be even profound when I would return home to an empty house—I'd be depressed and overwhelmed. That's a perfect description of what happened!"

With so many elements of her life seemingly out of control, the woman was genuinely anxious, panicky, puzzled, and incredulous about her impulsive decision. In light of the fact that all of these things are experienced as being out of control, the decision she made to make a formal offer to buy a new home in hindsight prompted her to feel as though she was even more out of control. Thus, although she felt almost euphoric upon visiting the new model, engaging in an impulsive behavior (i.e., without preparation for financing, not having even listed her home for sale, considering the pros and cons and discussing them with friends, family, etc.) prompted her to feel as though she was once again out of control, just like so many other elements in her life.

Underlying all of the nonlinear-listening categories listed above (i.e., congruence, absence, presence, inference, and resistance) is some level of client confusion or ambivalence. A therapist's job entails (1) detecting the ambivalence a client is expressing and presenting it appropriately to the client and (2) responding to the ambivalence in a way that facilitates a client engaging in therapy to sufficiently explore problems and arrive at an acceptable solution. In addition to the aspects of nonlinear listening identified above, responding in a nonlinear way also includes the following:

- Asking well-formed questions that elicit more information.
- Translating what it is that a client is saying.
- Relating what a client says to his or her past statements, one's past clinical experiences, and one's theoretical frame of reference.
- Forming and testing hypotheses.

The elements of nonlinear responding to be discussed are as follows:

- Responding to incongruence (i.e., "I hear that there is more than one side to this.")
- Responding to absence (i.e., "I see what you are not showing me.")
- Responding to presence (i.e., "I see what your body is saying, even if you may not.")
- Responding to inference (i.e., "I hear what you are not saying.")
- Responding to resistance (i.e., "I understand that you might not be ready for this.")

A key element in the domain of connecting with and engaging a client in treatment is conveying that therapy can sometimes be a daunting and scary experience, and a person may not be entirely ready to deal effectively with such a threat. At the same time, a therapist must communicate a sense of optimism, namely, that if a client perseveres with treatment, improvements can be made.

Nonlinear Responding to Incongruence (i.e., "I Hear That There Is More Than One Side to This.")

Recall that incongruent statements made by clients generally occur for one of two basic reasons: It is either misunderstanding or miscommunication between counselor and client, or because of unintentional deception on the client's part. Responding to incongruence is an attempt to understand the ambiguous meaning of what a client is saying. Because this is quite common, it is little wonder that Carl Rogers and researchers who followed him emphasized congruence (i.e., agreement between what is expressed and the manner in which it is said) as one of the basic principles of the therapeutic process[2] (Truax & Carkhuff, 1967). The important thing is, what does the client mean by what he or she says? If the answer is unclear, the therapist may want to respond in the following way:[3] "I know what I mean when I say _____, but I'm not sure what you mean by _____. Can you tell me what that means to you?" The clinical case example below might be helpful in illustrating this.

Clinical Case Example: A Man with a Drinking Problem and a History of "Bumps"

A man with an admitted drinking problem—who sought help on his own—came to therapy after voluntarily acknowledging to his wife that he could not handle alcohol and wanted to go to a hospital for detox. After detox, he accepted participation in a structured four-week program in recovery and sought psychotherapy to learn more about why he gravitated to drinking and eventually became addicted to the use of alcohol. In the second session of treatment, during the process of describing his early family life, he indicated that there were bumps while growing up in a good family atmosphere. The therapist heard this comment and became curious about the word *bumps*. He decided to follow up on this and responded, "I know that I had a few 'bumps' as a kid growing up and what that means to me. But, I'm not sure what having some 'bumps' means to you. Can you tell me what you mean by that?" Although everyone has encountered some bumps growing up, not everyone likely describes them in that particular manner. To this question, the client responded that his mother had become paralyzed when he was only a toddler and that he had to live with his grandparents many miles from his family home for a number of years. He then spoke in a very moving way about how being separated from his mother at an early age affected him. Of course, this is a very different narrative than the bumps the practitioner had experienced. Understanding what the client meant by bumps became a very important clinical understanding.

Obviously, the bumps described by the client in the clinical case example were of a significant nature and indeed much different from the bumps that the therapist envisioned in his own life. These events were significant in the early life of the client and became a significant issue in therapy. But consider what might have happened if the therapist had responded in a linear way (i.e., to content and information or to feeling). Imagine the vast amount of information that would have been missed. Nonlinear responding not only requires a client to slow down and elaborate on his story, but also closes the gap in understanding between client and therapist. Here is another example:

Therapist: "Could it be that there's a connection between the pain and sadness over your mother's death as a teen, and lashing out at coworkers and others now?"

Mike: "Maybe . . . I don't know. My fiancé thinks it's connected. It's been hard on her the last 6 months. I've been very moody, and we get into a lot of arguments."

Therapist: "Why? What happened 6 months ago?"

Mike: "My father passed away. He was driving home, and a truck ran a red light, he never saw it coming. He was killed instantly."

In this example, the therapist suggests a connection between two events (an anger problem dealing with coworkers and his mother's death when he was a teenager). Although he doesn't see that there is a connection, he drops a hint about something else that is a problem (his fiancée and 6 months ago). Using a sense of curiosity about these statements, the therapist learns that there is a more recent loss that might be contributing to the client's problem (his father's death 6 months ago).

Sometimes, incongruence or discrepancies are a matter of deception (either self-deception or deceiving the therapist). Remember the example in Chapter 2 of the man who said that he *hated* his son and his son's drug abuse? His statement was "I think I hate my son! I'm ashamed to say that!" The question that lingered was "Does he really *hate* his son, or is he expressing his pain and anger over what has become of his son?" If he literally hates his son, then there are different issues to deal with than if he merely hates what is happening to his son. One meaning—that he hates his son's behavior—perhaps offers the man hope and a sense of redemption from the guilt and embarrassment he is feeling. The other offers him a bad feeling about himself for hating his son and a sense of unredeemed guilt. Furthermore, the man states that he think(s) he hates his son. Such an expression suggests that he isn't certain or is deceiving himself in a way that doesn't allow him to reach out to his son. So how might one respond to him? Rather than accept his comment at face value, the therapist can ask, "I know what I mean when I say, 'I hate someone or something,' but I'm wondering how *you mean* that you hate your son?" By both listening and responding to incongruence, the therapist can be encouraging to a man who is obviously discouraged and embarrassed by his self-disclosure. The therapist can compliment the man on his honesty in expressing feelings and his integrity in saying something that must be incredibly difficult to divulge. Inquiries stated in that way say to the client, "I hear that there is more than one side to this." It communicates a level of interest in the client and can foster a positive, deeper measure of engagement.

But Don't Take Our Word for It! Master Example

Consider this example from master practitioner, Scott Miller (coauthor of *The Heart and Soul of Change* and creator of Feedback Informed Therapy, FIT), and how he responds to Scott's incongruence in a way that helps Scott connect (Allyn & Bacon, 2000e).

Scott Miller: "Okay. So when you have that feeling of things kind of burning inside, one way you take care of it is by getting off to yourself. That helps you I guess to keep from what?"

Client Scott: "Yeah. It keeps my temper under control."

Scott Miller: "Okay. Where'd you learn this?"

Client Scott: "Well, I don't know. It was something that Nancy or somebody was telling me. She always told—one or her girlfriends read it in a book, you should—one of them should always walk away."

Scott Miller: "Okay."

Client Scott: "Well, that didn't always work because, I'd think 'well, I walked away the last three times we've had a discussion. Well, it's your turn to walk away.'"

Scott Miller: "Okay."

Client Scott:	"Or she'd follow me right out to the garage."
Scott Miller:	"Right."
Client Scott:	"You know. But I, I'd do it at work if, you know, if things were going bad or whatever, I'd just go to the water cooler and get a drink. And just stay away from everybody for a couple of minutes, come back, and we'll hit it hard again."
Scott Miller:	"Okay."
Client Scott:	"Boss and me will discuss what, you know, we need to do and we'll go from there. That way nobody gets hurt and it's the safest way to do it."
Scott Miller:	"So there's a combination of things that I'm catching here that, that you, you not only sometimes take a break and say, 'I got to get away.' But there's also times where you discuss it?"
Client Scott:	"Yeah."
Scott Miller:	"How do you make the decision between the two? I mean, I'm sort of struck by that."

So by Miller catching Scott's incongruence about how he deals with his frustration, it opens him up to exploring how he has control over his reactions, and its impact on other relationships in his life.

Nonlinear Responding to Absence (i.e., "I See What You Are Not Showing Me.")

Listening for and responding to absence make up one of the hallmarks of a nonlinear approach to counseling. It is the process of seeing beyond what is present to what is absent. It is stimulated by therapist curiosity about what a client isn't saying or discussing. A therapist wondering and asking herself why something is not being discussed may very well be the clue that something is amiss and conspicuous by its absence. How does a therapist respond to this type of absence in a nonlinear way? Sometimes not responding is the appropriate response, whereas other times stopping the client in the moment is the best thing to do; it is a matter of timing.[4] Nevertheless, when a therapist interprets or brings up the topic of avoidance, it should always be done tactfully, affably, and perhaps *contritely* (see Information Box: The Columbo Approach).

Information Box: The Columbo Approach[5]

The detective character developed by the actor Peter Falk in the nationally acclaimed TV series *Columbo* can be seen as a caricature of a manner that partly resembles the way in which the topic of interpretation or avoidance can be advanced. In psychotherapeutic terms, the *Columbo approach* is similar to adopting a *not-knowing* stance (common in family therapy). Such an approach requires therapists to thoroughly understand a client's perspective by not taking for granted that they understand what clients mean in telling their story. Instead, they must listen deeply and stimulate clients to make the meaning of their statements very clear. If this is done well, it helps to maintain the therapeutic alliance by saying, "I may not be clear on this point—can you help me?" or "I'm confused. Could you help me to understand how it is that . . . ?" Another version of this is to use words such as "I noticed . . . ," "I'm curious . . . ," "I couldn't help but notice that . . . ," and "That's the third time I've heard you take such a big sigh when we talk about . . . " This stance communicates the following messages simultaneously: (1) "I seem to have noticed something that for whatever reason you are not showing me"; (2) "I could be wrong, but this is my observation"; (3) "I seem to be a little slow here, but it seems to me that what you are saying is . . ." Such nonlinear responding gives a client a certain amount of space either to more thoroughly align understanding between therapist and client, to acknowledge what is conspicuously missing, or to correct an oversight or misperception. For example, in the section on listening for absence in Chapter 2, regarding the woman who talked about only one child but not the other: A nonlinear response to that may be "I noticed that when you talk about your children, you only seem to talk about your older child but not your younger child. I was curious about that." The client may acknowledge that the younger child either is or is not her favorite, that the younger child is a perfect child, or that the client didn't think to mention the younger child because the problem didn't affect him. Regardless, responding to this absence communicates that the therapist is sensitive to things about which the client may not be cognizant.

There are clients who appear to talk incessantly about certain topics (e.g., land mines, rabbit holes, and red herrings, discussed in Chapter 2), which is another aspect of nonlinear listening and responding to absence concerns. Recall that these may be more active attempts to distract a therapist from addressing underlying issues. Perhaps the least effective way to respond to such behaviors is to make an effort to tackle them head-on (i.e., in a linear way) and attempt to work on that issue. Such an approach is likely to result in devoting time to topics that are unproductive. An example of this is the client (described in Chapter 2) with the land mine explosive temper that was triggered by the topic of his stepdaughter. A therapist who attempts to work on the issue by forcing the client to talk about the stepdaughter runs the risk of forcing the client out of therapy. A linear approach to such a land mine tends to feed the client's desire to not talk about the stepdaughter. A nonlinear response to this client would be to talk about the process that is going on in therapy at that moment (see the Information Box). For example, a counselor may say,

> I can't help but notice that although she is a key reason for why you are here, whenever we try to talk about your stepdaughter, you get very angry and I change the subject. Now, I know that her behavior has hurt you in the past, and that you're not eager to discuss your relationship with her, but we are going to have to talk about it civilly at some point. Let's see if we can figure out how and when to do that.

The conversation and the therapeutic challenge have shifted from (1) the topic of the stepdaughter to being about the dynamic process represented by the client and counselor and (2) avoiding a difficult subject altogether to discussing when and how to talk about the relationship with the stepdaughter. Or continuing with the case of Mike:

Therapist: "Pretty impressive. You know, I couldn't help but notice that you hadn't talked about your mom when I asked about frustration. Could it be that she frustrates you?"

Mike: "Oh totally! Both she and my dad did. I was always a little hyper. I remember growing up, my window opened onto the roof of the garage. I was on the second floor, and the garage was only one story, so it was easy to crawl out onto it. Well, I used to love to go out there and pretend that I was having all sorts of adventures. My mom used to freak out, she was afraid that I was going to fall."

The same principles of using the Columbo approach, namely, "I noticed . . ." statements and talking about the process, rather than the content, apply to rabbit holes and red herrings where the conversation does not move the therapy forward. Too often, Level I counselors either want to follow clients on these detours or create new detours (i.e., talk mindlessly about distracting subjects like how the week was)[6] rather than get more to the heart of the matter. Responding to absence does just that.

Information Box: Content versus Process in Therapy

At every moment in counseling, there are two distinct levels that are occurring simultaneously: the content level and the process level. Should the reader ask, "Exactly what does the term *process* mean?," we offer the following brief explanation. Dialogue between two individuals (or in a group of individuals) can focus on the content of what is being discussed (e.g., family of origin, marriage, health status, money, and parents), or it can focus on process (e.g., what manner of transactions are occurring between the participants, which means how transactions are being conducted—friendly, competitive, antagonistic, hostile, avoidant, blaming, humorously, etc.).

A therapist who thinks in a nonlinear manner is aware of both of these levels and is able to operate on both levels. At Level I, however, although this may appear daunting and unfamiliar, it is suggested that most people have been aware of these two levels in a relationship they have had at some time in the past. Being aware of the content and process levels of interactions does require some conscious effort or discussion with a supervisor. There are many dimensions to examining the processes that go on between the participants in a dialogue. They are detailed further in Chapter 4. As therapists move toward greater mastery (i.e., Levels II and III), they find that their interventions work on the content and process levels simultaneously. It is helpful for the Level I therapist to know that nonlinear thinking is useful in determining a better understanding of what is being transacted in therapy, so he or she should ask, "Is this process or content? Do we need to be discussing this content or this process?"

Nonlinear Responding to Presence (i.e., "I See What Your Body Is Saying, Even if You Don't.")

Much like the other nonlinear responses outlined above, responding to presence requires that the therapist go beyond what is being spoken to what is being communicated. Therapists must reflect on what they have heard, interpret a client's implied meanings, and express in a way that neither insults nor assaults. When therapists respond to presence, they must make accurate observations of both a client's verbal and nonverbal behaviors and give voice to what a client does not actually verbalize. Clients have to bring up material that is often difficult to discuss with the therapist (i.e., someone who is a stranger), especially early in the therapy relationship. There may be a disconnect between what a client says verbally and his or her body language. For example, when a client discusses a painful subject (e.g., rape, torture, other horrific abuse, a perceived failure, or a painful divorce) in a monotonous, matter-of-fact tone, punctuated with deep sighs, eyes welling up with tears, and significant pauses, it undoubtedly suggests the presence of something deeper. A therapist, observing such subtle behaviors, can empathically comment, "Those deep sighs (or tears welling up, etc.) as you describe this suggest how really painful and difficult this was for you, and still is. Can you tell me about those tears?" Such emotional punctuation marks are behaviors worth noting and commenting on. They can be a significant source of building both rapport and the therapeutic alliance.

Other behaviors such as facial gestures that occur whenever a certain topic is discussed can also be addressed. Again, using "I noticed . . ." statements can be particularly useful in these circumstances. For example, "I notice the way you wrinkle your nose every time that the topic of your mother comes up. I'm not sure what it means when you do that." Clients can then either admit that there is something underlying the noted behavior or express amazement and claim that they were unaware that this occurs! However, the next time that it happens, and it is tactfully pointed out to them, it will be harder to deny. This amounts to a variation on a wise theme that advises watching others' feet, not their words, as the most reliable indication of what their actual intentions and meanings are. Again, an illustration:

Ashley:	"Yeah, wishing someone would see me, see that I'm alone . . ."
Therapist:	"And that you need help?"
Ashley:	(Reluctantly) "Yeah."
Therapist:	"Did I hear some hesitation in your voice when I suggested that you needed help?"
Ashley:	"Yeah, I just cringed inside. I felt a lump in my throat."
Therapist:	"What was that lump all about?"
Ashley:	"What was it?" (Doesn't quite get the question.)
Therapist:	"Yeah, Where do you think it came from?"
Ashley:	"Fear."
Therapist:	"Of needing help?"
Ashley:	"Yeah, and asking for it."
Therapist:	"I see. So just thinking of the possibility of asking for help is enough to bring up the old fear of being replaced?"

As mentioned above, as the work of therapy proceeds, it is necessary for clients to describe painful, embarrassing, and clearly difficult personal circumstances, catastrophic events, failures, and mistakes. Discussion of such material often stimulates associative thoughts not necessarily shared with the therapist immediately. Not sharing such thoughts is not necessarily an indication of resistant or uncooperative behavior in therapy. When dialogue is interrupted for some reason, clients can sometimes be found to be staring away, defocusing, focusing upward, or staring down. Just like the emotional punctuation marks noted above, such staring behaviors can also be very revealing. No matter what the therapist had intended to say, it is generally much more profitable therapeutically to ask the client, "What were you thinking just then?" This is referred to as "using (the process of) immediacy" (Egan, 2009), meaning that whatever is happening now becomes the topic of discussion (in this case, the staring). The staring, defocusing, and other behaviors are typically indicative of ongoing thinking processes. The nonlinear-thinking therapist is quick to detect these therapeutic jewels and utilize them for the client's benefit. Responding to the presence of such thinking processes can be pursued as opportunities to further therapeutic connecting and engagement and later movement through the stages of change.

Nonlinear Responding to Inference (i.e., "I Hear What You Are Not Saying.")

When clients tell therapists what they don't want or what they don't want someone else to do, in a sense, they are indicating what they want. They are doing so, however, in a way that fundamentally limits a counselor's ability to help clients achieve change. This is because clients are asking a counselor to either (1) prevent something from happening or stop something that is currently happening (e.g., "I don't want to be depressed" or "I don't want to end up like my mother") or (2) stop someone else (or life) from doing something to them (e.g., "I don't want my wife to work such long hours"). These are limiting because counselors are powerless to influence things outside of the therapy session. Instead, what a therapist can do is help clients to shift their focus from struggling with their problem to the solution—that is, shifting from what other people are doing to the empowerment of what the client can do (e.g., accepting something or calming down) and from what the client doesn't want to what the client wants and how to achieve it.

By responding to inference, counselors can provide the impetus for clients to look at these issues from another point of view. Oftentimes, this can take the form of statements like "You know, a lot of times people don't know what they want. You at least have half the battle won; you know what you *don't* want! However, I am not sure how I can help you until I know what you *do* want." Or (responding to absence), "I can't help but wonder, I hear what you don't want other people to do, but I don't know what you want to do. . . . I haven't heard you say what you are going to do or can do about it?" Another response, called the *miracle question,* is also a way to help clients focus on goals or what would happen if they got what they wanted. (The miracle question is discussed in greater detail in Chapter 13.) Consider the following example from the case of "Ashley":

Ashley: "Well, he takes care of the car and the lawn outside, but that doesn't take too long. On weekends, he usually goes fishing. He likes to be outdoors."

Therapist: "What about you? Do you like outdoor activities?"

Ashley: "Oh yeah, but I really don't like fishing. My husband tried to get me involved, but it is a lot of doing nothing and if you catch a fish it is gross. I know fishing is his thing, but I wish . . ."

Therapist: "Wish what?"

Ashley: "I wish he wouldn't spend all of his time doing that. I mean, I know he works hard and deserves it, but it seems like every weekend he's on the water."

Therapist: "So let me ask, are you saying that you wish that he spend more time with you and/or you and the kids, or are you saying that you wish you had more time for yourself?"

All of these nonlinear responses help clients to disengage from what they are obviously preoccupied with (despite being phrased as negative; e.g., "I don't want to . . .") when describing their problem. Recall the case of the woman in Chapter 3 who gets anxious, particularly when riding in cars. Her statements of "It would be nice to not have to worry about what could happen! It would be nice to not be so nervous in the car" told what she didn't want. A response to the absence of what she does want might be to invite her to look at the other side, namely, "I hear that you don't want to be anxious all the time, but I wonder what you do want?" On the other hand, a response may be more direct, such as "What would you do with yourself if you didn't worry all the time?" In answering these questions, she might be inclined to give information about what it is that she is avoiding (or gaining, such as others' attention) by worrying all the time, or that she likes control, or that life makes her nervous. Each of these answers would be a stepping stone to formulating treatment goals for her (discussed in Chapter 5), once she has fully engaged in treatment.

But Don't Take Our Word for It! Master Example

Consider this example from master practitioner, Steven Andreas (creator of Neurolingusitic programming, NLP) and how he responds to Melissa's inference (Alexander Street Press, 2012).

Steven Andreas: "So the question is, how would you like to respond to this?"

Melissa: "I don't wanna blow up by people."

Steven Andreas: "Yeah! So?"

Melissa: "I don't like to do it."

Steven Andreas: "Okay! Now, if I got on a bus here and I said, I don't wanna go to Milwaukee, and I don't wanna go to New Orleans, and I don't wanna go to San Francisco, how would the bus driver know where to take me?"

Melissa:	"Unless you tell him?"
Steven Andreas:	"Yeah! So, where would you like to go? What would you like to do different rather than blow up?"
Melissa:	"Tell people what the problem is."
Steven Andreas:	"Okay!"

Nonlinear Responding to Resistance (i.e., "I Understand That You Might Not Be Ready for This.")

Like the other nonlinear responses, responding to resistance requires that a therapist be aware that clients may be feeling ambivalent about making changes in their lives. Being ambivalent, clients will resist attempts to move them too quickly to make decisions when they feel ill-prepared. At other times, a client may be more direct in verbalizations that indicate resistance, such as those discussed above (e.g., "I'll try . . . ," "I should . . . ," and "Yes, but . . ."). Often, a therapist may be aware of her or his own feelings of confusion regarding a client's behavior, or perhaps irritation at a client's lack of commitment. When responding to these various statements of resistance, it is appropriate for counselors to gently probe for more information, but not to challenge too early in the therapeutic relationship because it is counterproductive to the essential process of connecting with and engaging the client. Sometimes merely agreeing with the client's point of view is sufficient:

Mike:	"Alright . . . But look, when I was a teenager, I was forced to go to counseling, and it didn't do anything. The woman I went to see was all 'touchy-feely' and had candles and incense . . . I thought she looked more like a gypsy or a fortune teller! Anyway, I said enough of this and bolted."
Therapist:	"Yeah, I've known a few folks like that in my time. Sometimes people just don't mesh. Their styles don't match. So, if that starts to happen with us, you'll let me know before you bolt? If you do, I promise no incense and candles . . ."
Mike:	"Okay."

The nonlinear-responding strategies presented above, such as the Columbo approach, clarifying ("I know what I mean when I say ____, and I wonder what it means for you?"), or responding to the nonverbal behavior ("I can't help noticing that this is difficult for you . . ."), can help. More sophisticated examples of responding to resistance are discussed in Chapters 6, 12, and 13, and handling ruptures to the therapeutic relationship is discussed in Chapter 4.

But Don't Take Our Word for It! Master Example

Working with a victim of domestic violence who is considering leaving an abusive relationship can evoke a lot of fear and resistance in the client. As a result, it is important to put safety as the primary consideration. In this example from master practitioner, Leigh McCullough, she helps Marcy clarify what is important and address her resistance (Alexander Street Press, 2012).

Leigh McCullough:	"You keep going back into the stories about asking him."
Marcy:	"I know."
Leigh McCullough:	"And also, you tell me about the men who were, uh, kind to you. That . . ."
Marcy:	"Before him? Before Miguel?"

Leigh McCullough:	"Yeah and that, that you pushed away and, you know, you, you did a really good thing by coming here tonight because you said you were gonna start counseling, and we need to help you get counseling and get support and get active support, um, on this. It's tremendously hard to leave these situations. What's the likelihood that you will be able to go?"
Marcy:	"I don't know. Probably. I, I want to."
Leigh McCullough:	"Part of you? What, what percent wants to? Is it 50/50, or are you riding the fence?"
Marcy:	"No. It's more that I want to. I need help. I know I do."
Leigh McCullough:	"Uh-huh. It's more than 50/50?"
Marcy:	"Oh yeah. It's, I know I need . . ."
Leigh McCullough:	(crosstalk) "Except you're still there."

Clinical Exercise: Counselor's Experience of Connecting with and Engaging Others

Think of a time when you had to start something new that involved interacting with people who you didn't know (such as the beginning of a class or the start of a new job).

- How did you feel when you started?
- What made you feel more comfortable?
- How did you begin to engage with the other people?
- What helped you to begin to connect with others?
- Or, if this did not happen, what prevented you from feeling connected with or engaged in the group?

In class: Form dyads or small groups and discuss these experiences. Were there experiences in common that helped (or hindered) your ability to engage or connect? How can you apply this to working with clients?

Conclusion

What is the purpose of emphasizing linear and nonlinear listening and responding? The answer is as follows: to connect with and engage a client, encourage the client to tell his or her story, and become involved in the process of therapy. In order for someone to *tell* his or her story, he or she needs an appropriate atmosphere (i.e., a set of circumstances) that is conducive to doing so. In turn, such connecting with and engaging can be greatly facilitated if a therapist is aware of the many subtleties of both linear and nonlinear listening and responding that influence those processes.

The purpose of this chapter has been to discuss the elements of the domain of connecting with and engaging the client for treatment. This domain is the foundation of establishing a strong *therapeutic relationship and alliance* with a client (discussed in Chapter 7). Connecting with and engaging a client through listening and responding are the major ways of creating that atmosphere. In turn, once that story begins to unfold, a therapist is in a better position to understand the dynamics underlying a client's story and arrive at a starting point for treatment. In turn, that is the purpose of the interview, which has both linear and nonlinear aspects to it. From here, once the client's story has begun to unfold, and she is participating in therapy, the next step is for assessment and goal setting to take place.

Issues in Diversity Box: Contextually Cultural

There is a growing professional literature on the developing multicultural competencies (e.g., Delphin & Rowe, 2008; Sue, Arrendondo, & McDavis, 1992; Sue et al., 1982, 1998) in the therapy and counseling profession to enhance effectiveness in therapists' work with clients from diverse cultures with diverse ethnicity. With so many diverse cultures, what is a Level I therapist to make of such issues in meeting with clients who may have not only diverse backgrounds but also equally diverse problems? To discuss this question, we cite the following.

In the science fiction television series of the 1980s and 1990s, *Star Trek: The Next Generation,* one of the main characters was an android, Lt. Commander Data. He was a benign figure who, although he possessed superior cognitive and physical capabilities, yearned to be more human. In one particular episode, Data discovers after having an accident that he has a *Dream Subroutine* written into his programming. The Dream Subroutine was programmed to be activated when Data had reached a certain level of development.

As he explored his dream programs, like many of us, he encountered bizarre images that didn't make sense to him. In an effort to understand these disjointed and often puzzling visions, he sought out the computer's database filled with information from thousands of cultures for help. He discovered that certain images meant different (and often conflicting) things in different cultures, which brought him no closer to the truth about the messages that his dream metaphors were telling him.

Frustrated by this lack of progress, he sought out his captain's input. The captain sized up Data's approach to the problem and asked, "Why are you looking at all these other cultures?"

Data replied, "The interpretation of visions and other metaphysical experiences are almost always culturally derived. . . . And I have no culture of my own."

The captain then seized on the moment and said, "Yes you do. You are a culture of one. And that's no less valid than a culture of one billion." He then encouraged Data to explore what the meanings of his dreams are for him, rather than fitting them into a context that isn't his own.

In many ways, the practice of culturally sensitive or multicultural counseling presents the same dilemma for counselors. In fact, there are both linear- and nonlinear-thinking aspects to incorporating cultural sensitivity in the practice of psychotherapy, and care must be taken to successfully traverse what can be a confusing issue.

Many times, Level I or linear-thinking therapists adopt the same strategy as Data for understanding clients of a different culture by absorbing as much information about as many different cultures as they can. The thinking demonstrated in such an approach is that knowing about a culture will translate directly into a linear way of knowing how and what to say to an individual because she is from a particular culture. Part of the difficulty of this linear approach is that there are literally hundreds (if not thousands) of human cultures and subcultures. It is impossible to be familiar with all cultures. This leads to a thornier dilemma, namely, overgeneralization.

Consider for a moment some of the broad categories that we use for ethnicity: African American, Asian American, Asian, Caucasian, Hispanic/Latino, and so on. Now consider the following: Are all the members of these groups the same? Are all Asians the same? Are individuals of Chinese descent the same culturally as those of Japanese, Korean, Laotian, or Vietnamese descent? What about their cultures? Are they interchangeable? Clearly, the answer to these questions is an emphatic no! Although many texts relate somewhat broad generalizations about people from different cultures, care must be exercised in applying those generalizations without determining if they are relevant to the individual client.

Nonlinear thinking about cultural sensitivity extends to other areas of human beliefs and values, such as religion, ethnicity, race, and gender. The nonlinear-thinking therapist asks, "How important is this particular client making the issue of his or her culture (or religion, ethnicity, race, or gender) in describing the troublesome issues for which he or she is seeking treatment?" Culture (or religion, ethnicity, etc.) may play a great role, a small role, or no role for this particular individual seeking treatment for this particular issue.

Instead, we tend to endorse a nonlinear-thinking approach much like the captain's. When clients from a different cultural (or ethnic, racial, religious, etc.) background seek treatment, it is preferable to start with the flexible position that this is an individual who is a culture of one. As a clinician, it is incumbent upon a therapist to explore how a client's cultural (religious, ethnic, etc.) heritage potentially relates to him or her and the problem for which he or she is seeking help.

Clinically, this not only suggests considering the client's heritages (because many individuals come from family backgrounds with multiple cultural influences) but also means taking his or her developmental stage as well as the time (era) in which the client has lived into consideration as well. The therapist must ask such questions as and listen nonlinearly for the following:

"What does it mean to be who you are?"

"What does it mean to you to be where you came from?"

"What does it mean to you to have grown up and developed during particular periods of time (e.g., childhood, preteen, adolescence, and early adulthood) in your life?"

"Are these experiences (e.g., cultural, religious, and ethnic) a source of pride or embarrassment?"

"Is this heritage a source of strength that you can draw from?"

"What role does your heritage play in your thinking about the problem for which you are seeking help?"

By adopting a nonlinear-wondering stance (or not-knowing stance), both the client and counselor are invited to jointly explore the issue of heritage and derive a richer meaning of it from the client's perspective rather than a preconceived perspective being imposed by the counselor. This is what we mean by being *contextually cultural*. It does not mean that the counselor is blind to cultural differences, but rather expands upon them and embraces them as valuable client resources (or, at the very least, artifacts). There are applications of this in each of the seven domains that we present that demonstrate this perspective and challenge the reader to consider some of his or her own cultural dynamics.

Answers to the Spoonerism Exercise

1. Save the Whales.
2. I hit my funny bone.
3. Master Plan.
4. Doing the chores.
5. Washington's Birthday.

Notes

1. The solar plexus is a group of nerves and nerve endings in the abdomen that create radiating sensations throughout the body that many people associate with positive and negative emotions.

2. A basic element of good mental health is for the client to express truthfully and accurately what he or she felt and meant. Thus, to help a client accomplish this, it is important for a counselor to model congruence in his or her statements to a client (Carkhuff, 2009; Rogers, 1951; Truax & Carkhuff, 1967). This is discussed in Chapter 7 as well.

3. Please note that these statements are not meant to be rigidly copied by the reader but are meant as general guides for formulating your own responses that fit the situation, and reflect your own style of speaking.

4. *Timing* is the art of knowing when and how to interpret or bring up something that a therapist believes a client may be avoiding. It is a difficult and sensitive expertise to develop and is nurtured by the development of what is called clinical judgment, which we discuss later in this book.

5. For examples of the Columbo approach, search YouTube for "Peter Falk Columbo," and several clips from the television series or movies will appear.

6. Please note that there are many times when this is a legitimate topic for a therapy session, especially in the first few minutes of the session to discuss any recent developments in the client's life. However, when it is used to fill up time, then it becomes mindless.

4

The Domain of Assessment

Clients' Symptoms, Stages of Change, Needs, Strengths, and Resources

Introduction: Every Story Must Have a Beginning, Middle, and an End

Since 2005, the cable network Discovery Channel has chronicled the lives of crab fishermen in the Bering Sea off of Alaska in their smash-hit television show *Deadliest Catch*. And although the allure of the original premise was the danger (crab fishing is one of the most dangerous professions) and the exotic location (working for months at a time in the frigid waters off the Alaskan coast), the staying power for the series is not the success or failure of the fishing itself, but the lives of the men in the series who have become familiar to viewers. Now in the beginning of the series, this was not an easy thing to capture. A film crew was embedded with each of several boats to document their lives, and their presence was not always welcomed by the uncensored and sometimes unsavory crew (who were used to saying and doing what they wanted, without a TV crew sticking cameras in their faces when they were embarrassed or upset). This was especially true of one captain, Captain Phil Harris.

Like everyone else, Phil Harris was gruff, cranky, stubborn, and demanding. At the same time, he could also display caring when it came to his crew—especially his two sons on board (whom he admitted he had not been much of a father to in their childhood, but was making up for by teaching them to be crab fishermen). During the 2009 season, Phil experienced a medical crisis on board—a pulmonary embolism, or blood clot in his lung. This potentially fatal illness required emergency treatment, and it was all captured on film, which he was not happy about. The director of the show explained to him that it was part of the story and that "every good story has a beginning, a middle, and an end." His illness and recovery shot up the ratings and made him a fan favorite on the show. As a result, he (along with the other captains) realized that their stories were not just a part of the show, they *were* the show.

The next year, in 2010, once again Phil Harris had another, more serious crisis. This time, another embolism caused him to have a stroke, and once again, the TV crew was there to document it. At the hospital, the crew sensed the serious nature of Phil's condition and were reluctant to record the events. This time, it was the seriously ailing Phil who told the director to roll the cameras saying: "every good story has a beginning, a middle, and an end." They documented his deteriorating state, and shortly thereafter, he died. The story of Phil Harris's passing drew the biggest audience that the show had received ever and has placed it as one of the highest watched shows on cable.

As clinicians, we must recognize that our clients are coming in with their story, and our job is to understand and sometimes help them tell it. As such, we have to listen and assess for all the important elements of it (the beginning, the middle, and the end), as well as the sweeping arc of the story.

As discussed in Chapters 2 and 3, a therapist who uses both linear and nonlinear methods of listening and responding substantially increases the likelihood of connecting with and engaging a client. Engaging a client in the treatment process overcomes potential reluctance about telling a complete stranger the intimate details of his or her story. A client's story provides a wealth of information for a clinician to work with, but most often the information initially presented is not enough to begin to work toward definable goals. Sometimes, more detailed information is missing (e.g., "How long have you felt this depressed? Have you ever felt this way before? If so, what did you do about it back then? How did you get yourself out of that depression?"). Sometimes, there may be substantial gaps in a client's story (e.g., "You told me a lot about your childhood, but I'm not clear on how you see that affecting you today"). In other words, a client tells only the conscious part of a story, or the part of the story that is least anxiety producing. Thus, a master practitioner of necessity conducts a very thorough assessment of a client's history, needs, strengths, and goals to get the full story (beginning, middle, and end) before more definable therapeutic interventions can be considered and implemented.

When conducting an assessment, a master practitioner looks for connections, hypotheses, themes, patterns, resources, and so on to guide his or her understanding of and work with a client. A therapist can then be more responsive to the needs that the client's themes represent for therapy to proceed in a positive way. Thus, the basic elements of the assessment domain are as follows: (1) An inventory of a client's story is made to allow for a thorough accounting of his or her history and needs (both known and unknown), as well as a reckoning of the strengths and resources that the client brings to the therapy; (2) therapists use nonlinear thinking (even at Level I) and understand that not all clients seeking treatment have the same motivation or readiness for change, and every client's level of readiness for change must be taken into account before setting goals and initiating treatment; and (3) therapists assess for themes in a client's narration to greatly facilitate an understanding of the meaning behind the more conscious story. Once these elements are put in place (in conjunction with the domain of connecting with and engaging the client), a client and counselor can arrive at mutually agreed upon preliminary goals for treatment (i.e., the particular direction that their collaborative efforts will take). At the same time that preliminary goals for therapy are established, there is an explicit understanding of the fact that those goals might be changed in the future. But at least the initial goals provide a direction for the course of the treatment. This maximizes the potential benefits of and satisfaction with treatment. Another exceptionally important variable in achieving agreed upon goals is to elicit client feedback. The first step in this process is to assess the client's symptoms, diagnoses, strengths, and untapped resources.

Assessing the Client: Symptoms, Diagnoses, Strengths, and (Untapped) Resources

Recall from Chapter 1 Lambert and Barley's (2002) analysis of effective therapy—40% of the explained variance for what accounts for successful treatment comes from "client factors." Chief among these are personal resources, strengths, and social supports. Too often in a client's life, these factors are downplayed or not actively utilized. Likewise, in therapies that focus solely on the problems, symptoms, and diagnosis of the client (i.e., a linear approach), strengths and resources are not featured prominently. Nonlinear-thinking therapists, however, recognize the value of these strengths and resources, and utilize several methods for including them in the therapeutic dialogue. There are several ways that therapists assess these untapped resources (both linear and nonlinear). We begin with the linear assessment of a client's symptoms, problems, strengths, and resources.

Linear Methods of Assessment: Looking for Symptoms and Diagnoses

Whether it is conflict with loved ones, problems at work, perceived failure, coping with substance abuse, dealing with life-threatening or chronic illness, or managing their own lives and well-being, human beings encounter problems in their lives.[1] It is an individuals' inability to find constructive solutions for those problems that prompts the development of symptoms. One straightforward (i.e., linear) aspect of a clinical interview is evaluation: making an assessment of a client's clinical symptoms. It is akin to the following:

Physician: "What is it that prompts you to come and see me today?"
Client: "I have been having night sweats, a fever, chills, a feeling of being weak all over, and I have no energy."

The client's job is to report what he or she is experiencing and what is troubling for him or her. It is the doctor or therapist's job to make sense out of what is troubling the client. In order to make sense out of symptoms that a client reports, the clinician first develops a linear understanding of what the client reports as being the problem. So to reach a linear understanding of a client's problem, a great deal of factual information must generally be collected. This is accomplished through a traditional diagnostic or psychosocial interview. A diagnostic interview is a structured (or semi-structured)[2] process that addresses numerous areas of a client's present life (e.g., biological health, and psychological and social functioning), as well as the person's history (e.g., family of origin, education, employment, previous illness, and prior treatment). In addition, the psychosocial interview includes specific questions related to a client's present cognitive and emotional functioning, along with symptoms and the etiology (development) of his or her presenting concern.

The psychosocial assessment, also referred to as an *initial assessment* or an *intake assessment*, provides essential broad-spectrum information that is useful in arriving at both a formal DSM-5 diagnosis (American Psychiatric Association, 2013) and what is called a brief *dynamic formulation*. The dynamic formulation relates to information discovered in the psychosocial assessment regarding the development of the client's problem. A simple example might be a man in his mid-60s whose wife accompanies him to a clinic setting. They are interviewed together, and the wife reveals that since her husband retired from the job he held for 40 years, he has become increasingly sullen, withdrawn, and uncommunicative; he has lost weight, sleeps a lot, and so on. Clearly, after ruling out other possible factors (e.g., he has had a recent physical exam that revealed he is healthy), the loss of his job potentially looms as the significant factor in the development of his symptoms of depression. Until a thorough psychosocial assessment is done, however, this cannot be determined. Information Box: Sample Information Collected in a Biopsychosocial Assessment details traditional areas that are assessed as a part of a psychosocial interview. The reader will note the extensive nature of the topics that are covered. A linear approach to the psychosocial assessment collects information in a rapid, staccato firing of questions and a simple collection of answers. In some settings, much basic information is collected via a computer terminal or a form. Gathering information in a conversational manner is a nonlinear approach that encourages a sense of relationship.

Information Box: Sample Information Collected in a Biopsychosocial Assessment

Demographic Data
Date of Assessment, Name, Address, Date of birth, Social Security number

General Information
Clinic information, Insurance information, Requisite insurance information, Referral source, Required signatures

General Assessment

Current living situation, Employment (present and history), Family background, Educational background, Cultural factors, Military experience, Religious preference

History of Present Illness

Stated purpose of visit, How problem developed, Previous history of similar problem, How was that problem resolved?

Previous History of Problems

If no previous history, does client mention anyone who had a similar problem and how that person resolved it? Does client have expectations about how he or she thinks the problem will be resolved (i.e., the client's model of change)? Past use of psychiatric (and other) medications? History of abuse (physical, mental, or sexual)

At Risk for

Self-injury? (Suicidal thoughts? Suicide plan? Adequate controls?) Injury to others? (Homicidal thoughts? Homicide plan? Adequate controls?) Previous history of risk for injury to self or others? Vulnerable (e.g., handicapped or elderly)? Abuse by others?

Substance Abuse

Present use, Past history of use or abuse, Past treatment for substance abuse, Past participation in self-help (e.g., AA)

Medical-Physical Health

Current health or health problems? Has he or she obtained a physical exam by a physician? Need for immediate medical attention? Need for hospitalization?

Mental Status

Memory, Judgment, Orientation, Intellectual ability, Affect, Mood

General Appearance

Neat and well-groomed, Careless and indifferent, Disheveled or unkempt, Bizarre and eccentric, Appears to be stated age, Need for medical attention, Under the influence: alcohol and/or drugs?

General Attitude

Attitude toward appointment, Attitude toward therapist, Attitude toward problem

Behavioral Observations

Normal behavior, Peculiar behaviors, Agitation, Tremors, Depression, Anxiety, Signs of neurological dysfunction, Gait

Spontaneous Speech

Fluency, Syntax, Grammar, Awareness, Dysarthria, Repetition, Difficulty naming objects, Comprehension, Expression

Goals of Treatment

"I'd feel better!" What concrete, visual goals does the client have (i.e., something behavioral)?

Thought Processes

Intact, Circumstantial, Flight of ideas, Clang associations, Thought blocking, Looseness of associations, Obsessive thinking, Speed of thoughts

Thought Content

No abnormal thoughts, Delusions of persecution, Delusions of guilt, Delusions of disease, Delusions of religiosity, Delusions of poverty, Ideas of reference, Paranoid thoughts

Emotions

Anxious, Fearful, Depressed, Manic, Angry, Jealous, Affect, Normal affect, La Belle indifference, Euphoric, Inappropriate, Labile, Flat affect, Depressed

The Goal of the Biopsychosocial Interview

A useful way of viewing the biopsychosocial interview is to understand that it has both a formal and an informal goal.[3] The informal goal (i.e., nonlinear in nature) is to connect with a client by collecting the necessary diagnostic information. This is especially important if the person conducting the initial psychosocial assessment will also become the person's therapist. If, however, that is not to be the case, it is still important to connect with clients during the initial assessment process because it can both calm clients and prompt them to be more receptive to the idea of receiving help even if their treatment is to be conducted by someone else.

The ultimate formal goal (i.e., linear in nature) of the psychosocial interview is to arrive at a diagnosis. Because symptoms can be grouped into certain categories such as anxiety, depression, or psychosis, it becomes the clinician's task to determine the specific kind of disorder in question. The ability to recognize the patterns of such groupings is obviously helpful and useful (e.g., different kinds of depressions, anxiety disorders, adjustment disorders, and personality disorders). A formal diagnosis is defined as the process of identifying a client's signs, symptoms, and syndromes (i.e., the grouping of symptoms or signs that tend to be found together) and determining what criteria for a particular category of pathology they match as expressed in the DSM-5 (American Psychiatric Association, 2013). The purpose of the DSM-5 is "to serve as a practical, functional, and flexible guide for organizing information that can aid in the accurate diagnosis and treatment of mental disorders" (American Psychiatric Association, 2013, p. xli). The DSM-5 is a complex, detailed, and empirically derived method of classifying mental, developmental, and behavioral disorders. In any given diagnostic category of the DSM-5, numerous criteria are required for a client to be accorded a particular diagnosis. This is necessary for a variety of reasons, such as the need for a common medical terminology, third-party reimbursement, government regulations, procedural requirements, the need for clinic documentation, and conducting research, among others. In fact, the DSM-5 is not only a standard compendium of psychiatric conditions but also a means of establishing a common, mutually understood language among practitioners and agencies, clinics, regulatory bodies, and insurance companies. Although the DSM-5 has many benefits and establishes a uniform way of talking about different disorders and decreasing the frequency of misunderstanding, when it comes down to the treatment of a single unique individual, Norcross (2002) has adroitly pointed out,

> In the behavioral medicine vernacular, it is frequently more important to know what kind of patient has the disorder than what kind of disorder the patient has. . . . Research studies problematically collapse numerous patients under a single diagnosis. It is a false and, at times, misleading presupposition in randomized clinical trials that the patient sample is

homogeneous. Perhaps the clients are diagnostically homogeneous, but nondiagnostic variability is the rule, as every clinician knows. It is precisely the unique individual and singular
context that many psychotherapists attempt to treat. (p. 6)

Bolstering this point of view, Beutler, Moleiro, and Talebi (2002) indicated,

While it is certainly advantageous to cluster patients into homogeneous groups in order to better observe the effects of treatment, sharing a diagnostic label is probably a poor indicator of
how similar or different patients are from one another especially as pertains to predicting the
effects of psychological treatments. (p. 129)

In other words, DSM criteria are useful in the aggregate for diagnoses, but those criteria have
somewhat less dynamic relevance for individual treatment. This is due to the fact that DSM-5 criteria
alone cannot fully describe the unique nature of individuals and the particular circumstances that
have led to the development of their disorders. At the same time, it is very easy to see how the Level
I practitioner may be tempted to revert to linear thinking in this regard. Linear thinking is reflected
in simply collecting diagnostic information as an antidote to feeling overwhelmed about the initial clinical session. That especially includes times when the Level I practitioner is also focused on
(1) making the therapeutic experience as beneficial as possible to a client (i.e., establishing rapport,
being empathic, and connecting with and engaging a client, etc.), (2) minimizing the likelihood of
premature dropout, and (3) obtaining information from a client that maximizes therapeutic impact.
Thus, overreliance on the linear-thinking methods of the psychosocial interview and fixating on
making the right diagnosis—at the expense of nonlinear-thinking methods of working to connect
with a client and establish a therapeutic alliance—are precisely the wrong (i.e., least therapeutically
effective) things to do (we discuss more about case formulation in Chapter 9).

Linear Methods of Assessment: Looking for Strengths and Resources

For the linear-thinking Level I counselor, once a diagnosis is determined, the next logical step is
setting goals (usually a straightforward reduction of symptoms and the discomfort that accompanies them) with treatment immediately commencing along a logical trajectory toward a cure. In
reality, however, this is seldom the case with clients. A beginning counselor might wonder, "Why is
this? Shouldn't a 'good' psychosocial evaluation contain all relevant client information that a therapist needs?" There is more to a unique human being than a collection of facts and a diagnostic
assessment—even though these are useful and fundamental. Nonlinear-thinking therapists recognize that there is other information that may be even more important to successful treatment than
a client's symptoms or diagnosis. Hence, whereas a linear-thinking therapist sees a client in a single
dimension only (i.e., problem, symptoms, and diagnosis), it is the therapist who utilizes nonlinear
thinking that integrates both a client's problem and symptoms as well as his or her strengths and
resources when forming a multidimensional picture of a client.

At the same time, there are linear methods that are at a clinician's disposal. The most common
linear way to look for client strengths and resources actually derives from a basic intake interview,
as described above. The intake interview is a historical narrative of what a client has been doing in
his or her life. It is a recounting of what a client has accomplished and experienced in such areas as
education (e.g., how many years of formal education), employment (e.g., a steady work history that
demonstrates growth or an irregular one that could have a number of different causes), marriage
(e.g., a successful marriage or numerous divorces), and health history (e.g., relatively healthy, major
illnesses, or catastrophic illness). It can also be an indication of what the client can perhaps realistically accomplish in the future.

The intake evaluation also reveals very important information about a client's current functioning—mental status, marital status, income, employment status, physical health, friends, and other resources. All of these have been shown to correlate with health, wellness, and level of functioning (Sperry, Carlson, & Peluso, 2006). Directly asking a client questions about her successes, what makes her happy, who she gets support from (friends, family, fellow church members, coworkers, etc.), and what she does to relax or have fun are all good examples of ways of getting information about strengths and resources. The question is, why keep all of these things in mind?

The simplest answer is that all strengths and resources become assets that can directly or obliquely be called upon to help a client to overcome a particular problem. Resources and strengths reside within a client or are within his or her purview. However, they are perhaps not psychologically available to the client at a particular time because the client is currently overwhelmed and preoccupied by difficulties. Clients may also not be particularly aware of strengths and resources. However, that linear information can also translate into a nonlinear understanding of a client that we elaborate upon below.

Domain 2 Nonlinear Thinking Exercise—Galileo's Paradox "To Infinity and Beyond!"

In this domain, we are exploring the traditional method of assessment (symptoms, diagnoses, etc.) along with its opposite (strengths, resources, etc.). Both of these elements are very different from each other, but despite their differences, are they both equal? To answer this question, we go back to the 17th century and the work of Galileo Galilei. In addition to his work in understanding gravity and the cosmos, he was also a mathematician. In one of his more popular mathematical (and we think nonlinear) problems, he considered whether two different sets of numbers could ever be equal. First, he considered the set of natural numbers $(1 \ldots 2 \ldots 3 \ldots 4 \ldots 5 \ldots 6 \ldots 7 \ldots 8 \ldots 9 \ldots 10 \ldots)$ and then the set of square numbers $(1 \ldots 4 \ldots 9)$. For the first 10 natural numbers, there are only three square numbers. So when he asked "could they ever be equal?," it is clear that the first set of numbers has 10, whereas the second set only has 3. As a result, they are not equal.

In fact, as you go higher in the number of natural numbers (say to 100), the ratio of natural numbers and square numbers gets even smaller. The set of square numbers is ten $(1 \ldots 4 \ldots 9 \ldots 16 \ldots 25 \ldots 36 \ldots 49 \ldots 64 \ldots 81 \ldots 100)$. So the ratio goes from 30% (3 in 10) to 10% (10 in 100). Clearly the set of natural numbers is greater than the set of square numbers, and the trend is for it to get smaller and smaller. But even though we have demonstrated this, it is not settled, because this is not the only way to look at this!

Another perspective on the same question will lead you to the conclusion that the set of natural numbers $(1 \ldots 2 \ldots 3 \ldots 4 \ldots 5 \ldots 6 \ldots 7 \ldots 8 \ldots 9 \ldots 10 \ldots)$ is equal to the set of square numbers. You see, every natural number has a square number (1–1, 2–4, 3–9, 4–16, 5–25, 6–36 . . .). Therefore, there must be an equal number of square numbers to natural numbers. How can this be? How can one set be reasoned to be greater than (in the paragraph above), but then reasoned to be equal in the next paragraph! This is where Galileo and infinity comes in! In fact, he said that as one gets closer to infinity, both sets are demonstrably equal because both are infinite, even though the ratio of natural numbers to square numbers gets smaller and smaller! Now ask yourself these questions:

1. What has more numbers, the set of natural numbers or the set of odd numbers?
2. What has more numbers, the set of natural numbers or the set of even numbers? *Please see the end of the chapter for the answers!*

Now for practitioners, sometimes from the client's view, the problem is like the set of natural numbers while their strengths and resources are like the set of square numbers. The client sees the problem as greater than their strengths, and from their point of view, they are right. However, a nonlinear clinician helps the client to see their problems and resources as more evenly balanced like in the second paragraph. Thus, assessing client's strengths and resources are just as important (if not more so) in order to provide a more balanced picture of the client.

Adapted from Hayden and Picard (2009).

Nonlinear Methods of Assessing for Strengths and Resources

By contrast, one of the things that makes for a nonlinear-thinking therapist is to constantly look for the opposite of what seems logical. For example, to find client strengths, linear thinking might not prompt one to ask a client about the most painful or traumatic moments of a person's life. But that may be exactly what is called for. The most common nonlinear methods are looking for unused or misused power and connecting with untapped social supports.

Looking for Unused or Misused Power

An old expression states that everyone has power and everyone uses power. From a child throwing a temper tantrum in a checkout line at a local supermarket, to a tycoon who is about to acquire another corporation, everyone has some form of power. The issue is more a matter of individuals' awareness and appreciation of the power that they have to influence their circumstances in life (i.e., empowerment). Some individuals know how to use their power (i.e., they feel empowered and aware of their choices, resources, strengths, understanding, and ability to influence others and the world) to sway the direction of their lives.

Another adage says, "choosing not to decide is still making a choice." Hence, even when someone gives up power, it is a choice. This can often be the first, most basic step in working with someone who feels so discouraged, demoralized, or victimized that he no longer believes that he has a choice. Perhaps Victor Frankl[4] (1963) summed up best the power that everyone inherently has: "Everything can be taken from a man but . . . the last of the human freedoms—to choose one's attitude in any given set of circumstances, to choose one's own way" (p. 104). Stimulating awareness of empowerment can help clients recapture their "attitude in any given set of circumstances."

Symptoms as Solutions: Misused Power

Creativity in solving life's problems is another form of power. Many times, however, the solutions that individuals find for their problems are not constructive and may even seem to be eccentric or downright crazy! Such solutions are called symptoms, misguided behaviors, inappropriate or unregulated emotional responses, defense mechanisms, and the like.[5] Nevertheless, these maladaptive solutions are assets that enable clients to get things done—they excuse; absolve from responsibility; save face; achieve privately useful goals (but not goals useful to others); allow an individual to function, albeit to her own (as well as others') detriment; and so on.

But Don't Take Our Word for It! Master Example

In this transcript, master clinician and author Bradford Keeney is interviewing a female client who is struggling with her relationship with her husband. In this brief exchange, he begins to uncover some misused power from both partners (Alexander Street Press, 2012).

Bradford Keeney:	"So, let's think. What if you . . . if you could only create I don't know 5 minutes, 10 minutes maybe that's too ambitious, maybe 1 minute where that . . . where he did not relate to you as a . . . as a 38-year-old, 15-year-old and you did not relate to him with your mothering skills, where the two of you not as equals in the way you did as a couple before you were married, before the funeral, before all this crazy wake, before all these things started to happen. What . . . what would it be, what could we create that it would just be a moment, is there anything?"
Client:	"I don't know, but I . . . I do honestly miss not having him to talk to. When we met, we thought we were soul mates, I still sometimes feel I could connect with him. We almost think . . . we could almost think for each other at times, it sounds very weird as much as I could strangle him at times. I also feel like you know he is going to say, before he is going to say it. I don't know we didn't really date for very long, we only dated for six months before I married."
Bradford Keeney:	"Where did you go for fun? Did you go to movies, did you go to restaurants, did you go bowling?"
Client:	"A bar."
Bradford Keeney:	"A bar? Anything else?"
Client:	"We used to take a walk; we used to live downtown about two blocks from Lake Michigan; we used to get up in the morning on weekends and walk along the lake with cappuccinos."
Bradford Keeney:	"So walking and coffee."
Client:	"Yeah. Yes."

These maladaptive solutions are, nevertheless, based in the resources that all people need to accomplish the tasks of life. Among others, they include such things as personal attributes, intellectual ability, education, emotional sensitivity, a work ethic, honesty, a sense of humor, religious faith, a positive moral sense, not giving up, a sense of responsibility, and enjoyment of people. The list of potential assets is limited only by the nonlinear-thinking therapist's sensitivity and imagination. However, a nonlinear-thinking therapist recognizes the power that is bound up in negative client solutions. Therapists can encourage clients to see that their neurotic behaviors are actually misapplied or misguided strengths (i.e., attempts to problem solve but not in the most constructive way). Some of the nonlinear-listening and -responding methods (from Chapters 2 and 3) of absence ("What is it you are not telling me?"), inference ("What am I supposed to read into this behavior?"), and presence ("What is it that you are demonstrating or showing me?") are useful in getting at these unused or misused sources of client power.

Other Examples of Misused Power

Passive-aggressive behavior is also a demonstration of power, as anyone who has been victimized by it can attest. People acting in a passive-aggressive manner do not directly confront anyone if they disagree, but rather disagree by behaving poorly, forgetting, or being late when you are counting on them. Many times, such behaviors are done unconsciously (i.e., the perpetrator is unaware). Therapists at all levels of development are vulnerable to being manipulated in the course of treating passive-aggressive clients. Being alert for this emotional manipulation and knowing how to deal with it effectively are the mark of a master therapist (and are discussed further in the Level II and III sections).

Linear thinking is mostly ineffective with such clients and, more often than not, perpetuates the behavior. If such individuals are asked directly about their behavior or motives, they will deny them and even feel offended. Nonlinear methods of listening for and responding to congruence, presence, and resistance can be useful in working with such individuals. (Other methods related to this are discussed later in this chapter under the *precontemplation stage* as well as in our advanced text.)

Personal strengths and deficiencies are not absolute in nature. Nonlinear thinking reveals that strength can be a weakness, and weakness can be a strength, given the appropriate circumstances. It falls to the therapist to be able to identify those characteristics in the client's particular circumstances that may serve as assets. Likewise, positive attributes can serve as liabilities. For example, above-average intelligence can lead to intellectual pride that doesn't allow a client to accept another person's point of view. She believes that she is right, and others are just plain wrong. Likewise, a generally perceived negative characteristic such as passivity can be seen as containing a gentleness that does not threaten others. Nonlinear listening suggests that a therapist be aware of the general resources, strengths, and assets that a client brings to treatment.

Connecting with Untapped Social Supports

Human beings are social and communal in nature—we live in groups organized in a variety of different ways (e.g., family, church, town, city, state, and country). As such, human beings seek to affiliate—that is, they want to belong. The social dimension in human personality (McAdams & Pals, 2006) and the need to belong are primary factors in understanding human needs (Peluso, 2006). At times, clients become isolated through their own misbehaviors and estranged from family members and coworkers. It is absolutely essential for therapists to assess the extent to which clients feel connected to groups that are important to them such as family, friends, and church, synagogue, or mosque. Feeling connected in a meaningful way to a group or groups is important for a client; it is a fundamental human need and a distinct asset that can help them in their efforts to feel valued, functional, and optimistic.

Most clients have meaningful support systems in their lives; the problem is that they are frequently underutilized. At times, some clients (e.g., substance abusers) may feel that they have burned their bridges to others that they formerly could have counted on. Nevertheless, it is all too common for clients to fail to recognize that there are vast people resources that surround them. This might be due to personal feelings, attitudes, or beliefs such as the following: To ask for help is somehow weak; people have to pull themselves up by their own bootstraps; or "I've done something just too terrible for others to accept me." Such views represent *schemas,* a topic to be discussed in Chapters 8 and 9. Another reason may be a lack of trust, particularly if the client has been significantly disappointed by others or is characterologically averse to placing trust in another human being.

One method for helping clients identify and activate a myriad of resources is the genogram. A genogram is a powerful tool used by family therapists for both understanding the influence of a client's family of origin as well as providing feedback about family dynamics (McGoldrick, Gerson, & Shellenberger, 2008). Genograms are "a simple, graphic way to trace the multi-generational influences on an individual or family's present-day functioning" (Sperry et al., 2006, p. 251). They can also provide a picture of people surrounding the individual, which might make it easier for a client to reconnect with them. McGoldrick et al. (2008) provided the most comprehensive discussion of genograms and their application.

Although having people in our lives to provide emotional support is generally an asset, there are individuals who can be toxic. Such individuals are a net drain on our general sense of well-being and ability to cope. A clinical assessment must contain an evaluation of the client's social support and whether or not it is available. This clinical case example might prove useful.

Clinical Case Example: A Mother with Preschool Children

A talented and professionally successful young woman with three preschool children sought help from a specialist regarding her youngest child's behavior. Although the woman obtained expert counsel from her family physician, a neurologist, and learning specialists regarding her child's developmental disabilities, she wanted specific advice regarding appropriate discipline methods for her child's behavior. She said, "I don't want to be too harsh, but sometimes I feel like I have no choice. I just don't want to do any long-term damage, but I know that I just can't let things go unpunished or uncorrected. I don't want to be a failure as a parent, and I don't want to ruin my kids!"

Questions:

1. What is the main problem or presenting concern?
2. What information did you get from a linear approach to this case?
3. What information did you get from a nonlinear approach to this case?
4. What forms of nonlinear listening did you use?

As part of the assessment process, the counselor wisely asked the woman if her husband was supportive (i.e., social support) and involved regarding the general rearing and disciplining of their child. When the woman replied that for the most part her husband was not, the counselor sagely commented, "It's best if you are clear about some things. In this instance, it seems that you are for the most part alone in disciplining your child." To this feedback, the woman replied sadly, "I've come to realize that."

Questions:

1. What are the untapped social supports?
2. What power (used or misused) do you think the client has?
3. What would you suggest to help her use her power or tap her social supports?

Sometimes, it is difficult for a client to acknowledge strengths, especially if this entails reliving traumatic or painful events. A nonlinear-thinking therapist, however, can find it extremely advantageous to operate from a "not-knowing" stance (see Chapter 3) in helping clients identifying strengths. Expressing confusion and asking for clarification can help clients to become clearer in what they are expressing and feeling, thus moving along the therapeutic process. When progress has been made and a client has been able to cope quite well with circumstances that previously might have been considered problematic, a therapist can ask in a confused way (e.g., "Can you help me to understand how you managed to . . . ?"). This can help clarify how the client was instrumental in bringing about improved circumstances. Still another way of presenting the same therapeutic challenge can be seen in the following: "How on earth did you manage to . . . ?" Again, this stimulates a client's thinking to make clear his own instrumentality in bringing about desired changes. Just as clients bear a responsibility for maintaining self-defeating attitudes and patterns of behavior, so too must they become aware of and get credit for having improved their circumstances. On the way, they may discover strengths and supports that they didn't know they had. It also minimizes the therapist's expertise as someone who is supposed to have "all the answers."

Clinical Case Example: Putting It All Together

A recently married and now pregnant woman in her mid-30s called for an appointment with her therapist. They had a therapy relationship going back 8 years, during which time the therapist saw the client a total of 41 times. Half of all the therapy visits occurred within the first 2 years. During the early part of the treatment, she was hospitalized for an acute episode of anxiety that would not subside and was accompanied by thoughts of suicide. She recovered and resumed her career and a fully productive life.

The number of therapy visits she felt she needed steadily declined as the client achieved a greater sense of effectiveness in coping with chronically nagging issues. She carried a diagnosis of a generalized anxiety disorder. She presented herself for the latest episode of treatment because, as she stated, "There's so much going on. . . . Our lives have been constantly changing since I met my husband." Among other things that had changed, the client had not been working for the past year after being a stellar career woman who began as an 18-year-old high school graduate who moved out of her family's home and put herself through undergraduate and graduate school as well. Working full-time, she not only put herself through college without incurring debt but also managed to buy her own home. She had spent the last year making a major move, selling two properties that she owned, and preparing for motherhood. Her husband had also changed jobs, and at times, she felt that they didn't communicate very well.

From her previous treatment, the therapist has condensed a major cognitive theme in the client's life as being "Life makes me nervous." Several weeks before calling to make an appointment, she "caught" herself "spiraling down" (i.e., became aware of being "depressed"), not sleeping well, not eating, being fearful as well as "paranoid" (i.e., easily feeling attacked and criticized, and very insecure due to losing an attractive figure while pregnant), and battling with what she called "panic attacks."

She summarized her current position by stating, "There are so many things I'm afraid of . . . I realized that I couldn't take any medication like in the past because of the baby. . . . I was in that mode of everything falling apart and that triggered, 'It (i.e., being anxious) is a state of mind, like I learned about in therapy.' One day I got so mad! I was sick of this being anxious, being afraid, sick of the negativity, and I refused to feed it. I just woke up and said, 'That's it!' I was catching myself, being more proactive versus allowing this stuff to take over and snowball. I decided to call you and set up an appointment. I think it's taken a lot of effort to confront it. It's like a creeping vine that's starting to grow. It's something that's said or that I see, and if I don't chop it off, it takes over!" When asked to evaluate what was to be a single session of therapy at this time, she responded, "This relationship has always been a *safe* place for me!"

Exercise

1. What would you say this client's problems or needs are?
2. What are the client's strengths and resources that can be determined linearly?
3. What are the client's strengths and resources that can be identified nonlinearly? Any unused or misused power? Any unused social supports?
4. How might you help this client see her "problem" in a more positive light?
5. What form(s) of encouragement do you believe that the clinician might best utilize with this client?

It is clear that the woman in the clinical case is feeling anxious and overwhelmed by so many recent changes. Linear thinking might suggest getting to the bottom of her difficulty with anxiety and curing her of it. On the other hand, nonlinear thinking suggests emphasizing the positive and helping her to reevaluate: She has done a wonderful job of catching herself beginning to engage in a characteristic pattern (i.e., "Life makes me nervous"). Furthermore, she called for an appointment to reinforce her own efforts with those of the therapist whom she trusts and has known for a long time. The origins of her long-term (i.e., chronic) anxious disposition are less important in the present context than reinforcing what she has already done and continues to do to help calm herself down—not only now but also on a more consistent basis in the future. This could have a carry-over effect to her physical health as well (i.e., during her pregnancy). Hence, this strengths-based positive focus for therapy is likely to produce more satisfying results for this client in gaining perspective regarding recent events.

Assessing a Client's Readiness for Change: The Stages of Change Model

For many years, clients have been described in the psychotherapy literature as if they all had the same level of motivation and were equally prepared for making changes. As a result, therapists would typically proceed from the assumption that anyone with a given problem wanted it solved and was prepared to do what it takes to solve it. When a client did not "get with the program" (i.e., do what the therapist thought was best), he would be labeled as resistant (which we discuss in greater detail in Chapter 12). This represents a linear view of clients and therapy. Real and lasting change does not necessarily come easily for human beings.

In the last few decades, a more comprehensive model for understanding the change process has emerged, primarily from the work of Prochaska, DiClemente, and their associates (Prochaska & DiClemente, 1982, 1984, 2005; Prochaska, DiClemente, & Norcross, 1992). They derived an understanding of how people change (i.e., the processes) via development of a transtheoretical model called the *stages of change* (SOC) model. Table 4.1 outlines the five stages of change (precontemplation, contemplation, preparation for action, action, and maintenance) as described by Prochaska and DiClemente (2005). The SOC model suggests that people are not uniform in their understanding of problematic behavior and the need for change, or their motivation to make changes.

In our estimation, the SOC model represents a nonlinear-thinking approach to assessing a client's motivation for therapy. As such, the SOC model proposes that treatment interventions are not necessarily linear and straightforward but rather must correspond to and be in harmony with a particular

Table 4.1 Transtheoretical Stage Model of Client Readiness for Change

Stage	Description
1. Precontemplation	The client has no intention to change behavior in the foreseeable future. Many individuals in this stage are unaware of their problems, or greatly minimize the severity of the problem.
2. Contemplation	Clients are aware that a problem exists and are seriously thinking about overcoming it in the future, but have not yet made a commitment to take action.
3. Preparation for action	Clients in this stage intend to take action in the next month and/or have unsuccessfully taken action in the past year.
4. Action	Clients modify their behavior, experiences, or environment in order to overcome their problems in this stage.
5. Maintenance, or relapse or reversal	Clients work to consolidate the gains attained during the action stage and prevent the relapse of problem behavior.

Source: Adapted from Prochaska, DiClemente, and Norcross (1992).

person's phase of preparedness to embrace change. Many failures in difficult areas to treat (e.g., obesity, smoking, alcohol, safe sex, and cocaine use) can be attributed to a mismatch between a client's stage of change and a therapist's set of interventions (Norcross, Krebs, & Prochaska, 2011). An often-cited illustration of this is in the area of substance abuse treatment. For many reasons, perhaps 90% of treatment programs in existence today are appropriate for clients in the action stage. But of the clients seeking treatment in such programs, 90% are most likely in the precontemplation or contemplation stage of change. Hubble, Duncan, and Miller (1999) cited that the SOC model outpredicts other variables such as demographics, the type of problem, and the severity of the problem in determining who stays in treatment and who drops out early.

Brogan et al. (1999) compared standard psychotherapy client characteristic variables with variables derived from the SOC model to determine which of the two more accurately predicted clients who would terminate prematurely, stay in therapy, and terminate appropriately. In fact, the SOC variables correctly classified and predicted 92% of the clients, an astounding percentage in which other studies have indicated that more than 40% of clients terminate prematurely. In addition, clinical research (Norcross et al., 2011; Prochaska & DiClemente, 2005) using the SOC to determine initial readiness for change has shown a direct link between a client's stage prior to treatment and the amount of progress made after treatment (i.e., "does the change last?"). In fact, according to Prochaska and DiClemente (2005):

> During an 18 month follow-up, smokers who were in the precontemplation stage initially were least likely to progress to the action or maintenance stages following intervention. Those in the contemplation stage were more likely to make such progress, and those in the preparation stage made the most progress. (p. 164)

Such findings are a powerful, research-based testament to the efficacy of the SOC model. Complementing data derived from the SOC model, Fisch, Weakland, and Segal (1982); de Shazer (1985, 1991); and Johnson (1995) distinguished between visitors to treatment (i.e., those who are mandated to go for treatment), window shoppers (i.e., those expressing significant ambivalence about whether or not they have a substance abuse or other problem), and customers (i.e., those seriously interested in and preparing themselves for action). We turn our discussion to a description of the five stages of change, followed by a discussion of how to utilize elements of linear and nonlinear thinking to begin to work with clients in the various stages.

Precontemplation

Precontemplation represents a stage of change in which clients are essentially blind to having a problem. According to Prochaska (1999), clients in this stage "underestimate the benefits of changing and overestimate the costs" of continuing their behavior (p. 229). These clients may or may not be consciously aware that they are engaging in problematic behaviors, that is, behaviors that they see as causing them a problem. This lack of awareness makes treatment difficult (if not impossible) and significantly interferes with a person making changes. In turn, that allows for more damage to be done to themselves and others around them. Such clients may have been mandated (e.g., court-ordered) to come for treatment, feel coerced (e.g., were told by their lawyer to go for treatment because it will look good in front of a judge, were told by a spouse that they either go for treatment or else, or warned by a physician that they had better go for help or else), or believe that it is someone else in their life who needs to change (e.g., a boss who is impossible to get along with, a spouse who is miserable or difficult to live with, or a fiancée who won't listen). The person in this particular stage of change has most likely encountered someone of significance in the client's life who has told him or her, "*You have a problem, and I insist that you go and do something to fix it!*" A client in the precontemplation stage of change clearly demonstrates that he or she is not seeing a problem or, as Prochaska has suggested, is overestimating the costs of change and underestimating the benefits. Some might call this stage of change denial, as reflected in the general attitude "It's not me—it's someone else. . . . I don't have a problem . . . It's 'them.'" According to DiClemente and Velasquez (2002), there are four types of precontemplators: reluctant, rebellious, resigned, and rationalizing.

Reluctant precontemplators "are those who, through lack of knowledge or perhaps inertia, do not want to consider change . . . the effect of their problem behavior has not become fully conscious" (DiClemente & Velasquez, 2002, p. 205). Reluctant precontemplators tend to be comfortable where they are, fearful of change, and more likely to be passive in their reluctance, and they either tend to repeat "Yes, but . . ." in responses to their therapist or blame someone else for their problem. They don't have the necessary information about how big the problem is, or what impact it is having. As a result, they don't think that change is needed. They often will respond well to feedback that is given in a sensitive nonconfrontational way about the impact their behavior is having on themselves or the people around them.

Rebellious precontemplators are the opposite from reluctant precontemplators because they "often have a great deal of knowledge about the problem behavior. In fact, they often have a heavy investment in their behavior. They are also invested in making their own decisions" (DiClemente & Velasquez, 2002, pp. 205–206). The rebellious precontemplator is perhaps the easiest to recognize. Such an individual will often argue with the therapist, disagree with many comments a therapist makes no matter how innocuous, make it obvious (verbally or nonverbally) that he or she doesn't want to be in treatment, and generally provide reasons why he or she is not going to change (e.g., "I have a high-stress job, and pot relaxes me," or "Getting that driving under the influence/DUI was a fluke; I didn't have that much to drink"). In addition, they don't like being told what to do, and clinicians who try to be heavy-handed or confrontational will find such clients to be hostile, argumentative and in disagreement, and highly resistant to change. The key with these clients is that they fear losing control over their lives (and their behaviors), so they resist any attempt at coercion or control. Clinicians working with these clients must try to get the client to shift their focus from having their control taken away from them toward having the control to make change. Emphasizing a person's control for making sound choices is important.

On the other hand, resigned precontemplators have "given up on the possibility of change and seem overwhelmed by the problem" (DiClemente & Velasquez, 2002, p. 206). Such individuals come to treatment with an overwhelming sense of hopelessness, the feeling that they are caught in the grip of the habit or behavior (which controls them) and the belief that it is far too late for them to change (e.g., "I have tried to control my weight for years, and I can't keep it off. It's only a matter of time before I have a heart attack or a stroke!"). These clients may have tried to change several times but became demoralized after several failed attempts (Prochaska, 1999). They may also feel overwhelmed at the amount of effort that they think it will take to change. Many times they have an all-or-nothing or black and white way of thinking, and feel that if they have failed in the past to make a change, that they will always fail. Or they may think that if they can't do something completely or perfectly, then they mustn't try to do it at all. Another area where this can also be manifested in is in a relationship where one person tries to change another or get another person to change, but has failed. With resigned precontemplators, clinicians have to work hard to find small successes to build on (i.e., misused power, untapped social system or resources) and instill hope. Helping to set realistic goals is also important to minimize failure or catastrophic thinking ("What's the use, I'll never be able to do it!").

Rationalizing precontemplators are different from resigned precontemplators: They seem to have an answer to every challenge to their behavior. "These clients are not considering change because they often think that they have figured out the odds of personal risk or believe that their behavior is the result of another's problem, not theirs" (DiClemente & Velasquez, 2002, p. 207). In other words, even if the behavior is risky (i.e., drugs), they are overconfident in their ability to handle it, or beat the odds even if the negative consequences (DUI's, loss of job, family, etc.) have started to pile up. These clients tend to debate therapists on a cognitive level, often dismissing facts, common sense, or their own feelings of ambivalence in order to make their point and carry the day. In order to work with these clients, nonlinear listening and responding is critical. Listening and responding for congruence, absence, and inference can help to uncover the client's concerns over their behavior. Listening for (and responding to) presence and absence will help you see how much the client is willing or able to tolerate. (Chapters 13 and 14 introduces more sophisticated tools to use with a client in the precontemplation stage.)

Despite differences among these precontemplators, what links them are the unmistakable facts that they are not interested in, prepared for, or willing to change, as demonstrated in the following clinical case examples.

Clinical Case Example: A Case of Stopping Smoking!

An elderly man consulted a therapist who uses hypnosis. He says that he has been smoking for 40 years and has emphysema. Five years ago, he had a heart attack and quit for a year afterward. However, he went back to smoking saying, "I missed it." Now, however, "all my wife does is nag me about it. I don't do it around her, but that's not good enough anymore!" He described his purpose for coming for help as follows: "I want you to make me want to stop smoking because my wife wants me to quit."

Questions:

1. What kind of precontemplator is this client?
2. What kind of linear listening helped you determine this?
3. What kind of nonlinear listening helped you determine this?
4. What kind of responses would be disastrous to use with this client?

For many beginning therapists, this might seem to be a straightforward and sensible client request for any number of reasons (e.g., the client has come to a therapist's office, smoking is bad for one's health, and the man is listening to his wife and requesting hypnosis to help him quit). It is easy enough to believe, on the surface, that the client is motivated to follow through with the treatment, but is he? This, however, would be an example of a linear-thinking approach to the problem (i.e., "The client said he wanted to stop; therefore, he wants to stop"). On the other hand, if the therapist utilizes nonlinear listening (i.e., listening for congruence, absence, or resistance), she may begin to believe that the client is a reluctant precontemplator. She may try to respond to this client in a nonlinear way (e.g., "I can't help but notice that it is your wife who wants you to stop smoking, but I am not sure what it is that you want"). By asking that question, the counselor would learn that this gentleman actually enjoyed smoking immensely and was well aware of the health hazards, which he had (up to now) never experienced. As a result, it might very well prove to be quite futile to recommend that the person undergo hypnosis, use the nicotine patch, or undergo some other standard treatment. The SOC model would recommend addressing issues at the precontemplation level by supportively helping a client begin to address how he felt about the many health factors associated with stopping smoking, what he thinks about his own smoking (e.g., what he believes that it does for him), what he thinks and feels about his wife telling him to stop smoking, and so on. Specific strategies for doing this are discussed later in the text (see Chapters 8–13).

Clinical Case Example: A Case of DUI

A client came for therapy after being charged with his third arrest for DUI within a 12-month period. He didn't think that he had a problem with drinking, and the only reason why he came to therapy is because his lawyer thought it would be a good idea. The therapist asked the client to reflect on what he thought about someone who has been arrested three times in a short span. He replied, "I have never missed a day of work. I take care of my family. I don't beat my wife. So, I am not an alcoholic, and I am not going to stop drinking."

When the therapist began a traditional substance abuse inventory, which includes such questions as "How much do you drink?," "How often do you drink?," and "How does drinking affect others in your life?," it became clear that the client did have a significant drinking problem according to standard criteria. When the counselor tried to delicately bring this to the client's attention, the latter immediately retorted, "You're just trying to convince me that I'm a drunk. You're like the lawyers and judges: You want me to wind up paying more money. It's a scam! Besides, what about all the health benefits of alcohol, huh? Do you ever drink? Have you ever drunk too much? Does that make you an alcoholic?"

Questions:
1. What kind of precontemplator is this client?
2. What kind of linear listening helped you determine this?
3. What kind of nonlinear listening helped you determine this?
4. What kind of responses would be disastrous to use with this client?

Clearly, this case example is about a rebellious precontemplator. The client's verbalizations betray the fact that he does not agree with the determination of others (i.e., his family, the court, his attorney, etc.) that he has a problem. If the therapist tries to fight the client and coerce him to acknowledge that he is an alcoholic, it will quickly lead to a therapeutic impasse and a failure to build and maintain a therapeutic alliance. Obviously, under such conditions, it is difficult to connect with and engage the client.

Such impasses result from a therapist's linear thinking (i.e., "Don't question me! You're the problem; you need to get help and fix it"). Instead, a therapist may consider the explosive nature of the client's rebellion (i.e., a land mine, discussed in Chapter 2) and utilize the methods of nonlinear listening and responding for absence. For example, the clinician may wish to adopt the Colombo approach of "I'm confused. . . . Tell me some more about how that works for you" or "I'm confused. . . . How did a nice guy like you ever get into such a mess with lawyers, courts, and psychologists telling you that 'you're this,' 'you're that.'" Another approach might be for the therapist to comment on the process that is going on between the client and the counselor. For example, "You know, I'm not sure what we are supposed to accomplish here. Every time I ask you about drinking, you get very upset. Perhaps you feel that this is a quick way to get me off your back? There really is nothing in it for me to make you upset!" This allows the client to vent his frustration in a more constructive way and gives the therapist an opportunity to win over the client to at least continue the conversation in a less combative way.

In each of these examples, once a practitioner grasps the general thrust of what the client's precontemplation is about, it is easier to resist the linear-thinking temptation to exhort, admonish, subtly threaten, or otherwise coerce clients into owning (or at least exploring) problems that at the present moment they are not prepared to own. Coercive comments simply do not match the client's view of self, life, or circumstances, and do not facilitate ownership of whatever problem the client may actually have. If the clinician continues to push a client into adopting a problem that the client refuses to see, this will only lead to further resistance and premature termination. When the therapist recognizes this stage of change, however, it allows her or him to avoid the trap of trying to make the client own the problem, just as other people in the client's life have tried to do with no success. In the frame of reference proposed here, identifying the fact that the client sees no problem in responding to the client accordingly represent nonlinear thinking. It is nonlinear because it is counterintuitive to what everyone (i.e., an important person(s) or authority figure) has told the client. It allows for an opportunity to connect with and engage the client, as discussed in Chapters 2 and 3, and facilitates development of a working alliance between the client and therapist (to be discussed in Chapter 7). One particular method that is used to discuss issues and help a client move out of a precontemplation stage is motivational interviewing (see Chapter 13).

Contemplation

Contemplation is the stage of change in which an individual recognizes that a distressing set of life circumstances exists; the client is interested in exploring whether or not his or her problems are resolvable, and perhaps counseling could be useful to the client in that regard (DiClemente & Velasquez, 2002; Norcross et al., 2011). At this stage of change, a client is assuming greater awareness of and perhaps a need for work on a particular aspect of life. As such, the client may be expending considerable time and energy thinking about his or her problem. The thinking may show itself by increased consciousness raising and attempts at decision making (DiClemente & Hughes, 1990). At this stage, for practical purposes a person is acknowledging that a problem exists. Although not exactly certain what to do about it, the individual is demonstrating a marked shift from precontemplation. However, clinicians should not be lured into a feeling of complacency that change will automatically follow just because a client has acknowledged that he or she has a problem. Clients in the contemplation stage are reminiscent of St. Augustine's famous quote, "Oh Lord make me chaste . . . but not yet!"[6]

A clinician can recognize the contemplation stage in many instances when a client is expressing great ambivalence regarding the issue(s) at hand (Prochaska, 1999). Ambivalence is reflected in client sentiments such as "I may have a problem, and if I do, I'm not quite certain that I am prepared to tackle it." Or, a client may feel that solving a problem in a direct fashion might result in failure of one sort or another. Such unconscious recognition may prompt considerable anxiety because it puts a client in a double bind (see Chapter 5): "If I address this problem directly, the way I should, it could result in failure.[7] If I don't address this problem, I'm going to have continued difficulty in this area of my life!" It is as if he is in a love-hate relationship with his dilemma. This level of ambivalence, or double bind, can keep a client stuck in the contemplation stage for a long time, becoming what Prochaska (1999) called "chronic contemplation or behavioral procrastination" (p. 230).

A linear-thinking therapist may grow impatient as a client vacillates between feelings of changing and remaining the same, and may attempt to put undue pressure on the client (e.g., "What do you mean you are going to stay with your wife? Just last week, you were convinced that you were going to leave. Make up your mind!"). On the other hand, a nonlinear-thinking clinician recognizes and utilizes the listening and responding to incongruence and resistance methods discussed in Chapters 2 and 3 to help draw out different options and guide a client toward making a decision that he or she is prepared to see to completion.

But Don't Take Our Word for It! Master Example

In this transcript, William Miller (one of the cocreators of motivational interviewing) is interviewing a male client who is aware that his drinking is becoming a problem, but he has not completely committed to doing something about it (Allyn & Bacon, 2000b).

Client:	"It's, it's still addiction, so you're stupid, so you keep on playing at it. You know?"
William Miller:	"It is amazing how long you kept it going."
Client:	"Yeah."
William Miller:	"But with alcohol, you're kinda getting to a point where, 'No, this isn't worth it anymore.'"
Client:	"Yeah. Yeah. But I'm not, it, it's not because, it's not because anyone is telling me for the outside. It's not because I'm being forced to do that. It's just because I got to wake up in the morning, and I know how I feel, period. Okay? And I, I think what has happened is ah, before I used to drink, drink, drink-all the time, and I was, I was, I was always drinking, then I, then I stopped. Then I thought of how good I felt."
William Miller:	"Uh hmm."
Client:	"Okay? Now, I have a compare and contrast."
William Miller:	"Uh hmm."
Client:	"Whereas before, I never had a compare and contrast."
William Miller:	"Now you know."
Client:	"Now you know. Yeah, now you know. Hey, wait. Wasn't it a lot better; I was more clear-headed than when I was,' you know." (crosstalk)
William Miller:	"Uh hmm."
Client:	"So and, ah, ah, to me, then, then it does become a problem, because now you, at least you have something you can, you know."
William Miller:	"Right."
Client:	"You can relate to. You can say, 'This is, this is how I am without it, this is how I am with it. This is my performance without it, this is my performance with it.' You know?"
William Miller:	"It's only when it's a problem for you really that it matters."
Client:	"Right. Alright."
William Miller:	"If somebody else is telling you."
Client:	"Yeah, it doesn't work."

As such, the type of questions and interaction that a clinician utilizes will be quite different from those used with a client who does not accept the idea that he or she has a problem (i.e., is in the precontemplation stage). Such a client may feel that he lacks the resources (e.g., courage and skills) to deal with the problem, does not know how to go about addressing it, simply wishes to explore, or may simply need to talk about the problem with a professional. Frequently, a client will express the contemplation stage of change by stating, "I'm sorry for being so scattered in my thoughts . . . I don't know if I'm making any sense . . . I don't know if I have a problem or not." Most often because of the feelings involved in coming to see a therapist (e.g., embarrassment, anxiety, confusion, defensiveness, or failure), it is difficult for a client to present what he or she believes is a coherent narrative regarding his or her particular problem. Although this is perhaps true of a client, the story being told will make a great deal more sense to a nonlinear-thinking practitioner.

Preparation for Action

Preparation for action represents a decision-making stage of change. The client is literally gearing up for action. The gearing-up process is demonstrated by decisions actually being implemented to take constructive steps, make inquiries, check things, and incorporate a need to do something about one's life situation in the near future (e.g., within the next month). Clients in this stage may also have taken some concrete positive steps toward change in the last year, and in the process, they have most likely learned lessons for the upcoming change (DiClemente & Velasquez, 2002; Prochaska, 1999). DiClemente and Velasquez noted, "Individuals in this stage of change need to develop a plan that will work for them" (p. 210).

The most significant feature of the preparation for action SOC is that change is contemplated in the near future, and often a specific target date is set. In Western culture, it is commonplace to make New Year's resolutions. This phenomenon dictates that in early January, a person commits to quit smoking, stop drinking, go on a diet, and begin exercising on New Year's Day. Individuals with self-defeating patterns of behavior that involve chemicals (i.e., alcohol or drugs) or habits or addictions (e.g., gambling, eating disorders, spending, shopping, or some kind of sexual behavior) may decide to take steps to demonstrate that they are preparing for action (e.g., setting a target date to change their behavior and taking preparatory steps toward that end). Clients may practice self-management techniques to reduce the frequency of the self-defeating behavior in preparation for actually stopping it completely on the target date. They may also take deliberate steps to rearrange their environment, thus making unwanted behaviors more inconvenient (e.g., not smoking with a cup of coffee or while driving). Some individuals may put in place concrete steps such as depositing notes in key locations of the house, car, or work area to remind them of the advantages of making a change in their behavior to ensure ambivalence resolution. They may go public, announcing their intention to change and thus enlisting significant others' cooperation and support but without the benefit of some sort of counseling from a practitioner. A commitment to consult a professional is not necessarily part of their resolution. Such *resolvers* may start out well on New Year's Day, but without sufficient preparation or professional help, they soon fall prey to human nature and typically fail to successfully implement their resolutions.[8] Individuals who never even take the first step other than making a declaration are simply expressing good intentions.

Work with clients in this stage must be supportive as well as provide them with guidance or skill building. But DiClemente and Velasquez (2002) cautioned, "Commitment to change does not necessarily mean that change is automatic, that change methods used will be efficient, or that the attempt will be successful in the long term" (pp. 10–11). Practicing self-management techniques and environmental management strategies strengthens confidence in the desire to change. Going public with the intended change strengthens commitment because a plan shared with others is more likely to be kept by the person. Clients who make good use of preparation time, and don't leap into the action stage prematurely, are more likely to be successful with their change (DiClemente & Velasquez, 2002).

Action

In the action phase of the SOC model, a client demonstrates active steps toward changing something that he or she deems pertinent to the defined problem and seeks help to accomplish implementing the action strategies. According to DiClemente and Velasquez (2002), clients in this stage "overtly modify their behavior. They stop smoking . . . pour the last beer down the drain. . . . In short, they make the move and implement the plan for which they have been planning" (p. 211).

The action stage is the most active and obvious stage of change. Everyone in a client's immediate circle knows that some sort of change has been made. As a result, during the action stage, a client generally receives recognition and support, although not always. Sometimes, friends and family members subtly tell clients that their change is too radical for them to handle. Not infrequently, clients will hear such things as "I liked you better when you were stoned" or "(Sigh) I wish you would have a cigarette and lighten up already!" When clients hear these *change-back*[9] messages, therapists must be supportive to help a client gain perspective on what he or she is hearing from loved ones (DiClemente & Velasquez, 2002; Prochaska, 1999). This clinical case example shows a client in the action stage of change.

Clinical Case Example: Action in Dealing with Anxiety

A man in his early 30s sought help from a psychologist. When asked what sort of difficulty prompted him to come for help, he replied, "I've been thinking about going and talking to someone for quite a while (contemplation). I mentioned that I've been thinking about going to see someone (preparation for action) to my boyfriend, and he gave me your name as someone that he could recommend. I had talked to several other therapists (preparation for action) on the phone, but they either didn't appeal to me, didn't call me back, or were not on my insurance list of preferred providers. I called you, and you were so nice to talk to, so I scheduled an appointment."

Then the man began talking about his "suffering from anxiety." His anxiety was especially pronounced when driving in his car and being preoccupied with potential dangers. Furthermore, he noted that the problem can increase in intensity when someone whom he does not know well is driving.

When asked how it came to pass that he decided to come to therapy now, the client indicated that he became more comfortable in discussing his nervousness with his family members. Those discussions led the client to conclude that experiencing anxiety wasn't normal. He then said, "I want this to be fixed!"

Further along, the therapist asked what sort of things he had done to deal with the problem of being anxious while driving or being a passenger in someone else's car. He responded, "I play this game and say, 'Okay Marc, you're not going to get concerned about the person driving.' I also try to look at the road, and if there is something scary, I look away. At other times, I won't look at the road at all. I also concentrate on breathing, and finally I concentrate on staying calm."

The young man spontaneously added, "I don't like to take medications. I just don't want someone to say, 'Take pills.' I want to find out why I am this way."

This clinical case example is very instructional, as are the client's attempts at managing his anxiety himself. In fact, the vignette makes several important points to be noted for the Level I practitioner. To begin with, the young man is attempting to do something to help himself—he takes action, albeit inconsistent in its effects at ameliorating his anxiety (i.e., action stage of change). The therapist praised his efforts at what he had been doing and noted that perhaps therapy could help make his own efforts more consistently effective. This represents an attempt to encourage him, build on his assets (i.e., the coping he was already familiar with), and strengthen a sense of therapeutic alliance— "I'm on your side; you're doing some positive things. Let's work together on this!" Finally, this man is telling the therapist what he is uncomfortable with and does not want to hear (listening for inference). To paraphrase it, he said, "Don't tell me to take pills to make this go away!" After hearing such a declaration, it would be extremely imprudent of anyone to tell the client that he needs and must take medication. It would have the impact of saying, "I really don't care what it is that you want; you have to take medications." At the same time, if a practitioner believes that a client is in need of a medication evaluation, there is a professional obligation to tactfully point out that medication is an option. At which point, you would need to shift strategies and realize that, on the issue of medication, the client is probably a reluctant precontemplator.

Maintenance

An individual must consolidate and integrate changes once they have been made (the action stage can be up to 6 months of active changing or more). At this stage, according to DiClemente and Velasquez (2002) and Prochaska (1999), clients realize that they no longer have to be as active or conscious in their changed behavior, but they do have to pay attention to it. Even a recovering problem drinker participating in AA with years of sobriety will refer to maintaining sobriety as one day at a time. They are mindful of the need to keep an eye on their sobriety but also get on with the business of life. As time passes (between 6 months and 5 years), the positive behavioral habits take hold, and clients become more confident that they are being successful in implementing long-term changes.

Perhaps the easiest way to appreciate the maintenance stage of change is to ask yourself (or someone you know) if you have ever lost a significant amount of weight. It takes as much as a year and longer after the weight loss for the permanent sense of a new me to emerge with more sensible nutritional habits, activity patterns, and mental attitudes toward food than were previously held. Perhaps that is one of the major reasons why up to 95% of those who have lost a significant amount of weight gain it all back and then some.

At times, clients who have attained their treatment goals are reluctant to terminate therapy. In effect, they believe that therapy and the therapeutic relationship serve as a sort of rabbit's foot, and they are hesitant to relinquish it. For some clients, this dilemma is easily resolvable by a therapist suggesting less frequent visits to see how things go. Thus, a client can continue holding his or her rabbit's foot until he or she is more confident and comfortable in getting on with life without the therapy relationship.

Relapse

Once an individual has made substantive changes, it is clear that it is not always a simple matter to maintain the gains made regarding a problem, a problematic behavior, or difficult relationships. According to Prochaska (1999), the main reason for relapse in the early action stage is because the client did not prepare well for change in previous stages. Such clients tend to underestimate the effort that will be needed or overestimate their own capabilities for coping with the stresses associated with real and lasting change. As a result, they give up easily at the first sight of trouble and head toward relapse. Anyone who has stopped smoking, lost weight, done something about overcoming anxiety or depression, or reengaged in an on-again/off-again relationship that is going nowhere knows that life does not necessarily cooperate in helping one to maintain resolve and preserve the gains that have been made. Sometimes, the cravings, urges, old habits, or other self-depictions of falling off the wagon are difficult to eliminate permanently. Other times, a client's support network fails to accept the change in a client (i.e., change-back messages). In some instances, a client becomes complacent about maintaining his or her gains and backslides into his or her old behaviors.

Linear-thinking therapists might see relapses as nothing but treatment failures, because a client was not able to permanently maintain treatment gains. Because it often takes clients several instances of reaching therapeutic goals and relapsing before finally arresting problem behavior, nonlinear-thinking therapists will often view slips as sometimes necessary steps backward toward the longer term goal (DiClemente & Velasquez, 2002; Norcross et al., 2011).

Linear-thinking therapists might also see a client's plateau (i.e., a period of no apparent further therapeutic gains) as a sign of resistance. A nonlinear-thinking therapist is not only likely to consider viewing such a plateau as a period of consolidation of gains made but also likely to convey such a suggestion to the client in order to be encouraging.

It is the nonlinear-thinking therapist who also views instances of relapse as opportunities for the client to delineate lessons learned. Instead of giving up on a client, it is at this time that the client most needs a therapist as a trusted person to provide support, reenergize him or her, and motivate him or her once again. Another nonlinear-thinking strategy to implement with a client who has relapsed is to point out that "no one can take away what you were able to do—and hopefully what you will be able to do again." The clinical case example below illustrates movement between stages of change.

Clinical Case Example: A Woman Making Movement

An attractive, divorced woman in her early 50s became involved with a manipulative, and emotionally abusive man. After several sessions of therapy, she stated that she understood the man's original seemingly hypnotic-like appeal. It was a tearful and painful acknowledgment to make to herself and the therapist. But her acknowledgment of what she had previously been unwilling or unable to admit precipitated a number of declarations about no longer wanting him in her life. Despite these declarations, however, she felt manipulated by his friends and family, who lived less than a mile from her, to maintain contact with him and help him when he became ill with a virulent, long-lasting winter virus. She began taking friends' advice, resolving to get out of any contact with him. As a result, at the conclusion of one session she stated, "If I have to move (i.e., change residences) to get out of harm's way, that's what I'll do!"

The following session was spent in discussing past experiences in which she had difficulty in setting limits and establishing boundaries as well as an episode of involvement with the man currently the focus of her concern to which she said, "I don't know how to set boundaries." But during the following session, she indicated, "It's not over, but I feel stronger!" In subsequent months, she took concrete steps of removing some of the man's possessions that he had been storing at her home as well as other concrete demonstrations of movement to permanently end the abusive relationship.

The therapist, mindful of the stages of change, indicated to the woman that relationships such as she had been struggling with seldom end in a precipitous, well-defined manner. Rather, they end over time with greater resolve, further concrete steps taken, setbacks and self-recrimination about felt failure, more resolve, still further concrete steps, and planning for the future. Verbalizations in different sessions included, "I've been scammed by him one too many times (preparation for action). . . . ," "I haven't given myself permission to say, 'I don't want to talk to you' (preparation for action). . . . ," "I'm sick of all this. . . . I think I'm starting to put my self-respect back together again (action). . . . ," and "I'm learning how to set boundaries (action). . . ."

After several months, the woman successfully rebuffed several attempts by the man to reenter her life. To reinforce the changes she had made, the therapist asked her how she thought that she had been able to accomplish her stated objective. Although she gave credit to God, friends, and the therapist, the therapist stressed her efficacy, strengths, hard work, resolve, and willingness to take risks in bringing about the change.

How to Identify a Client's Stage of Change

There are linear and nonlinear methods of listening, responding, and interviewing in order to determine where a client is currently along the SOC continuum. Linear methods include listening and responding to content and information and to feeling, as well as an assessment tool (see Information

Box: Sample Information Collected in a Biopsychosocial Assessment). As mentioned above, nonlinear methods of listening and responding (described in Chapters 2 and 3) are also powerful means for determining a client's stage of change.

Although a stage of change is easily described, identifying it often is not (particularly for the Level I therapist). Clients do not move in a neat, orderly, and linear fashion from one SOC to the next, but may move back and forth on the readiness to change continuum. Clients well into the maintenance SOC for months may have fleeting episodes of ambivalence from time to time that may or may not be recognized by a clinician. It is clinically vital to use both linear and nonlinear listening to monitor and be sensitive to a client's struggles with the particular stage of change at that time. For example, although relapse is (strictly speaking) not a stage of change, it is unfortunately a common occurrence in treatment, regardless of the particular problem. It is not unusual for someone to be doing well in treatment for months (i.e., being well in the maintenance stage of change) and then to encounter a highly emotionally charged and perhaps unexpected life circumstance (e.g., a death in the family or a threatened job loss). Such circumstances may precipitate treatment reversals and noncompliance for weeks or even months. If a client has successfully completed treatment, it may be necessary for her to reenter therapy. A client abstinent of alcohol for many months or even several years could relapse and enter a detox program with plans to return to a specific AA meeting on the day of discharge from that program. Such behavior is seen as a sign of the preparation for action or even the action stage of change. Some clients in therapy for the first time may still be struggling with ambivalence and contemplation. As with any client, assuming that each individual in detox is in the same place regarding his stage of change represents linear thinking. And, in addition, it is clinically unwarranted.

Moving through the Stages of Change

What motivates a client to move from one SOC to another? According to Prochaska (1999), no inherent motivation exists for people to progress from one stage of change to the next, but Prochaska and his colleagues identified two dynamisms that seem to be a part of such motivation. The first concerns developmental events (i.e., turning a certain age or passing a certain milestone). The second dynamism concerns environmental factors (i.e., an event occurs—9/11, a friend dies, a divorce, an anniversary, a significant accident, an unexpected bout of severe illness, or any event that impinges upon a client in a significant way). A therapist's task is to constantly monitor a client's SOC and capitalize on environmental factors to direct therapeutic interventions and assist his or her client in moving to the next SOC.

Norcross et al. (2011) found that each stage of change had an optimal therapist approach. In order to facilitate clients' movement between stage, they recommend matching the appropriate therapist approach to the client's particular stage of change. For example, they recommend:

- For clients in the precontemplation stage, a nurturing parent role is important.
- For clients in the contemplation stage, a Socratic teacher role is important.
- For clients in the action stage, an experienced coach role is important.
- For clients in the maintenance stage, a consultant role is important.

Both identifying a client's stage of change and identifying movement (or lack of it) between stages require linear and nonlinear listening and responding. The following are indications of change being underway to which a therapist can direct comments:

- Verbalizations that small initiatives have been undertaken.
- Client expressions of failure to take bigger steps to change.
- Comments that steps taken were discouraging or aborted.

- Feelings of taking two steps forward and one step back (or one step forward and two steps back).
- Expressions of having undertaken something new or different.
- Avoidance of, or declining, opportunities to regress.

Listening for and attending to such client verbalizations, complaints, feelings, sentiments, and self-assessment can be fruitful for the client and the therapy.

Conclusion

Knowing clients' symptoms, strengths, and resources as well as their stage of change gives the therapist a lot of information. It guides a therapist's initial interventions so that they are in keeping with a client's current position (i.e., stage of change, and client, patient, or complainant status) relative to achieving therapeutic goals. That is, if a therapist is dealing with a client, that person is at least past the precontemplation stage and perhaps at either the contemplation or preparation for action stage. Accordingly, a therapist will want to employ certain strategies to specifically engage such a person. It is at this point, however, that master therapists find ways to pull together the client's narrative into a coherent whole, or theme. Once all of this information is gathered, the client and counselor can begin to move from assessment toward setting some goals for treatment. It is to these topics that we turn our attention.

Answer to Nonlinear Thinking Exercise: If you answered "Neither, both are equal" to both questions, then you have just used nonlinear thinking!

Notes

1. The reader should note that these subjects (symptoms, psychosocial evaluations, mental status exam, and diagnosis) are each topics for entire texts that are beyond the scope of the present text. We present them briefly here as they pertain to the domain of assessment, although more formal and thorough training in these areas is necessary. For example, for a delineation of how to conduct a clinical interview, see Othmer and Othmer (1994).
2. The terms *structured* or *semistructured* refer to required or essential categories of information or topics that need to be surveyed and questions that need to be asked in order to fulfill the professional obligations that clinicians have to their clients. As an analogous example, a physician conducting a physical examination has certain required categories or systems (e.g., heart, lungs, kidneys, liver, senses, glands, and history of illnesses and surgeries) that must be evaluated because they can have a bearing on what it is that the patient is complaining of at the time of the evaluation. For a physician not to listen to a patient's heart when the patient is complaining of chest pains or shortness of breath would be irresponsible.
3. We encourage students to find a standard biopsychosocial assessment tool and practice collecting information in a conversational way with fellow students in class in order to feel more comfortable with the process.
4. Dr. Frankl's expertise in this area stems from his personal experience in the Nazi concentration camps. His book *Man's Search for Meaning* (Frankl, 1963) remains a classic for any therapist to read.
5. Some symptoms are decidedly the result of disordered biology and not the creation of the individual. Discerning the difference between symptoms of chest pain motivated by someone having "a lot on their chest" and someone experiencing cardiac insufficiency, angina, or a heart attack at times can be challenging to discern.
6. From St. Augustine's *Confessions* (397/1909–1914), Augustine's famous prayer when he begins to realize that he has been living a sinful life, but doesn't want to abandon it yet!
7. Failure is defined as a set of circumstances that might result in a client's efforts falling significantly short of the ideal or expected at some venture, thus losing prestige, losing face, being embarrassed, feeling rejected, and so on.
8. This may also account for the abysmal failure of New Year's resolutions. Although a target day is set to initiate change, there may be little preparation to build confidence or strengthen commitment to change. In fact, approximately 88% of New Year's resolutions fail with over one third failing by the end of any given January.
9. Developed from family systems theory, these are subtle messages sent by friends and family members that are the product of their anxiety over the changes that the client has made. It is as if these people are saying, "We are unsure about this 'new you.' We felt more comfortable the way you were, so please change back now."

5
The Domain of Assessment
The Theme behind a Client's Narrative, Therapeutic Goals, and Client Input about Goal Achievement

Introduction

In the last chapter, we discussed some of the common elements of assessment, including the client's symptoms and diagnoses as well as the client's strengths, resources, and stage of change. But assessment is really about understanding the story of the client's problem. As a result, a client's story has two basic elements that therapists must assess. There is the first element that consists of the facts of the story (which we covered in the last chapter), and the second element (which incorporates the first element): the theme or meaning behind the story. Awareness of an underlying theme can be enormously useful in appreciating what the problem is and what a client really wants (or needs) from therapy. In turn, knowing what areas may be more important and what areas are less important to a client is helpful to a therapist. We will describe each of the seven common themes below, how to assess for these themes, and present examples and suggestions for how linear and nonlinear listening (and responding) may be helpful in working with clients with these underlying themes.

Assessment: The Theme behind a Client's Narrative

A master practitioner automatically listens for a client's narrative theme—much like being intimately involved in absorbing and understanding the plot in a movie or a novel. At Level I, the common themes are focused on the problem itself. As a therapist progresses to Levels II and III, assessment delves into deeper patterns in the client's life (i.e., schemas, to be presented in Chapters 8 and 9). However, it is important for the beginning therapist to begin to rapidly assess for some of the more common themes that are present when a client tells his or her story. Although we have attempted to arrange them in a descending order from the most obvious to the most subtle, human ingenuity demands that we caution the following: These are not the only way to look at themes. They are as follows:

1. Theme of desperation: "I have a problem that I need to work on!"
2. Theme of helplessness: The symptom is out of control ("I can't help myself").
3. Theme of hopelessness: "I have a chronic problem."
4. Theme of defensiveness: "Who or what is the problem? (Cause it's not me!)"

5. Theme of exhaustion: Being overwhelmed (physically, emotionally, and/or psychologically).
6. Theme of despair: The experience of loss.
7. Theme of fear and confusion: Double binds.

In order to assess for these themes, it is important to use both linear and nonlinear listening and responding (i.e., congruence, absence, inference, presence, and resistance). A client may not even realize what the underlying theme is, but an effective (i.e., nonlinear-thinking) therapist soon discovers it.

Theme of Desperation: "I Have a Problem That I Need to Work On!"

Many times, clients will come into therapy in a state of crisis. These clients are often clear (initially) about what the problem is that they need help with ("I have a problem that I need to work on!"), and they are often desperate to have the problem cured. Clients with extreme phobias—like the fear of flying—that prohibit them from engaging in their routine tasks are one example. People addicted to alcohol or drugs who have hit bottom are another. This level of desperation often gives beginning therapists hope that the client is sufficiently motivated for change, and will be responsive to treatment.

On the one hand, it is obvious from such a client's statement that what he or she is pointing to is the problem. If the therapist helps him or her with that problem, the client will be able to live life happily. Sometimes that is the case, and treatment is straightforward. But to treat everyone in that way is a linear way of thinking. Many times, things are never quite as simple as they seem and generally require a therapist to probe a little deeper. The starting point, however, is right at the surface. The clinical case example below illustrates.

Clinical Case Example: "The Sky Is Falling!"

A married woman age 53 sought therapy due to a psychologically devastating set of circumstances. As a professional dance instructor, she was exceptionally talented, fit, and attractive with a wide following of students who eagerly sought her services. By every possible contemporary standard, she and her husband, a very successful entrepreneur, were happy and just a few weeks prior celebrated their 30th wedding anniversary with an opulent party. Somewhat ironically, she explained the reason for coming to therapy concerned her marriage of 30 years. She explained that she received a phone call at work from her cleaning lady whom she had known for many years. The cleaning lady told her that she needed to come home immediately. When asked "Why?," the cleaning lady would only repeat that it was necessary for her to come home immediately. The woman left her dance studio and when she arrived at home, the cleaning lady escorted her upstairs to the master bedroom. It was there that she discovered a note from her husband on her dresser. Before opening the note, the cleaning lady led the woman to her husband's closet. It was completely empty—not a single shirt, suit, or pair of shoes remained, where only hours before the closet was completely filled with clothing commensurate with a corporate executive. When the woman opened the note from her husband, it read simply, "I have filed for divorce. Please do not attempt to contact me; any communications that you might have you can conduct through my attorney."

There were no arguments prior to this time that would have left the woman to suspect that divorce was even remotely a possibility. Imagine the impact you would feel upon confronting such circumstances. The woman was devastated; she simply did not know what to do. To put it simply, she was in crisis.

Crises both catastrophic and miniscule are probably one of the most common clinical encounters that practitioners face. Intuitively, it is easy to see why this might be the case: the blunders that people make (e.g., an affair is discovered by a client's spouse) can catch up to them; life can be quite impartial and indiscriminate in dispensing unexpected misfortune (e.g., a client loses their job just after having received exceptionally positive reviews and purchasing a new home); and miserable tragedies can befall anyone (e.g., being diagnosed with cancer, a loved one being diagnosed with cancer, being severely disfigured by injury, etc.).

When under the spell of a crisis, human beings typically want to do something to alleviate their suffering. For example, it is not difficult to understand why people suffering terrible pain want to be relieved of it or why some clients in very psychologically adverse circumstances ask their therapists, "What should I do?" Under such conditions, doing something—including therapy—gives us the illusion that we will once again be in control of our lives as opposed to being victimized by a life of circumstances not of our choosing. This is where understanding the client's stage of change is important. If this client was in the action stage, the therapist may be able to intervene quickly as the crisis would be a motivation for change. However, if the client is still in shock by her husband's news, then she may be a reluctant or resigned precontemplator. At which point, the therapist would want to proceed more slowly and help the client move past the shock and out of the precontemplation stage (these are covered in more detail in Chapters 10–13).

Theme of Helplessness: The Symptom Is Out of Control ("I Can't Help Myself")

Another common theme is one in which a client, directly or indirectly, acknowledges feeling out of control. Verbal expressions that tend to signify such difficulty are often represented by comments such as "I can't help myself," "I don't know what comes over me," "I feel out of control," "Something comes over me," "It comes out of nowhere," and "I don't know what's going on." One particular client, feeling particularly out of control, described his work environment as follows: "I feel like I'm behind the controls of a 747, and I know it's going to crash and there's nothing I can do about it!" Of course, clients don't always necessarily express themselves quite so clearly, but sentiments of being out of control—or ill-equipped to cope—can be discerned in the narrative story that a client relates. From compulsive shopping, to obsessive thoughts, to an inability to stop drinking, the underlying theme is that a client feels helpless in the face of her compulsion, illness, or symptom. Consider the clinical case example below.

Clinical Case Example: Pregnant and Anxious

A 34-year-old recently married woman who is 6 months pregnant called for an appointment with a psychologist because she has developed a paralyzing fear of needles. When she appeared for her appointment, the therapist asked how he might specifically be of assistance to her. The young woman replied, "I've been under a great deal of stress! Everything imploded at once. When we were preparing for the wedding, I had the perfect wedding dress, the perfect invitations, and the perfect reception hall. Everything was going along just perfectly. Then, 3 weeks before the wedding, I found out that I was pregnant. I had just changed jobs for advancement in my career and found out that I would unfortunately be let go because the person who was supposed to be leaving was now intending to stay. I had to temporarily go on public aid until my husband's insurance covered me. And now I'm feeling every symptom from the pregnancy that you can imagine!"

The therapist noted that she said absolutely nothing about needles, which she had discussed in their conversation on the telephone! This represented a significant disconnect (or incongruity) between what her original statement was and what she was now complaining of. When specifically asked about the fear of needles discussed on the phone, she revealed that as a very young child, she had been quite ill and required hospitalization with numerous IVs, injections, and blood tests. She summed up her childhood reactions to these experiences as "It never fazed me. I was a little squeamish but never afraid. They even drew blood twice a day and did a spinal tap."

More recently, in a routine blood draw regarding pregnancy health, a nurse collapsed a vein. Until that time, she had not contemplated any inherent difficulty (i.e., no problem) with giving her obstetrician permission for the use of an epidural[1] anesthetic for delivery, or any other medical procedures to assist in the delivery. But the client stated when her sister-in-law delivered a baby several months earlier, she had serious panic feelings. "When they said they were sewing her up, I lost it!"

In dealing with all of these many things, she stated powerfully that "the biggest mistake I made was to go for my blood test by myself. I've always been someone who says, 'I might as well do it myself.' I'm used to getting what I want not because I'm spoiled but because I go out and work for something and can usually get it. My parents always said, 'If you want something, work for it and you can have it. Don't expect anyone to give it to you.' I like to be prepared along the way, but when I expect things to go one way and they go another way, it bothers me. I don't like surprises. I then think to myself, 'What happens if I'm all positive and I'm having trouble?'"

When asked what she would like to realistically accomplish through treatment, she indicated that she would like to get through her labor, have a healthy child, and not hurt her baby. "My goal is not just to get blood samples or vaccinations. . . . I'd like someone to see me through a successful delivery . . . and go through the delivery like an adult!"

In this clinical case example, the obvious problem the client presents is that she needs to have regular blood tests as part of her prenatal care, but this is seriously distressing to her. At first glance, there appears to be a straightforward complaint and a reasonable request for a particular treatment (i.e., using therapy to deal with fears). Despite this, an assessment of the underlying themes is perhaps one of the most important things a clinician can do, even in the most straightforward linear cases. In this case, it makes a major difference in the effectiveness of her treatment.

The therapist allowed her to tell her story, and the way that it unfolded pointed to the underlying theme. On the surface, the client's fear of needles placed her in such a state of anxiety that she felt unable to control it. She felt helpless. But, initially she did not seem to place much importance on her fear of needles. Even though the fear of needles was not in the forefront, the theme of helplessness remained throughout her story.

The bottom line for this client is that she felt out of control about her situation and helpless to do anything about it. She clearly had beliefs about the way "things ought to go," but her life circumstances took her another way. Many times these clients are accustomed to having control (as she did when she was employed and planning her perfect wedding), but the control has since been lost (once the pregnancy began). In addition, she has lost her identity (from a single, employed, self-reliant woman to an unemployed, pregnant newlywed). Although she does have her husband's support, it is limited by his preoccupation with a new job and being tired after working long hours. She feels alone and helpless. Her symptomatic fear of needles becomes a metaphor for her helplessness and sense of loss of control (i.e., "I have no choice in the matter"). Hence, it is clear from her statements that she will be disappointed if she is treated linearly (i.e., the therapist-hypnotist deals strictly with her announced fear of needles) and sent on her way. She will not be satisfied, and her problem will probably not go away.

Nonlinear listening for inference informs the therapist about what the client does not want. In addition, there are some statements that reflect incongruence (e.g., wanting to go through the labor as an adult, but depending on her husband and family that are not there for her). As a result of this underlying context, the client focused on scaring herself through a fear of needles to bring her into therapy. In fact, the metaphor of getting stuck by the needles may have a double meaning: getting stuck (by the injections) and getting stuck all alone and helpless to handle the pregnancy. Thus, the woman has treatment objectives (i.e., "I will find someone to help me go through this and not feel helpless"), even if she is not consciously aware of it. Once goals and expectations are clarified, collaboration between the client and therapist can work out the specific details of how they will accomplish them. Notice how nonlinear listening for inference also can help a therapist to identify where along the stages of change spectrum the client seems to be stuck. Setting goals and expectations for treatment are discussed later in the chapter.

Theme of Hopelessness: "I Have a Chronic Problem"

Some individuals come for treatment with what is obviously a chronic problem—something they have struggled with (e.g., a chronic mental health issue such as depression or anxiety) for many years, sometimes more successfully and sometimes less so. On the surface (linear), the condition may be either exotic or routine, and it may be tempting for the counselor to try to address or even treat the condition by giving the client advice.[2] However, with chronic conditions (especially ones that the client has dealt with for years), very often a therapist is much more constrained in what can be done to alleviate the condition. When the client's chronic condition is making her life difficult, there is usually a theme of hopelessness that is below the surface. The therapist will likely listen for and respond to themes of chronic complaints with all the nonlinear elements (congruence, absence, inference, presence, and resistance). If a therapist can assess and intervene with the client to offer support and revive her or his own sense of hopefulness, then the client will generally get back on track and manage the condition more successfully. This clinical case example may be helpful as an illustration.

Clinical Case Example: On-and-Off Treatment for Years

A widow in her 60s with a long history of on-and-off treatment with several therapists was transferred from one therapist who was retiring to another. She dressed in somewhat plain clothing, wore no makeup, was mildly overweight, and appeared older than her stated age. Nevertheless, she was neat in her appearance and well groomed.

When presenting her story, she is articulate and logical, and demonstrates an impish, off-the-wall sense of humor of which she seems quite proud. Although she has little income, she works part-time and is adamant that she always pays her bills. In her first interview, she described herself as semiretired and about to quit her latest part-time job because it was not working out. She also described herself as very sensitive, chronically depressed, angry, chronically annoyed, and wanting to stay in bed, but "I'm not suicidal."

She described childhood as being laden with criticism of her, with high parental expectations but little demonstrable love, affection, or positive reinforcement, especially when compared with her siblings.

Because the woman in the clinical case example is someone who has a chronic problem does not mean that she is not doing some things that are positive and adaptive. In fact, she is not describing that she is in crisis but simply feels the need for someone to be supportive, point out some of her positive attributes, and thus stimulate her sense of hopefulness. Often, this can take the form of assessing for strengths (discussed below). In this case, the client might be asked in a nonlinear way how she has done so well (e.g., manages to work, financially keeps herself in her own home after becoming a widow even though she realistically has little money, looks after an aging parent, contributes as a volunteer in her local community, and maintains her sense of humor) despite life and family circumstances having been so unkind to her. Reminding clients of their constructive and adaptive behaviors that support healthy coping with their condition is often a crucial first step in helping them regain their sense of equilibrium and hope—even with a chronic mental health complaint.

But Don't Take Our Word for It! Master Example

In this example, master clinician Leigh McCullough works with a woman who is in an abusive relationship. In this brief segment, the client expresses her theme of hopelessness, as she discusses the abuse that she endures and how she perceives it (Alexander Street Press, 2012).

Marcy:	"Yeah. I hate my son seeing me get hit."
Leigh McCullough:	"Yeah."
Marcy:	"That's the thing that hurts about me, not me getting hit. Him seeing it."
Leigh McCullough:	(crosstalk) "Yeah. Why doesn't it matter that you get hit?"
Marcy:	"Cuz I don't care. I just, I don't care about myself."
Leigh McCullough:	(crosstalk) "You don't care?"
Marcy:	"I really don't care if it, you know, if anything happens to me. I just, I sit."
Leigh McCullough:	(crosstalk) "You don't care if anything happens to you?"
Marcy:	"No."
Leigh McCullough:	"Why not?"
Marcy:	"I don't know."
Leigh McCullough:	"Well, just stay with that . . . You don't care if anything happens to you?"
Marcy:	"Not anymore."
Leigh McCullough:	"Were you always like this?"

In this case, the client is not only expressing the theme of hopelessness about her situation (to the point where she doesn't even care about being hit by her husband), but clearly she is a resigned contemplator. She has come to the conclusion that she cannot do anything to change the situation—or at least that would be one way of looking at her present circumstances. And if that was the only way to look at the theme of hopelessness for a resigned precontemplator, then it would be a very dismal prognosis for therapy (and a very linear one). If, however, one takes into consideration that despite the hopeless theme to her story, and that she seems to be resigned to her fate, she has come to therapy to find help. A nonlinear thinking therapist takes both sides into account—her theme and stage of change—while aligning with her hope that things could be different or change (which is what drove her to therapy). This is a common dynamic in therapy, and it is important for therapists to be a collaborative partner (more on this later in the chapter), and help instill hope that things can be different.

Theme of Defensiveness: "Who or What Is the Problem? (Cause It's Not Me!)"

It is tempting to think that just because someone comes to see a therapist that he is acknowledging that he has a problem. The fact is that many people come to therapists because they believe that someone or something else is the cause of their problems. Parents who bring their children to a therapist in order to be fixed represent a vivid example of this (see Peck, 1983). The child may be exhibiting behaviors that create discipline problems in school, or is constantly seeking (negative) attention. Some children brought for consultation to therapists may have legitimate problems of autism, or some other pervasive developmental disorder. However, it is not uncommon for children brought in (usually against their will) to therapy to get fixed to have parents who are abusive, addicted, or lack effective parenting skills. Yet to suggest any role or part in the child's behavior to the parents usually results in anger and defensiveness. In these circumstances, it is important for the therapist to be listening for and responding to congruence, absence, inference, and resistance in order to determine who the client really is. The clinical case example below may be helpful.

Clinical Case Example: Abandoned by a Daughter

A 68-year old woman with no previous psychiatric history and her 71-year old husband consulted a psychologist because of a series of events that had recently culminated in an adult daughter no longer wanting very much to do with her with no explanation of any sort. The woman looked her stated age and was pleasant but mildly depressed and clearly anguished by the lack of contact with her daughter, often causing her to break down in tears during the session. She was also greatly distressed because her daughter now tightly controlled access to her grandchildren. Her husband had washed his hands of the matter and refused to talk to the client about their daughter. As far as he was concerned, the daughter was ungrateful for the help that he and his wife had provided through the years. So for him, the issue was dead. "If that's how she feels about us" he declared bitterly, "then she can live without us!" Furthermore, the woman did not want to bring up this issue with her daughter for fear of further limitations being placed on her access to her grandchildren.

At the time of treatment, the client was incredulous regarding her daughter's behavior. She declared her daughter's complaints were vague and untrue. According to the client, her daughter would say, "Mom, you didn't support me!" The client perceived herself as making many sacrifices on behalf of her daughter (e.g., giving up her job to be a caretaker for her grandchildren, keeping accurate diaries of their development, moving closer, etc.). The client proclaimed innocence regarding having wronged her daughter. She decided that therapy was her last hope to figure out, "What's wrong with our daughter? Why is she doing this?"

In the clinical case example, if using just linear listening for content, the therapist will be led to the same conclusion as the client: The daughter is the problem—something is wrong with her daughter, but no one seems to know exactly what. According to the client, she had curtailed her own career to be the primary caretaker for her grandchildren without any recompense while the daughter worked. However, now the daughter is claiming that the client was unsupportive and is unworthy of having access to the grandchildren. Hence, the purpose of therapy (from a linear perspective) would be to help the client change her daughter. But at this point, it is important to ask oneself: Exactly who is the client and who is the problem?

At this point, your natural curiosity may be aroused, and you may be wondering "what did happen?" We are keeping the details vague for two reasons:

1. Many times, clients will not tell you the full story, or they may tell you the story from their point of view. How do you handle a situation where you may not get the whole story? How would you go about getting the full story?
2. We want you to use your imagination and fill in the blanks. Imagine what scenario or situations might cause a daughter to withdraw from her parents like this. Imagine scenarios where the

daughter is justified in doing so. What are those? Finally, ask yourself what would you do to help this couple and their entire family? (Variation: Brainstorm with classmates the answers to these two sets of questions).

Nonlinear listening reveals incongruence between the client's story (i.e., "I am a good mother and grandmother") and the reality of the situation (i.e., her daughter didn't feel supported and doesn't want anything to do with the client). In addition, listening for inference reveals the client's indignation at being marginalized by her daughter. Furthermore, listening for resistance indicates that the client feels that she has done all of the work and that it is her daughter's responsibility to act (not hers). In terms of the stages of change, she would be a precontemplator. All of this points to a theme of defensiveness regarding her relationship with her daughter.

The therapist must pay careful attention to the client's defensiveness and not enter into a linear-based discussion of what the mother and father did or didn't do. Such a discussion would begin to ascribe responsibility for the breach in the relationship with their daughter to the mother and father. This would likely result in a power struggle with the client, the therapist would be alienated from the client, and there would be a likely premature termination. Consider the following example from a master therapist.

But Don't Take Our Word for It! Master Example

In this example of a transcript with a master practitioner, Steven Andreas (creator of Neuro-linguistic programming, NLP), works with a woman who is dealing with her anger issues at everyone else, but herself (Alexander Street Press, 2012).

Melissa: "That . . . It's . . . It's their fault and since they are the one to blame."
Steven Andreas: "Oh you wanna blame somebody?"
Melissa: "Yeah!"
Steven Andreas: "Oh!"
Melissa: "I wanna yell at somebody, I wanna scream."
Steven Andreas: "What does . . . What does blaming do for you, blaming somebody else?"
Melissa: "It makes people see what they did wrong."
Steven Andreas: "Well, they're just following the rules. What are they doing wrong?"
Melissa: "I'm not talking about just that situation, I'm talking about everything, like other instances."
Steven Andreas: "Okay! Now, you'd like them to understand that there could be a different way of doing things . . ."
Melissa: "Hmm . . . hmm . . ."
Steven Andreas: ". . . they'd be more respectful of you."
Melissa: "Right!"
Steven Andreas: "Is that right? Is that a good way of playing it?"
Melissa: "Hmm . . . hmm . . ."
Steven Andreas: "Okay! Do you think they're gonna listen to you better if you blow up and get outraged at 'em or if you were calm?"
Melissa: "If I was calm."
Steven Andreas: "I think so. So if you really wanna change your bureaucracy or if you wanna change some other situation or to say somebody else is disrespectful of you, wouldn't it actually be easier if you could just be calm and centered and self-composed and say, 'look, I didn't like what you did. That doesn't fit for me. I want you to change it.'"

Melissa:	"But they don't listen. They're never gonna listen."
Steven Andreas:	"Sometimes they won't listen. Do you think they're gonna listen better if you're angry or if you're calm?"
Melissa:	"Well, how about if I start off calm, then I can get angry if they don't listen?"

The type of nonlinear therapeutic intervention needed in such instances requires that the therapist acknowledge the client's hurt and simultaneously provide the client with an acceptable rationale that potentially explains the other person's seemingly irrational behavior, which can help them change their stance toward them. In both cases above, the parents and Melissa, this is an appropriate strategy. Such an intervention can only be provided through nonlinear-thinking processes, which are described in the latter portions of this book, as well as more fully in our advanced text. At this point, however, accurately assessing the clients' themes and understanding that they are in the precontemplation stage are the most important things in building a therapeutic alliance.

Theme of Exhaustion: Being Overwhelmed (Physically, Emotionally, and/or Psychologically)

There is no question that life is extremely demanding at times. In fact, at times it can be brutally cruel, overwhelming, and randomly tragic. The trauma of experiencing war as a combatant or as a civilian victim, surviving a natural disaster and being dispossessed of one's home and possessions, being a traumatized first responder to a disaster, and being a victim of physical, verbal, and sexual abuse are all examples of this. When such events transpire, the psychological aftermath can be as disabling and immobilizing as the theme of hopelessness presented earlier. Such individuals are different, however, because the underlying theme is exhaustion, rather than hopelessness. Consider the dialogue from the case of "Ashley" below:

Therapist:	"What do you mean when you say 'a mess?' Just a moment ago, you said that you have won awards for efficiency and productivity. How do those two reconcile?"
Ashley:	"That's usually because I pick up the slack and make sure everything gets done."
Therapist:	"Even though it is not your job?"
Ashley:	"Yes."
Therapist:	"So tell me what you mean when you say that it is a mess?"
Ashley:	"Well, my coworkers don't take their jobs seriously. They are sloppy with their paperwork. When this happens, bills don't get submitted correctly, and we don't get paid. This puts the hospital in jeopardy! No one seems to care, so I usually have to go and correct all of their mistakes before we submit the claims."
Therapist:	"I am confused, why don't you send it back to them."
Ashley:	"Because it would delay payment."
Therapist:	"And if you just let the errors go through as is?"
Ashley:	"It would get denied and that's a whole other set of procedures and paperwork to correct it. So it is just easier if I correct it before it gets submitted. That way I save myself the work of doing the corrections and the headache of hearing from the CEO that the, that the billing department is inefficient and hopeless."
Therapist:	"Okay, so you do all this work up front (other people's work) so you don't have to do it later, but it comes at a cost."
Ashley:	"Yeah!"
Therapist:	"Yeah, your coworkers never have to take responsibility, you take all the responsibility, and they get the reward?"

It is also important to inquire how the client was able to accomplish certain things to emphasize the fact that she was instrumental in such accomplishments. It is important to assess clients for strengths and help them see that their efforts are not routine but (often) extraordinary. This level of assessment can motivate them to move into the action stage of change.

Theme of Despair: The Experience of Loss

Unquestionably, human beings are extraordinarily vulnerable to grief subsequent to the loss of a loved one. Deep affection, intensely interwoven lives, interdependence, and shared experiences are all part of the things that an individual loses when he or she experiences the death of a loved one. Human beings can also experience grief, uncertainty, and a sense of loss upon retirement, being let go from a long-held job, the breakup of a romantic relationship, profound changes in a company's employment philosophy, the death of a dearly loved family pet, an extreme reversal in health status, or financial loss. The point is that individuals react with grief when they experience an important loss, and very frequently they do not recognize what they are experiencing. Although they may realize that they are depressed, blue, or down, they may not understand that they are grieving.

Because deeply felt losses are not necessarily a daily occurrence, individuals often have no comparable experience with which they can relate their current loss. They lack a template of understanding for what they are experiencing and how to deal with it. A therapist will want to look for nonlinear aspects such as absence (i.e., what part of your life has not been touched by the loss?), inference (i.e., when the client says, "I don't want to let go"), presence (i.e., subtle body language that betrays emotion), and resistance (i.e., not wanting to move forward with life).

Long ago, Kübler-Ross (1969, 1975, 1981) identified four stages often found in individuals who are dying, namely, denial, anger, bargaining, and acceptance. Worden (1982) discussed the stages of grief that individuals experience after a significant loss, namely, accepting the reality of the loss, experiencing the pain of the grief associated with the loss, adjusting to a world and an environment in which the deceased is absent, and disinvesting emotional energy from the lost person and reinvesting it in other relationships. These processes represent approximate templates. The processes are similar for everyone, but at the same time distinctly different for each individual. Each individual's grief lasts according to his or her own time frame. The different stages are unique for each individual; some find one stage harder to deal with than others, and so on, but all individuals go through all the stages to a greater or lesser extent when successfully recovering from losses and moving on with their lives (a more thorough description of how to work with complex emotions is discussed in Chapters 10 and 11).

It can be useful to the Level I clinician to understand that linear empathizing with the client's loss is both essential and helpful. Giving advice about what to do to get over one's grief represents linear thinking. Instead, helping the client to understand that he or she will have to live with the loss for the rest of his or her life, and validating the client's despair without trying to make it all better or helping the client get over it, can be the most therapeutic thing that a therapist can do. It helps to focus the client on the real fear: not being able (or willing) to go on in the face of the loss. Therefore, it is sometimes necessary to counsel people dealing with loss not to move too fast. The clinical case example below is illustrative.

Clinical Case Example: Loss of Spouse

A professional man with a distinguished career sought counseling after the death of his wife, whom he loved dearly. By all measures, he was going through the stages of the grieving process and found himself going to the cemetery almost daily to visit his wife's grave. At the same time, he had also begun casually keeping company with a coworker whom he had known on a friendly basis for many years. Within a period of about a year, they found their mutual interests, enjoyment of each other's company, and mutual fondness to be sufficiently developed to talk about getting married. It was approximately at that time that he sought counseling.

The man explained that he felt he was gradually getting over the loss of his wife, but that he just didn't know if getting married was the right thing to do at this time. At the same time, he didn't want to lose this woman who comforted him regarding the loss of his wife and understood his grief. She was also fun to be with and a good companion, and they had a mutual interest in their profession. His loyalties appeared divided to him because he was still going to the cemetery to visit his wife's grave. The woman was strongly signaling that if he didn't know what he wanted, she needed to move on with her life because of her advancing age and desire to be married as she moved closer to retirement.

In the clinical case example, it appeared clear that the theme of this counseling was loss and the fear of its aftermath. Listening for presence (client's physical reactions) and listening for absence (what is not being said) can help to assess for this theme. The therapist assessed that the theme of the client's story was loss. The therapist pointed out that the client was caught between two areas of loss. The first area was the death of his wife, and the second area of loss was the potential loss of his new companion (who he could see building a future with). The therapist explored the feelings underlying both losses. For the first, the client was feeling guilty that he was moving on without his wife, and for the second, the client admitted feeling fear at potentially losing a person he had come to really care about. As a result, the client felt ambivalent and stuck regarding the possibility of moving forward with his life and investing in a new relationship.

But Don't Take Our Word for It! Master Example

In this segment, master clinician Francine Shapiro (developer of Eye Movement Desensitization and Reprocessing [EMDR] Therapy) talks to a client who is struggling to deal with the death of her partner and begins to set some reasonable expectations and goals for the session (Alexander Street Press, 2012).

Francine Shapiro:	"So what would . . . what would you like to accomplish by the end of the hour, if we could, so that you would know we were successful."
Client:	"I can't make it stop hurting . . . In a way . . . I just wish it would stop hurting sometimes."
Francine Shapiro:	"Okay or make it softer."
Client:	"Yeah."
Francine Shapiro:	"Yeah, okay so you talked about that feeling like there was a hole that goes along with that feeling of pain?"
Client:	"Yeah."
Francine Shapiro:	"Okay."
Client:	"When something gets ripped out it hurts."
Francine Shapiro:	"Yeah . . . yeah okay you know mourning and grieving is a natural process if someone dies. But with the method I use, it can sometimes help take the knife out of the heart, something just makes it softer, but it is a natural process to have. So I wouldn't want you to think that at the end of the hour, the

	goal would be that you wouldn't miss her, yeah, but if you are up for seeing if we can deal with some of the pain then we could . . . we could try that."
Client:	"Okay . . . Okay yeah alright."

Theme of Fear and Confusion: Double Binds

A *double bind* is an expression used to describe a client's experience of being stuck between two unpleasant choices ("I'm damned if I do, and I'm damned if I don't"). Other people or external forces create a dilemma and constrain a person's behavior to the point where if they choose to obey one directive, they must disobey another. These double binds are often used to control or manipulate another person, and because of the confusion and fear that the person experiences, the reality or truth of the directives cannot be questioned (Gibney, 2006). For example, if someone says: "Be spontaneous!" it creates a dilemma because if the person is spontaneous, the individual is following the command to be spontaneous (and thus, is not being spontaneous). But if the individual is not spontaneous, then he or she is disobeying the command and "thinking about it too much" (hence, ruining any spontaneity). Another example of this is bullying, where one child hurts or causes pain to another and then threatens the victim to hurt them even more if they tell, even though that is the proper course of action. The bullied child feels trapped, afraid, and confused. In other words, it is a no-win scenario! (We discuss more about double binds and no-win scenarios in Chapters 12 and 13, as well as in the advanced text.)

Although double binds are a clinically significant dynamic, they are not always easily discernible. In fact, it can often take a while for beginning therapists to discover that the client is exhibiting characteristic signs of double binds. Because of their complexity, therapists generally are required to utilize all of the nonlinear forms of listening and responding (i.e., congruence, absence, inference, presence, and resistance) to assess for double binds. It is important to remember, however, that the theme underlying a double bind is fear and confusion—fear of change or making a mistake, and confusion from an inability to commit to a decision. These clients are often in the contemplation or preparation for action stage of change. This can lead to a frustrating sense of lack of progress in therapy. The clinical case example below illustrates.

Clinical Case Example: The Aftermath of an Affair

A woman who caught her husband participating in an extramarital emotional, nonphysical affair became literally enraged and threw him out of the house. She sought therapy to help herself determine what she should do—divorce him or try to work things out. Over a period of several months, she managed to calm down significantly. Nevertheless, it was clear that she occasionally had difficulty coping with the reality that her husband had cheated. She kept vacillating: On the one hand, she would experience harmonious and intimate moments with her husband motivated by desperately believing in marriage and wanting to keep hers going. Equally profoundly, upon exposure to any references to infidelity, divorce, prostitution, and the like in any media, she would impulsively become enraged, scream obscenities at her husband, and make unfounded accusations.

During one session, the therapist asked her what she had learned about herself in the process of doing her homework (i.e., thinking about/being mindful of her uncontrolled swings of mood and behavior). She replied, "It's not like I've had a huge revelation, but there are two things that I've figured out. One is that I've always said I would never put up with infidelity—if it happened, I'd get divorced. The second thing I figured out is that I totally believe in marriage and in always working things out. These two things are in conflict. I always try to do the right thing."

In the clinical case example, it is clear that the client's uncontrolled bouts of rage and moments of working things out are reflections of her belief system and values. Staying in the marriage represents one side of the double bind (i.e., "totally believ[ing] in marriage" and "always working things out"), and screaming and raging represent the other side of the double bind (i.e., "I would never put up with infidelity"). Her behavior can be seen as wanting to have her cake and eat it too. She wants to stay married (i.e., she views divorcées as losers), and at the same time, she is totally intolerant of the fact that her spouse had cheated (i.e., she has long maintained that she would get divorced if her husband was unfaithful). She is afraid to make a mistake by leaving, and she is equally afraid to stay. This leads to her apparently confusing behaviors. From a nonlinear perspective, however, the behavior does make sense.

In terms of the nonlinear listening involved, her vacillation was a sign of incongruence and some resistance to dealing with the subject. Also there is an absence of her own part in the marital dyad that may have contributed to the infidelity, plus her strong emotions are clearly a presence in the therapy that contradicts many of her incongruent statements. In addition, her declarations of what she would not tolerate allow the clinician to infer her goals for therapy. Clearly, for her to move into the action stage would mean that she would have to make a decision. Therefore, by vacillating, she is able to put off making a decision (although at a price!). We discuss the important subject of schemes, double binds, the ambivalences they generate, and nonlinear ways of dealing with them in greater detail in the later chapters of the book.

Clinician Attitude and Disposition: Collaboration

"Coming together is a beginning, staying together is progress, and working together is success."
—Henry Ford

Medicine at the turn of the 20th century was based on what is called *medical paternalism.* Contemporary therapy grew from that traditional paternalistic medical model (remember that Freud was originally trained as a physician). Even as late as a few decades ago, paternalism was the state of the art in the practice of medicine—a philosophy of "The doctor knows best—don't ask questions—follow my directions—it's doctor's orders—everything will be okay. . . ." This phenomenon was so profound that it led Cummings (1986) to note,

> It is a propensity of psychotherapy that every patient who walks into a therapist's office receives the type of therapy the psychotherapist has to offer. If the therapist is a Freudian analyst, he or she does not care what the patient has—alcoholism, marital problems, or job problems—that patient is going to get the couch. If the therapist is a Jungian analyst, the patient is going to paint pictures. If the therapist is a behaviorist, the patient is going to get desensitization. (p. 429)

As information has become more widely available, and as individuals have become more involved in their care, this idealized vision of the infallible doctor has gone away, and "(t)he field can no longer assume that therapists know what is best, independent of consumers" (Hubble et al., 2010, p. 36). In its place is *collaboration.*

What does it mean to adopt a strategy or disposition of collaboration? It is a democratic stance, but it does not mean that the clinician gives up their expertise in the clinical realm. It means that the therapist values the client's input and sees them as a partner in the therapy. It does mean that they don't believe that their knowledge is less important than their client's knowledge or information, either. Rather, "(c)ollaboration represents the active process of working together to fulfill therapy goals . . . Collaboration is a pan-theoretical concept that applies to all types of therapies" (Tyron & Winograd, 2001, p. 157).

In fact, Tyron and Winograd (2001) conducted a meta-analysis looking at studies that assessed collaboration in therapeutic settings. They found that in 89% of the studies they used, higher levels of collaboration were positively associated with treatment success. Ten years later, they conducted a follow-up meta analysis, and found a mean correlation of 0.33 between collaboration and outcome. This is considered a medium effect size, but important because they did not discover any moderating variables. The bottom line is that collaboration is a variable that is directly tied to positive outcomes, that is under the therapist's control. "This effect corresponds to a 2/3 standard deviation ($d = 0.68$) improvement associated with a 1 standard deviation boost in collaboration. Thus, patient experience and well-being appear to be considerably enhanced with a better quality collaborative relationship between the patient and the therapist" (Tyron & Winograd, 2001, p. 162).

Hubble et al. (2010) argued that for therapists to adopt a collaborative stance, it means that they have to "organize clinical services to clients: who they are, what they want, and what constitutes and influences the circumstances of their lives" (Hubble et al., 2010, p. 36). Tryon and Winograd (2011) suggest certain practices that clinicians might find useful in working collaboratively with clients toward their goals. These include:

- Working on problems only after the client and therapist agree on therapeutic goals and the methods to be used in reaching those goals.
- Pursuing input on what the client is seeking to achieve, rather than pressing the therapist's agenda. (We note that this requires linear and nonlinear listening.)
- Encouraging clients' "feedback, insights, reflections, and elaboration" (p. 164) as well as seeking information about their current functional status (i.e., how they are doing).
- Teaching clients about the importance of their contributions to the process of treatment.
- Encouraging the completion of homework assignments that directly relate to the goals of treatment.
- Making certain that client and therapist share the same understanding and check frequently about whether or not mutual understandings are in effect.
- Being flexible and willing to modify treatment methods employed in response to feedback from clients.

In the following chapters (especially in Domain 3), it will be apparent that collaboration is critical for building the therapeutic relationship. However, in assessment, it is especially important to adopt a collaborative stance when it comes to understanding the client's symptoms or complaints (e.g., "Tell me how *you* experience your sadness . . ."), as well as strengths and resources (e.g., "So how have *you* figured a way to get this far along . . ."). Most important, collaboration means being willing to admit that we are not always the expert. It means being willing to be influenced by the client's needs or agenda, and soliciting their feedback. Finally, when it comes to goal setting, collaboration means having a shared understanding of the client's story so far, as well as having a shared understanding of where the story is going to go in the future.

Therapeutic Goals

All therapy is a contract between the therapist and client. Goals are the agreement about what will be worked on and how it will be achieved. This agreement is called goal consensus, and it is vital to the success of therapy. In fact, Tyron and Winograd (2011) found that for every 1 standard deviation increase in goal consensus between a therapist and a client, there was a 0.75 standard deviation increase in therapeutic outcome. This is a powerful relationship (just as with collaboration) for client retention in therapy, as well as in successfully resolving client issues.

Establishing treatment goals is critically important if a client is going to be successful in therapy. There are a number of potential consequences as a result of not having clear goals in treatment. For example:

- The treatment sessions can and do wander somewhat aimlessly from session to session even though important material may be discussed.
- There can be little sense of making progress because there is no bench mark as to how much progress is being made toward what.
- Client satisfaction can diminish or disappear.
- Clients can drop out prematurely.

As a result, it is vital that the therapist and client establish clear goals for treatment and that their goals are in alignment. Otherwise, client and therapist work at cross-purposes. Perhaps the most cogent way to avoid this is to help a client develop more concrete (i.e., behavioral and visualizable) indications that the client either is approximating or has actually arrived at what it is that the client wants to accomplish. Oftentimes, a simple question can greatly help facilitate a client's development of specific goals, such as "How would you know that you had gotten what it is that you have come to counseling for?" The clinical case example below may prove useful.

Clinical Case Example: Art, Not Sex!

A handsome, middle-aged, well-educated, never-married retired man in excellent physical condition was participating in supportive psychotherapy on a monthly basis. He was well aware and accepting of his need for help in dealing with his propensity for overreacting to and obsessing about many of life's ordinary difficult circumstances. At the same time, he was taking a psychotropic medication designed to help calm him and manage his mood; this was prescribed by a physician who had known the man and his history for several years. Although the client was a multitalented individual who had casually dated attractive women for many years, he had never engaged in sexual relations. Consciously, he explained the reason for this as being because of religious hang-ups. When asked what these hang-ups might be, he explained that having sex outside of marriage was a sin, and he never felt prepared to accept (i.e., he felt overwhelmed by) the financial and psychological responsibility of being married with a family to support. His doctor told him off-handedly, "You should get laid!"

In the clinical case example, the client saw his therapist after this appointment with his doctor and confided that he was very upset. He began discussing what his doctor had told him and knew that he was obsessing about it. When asked if he felt prepared to pursue having a sexual relationship with a woman, he decisively indicated, "Definitely not!" He explained that pursuing such a goal would cause him no end of guilt and obsessive preoccupation at the expense of what he was interested in pursuing, namely, perfecting his considerable artistic abilities. With a strong therapeutic alliance, the therapist perceived the myriad problems that would result from this action, and agreed with the client that he had other preoccupations and that seeking a sexual encounter was not very high on his list of life priorities. In addition, as the client stated, the therapist supported the client's contention that having a sexual encounter with a woman was likely to generate further problems with guilt.

Obviously, a misalignment between a practitioner's goals (in this case, the client's physician) and the client's goals can easily cause significant problems. An active and clear discussion must take place of what issues are to be worked on and what are reasonably achievable goals. Perhaps Hoyt and Berg (1998), in discussing the development of solution-focused goals, put it most succinctly, stating that the best goals:

> are small rather than large; salient to clients; articulated in specific, concrete behavioral terms; achievable within the practical contexts of clients' lives; perceived by clients as involving their own hard work; seen as the "start of something" and not as the "end of something"; and treated as involving new behavior rather than the absence or cessation of existing behavior. (p. 316)

Such a discussion clearly lays out agreed upon expectations for and steps of therapy—that is, what will be discussed, what won't be discussed, identifying and evaluating signs of progress, identifying signs of regression, and finally the proper end point to the therapy itself (see Skovholt & Rivers, 2004). Without such goals, the course of therapeutic encounters can wander.

Making Good Therapeutic Goals

The question remains, what makes for good therapeutic goals? In addition to the factors listed above, effective goals should result from a careful examination of a client's needs and wishes. This does not mean, however, "Whatever the client says, goes." This is because sometimes clients do not know what they want, or feel coerced into therapy when they are neither ready nor willing to make changes (e.g., they are precontemplators). Still other clients come to therapy with unrealistic goals and expectations. Thus, a therapist has an important role to play in helping the client set appropriate goals. A therapist must take into account the resources (e.g., strengths, use of power, and social supports) that a client brings into therapy, and then focus the client on goals that are reasonable and realistic. Last, a therapist must also help to set an appropriate and reasonable time frame for the change to occur that encourages working toward desired changes, rather than failure (Skovholt & Rivers, 2004). In order to accomplish this, Tyron and Winograd (2011) recommend that therapists: "Be 'on the same page' with patients. Check frequently with patients to make sure you understand each other and are working towards the same ends . . . Modify your treatment methods and relationship stance, if ethically and clinically appropriate, in response to patient feedback" (p. 165).

Although a therapist's role is important, a client's role in the goal-setting process is equally valuable. Clients must be willing to challenge themselves, commit to the change process, and confront whatever core issues may arise as a result. They must recognize and identify a significant life issue that they want to change. In addition, both therapist and client, when setting goals, need to focus on positive, not negative change and provide for the necessary checks along the way (i.e., short-term and midrange goals on the way to longer term goals). Whatever goals client and counselor agree upon in the collaborative process, such goals must be consistent with the client's needs and the counselor's capabilities to help (Skovholt & Rivers, 2004). Last, goals should be open to change, revision, and evolution as the therapeutic process moves forward, therapeutic milestones are reached, and new elements emerge.

Information Box: Questions for Client and Counselor in Considering Goal Setting

Questions to Ask Clients for Setting Goals

- How would you like for things to be different?
- What would you like to change in your life?
- What would you like to accomplish? How would you know that you had achieved what it is that you came to therapy for?
- How would you know that therapy was successful?
- If your problems were resolved and you were living the life you wanted, what would be different in your life (miracle question)?

Questions to Ask Oneself (as a Counselor) for Setting Goals

- Does the goal address the client's symptoms or problems?
- Does the goal match the client's readiness level for change?
- Is there a good purpose for the goal? Is it reasonable and measurable, with a time frame for completion? Is it achievable in the time frame with specifically defined action steps?
- Will treatment goals address core issues underlying the problem?

Exercise: Return to the second clinical case example in Chapter 4 and apply the questions above. Answer using case material that was given. Form dyads (or group of students) and discuss possible treatment goals.

Our Nonlinear Brain: Visualizing Goals

As we discussed in Chapters 2 and 3, most typically, when a client is asked what she might like the outcome (i.e., goal) of treatment to be, she replies, "I want to feel better . . . more relaxed. . . . I don't want to argue with my husband. . . . I want to be happier in life. . . . I don't want to be depressed. . . . I don't know. . . . I don't want to have these urges. . . . I want all of it to go away. . . ." All such articulations are understandable when someone is in the throes of suffering. But in terms of how the brain actually operates, it becomes difficult for a client to pursue feelings as an objective. Feeling good is the result of achieving a particular desired goal. On the other hand, pursuing a goal that is concretely visualizable is much more in keeping with how the brain actually works. For individuals to aspire to therapeutic goals, it is valuable and perhaps essential that they specify in concrete and clear—preferably visualizable—terms of what it is that they do want or how they want to be, to the extent that it could be seen on a TV monitor.

Pinker (1999) illustrated creative thinkers' use of imagination to solve complex problems:

Many creative people claim to "see" the solution to a problem in an image. Faraday and Maxwell visualized electromagnetic fields as tiny tubes filled with fluid. Kekulé saw the benzene ring in a reverie of snakes biting their tails. Watson and Crick mentally rotated models of what was to become the double helix. Einstein imagined what it would be like to ride on a beam of light or drop a penny in a plummeting elevator. He once wrote, "My particular ability does not lie in mathematical calculation, but rather in visualizing effects, possibilities, and consequences. Painters and sculptors try out ideas in their minds, and even novelists visualize scenes and plots in their mind's eye before putting pen to paper. . . . Images drive the emotions as well as the intellect. . . . Ambition, anxiety, sexual arousal, and jealous rage can all be triggered by images of what isn't there." (p. 285)

Research in neurobiology is revealing that "thinking in images engages the visual parts of the brain" and "images really do seem to be laid across the cortical surface" (Pinker, 1999, pp. 287, 289). Clinical hypnosis has historically utilized the subconscious relationship to visualization as a major factor in helping clients to achieve therapeutic successes: "There is a tendency on the part of the subconscious to carry out any prolonged and repeated visual image" (Cheek & Le Cron, 1968, p. 60). Kroger and Fezler (1976) and Hammond (1984) have compiled a series of images and metaphors designed to enhance clients' success in overcoming a wide range of human problems.

However, there is a cost and a caution from some neuroscience researchers. Often unrestrained goal setting and even moderate goals go unfulfilled. King and Burton (2003) caution to be restrained in goal setting, "The optimally striving individual ought to endeavor to achieve and approach goals that only slightly implicate the self; that are only moderately important, fairly easy, and moderately abstract; that do not conflict with each other, and that concern the accomplishment of something other than financial gain" (p. 68). More recently, Spunt and Lieberman (2013) using functional MRI scans reported findings that may account for these goal setting failures. They asked participants to think about *how* the people were doing a specific task or *why* the people were doing them. When participants thought about the *how,* specific regions on the left side of the brain such as the premotor cortex that are involved in tracking the location of oneself and others in space and planning motor movements were active. When they were asked to think about the *why,* an entirely different set of regions in the brain were activated. Areas like the right temporoparietal junction, the precuneus, and the dorsomedial prefrontal cortex—which become active when a person thinks about the states and intentions of others—were active. Perhaps most interesting was the finding that the two sets of regions were almost completely different from each other. In fact, there was even a suggestion (although not confirmed) that when one system is activated, the other system may be suppressed. As a result, when clinicians want to help move a client toward setting and achieving goals, it is important to activate the *why* system and the *how* system alternatively in order to get the client to think alternatively about both when determining their goals. This may be particularly useful when clients seem stuck or unable to either set or plan on achieving goals. Understanding the nonlinear neuroscience behind it can give clinicians the ability to help clients achieve their goals more effectively.

Treatment Plans

A *treatment plan* is an overview of the understanding between therapist and client as to the more formal agreement that they have. As a plan, it is an outline of what both parties can expect: goals, objectives, steps to be taken, time frames, and mechanisms for review. Clinics, inpatient psychiatric hospitals, outpatient treatment centers, substance abuse programs, and so on all require that a treatment plan is properly entered in the medical record and updated periodically. In fact, in some settings, multidisciplinary input is required, for example the Joint Commission on the Accreditation of Healthcare Organizations (JCAHO) or the Commission on Accreditation of Rehabilitation Facilities (CARF).

Treatment plans are meant to keep what happens in treatment on track.[3] As such, a formal treatment plan is a complement to such procedures as eliciting client feedback on therapeutic progress. Specifically, treatment plans cover what type of mental health procedures will be provided (e.g., marital therapy, cognitive behavioral therapy, or group therapy), for what problem, by whom, how often, and the desired goal (e.g., criteria). Formal treatment plans need to be signed and dated by the therapist, and reviewed and updated periodically to make certain they reflect changing client needs. We discuss this in more detail in Chapter 9 as we discuss treatment formulations.

What Happens When Goals Don't Align?

Despite the best efforts, there are times when a client's goals simply don't align with what the therapist believes the stated goals of treatment to be. When this occurs, it is usually because one or more of the elements presented over the last two chapters have been missed. Consider the following:

- Did the counselor connect with the client (i.e., listen and respond effectively to the client)?
- Did the counselor understand the underlying client dynamics and take into consideration the client's stage of change?
- Were strengths or resources overlooked or underutilized?
- Did the client's goals change during the course of the therapy without the therapist being aware of it?

Answers to such questions are important. For example, if a therapist was too eager to move a client toward a solution when the client demonstrated signs of being a reluctant precontemplator, then that therapist is contributing to the client's resistance. Likewise, if part of a treatment plan requires a client to use undeveloped skills or needs to rely on the support of other unavailable people, then the treatment plan will likely fail. When this happens, a therapist must review the treatment plan and look at the elements within it. Perhaps, the counselor missed an element, or perhaps the client was simply not ready to move forward. Slowing down treatment to review the treatment plan signals to a client that such things are valued—which can strengthen the therapeutic relationship.

Issues in Diversity Box: Contextually Cultural

Developing the expertise of a master practitioner for connecting with and engaging clients in treatment is an art. It is the master practitioner who engages in a lifelong process of learning about human nature, the world we live in, and how to be oneself while relating to a wide spectrum of different individuals. In that process, they learn that all individuals share much in common by virtue of the fact that human beings are social creatures by nature.[4] At the same time, living in different regions of the world, in different climates, and with different geographical conditions, customs, languages, and values, human beings have clustered themselves into racial, ethnic, nationalistic, religious, and tribal groups. These clusters make for the development of different customs, values, and cultures (i.e., ways of seeing and doing things) between groups. Given human beings' felt sense of inferiority and natural competitive strivings, ultimately, perceived differences in one's position above others (i.e., feeling included and superior) or below them (i.e., feeling excluded and inferior) make fertile ground for the development of barriers, discriminations, tensions, and aggressions between groups.

The master practitioner has trained him- or herself to be sensitive to the differences between his or her own cultural underpinnings and those of the clients seen in treatment. It is incumbent upon clinicians to keep in check their own biases and simultaneously be open to different values that are represented by different ethnic, racial, cultural, and religious groups.

A clinician's own biases can undermine the capacity to connect with and engage a client in treatment. Therapists' fiduciary responsibility to put the interests of their clients above their own interests demands this. The extent to which practitioners can relate to clients from a group different from their own is a function of their flexibility, exposure to different groups, and willingness to learn about others with diverse origins.

Understanding such enormous subtleties helps therapists connect to clients from backgrounds different from their own. Master practitioners have trained themselves to be exquisitely sensitive to human individuality and its potential for impacting the therapeutic encounter.

Conclusion

This chapter has outlined the elements of the domain of assessment regarding client needs, strengths, and goals. In many respects, this has become a standard practice in therapy because of the contemporary requirements that managed care insurance companies and other regulatory bodies impose on clinicians and the treatment process. As we have noted, however, there are both linear and nonlinear methods for assessing clients. The master therapist is able to utilize both in order to get the most complete picture of a client and focus for treatment. We contend that practitioners at Level I can become adept at using these methods in order to increase their effectiveness. The key is to remember that the focus must be on and proceed from the client. Perhaps Tallman and Bohart (1999) put it best:

> Clients then are the "magicians" with the special healing powers. Therapists set the stage and serve as assistants who provide the conditions under which this magic can operate. They do not provide the magic, although they may provide means for mobilizing, channeling, and focusing the clients' magic. (p. 95)

Among the most important means that master practitioners have for eliciting the healing powers that reside within clients is their ability to establish a meaningful relationship with them. Although connecting with and engaging a client in the beginning stages of treatment is essential for limiting the chances of a premature termination, establishing and maintaining a positive working therapeutic relationship—the therapeutic alliance—are essential for successfully conducting and completing the work of therapy. It is to a discussion of the therapeutic relationship that we now turn our attention.

Notes

1. An epidural, as it is called, is a regional anesthetic (i.e., it produces numbness to an entire region of the body) and consists of an anesthetic agent being injected into the peridural space of the spine.
2. Please note: It is *never* a good idea to give medical advice if you are not medically trained.
3. For more information on treatment planning, see Adams and Grieder (2005).
4. The term *social* when used in this context refers to the fact that human beings live and work in groups and are interdependent upon one another for survival. It also means that human behavior must always be interpreted within its social context.

6

The Domain of Establishing and Maintaining the Therapeutic Relationship and the Therapeutic Alliance
Relationship Building

Introduction: *The King's Speech*

Albert, the Duke of York (and future King George VI of England), had a problem. He had a stammer that no one seemed to be able to cure. This was an embarrassing problem that was made worse by the fact that he was living in the 1930s during the heyday of radio—where speaking publicly and directly to the subjects of the British Empire was a necessity for a member of the Royal Family. In 2010, his plight (and the powerful story of how he overcame it) was made into the Oscar winning film *The King's Speech.*

In the movie, Albert is a resigned precontemplator who feels that his stammer is hopeless. His wife finds an unconventional practitioner in a frustrated Australian actor who helps people with speech defects named Lionel Logue. Logue had no credentials or degrees, but what he did have was a method that worked: "When the Great War (World War I) came, all our soldiers were returning to Australia from the front, a lot of them shell-shocked, unable to speak. Somebody said, 'Lionel, you're very good at all this speech stuff, you think you could possibly help these poor buggers?' I did muscle therapy, exercises, relaxation, but I knew I had to go deeper. Those poor young blokes cried out in fear. No one was listening to them. My job was to give them faith in their own voice, and let them know a friend was listening."

He also had another rule: "I must have total equality." For a royal prince, this was almost impossible! From the beginning, however, Logue insisted that the prince calls him "Lionel" and that he call the prince "Bertie" (a name that only family members call him). He builds a relationship with Bertie and, while resistant at first, he does reveal that his stammer was the result of a traumatic upbringing (deprived of food and abused by his first nanny, bullied by his father and older brother, forced to learn to write with his right hand when he was naturally left handed). While the relationship deepened, and Bertie was able to start to give speeches, it was not always smooth! There were ruptures when Lionel pushed Bertie too far, which estranged them. But when Bertie's brother (King Edward VIII) abdicated the throne in 1936 to marry a divorced American woman (a scandal that could not be tolerated), he becomes the next king of England. Terrified at this prospect, he turns to Lionel to help him find the courage to carry out his duties. At one point—while rehearsing for his coronation—Lionel confronts Bertie by sitting on the coronation throne. Bertie is outraged and tells him to get off the throne, but Lionel refuses. "Listen to me!" Bertie commands, "I am your king!" Logue tells him

"No you're not, you just told me you didn't want it. Why should I waste my time listening to you?" Bertie responds: "Because I have a right to be heard. I have a voice!" Lionel, having gotten Bertie to clearly and genuinely *own* his voice, gets off the throne and gently tells him, "Yes, you do. You have such perseverance, Bertie. You are the bravest man I know. You'll make a bloody good king."

Finally, the movie turns toward the beginning of World War II in 1939. On September 1, Hitler's army invaded Poland, which forced England to declare war on Germany. The king must address his people across the globe on the radio and rally them for war. This is the most important speech that he has ever given, and he summons Lionel to be with him. As the king is rehearsing and begins to stammer, he begins to despair. Lionel looks at him and says "Bertie, forget about the microphone and everything else. Just speak to me." At which point, he is able to get through the speech flawlessly. What becomes apparent is that although many of the techniques are helpful to Bertie, it is the relationship—the *therapeutic relationship*—with Lionel that allows him to assume the throne, communicate with his people, and effectively lead them through the darkest period of World War II to victory.

Research Findings: The Therapeutic Relationship and the Therapeutic Alliance

No one in the counseling profession has been more directly linked to the importance of the therapeutic relationship than Carl Rogers. He famously proposed that certain conditions were necessary for growth and change to occur in therapy: unconditional positive regard, accurate empathy, and congruence of the therapist (Rogers, 1957). These qualities facilitated removing obstacles that interfered with clients' ability to resolve their problems:

> The most impressive fact about the individual human being seems to be the directional tendency towards wholeness, toward actualization of potentialities. I have *not* found that psychotherapy … [is] effective when I have tried to create in another individual something that is not there, but I have found that if I can provide the conditions that make for growth, that this positive directional tendency brings about constructive results. (Rogers, 1957, quoted in Bien, 2004, p. 493)

Rogers suggested that the way to achieve this is through the therapeutic relationship. Indeed, without a relationship between client and counselor, nothing would be accomplished in therapy. Since Carl Rogers, theorists, researchers, practitioners, and Rogers himself have stated that the conditions of therapy and therapists that he articulated (i.e., congruence, accurate empathy, and unconditional positive regard) were necessary but insufficient conditions for change. Norcross and Lambert (2011), reporting on the American Psychological Association's Interdivisional Task Force on Empirically Supported Therapy Relationships[1] defined the psychotherapy relationship as "the feelings and attitudes that therapist and client have toward one another, and the manner in which these are expressed" (p. 4). These general characteristics have come to be identified under a more global theme as components of the therapeutic relationship.

The clinical research literature has traditionally tried to describe the salient qualities of the common factors in therapy by referring to the therapeutic relationship. Indeed, without a positive therapeutic relationship between client and counselor, nothing significant would be accomplished in therapy. Even though it is a professional engagement between a client and a practitioner, at the core, the therapy relationship is a human encounter.

In the following sections, we discuss the salient factors that contribute to a clinical understanding of the therapeutic relationship. According to Norcross and Lambert (2011): "The therapy relationship is like a diamond, a diamond composed of multiple, interconnected facets. The diamond is a complex, reciprocal, and multidimensional entity" (p. 6). We propose to elaborate on some of these facets that make up a therapeutic relationship. They are amazingly intertwined, continuous, fluid, and are accomplished in a seemingly effortless manner by the master practitioner. Identifying more discrete processes as part of their larger context will facilitate the Level I practitioner's understanding of the domain of establishing and maintaining a therapeutic alliance. We will be guided by the best and latest research findings about the therapeutic process. We present exercises designed to have readers reflect on their personal experiences related to relationship building. Furthermore, we believe that no two therapists will create or maintain a therapeutic relationship in the same way. Instead, we present guidelines that readers can practice on their own, with classmates or clients. As with the other domains, there are both linear and nonlinear ways to work within this domain.

Factors that Contribute to the Therapeutic Relationship

In 2002, John C. Norcross chaired the American Psychological Association's Task Force on Empirically Supported Therapy Relationships. In his report, published as the book *Psychotherapy Relationships that Work,* distinguished researchers in the field were assembled "to identify, operationalize, and disseminate information on empirically supported therapy relationships" (Norcross & Lambert, 2011, pp. 3–4). They performed exhaustive literature reviews on variables and presented their results. Almost 10 years later, a second task force was appointed, again to review the literature on the therapeutic relationship. This task force (again chaired by Dr. Norcross) updated the research literature and commissioned meta-analyses to be performed on the aspects of the therapeutic relationship to determine their relative contribution to the effectiveness of the therapeutic relationship. A meta-analysis is a method to study the overall effects of particular variables across numerous studies which produces an effect size (ES) (see Lipsey & Wilson, 1993).[2] We summarize some of the findings of the first task force, and then discuss some of the findings of the second task force, below.

In 2002, Lambert and Barley summarized available research and concluded that certain variables contributed significantly different percentages[3] to successful outcomes. These factors (and their percentages) represent the *explained* outcome variance in psychotherapy (but not the *total* variance), and are as follows: expectancy (i.e., hope for change or the placebo effect) contributes 15%, technique contributes 15%, extratherapeutic change contributes 40%, and common factors contribute 30%. Norcross and Lambert (2011) attempted to quantify the *total* variance of therapeutic factors that contribute to outcomes in psychotherapy, which includes the explained and unexplained variance. In their model, 40% of the variance is unexplained[4] (this can include measurement error as well as the complex nature of human behavior that cannot be quantified at this point in time), 30% is patient contribution, 12–15% is the therapeutic relationship, 8% is attributable to treatment method, 7% to the individual therapist, and 3% to other factors. In this model, the common factors are spread across different therapeutic factors.

Selected Findings of the First Task Force (2002)

Lambert and Barley (2002) carefully pointed out that the data accumulated from psychotherapy research demonstrate that "specific techniques contribute much less to outcome than do important interpersonal factors common to all therapies" (p. 21), such as empathy, warmth, and acceptance. These conclusions are highly instructional for the Level I practitioner but also apply to all levels of practitioner. In the absence of confidence and experience, the Level I practitioner is more likely to gravitate toward such things as the use of techniques or honing micro skills in psychotherapy as an approach to treatment. Techniques typically provide an illusion of expertise and control (i.e., "If I do the 'techniques' the 'right way,' then I'll get a positive outcome"), which comforts the Level I practitioner's anxiety. By comparison, developing a way of thinking about what is required for effective therapy can be more unfamiliar and uncomfortable. Thus, Level I clinicians may feel less certain that merely developing a therapeutic alliance with a client will be effective, despite the evidence that those relationship factors contribute nearly twice as much to successful therapy outcomes as techniques.

Centorrino et al. (2001) demonstrated how important the therapy relationship is in determining successful treatment outcomes. They investigated factors associated with outpatient mental health treatment compliance (e.g., keeping scheduled clinic appointments) versus noncompliance (e.g., failure to keep appointments and treatment dropouts). Only three factors contributed to treatment compliance: (1) the perceived warmth and friendliness of the therapist, (2) talking to the client about something that was of importance to the client, and (3) talking to the client in a structured manner. These three (relational) factors were shown to be more important in determining outcome than client diagnosis or demographics. Last, clients who felt that they were going to be listened to by a therapist, rather than merely treated by a medical professional with medications, were more likely to be compliant (a prerequisite for eventual success in therapy). Lambert and Barley (2002) summarized what this study and others demonstrate:

(1) Psychotherapy is a successful therapeutic endeavor as determined by an average of 80% of clients [that] are better off than individuals not treated. (2) Studies that compare different therapies support the conclusion that they are relatively equivalent in promoting change in clients. (3) The therapeutic relationship *consistently* is more highly correlated with successful client outcomes than any specialized therapy techniques. Associations between the therapeutic relationship and client outcome are strongest when measured by client ratings of both constructs. (p. 26)

Clinical Example: The Healing Power of the Relationship

A 19-year-old female client entered therapy with a severe anxiety disorder and symptoms of Trichotillomania (recurrent episodes of pulling out one's hair resulting in noticeable hair loss). The client came from a family where there was a lot of violent verbal and physical conflict between her mother and father. She felt like her parents concentrated all of their attention on their failing relationship and neglected her and her sister. As a result, she feels like she was *damaged* by them: "I hate them! Because of them, I can't feel love. I'm not normal."

However, the client is able to connect with children, elderly people, and pets. She enjoys helping and frequently volunteers at a local animal shelter that has an outreach program to a nearby nursing home. "I don't get it, I feel so much rage when I am on my own and thinking about my past, but when I am working with these pets, or when I see an old person smile when we bring the animals, I feel calm and normal." The therapist asked: "Where did you find nourishment (emotionally) when you were growing up and your parents couldn't give it to you?" The client answered that there were a few people around, but no one to whom she felt connected or safe. "So you need to create the family that you never had. You were born to an abnormal, dysfunctional people. People do the best they can do, but sometimes it is not enough. You may have to abandon the family that abandoned you." The client agreed with this concept and realized that she had been creating a new family with the elderly people she knew and the people she worked with.

Over the course of three months of therapy, her Trichotillomania symptoms subsided completely, but she still was prone to feeling rage at her family. "When will I get over this?" she asked the therapist. The therapist suggested that: "You will know that you have gotten to a place of healing when you can place your family in their proper context. When you realize that *they* were the 'damaged' people, not you." Gradually, the client began to shift her focus away from the idea that she was "damaged" to the idea that her parents were. Her episodes of rage began to calm down, and she was able to establish some contact with her sister. At termination, the client reported that being able to have a family outside of her own family of origin, that is to create healthy relationships, allowed her to feel less anxious and damaged by her upbringing.

Table 6.1 Findings of the Second APA Task Force on the Psychotherapy Relationship

	Relationship Elements	Methods of Adapting
Demonstrated Effective	Therapeutic Alliance (Chapter 6) Empathy (Chapter 6) Collecting Client Feedback (Chapter 6)	Reactance/Resistance (Chapter 7) Client Preferences (Chapter 7) Culture/Religion/Spirituality (Chapter 7)
Probably Effective	Goal Consensus (Chapter 5) Collaboration (Chapter 5) Positive Regard (Chapter 6)	Stages of Change (Chapter 4) Coping Style (Domain 5)
Promising, but Insufficient Research to Judge	Congruence/Genuineness (Chapter 7) Repairing Alliance Ruptures (Chapter 7) Managing Countertransference (Chapter 7)	Expectations (Chapter 7) Attachment Style (Domain 4)

Note: Where each element is covered in this text is in parentheses. Adapted from Norcross and Wampold (2011).

Selected Findings of the Second Task Force (2011)

In 2011, owing to the frustrations of the movement to establish empirically validated treatments (see Chapter 1), Norcross and Lambert (2011) criticized practice guidelines and treatment manuals that devote only a short paragraph to the therapeutic relationship saying that it is important but then offer no guidelines "on which therapist behaviors contributes to the therapeutic relationship . . . few specify which therapist qualities or in session behaviors lead to a curative relationship" (p. 9). As a result, the second task force compiled the results of the meta-analyses and divided them along the criteria of "Demonstrably Effective," "Probably Effective," and "Promising, but insufficient research to judge" (Norcross & Wampold, 2011). In doing so, they have provided some of the most comprehensive listing of the best-researched elements of the therapeutic relationship. These include elements like the therapeutic alliance, empathy, and collecting client feedback (to name a few).

In addition to the relationship elements, they also list methods of adapting (or tailoring) the therapeutic relationship, based on the client needs. According to Norcross and Lambert: "(t)he relationship does not exist apart from what the therapist does in terms of method. We cannot imagine any treatment methods that would not have some relational impact. Put differently, treatment methods are relational acts" (2011, pp. 4–5). As a result, therapist sensitivity to client needs in choosing how to intervene is an important relationship factor that a nonlinear thinking therapist takes into consideration. Some of these adaptations include client reactance; client preferences; and issues of culture, religion, or spirituality that must be considered by the therapist when creating a therapeutic relationship.

In Table 6.1, we list the relationship elements plus methods of adapting according to the level of demonstrated research support. We have reorganized this domain using the findings of the second task force as a guide. We agree that trainees should be exposed to those elements that are demonstrably effective, as well as the methods of adaptation. Lastly, Norcross and Wampold list what doesn't work in the therapeutic relationship. We discuss some of those elements at the end of the next chapter.

Demonstrably Effective Element of the Therapeutic Relationship: The Therapeutic Alliance

Like many concepts in psychotherapy, it is difficult to arrive at a consensus definition of a therapeutic alliance. Drawing on 20th-century history, during World War II, Britain and the United States formed an alliance to defeat the Axis powers (Nazi Germany, Imperial Japan, and Fascist Italy). In this alliance, they agreed to share their strengths and ally their efforts toward the goal of winning the war. They planned their troop movements and battle strikes as joint enterprises. As a result of working together cooperatively (although not always harmoniously), they were able to fight a war on several continents throughout the world and gain total victory. Martin, Garske, and Davis (2000) approached their study of the therapeutic alliance by acknowledging the diversity of "alliance conceptualizations" (which seems to match our historical exemplar) and concluded that:

> most theoretical definitions of the alliance have three themes in common: (a) the collaborative nature of the relationship, (b) the affective bond between patient and therapist, and (c) the patient's and therapist's ability to agree on treatment goals and tasks. (p. 439)

Although the concept of a therapeutic alliance (working alliance or helping alliance) appears to loom large as an important variable in determining successful outcomes across different forms of treatment, Horvath et al. (2011) carefully pointed out that the term still seems to lack a universally accepted definition. In an attempt to encapsulate prior theoretical work (e.g., Barber, Connolly, Crits-Christoph, Gladis, & Siqueland, 2000; Horvath, 2001; Martin et al., 2000) and convey what appears to be a consensus clinical definition of the term therapeutic alliance emerging in the literature, Horvath and Bedi (2002) proposed the following definition:

> The alliance refers to the quality and strength of the collaborative relationship between client and therapist in therapy. This concept is inclusive of: the positive affective bonds between client and therapist, such as mutual trust, liking, respect, and caring. Alliance also encompasses the more cognitive aspects of the therapy relationship; consensus about, and active commitment to, the goals of therapy and to the means by which these goals can be reached. Alliance involves a sense of partnership in therapy between therapist and client, in which each participant is actively committed to their specific and appropriate responsibilities in therapy, and believes that the other is likewise enthusiastically engaged in the process. The alliance is a conscious and purposeful aspect of the relation between therapist and client: It is conscious in the sense that the quality of the alliance is within ready grasp of the participants, and it is purposeful in that it is specific to a context in which there is a therapist or helper who accepts some responsibility for providing psychological assistance to a client or clients. (p. 41)

Using Horvath et al.'s (2011) modified definition—(1) positive affective bond, (2) therapeutic tasks, and (3) a consensus on goals—we highlight the following.

Positive Affective Bond

A positive outcome for therapy is contingent upon the quality and strength of the alliance. In more human terms, this means that there is a positive affective bond between therapist and client. In turn, that positive affective bond is composed of the qualities discussed previously about establishing a working relationship—mutual trust, positive regard, liking, respect, and caring. It is an attachment relationship between the client and counselor that has depth and feeling. At the same time, it is a professional relationship that is governed by rules, ethics, and so on (we discuss these aspects below). Because it is an attachment relationship, the therapist brings her personal style to it. This includes her personality characteristics and personal history. As a result, no two therapists display caring, respect, or other responses in identical ways, nor will any two clients perceive a therapist's efforts in this regard in the same way.

Therapeutic Tasks

A second factor in their definition of a therapeutic alliance is therapeutic tasks. This refers to a mutual understanding and agreement on the scope of change the therapist and client are striving for, which was discussed as collaboration in the previous chapter. Although it is quite human, all too often, clients seek relief from suffering but have no clear idea of what specific behavior(s) to engage in (e.g., thoughts or actions) that would provide them with that sense of relief. Agreeing on the therapeutic tasks insures that there is a mutual understanding (and no surprises) about what issues will be worked on in session. As a result, a client is obligated to be the one to do the work of making changes. Often, these obligations create inevitable friction, even to the best built therapeutic alliances. When these frictions occur, a therapist must understand either how to maintain positive momentum in therapy (if the friction is minor) or how to repair the alliance (if the friction is major). Having a clear agreement on the therapeutic tasks can facilitate this without disrupting the therapeutic alliance.

Consensus on Goals

Part of the therapeutic alliance also includes commonly agreed upon means of achieving particular goals as part of the therapeutic alliance. In Chapter 5, we discussed the importance of setting realistic and achievable goals. Once the goals are agreed upon, then the client and therapist must consciously work toward achieving them. We have encountered innumerable instances of therapists of all levels of experience attempting to impose a particular treatment method on their clients. One example can be seen in a client coming for treatment for a phobia that the clinician believes would best be treated by hypnosis. Some clients don't like the idea of hypnosis due to the fear of not being in control of themselves when in a hypnotic trance. Insistence on the use of hypnosis with these clients would be imprudent. Especially in this regard, it is important that therapists disabuse themselves of trying to change a client. Although a therapist is a *change agent* (i.e., advocating that the client does things differently than before), being one means that he develops the conditions under which it becomes possible for the client to make positive decisions and alter behaviors, attitudes, and emotions. It also requires that both therapist and client recognize that there is a purpose to the therapeutic endeavor. Although some clients do come to therapy purely to find themselves and explore their life's experiences, it is more often the case that clients have a specific agenda to pursue. A therapist is also accountable in that he or she accepts responsibility for being a helper to a client and holds the client accountable for making changes.

This definition for a therapeutic alliance can serve as a useful template and clinical guide for the Level I therapist—a conceptually useful starting point for understanding and working with a client to develop a therapeutic alliance (i.e., goals, tasks, and bond). With experience, understanding of the sentiment of the definition hopefully becomes an automatic disposition that is expressed in the art and science that is therapy. The definition is not formulaic and must ultimately be integrated into one's thinking (both linear and nonlinear) about therapy and behavior. The clinical case example below illustrates the challenges of establishing a therapeutic alliance.

Clinical Case Example: Husband versus Wife over Internet Porn

A middle-aged man and his wife entered couples therapy after the wife discovered him watching pornography on the Internet. He complied with her request that he leave the family home due to how intolerably upset she was with his behavior after many years of marriage. While living alone, the man spent many lonely hours in a tiny apartment committed to writing a diary of his thoughts, his feelings, and things that he apparently wanted to talk about with his wife (this had been recommended to him by another therapist). When the husband brought the notebook to therapy to discuss its issues with his wife, she expressed considerable trepidation regarding whether or not she wanted to do so.

In discussing the contents of the notebook, the husband revealed that there were many sexual fantasies that he wanted to present to his wife. It was abundantly clear that the wife cringed at any such discussion because she had been sexually abused in childhood, and it was clear that their inability to communicate about sexual fantasies was an ongoing issue between them throughout the marriage. In terms of the stages of change, the wife was between the contemplation and preparing for action phases, whereas the husband was in the action stage. They appeared stalemated.

Questions: Before reading further, consider the following questions.

1. What are the issues presented in this case?
2. Describe, as you see it, the bond to be established, tasks to be performed, and the goals to be agreed to that would define the therapeutic alliance?
3. Discuss how the issue presented above poses a challenge to the elements of the therapeutic alliance (goals, tasks, and bond)?
4. How can the therapist intervene in a way that preserves the therapeutic alliance?

In the clinical case example, it is clear from the outset that there is a real threat to the early therapeutic relationship and therapeutic alliance. It is important to be sure that there is clear agreement on the bond between the couple and the therapist, the tasks to be accomplished, and the goals of the therapy. In order to preserve these, the therapist suggested that perhaps he could look at the diary and then offer a suggestion as to whether or not discussion of the material was presently relevant to what they had described originally as their problem. Upon reviewing the manuscript before their next therapy session, the therapist determined that a discussion of the material had the potential to lead treatment in an unfruitful direction—a therapeutic rabbit hole. The diary was largely filled with very pornographic, titillating, and very explicitly lewd fantasies. A frank discussion of such material would not have been very productive, especially in the light of the wife's current stage of change (i.e., reluctant precontemplator as well as her sense of unpreparedness).

On the other hand, the therapist reviewing the diary accomplished several therapeutic objectives: (1) He legitimized and honored the husband's desire to introduce the material into the therapy, and by reviewing it, the therapist was acknowledging, validating, and respecting the husband's wishes that the material be introduced into the therapy; (2) it honored the wife's felt sense of unpreparedness to deal with such issues and her sensitivities about them as a victim of childhood sexual abuse; and (3) it provided the therapist with an understanding of the husband as an excitement-seeking individual whose lifelong pursuit of exciting adventures (e.g., sky diving, scuba diving, drugs, alcohol, a high-stress and fast-paced professional career, and pornography) had often exposed him to very dangerous situations sought for the rush they produced. That understanding of the husband proved advantageous for both him and his wife in the treatment that followed. Many of the husband's other exciting pursuits became much more understandable to him and his wife. At the same time, introducing the material in the diary into the therapy did not prove to be a distraction from the larger issue at hand, namely, helping the couple to reconnect and once again build on the positive and successful relationship that they had had for many years. Refraining from a frank discussion of the fantasy material in the early phase of therapy also helped the alliance with the wife, who was clearly not prepared for any such discussion. In the meantime, with the help of the therapist, the couple demonstrated an ability to talk about talking about a problem in a nonconflictual way—a desirable therapeutic outcome.

This is a couple that had problems talking to one another about other issues, let alone discussing sexual fantasies. But both spouses felt that the therapist had not taken sides. The husband had the material introduced and respected by the therapist as potentially valuable in providing a greater understanding of some of his concerns; the wife felt respected by not having to discuss material that she was far from prepared to discuss. Hence, the elements of the alliance (bond, tasks, and goals), as well as the overall alliance with both, was preserved. It also allowed for a discussion of the material at a later time when both partners were prepared to work on it.

Now the therapeutic relationship doesn't always go smoothly, in a perpetual, linear, ascending arc of positivity or quality. In fact, the consensus opinion is that there will be flux or change from time-to-time, particularly in the middle phase of therapy. Horvath et al. (2011) also reported that despite the knowledge that fluctuations will occur in the quality of the therapeutic alliance, there is no agreed upon pattern of ebb and flow for the therapeutic alliance. Therefore, master clinicians must be prepared to have the alliance challenged or change at certain points in the course of therapy, but not to be threatened by it. This is where nonlinear thinking comes in (i.e., "sometimes to go fast, you have to go slow"). What is important is the overall trajectory of the quality of the therapeutic alliance. If it is positive, then it can tolerate any pullback. If it is negative, then the shifts that are detected may be fatal to the therapeutic relationship. Again, this is where master clinicians know how to assess this and be able to actively engage the client to manage the relationship.

Research on the Therapeutic Alliance

So just how important is the therapeutic alliance? In their meta-analysis of 79 studies of psychotherapy outcome, Martin et al. (2000) determined that the relationship between alliance and outcome is consistent no matter what variables have been proposed as possibly influencing it.[5] They also concluded that the relationship between alliance and outcome seems to represent "a single population of effects." That suggests that there likely aren't any moderator variables[6] that might explain the relationship between alliance and outcome. Furthermore, Martin et al. (2000) suggested that there is a therapeutic and healing effect in the alliance itself, and that if an appropriate alliance is established, a client will experience the relationship as therapeutic regardless of other psychological interventions. These results have been consistently reported in various degrees of refinement over a considerable span of years (e.g., Fiedler, 1950; Horvath, 2001, 2006; Norcross, 2002; Rosenweig, 1936) of empirical and clinical research.

Another powerful conclusion from Martin et al. (2000) is that the strength of the therapeutic alliance predicts outcome whatever the psychological component underlying the relationship between alliance and outcome. In other words, other variables do not seem to influence the relationship between outcome and alliance. Variables that don't affect the relationship between the outcome and the strength and quality of the therapeutic alliance include the type of measure that is used to evaluate outcome, when during the course of treatment, the alliance assessment is taken, the rater making the estimate of the strength of the alliance and the type of treatment provided.

Lastly, Horvath et al. (2011) conducted one of the most thorough meta-analyses to date. Using over 200 studies that looked at approximately 14,000 patients, they found a modest, but robust relationship between alliance and treatment outcome. In fact, they found a median $r = 0.28$ (which translates into an effect size of $d = 0.57$), which is impressive, but does not take into account all of the factors that account for the effect of the therapeutic relationship on treatment outcomes ($d = 0.80$). Still, it affirms earlier findings of the importance of the therapeutic alliance.

Conclusions on the Therapeutic Alliance

It is clear from the empirical evidence that a strong relationship resulting in a consistent therapeutic alliance is an important vehicle in determining successful treatment outcomes. But the essentials of how to create this alliance are not easily described. Horvath et al. (2011) conclude with the following clinical suggestions:

1. The alliance is not synonymous with the therapeutic relationship. "The relationship is made of several interlocking elements (empathy, responsiveness, creating a safe secure environment, etc.). The alliance is one way of conceptualizing what has been achieved by the appropriate use of these elements" (p. 56).

2. The alliance is not separate from the interventions that a therapist uses. Rather, it is "influenced by, and is an essential and inseparable part of, everything that happens in therapy" (p. 56).

3. Adapting the tasks of therapy to fit the client's needs or expectations is important, especially in the formative stages of the therapeutic alliance.

4. In the face of client negative affect, or hostility, therapists must respond nondefensively in order to maintain a good working alliance. "Therapists ought to neither internalize nor ignore client negative responses" (pp. 56–57).

Hubble et al. (2010) provide important guidance to Level 1 clinicians as well: "Therapists cannot presume that given enough time, a good alliance will develop. Instead, they must ensure that from the first moments of the therapeutic encounter, the client is experiencing the relationship as meaningful and positive" (p. 38). As a result, we turn our attention to another important, and demonstrably effective, element of the therapeutic relationship: Empathy.

Domain 3 Nonlinear Thinking Exercise—The Prisoner's Dilemma

"Men are not prisoners of fate, but only prisoners of their own minds."

—Franklin D. Roosevelt

"Only free men can negotiate; prisoners cannot enter into contracts. Your freedom and mine cannot be separated."

—Nelson Mandela

Perhaps one of the most famous games from social psychology is the Prisoner's Dilemma. It tests what the best outcome could be for two people given a choice to either cooperate with each other, trust each other, or betray one another. The setup for the game is this:

> You and a partner are criminals who work together, and you are arrested for a crime. You are both isolated from one another and cannot talk to each other or know what the other person is planning to do. The detectives do not have enough evidence to convict both of you on the most serious charge, but they can convict both of you on a related (though lesser) charge, which carries a one-year prison sentence. But, if they can get one of you to confess and implicate the other, then the one who confesses goes free and the other will go to prison for five years. But, if both people testify against each other, then both will be sentenced to a two-year prison term (adapted from Hayden & Picard, 2009).

> So, (before reading on) decide what you would do?

The conventional wisdom is that if you want the best outcome, then confessing and implicating the other person (i.e., "ratting out your partner") gives you the best opportunity for the best option (going free). But it is a high-risk/high-reward option because it puts you in danger of getting the higher sentence (2 years) than if you keep quiet (1 year). However, keeping your mouth shut has risks as well. You could get the maximum (5 years) if your partner betrays you, but if you both work together for your mutual interest (i.e., both keep your mouth shut), then you will have to serve some prison time, but it won't be the maximum. So what do you do? The reality is that if everyone works for their own self-interest (rat), they won't get the *best* outcome. However, if everyone works for the common interest, then the outcome may not be the most optimal (you will still be in prison), but it won't be as bad as the self-interested option (1 year versus 5 years). As a result, it is an example of nonlinear thinking because to do the best (for yourself), you can't pick the best option, and if you try to do the best (for yourself), you will probably do worse! (As a variation, find a group of people and pair them up. Give them the Prisoner's Dilemma scenario and see what they choose and why.)

So what does the Prisoner's Dilemma have to do with the therapeutic relationship? It underscores the importance of seeing how collaboration and working together is the best strategy. It is nonlinear because it requires the person not to act in self-interest and work together in order to get the best outcome (which in the end, is in one's own best interest!). Using the exercise of the prisoner's dilemma helps the emerging nonlinear thinking therapist to see this in action and provide a framework to help clients reach the same conclusion! Trying to work alone won't work in getting a better prison sentence, nor will it create a positive therapeutic relationship!

Demonstrably Effective Element of the Therapeutic Relationship: Empathy

The concept of empathy is used ubiquitously when discussing the processes of counseling; however, little time is typically taken to thoroughly examine its complexities. Rogers (as cited in Elliott, Bohart, Watson, & Greenberg, 2011) defined empathy as: "the therapist's sensitive ability and willingness to understand the client's thoughts, feelings and struggles from the client's point of view. [It is] this ability to see completely through the client's eyes, to adopt his frame of reference" (p. 133). It may be relatively easy to intuitively understand the importance of being empathic and expressing it sensitively in establishing and maintaining the therapeutic relationship. On the other hand, a master practitioner understands that it is the level of empathy perceived by the client that is the deciding factor, regardless of how the therapist thinks the client may be expressing it.

In fact, Level I of counselor development is an ideal time to learn the importance of empathy in all its forms and complexities. From a research perspective, empathy is one of the most important elements of the therapeutic relationship. In their meta-analysis of 57 studies, Elliott et al. (2011) found one of the highest effect sizes for empathy (accounting for 9% of the variance in treatment outcome). In order to describe the concept more precisely, Elliott et al. (2011) characterized three modes of therapeutic empathy. Although these may be distinct facets to empathy, they are quick to point out that they also overlap or interlock with each other. They are empathic rapport, communicative attunement, and person empathy. First, we discuss *empathic rapport*.

Empathic Rapport

An example of a master practitioner demonstrating the art of establishing rapport taken from a popular film may be helpful. In the film *Don Juan DeMarco* (Leven, 1995), Marlon Brando plays an aging psychiatrist who is consulted about a young man wearing a mask, dressed as an 18th-century Spanish nobleman, brandishing a sword atop a billboard, and threatening to jump to his death! The young man, played by Johnny Depp, claims to be the great fictional lover, Don Juan. He further declares that he is awaiting the return of another nobleman whom he intends to challenge in order to win back the lost love of his life. Brando introduces himself as Don Octavio De Flores, another Spanish nobleman, and invites Don Juan to come to his villa and await the return of the nobleman. Don Juan accepts this gentlemanly gesture and agrees to accompany Don Octavio to his villa. The villa, of course, is the state psychiatric hospital where Brando works.

For the remainder of the film, Brando works with Don Juan by having him tell his story, never doubting that Don Juan is who he says he is. In fact, Brando even begins to entertain the possibility that, in some strange way, Depp could be Don Juan himself! The result of the accepting relationship that is built between the two is that Don Juan is slowly able to tell Brando the true story of his life, without having to sacrifice his persona. Meanwhile, Brando is able to convince Depp to embrace his true self (which includes his Don Juan persona) and convince a psychiatric board that Don Juan is not insane and should not be committed.

What does this film have to do with building rapport and nonlinear thinking? Actually, a great deal! Brando's character is able to use what we have designated as *nonlinear* thinking to establish rapport with and respond to Depp's Don Juan persona, and the nonlinear thinking that the character demonstrates. Although logical to Don Juan, the thinking he demonstrates is only privately logical (i.e., that he is Don Juan, the famous lover from the 18th century, and is awaiting an adversary to fight him for a fair maiden's hand—all the while perched on a modern-day billboard). To the rest of the world, the thinking he demonstrates is not rational or logical. Thus, Don Juan's thinking is nonlinear: not based on straightforward commonsense (i.e., consensually validated) thinking and rigidly adhered to. As a result, Brando as the therapist must choose between either (1) staying within his own perceptual frame, using consensually validated linear thinking to persuade Don Juan out of his delusion and to come down from the billboard; or (2) finding a way to engage, connect with, and meet Don Juan where he is, thus perceiving the world through his eyes in order to establish rapport with him. By presenting himself to Don Juan as a Spanish nobleman himself, he chooses the latter path. In choosing to accept Don Juan's frame of reference, Brando has engaged and connected with his client by responding to him in a nonlinear way, as described in Chapter 3.

As a result of choosing to enter Don Juan's perceptual frame, Brando also poses a double bind to Depp: If Don Juan says, "Oh come on, you are not Don Octavio, there is no such person, and you do not have a villa. This is the 21st century!," then he has broken character and must admit that maintaining he is Don Juan is just an act. If, however, Don Juan accepts that Brando is a nobleman, then he must treat Brando with respect and courtesy as a gentleman. He must listen as well as be heard. By posing the double bind (see Chapters 5 and 12), Brando has created conditions that establish rapport with Don Juan. Such rapport can lead to a therapeutic relationship with him on terms acceptable to Don Juan, thus successfully bypassing much potential resistance. That is, a power struggle could easily erupt over the Don Juan persona issue, resulting in such dialogue as "You are not Don Juan; he doesn't exist." "Oh yeah, I am Don Juan, and you can't tell me otherwise." That is, Brando uses nonlinear-thinking processes that mirror Don Juan's exceptionally idiosyncratic nonlinear thinking as a vehicle for achieving therapeutic goals and progress.

What is abundantly clear in the film is that Brando's use of nonlinear thinking renders him eminently more successful than other therapists in the psychiatric hospital who use more linear approaches with Don Juan to no avail. He gave his *permission* for Don Juan to have the symptom (nonlinear thinking) rather than struggle with his client to eradicate it (i.e., linear thinking).

Clinical Exercise: *Don Juan DeMarco*

1. After reading this entire chapter, rent the film *Don Juan DeMarco* and note the various ways in which Marlon Brando demonstrates nonlinear thinking in the service of establishing rapport with a man who appears to be mentally disturbed.
2. Distinguish between the traditional psychiatrists' linear thinking and Brando's nonlinear thinking.
3. Do an analysis of what you believe to be the benefits and shortcomings of both methods of thinking.

The example of *Don Juan* may seem to be an extreme illustration of the use of nonlinear thinking in building empathic rapport. The film is very instructional, however, about ways that nonlinear thinking can be used to quickly and effectively build rapport with clients in a way that encourages a greater likelihood of success in therapy.

Communicative Attunement

A simple experiment from an elementary school science class may also demonstrate what empathic attunement is about. If a tuning fork is struck, it vibrates. If the vibrating tuning fork is then moved close to a nonvibrating fork of the same (or similar) frequency, the nonvibrating fork will begin to resonate with the frequency of the vibrating fork (without ever directly contacting the vibrating fork). In other words, the vibrations in the air are picked up by the second tuning fork, causing it to vibrate in synch. Consider also the opposite situation, as when a vibrating fork is brought near another tuning fork that does not have a similar frequency—the second fork will barely vibrate or not vibrate at all.

Clients frequently come for therapy feeling defensive about their circumstances and a little wary about the therapist or therapeutic process. They may be alert for any indication that the therapist understands them on a deeper level. Procedurally, in order to accomplish this, the therapist must use the linear and nonlinear listening and responding methods outlined in Chapters 2 and 3. A therapist using both linear and nonlinear thought processes acts like a tuning fork that sympathetically vibrates in response to a client and communicates a sense of connection and understanding. Listening for and responding to information or content, feelings, congruence, absence, presence, inference, and resistance all combine to help a client feel more at ease and establish a connection. A therapist who can follow the nonlinear (i.e., privately logical) aspects of a client's thinking process is more likely to stimulate a client to feel connected and understood: "You get it. You understand!" Also, the feeling of connectedness occurs simultaneously on the cognitive, relational, and emotional levels. Clients want to know that you are in tune with them!

Specifically listening for the issues that relate to a client's theme or *underlying dynamics* (e.g., "None of these problems I'm having are my fault") and stage of change (see Chapter 5) provides an enormous advantage to the practitioner in establishing rapport. For example, if a client is in the precontemplation stage and feels that he does not believe that he has a problem, then a clinician may respond by saying: "So, if I understand you correctly, I can see how you really feel that you haven't done anything to be getting all of this flack" or "I can see how really blameless you feel about this situation while others are definitely pointing the finger at you." This can be very effective in establishing rapport and validating the client. The therapist, as a person, is validating the client. It is an exchange that says, "I see your point of view!" It also says, "I, as a therapist and authority figure, am not going to impose my point of view on you." It does not imply that the therapist agrees with the client's interpretation. However, such validation is fundamental to the process of empathic attunement, a therapeutic relationship, and ultimately an alliance that allows the work of therapy to be accomplished successfully.

Part of empathic attunement, from a nonlinear perspective, is the therapist's ability to attend to what is said and not said: "or that which is at the periphery of awareness as well as what is said and is in focal awareness" (Elliott et al., 2011, p. 146). This is the essence of our concept of linear and nonlinear listening and responding that was introduced in Chapters 2 and 3. However, nonlinear thinking therapists also have to be sensitive "to know when—and when not—to respond empathically. When client's do not want therapists to be explicitly empathic, truly empathic therapists will use their . . . skills to provide an optimal therapeutic distance in order to respect the client's boundaries" (Elliott et al., 2011, p. 146). Because it is the client who is consulting and paying for the therapist's services, it is professionally incumbent and obligatory upon the therapist to adapt his or her behavior to make certain that he or she is empathically attuned with the client in order to form a solid therapeutic relationship. Empathic attunement, therefore, is an important precursor to change and a preliminary element of the domain of establishing and maintaining the therapeutic relationship.

But Don't Take Our Word for It! Master Example

Consider this example from master practitioner, Scott Miller (coauthor of *The Heart and Soul of Change* and creator of Feedback Informed Therapy, FIT), and how he demonstrated empathetic attunement to Scott's frustrations to build the therapeutic relationship (Allyn & Bacon, 2000e).

Scott Miller: "Okay, so you're the kind of guy who carefully weighs a decision, considers the options . . ."

Client: "Tries to anyhow. Uh-huh."

Scott Miller: "Sometimes that works and sometimes it doesn't . . ."

Client: "Yeah. Sometimes I wonder if you're better off just to go to with your gut feeling and go for it."

Scott Miller: "Okay. Do you do that sometimes?"

Client: "Once in a while."

Scott Miller: "When you've done that, the results aren't as . . ."

Client: "They're not as good."

Scott Miller: "Okay."

Client: "Yeah, it, I don't know, lots of times, it—plans get changed. 'Dadgummit, here we had this all planned out to go and it don't go.'"

Scott Miller: "Okay."

Client: "Somebody threw a wrench in the pile and there—now we're sitting."

Scott Miller: "'Well, you didn't plan careful enough that time.' Is that the sort of thought that comes back to you?"

Client: "Right."

Scott Miller: "And maybe you then, you think 'I should plan more carefully in the future.'"

Client: "Yeah."

Scott Miller: "Okay."

Client: "And I'm always trying to look out for everybody else instead of myself."

Person Empathy

According to Elliott et al. (2011), the third facet of empathy, person empathy:

> consists of a sustained effort to understand the kinds of experiences the client has had, both historically and presently, that form the background of the client's current experiencing. The question is: How have the client's experiences led him or her to see/feel/think and act as he or she does? (p. 134).

This level of empathy is also contained in Domain 4—Schema Dynamics, as we describe how to understand a client's view of self, view of others, and view of the world, but we discuss some aspects of it here.

For example, a linear expression of person empathy would be to tell a client, "I understand what you are going through," or to merely verbatim repeat or parrot feelings that the client had just expressed. But such an expression would be devoid of genuine feelings and not the kind of sustained effort that Elliott et al. describe above. Chances are that the client would not feel the sense that "this person knows what I've been experiencing" (i.e., the client does not feel in synch with the therapist).

Master practitioners understand that person empathy is an art. They transform mere client facts, experiences, and expressions into the transmission of a common bond by conveying truly shared meaning. Telling someone, "I understand," can, in fact, at times be countertherapeutic! Some narratives told in therapy defy understanding, such as experiences of the horrors of war, childhood sexual abuse, rape, or the loss of a child.

When clients relate their sometimes extremely tragic experiences, comments such as "I can't imagine what it was like for you to discover . . . ," "You must have been totally overwhelmed and exhausted when . . . ," "It must have seemed as though it would never end . . . ," and "It's as though a bomb has gone off in your life. . . ." can be helpful, nonlinear expressions of person empathy. They are nonlinear because it is the opposite of saying, "I know how you feel," but it conveys a sense that the therapist grasps (as closely as possible) the essence of the client's traumatic experience. This is done despite the fact that the therapist has not gone through the same experience. When the therapist demonstrated this kind of nonlinear person empathy, the client's can acknowledge: "Yes! That's it! That's how I feel—like no one could know what it was like to go through such a horrible thing." In turn, this strengthens the therapeutic relationship.

But Don't Take Our Word for It! Master Example

Consider this example from master practitioner, John Norcross (chair of the American Psychological Association's Task Force on Empirically Supported Therapy Relationships and editor of the book *Psychotherapy Relationships that Work*) and how he demonstrates person empathy attunement to the client when he misspeaks in a way that builds their therapeutic relationship (Allyn & Bacon, 2000d).

John Norcross: "What would you really dislike from me as a therapist, something that really annoys you I should know about?"

Smith: "Well, when I was, when I was in treatment before like what, what used to get me really annoyed was like they asked me how I feel or this and that all, you know. Like one time this guy asked me how I feel, I told him, I said, 'Great.' He said, 'No, you can't feel great.' How can you tell me how I feel or how I am supposed to feel, you know, because I know how I feel, you know, just."

John Norcross: "So, respect you . . ." (crosstalk)

Smith: "Right."

John Norcross: ". . . in what you say. I take . . ." (crosstalk)

Smith: "I won't, I won't, you know, you ain't got to take it, you don't know how to believe just that I have no reason to, to tell you anything else but than in an other way. You know, I just tell you the way I feel."

John Norcross: "And thank you for correcting right there. That worked fine. I kinda missed what you told me and you corrected me. We're off to a good start here, I think."

Ultimately, as a master practitioner, the therapist's goal in empathy is to use nonlinear processes to see things that aren't said, hear things that aren't seen, and feel things that are ethereal (e.g., listening and responding to absence). Sometimes, however, the best response that a therapist has to convey is to say, "I couldn't possibly know how you feel. . . ." On the surface, this seems like the opposite of empathy, but from a nonlinear perspective it conveys that you understand a client has experienced something so profound and tragic that it is something beyond the counselor's ability to grasp.

Nonlinear thinking provides still another way of understanding empathy, namely, by looking at its opposite. Challenges to a client's sense of being worthwhile, disbelieving the client, negating her feelings, and relating to the client in a plastic manner (i.e., with little feeling or personal regard) are all manifestations of a lack of empathy, or (at the very least) of rapport that is being eroded. When this happens, the foundation for the development of resistance or premature termination (both evidence of poor therapeutic outcomes) is set. To treat a client's experience casually or to assume an understanding of what a client is feeling can be devastating to the relationship. We cite the clinical case example below to illustrate.

Clinical Case Example: A Mother in Distress

A mother in her 50s was attending to her critically ill, unconscious son in an intensive care unit. Her son, a formerly brilliant, vibrant, and successful man in his mid-20s, had been reduced to clinging to life by a rare illness. Multiple surgeries, innumerable instances of being placed on a ventilator, and exotic and powerful steroidal medications with profound side effects were all part of his daily routine only to be succeeded by the next life-threatening crisis. This had gone on for *several years*. An experienced mental health practitioner[7] was called to evaluate the client for a possible change in the young man's anticonvulsive medication. Not knowing the background of the client, the psychiatrist asked the client's mother about her unconscious son's history. She related a gut-wrenching, condensed version of the facts as tears welled in her eyes. She then expressed how helpless and frustrated she felt at not being able to help her son, especially with the very real prospects of death looming daily for 3 indescribably long years. At that point, the well-meaning practitioner replied, "I know how you feel."

Later, as the mother related the experience to her therapist, she stated her reaction to the psychiatrist's comment as "How dare he tell me after 5 minutes of listening that he knows how I feel!"

The vignette in the clinical case example conveys a powerful example of how important it is to be cautious when putting oneself in the shoes and skin of another human being who is experiencing unimaginable circumstances. Can we really imagine what it would be like to have one's adult child suffering over a period of years and routinely facing death? Obviously, the mother felt her experience had been trivialized. The professional made an attempt at linear empathy, and it turned the mother away from the practitioner rather than toward him. One of the authors has worked extensively with family members who have had a loved one killed by homicide or suicide. The tremendously painful emotions such clients felt and experienced are extreme, to say the least (working through emotional issues like this is discussed in Chapters 10 and 11). But despite having specialized training in complicated, traumatic grief, the therapist did not have the personal experience of having a direct family member die by suicide or homicide. The therapist could either attempt to empathize linearly by drawing on the experience of losing loved ones to illness and old age, or acknowledge that he did not have these experiences, but would be guided by the client's experiences. In every instance, when disclosing that he had not had that experience, family members would express gratitude that the therapist would not try to tell them that he "knew how they felt." A seemingly counterintuitive nonlinear approach to empathy actually fosters a therapeutic relationship.

Nonlinear thinking also reveals empathy to be something other than one-dimensional. Bachelor (1988) noted that empathy is perceived and experienced in different ways. For certain clients, a therapist expressing what the client felt was experienced (i.e., received) as empathy. On the other hand, other clients believed that the therapist feeling what the client was relating was most meaningful and empathic. Still other clients experienced a nurturing response or the therapist disclosing some personal information as empathic. Specifically what constitutes an empathic response for a client is as yet unknown. But it is clear that empathy is best understood in nonlinear ways rather than the linear understanding of one size (i.e., type) of empathy fits all.

Our Nonlinear Brain: The Brain, Empathy, and Culture

Social neuroscience explores the biological underpinnings of empathic concern and more generally interpersonal sensitivity, using an integrative approach that bridges the biological and social levels. According to Elliott et al. (2011), "The most important development in the past 10 years, however, is the emergence of active scientific research on the biological basis of empathy, as part of the new field of social neuroscience" (p. 132). In addition, there is no question that functional magnetic resonance imaging (fMRI) technology has made diagnosis in medicine much more precise. Use of fMRI has made it possible to unravel more and more secrets of brain functioning more quickly than the more traditional methods of neuroscientists in the past (e.g., LeDoux, 1998).

Gibson (2006) described empathy as not only a "basic human impulse" that has affected "the course of history, culture and personal connections" but also a "neurological fact" (p. 34) whose secrets are being divulged through the focused study of neuroscience. As an example, Jackson, Meltzoff, and Decety (2005) studied one component of human empathy, namely, the "interpersonal sharing of affect" (p. 771). Subjects in their study were shown a series of still pictures "of hands and feet in situations likely to cause pain" and a matched set of control pictures devoid of any discernible painful events. They were then requested to evaluate online what they believed to be the pain level of the person in the pictures. Jackson et al. (2005) found that there were significant bilateral changes in the brain's electrical and metabolic activity in a number of areas, including the anterior cingulate, the anterior insula, the cerebellum, and to a somewhat lesser degree the thalamus when subjects were asked to evaluate (from pictures) the pain level of people whose hands and feet were in situations likely to cause pain. From previous research, it is known that these same regions of the brain participate significantly in pain processing. They also observed that the subjects' ratings of others' pain was strongly correlated with activity in the anterior cingulate. They concluded that there is an overlapping of areas in the brain that process perceptions of pain in others and experiences of our own pain. The brain is inherently sensitive to the differences between our own and someone else's pain.

In another study, Jackson et al. (2006) proposed, "When empathizing with another individual, one can imagine how the other perceives the situation and feels as a result. To what extent does imagining the other differ from imagining oneself in similar painful situations" (p. 752). Once again, participants were given pictures of people with their hands or feet in painful or nonpainful circumstances with directions to "imagine and rate the level of pain perceived from different perspectives," namely, those of both the self and other. Both perspectives yielded the activation of portions of the neural network that have been demonstrated in pain processing, including the parietal operculum, anterior cingulated cortex, and anterior insula. But the self-perception of being in painful circumstances versus the other person being in pain also yielded differences in the areas of the brain that were activated. Jackson et al. (2006) concluded not only that there are similarities between the self's and others' pain, but also that there are distinct and *crucial* differences: "It may be what allows us to distinguish empathic responses to others versus our own personal distress. These findings are consistent with the view that the empathy does not involve a complete 'Self-Other' merging" (p. 752).

Lydialyle Gibson (2006) did an extensive interview of Jean Decety, one of the neuroscientist coinvestigators of the studies cited above, who said that the implications of these findings for therapists are not casual:

> [E]mpathy requires emotional control—the capacity to distinguish self from other. People who lose themselves in other people's pain . . . experience "personal distress." While empathy is "other-oriented," personal distress turns inward. It drowns the impulse to assist. "If you are in the same state of distress, I don't know how you can help the other person," Decety says. "But if you are able to separate yourself, then the non-overlap in the neural response frees up processing capacity in the brain for formulating an appropriate action." (p. 36)

This is what we believe master practitioners who use nonlinear thinking are doing when they can be completely present and attuned with a client, while at the same time detached and analytical about the case at hand. It is an important state of mind that aspiring master practitioners must achieve.

Demonstrably Effective Elements of the Therapeutic Relationship: Collecting Client Feedback

Historically, therapy has been regarded as a procedure that has been done to or done for a client—rather than something done with a client. Such misplaced emphasis appears to be a holdover from and a direct result of the historical origins of contemporary therapy in psychoanalysis. Even the name psychotherapy is an enduring holdover from the historic days of Freud. The analyst psychoanalyzed the client (or patient, as they were known in psychoanalysis). It was the analyst who held the key to successful treatment through conducting an analysis of the client's *free associations,* interpreting the client's dreams, working through the client's resistance, and analyzing the transference relationship. The client, or rather patient, came to the therapist, who analyzed his or her condition.

In the past 40 years, researchers like Norcross, Lambert, Miller, Duncan, and Hubble (and their colleagues) have conducted revolutionary outcomes therapy research. The central thread running through their research findings has been that it is the client rather than the therapist who is the primary agent of change in therapy. Although this might seem to be a common sense statement, it flies in the face of over 80 years of tradition and training that emphasized therapist techniques and skill as the conditions for eliciting client change. Most outcome research, however, has revealed that a client's experience of and participation in the therapeutic endeavor are significant predictors of successful outcome in therapy (Duncan, Miller, & Sparks, 2004; Hubble et al., 2010; Lambert & Shimokawa, 2011; Miller et al., 2005). Accordingly, as we have advocated, much of the thinking about and informed understanding of the practice of therapy have shifted toward connecting with, engaging, involving, and collaborating with rather than doing something to a client that would supposedly produce (i.e., elicit) cognitive and emotional change. Yet, despite this (as mentioned in Chapter 1), the training of therapists has continued to emphasize specific fragmented approaches and techniques, and has pretty much ignored the value of seeking and using feedback from clients to guide the therapeutic process (Miller et al., 2005).

As an indication of the importance of eliciting feedback from a client, consider the therapeutic task of goal setting. In addition to providing an appropriate collaborative structure to the therapy, setting goals that match a client's needs also leads to better therapeutic outcomes. According to Miller et al. (2005), "Congruence between a person's beliefs about the causes of his or her problems and the treatment approach results in stronger therapeutic relationships, increased duration in treatment, and improved rates of success" (p. 46). Orlinsky, Grave, and Parks (1994) found that positive client outcomes were associated with how clear the goals of treatment were and the level of counselor–client agreement about treatment goals. Mutually agreed upon goals are more likely to keep clients engaged in the process of therapy (Miller et al., 2005). We believe this is a function of the convergence of several elements: nonlinear listening and responding, understanding the underlying dynamics of client concerns (i.e., those things a client can't articulate directly such as the double bind she feels or the ambivalence she expresses but doesn't recognize), ascertaining a client's readiness for change, and appreciating particular strengths and resources.

Miller and his colleagues (Miller, Duncan, & Hubble, 1997a; Miller et al., 2010), however, have placed the active solicitation of client feedback as a central component of each and every therapeutic session. They have found, "Clients whose therapists had access to outcome and alliance information were less likely to deteriorate, more likely to stay longer (e.g., remain engaged) and twice as likely to achieve clinically significant change" (Miller et al., 2005, p. 45). As a result, they have focused on and developed a "client-directed, outcome-informed approach" that actively engages the client as the director of the therapeutic process. Treatment is based on and tailored to a client's needs and wishes for therapy, rather than a fixed, one-size-fits-all approach to treatment. In order to accomplish this, a therapist must not only involve a client in the assessment and goal development process, but also conduct an ongoing assessment of client perception of and satisfaction with the therapeutic process (Miller et al., 2010).

The client-directed, outcome-informed approach is both linear and nonlinear in its underlying conceptualization. It is linear in that the methods that are used to solicit the client's feedback are, for the most part, straightforward (i.e., a client fills out the instruments, and the results are clear). Indeed, periodically, clinicians solicit client feedback (through standardized instruments or by directly questioning clients), and assess what is working, and (possibly more important) what is not working in the therapy (Lambert & Shimokawa, 2011). On the other hand, it is nonlinear in its emphasis of a client's role as not just the primary agent of change, but also the primary source of treatment effectiveness. This places a client's perceptions of change as the "sine qua non" of therapy. And yet, even clients who are ambivalent about therapy or are in a precontemplation or contemplation stage of change may not have the same perceptions of (and, hence, goals for) treatment as a therapist or other entities (family members, the justice system, the workplace, etc.). As a result, establishing workable goals for a client, regardless of his or her stage of change, must focus on the perceptions of change. Even the most chronic psychiatric patients recently released from a long-term care facility can participate in the development of a goal such as "doing whatever it takes to stay out of the hospital." Although such a global goal can be refined (e.g., take medication regularly, develop methods to insure adherence to a medication regimen, and attend supportive aftercare meetings) and may not appear very dynamic, it can be extremely effective. Consider an example from the case of Ashley.

Therapist: "I see. So just thinking of the possibility of asking for help is enough to bring up the old fear of being replaced?"

Ashley: "Uh-huh."

Therapist: "So then to move too fast, and for me to say, 'Okay, so tomorrow you are going to ask everyone at home and at work for help' probably isn't going to feel as good, and probably won't work, right?"

Ashley:	"Probably, yeah."
Therapist:	"But you can agree with me that it is a goal to work towards."
Ashley:	"Yeah." (slowly)
Therapist:	"Okay, I heard the hesitation again. How about if we worked on the goal of helping you lower your fear of being replaced? Help you feel less lonely, would that be better?"
Ashley:	"Yeah." (Nodding)
Therapist:	"Okay, the bad news is that you will have to work on all areas of your life, but the good news is that we can take it slowly—a little at a time. But it is going to mean that you have to decide which area you want to work on first: relationship with your husband or work."
Ashley:	"I think I would like to work on my relationship with my husband."
Therapist:	"Okay, fair enough, but just to let you know, that at a future date, we will address work, Okay?"
Ashley:	"Okay."

Lambert and Shimokawa (2011) conducted a meta-analysis of studies that investigated collecting client feedback. One of the challenges was the relatively few studies that have client feedback as a variable. However, of the nine studies that were analyzed, the medium effect size (approximate $d = 0.5$) that was discovered led the researchers to conclude that there was a reliable relationship between client feedback and outcomes. In fact, Lambert and Shimokawa claim that collecting client feedback (and responding to it appropriately) reduces the chance of at-risk clients from deteriorating (or getting worse, prematurely dropping out of therapy) by one half. As a result, the APA task force decided that this was a demonstrably effective element of the therapeutic relationship (Norcross & Wampold, 2011).

Probably Effective Elements of the Therapeutic Relationship: Positive Regard

As noted in Chapters 4 and 5, therapists are required to assess (i.e., evaluate) clients. But it is important to note that therapists must be aware of and carefully distinguish between assessing a client's symptoms, complaints, and clinical and life circumstances and the personhood of a client. Regardless of the bizarreness, peculiarity, or severity of clinical and symptomatic features that a client presents, it is incumbent upon the therapist to convey a sense of respect for a client's personhood or a positive regard for them. There are three reasons for such respect: Human beings inherently deserve respect; respect for personhood is a core element in building a therapeutic relationship and a nonnegotiable expectation that therapists must fulfill; and we note emphatically that if therapists presume to evaluate clients, clients are also indisputably evaluating their therapists. Although positive regard is considered to be a central element to Rogerian or Person-Centered Therapy, "nearly all schools of therapy now either explicitly or implicitly promote the value of this basic attitude toward patients" (Farber & Doolin, 2011, p. 168).

The evaluations a client makes of his or her therapist are generally of two kinds. The first has to do with the therapist's competence. Competence has to do not only with a therapist's professional qualifications but also with a client's belief in the therapist's ability to be helpful. That is, a therapist may have wonderful professional credentials and look good on paper, but if a client doesn't believe in the person with those credentials, a credibility gap exists that can significantly impinge upon the ultimate effectiveness of a therapeutic relationship. The work of Miller et al. (2005) on the importance of clients providing feedback to therapists about satisfaction with their therapy is precisely the sort of evaluation clients make with or without formal feedback.

The second evaluation that a client makes of the therapist has to do with respect, caring, and liking. That is, a client reads the therapist and asks, "Does this therapist really respect, care about, and like me—or is this therapist judging me?" People reading one another and situations are an inescapable part of human functioning and reflective of how the brain works in making its intuitive emotional appraisals. This is exactly what a client does in the setting with a therapist. The client is reading or appraising unconsciously whether or not he or she feels a tendency toward the therapist as good or away from the therapist as bad. The good and bad referred to are not moral judgments but elemental intuitive appraisals made by the inner workings of the limbic system in the midbrain.

Respecting, caring about, and liking someone are conveyed as part of a significant body of information that is exchanged between client and therapist at a nonverbal level. What does it mean to care about another human being? It means that a therapist is concerned for his or her welfare and above all is respectful. Sincerity in caring about clients is essential and achieved via the congruence discussed in Chapter 2. Sincerity and caring cannot be faked. If it is, sooner or later the clinician will be exposed. The foundations for sincerity and genuine caring are found in empathy, that sense of asking oneself: "What would it be like to be in this client's shoes?" Caring about clients, however, does not suggest that the cautions regarding boundaries and dual roles be disregarded for the sake of caring. It is possible to convey a genuine sense of caring for one's clients and be a guardian of appropriate boundaries.

It thus is incumbent upon therapists to act in accord with clients' interests. But can an egalitarian relationship exist between client and therapist? The answer is, of course, that client and therapist are of equal worth, and each is deserving of equal respect from the other. The power, prestige, status, and success of a therapist's position, however, can distort and erode that sense of equal worth. Therapists must disavow exercising any power of their office such as superior authority, superior knowledge, correct decision making, and knowing what's best, which can easily render a client feeling arbitrarily diminished.

Liking a client may in some instances be difficult because clients can engage in very disagreeable behaviors. One way of helping Level I therapists to deal with the issue of liking a client who demonstrates such disagreeable behaviors is to understand the difference between a client's behavior and his or her personhood. Some therapists may find it difficult to work with certain types of clients (e.g., antisocial personality, borderline, or narcissistic personality disorders), and yet other therapists not only treat and enjoy working with such clients but also specialize in treating them.

But Don't Take Our Word for it! Master Example

Consider this example from master practitioner, John Norcross (chair of the American Psychological Association's Task Force on Empirically Supported Therapy Relationships and editor of the book *Psychotherapy Relationships that Work*) and how he demonstrates positive regard to the client (Allyn & Bacon, 2000d).

John Norcross:	"Uh hmm. Well, so tell me about the ah, cocaine. You've been in recovery for that for some time?"
Smith:	"I'd went to a recovery. I went to, was in three different programs, you know, like ah, this. I guess to me, ah, it really didn't work out. I just wasn't ready for that at that time. Like one time I was off of it for three years and right now, I haven't done it for over a year now."
John Norcross:	"Over a year?"
Smith:	"Right."
John Norcross:	"Congratulations."
Smith:	"Thank you."

John Norcross:	"How'd you do that?"
Smith:	"Well, I just got tired. Got tired of being broke and disgusted (chuckles) . . . and it wasn't, I wasn't going nowhere with it. The more I use the further behind I get I knew I would never break even or get ahead, but the alcohol, I just, you know, keep taking alcohol though."
John Norcross:	"Then I suspect within you is even the answers for your alcohol. If you've been able to stay a year clean from the cocaine. Let's talk if, if it's all right with you for a moment about how you specifically did that?"
Smith:	"Not do it, stay away?"
John Norcross:	"From that cocaine, did you change your friends, change your thinking? What happened?"
Smith:	"Well I still, I goes around, you know, these with people sometimes I was messing around with. But it just, I got tired of the feeling all tired and run out, and come out of the house with $300 to $400 in your pocket, and I don't have a car fare to get back home or can't buy cigarettes. You know, I just, I just got tried, and you'd be so embarrassed; I'm scared to go home and face anybody. I'd stand on the street all night, you know, it, it just, it just took its toll on me."
John Norcross:	"Okay."
Smith:	"I got tired of being run down."
John Norcross:	"And how confident do you feel that you won't slip back into the cocaine now?"
Smith:	"Well, I feel pretty confident. Well, I guess the, that was the effort three years before, you know, and the only thing I say now is everyday I just try to stay away from it . . . I'm not going to guarantee that I won't do this, and I won't do that, and I will only try to just keep doing something to keep myself busy that way I won't fall back on it."
John Norcross:	"I got it. Well, so you're on a different stage, what we called maintenance for the cocaine, but you are actively drinking now and that bothers you?"

In this example, Norcross uses the positive regard that he has for the client and builds on the therapeutic relationship to the point where he can begin to address a subject that he is hesitant about, namely, drinking.

Conclusion

Horvath and Bedi (2002) reported research that demonstrates one of the major reasons for premature termination is a failure in the therapeutic alliance. That is, on some level (cognitively, emotionally, or relationally), the therapist who failed to connect with and engage the client in the collaborative work of therapy has lost a connection with the client (i.e., suffered some form of therapeutic rupture; see Chapter 7). From our perspective, such therapeutic failures can be avoided by appreciating clients' nonlinear thought processes and working through such thinking and helping clients prepare for change. As we discussed in Chapter 4, the result of misjudging clients' *stage of change* is that therapists use interventions that are essentially more appropriate for another stage of change. Such interactions with clients are likely to result in poor therapeutic outcomes. Thus far in this domain, we have discussed the basic ingredients for building a therapeutic relationship, as well as their demonstrated importance in achieving effective therapy. We next turn to a discussion of additional elements of the therapeutic relationship that have been demonstrated to be effective and how the therapeutic relationship can be adapted to bring about therapeutic change.

Notes

1. In doing so, they adopted Gelso and Carter's (1985, 1994) definition of the therapeutic relationship.
2. Meta-analysis is a research procedure that examines all (or many) research studies conducted on a particular topic (e.g., psychotherapy outcomes). Thus, the different studies serve as the subjects to be sampled in the investigation, and the data from these studies are analyzed similarly to data in other quantitative studies. Effect size (ES) is the term used to describe a class of indices whose function is to calculate the magnitude of a particular treatment effect. It differs from a test of significance in that ES indices are statistically independent of the size of the sample studied. In today's psychotherapy outcome studies, ESs are the measures derived from the meta-analysis of studies to describe how much influence a particular treatment variable (e.g., the therapeutic alliance) under investigation has on outcome.
3. The percentages derived were not formally derived as a result of meta-analytic techniques but "characterize the research of a wide range of treatments, patient disorders, dependent variables representing multiple perspectives of patient change, and ways of measuring patient and therapist characteristics as applied over the years. These percentages are based on research findings that span extremes in research designs, and are especially representative of studies that allow the greatest divergence in the variables that determine outcome. The percentages were derived by taking a subset of more than 100 studies that provided statistical analyses of the predictors of outcome and averaging the size of the contribution of each predictor made to final outcome" (Lambert & Barley, 2002, p. 18).
4. According to J. Norcross (personal communication, February 16, 2013), this is better than medicine or education, where the unexplained variance that accounts for outcomes is closer to 50%.
5. They found an overall ES of 0.22, which is generally considered to be a modest, although significant, effect.
6. A moderator variable is any variable that can affect the strength of the relationship between two variables. For example, if the therapeutic relationship was stronger for women than men, then sex would be a moderator variable.
7. Not one of the authors.

The Domain of Establishing and Maintaining the Therapeutic Relationship and the Therapeutic Alliance

The Therapeutic Alliance

Introduction

We continue to discuss the domain of establishing and maintaining the therapeutic relationship. We start this chapter with two elements of the therapeutic relationship that Norcross and Wampold (2011), speaking for the task force called "promising but insufficient research to judge." These are elements of the therapeutic relationship that have been traditionally thought of to be important, but do not have the research base (or what research base there is has serious limitations) to be more definitively linked. However, the three that are presented, congruence/genuineness, managing transference and countertransference, and repairing alliance ruptures, we feel are important enough to discuss here. Next, we discuss some elements of adapting the therapeutic relationship based on the task force's recommendation, including resistance/reactance, client preferences, and culture/religion/spirituality. We conclude with some discussion of managing the boundaries of the therapeutic relationship in an ethically sensitive manner, and look at elements of the therapeutic relationship that are demonstrated *not* to work!

Promising Elements of the Therapeutic Relationship (But Insufficient Research to Judge): Congruence/Genuineness

Probably the most fundamental of Carl Roger's facilitative conditions is congruence or genuineness. In fact, Roger's other two facilitative conditions, empathy and positive regard (which have demonstrable effects on the therapeutic relationship), cannot be communicated unless the therapist is seen to be genuine by the client (Kolden, Klein, Wang, & Austin, 2011). There are two important elements to the concept of congruence. First is the therapist being personally aware of him- or herself in the relationship as a person. This is a concept reflected in Gelso (2011)'s conceptualization of the *real relationship* of two human beings in contact with each other as part of the therapeutic relationship. The second is the ability of the clinician to share aspects of him- or herself—feelings or experiences—with the client. This is important, but must also be viewed in light of the issue of self-disclosure, which we discuss later in the chapter.

As a topic of research, however, the scientific study of congruence, has declined, and of the current studies, many have inadequate methods and small n's, (i.e., research conducted with few subjects). However, in a meta-analysis of 16 studies Kolden et al. (2011) found a correlation between genuineness and client outcomes (mean $r = 0.24$), with a higher ES (for effect size) for older, more experienced therapists. They conclude that:

> Congruence appears to be especially apparent in psychotherapy with more experienced (often older) practitioners. Perhaps therapists come to relax the pretense of role-bound formality and give themselves permission to genuinely engage their patients as they gain experience and confidence. Moreover, experienced therapists may recognize and more carefully discern a patient's need for relational congruence. (p. 200)

There is some evidence that congruence may be important for younger patients (e.g., teenage and college-age), as they may feel more sensitive to inauthenticity and require a level of acceptance from their therapist.

Congruence and genuineness on the therapist's part is also important when listening and responding to congruence in the client. By being genuine and congruent, it helps when having to point out incongruence. Clients are less likely to be dismissive or suspicious of the therapist's motives: "(c)ongruent responses are not disrespectful, overly intellectualized, or insincere, although they may involve irreverence. They are authentic and consistent with the therapist as a real person with likes, dislikes, beliefs and opinions" (Kolden et al., 2011, p. 199). As Rogers et al. (1967) put it, a congruent therapist: "comes into a direct personal encounter with his client by meeting him on a person-to-person basis. It means that he is *being* himself, not denying himself" (p. 101, as cited in Kolden et al., 2011). As a result, it is an important element to the therapeutic relationship that master practitioners actively pursue.

Promising Elements of the Therapeutic Relationship (But Insufficient Research to Judge): Managing Transference and Countertransference

Transference and countertransference were initially psychoanalytic terms developed by Sigmund Freud. The term *transference* referred to the affective material arising out of the client's unresolved conflicts that were projected onto the analyst by the client, which was analyzed and interpreted for the client. It was the psychoanalyst's job to detect such transference feelings, analyze them, and interpret them to the client. For present purposes, we define transference as thoughts, feelings, and behaviors that (1) a client brings to the therapy, (2) a client attributes to a therapist, (3) may have little to do with actual therapist behavior or intentions, and (4) may need to become the focus of attention for the therapeutic relationship.

With the ultimate decline of psychoanalytic preeminence and relevance (see Hobson & Leonard, 2001), and the development of brief methods of therapy (e.g., cognitive and behavioral psychology), the idea of transference as a therapeutically useful construct was diminished or forgotten altogether (Gelso & Hayes, 2002). Today, however, an interest in some elements of transference (e.g., relational factors) impacting therapeutic outcome has been resurrected (Crits-Christoph & Gibbons, 2002).

For example, if a client begins to feel, and discloses, romantic (or parental) feelings toward a therapist, it is the therapist's job to reinterpret those feelings as not really directed to the therapist (because the therapist cannot return such feelings), but as feelings that contain important information for the therapy itself. In order to tactfully (i.e., without disrupting the therapeutic alliance) deal with this situation, the therapist may ask, "What is it about our relationship—that we have created together—that you find fulfilling?" If that discussion is productive, a variety of follow-up questions can be added, including, "Do you still really need to have that done for you, in your life, etc.?"

Further follow-up could proceed along the lines of "If you, indeed, still need that in your life, how might you go about appropriately eliciting that from someone in your life?" or "What is it about our relationship—that we've created together—that you find nurturing that you can ask from someone else, if not yourself?" This allows for the therapy to move forward constructively, compared with a linear approach that many novice therapists might take with this situation (e.g., "Um, it is not appropriate for you to feel these things for me. The ethics code tells me to tell you that we cannot have sex"). A linear approach, although technically correct, in the long run can be the least effective means of sustaining the therapeutic alliance, particularly if it causes the client to withdraw from any future therapeutic endeavor.

Clinical Exercise: Transference

Brainstorm the following client scenarios arising in therapy. Does the issue at hand revolve around a transference theme? If so, why? If not, why not?

- Client expresses attraction for you.
- Client suggests getting together with each other's spouses or partners for dinner and a movie.
- Client offers to hire your child to babysit her children.
- Client begins to yell at you, "All you do is just sit there; you don't *help* me!"
- Add your own scenario.

1. How would the interaction between client and therapist be scripted?
2. How would you respond in a way that preserves the therapeutic alliance?

Additional suggestion: In a group setting, share your responses, imagine that you are giving each other peer supervision, and get feedback on how you might handle these situations.

Countertransference

Countertransference refers to affective material arising out of a therapist's unresolved conflicts and personal sensitivities that may be projected onto a client. Countertransference was seen as a significant threat to the psychoanalytic process. It even earned the scorn of Freud (1910, as cited in Gelso & Hayes, 2002), who proclaimed that any analyst who experienced countertransference and failed to "produce results in a self-analysis of this kind may at once give up any idea of being able to treat patients by analysis" (p. 267). As a result, countertransference as a therapeutic issue was grossly minimized by the analytic community for decades out of fear that the therapist would be judged inadequate. In subsequent years, therapists from nonanalytic traditions began to utilize their emotional reactions to a client as an important source of therapeutic information about the client. As a result, countertransference (like transference) found a resurgence (Gelso & Hayes, 2002).

A therapist's feelings generated by interaction with a client need to be processed as part of the therapy, if appropriate. The important caveat is *if appropriate*. By this, we mean that if a therapist's feelings, generated by a client's behavior, stem from unresolved childhood conflicts (e.g., "You tick me off the same way that my sister does, and I haven't spoken to her in 6 years! And you really are a jerk, just like she is!"), then it is probably not appropriate for a therapist to relate this to a client. Instead, such issues need to be discussed in supervision, in the therapist's own therapy, or perhaps both. If the therapist does not pay attention to such feelings, conflicts, and the like, then he runs the risk of acting inappropriately with a client. If it does not come from the therapist's unresolved childhood conflicts (i.e., the therapist uses his or her emotions as a "barometer"—as mentioned in Chapter 2), then there could be valuable (if not critical) information that needs to become the focus of the therapeutic relationship.

As a brief example of what is meant by a therapist appropriately using feelings generated by a client's behavior as an important source of therapeutic information, see this clinical case example:

Clinical Case Example: Therapist Frustration

A successful businessman in his early 50s sought therapy in order to better understand how to respond to his angry wife. He was very open to suggestions made by the therapist and discussed how he could easily improvise and improve on them. At the same time, he seemed to derive few original ideas of how to proceed in relating better to his wife. The therapist felt frustrated and that he was working harder at the therapy than the client. When this was disclosed to the client in a friendly and collaborative way with the question "What do you think and feel about that?," it opened an entirely new area of discussion. The client's first reaction to the therapist's observation was "As a child, I was told that children are to be seen and not heard. I gave my opinion only when I was asked for it—otherwise, I kept my mouth shut or paid the consequences!" At the conclusion of the session, the client spontaneously offered the observation that he would have never thought that the discussion would have gone in the direction that it did. He had prepared some things that he wanted to discuss, but instead found an entirely new understanding of his characteristic way of relating not only to the therapist but also to his wife. In fact, he indicated that one of his wife's constant comments to him was "You don't talk to me!"

Managing countertransference, according to VanWagoner, Gelso, Hayes, and Diemer (1991), consists of five related factors: self-insight, self-integration, empathy, anxiety management, and conceptualizing ability (see Table 7.1). Taken together, these factors create a matrix wherein countertransference material can be sifted, understood, and utilized. Again, the key is that the therapist must be aware of his or her own feelings and conflicts, and has a handle on his or her propensity for acting upon them in an unconscious way. Hayes et al. (1998) put it best: "The more resolved an intrapsychic conflict is for the therapist, the greater the likelihood that the therapist will be able to use his or her countertransference therapeutically (. . . to deepen one's understanding of the client)" (p. 478).

Table 7.1 Five Countertransference Management Factors

Factor	Definition
Therapist Self-Insight	Therapists' awareness of their feelings, as well as their underlying basis.
Therapist Self-Integration	The integrity of therapists' character structure, ability to maintain boundaries, and ability to differentiate themselves from others.
Anxiety Management	Therapists' ability to experience anxiety—their own and other people's—without being overwhelmed.
Empathy	Therapists' ability to identify with the feelings of others.
Conceptualizing Ability	Therapists' ability to draw on theory to understand the client's dynamics relative to the therapeutic alliance.

Source: Adapted from VanWagoner et al. (1991) and Gelso and Hayes (2002).

For example, if a therapist finds himself feeling irritated by a client's subtle intellectual bullying in the same way that he used to feel when his big brother would tease him, but the therapist had dealt with these issues long ago, he could utilize them in session to say, "Hmm, it seems like you need to wrestle with me in order to feel connected to this process. Could it be that you really believe, in your heart of hearts, that you are right, and you are trying hard to convince me of that? In addition, could it be that the more that I fail to (or *refuse* to) agree with you, the angrier you get and the more passion you feel for this subject?" Again, the therapist's feelings (e.g., "Why is this person being such a jerk?") are formulated in a therapeutically appropriate way (e.g., "Hmm, it feels like this man is attempting to bully me because he is threatened about losing his prestige") and allow for more of a constructive (and nonlinear) strengthening of the therapeutic alliance.

Direct personalizing of countertransference feelings may be damaging to the therapeutic alliance. In such instances, the countertransference interpretation can still be used, but as indirect, third-person statements. In the example above, feedback might be "Sometimes, it can feel overwhelming to come to therapy and not know what you may hear. It's only natural that you may be on guard so that you won't be surprised. If this is your concern, I'll look out for it as well, and we can discuss it. Therapy can be a somewhat unpredictable process, but it doesn't do any good to be uncomfortable the entire time. Should you start to feel that way, or I sense that you might be feeling that way, we can pause what we are discussing and look at those feelings. What do you think?"

With the responses suggested above, the client is arousing defensive and hostile emotions in the therapist because he is threatened by and unsure of the therapeutic process. The therapist utilizes all five of the factors for managing the countertransference feelings: self-insight (i.e., "I am feeling angry! Why?"), self-integration (i.e., "This isn't about me"), anxiety management (i.e., "I don't have to feel threatened by this"), empathy (i.e., "What is the person feeling?"), and conceptualizing ability (i.e., "What is it that this person's feelings of anger and fear are telling me?").

But Don't Take Our Word for It! Master Example

This excerpt is taken from a family therapy session with Leigh McCullough, (pioneer of short-term dynamic psychotherapy, STDP) as she works with a battered woman who is concerned for her son, but seemingly not about herself. Notice how Leigh McCullough uses her countertransference feelings to help the client see the seriousness of the situation (Alexander Street Press, 2012).

Leigh McCullough:	"And what about your son being without a mother?"
Client:	"That's true, but, you know, it's like, I have no self-esteem. I mean, I don't have any, I care about my son a lot. I do love him."
Leigh McCullough:	"Mm-hmm."
Client:	"And I know people say, 'How can you love him, but you don't love yourself?' I will do anything for my son. And there's nothing . . ."
Leigh McCullough:	"You'll do anything for your son?"
Client:	"Yes, I will and I'm trying to get out of there."
Leigh McCullough:	"Yeah, but what is your son going to do if he's, if he's left only with your, your husband?"
Client:	"Yeah."

Leigh McCullough:	"You said he was hitting you so much in the head that you didn't know if you were going to wake up."
Client:	"Yeah, it happens a lot. I mean . . ."
Leigh McCullough:	"That happens a lot. Where you don't know if you're going to live . . ."
Client:	(crosstalk) "He's a black belt in karate. I mean, there's no way I can protect myself from him. Not at all."
Leigh McCullough:	"Uh, that's, this is hard for me to hear. That's, you know and I'm in the business of listening to painful stories. Uh, what is it like for you hearing that from me?"
Client:	"It's scary."
Leigh McCullough:	"It's scary?"
Client:	"Yeah."

What is clear in this transcript is that the client is so discouraged that she is desensitized to her own level of danger in the situation (thus, a resigned precontemplator) and has the theme of hopelessness. The only thing that motivates her is her fear for her son, and Leigh McCullough uses her own feelings of countertransference to try to impress on the client how dangerous the situation really is.

In terms of the research base, Hayes, Gelso, and Humel (2011) found relatively few articles to conduct their meta-analyses. As a result, the task force had to list managing countertransference in the "Promising, but insufficient research to judge" category (Norcross & Wampold, 2011). What Hayes et al. did find was across 10 studies, a small ES negatively correlating countertransference and therapy outcomes, but in 7 studies that looked at successfully managing countertransference, there was a moderate effect size between outcome and countertransference. Clearly, transference and countertransference are potent therapeutic factors that can potentially erode a therapeutic alliance. Managing this material effectively can not only protect but also strengthen the alliance and lead to more successful outcomes (Gelso & Hayes, 2002).

Promising Elements of the Therapeutic Relationship (But Insufficient Research to Judge): Ruptures to the Therapeutic Alliance

Sometimes, despite the best efforts by a therapist to positively manage the therapy relationship, threats, breaks, or ruptures to the therapeutic alliance can occur. According to Safran, Muran, Samstag, and Stevens (2002), a rupture in the therapeutic alliance is defined as "a tension or breakdown in the collaborative relationship between patient and therapist" (p. 236). Such breaks can be precipitated by any number of factors, as previously noted: failing to engage and connect with the client (Chapters 2 and 3), failure to consider the client's stage of change, or incompletely assessing client needs and goals for treatment (Chapters 4 and 5). All such missteps lead to a failure to establish rapport (i.e., resonating together), as well as a failure in forging and maintaining the therapeutic alliance. Coutinho, Ribiero, Hill, and Safran (2011) conceptualized three major sources of ruptures: differences between therapist and client about the tasks of therapy, differences between them about the goals of treatment, and *strains* in their connection.

The theoretical foundation for their thinking stems from Bordin's (1979) pioneering transtheoretical understanding about ruptures in the alliance. Bordin suggested that negotiations were constantly being conducted between client and therapist about the three major areas (i.e., tasks, goals, and bond) in two dimensions: a conscious level (i.e., surface meaning) and unconscious level (i.e., underlying meaning). Disagreements may be expressed explicitly and sometimes implicitly. However, when ruptures occur, the process of negotiation must be moved front and center in therapy.

Therapeutic Ruptures and Nonlinear Thinking

When ruptures occur, given the prime importance of the therapeutic alliance, it is essential that it be repaired. Much like the discussion above regarding transference and countertransference, repairs can be addressed in a variety of ways that actually strengthen the alliance. In keeping with a major emphasis of the present text, Safran et al. (2002) suggested that there are direct and indirect means of dealing with disagreements. For example, more direct means might be exploring the possible meaning of a client's refusal to do a homework assignment, clearing up misunderstandings, or reiterating tasks and goals in different words to assure greater clarity. *Indirect means* bear strong resemblance to the present authors' nonlinear thinking. For example, a therapist can ally herself with a client's resistant behavior or can begin to define uncooperative behavior as a useful indicator of a new way of experiencing the therapeutic relationship, which we discuss in more detail in Chapters 12 and 13. In addition, the depth of the rupture is important to consider. Some ruptures are manifested at a surface level (e.g., disagreements about topics being discussed or procedures being followed) or on the underlying meaning level (e.g., relationship issues such as transference and countertransference or boundary issues).

Identifying Ruptures to the Therapeutic Alliance

Regardless of the underlying issues, once a rupture in the alliance has occurred, it is the responsibility of the therapist to attempt immediate repair. In order to do this, the therapist must first recognize that a rupture has occurred. The two types of behaviors that seem to indicate that a rupture has occurred are *withdrawal* behaviors and *confrontation* behaviors (Safran & Muran, 2000). Withdrawal behaviors are any actions that seem to limit the client's participation in therapy and signal his or her disengagement. Confrontational behaviors are expressions of anger, frustration, or resentment toward the therapist or the therapeutic process. Each of these types of behaviors is designed to stop the therapeutic process and force the therapist to react. The therapist's reaction will generally determine whether the rupture will become a breach in the alliance (and effectively end the therapy) or will be repaired in an attempt to salvage (and possibly strengthen) the alliance (Coutinho et al., 2011).

Repairing Ruptures to the Therapeutic Alliance

Following a decade of research, Safran and his colleagues (Safran et al., 2002) developed a conceptually useful four-stage framework for repairing alliance ruptures that is effective in maintaining the therapeutic alliance. Briefly, these stages are (1) attending to the rupture behavior (i.e., withdrawal or confrontation), (2) exploring the rupture experience, (3) exploring the client's avoidance, and (4) the emergence of a wish or need (see Table 7.2).

There are several topics that Safran and his colleagues (Safran et al., 2002) suggested exploring in the repair process, namely, core relational themes (e.g., a client's experience of the therapist and strains in the relationship): clarifying misunderstandings, reframing the meaning of tasks or goals, and allying with the resistance. In particular, some research findings related to therapeutic ruptures suggest that clients frequently have negative feelings about the therapist or therapy but do not give voice to them. In fact, it is generally not until the end of the therapeutic endeavor, when a client terminates therapy, that most will express any negative emotions or experiences to the therapist. In general, research has revealed that the reasons for clients not to express negative feelings concern fears regarding the therapist's reactions. As a result, a therapist must be sensitive to this general

Table 7.2 Stage Process Model of Repairing Therapeutic Rupture

Stage	Definition
1. Attending to the rupture behavior.	Therapist recognizes behavior that signals the therapeutic rupture (either client withdrawal or increased confrontation toward the therapist and therapeutic process).
2. Exploring the rupture experience.	Allowing a client to discuss feelings of dissatisfaction or hurt and resentment regarding the therapist's action, while the therapist facilitates the experience in a nonthreatening way and offers his or her perspective.
3. Exploring the client's avoidance.	Exploration of any actions or feelings of client withdrawal or avoidance, defensiveness, and inability to discuss these openly with the therapist.
4. Emergence of wish or need.	Client expressing the desire to express negative feeling or having the power to alter the course of therapy.

Source: Adapted from Safran et al. (2002) and Safran and Muran (2000).

situation (not wanting to voice negative comments) and be the *first* to talk about it in order to set the stage for clients to talk about these feelings when they (inevitably) arise (Safran & Muran, 2000; Safran et al., 2002).

Clinical Exercise: Repairing Alliance Ruptures

Examine the following scenarios of ruptures in progress and create a rupture repair rationale (including the possible reasons for the rupture) utilizing the four-stage model outlined above.

1. A depressed client has been in treatment for six sessions. He has begun to make progress when suddenly he skips his last session, calling at the last minute to say that he couldn't make it.
2. A client who is a single parent has initiated therapy to develop better methods of parenting her two preteen children. You have seen her three times, and in the last session you pointed out that she was making some progress. In the next session, she complains bitterly that her children still won't listen to her and states, "This is just a waste of my time; we aren't getting anywhere!"
3. A client has been in therapy for approximately 1 year. During one session, you notice that his attention has started to wander and that he tends to give one-word or very brief answers.

Additional suggestion: Share responses in small groups, imagining that you are giving each other peer supervision. Get feedback on how you might handle these situations as well as why you might handle them in that way.

What essentials can a Level I practitioner take from this discussion about the practice of therapy? As noted previously, client feedback to a therapist about the therapy is important in facilitating a positive treatment outcome. That feedback should also include negative feelings as well as any different perspective that the client may have. Although this might seem counterintuitive (or nonlinear), the process of discussing a client's expression of negative feelings and thoughts can be a source of growth while simultaneously helping to resolve a possible therapeutic rupture. Therapists also need to be mindful of the possibility that perceived attacks by a client can prompt retaliation using expressions of veiled hostility or defensiveness. Such interactions can ultimately result in further deterioration of the alliance and a premature termination.

Safran et al. (2002) ended their discussion with sobering advice to clinicians derived from relevant research: It can be difficult to train therapists to constructively deal with a client's negative expression toward the therapist that, in turn, can precipitate hostile, negative, and/or defensive reactions in the therapist. For the Level I practitioner, we add the following two other points regarding client expressions of negative feelings: (1) The use of a linear, friendly, and cooperative discussion of the client's disagreement with the therapist is legitimate and (2) nonlinear thinking about a client's disagreement, as mentioned above, can promote growth and a strengthening of the therapeutic alliance.

But Don't Take Our Word for It! Master Example

This excerpt is taken from a family therapy session with Monica McGoldrick, (author of *Genograms* and *Ethnicity and Family Therapy*) as she works with a teenage daughter, her father, and her step-mother (Psychotherapy.net, 2006).

Monica McGoldrick: (to daughter) "So it sounds like you were very close to your grandmother. Were you?"

Father: "Uh, excuse me, Monica. Uh, I really have to ask the question again where this is leading. I mean, we've, we've really wasted most of this session going back on this ancient history, and I, I'm—what I'm really afraid of is that we're not going to focus on the problem that we came in here to, to address, which is Michelle's misbehavior. And I –I'm, I'm very concerned that she's going to take this as a cue, cue that this is some sort of an excuse."

Monica McGoldrick: "Was there something about that that got, I don't know."

Father: "No, it's just that, you know, she really wasn't very close to her grandmother, that's the point of fact, and I, I just am afraid that if we just keep harping on this, this, this, this stuff here, we're not going to deal with what's going on with Michelle at school."

Monica McGoldrick: "Uh hmm, Uh hmm."

Father: "Now, I, I really feel like, if we're going to go on with this—ah, I need to know how long this is going to take, and I mean, I'm, you know, I'm a lawyer and I work with contracts. And I have, and we have to tell clients how long something is going to take and, and what it's going to cost."

Monica McGoldrick: "Uh hmm. Well, in some ways this is a little bit different situation, you know. But it's very hard until I get a sense of what the story is, to know how to, exactly help you to figure."

Father: "I'm thinking you give us a ballpark figure?" (crosstalk)

Monica McGoldrick: "Sure, sure, sure. And I feel very strongly about being accountable to you, so I, you know, you're gonna have to feel okay with the process. In a general way, that's going to take us a few sessions. You know, what I would say is if, after we've met three or four times, you feel as you do now, that this is, you know, what did this have to do with anything, then I would say, let's really talk about it. But until we get a sense of what the history is, and how that may relate to whatever is happening right now, both in your family and for her at school, I, kind of, need to get oriented to this."

Father: "All right, well, I, I think we have to think about it."

Step-Mother: "Dear, I think, I think we should do it, all right?"

As you read the transcript above, can you see the elements of a therapeutic rupture in the father's challenge to Monica McGoldrick? See also if you can figure out the unexpressed wish that the father has about the therapy process. Do you think that Monica McGoldrick handled the rupture effectively? Which of the four-stage model did you see her utilize in repairing the rupture?

Methods of Adapting the Therapeutic Relationship

In addition to the elements of the therapeutic relationship that APA's second task force on the therapeutic relationship found to be effective, they also identified since "a truly evidence-based psychotherapy will necessarily consider the person of the therapist, the therapy relationship, and the means to adapt or tailor that relationship to the individual patient . . . Otherwise, evidence based practice will prove clinically incomplete as well as scientifically suspect" 2011, (p. 10). In fact, clinicians who do this, are often more effective with clients than those who don't (Norcross and Wampold, 2011). Norcross and Lambert (2011), quoted Sir William Osler, the father of modern medicine, saying: "It is sometimes much more important to know what sort of patient has the disease than what sort of disease a patient has" (p. 9). In the spirit of this quote, we present in this section the elements of the therapeutic relationship that should be adapted depending on client factors that are demonstrably effective (see Table 7.3) including reactance, client preferences, and culture/religion/spirituality.

Demonstrably Effective Method of Adapting the Therapeutic Relationship: Reactance/Resistance

Client demonstrations of ambivalence have been well-known since the beginnings of psychotherapy. From Charcot and Janet to Freud, the earliest clients of psychotherapy displayed ambivalence (e.g., hysterical paralysis), and making sense of this behavior was often difficult. In his early work, Freud interpreted ambivalent behavior demonstrated by his clients as being a sign of noncompliance. Thus, when they would not comply with his therapeutic interventions, he called it *resistance*. In traditional psychoanalytic theory, resistance is a defense mechanism employed by the client in an effort to "repress intra-psychic impulses that conflicted with social expectations and self-perceptions" (Beutler et al., 2002, p. 130). As an unconscious process, resistance allows a client to avoid certain thoughts and feelings that may cause anxiety or embarrassment. Resistance is thus used in the service of protecting the ego (or "self") and is associated with a fear of change (Beutler et al., 2002; Hanna, 2001). Whether or not resistance is considered a sign of psychopathology (as in the analytic sense), it is certain that it can be disruptive to the treatment process. Information Box: Four Process Categories of Resistant Client Behavior presents some examples of classical resistance behaviors.

Table 7.3 Findings of the Second APA Task Force on the Psychotherapy Relationship

	Relationship Elements	Methods of Adapting
Demonstrated Effective	Therapeutic Alliance (Chapter 6) Empathy (Chapter 6) Collecting Client Feedback (Chapter 6)	Reactance/Resistance (Chapter 7) Client Preferences (Chapter 7) Culture/Religion/Spirituality (Chapter 7)
Probably Effective	Goal Consensus (Chapter 5) Collaboration (Chapter 5) Positive Regard (Chapter 6)	Stages of Change (Chapter 4) Coping Style (Domain 5)
Promising, but Insufficient Research to Judge	Congruence/Genuineness (Chapter 7) Repairing Alliance Ruptures (Chapter 7) Managing Countertransference (Chapter 7)	Expectations (Chapter 7) Attachment Style (Domain 4)

Information Box: Four Process Categories of Resistant Client Behavior

Arguing: challenging: challenging the accuracy of what the counselor says; discounting: questioning the counselor's personal authority; hostility: expressing direct hostility at the counselor
  Interrupting: talking over; cutting off
  Negating: blaming: other people are at fault for the behavior; disagreeing: "Yes, but . . ."; excusing; claiming impunity: client claims not to be in danger; minimizing; pessimism; reluctance: expresses reservation; unwilling to change: lack of desire to change
  Ignoring: inattention; nonanswer; no response; sidetracking

Source: Taken from Chamberlain, Patterson, Reid, Kavanaugh, and Forgatch (1984), as cited in Miller and Rollnick (2002, p. 48).

Reactance

Many nonpsychoanalytic or psychodynamic therapists found it difficult to adopt constructs from a dynamic perspective. The assumptions and implications of these constructs simply do not match up with their view of the therapeutic process. In the process of encountering client ambivalence, however, many nondynamic therapists have needed a way to understand it and address it. One construct that has been adopted from social psychology by cognitively or behaviorally oriented clinicians was the construct of reactance. Resistance refers to being easily provoked and responding in opposition to external demands (Beutler, Harwood, Michelson, Song, & Holman, 2011). Reactance in a person occurs:

> whenever he or she believe[s] that free behaviors are being threatened with elimination. Thus, even normal reactance tendencies are both differentially responsive to an individual's disposition to perceive threat and motivational in that they direct the individual toward restoring the threatened behaviors. Once activated, reactance is observed in oppositional behavior, noncompliance, and rigidity. (Beutler et al., 2002, p. 130)

In other words, reactance occurs as a typical response that human beings demonstrate to threat or coercion, not a response that arises from more unconscious processes that prevent thoughts or feelings from being expressed. This explanation has allowed for nonanalytic therapists to devise methods for working with this manifestation of ambivalence.

In therapy, reactance can be thought of as a naturally occurring process. As described above, at some level a client intuitively senses that a therapist will try to persuade him to change his usual pattern of behaviors—and that may be perceived as a threat to the client's freedom (Beutler et al., 2002). According to Hanna (2001), clients who are actively engaged in therapy may feel the ambivalence of giving up control of their lives: "People who actively fight beneficial change do so because their beliefs and general outlook are so delicately in balance that change appears as a threat" (p. 21). Resistance may be thought of as a state, but reactance is more like a trait. It is a client marker for the optimal degree of therapist directiveness. It exists on a normally distributed continuum from compliance to defiance. How directive one is depends on the client's level of reactance! Matching therapist directives to reactance improves patient outcomes in 80% of the identified studies. A meta-analysis of 12 studies (with over 1,000 participants) found a large effect size ($d = 0.76$) for matching therapist defectiveness to patient reactiveness (Beutler et al., 2011).

This suggests a paradoxical phenomenon: Even clients who voluntarily come for counseling or psychotherapy will demonstrate reactant behavior(s). Linear thinking suggests that this contradiction is confusing: If clients want the help of a therapist, why would they be resistant to such help? However, a nonlinear thinking therapist realizes that, just as clients come to therapy at different stages of change, clients come to therapy with different levels of reactance. As a result, they have to adapt their approach based on the client's reactance level. A client who has higher levels of reactance may benefit from more self-control methods, minimal therapist directiveness, and paradoxical interventions, whereas clients with lower levels of reactance, benefit more from therapist directiveness and explicit guidance (Beutler et al., 2011).

Demonstrably Effective Method of Adapting the Therapeutic Relationship: Client Preference

Have you ever had this happen to you? You go in to get a haircut, and the stylist asks you how you want to have your hair cut. You tell them and they give you *exactly* what you want. It is the perfect haircut. How did you feel? What did you think of the stylist? Chances are, you felt wonderful and you probably declared that you would never get your haircut from anyone else! Now what about the opposite case? Have you ever gone in and asked for one hairstyle and came out with your hair cut too short, or unevenly? Again, how did you feel and what were your thoughts about the stylist? Let's consider another example in a different context. Have you ever been in a restaurant, and the waiter asks: "How would you like that cooked?" Suppose you say ask for your dinner cooked medium well, and it came out almost raw? In other words, the meal is completely ruined! Chances are you would decide not to go back to the restaurant, nor would you recommend it!

So what does this have to do with counseling or psychotherapy? It turns out, plenty! All of us—including clients—have preferences. That is, we have certain expectations and a certain way that we like things. From our hairstyle to our food order to the way we want a physician (or therapist) to treat us, we all have preferences. Some people are quick to let others know what their preferences are: "I don't want to take pills," "I want direct answers," and so on. Some people know their preferences because they have had bad experiences. Take this example from the case of Mike.

Mike:	(wearily looks over the top of mirrored sunglasses) "Alright . . . But look, when I was a teenager, I was forced to go to counseling, and it didn't do anything. The woman I went to see was all 'touchy-feely' and had candles and incense . . . I thought she looked more like a gypsy or a fortune teller! Anyway, I said enough of this and bolted."
Therapist:	"Yeah, I've known a few folks like that in my time. Sometimes people just don't mesh. Their styles don't match. So if that starts to happen with us, you'll let me know before you bolt? (silence) If you do, I promise no incense and candles . . ."
Mike:	(laughs) "Okay."

The reality is that all clients come to therapy with their own set of preferences and their own ideas of what kind of therapy they will feel comfortable with, many will not directly tell their therapists. A more troubling reality is that many therapists will not ask their clients explicitly about their preferences. Instead, many therapists assume that delivering their own, unique version of therapy is good enough, and that clients will let them know if they don't like something that the clinician is doing. However, this is a linear way of employing a one-size fits all approach. Master practitioners use a more nonlinear approach and realize that just as not all clients come in at the same stage of change, not all clients have the same preferences for therapy. As a result, the therapist needs to adjust to client preferences.

First, from a clinical perspective, what are client preferences, exactly? Actually, according to Swift, Callahan, and Vollmer (2011) client preferences "represent what clients would want the therapy encounter to be like if the choice were left to them" (p. 302). In the clinical literature, there are three broad types of preferences: role preferences, therapist preferences, and treatment preferences. Role preferences include the activities and behaviors that take place in the therapy. These can include the level of activity or passivity of the therapist. Therapist preferences include desired characteristics of the therapist (i.e., number of years of experience, level of training, cultural or gender similarity or difference). Treatment preferences are more specific things about the treatment that the client wants from the type of treatment ("trauma work," cognitive-behavioral therapy) to methods of treatment (psychopharmacology versus psychotherapy alone).

So what is the best way to elicit these preferences? It may sound counterintuitive to everything that we have discussed relevant to nonlinear thinking, but a linear approach is often best. That is, a clinician merely asking the client what his or her preference is for therapy or for them as a therapist. Vollmer, Grote, Lange, and Walker (2009) formalized this process by creating the Treatment Preference Interview, which allows clinicians to be able to quickly gather this information during an intake session. It includes questions for all three types of preference (role preference, therapist preference, and treatment preferences) and can quickly provide the therapist with a client's desires.

But Don't Take Our Word for It! Master Example

In this brief exchange, John Norcross shows how he uses eliciting client preferences (specifically therapist preferences) to build the therapeutic relationship (Allyn & Bacon, 2000d).

John Norcross: "Alright. And so if I have something on my mind, just bring it straight out."
Client: "Oh yeah."
John Norcross: "Yeah. Alright. And if I brought it out a little too harshly, you think you'd be able to tell me?"
Client: "Yeah. I think I could tell you."

In a meta-analysis of 35 studies comparing outcomes of clients who were matched in terms of their preferences versus those who were not matched according to their preference, Swift et al. (2011) found an ES of 0.31, which was considered to be small, but significant. In fact, clients who received their preferences were one-third less likely to drop out of treatment prematurely than those who did not. Even if the clinician could not necessarily deliver the client's preferred mode of therapy, the act of *asking* the client was positively associated with successful outcome. This was considered to be a robust finding of the meta-analysis.

Demonstrably Effective Method of Adapting the Therapeutic Relationship: Culture/Religion/Spirituality

Closely related to the construct of client preferences are the issues of culture, religion, and spirituality. Each of these are personally relevant to the client in singularly unique ways. As a result, these must be treated in such a fashion. In fact, master practitioners understand that just as clients with the same diagnosis have very different presentations and motivations, so too do clients of the same culture, religion, or spiritual belief. Adapting therapy in a culturally sensitive and appropriate way requires an understanding of the client's context relative to these factors.

Unfortunately, although the field of mental health has tried to emphasize cultural sensitivity, clients from ethnic minority subgroups are still often underserved (Gonzalez et al., 2010). Many times if clients from nondominant ethnic groups do come to therapy, they drop out because they do not feel safe enough to engage with the therapist. Treatments that are successfully adapted to different cultures have several factors in common. They include cultural adaptations based on language. In fact, conducting all therapy in a client's native language (if other than English) is twice as effective as therapy conducted in English. So if it is at all possible to match a client with a clinician who can speak in the client's native tongue that is more effective. Another factor is the use of metaphors and concepts that are appropriate to the client's culture. This includes sayings, stories, constructs, or symbols that have particular relevance to the client's culture (e.g., *Marianismo* in Hispanic cultures or *Enquing* in Asian cultures), but that may not have an equal in the dominant culture (Ng, Peluso, & Smith, 2010; Peluso, Miranda, Firpo-Jimenez, & Pham, 2010). Also issues of context are potentially relevant to culturally adapting the therapeutic relationship. This can include broader culture-wide issues like acculturative stress, economic disadvantage, migration issues for the client or the client's family, and lack of social supports.

Clients who are highly religious or spiritual can provide unique challenges and opportunities to the clinician. These issues can significantly impact the therapeutic relationship if they are not attended to. Worthington, Hook, Davis, and McDaniel (2011) found wide variability in the definition of religion and spirituality, but offer the distinction that religion refers to adherence to a set of spiritual beliefs or traditions rooted in a community of believers, whereas spirituality is "a more general feeling of closeness and connectedness to the sacred" (pp. 402–403). They note that religious connection or spirituality can offer potential strengths for the client to help overcome problems, or can be the source or impetus to change. However, they can also be rigidly applied as punishers for clients who see themselves as bad or failing to uphold a spiritual ideal. In these cases, employing religious or spiritual practices that incorporate forgiveness strategies or redemptive narratives can be a useful addition to traditional psychotherapeutic approaches when clients hold strong religious or spiritual views. Therapists who are able to adapt treatment to include these can foster a stronger therapeutic relationship than those who do not.

In terms of the research on these constructs, there is evidence that culture, religion, and spirituality have an impact on the therapeutic relationship. Smith et al. (2007) conducted a meta-analysis of 65 studies (with over 8,000 participants) to look at the impact of culturally adapted treatments compared with treatments that were not culturally adapted. They found that when clients received a culturally adapted treatment, their outcomes were greatly improved ($d = 0.46$). The most frequent adaptations included incorporation of client cultural content or values, use of client's native language, and clinicians of similar ethnicity. In terms of religion and spirituality issues, the results were mixed. Worthington et al. (2011) found that in 29 studies, clients in treatments that had a religious or spiritual approach incorporated into them showed greater improvement in both psychological outcomes and spiritual outcomes. However, in 11 other studies that used rigorous dismantling designs (where the specific elements of religion and spirituality could be controlled), there was no difference in therapies that were specifically religious or spiritual compared with comparable treatments (with the same theoretical orientation) for psychological outcomes, but there were significant improvements for spiritual approaches with spiritual outcomes.

Again, just as with culture, matching client preferences for religion and spirituality seems to be the most important factor in determining the effectiveness of these factors to clinical success. In fact, routinely matching therapists to clients based solely on either gender, ethnicity, or religion/spirituality does not seem to be supported by the literature unless there is a preference expressed by the client (Norcross & Wampold, 2011).

Clinician Attitude and Disposition: Optimism and Hope

"All hope abandon, ye who enter here."

—Dante, *The Inferno*

"Optimism is the faith that leads to achievement. Nothing can be done without hope and confidence."

—Helen Keller

As he enters the gates of Hell in the Divine Comedy, the Narrator, Dante reads the quote above on a sign over the gates. The tenor of this brief sentence is indeed truly menacing. For clients facing overwhelming life circumstances, however, it might be a fitting description of their lives. By contrast, Helen Keller's words are the antidote. As a result, the best thing that a therapist can offer their clients is a sense of hope. Frank (1961) in his book *Persuasion and Healing* wrote that a sense of hope must be mobilized in the client by the therapist for any positive movement to occur. "According to Frank, patients enter therapy because they are demoralized, and restoring their hope and positive expectation is a powerful ingredient (Constantino, Glass, Arnkoff, Ametrano, & Smith, 2011, p. 354). Therapist encouragement can reasonably convey and instill belief that a client's condition and circumstances can improve. Even under dire clinical circumstances, a therapist's attitude that conveys, "Let's put our heads together and see what we can work out," goes a long way toward instilling hope without making outrageous predictions of client success. Conveying hope must also take into consideration the particular stage of change in which a client enters treatment. For example, if a client is in a precontemplation stage of change and thus isn't certain that she has a problem, care must be exercised in the messages conveyed.

However, an optimistic and hopeful stance is not synonymous with being "Pollyannaish." Although a therapist may offer a sense of hope that a client's condition and circumstances can be improved, a therapist must also be careful to avoid making outrageous and irresponsible promises or guarantees of success. Such guarantees are not only prohibited by codes of ethics but also defy sound principles of therapy. Most importantly, such guarantees are likely to negatively impact the therapeutic relationship. In fact, Constantino et al. (2011) caution that therapists should:

> tread lightly and empathically in using strategies to enhance outcome expectations. Make a concerted effort to use hope-inspiring statements that neither too quickly threaten a patient's belief system or sense of self . . . The therapist can also express confidence and competence in such statements as, "I am confident that working together we can deal effectively with your depression" while maintaining a sense of understanding that the patient might not fully believe this statement at the outset. (p. 370)

So what does it mean to have hope or be optimistic? In part, it means believing in the process of therapy and then imparting this to the client. There is a common saying that most beginning clinicians are taught: *Trust the process*. It means that even when the therapist might not necessarily know what to do or say next, which technique to employ, or what avenue of discussion to pursue, that having an innate, optimistic belief that the therapeutic process will produce some result. It calls for the therapist to be patient and to not feel that they have to force something to happen in session. Instead, embracing many of the factors described in the last two chapters (empathy, congruence, positive regard, etc.) require that the clinician begin with the optimistic ideal that anyone can learn to improve their lives and their conditions. It also means never giving up hope about the client's ability to make changes. Although clients are often very modest in terms of what they expect from therapy, Kirsch and Lynn (1999) have pointed out,

> [I]t has long been recognized that positive expectancies about treatment outcome play an important role in stimulating behavioral change in psychotherapy . . . virtually all schools of psychotherapy acknowledge the importance of bolstering positive expectancies to maximize treatment gains and minimize noncompliance . . . (it includes) encouraging clients to recognize that pessimistic attitudes are unrealistic, and singling out a readily changeable behavior to maximize optimism about positive therapeutic outcomes. (p. 511, parentheses added)

Indeed, this is the essence of Helen Keller's quote above, and it is something that all master clinicians pay close attention to, regardless of theory or technique when developing and maintaining the therapeutic relationship. As you watch excerpts of master therapists at work, see if you can detect elements of optimism and hope across different therapists. How do they communicate this to clients? How effective are they with clients, as a result?

Ethically Maintaining the Therapeutic Relationship

Creating a therapeutic relationship is a crucial skill that therapists of all developmental levels—and all theoretical persuasions—must achieve in order to be effective with clients. Although the elements of the therapeutic relationship and the methods for adapting it, as outlined by the task force are important, there are still some additional topics that we think are important to cover as well. They are topics about ethically maintaining a therapeutic relationship.

Too often, beginning (and some advanced) therapists feel that merely creating the therapeutic alliance is sufficient for moving a client forward in accomplishing the therapeutic goals. This linear view implies that the alliance, once established, is a static (or unchanging) entity that does not need attention. The therapeutic alliance, however, is a dynamic (and often nonlinear) function of the therapeutic endeavor that requires a therapist's constant monitoring and attention. It is akin to the carnival act that has a row of five plates spinning at the top of broomstick handles. As long as the performer pays attention to the plates and keeps them spinning, they will not fall off the broomsticks. Similarly, a therapist must be aware of the state of the therapeutic alliance, understand what issues threaten it, and be skilled in how to repair ruptures to its fabric. Although there are literally *thousands* of ways that an alliance can be threatened, we will address several of the more common issues that Level I therapists confront that can jeopardize the therapeutic alliance: boundary issues, multiple relationships, and self-disclosure (in subsequent chapters, we discuss further threats to the therapeutic alliance and ways to maintain it relative to Level II and Level III domains).

Boundary and Role Management I: Boundaries

All relationships are guided by boundaries. That is, within a given type of relationship (e.g., parent-child, husband-wife, teacher-pupil, doctor-patient, and supervisor-supervisee), there are certain behaviors and actions that are *prescribed* (i.e., must take place) and certain behaviors and limits that are *proscribed* (i.e., must not take place). When these boundaries are maintained, the function and the purpose of the relationship can take place more or less smoothly. Violations of prescribed and proscribed behaviors, on the other hand, represent boundary crossings, which can disrupt the normal flow of the therapeutic alliance. Although such boundary crossings can occur on the part of either individual, Poon, Mozdzierz, Douglas, & Walthers (2007) indicated that in a professional relationship such as between counselor and client, it is *always* the professional individual who has responsibility for making certain that appropriate boundaries are maintained. Sommers-Flanagan, Elliott, and Sommers-Flanagan (1998) put it this way: "The challenge to the professional and, we argue the moral obligation of the more powerful person in any relationship, is to be conscious of all boundaries and willing to extend or hold firm, depending on circumstances" (p. 39).

Take for example the following scenario. After several successful sessions, a client suggests that you and she should go into business together because "We make such a great team." This is clearly a boundary crossing that is prohibited—a therapist cannot maintain a therapeutic relationship and a business interest with a client. Such a dual relationship has the potential to damage a therapeutic alliance because (1) it misunderstands the essence of the therapeutic relationship—"We make such a great team because it is a professional relationship that is governed by rules, not because of our compatibility" and (2) to introduce the dynamic of business partner into the therapeutic endeavor would create confusion about a number of issues. Consider the following.

In any business venture, disagreements between partners are inevitable. How would a therapist and client *ever* be certain about whom they were relating to in such a disagreement? Would a client be disagreeing with her therapist or her business associate? Would a therapist be disagreeing with his business associate or with his client? In addition, a therapist's motives come into question. As a therapist, one's fiduciary responsibility is to put a client's interests first, before one's own interests. When a therapist's business and financial interests are involved, such interests are likely at some point to come into conflict with a client's best interests, thus prompting self-interest to take precedence over a therapist's fiduciary responsibilities. Hence, linear thinking about boundary crossings would suggest that any boundary crossing is an ethical violation. This is primarily true of the Level I practitioner, who is concerned about jeopardizing the therapeutic alliance or violating any ethical standard.[1]

Nonlinear thinking, on the other hand, gives rise to the question as to whether all boundary crossings actually represent ethical violations. Although the answer is "no," such boundary crossings, nevertheless, have the potential to be ethical violations, and hence in a therapy relationship, boundaries must be carefully monitored. Peluso (2007) described this issue particularly well as it pertains to Level I counselors:

> Any alteration, extension, or crossing of the relationship boundary either may temporarily or permanently change the nature of the therapeutic relationship positively or negatively. This can occur even if the violation or crossing is inadvertent. Even if the therapist's intentions are good, she cannot know how the client will react to a particular crossing, which will necessarily cause a shift in their perception of the client. This may affect the amount and type of information that is shared in therapy, and even how the client feels about the therapeutic process itself. Of course, this does not mean these changes cannot be incorporated into the relationship, nor does it mean the boundary violation or crossing is automatically damaging to the therapeutic relationship. (p. 36)

Ethics and Boundaries

To help guide therapists in maintaining appropriate boundaries, various professional organizations, including the American Counseling Association, the American Psychological Association, and the National Association of Social Workers, have developed codes of ethical conduct to help define the therapy relationship and thus protect both client and counselor. As Sommers-Flanagan et al. (1998) argued, by helping to define this relationship, the ethical codes protect both the counselor and client:

> Professional ethics codes formally articulate professional relationship boundaries. As such, boundaries guide a host of potential interactions, some of which are more central to defining professional relationships, whereas other interactions are less specific, less impermeable, or less damaging to change. In professional relationships in which there is a clear power differential, there are boundaries of such clarity and precision that to violate them essentially redefines the relationship (i.e., sexual contact). (p. 38)

Concretely, what are some of the boundary issues that therapists should be concerned about? Obviously, a sexual relationship with a client is forbidden. A therapist who claims that he was seduced is not using a valid argument regarding such behavior. The harms accruing to a client from a sexual relationship with his or her therapist are numerous and significant. To begin with, given the intrinsic nature of client vulnerability, a sexual encounter is heinously exploitive. Individuals engaging in such boundary violations are hard-pressed to rationalize such encounters with clients as being for the client's benefit. Sexual encounters add confusion to client feelings about the nature of the relationship (i.e., from that of a helper and helped to one of romance). Furthermore, sexual involvement with a client clearly can aggravate psychosexual issues already patent within an individual.

Gift giving is another area with the potential for boundary violations. The question arises as to exactly when a gift from a client represents a boundary violation. A therapist accepting home-baked cookies by a grateful client during the holidays is a case in point. Poon et al. (2007) suggested that the operational criteria to apply in determining if a boundary violation has occurred are several—are the client's interests being served, and what is the potential for harm accruing to a client if the therapist accepts the gift of home-baked cookies? Acceptance of tickets to a playoff sporting event may be an ethical violation if the client harbors an expectation of a quid pro quo such as a preferred appointment time or an extended therapy session. Making relevant distinctions between small tokens of gratitude and expectation of a quid pro quo is not always easy, and the Level I clinician is well advised to seek consultation regarding gift giving if uncertainty arises in a particular situation.

Maintaining appropriate boundaries is essential in the service of a therapeutic relationship. An important bit of guiding wisdom says that therapists are not here to judge, punish, or be entertained by our clients but to assist them in figuring out how they are making themselves unhappy.

Clear boundaries guide transactions and can deepen the therapeutic relationship, leading to positive treatment outcomes—even when it is a client who acts inappropriately. Johnson (1995) has noted that a therapist has to be "disengaged from the emotional demands of the situation" (p. 75). Although this is difficult and at times impossible given the suffering that many clients experience when seeking help for traumatic experiences, losses, bouts of life-threatening illness, or end-of-life issues, it is most useful for therapists to monitor their emotions. This does not mean that a therapist is not empathic, however. It does mean that therapists do not respond to clients in the same way that clients' suffering, symptomatic, inappropriate, irritating, or manipulative behaviors typically precipitate in others. Johnson presented an example of an attractive female client who suggested that she and her therapist have a sexual relationship, so that she could resolve her sexual hang-ups with men like him. The therapist, with warmth and empathy, refused. Because the therapist's response made the client feel safe in the relationship, she "felt emboldened by his boundaries" (Johnson, 1995, p. 70) and pursued issues that she had previously avoided in treatment. It has been noted, "The only unique thing that therapists have to offer is that we don't try to meet our own needs in therapy. Everything we do should be with the intention of helping the client" (Johnson, 1995, p. 79).

The Level I therapist will note that the example cited by Johnson (1995) is demonstrative of nonlinear thinking regarding transference (discussed above). That is, a client's sexual advances and outright proposition might suggest that the therapist provide a linear response to be more careful about not provoking such behavior in the client (i.e., "I have to be more careful because this client might misinterpret some of my behavior as a sign of wanting sex with her"). Instead, the therapist declined the invitation with warmth and empathy. He did not change his behavior toward the client in the least. One could easily make the case that the therapist provided a safe place (i.e., one in which her usual behaviors would not provoke the response that they typically did). At this point, he could invite the client to explore what elements of the therapeutic relationship she found satisfying and find ways to get this level of satisfaction from her romantic relationships (i.e., redirecting the client's extra therapeutic feelings back into the therapeutic endeavor). Such counterintuitive behavior—not withdrawing warmth and empathy in the face of a client crossing appropriate boundaries—is distinctly nonlinear.

Boundary and Role Management II: Multiple Roles

A therapist having a *dual* or *multiple*[2] relationship with a client provides clear challenges to the therapeutic relationship. What is a multiple role? Perhaps the easiest way of setting the context for a discussion of multiple roles is an example.

A man who has developed a very successful business would very much like to have his son and daughter become involved in the business. Even under the best of circumstances, good intentions, and positive familial relationships, it will oftentimes be hard for the participants in such an arrangement to determine when they are relating to each other as business associates or when they are relating as parent and child. Directions or feedback that may be given by the father as the founder-owner of the company may be interpreted by his children as being harsh, unfair, or rejection by their father. Given this example, what constitutes a multiple role in the context of being a therapist?

Lazarus and Zur (2002) defined a multiple relationship as "any association outside the 'boundaries' of the standard client-therapist relationship—for example, lunching, socializing, bartering, errand-running, or mutual business transactions (other than the fee-for-service)" (p. xxvii). But there are other, more complicated variations of engaging in multiple roles with a client.

Karl Tomm (2002), a distinguished writer and practitioner of couples and family therapy, importantly differentiates between multiple relationships and exploitation:

> Exploitation in relationships is always exploitation, regardless of whether it occurs in a dual relationship, a therapy relationship, a supervisory relationship, or a research relationship. A dual relationship is one in which there are two (or more) distinct kinds of relationships with the same person. For instance, a therapist who has a relationship with someone as a client and who also has another relationship with that person, such as an employer, an employee, a business associate, a friend, or a relative, is involved in a dual relationship. While dual relationships always introduce greater complexity, they are not inherently exploitative. Indeed, the additional human connectedness through a dual relationship is far more likely to be affirming, reassuring, and enhancing, than exploitative. To discourage all dual relationships in the field is to promote an artificial professional cleavage in the natural *patterns that connect* us as human beings. It is a stance that is far more impoverishing than it is provocative. (p. 33)

Just like the brief example of the man involving his children in his business, there are circumstances in which a therapist engaging in two roles with a client would be inappropriate despite noble intentions or the particular therapist involved having the highest ethical standards. Examples of someone engaging in multiple roles include a psychologist providing therapy to a graduate student enrolled in the psychologist's course or a psychologist treating someone who is also a supervisee. The significant vulnerabilities of the student or supervisee render great power imbalances in such complementary relationships. With such imbalances, it becomes relatively easy for the student or supervisee to be subjected to unfavorable transactions. As Peluso (2007) has stated,

> When a therapist has more than one relationship with a client (i.e., business relationship, friendship, etc.), the ability to remain neutral, or act in the client's best interest[,] is compromised (or at least can be called into question). Thus, the prohibition against therapists having more than one relationship (that is, the professional, therapeutic relationship) is a boundary designed to protect both the clinician and the client(s) from manipulation, collusion, boundary confusion, and exploitation. (p. 313)

See Clinical Exercise: A Conflict of Interest for examples of therapists acting in multiple relationships.

Clinical Exercise: A Conflict of Interest?

An experienced and compassionate female therapist worked in a clinic that provided services to indigent clients. One of her clients was an unemployed car mechanic who was in debt and could not find work. The therapist contracted with the mechanic to do some work on her car and agreed to pay him for his services. When confronted with the impropriety of such a multiple role, the therapist's reply was that she was being helpful to someone who needed work.

1. Is this transaction appropriate? After all, wouldn't the man's earning money as a mechanic help him to pay some bills, improve his self-esteem, increase his motivation, and so on?
2. If this multiple role is inappropriate, what is it that is inappropriate?

Being a therapist is challenging whether at Level I or beyond. The clinical exercise is meant to challenge the Level I therapist and follow up on the case above by rendering a semifictitious case with circumstances still more complicated than those previously noted.

Flexibility of Boundaries

Clearly, the cases noted above can quickly become quite complex. Thus, there are some experts who have held the line and stringently maintained that *no* multiple roles are appropriate (Lazarus & Zur, 2002; Pope & Vasquez, 1998). In keeping with such a stringent position, they suggested that practitioners who engage in *any kind* of a multiple role should be subjected to professional review and have professional association memberships suspended and licenses revoked. But there are less complicated circumstances with more benign outcomes, as Peluso (2007) has illustrated:

> In the "real world" of most people's lives, there are individuals that have operated on more than one level at any given time. According to Coale (1998), these occasional dual roles can be "invigorating, healthy, and conductive to healing, as long as they are not secretive or skewed toward therapist interest at the expense of the client" (p. 103). For example, if a therapist is stranded due to car problems and a client drives by and offers to help (change a tire, give the therapist a ride)[,] should the therapist refuse based on the fear of violating the dual role boundary? Probably not, in fact the therapist would be silly to continue to be stranded. In fact, these occurrences can be empowering to the client, or humanize the therapist for the client. (p. 314)

The central construct regarding multiple relationships is a therapist's conflict of interests. As a human being, the therapist has interests in his own well-being (i.e., getting his car conveniently repaired without having to travel a great distance). But, a therapist incurs a responsibility to put the interests of his client *ahead* of self-interest.

As mentioned in the discussion of the need to maintain appropriate boundaries, the most egregious violation of a therapist forgoing his fiduciary obligation to a client is sexual involvement. Again, it does not matter that a client acts seductively toward a therapist. Such relationships are forbidden by ethical codes of conduct because of the blatant nature of exploitation inherent in the situation. The therapist is obtaining gratification at the expense of his client. That means that the therapist has clearly put his interests ahead of the client's interests. The trust implied in the fiduciary relationship between client and therapist has been broken. Rationalizations about having sexual relations with a client for the good of the client cannot stand the test of truthfulness.

The issue of multiple roles can quickly become murky in today's complex clinical practice. Baird (2006) illustrated this fact with the observation that anyone with considerable experience in clinical practice will have faced the dilemma of being requested to engage in couples therapy with a client being seen in individual therapy. Although there are many flattering arguments (e.g., faith in the therapist's ability, the client[s] would not have to start therapy from the beginning, and a trusting relationship has already been established) that can be offered in favor of proceeding with such a new therapeutic arrangement, there are many ethical principles that must be attended to as well (e.g., beneficence and nonmaleficence, fidelity and responsibility, and conflict of interest). In fact, one can make a case that referring a client to someone else increases the costs to a client, because of necessity she must start her marital therapy from "scratch." Perhaps the best caution is twofold: (1) A therapist must be alert for the conflicts that can arise when engaging a client in more than one role and (2) when in doubt, obtain consultation with a trusted colleague, mentor, or supervisor.

Boundary and Role Management III: Therapist Self-Disclosure

The value and propriety of self-disclosure (i.e., the deliberate revealing of thoughts, feelings, or personal information by a therapist to a client in treatment for therapeutic purposes) have been debated in the literature for decades. Such disclosure contrasts with the concept of the anonymous therapist (i.e., someone about whom a client knows nothing personal, such as marital status, age, and religious preference) long held by psychoanalytic proponents. Given the constraints and caveats noted in the discussions above on boundaries and multiple roles, we discuss the merits and limits of self-disclosure.

As briefly discussed earlier, therapy and counseling in their essence are human encounters. Appropriate self-disclosure can present the therapist as an authentic human being. Thus, there are many instances where well-timed self-disclosure is appropriate, and may actually strengthen the therapeutic alliance. Likewise, there are instances and types of self-disclosure that may be inappropriate. Therapy, as a human encounter, is subject to professional considerations, power imbalances, client vulnerability, misinterpretations, potential exploitation, and inappropriate therapist behaviors, all of which *can* detract from the therapeutic relationship. Thus, even now, self-disclosure is still the subject of discussion. For example, the Psychopathology Committee of the Group for the Advancement of Psychiatry (2001) suggested the following regarding this interesting therapeutic phenomenon:

> In mental health practice, a commonly held view is that therapist self-disclosure should be discouraged and its dangers closely monitored. Changes in medicine, mental health care, and society demand reexamination of these beliefs. In some clinical situations, considerable benefit may stem from therapist self-disclosure. Although the dangers of boundary violations are genuine, self-disclosure may be underused or misused because it lacks a framework. It is useful to consider the benefits of self-disclosure in the context of treatment type, treatment setting, and

patient characteristics. Self-disclosure can contribute to the effectiveness of peer models. Self-disclosure is often used in cognitive-behavioral therapy and social skills training and might be useful in psychopharmacologic and supportive treatments. The unavoidable self-disclosure that occurs in non-office-based settings provides opportunities for therapeutic deliberate self-disclosure. Children and individuals who have a diminished capacity for abstract thought may benefit from more direct answers to questions related to self-disclosure. The role of self-disclosure in mental health care should be reexamined. (p. 1489)

Obviously, self-disclosure must be considered carefully because of numerous factors that clients and therapists bring to the therapy relationship. Whether or not a therapist engages in self-disclosure is ultimately a context-dependent decision to make. Some contextual factors that a Level I practitioner might take into account about self-disclosure are as follows:

- For whose benefit is the particular information being disclosed?
- What is the rationale for the disclosure?
- Does the disclosure strengthen the therapeutic alliance (e.g., is the disclosure straightforward, commonsense, encouraging, and/or facilitating hope?), or does it inappropriately meet an unconscious psychological need of the therapist?
- Is *this* disclosure appropriate for *this* particular client at *this* particular time?

These are complex questions deserving of considerable thought. The Psychopathology Committee of the Group for the Advancement of Psychiatry (2001) has suggested that disclosure may make more sense in certain clinical settings such as clinician-facilitated self-help groups. Most often, clinician-facilitated self-help groups (e.g., for parenting, couples' communication skills, bereavement, or divorce support) are very focused, and self-disclosure is part of the sharing. A therapist may disclose past experiences as part of the ethic of sharing. As suggested above, such disclosure can help reduce a client's sense of shame and embarrassment, and provide positive modeling and normalization, particularly with regard to transference or countertransference material. Again, the key factor is the impact of the disclosure on the therapeutic alliance. What is the disclosure's potential for strengthening the alliance and leading to better outcomes, and what is its potential for creating a rupture in the therapeutic alliance, perhaps leading to premature termination?

Harm from Disclosure

At first glance, a linear-thinking approach to self-disclosure might suggest, "What's the harm?" To this, we respond with an anonymous description of one former therapy client's interpretation of self-disclosures by her therapist:

During my therapy with Dr. "X," he shared many of his own personal problems and conflicts, including information about his own therapy issues. I used to love it when he would talk about himself because it made me feel even closer and more special to him when he would share his problems and concerns with me. We also had a friendship away from therapy ["dual relationship"] and this enabled me to know even more about him and his life. His own disclosures in our therapy sessions and away from sessions led me to believe that I was truly the "*special friend*" he said I was in his life. Little did I know at the time that this was part of therapy exploitation—that *he was benefiting* from me listening to his problems and feelings and I was helping to meet his needs by expressing my care and concern for him. As the jury concluded, "it was like she was his therapist." (Kay, 2000)

Obviously, the above example is extreme. Nevertheless, it emphasizes that unreflective self-disclosure can lead to inappropriate boundaries and disastrous therapeutic results. Alternately, Mosak and Dreikurs (1975) stated that when a therapist reveals himself as a person, he is acting "authentically": "Self-revelation can only occur when the therapist feels secure himself, at home with his own feelings, at home with others, unafraid to be human and fallible and thus unafraid of this patient's evaluations, criticism, or hostility" (pp. 68–69). Nevertheless, self-disclosure must be approached thoughtfully because of the varied characteristics that individually unique clients and therapists bring to a therapy relationship.

Clinical Exercise: Self-Disclosure

1. Discuss particular formal diagnostic categories that might give you cause for concern about making self-disclosures.
2. Discuss information that you would consider easy to self-disclose if asked by a client. Why?
3. Discuss information that you would consider difficult to self-disclose to a client. Why?
4. Discuss information that you would consider inappropriate to disclose to a client. Why?
5. What is the rationale used for disclosure or nondisclosure in each instance above?

What Not to Do in a Therapeutic Relationship

Although the second task force was able to find important elements of the therapeutic relationship that does work, Norcross and Wampold (2011) also summarized what doesn't work to establish the therapeutic relationship (and may be harmful in therapy). The first and simplest answer about what doesn't work is do the *opposite* of what has been found to be effective! This includes things like a poor therapeutic alliance, lack of empathy, failures of consensus on goals and collaboration, and not responding to client feedback. In addition, therapists who won't adapt their treatment strategies to client preferences or characteristics is also a hallmark of what doesn't work in a therapeutic relationship.

However, in addition to simply avoiding the opposite of what had been found to be effective, Norcross and Wampold (2011) also listed specific qualities of the therapeutic relationship that have been demonstrated to be ineffective. Some of these include:

- Confrontations as a style (not specific areas or issues)
- Negative, hostile, pejorative, or critical comments about the client
- Assumptions about the client perceptions of satisfaction (without soliciting feedback)
- Therapist-centricity
- Rigidity of approach
- Using a one-size fits all (Procrustean Bed) approach

It is important for all clinicians to actively monitor and understand their own approach and attitudes toward the client and have the flexibility to be able to utilize as many of the demonstrably effective elements of the therapeutic relationship, as well as avoid those elements that do not work in order to create a positive relationship with a client.

Conclusion

This chapter concludes our discussion of Level I domains. Beginning therapists who have learned to master connecting with and engaging a client, assessing (i.e., client readiness for change, themes, needs, resources, and goals), as well as building and maintaining therapeutic alliances are aware that these tasks are essential for creating conditions under which change can occur. But they are ultimately insufficient by themselves for producing successful therapeutic outcomes. However, with such an understanding, Level I practitioners are prepared to help move clients forward by working through issues. In closing, we note Safran et al. (2002) and their sage counsel:

> The initial stage of treatment is a period when patients become mobilized and hopeful. They then experience a phase of ambivalence when they may begin to question what therapy can provide. If this phase is successfully negotiated, the alliance is strengthened and termination can be worked through. (p. 245)

In other words, the next level in counselor development and the therapeutic endeavor is to delve further into clients' issues and address their fundamental ambivalence for change in all of its manifestations.

Notes

1. We do not mean to imply that the Level I therapist is wrong to be concerned about ethical violations, especially when a boundary crossing would be an egregious violation.
2. Traditionally, the term *dual role* has been used to describe any set of conditions in which a therapist encounters a conflict of interest with a client. Recently, the term *multiple roles* has been favored in order to illustrate the multifaceted nature of the therapeutic endeavor and the potential for good and bad that these multiple roles place on the therapist (see Peluso, 2007).

The Level II Practitioner Profile

The Level II practitioner has reached a point where more obviously naïve considerations about clients have been dissolved. Those more unsophisticated understandings are replaced by much more sophisticated considerations, questions, and challenges. The Level II practitioner is also more at home in clinical settings, is more at ease with clients, and genuinely understands (and has experienced) the value of establishing rapport, developing therapeutic relationships, and even creating positive and enduring therapeutic alliances. The Level II practitioner's listening skills, both linear and nonlinear, and ability to more effectively read between the lines of what a client is saying have also improved markedly. Level II practitioners listen not just mechanically but also with the enthusiastic understanding that such listening serves the therapeutic relationship. In addition, a Level II practitioner is able to see a client's behavior as separate from (and not a reflection of) one's own performance or abilities. Level II clinicians are able to operate with sufficient competence in the three domains of Level I domains (see Chapters 2–7) to begin to work with a client and also calm any of their own fears or anxieties about themselves.

At the same time, this stage of development, with its palpably increased feelings of confidence and comfort, may be somewhat illusory or premature. The Level II practitioner may not have yet fully understood, appreciated, and integrated into everyday practice very significant subtleties, nuances, and intricacies of becoming a professional counselor. In fact, the Level II practitioner's use of non-linear thinking may be limited despite feelings of growing confidence and comfort. Such limitations are reflected when clients with more complex and obscure problems appear, and the Level II practitioners struggle to be effective. Thus, supervision at Level II is critical in facilitating the emergence of a more complete clinician. Even the most advanced practitioners consult with colleagues, an indication of a desire to learn, be open to blind spots, and serve the needs of one's clients.

Focus of Attention

As in Stoltenberg's (1993) model of supervision, perhaps the biggest change that occurs as practitioners evolve from Level I to Level II is a shift in the focus of attention. At Level II, the practitioner has learned to focus attention on a client's specific cognitions, emotional states, complaints, and motivations. Such a shift in orientation can take place only when a practitioner has an increased sense of calm, comfort, confidence, interest, and fundamental understanding of the nature of the work of therapy. Such a shift occurring with an increased sense of comfort and understanding greatly facilitates an increased ability to concentrate on a client and his or her concerns, purpose for seeking treatment, and goals.

Intuitively, increased feelings of confidence would appear to be inversely related to subdued levels of anxiety. As noted in Level I practitioners, such anxiety stems from feelings of inadequacy. At Level II, the practitioner's focus of attention remains notably inconsistent as cases emerge of increased difficulty (e.g., a personality disorder), complexity (e.g., a dual-diagnosis patient), threat (e.g., a client mentioning thoughts of suicide), and/or novelty (e.g., a request for assisted suicide). Nevertheless, Level II practitioners are much more comfortable with the requirements of engaging in the formal professional-level practice of therapy. They have ready an internal understanding of and access to the network resources of the agency (e.g., a hospital, clinic, counseling center, or community affiliate) in which they operate. They also have a greater fluid and intuitive understanding of and access to performing more formal diagnostic procedures as an aid in addressing more complex clients. Such increases in the professional level of functioning are seen to be directly correlated to a Level II clinician's greater sense of an emerging professional identity.

According to Stoltenberg, just as focus can fluctuate according to the case at hand, motivation can also fluctuate: When therapeutic *success* is high, motivation will be correspondingly high—and when therapeutic failure looms, motivation will likely diminish. The consistency–inconsistency continuum needs constant attention at Level II.

At Level II, consultations with a supervisor, consultant, or mentor are less threatening than they were at Level I and can serve as a partial antidote to inconsistencies arising from waxing and waning therapeutic outcomes. Stoltenberg (1993) and Haley (1996) have wisely observed that at times, trainee *reactance* is prominently observed in the context of supervision. Such reactance (i.e., resisting threats to autonomy) can come when therapeutic successes and corresponding feelings of independence run high only to be replaced by increased feelings of dependence when therapeutic failures loom. Through supervision, the growth of the Level II practitioner can be greatly enhanced as tolerance for greater ambiguity and case complexity grows. Encountering cases of clinical complexity beyond the Level II practitioner's competence (e.g., discussing end-of-life issues with a patient in a medical setting when the practitioner has little or no knowledge of biomedical ethical issues) can have discouraging results for the client as well as the therapist. Also, cases with severe emotional volatility can be daunting for the Level II practitioner and damage the sense of therapist confidence.

Decreased Level of Anxiety

Under conditions of greater confidence and diminished anxiety, a Level II practitioner has become more facile with the development of clinical understanding. At this level, there is a richer, more intricate, and more sensitive conceptualization of clients' symptoms, circumstances, and personal formulation of their own difficulties. Concomitantly, a Level II practitioner is generally more adept at fostering, nurturing, and maintaining the therapeutic alliance. The overarching goal for a Level II practitioner is an increased sense of autonomy and responsibility for treatment. Concomitant with a greater sense of autonomy and responsibility for treatment, Level II practitioners demonstrate significant improvement in the sense of clinical judgment as their confidence expands and experience base grows. Also notable at Level II is the managing of one's anxieties and countertransference issues, and a generally more effective and appropriate regulation of self-disclosure. The Level II clinician begins to understand the value of understanding oneself, what kind of clients one works best with, and what clients one does not work well with—and why that is the case. Regarding emotions, the Level II clinician has become more clinically enlightened. Although Level I therapists allow their feelings to distract and disrupt them from the task at hand, Level II therapists have the dawning nonlinear awareness of their feelings as an important source of information.

The Development of Understanding and Nonlinear Thinking

Beyond understanding the primacy of the therapeutic relationship, perhaps no other characteristic quite typifies the development of Level II practitioners more than the maturity they begin to demonstrate in their understanding of the therapeutic process and the nature, role, and value of nonlinear thinking. Such understanding and thinking represent a quantum leap from the Level I of the novice. At the same time, such understandings underscore that mastery will require more experience, supervision, study, and reflection. In effect, a Level II sadly learns that there are no shortcuts. Nevertheless, the application of nonlinear thinking reveals that such an awakening paradoxically can be quite liberating. That is, Level II practitioners can begin to relinquish their struggle to make something happen in treatment and instead let it happen—in other words, they become facilitators of things therapeutic. Master practitioners guide the process of therapeutic discovery, change, and the relief of suffering rather than being pushed to come up with the answer to a client's difficulties.

Understanding the distinctions and differences between making and letting becomes the gateway to the world of the Level III practitioner and the feelings of mastery. As such, the gateway is an entrance into the world of how master practitioners think differently about people, problems, and making changes. It is, in many respects, the world of nonlinear thinking.

Another insight to emerge from Level II has to do with choosing a particular theoretical orientation or frame of reference. Such a frame of reference may consist of a theory of therapy (e.g., cognitive-behavioral), a school of thought (e.g., systems), or a theory or personality (e.g., Jungian). Staunchly eclectic practitioners may decry the necessity for making such choices. In fact, this text proposes that regardless of theoretical orientation, there are universal principles of therapy to which master practitioners pay attention, albeit from their own theoretical frame of reference. The advantage of choosing a particular frame of reference is that it provides a particular metaphorical underpinning and understanding to the process of therapy and the way things work. The Level II practitioner begins to understand that there is value in knowing that research has developed universal principles of effective therapy and in having a specific theoretical orientation that reflects particularly interesting nuances and appealing constructs. In a sense, such an understanding allows for a practitioner to have his or her cake and eat it too—the best of both worlds!

The integral relationship between clinical concepts comes to be understood by the Level II practitioner. Foremost among such awakenings within Level II clinicians is the view that things are not necessarily what they seem. That is, cognition may appear quite distinct from emotion, but functionally they are not necessarily separate from one another. To elaborate, cognitions are easily definable as thoughts based on a schema. Obviously, clients are routinely troubled by thoughts that they harbor, and many times they are reluctant to reveal them to their therapists. It is equally obvious that clients express feelings and emotions and vividly describe them in poetic terms such as overwhelming, dismal, and terrifying. How can two such human functional activities, thinking and feeling, not be separate?

We propose very simply that the Level II practitioner begins to understand that human experience is truly integrated—a person is a functional unit, not a conglomeration of disparate parts or systems. This is not mere speculation but rather is demonstrated in the experience of everyday living and in the delicate and painstaking research of neuroscience. Hence, an informed understanding of cognition and emotion emerges as being part and parcel of the process of integrating human experience. What sort of integration are we proposing? In a truncated manner, we propose that the Level II therapist begins to understand the following elegant and complex relationship between cognition and emotion supported by clinical and neuroscience research:

- Schemas are assumptions, understandings, and representations about major aspects of the world. Individuals have schemas about the self, life, the world, people, and so on.
- Schemas are organized into holistic themes that provide unique qualities to an individual that are reflected in his or her thoughts, feelings, and actions; that holistic theme is called the *personality*. Schemas are difficult to change.

- Perceived threats to schemas are stressful. Typically, the more rigidly held they are or the more outlandish schemas are, the greater the reaction to a perceived threat. Perceived enhancements to schemas are often pursued in one manner or other.
- Reactions to perceived demands or threats from the environment (e.g., interactions with others or circumstances) to schemas that are held dear to the personality will generate strong feelings and emotional reactions.
- When demands upon or threats to core schemas do not recede and core schemas are maintained without modification, their interaction creates and is experienced as ambivalence.
- Ambivalence is a core dynamism commonly operative in clients who want to maintain their core schemas that are, however, incompatible with the perceived demand or threat from life that does not recede.
- The resolution of such ambivalence becomes the major challenge and focus of therapy.

A discussion of schema dynamics, emotions, and their relationship to one another is a major focus of attention in this section of our text. First, we present the domain of understanding clients' cognitive schema dynamics.

8

The Domain of Understanding
Clients' Cognitive Schemas
Foundations

Introduction: The Shawshank Schema

In the 1994 film, *The Shawshank Redemption,* Morgan Freeman plays the role of Ellis "Red" Redding—a convict sentenced to a life sentence at the eponymous Shawshank Prison. As a man with connections able to get items for fellow prisoners (for a fee), he befriends Andy Dufresne, the main character (played by Tim Robbins). The film follows their relationship over years of imprisonment. Toward the end of the film, Andy and Red talk about the unlikely possibility of one day getting out of prison. Andy asks Red if he thinks that he (Red) will ever be paroled: "Jesus, Andy. I couldn't hack it on the outside. Been in here too long. I'm an institutional man now." He describes how experiencing prison institutionalizes a person: "These walls are funny. First you hate 'em, then you get used to 'em. After long enough, you get so you depend on 'em. That's 'institutionalized.'" He further adds how his life in prison has defined who he is, "In here I'm the guy who can get it for you. Out there, all you need are yellow pages. I wouldn't know where to begin." This sense of loss and despair is confirmed for Red when he (surprisingly) is granted parole as an old man.

Having incorporated his new prison-based view of himself and the world, he must face a radically changed world, leaving him confused and overwhelmed. This is best exemplified in his new job as a grocery clerk. Bagging groceries, he nervously raises his hand asking his boss if he can use the bathroom. The manager angrily says, "Yes, you don't have to ask for permission *every time!*" Embarrassed and frustrated, Red tells himself, "There is a harsh truth to face. No way I'm gonna make it on the outside . . . Thirty years I've been asking permission to piss. I can't squeeze a drop without say-so." He also confesses that, "All I do anymore is think of ways to break my parole . . . All I want is to be back (in Shawshank prison) where things make sense. Where I won't have to be afraid all the time . . . [It's a] terrible thing, to live in fear."

While living in Shawshank prison, Red had a sense of security, predictability, and identity. He knew with *certainty* what the roles and boundaries were, what was expected of him, as well as what he could expect from others. While knowing how to use the system to get things and grant favors, he also knew how far to push things to avoid getting into trouble with guards or other inmates. Of course, none of this was written down anywhere. *Knowing* it without knowing it, Red was following a blueprint for life that he learned as an adult. Clients often operate on the basis of internalized schemas, that is, abstractions about life (i.e., beliefs, convictions, and values) that they learned in childhood, which stimulates their spontaneous emotional reactions to life circumstances and guide their actions. This chapter presents an overview of the Domain of understanding cognitive schemas: what they are about, where they come from, how there is a substantial convergence and overlapping agreement of different theories about them, and why it is important to understand them. Second, this chapter presents an overview of some of the skills that are useful for discovering *what* a client's schemas are. That process of discovery seeks to determine the content and organization (i.e., the patterns of thinking and reasoning) of a client's beliefs, convictions, and values by which that client operates in the world. This chapter also presents a framework by which a practitioner can understand and assess the patterns in a client's thinking.

In discussing the domain of schemas, we wish to accomplish four things. First we present an understanding of the theoretical background of schemas (i.e., what they are, where they come from, their general and specific characteristics, organized into patterns, etc.) and prepare the reader for the next chapter in which we discuss more specific means of clinically working with clients' schemas. Second, we connect an understanding of schemas with the ability to think in both linear and nonlinear ways. That is, knowing about a client's schemas and how they are organized into patterns is important because it helps a practitioner to put him- or herself into a client's shoes: "If I believed what this client believes (i.e., 'If I had their schemas'), then I would feel and act the same way that they do . . . since I know that about this client but *do not* believe what they do, this is how I can begin to help them." Third, we wish to demonstrate how an empathic understanding of a client's schemas can facilitate not only how a client is thinking (i.e., their *logic*, as skewed as it may be) but also can help build and strengthen the therapeutic alliance. Finally, in this and the following chapter, we: introduce specific clinical concepts (i.e., how to recognize dysfunctional beliefs/belief systems; what some of those beliefs/systems are and interventions to deal with them) that guide client behavior; and skills for helping clients challenge and alter distorted perceptions of the world around them.

What Are Schemas? Where Do They Come from?

Schemas refer to patterns of cognitions, ideas, or beliefs and the thinking processes that stem from them. They are created in childhood. Each human being creates schemas as a result of childhood experiences. The childhood experiences can be, but are not necessarily, dramatic in nature, but they do represent a child's interaction with the world, life, and other people. Although we may not think of it much, it is obvious that the brain is the basis for creating schemas. The normal brain has built into it the neural circuit boards or anatomical structures necessary for making abstractions and coming to conclusions about experiences encountered. Those abstractions/conclusions are then called schemas, which, in turn, decidedly influence our perceptions (i.e., how we see and interpret things and not how things actually are). Schemas have certain general characteristics that pertain to what they do.

Three General Characteristics of Schemas

First, collectively schemas represent sort of a cognitive filter that colors our experience in one way rather than another. Because they filter our experiences, the abstractions, conclusions, and heuristics represented by schemas are basically biases. In turn, because the biases from our schemas exert influence on the perception of events in our lives, they end up guiding our action tendencies (i.e., inclinations) and behavior. Contemporary psychology might refer to the abstractions and conclusions contained in schemas as learned behavior. That is, as children experience repeated exposure (or in certain instances even a single exposure) to certain types of circumstances and experiences (with similar outcomes) that are accompanied by emotions (i.e., fear, anxiety, joy, sadness, etc.), they unknowingly (i.e., unconsciously) come to certain conclusions, whether those conclusions are accurate (i.e., accuracy refers to concordance with reality and common sense) or not. We emphasize that children are in general very good observers but poor interpreters of events. The conclusions that they draw about certain major categories of life experience (e.g., self-concept, what kind of place the world is, what other people are like, etc.) that blame negative events on themselves, without fully understanding the *context* of the event (e.g., "mommy and daddy fight about a lot of things, I must really be a lot of trouble." vs. "Mommy and Daddy don't know how to resolve their marital conflicts with each other").

Second, besides being a cognitive filter, schemas represent a *template* or reference manual that each individual has on how to deal with life. The reference manual helps us to appraise and interpret experience while mediating and guiding emotional responses, attitudes, action tendencies, and behaviors in general and problem solving in particular. However, as with all reference manuals, schemas are very functional but simultaneously limited. Obviously, they have proven useful in accomplishing whatever we have accomplished but limiting because they cannot constructively address all circumstances that life generates. In this regard, another limitation of schemas is that they tend to be vulnerable to a sort of *perceptual neglect*. Perceptual neglect is that phenomena that pays attention to certain information at the expense of ignoring certain other information that might not only be relevant but essential (i.e., parent's ongoing marital problems). Goldfried (1989) suggested a clinically useful description of a schema:

> [A] schema refers to a cognitive representation of one's past experiences with situations or people, which eventually serves to assist individuals in constructing their perception of events within that domain. Although there are varying definitions of a schema, most reflect three basic assumptions: a schema is said to involve an organization of conceptually related elements, representing a prototypical abstraction of a complex concept. From a clinical vantage point, these complex concepts are likely to consist of types of situations (e.g., being criticized) and/or types of persons (e.g., authority figures). Specific examples are said to be stored in a schema as well as the relationship among these exemplars. Second, a schema is induced from the "bottom up," based on repeated past experiences involving many examples of the complex concept it represents. Finally, a schema is seen as guiding the organization of new information, much like a template or computer format allows for attending to or processing some information but not others. (p. x)

A third general characteristic of schemas is that they form a pattern. It is perhaps easiest to consider about the pattern aspect of schemas as thinking about ourselves as being consistent in our personality. Even though we may look different, sound different, and dress differently from when we were children, we still think of ourselves as being the same person. For each person, personal schemas contain patterns of important information that are useful and essential. Think of a cookie cutter stamping out the shape of a gingerbread man into cookie dough. The dough represents the experiences in a person's life, whereas the cookie cutter represents the schema that stamps into the dough in order to make sense of the experience. When individuals adhere to schema content, they can go through life with a sense of stability without being irrationally overwhelmed. Schemas guide the organization and interpretation of information from the world, as well as an individual's reactions to what is being evaluated. Individuals thus become more efficient, and life is made more predictable, more manageable, and, to a certain extent, safer. Schemas also provide a guiding sense of what it is that each human being seeks and strives for. In more primitive humans, the guiding and striving function of schemas increased chances of survival—obviously a good thing. In contemporary humans, schemas enhance not just physical survival but also a sense of personal worth (i.e., self-esteem), social significance, and avoidance of failure.

But when they are too rigidly applied or clung to by a person, they can cause problems (we discuss this more later in this chapter). Defined beliefs (conscious and unconscious) and set ways of thinking make up our worldview. But it is nothing more than a *map*, a construct, or a systematic theory for how the world works (Kelly, 1955; Shepris & Shepris, 2002). Each individual constructs a worldview based on his or her own perception of self, others, and the world. The worldview isn't the way the world really is but rather an interpretation of the world constructed by each individual. Thus, everyone functions according to a set of rules or expectations about the way the world operates and how we believe it should operate. This is how a person's schemas work. We follow our schemas (i.e., our interpretation of the world) with intense loyalty and it changes little, which provides us with a sense of continuity, stability, functionality, and predictability in life.

A Historical Overview of Schemas in Therapy

Mozdzierz, Murphy, and Greenblatt (1986) suggested that authors of widely different theoretical orientations have actually described, condensed, and summarized many similar observations regarding the thinking and reasoning processes of troubled individuals. Innumerable authors, regardless of their theoretical orientation (e.g., cognitive therapy, cognitive-behavioral therapy, control mastery therapy, psychodynamic therapy, rational emotive therapy, Adlerian psychotherapy, attachment theory, neurolinguistic programming, or dialectical behavioral therapy), basically have recognized that a client's dysfunctional belief system and distorted thinking play a major role in their misery and emotional dysregulation. We briefly demonstrate in Information Box: A Brief History of Schemas that schemas are an important *pan-theoretical* concept that all master practitioners understand and work with in order to be effective.

Information Box: A Brief History of Schemas

Theorist and Their Formulations Regarding Cognitions/Thinking

Adler (1927, 1929, 1956): Failure in the "logic of communal living"—how a person thinks can only be understood in terms of their relationship to others.

Horney (1945, 1950): Neoanalytic "over-driven attitudes" (i.e., unrealistic expectations, egocentricity, disconnect between expectations and adequate efforts, a strong potential for vindictiveness—overt or covert—if wronged, "tyranny of the shoulds").

Kelly (1955): Socialpsychological "personal constructs."

E. Berne (1966): "Scripts."

Bandler and Grinder (1975): The neurolinguistic programming and the role of an impoverished understanding of the world represented by generalizations, deletions, and distortions. "The map is not the territory."

Beck and Weishaar (1989): Therapy with a client's arbitrary inference, selective abstraction, overgeneralization, magnification and minimization, personalization, dichotomous thinking.

Ellis (1955): Rational Emotive Therapy.

Dreikurs (1973): Adlerian based "basic mistakes" in one's "life plan."

Shulman (1973): "Oversimplification, exaggeration of one part of life at the expense of others and mistaking a part of the whole" (p. 20).

Seligman (1990): Explanatory style.

Millon (1996): "Functional processes" and "structural attributes" of personality disorders.

Young, Klosko, and Weishaar (2003): Schema Focused Therapy.

Bowlby (1969, 1988), and Greenberg and Johnson (1986): Attachment style, internal working models of self and others.

Schemas Help Guide Our Responses to New Experiences

Without schemas, life would be a constant series of challenges or threats that a person would not know how to respond to. It would be very similar to patients with head traumas who suffer with anterograde amnesia (i.e., they can't form new memories). If a new person or new situation comes into their lives, they have no way of remembering anything about them (or the situation). When that new person (or situation) arises, the amnesic patient acts as if he or she is meeting the person (or doing an activity) for the first time, even though the patient may have encountered them dozens of times.[1] Although this plot device has been used in multiple films to create humor (e.g., *50 First Dates*) or add tension and drama (e.g., *Memento*), in reality this is a serious problem that impedes a person's ability to move through life. Schemas help us to recognize patterns of encounters in life so we don't have to treat everything as new and unfamiliar, which would be time-consuming and energy wasting; they protect us from entering harmful situations or becoming involved with people who may take advantage of us.

Although schemas are efficient, they often contain information that does not address life circumstances appropriately. In such instances, understanding the information that schemas contain becomes very important. If an individual begins to understand her schemas, she can hopefully do something constructive about them; she can become more open to new experiences and flexible enough in her thinking to grow and change. When a person does not, the person runs the risk of encountering the same problem over and over again.

Domain 4 Nonlinear Thinking Exercise—Gambler's Fallacy

Although our schema dynamics allow for us to remain safe in the face of danger, adapt to new situations by falling back on old strategies that worked in the past, or just help us to make sense of the world, there can also be a serious drawback to them: They can cause you to lose, BIG! This is because people often will try to draw connections to things that are not connected based on their belief of what is going to happen. In other words, their overreliance on a particular schema dynamic causes them to believe that something must happen, because of what has happened in the past. It's like being at a craps table or blackjack table and saying, "I've lost 20 times in a row, my luck *has* to change." Or after winning 20 times in a row and saying "I'm on a hot streak, but it can't last, I'm going to quit while I'm ahead!" In the first case, the majority of the time, the person will lose. However, in the second case (although it might be a *prudent* thing to do), their belief may also not be correct. This is because they are using the Gambler's Fallacy.

The Gambler's Fallacy is "a very common belief that random events will even themselves out over time" (Hayden & Picard, 2009, p. 84). In other words, people believe that because a random event has happened in the past, it will have an influence on another random event in the present or future. For example, rolling an unbiased six-sided die has only a one in six chance of coming up with the number "six." Even if it has come up six 20 times in a row, on the next roll, the chances are still one in six. What was rolled before makes no difference in influencing what will be rolled next. But if you ask people which number is likely to come up next, many will say "six" because it was what they have seen reliably come up before. But the Gambler's Fallacy doesn't stop there!

Let's make a nonlinear deal!

Take the following scenario that comes from a common game show, called the "Monty Hall Problem," named after the long-time host of the game show *Let's Make a Deal*. On the show, there would be three doors, and behind one door was a car and behind two other doors would be loser prizes (goats, wheelbarrows, etc.). The contestant would select one of the three doors, and the host would then open up one of the two doors that they had not selected. Always, the door would contain one of the loser prizes. The contestant would be relieved, knowing that they still had a chance to win the car! At this point, Monty would turn to the contestant and ask:

"Would you like to stick with your choice of the door, or switch it to the other door?"

What would you do? Which provides you the best chance of winning: sticking with your choice or changing your mind? A linear-thinking person might say: "With two doors, I have a 50–50 chance of winning!" However, that would be a false sense of security (as well as statistics). The reality is that you still have a one in three chance of winning, the same as when you first chose. But here is the nonlinear part: if you switched your choices and picked the other door, you improve your chances to two in three. That's right, if you stay with your choice, you only have a 33% chance of winning a car. If you switch, you actually have a 67% chance of winning!

But don't take our word for it! Heck, don't even take the statistics word for it!! In a 2011 episode of the Discovery channel show *Mythbusters,* a simulation was run 50 times to see whether switching doors or sticking with the original choice was best. Overwhelmingly, switching won (about 67% of the time!). However, the episode didn't stop there. The hosts then brought in 20 people to play the game for real (minus winning the car), and when asked if they wanted to switch their choice, or stay with their original choice, all 20 stuck with their original choice (losing about two-thirds of the time)!

So what's the point of all this? First, most people feel very comfortable with their choice and will stay with their choices, even if the odds are against them! This is true with their beliefs and behaviors that are based on their schemas. Second, they will use linear thinking to justify their decision to stick with their original choice (e.g., "I have a 50–50 chance now of winning!"), even if it is a losing strategy. In other words, their decision, which was based on their understanding (or belief) of the situation, allowed them to rigidly cling to their original decision. However, reality was different than their belief. Clients who are fearful or anxious typically act in a similarly rigid way. Nonlinear thinking, on the other hand, means looking at the situation and considering the possibility that one's original choice was wrong, or taking in the new information (the opening of the door changes the odds), and acting on the new reality rather than clinging to our old way of looking at things. Master practitioners know that one of the most difficult jobs is to get clients to accept new information and adopt a new way of thinking about things even if they run contrary to their expectations or beliefs. They often have to convince clients to look at things in counterintuitive ways that wind up being true. However, just as with the Gambler's Fallacy and the Monty Hall Problem, nonlinear thinking is a winning strategy!

Personality Development and Core Schema Dynamics

Considering how important schemas are, where do they come from, and what do they contain? The simple answer is that schemas are built from a person's experiences, especially those in childhood. In turn, childhood experiences typically shape the three core elements of a person's schema dynamics: the view of self, the view of others, and the view of the world and life.

Children use their innate creative capacity of human beings to make meaning, interpret their experiences, and draw conclusions that may not be (and frequently are not) accurate. For example, a child believes that his father drinks because the child gets into trouble in school, or that the world is unfair because a sibling was born, taking the parent's attention away. Thus, although children are makers of meaning, the meanings that they make (schemas) might not necessarily be valid because they do not have the maturity to understand very complex topics such as self-concept, the world, life, other people, virtue, success, failure, and so forth. Instead, they have characteristics of private (i.e., nonlinear or not commonsense) meanings. Although an individual's private meanings (i.e., schemas) make them more efficient in functioning (because they act as a roadmap, a guide through life, etc.), they are often skewed and do not necessarily render them more effective at getting along with others or meeting life's diverse challenges.

Obviously, parents play a big role in shaping and guiding the development of the meanings children give to their experiences. How parents respond to children, their attitudes toward children, and their behavior in general are all reinforcers that help shape their children's schemas (see Gottman & DeClair, 1997, for a practical description of the different ways in which parental responses to and interactions with children affect child development, self-image, emotional competence, etc.). Likewise, sibling relationships and other experiences in the family are powerful influences in the creation of an individual's view of self, view of others, and view of the world and life. These are discussed further in this chapter.

Culture also plays an important role as the context in which a person forms her or his schemas. The particular culture in which a child is raised frames and guides the development of the meanings children give to many important issues. Particular meanings and values held for countless generations change only slowly (e.g., the value of male over female children, religious beliefs, and the concept of arranged marriages held by some cultures). In addition, emotionally charged situations that are repeated can become the basis for children drawing erroneous conclusions that become part of the client's schema dynamics. For example, how a child interprets (i.e., appraises) what siblings and others attribute to him can and does contribute to a child's view of self, view of others, and view of life and the world.

One's view of self, view of others, and view of life and the world represent core schemas or a map of the world. The most typical problems for which individuals seek treatment relate in some way to these core schemas. The master practitioner understands and pays attention to the fact that this particular person with this *complaint* or *problem* sees himself as _____, sees others as _____, and sees life and the world as _____. The problems that a client experiences are derived, in part, from the way in which the client sees him- or herself and others, or how he or she sees the world. Thus, any effective therapist must work on the schema level and help clients see where their flawed thinking gets them into trouble. Clients in trouble are often unaware of the skewed nature of schemas that are relevant to their problems. In the next few sections, we discuss, in detail, the components of schema dynamics: view of self, view of the world/view of life.

View of Self

A core element of a client's schema is the view that a person has of him- or herself. This takes the form of definitional statements about the self, and answers the question "I am . . . ?": for example, "I am stupid," "I am smart," or "I am clumsy." More than anything, a view of self[2] contains a *subjective evaluation* that may or may not bear any resemblance to factual information. As such, it contains subtle nuances and implications that are difficult to verbalize and can be either realistic or unrealistic.

Seligman (1990) has described this view of self in terms of how an individual thinks about the causes of the unfortunate and misfortunate events, whether big or little that befall everyone. He called this view of self an "explanatory style":

> Some people, the ones who give up easily, habitually say of their misfortunes: "It's me, it's going to last forever, it's going to undermine everything I do." Others, those who resist giving in to

misfortune, say: "It was just circumstances, it's going away quickly anyway, and, besides, there's much more in life." Your habitual way of explaining bad events, your explanatory style, is more than just the words you mouth when you fail. It is a habit of thought, learned in childhood and adolescence. Your explanatory style stems directly from your view of your place in the world—whether you think you are valuable and deserving, or worthless and hopeless. It is the hallmark of whether you are an optimist or a pessimist. (pp. 43–44)

Clinically, consider the example of someone who is intellectually gifted as measured by standardized IQ and achievement tests in school. If a person is repeatedly exposed to negative parental reinforcement regarding how stupid she or he is, the self-view that can easily emerge via underdeveloped abilities to reason effectively can be one of "I must be stupid because my father says I'm stupid. . . . I am stupid." Furthermore, such an individual will scan the environment for evidence confirming his or her negative self-evaluation and ignore those instances (e.g., good grades in school or encouragement by the teacher) that do not fit such a negative self-evaluation.

An example of a realistic view of self might be a person who enjoys playing the piano for recreation, but doesn't have the passion or discipline to play at a professional level. She still enjoys it, but does not delude herself into thinking that she will play at Carnegie Hall. Such a person is able to put her ability (and lack of ability) into a realistic context in harmony with other aspects of her life. People with a realistic view of self are able to take a more balanced look at themselves and be able to see their good qualities and shortcomings (i.e., "I know I tend to procrastinate and wait until the last minute"). They are also less likely to be dependent on others' opinions to determine self-worth. Individuals with unrealistic views of self may tend to discount their own perceptions (i.e., they can't trust in themselves) and buy in to others' opinions more easily—the client who appears to be appropriately dressed and groomed claims that she is a mess because her mother says so (or see the example of the stupid person, above).

Another element of schema dynamics is the degree of flexibility or rigidity in the particular schema dynamics (e.g., view of self). Rigid, inflexible schema dynamics can lead to interpersonal problems and are a signature feature of personality disorders (see below). Conversely, individuals who are more flexible tend to be able to cope with change, or with the disappointment of life, whereas individuals who are more rigid can not. Ultimately, these individuals will try to change reality to fit their schema, rather than adapt to the circumstance. This can be manifested in a number of ways in a person. Most commonly, clinicians will hear words like always and never when people describe their particular schema dynamics. For example, they may say: "I always arrive on time. I am never late." These are indications of rigidity in a person's view of himself. People who are more flexible are open to exceptions and can tolerate changes based on circumstances ("I like to be on time, but sometimes there are things that you can't control").

View of Self and Optimism

A view of self can also be globally positive or negative, as well as realistic or unrealistic. Individuals with a positive view of self are generally more optimistic about their own abilities and talents. Schneider (2001) suggested that cognitive and motivational processes such as realistic optimism contribute to a sense of well-being in life:

> Within our reality, we may often be able to discover a positive perspective on our situation—not a distortion or illusion, but a legitimate evaluation, within reasonable limits of what we do and do not know about our reality—that helps us to achieve peace of mind, appreciation for our experiences, and mobilization for future endeavors. This perspective invites emotions such as hope, pride, curiosity, and enthusiasm, which are likely to be powerful contributors to the essence of meaning, as well as powerful

motivators. . . . The illusion of the good life is likely to break down for those who lull themselves into complacency with self-deceptive beliefs, but the illusion is likely to become reality for those who are optimistic within the fuzzy boundaries established by active engagement in life. (p. 261)

Individuals with a more positive and optimistic view of self tend to believe in their ability to accomplish tasks. Correspondingly, individuals with a negative view of self will tend to be more pessimistic and downgrade their strengths, accomplishments, or capability to do things. When combined with whether a person is realistic or unrealistic, the schematized view of self exerts powerful influences over a person's action tendencies, attitudes, engagement with life, and behavior.

If a person is realistic, flexible, and positive, the individual may be appropriately self-critical, but generally optimistic, nevertheless. The individual has the capacity to set and obtain goals and is not generally self-destructive. Individuals with a negative, flexible, and realistic view will tend to self-denigrate or downplay others' expectations of them. Such individuals may indeed be successful and capable, but generally refuse to see these qualities in themselves, preferring to see any accomplishment as a matter of luck rather than skill or hard work. Individuals with a positive, rigid, although unrealistic, view of self may seem overly optimistic and inflated in self-appraisal of their ability. They may feel that they can do anything and cannot see the remote possibility of failure. Extreme forms of this could be seen in mania. Some individuals may feel a high sense of entitlement or that they should get what they want.

Conversely, individuals with negative, rigid, and unrealistic views of self can be pessimistic to the point of self-loathing. They often cannot see anything positive about themselves, despite overwhelming information to the contrary. This contrasts with individuals who have a negative, flexible, and realistic view of themselves, who can at least be persuaded by the results of their work that they have talent. Negative, rigid, and unrealistic individuals may seem to lack motivation to do things (i.e., give up on themselves) and may even exhibit signs of severe depression. Clinical Exercise: View of Self gives some examples of these.

Clinical Exercise: View of Self

Directions: Read each statement. Decide if the individual's view of self is realistic or unrealistic, flexible or rigid, and whether it is positive or negative. (Answers at the end of chapter.)

1. A client comes to therapy to address her fear of public speaking. She is interested in pursuing a career as an executive and knows that this is an important part of attaining her career goals. She also understands that this will entail some skills training on her part that might make her uncomfortable.

2. A woman comes to a therapy session complaining of depression following a recent layoff from her job as an accountant. She states, "I am good at what I do, but I knew when I heard the rumors about layoffs, it would happen to me. All my life, stuff like that seems to happen to me."

3. A man comes for counseling because his family is concerned that he was becoming depressed. He is a highly intelligent, although aloof computer programmer who was working as a convenience store clerk because he was waiting for the right job. The client was asked what he has done to find it, and replied, "I've e-mailed my résumé, but no one has called me. I figured I wasn't good enough."

4. A client tells his therapist that his wife sent him to counseling in order to deal with his anger problem. He states that he resented his wife for thinking that he has a problem: "It's not me. I know that I always give people a fair chance. Ask anyone who knows me, and they will tell you that I only get angry when the idiots around me do stupid things!"

Variation: Once the elements of the view of self (positive or negative, flexible or rigid, and realistic or unrealistic) are determined, discuss how this might impact or influence the therapeutic process. Form small groups or discuss as a larger group.

View of Self and the Family of Origin

Each of these elements of the view of self (i.e., positive or negative, flexible or realistic, and realistic or unrealistic) is shaped by an individual's early experiences, especially in the family of origin. Most people would agree that an individual's family of origin is an important influence on his or her perception. The family, however it is defined (from a traditional two-parent household to a *kibbutz*, orphanage, stepparents, etc.), serves as an individual's first exposure to life, the world, and others. As a result, a person chooses[3] to take a realistic or unrealistic, flexible or realistic, and positive or negative, view of self, in part based on what was modeled to him or her. Consider this example from the case of Ashley:

Ashley:	"That's why I got so fed up the other day with the kids. I just felt like it didn't matter what I did; nothing was going right. I felt like the house was collapsing on me, and I was trapped underneath."
Therapist:	"You've felt this way before? That no matter what you did, nothing would 'go right'?"
Ashley:	"Yeah, when I was younger."
Therapist:	"Can you tell me what happened then?"
Ashley:	"Well, I was in third grade, and my parents got a divorce."
Therapist:	"And that was difficult . . ."
Ashley:	"My father had an affair with my mother's friend. It was so messy. My mother cried for weeks. My father was apologetic, but he said that he loved the other woman. Then he married her, which made things so weird for a long time. I loved him—still do, but I never saw him the same way again."
Therapist:	"And what happened to you. How were you 'replaced'?"
Ashley:	"Sara, his new wife, had two younger children, and then they had two more children together, so he spent more and more time with them and less time with me."
Therapist:	"Wow, that must have really been painful . . ."
Ashley:	"Yeah. I tried to be the perfect daughter—got straight As, never got into trouble, and I thought if I didn't cause problems, he might just want me . . ."

Seligman (1990) suggested there are three crucial dimensions to an individual's explanatory style: permanence, pervasiveness, and personalization. He described the permanence dimension as being characteristic of individuals who believe that causes of bad events and circumstances that occur are permanent (i.e., bad events are unrelenting and will continue to linger), causing them to give up easily. Pessimistic, easily discouraged individuals also believe that negative events are more pervasive and universal than they are episodic, specific, and transient. Finally, Seligman indicated that pessimistic individuals personalize:

When bad things happen, we can blame ourselves (internalize) or we can blame other people or circumstances (externalize). People who blame themselves when they fail have low self-esteem as a consequence. They think they are worthless, talentless, and unlovable. People who blame external events do not lose self-esteem when bad events strike. On the whole, they like themselves better than people who blame themselves do. (p. 49)

Children's values and explanatory styles (i.e., what is important, not important, to be strived for, and to be avoided) are influenced by the modeling of parents and culture (as in the case of Ashley above). Those values strongly influence children's unconscious choices about how they see themselves, how easily they give up or persist, what they will strive for, and what they will avoid. We revisit a case from Chapter 5 (Theme of Hopelessness: "I Have a Chronic Problem") to illustrate this in the clinical case example below.

Clinical Case Example: A Chronic Problem

Recall from Chapter 5 the widow in her 60s with a long history of treatment. She presented as neat and well-groomed, although dressed in somewhat plain, out-of-style clothing and mildly overweight. She was articulate and logical, and demonstrated an impish, off-the-wall sense of humor. Her presenting concern was a chronic depression she has struggled with her entire adult life. She furthermore described herself as supersensitive, angry, chronically annoyed, and wanting to stay in bed, although she forces herself to go to work. She denied she was suicidal.

In reviewing her history, her childhood was laden with criticism by her parents with high expectations but little demonstrable love, affection, and positive reinforcement (especially when compared with her siblings). She describes failure to thrive over the years (i.e., her depression and symptoms of problem drinking) as being due to the many years of deprivations and hardships in her family of origin.

It is easy to see that she has a negative and unrealistic view of self. Growing up in her family, she was presented with a set of standards that she believed was too high for her to reach. In addition, the little physical affection, warmth, or other demonstrations of love she received were too sparse for her to encourage efforts to even attempt to excel at anything, which added to a negative view of self (i.e., someone not worthy of being loved). The essence of these experiences was "I am ordinary," "I am not (able to be) successful," or "My only claim to fame is to be critical, irascible, outspoken—that's who I am." This view of self is unrealistic because it is so pervasive and renders her unable to see positive attributes or accomplishments (e.g., she had a successful marriage, maintained steady employment, helped others less fortunate than herself, and engaged in volunteer community activities) as sufficient to warrant a self-view of "I'm okay—not perfect, but okay." She did have numerous other positive traits, including a sense of humor and anger (which can be a positive trait and is discussed in the next chapter) that allowed her to form a positive therapeutic alliance where these strengths were revealed.

But Don't Take Our Word for It! Master Example

In this example of a transcript with a master practitioner, William Glasser (creator of Reality Therapy) works with a woman who is deciding about whether to commit to a relationship or not (Alexander Street Press, 2012).

Ann Mary:	"No, and I just had kind of given up on the whole idea you know and decided that I was going to live my life alone, and I would still have a good life and you know he wasn't very comfortable with that idea for the last five years."
William Glasser:	"You don't consider yourself a real needy person then?"
Ann Mary:	"No, I don't."
William Glasser:	"Yeah, I mean, you can take care of things. You're not desperate to have a child today or tomorrow?"
Ann Mary:	"No, I'm not even sure."
William Glasser:	"Your biological clock is at the top of your mind now."
Ann Mary:	"No . . . no . . . no."
William Glasser:	"Okay."

And for a *two-fer*, we present master Cognitive-Behavioral Therapist Michael Yapko. Read to see how he elicits the client's view of self.

Michael Yapko:	"And so with that kind of pretty nasty background, how does it affect the choices that you're making today?"
Mike:	"It seems, a lotta times that I second guess myself all the time, you know, I'm not really sure exactly which way to move without constant replaying things in my head. Or, you know it just seems like I'm kinda stuck in the gutter. You know, and can't get out. And so—"
Michael Yapko:	"Stuck in terms of your ability to do what?"
Mike:	"Function a lotta times. It seems like a, it weighs me down, and, uh, you know I'm married and I have two children, and it seems to affect them also, you know. Um, where there's an emotional distance a lotta times."

Take a moment and reflect on the clinical examples above. How would you describe the client's view of self (positive or negative, flexible or rigid, and realistic or unrealistic)?

Before leaving this section, we wish to address how clinicians can reflect back to a client's view of self. Although the classification of positive or negative and realistic or unrealistic is useful for a clinician to organize his or her thinking, it may not prove very useful for a client to hear such feedback presented in that way. We suggest that a clinician needs to translate this conceptualization into an easily understandable format that is more personally relevant to the client. This would be in the form of "Perhaps you believe, 'I am . . . ,'" "You seem to see yourself as . . . ," or "Could it be that you see yourself as . . . ?" thus representing a summary statement of a client's view of self that is easy to understand and perhaps reflected in daily life. The goal of the first phase of therapy would be to move the client from a rigid stance toward a more flexible view of him- or herself. A statement can be in the form of a theme or a metaphor,[4] drawn from a client's own statements, or it can be derived from the therapist's imagination based on discussions in therapy. It also highlights individually unique qualities while placing them within a more standard format. In Clinical Exercise: View of Self (Continued), we revisit the previous clinical exercise to practice translating view-of-self categories into "I am . . ." statements.

Clinical Exercise: View of Self (Continued)

Reread the statements in Clinical Exercise: View of Self, take the view-of-self categories, and translate them into "I am . . ." or "You seem to see yourself as . . ." statements.

Example: A client comes to therapy to address a fear of public speaking. She is interested in pursuing a career as an executive and knows that this is an important part of attaining her career goals. She also understands that this will entail some skills training on her part that might make her uncomfortable.

Suggested answer: "I am a cautious person, but I like stepping out on a limb if it will help me grow."

Variation: Form small groups, and compare "I am . . ." or "You seem to see yourself as . . ." statements.

View of Others

An individual's schema regarding view of others conforms to many of the same structures as one's view of self. Again, more than anything, a view of others contains a *subjective evaluation* that may or may not bear resemblance to factual information. Whether one's view of fellow human beings is realistic or unrealistic, and positive or negative, it is uniquely influenced by an individual's early life experiences, particularly in the family of origin, culture, and society. For example, closely knit cultures, tribal and insular in nature, will tend to convey meanings regarding others transmitted from one generation to another—likewise for such cultural phenomena as racial and ethnic prejudice.

Fundamentally, the view of others guides individuals through life by answering the statement "People (or others) are . . ." As examples, we cite, "Others are out to get you," "Other people genuinely want to help you," "You can never trust a . . . ," "Other people are supposed to make things easy for me," and "*Those* people are no damn good." One's view of others can be reflected when negatively describing someone's character, name calling, or suspecting his or her motives. This negative view of others might take the form of "They are *always* _____" (dishonest, incompetent, bad, weak, mean, etc., or a derogatory term). Such a negative view of others is also unrealistic as it globally describes the person's character or motives, rather than describing a specific event, encounter, or situation. It may be more rigid (as with prejudice) and not allow for exception (in their mind). In turn, a negative view of others tends to shape an individual's action tendencies. Of course, as with other elements of a client's schema, subjective evaluations of other people contain deficiencies and omit essential information. A key component to this is whether this view of others is realistic or unrealistic.

A more realistic and flexible view of others may contain beliefs such as "Although you can't be too trusting of strangers, friends who demonstrate that they are trustworthy can be relied upon to be loyal," or "Family members are more likely to stick by you; look out for them, and they will look out for you." In other words, even though the client may be cautious he or she is open to the possibility that people can be good. More unrealistic views of others might be reflected in such qualities as excessive gullibility (e.g., "Everyone likes me," "No one would want to hurt me," and "Everyone has some good in them")[5] or excessive suspiciousness (e.g., "You just can't trust anyone," "Do unto others before they do unto you," "Other people wait to take advantage of you," and "Others do it to me, so I'm going to do it to them").

People with realistic views of others encounter trouble when others violate these personal rules (e.g., a friend runs off with your spouse, your brother steals your TV to feed his drug habit, or your best friend doesn't show up for your birthday party and doesn't call to explain). However, these individuals are able to put such unfortunate events in proper perspective (e.g., "It was one person, and he was sick," or "He was just a bad apple, but most other people are honest"), and bounce back after a period of disequilibrium. On the other hand, people with an unrealistic view of others can create problems all their own (e.g., regularly getting taken advantage of or adopting a paranoid stance and having difficulty relating to others).

View of Others: Positive or Negative

Another aspect of the view of others is whether it is generally positive or negative. Individuals with positive views of others often adopt a belief that people are generally good and that the motives for their behavior are benign. This allows individuals to generally relate well to others and establish positive working relationships. If the individual also has a realistic view of others, then relationships with others will usually be mutually satisfying and based on trust. An individual with a rigidly positive view of others, however, may demonstrate a Pollyannaish or innocent disposition—believing people are incapable of malevolent motives, especially about oneself. This can lead to being taken advantage of, or (at worst) victimized. Such a view can also be adaptive, however, because sometimes it inoculates individuals from being too disappointed by the actions of one person, thus giving credence to the idea that ignorance is bliss. Such bliss can be protective. Conversely, a negative view of others most often translates to a generally defensive posture toward others. If realistic in orientation, a person may be slow to warm up to people but can and will eventually form and establish relationships. Consider this excerpt from the case of Mike:

Therapist:	"Okay, so who *really* got you frustrated growing up? C'mon, there has to be somebody . . ."
Mike:	"Teachers, mostly. I hated school. It bored me. I actually had this programming teacher in high school who said that I was really into it, and I asked her what I should do, you know, to go further?"
Therapist:	"Uh-huh."
Mike:	"And she said, 'Aw, programming is dead. It won't do you any good to go further. It's pretty well-automated, so you don't have to know the language, and it is all outsourced overseas, anyway.' I was so pissed. I was like 'What the hell? Why are you teaching this?' I later found out that she had no idea what she was talking about; she was full of it, you know? Programming wasn't being outsourced or whatever. The web was just getting started, and it was the right time to learn programming languages! People needed programmers. She was just an idiot. It was around the time that my mom started to get sick, and I dropped out of school for a while."

If an individual maintains an unrealistic, as well as negative view of others, however, he is more likely to be both reticent and unwilling to engage or possibly adopt an aggressive stance toward others (like Mike above). For example, a person may say, "People are dangerous; if you let your guard down, they'll take advantage of you." Likewise, such a person may be more likely to act in ways that would turn people off (e.g., being aloof or cold toward others), thus missing out on opportunities to make lasting friendships. Ample research has long shown that a lack of satisfying close affiliation and support from others can have a detrimental effect on both physical and mental health (Myers & Diener, 1995; Reis, 1984). Clinical Exercise: View of Others offers some examples of these different views of others.

Clinical Exercise: View of Others

Directions: Consider that each brief statement is from an initial assessment of a client regarding social support (family, friend, etc.). Read each statement and decide if the individual's view of others is realistic or unrealistic, and positive or negative (Answers at the end of the chapter).

1. "I don't have much use for friends. Anyone that I have gotten close to winds up hurting me, screwing me over, or leaving me in the end. I figure, 'Why bother?' I leave them alone, and they leave me alone."

2. "I have some very good friends that I can rely on. I have always been fortunate in making friends. Sometimes, I have had people who weren't good to me or for me, but I usually end those relationships quickly."

3. "I have a ton of friends! People are always helpful and so nice to me. I love helping back, too. I can't think of anyone that I have had a problem with. I am sure that I must have, but I can't remember it."

4. "It is tough for me to get to know people. I have a really busy schedule, and I don't have many friends, outside of a couple of guys I've known since childhood. At work, I generally get along, but I don't like to get too personal."

Variation: Once you have determined the elements within the schema called view of others (positive or negative, and realistic or unrealistic), discuss how this might impact or influence the therapeutic process. Form small groups or discuss as a larger group.

View of Others and the Family of Origin

As with the view of self, each person has unique factors that make his or her view of others truly his or her own. These primarily arise out of early-childhood and family-of-origin experience. For example, if a family is wealthy or poor, abuses drugs, has social status or not, or is from a minority group, all can contribute to not only one's view of self but one's view of others as well. Attitudes about the role of men and women in society are created and passed along within a family and cultural context.[6] As mentioned earlier, culture also greatly influences one's view of others. It is a transporter of value and meaning, whether good or bad. Together, family of origin and culture provide the context for the development of lifelong feelings and attitudes of racial, religious, and ethnic biases and prejudices. Such biases can be (and oftentimes are), unfortunately, the foundation for the development of racial prejudice, overt hatred, and violence toward people from other groups. Even promulgating the value of boy versus girl babies is a means of promoting gender bias and the pseudo-inferiority of women.

But Don't Take Our Word for It! Master Example

In this example of a transcript with a master practitioner, William Glasser (creator of Reality Therapy) works with a woman who is deciding about whether to commit to a relationship or not (Alexander Street Press, 2012).

Ann Mary: "But I don't know. I just don't know, I mean I've had a lot of disappointment in the past, and I've been around a lot of bad relationships in my life growing up I've seen you know."

William Glasser: "Uncles, aunts and cousins and . . ."

Ann Mary: "Grandmother and grandfather and everything and I don't, oh yeah they did. I mean I remember I didn't know that, I thought for the one time that married people weren't supposed to talk. I really thought that."

William Glasser: "Right."

Ann Mary: "And I went to one of my friend's house and like, her parents were speaking to each other and I was amazed because I didn't, do you know that's how my family was, I didn't know they talked."

William Glasser:	"You're an only child with the mother and father who didn't talk a great deal either?"
Ann Mary:	"Eh, no, my parents were divorced when I was very young, and we've lived with my grandmother and my grandfather; my mom and I did."
William Glasser:	"I see."
Ann Mary:	"And they didn't talk at all."
William Glasser:	"You don't have any real big long term closeness with your father then?"
Ann Mary:	"No not at all."

As mentioned earlier, relationships with parents and siblings, culture, social position, as well as birth order can all play roles in the development of any particular individual's view of others. It is a client's perspective, interpretation of, and attitude toward such factors, however, that matter the most. Although some clients will unquestioningly accept family or cultural influences on their view of others, others may reject them and adopt an opposite view. Each of these instances are clinically valuable for therapists to explore.

Again, as with the view of self, the conceptualization of the view of others (positive or negative, and realistic or unrealistic) is helpful for a clinician. In order to personalize the view of others that a client holds, clinicians may use statements such as "Others are . . ." or "You seem to see others as . . ." Clinical Exercise: View of Others illustrates this point.

Clinical Exercise: View of Others

Return to the statements created in the clinical exercise on the view of others and translate each of them into "Others are . . ." or "You seem to see others as . . ." statements. When you have finished, form small groups and share your responses. Then discuss with the class.

View of the World and View of Life

An individual's view of the world in many respects is very similar to his or her view of others—but it has a somewhat broader scope. The view of the world refers more to an individual's perspective on living life itself. A view of the world and/or life addresses the following questions: "What is it like to live life on this Earth?" and "What kind of a place is the world?" A Level II practitioner must suspend his or her own beliefs about such issues and assume the challenge of learning about someone else's view of life and the world. Does a client believe that life is a struggle, painful, dangerous, a piece of cake, sucks, my oyster, a jungle, hell, survival of the fittest, a race, exciting, uncertain, or something else? Developing an understanding of a client's view of life has multiple implications. Whatever the *theme* of an individual client's narrative, the view of life and the world addresses the stage and setting in which that person believes he or she must live out his or her particular drama and pursue his or her goals. If the client believes that life is a jungle, then it follows from his or her nonlinear logic that the survival of the fittest (e.g., only the strong survive) may very well apply. On the other hand, an individual who believes life is a jungle may also believe that he or she is not the strongest creature in the jungle and that the only way to survive is to carry a low profile and go largely unnoticed by the predators in the jungle. A person's behaviors must be understood from his or her particular point of view.

Again, like the other components of a person's schema, it can be realistic or unrealistic, flexible or rigid, and positive or negative. In the instance of a client with a view of life and the world as a jungle, it might be more accurate (i.e., realistic) to say that there are many things in life that are competitive, but not accurate (i.e., unrealistic) to say that there is no place for those who are not particularly competitive (i.e., rigid). Unique experiences from an individual's early upbringing help to shape a person's view of life and the world. Individuals with a realistic view of the world see life, society, and so on in a balanced, realistic way. Such a view allows individuals to be able to see the world as it is (i.e., realistically, both good and bad), rather than in a particularly skewed way or how they would want it to be. An individual with a view of the world may have views that depart significantly from reality. If they are rigidly clung to, these beliefs can lead to a kind of behavioral paralysis that may *protect* the individual, but can also lead to the person missing out on important experiences of life. Individuals holding unrealistic views can easily distort reality to conform to their view in ways that cause many problems. As such, to the ordinary (commonsense) person, individuals with unrealistic views of the world may hold seemingly idiosyncratic beliefs, perverted values, extreme biases, and so on. Consider the example with a master practitioner below.

But Don't Take Our Word for It! Master Example

Consider this example from master practitioner, Steven Andreas (creator of Neurolingusitic programming, NLP) and how he responds to Melissa's view of the world (Alexander Street Press, 2012).

Melissa:	"That . . . It's . . . It's their fault and since they are the one to blame."
Steven Andreas:	"Oh you wanna blame somebody?"
Melissa:	"Yeah!"
Steven Andreas:	"Oh!"
Melissa:	"I wanna yell at somebody, I wanna scream."
Steven Andreas:	"What does . . . What does blaming do for you, blaming somebody else?"
Melissa:	"It makes people see what they did wrong."
Steven Andreas:	"Well, they're just following the rules. What are they doing wrong?"
Melissa:	"I'm not talking about just that situation, I'm talking about everything, like other instances."
Steven Andreas:	"Okay! Now, you'd like them to understand that there could be a different way of doing things . . ."
Melissa:	"Hmm . . . hmm . . ."
Steven Andreas:	". . . they'd be more respectful of you."
Melissa:	"Right!"

An individual's view of the world can also be either positive or negative. Those who have a positive view of the world are fairly optimistic and believe that the world is a relatively safe place. Individuals who have a negative view of the world tend to see the world somewhat as a dangerous place that requires an individual to be vigilant. On the surface, it may seem that individuals with a negative view of the world might be misanthropic and chronically troubled. It is possible, however, for a person to have generally positive views of self and others that are realistic, but to also have a negative view of the world. For example, if someone believes life requires survival of the fittest, he may also feel confident about his ability to survive as well as have meaningful relationships with others. Clinical Exercise: View of Life and the World provides examples of different views of life and the world.

Clinical Exercise: View of Life and the World

Directions: Read over each statement. Decide if the individual's view of life and the world is realistic or unrealistic, flexible or rigid, and whether it is positive or negative (Answers at the end of the chapter).

1. Client focuses on terrorism, security, killer storms, disease, and threats, and states, "If you aren't careful, you could be injured by a comet or global warming."
2. Client comes to session and states, "Life is a struggle. People should get ahead by hard work. However, many times *who* you know wins out over what you can do. You have to seize opportunities when they come to you."
3. Client states, "Life is good. If you just take it easy, things will work out. There is no need to get so worked up about things."
4. Client comes to session and states, "There is a balance in life, but no guarantees. Hard work and good faith attempts will usually turn out well, but that is not always certain. However, cheating isn't a good option, because that never works in the end."

Variation: Once the elements of the view of life and the world (positive or negative, and realistic or unrealistic) are determined, discuss how this might impact or influence the therapeutic process. Form small groups or discuss as a larger group.

View of Life and the World, and Family of Origin

A person's view of life and the world is also shaped in large measure by perceptions a child makes while living in her family of origin. If parents were overprotective and instilled a great deal of fear, then their children are likely to develop a tentative, negative, rigid, and/or unrealistic view of the world. They are prone to be anxious about perceived threats and fear that they will not be able to cope with them. As a result, such individuals often adopt a self-protective, cautious stance. Many times, this can manifest itself as generalized anxiety, or even a sense of entitlement. In either case, such individuals feel that the world is dangerous. This development can be seen early in life with very young children, even in preschool.

Consider the case of a child accustomed to getting his way at home by throwing temper tantrums, a display of helplessness, withdrawal, and so on. Such a child is likely to believe that other adults and children should give him what he wants (e.g., toys or his way) when he wants it. Some children will be successful in fulfilling this schematized view by bossing others around, whereas other children may not be successful (because other children resist, or a teacher intervenes). These children may then adopt a view of the world that "Life is unfair," "No one understands me," or "Grab what you can at all costs, because you aren't guaranteed anything!" If a person has had consistent and balanced role models, however, her view of the world is likely to be more realistic (e.g., "Life is balanced, though not always fair. No one gets what they want and wins all the time").

Again, as with the view of self and view of others, a more personal translation of the view of life and the world for clients is characterized by statements such as "You seem to see life (or the world) fundamentally as . . ." Again, this is informed by the classification of the view of life and the world as well as the unique elements of the client. We present Clinical Exercise for you to practice understanding the view of life and the world.

Clinical Exercise: View of the World and Family of Origin

Return to the statements created in Clinical Exercise: View of Life and the World, and translate each of them into "The world is . . ." or "You seem to see life as a . . ." statements. When finished, form small groups and share your responses. Then discuss with the larger class.

A realistic view of life allows an individual to contend with the ups and downs that are inherent in everyone's life. We revisit a case from Chapter 4 to illustrate this in detail.

Clinical Case Example: A Woman Tired of Being Anxious

Recall from Chapter 4 the case of a pregnant woman with a diagnosis of a generalized anxiety disorder that included hospitalization and suicidal ideation. She eventually found relief and resumed a normal life. She presented herself for treatment because of several major life changes that triggered her anxiety (e.g., not working following a period of success in her career, incurring debts, having problems with her marriage, and being several months pregnant). She moved out of her family's home at age 18 and put herself through undergraduate school and graduate school as well. Several weeks before calling to make an appointment with her therapist, she caught herself spiraling down (i.e., became aware of the fact that she was depressed) due to her not sleeping well, not eating well, being fearful as well as paranoid (i.e., easily feeling attacked or criticized and very insecure due to losing an attractive figure while pregnant), and battling with what she called panic attacks.

She summarized her current position by stating, "There are so many things I'm afraid of . . . I realized that I couldn't take any medication like in the past because of the baby. . . . I was in that mode of everything falling apart and that triggered, 'It's (i.e., being anxious) a state of mind, like I learned about in therapy.' One day I got so mad! I was sick of this being anxious, being afraid, sick of the negativity, and I refused to feed it. I just woke up and said, 'That's it!' I was catching myself, being more proactive versus allowing this stuff to take over and snowball. I decided to call you and set up an appointment. I think it's taken a lot of effort to confront it. It's like a creeping vine that's starting to grow. It's something that's said or that I see, and if I don't chop it off, it takes over!"

Exercise

1. What might be this woman's view of life and the world?
2. How have such a life view and worldview manifested themselves?
3. Hypothesize about other elements she may hold within her schema of life and the world.
4. How might her previous experience in therapy help her to understand her present situation?
5. How might her schema dynamics be employed to help her?

Few people would argue that an individual's family of origin does not influence one's perception. The family, however it is defined (from traditional two-parent households, to a *kibbutz*, orphanage, etc.) serves as an individual's first exposure to life, the world, and others. The person chooses to take a realistic or unrealistic, positive or negative view of self based, in part, on what was modeled to him or her. Children also learn about values (i.e. what is important, what is not important, what is to be strived for, and what is to be avoided) from their parents who hold particular values and have different methods of reinforcing them. Those values strongly influence children's unconscious choices about what they will strive for and what they will avoid. In the clinical case example below, we present a historical example of how these schematized values produced three senators and a president of the United States.

Clinical Case Example: The Kennedy Family: Transmission of Schemas from One Generation to Another

Joseph P. Kennedy, Sr. was the powerful patriarch of the famous Kennedy clan. His grandparents emigrated from Ireland fleeing the great Irish famine of the 1840s. But the Boston environment in which he grew up was not very hospitable to Irish immigrants. It is well-known, that the Irish were overtly subjected to flagrant discrimination by the Yankee WASP establishment and laws that flagrantly banned Irish Americans from holding a great number of jobs in a variety of businesses. Nevertheless, his father had become very prosperous having done well in the liquor business. Two values being expressed in the family at the time thus were: being Irish makes one unpopular/discriminated against by the larger society and being successful in business makes you not only more acceptable, it can make you wealthy and you don't have to worry about not getting a job—you're the boss!

Having attended the most prestigious public high school in Boston, but not being a scholar of note, Joseph Sr., nevertheless, was a very popular young man, had strong leadership qualities, and became president of his high school senior class. He also graduated from Harvard University, but it was there that he encountered both positive experiences (e.g., popularity, admission to the prestigious Hasty Pudding Club, membership in a good fraternity, etc.) and a very bitter experience—a fraternity rejected him. He was convinced that it was Irish prejudice that was at work in his being rejected. This perceived (or perhaps real) rejection of him because he was Irish left him embittered for the remainder of his life.

The themes of popularity (i.e., being accepted by making friends) versus being hated, looked down upon, and discriminated against (i.e., being flagrantly discriminated against in work and business opportunities by law) can be seen as a fundamental schema by which he acted repeatedly throughout his life. It can also be seen as a consideration that factored in his decisions and actions in life namely, becoming as outgoing and popular as he was. With another related schema as to how to function in the world and not be a victim of discrimination, he emulated and exceeded the success of his father many times over by becoming a shrewd businessman with an eye for value investing.

The same schema (i.e., being popular and successful) can also be looked at as the basis for his entering politics. Although he personally did not seek office, he was early on a supporter of the Democratic Party, a political organization that supported the causes of the little guy against the establishment. Politics was an endeavor in which the most popular candidate wins. Recall, how early in his life he sought popularity in school versus working to be an academic standout. Perhaps this reflects unconscious psychological compensatory behavior for being a member of a group that was unpopular and overtly discriminated against. Politics was also an endeavor complemented by the money generated by business success; it is a well-financed and popular candidate that often wins an election.

We suggest that it was these schemas that he instilled in his children and grandchildren as values. Examples of how the family patriarch's values influenced his children started with his eldest son Joseph Jr. who was destined to enter politics when World War II concluded. But, as an aviator in World War II, Joseph Kennedy, Jr. volunteered for a very dangerous mission, even though he had completed the number of combat missions set as a requirement for pilots. Tragically his plane exploded and killed him.

Obviously other members of the Kennedy family entered politics and produced congressman, senators, an attorney general, and a president of the United States of America. It is interesting to note that in JFK's campaign for the presidency although it was the prejudice against an Irish *Catholic* candidate that was the focus of attention, it was his enormous popularity and a well-financed campaign that narrowly won him the election.

Likewise, Bobby Kennedy, the shortest of the Kennedy sons, can be seen to reflect popularity as a schema taken to heart. In his political life (e.g., as a senate lawyer, attorney general, campaign manager for his brother, senator from New York, taking on Jimmy Hoffa, J. Edgar Hoover, and mob bosses like Sam Gianconna, etc.), he was known to pursue goals that were popular with the citizenry. This prompted Joseph Sr. to remark that of all his sons, Bobby was the most like him. Joseph Sr. was perhaps observing that Bobby was most like him in his schema to overcome being discriminated against and looked down upon. If Bobby felt less than (i.e., he was the shortest of the brothers, teased about it, felt unpopular), he may have been determined to overcome his feelings about that by becoming popular to the masses through taking on popular causes.[7]

The Kennedy family's experiences are exemplars of the ability of these values to be transmitted from generation to generation, but manifested uniquely in each person. It would seem intuitive that positive exposures increase the likelihood of an individual deriving a somewhat positive outlook and likewise, negative exposures increase the likelihood of a somewhat negative outlook. Each child, however, makes a decision about how they will react to the particular family value. Either they accept it and incorporate it into their view of self (e.g., "I must be popular, I must be the best"), or they will reject it (e.g., "I can't seem to be as popular as my parents want me to be. I won't even try"). A child thus unconsciously abstracts certain elements from their experience and concludes, "This is the essence of . . ." the particular complex understanding that is the focus of attention. That becomes the individual's working model, *prototypical abstraction* or schema for that complex subject.

Another area of special interest for discovering a person's view of the world is the assessment of loss early in a client's life, primarily regarding divorce or the death of a parent. By no means do such events automatically create a negative or unrealistic worldview. On the other hand, a child's early experience of the totality and irrevocability of death, or the perceived reality of parental loss through divorce, can leave lasting impressions that the world is cruel, is unsafe, and does not conform to one's wishes or desires. Such realizations might then be incorporated (into one's schema) and manifested in a person's approach to the world.

Clinical Attitude and Disposition: Pattern Recognition

"What we call chaos is just patterns we haven't recognized. What we call random is just patterns we can't decipher."

—Chuck Palahniuk

"Perhaps we can recognize our way out of patterns rather than repeating our way out of them."

—Patti Digh

Pattern is a word that is synonymous with schemas (and their dynamics). As we have mentioned, they are the customary and often repeated way that a person behaves. Master practitioners know that everyone has some type of patterned or schematized behavior (that is, based on their schema dynamics), and they know that virtually all behavior reveals *something* about a person's schema dynamics. Therefore, they treat all information, stories, anecdotes, etc.—regardless of their seeming relevance—as important because they usually have an underlying, repeating pattern to them. So why is this important? Well, once a person's underlying pattern or schema dynamics are understood, then problem areas in their life—even if there seems to be no connection—may be linked together. When therapists can identify underlying themes, rules, beliefs, or values that govern a client's personality, they can make better sense of their attitudes and behavior (no matter how apparently lacking in sense or bizarre they may seem).

For example, instead of dealing with a person who had a fear of flying and difficulty completing his work on time (thus, two seemingly disconnected problems), a master practitioner would look for what these two problems have in common. One thing that they might see in common is that both issues are methods of *avoidance*. This can then become a focus of therapy. It can point to elements of a person's schema dynamics (e.g., globally negative view of self and world, and possibly negative view of others), and it can also help discover where they were developed (i.e., family of origin). It allows the clinician to begin to link other behaviors that are also examples of the central theme of avoidance (i.e., not dating, not finishing an MBA) and allows for some predictions to be made (e.g., "you will probably continue to avoid situations that make you uncomfortable, unless you make a conscious choice to change this pattern"). Last, these patterns can allow clinicians to also begin to speculate about how behaviors linked to the pattern are helpful in the client's life ("avoidance protects you from getting disappointed or hurt"). This gives the client the power to make different choices about his life. But this can only happen if the therapist is able to see the basic underlying pattern.

So how does a master practitioner recognize patterns? First, they look for and expect to find patterns (schema dynamics). By contrast, a linear-thinking therapist may feel lost in trying to understand a client's often contradictory or confusing behaviors. A nonlinear-thinking master practitioner, on the other hand, understands that everything derives its meaning from its context and starts his investigation there. Such a practitioner understands that knowledge of a client's context or worldview is what makes it possible to make sense of a client's behavior and attitudes, and be effective in treatment. Next, they use many of the linear and nonlinear methods that we have discussed in the Level 1 domains (listening and responding, assessment, as well as various elements of the therapeutic relationship). For example, they listen for congruence, absence, presence, inference, and resistance to piece together the larger patterns. Skill in this domain is a further extension and refinement of a clinician's ability to listen, respond, and think in both linear and nonlinear ways. Awareness and recognition of these patterns or how a client thinks build upon the clinical work accomplished in the Level I domains. Finally, they reflect on the following questions:

- A client's explanatory model for behaving the way he or she does (i.e., the reasoning and *private logic* of his or her symptoms)?
- A repetitious pattern(s) in a client's verbal expressions, thinking, and feeling reactions to events he or she is describing that represents indications of underlying schemas?

- Missing elements in a client's story (absence, inference) or those that do not fit (congruence, resistance)?
- Nonverbal behavior(s) conveying meaning, importance, or context to the narrative (presence)?
- Beliefs and reasoning regarding specific problem-solving situations, and how such thinking and reasoning are linked to the development and maintenance of problems and symptoms?
- What is the client's background (context, history, etc.)? What would it be like to come from such a background?
- A client's understanding of the impact of family-of-origin dynamics on present functioning?
- What are the client's needs at this particular time? Comfort, reassurance, someone on his or her side, or the like?
- Where does the client want to go? Is it realistic?

Let's consider the following exchange from the case of Mike to see where these patterns fit in.

Therapist: "So let me go back to something you said earlier. You said your fiancée also felt that coming here would be good. Why is that? What does she want you to get out of coming here?"

Mike: "Well, she complains that I am stubborn and that my temper can be explosive, and sometimes she gets the brunt of it, you know? She thinks that I need to learn to control it."

Therapist: "Let me guess, this happens when she won't listen to you?"

Mike: "Uh-huh."

Therapist: "Kind of like your coworker?"

Mike: "Yeah."

Therapist: "So there is a pattern here. You are following your father's 'philosophy?' (not to 'suffer fools gladly') And sometimes it gets you into trouble with the people in your life?"

Ultimately, it is the context or big picture (i.e., schemas) regarding a problem or complaint. Such knowledge can also be the starting point for Level II practitioners to make real and lasting interventions (i.e., second-order changes)[8] that impact a client's worldviews and alter his or her behavior. In the domain of understanding client schemas, master clinicians demonstrate their skills in utilizing nonlinear thinking to be helpful to some of the most difficult clients (e.g., those with a personality disorder). When a therapist understands a client's schemas (i.e., how a client operates as a result of how she views herself, other people, and the world around her), he knows what makes a client tick. By looking for the underlying pattern, and recognizing the pattern, master practitioners find the vital clues to work effectively with clients.

Universal Characteristics of Schemas

Now that we have defined the elements of schema dynamics, there are some important features to keep in mind as we end this chapter and introduce methods for working with schema dynamics in Chapter 9. According to Mozdzierz (2011), schemas have certain universal "operational" characteristics as to how they do what they do regardless of what they are about (i.e., view of self, view of others, etc.). Those operational characteristics are:

1. *Primitive* (i.e., they are not only among the oldest beliefs within us, but also represent partially informed conclusions—they are skewed by such considerations as excluding information, distorting information, and so forth, when formed—from a child's experiences because a child lacks broader exposure to and understanding of life).

2. *Powerful* (i.e., they represent dominant patterns for guiding a person through life).
3. *Unconscious* (i.e., most individuals are largely unaware of the content of their schemas).
4. *Automatic* (i.e., for the most part, individuals do not think about what their schemas contain, but they do come to certain conclusions and act as a result of them).
5. *High-Speed* (i.e., schemas are activated in milliseconds, and because they are automatic, there is most often little questioning or examining of them. The speed with which schemas are stimulated often account for why it is that people ask themselves, "I have no idea why it is that I acted that way!").
6. *Unchallenged* (i.e., the combination of the speed and automaticity of schemata potentiate to make them uncontested. Human beings use them, rely upon them, find them valuable, and reinforce them because they have those characteristics making them so much more powerful).
7. *Durable* (i.e., each individual has used essential schemas for the better part of their entire life. Thus the schemas used for such a long time are unwittingly treasured by each individual as being responsible for their successes in life. Whatever is deemed as being responsible for our successes is likely to be given up with great reluctance that is difficult to change. Like some politicians argue, our failures are due to other people, life, bad luck, etc. but not themselves!).
8. *Functional* (i.e., schemas are effective in doing what they do, but they can be wrong. They facilitate our operating as smoothly as possible in a complex world demanding many practical and spontaneous decisions without having to stop, ponder, question, and weigh risks/rewards and so forth. But the functionality of schemas can be called to question when they guide us incorrectly as, for example, when we decide something instantaneously because it has always worked for us, but the circumstances in which we are deciding something are different).

Given such characteristics, schemas represent very powerful linear cognitive processes. To verify this in terms of human experience, simply think back to some decision, judgment, or choice that you made without thinking through the consequences or implications for your life and impact on others.

The characteristics of schemas noted above reflect the way in which our clients and patients are thinking, that is, processing information. It is difficult for them to know how to think differently in part because they have been thinking in one particular way about a certain subject matter (i.e., self-concept, view of others, etc.) for a long time without necessarily realizing it. On the other hand, some clients and patients realize that they have been thinking in nonproductive, self-defeating ways and yet feel powerless to do anything about it. When dealing with clients who seem slow or impervious to recognize their schemas (i.e., how they think about certain things), it is important to remember the ten universal characteristics of schemas that Mozdzierz (2011) notes. In essence, so very many of the clients that we see are processing their experiences through the filter of their schemas without even realizing that there are schemas activated. They are thus thinking with the operational characteristics noted above in a linear way (i.e., experience → schemas → action tendency → reaction) but without any conscious reflection as to the validity, applicability, timeliness, and so forth of what they are thinking for the particular current set of circumstances in which they find themselves.

As an example of how schemas develop, consider the case of a little boy who is constantly reminded of how bad, terrible, or disrespectful he is (even though his bad behavior is simply that of being an energetic, curious, bright little boy, and not much more than that). As a result of the repeated criticisms directed toward him because of his energy, in angry ways by his father because his son's behavior annoys him, he cries. As a result of his crying, the response he gets from his father is further rebuke about being a cry baby. Unfortunately, he does not understand that his seemingly all powerful, god-like father is no such thing but rather a mere mortal misguidedly doing what he thinks being a father is all about. A consequence of all this can be that the little boy is less likely to develop a positive image of himself. He has unconsciously (i.e., out of awareness and without understanding in a conscious and rational way because he is too young to have the ability to do so) learned to interpret himself and his actions as being bad. He has further learned that expressing his feelings or crying, about being called bad, is additionally labeled as something even worse (i.e., a cry baby). From childhood on, he carries a belief about himself that is called a self schema. The brain has circuitry built into it with the ability to detect threat whether physical or psychological. Once the brain has detected threat from powerful authority figures, it begins to scan the environment for more and more of such phenomena. What are the chances that his self-schema will be something good? They are not good. Whatever negative, self-schema image he will have learned, it will be quite automatic (i.e., unconscious, unavailable to him, out of awareness, etc.), primitive, fast, automatic, powerful, and so on in its effects, thereby affecting his day-to-day interactions with others, life, and so forth.

A child cannot interpret the context and subtleties of life because he lacks a breadth and depth of experience. In the case of our fictitious little boy above, he does not know that his father is a bullying man with a drinking problem who has a history of being physically and emotionally abused by his father and thus not a reliable source to be making judgments that he (the little boy) is bad.

As he develops into manhood, our fictitious little boy has developed self-schema (and other schemas about important categories of experience such as others, life, relationships with women, etc. as well) that have become his instruction manual for making sense out of life but it doesn't necessarily contain the most adaptive set of instructions as to how to go about dealing with life! Nevertheless, it works. He goes on with his life, but his adaptation and handling of life's challenges, disappointments, or frustrations may be far from optimal. In a passage from his famous book *Zen and the Art of Motorcycle Maintenance,* Robert Pirsig (1974) describes this phenomenon as he describes how factories create instructions to put together something (in this case, a rotisserie grill):

> What's really angering about instructions of this sort is that they imply there's only one way to put this rotisserie together . . . their way . . . Actually there are hundreds of ways to put the rotisserie together and when they make you follow just one way without showing you the overall problem the instructions become hard to follow in such a way as not to make mistakes. You lose feeling for the work. And not only that, it's very unlikely that they've told you the best way. (p. 164)

Obviously, the rotisserie grill is a substitute for life, and the writer of the instructions is a metaphor for a child creating his or her own schema. As Pirsig's character indicates, instructions that come with the rotisserie are only one way of putting it together. Likewise, the schemas we develop are only one way of looking at the world. These schemas are adaptive and have many advantages that we describe, but they also have many disadvantages.

Clinical Exercise Answers:

(1) Realistic/flexible/positive; (2) Realistic/flexible/negative; (3) Unrealistic/rigid/negative; and (4) Unrealistic/rigid/positive.

Clinical Exercise Answers:

(1) Unrealistic/rigid/negative; (2) Realistic/flexible/positive; (3) Unrealistic/rigid/positive; and (4) Realistic/flexible/negative.

Clinical Exercise Answers:

(1) Unrealistic/rigid/negative; (2) Realistic/flexible/negative; (3) Unrealistic/flexible/positive; and (4) Realistic/flexible/positive.

Conclusion

We have defined the core elements, general and universal characteristics of a crucial domain that all effective clinicians utilize—client schemas. An understanding of the dynamic meanings underlying a client's schema give a practitioner vital clues to unlocking central themes that contribute to a client's concerns. Once a therapist understands the components of a person's schema (view of self, view of others, and view of life and the world) and the numerous sources of influence in their formation, there are two important questions to address. The first is, can an individual modify his or her schemas? In the next chapter, we discuss ways to both assess and use the information about a client's schema dynamics.

Notes

1. This has been used as a plot device in movies, such as *50 First Dates* (Segal, 2004) or *Memento* (Nolan, 2000).
2. The view of life and view of the world can be separated into two separate views for reasons specific to a particular client.
3. We briefly discuss first-order and second-order change later in this chapter and in more detail in Chapter 10.
4. For the purposes of this text, we do not differentiate between view of self, self-image, or self-concept.
5. The word *choose* may seem odd regarding a child choosing to take a positive or negative view of self. The word choose represents a constructivist viewpoint—it is the child who concludes whatever it is that she concludes about self. Thus, in effect, a child chooses. But because a child has an unconsciously determined and limited understanding of complicated things, she cannot be held fully accountable for the view of self that she develops. Despite such limited culpability, whatever is concluded about oneself in the view of self, it *is* the individual who concluded it and correspondingly must take ownership of it. The discouraging aspect of this incongruous conundrum is that we are all held responsible for conclusions about the self made as children. It is encouraging that by taking responsibility for childhood conclusions, we can influence and change them.
6. The subject of metaphors is discussed later in the chapter.
7. Adapted from http://en.wikipedia.org/wiki/Joseph_P._Kennedy,_Sr
8. This will be discussed in Chapter 9 and later in this text.

9

The Domain of Understanding Clients' Cognitive Schemas
Assessment and Clinical Conceptualization

Introduction

In Chapter 5, as part of the domain of assessment, we discussed the theme of a client's problem. This is one part of the client's overall story, but not all of it. Just like a person's career may come to identify them (e.g., "I am a doctor," "I am a lawyer," etc.), it does not completely define them. There are other things about the person that may be more central than their career choice ("I am a cancer survivor," "I am a mother or father of three children," etc.). The same is true of the theme of a client's problem. You can think of the theme as the story of the problem, but it is not the whole person. In the same way, one can think of the schema dynamics as the story of the person within whom the particular problem (i.e., theme) takes place. By putting these together, you begin to get a bigger picture of the client and their situation. In addition, putting together the story of the problem and the story of the person, a clinician can also begin to move toward a solution and make some lasting changes. These are all important parts of a clinical formulation or case conceptualization (Sperry & Sperry, 2012), and we discuss these, as well as how to work with schema dynamics using elements from the previous domains, in this chapter. First, we look at the connection between schema dynamics and their role in a person's perceptions and personality development.

Schema Dynamics and Cognitive Distortions

Spearheaded by pioneers such as Albert Ellis and Aaron Beck, practitioners in the 1960s and 1970s began recognizing and identifying certain definable automatic and unconscious (i.e., the client is unaware of) patterns of client thinking. By uncovering these automatic negative thoughts and pointing out their negative effects on clients, therapists were able to emphasize and establish client control over distorted and automatic thinking. Guiding behavior, such thoughts and thinking are so rapid and powerful that they prompt clients to believe they are beyond the threshold of control. By describing and highlighting such thinking, therapists are able to persuade and guide clients in refuting or arguing against such thoughts in order to stimulate acting differently (i.e., in a more positive way) or not succumb to these automatic thoughts. Using clients' schema dynamics, therapists can help clients gain an understanding into these cognitive distortions and begin to change how they react to such automatic thoughts. Common methods that clients use in distorting cognitions are listed in Information Box: Common Methods of Distorting Cognitions.

Information Box: Common Methods of Distorting Cognitions

Arbitrary inference: Making a conclusion that has no supporting evidence or contradicts existing evidence. Examples of this include catastrophizing or thinking the worst of any situation.

Selective abstraction: Drawing conclusions about events by taking information out of context or ignoring other information. This is also understood as mistaking a part for the whole.

Overgeneralization: The process of making a general rule on the basis of one or more isolated incidents and then applying it to unrelated situations.

Magnification and minimization: Involves viewing something out of proportion, as either less or more significant than it really is.

Personalization: Occurs when individuals attribute external events to themselves even when there is no evidence of a causal connection.

Labeling and mislabeling: Defining one's identity based on imperfections and mistakes made in the past.

Dichotomous thinking: Conceptualizing an experience in either-or terms (e.g., seeing a situation as all good or all bad).

Exercise: Take each of the cognitive distortions above and describe what schema dynamics (positive or negative, realistic or unrealistic, view of self, view of others, and view of life and the world) would contribute to its development.

Source: From Beck and Weishaar (2005), Corey (2005), and Nystul (2006).

Schema Dynamics, Cognitive Distortions, and Psychological Disorders

It is important for a nonlinear-thinking therapist to remember that it is not schemas themselves that become problematic, but how a client applies them to life's challenges. Problems arise when a client applies schema dynamics too rigidly to a given set of life circumstances that are not appropriate. People do this because of schemas' perceived effectiveness in the past. We represent a case study from Chapter 3 to elaborate.

Clinical Case Example: A Drinker with "Bumps" in His Childhood

Recall (in the section on nonlinear responding of Chapter 3) the example of a man with an admitted drinking problem who came to therapy. In the second session of treatment, during the process of describing his early family life, he indicated that there were bumps while growing up in a good family atmosphere. When the therapist followed up on this statement by asking, "I'm not sure what having some 'bumps' means to you. Can you tell me what you mean?" The client responded that his mother had become paralyzed when he was only a toddler and that he had to live with his grandparents many miles from his family home for a number of years. Obviously, the bumps he described were of a significant nature and indeed much different from the bumps that occur in most people's lives.

Exercise

1. What elements of the client's schemas (view of self, others, and the world) can be gleaned from this brief description of his situation?
2. What type of nonlinear listening and responding is utilized to discover schema elements?
3. Which cognitive distortions presented in the first part of the chapter does the client employ in describing his bumps?
4. Might this client's schemas be helpful in managing life? Might they get him into trouble?
5. How can you personalize the client's schema dynamics (using the "I am...", "Others are...", and "The world is..." statements)?

In the clinical case example, based on his experience with his mother's paralysis and his subsequent drinking problem, we hypothesize that his view of the world is generally negative (e.g., "Life is full of big problems, and most people have bigger problems than me; I'd better not complain"). In addition, he may also have a negative and unrealistic view of self (e.g., "My problems are never important enough to trouble anyone with"). His expressed view represents a pattern of cognitive distortion that arranges his life experiences to fit with his schema: *minimization.* By minimizing his own needs (e.g., for attention and affection), he decided to manage his life by not creating demands on his already stressed family. Such a schema was useful at that time. He took this to the extreme, which led him to suppress his needs, or distort reality to the point where his needs became virtually nonexistent. This might have helped him to get through the trauma of his childhood, but we cannot distort or suppress our needs as a permanent way of living. There is a cost for such distortion and suppression of needs. Cognitive distortions became hurtful, and the use of alcohol helped him to minimize his needs but only compounded his problems over time. In treating this person, a nonlinear-thinking therapist would begin by discussing the dual nature of his schema (i.e., how and where it is helpful, and where it is hurtful) and its particular distortions while exploring more adaptive approaches to one's needs and their expression.

Beck and Weishaar (1989) asserted that certain diagnoses have certain "systematic biases" (i.e., have similar schema dynamics) that impact the client's way of thinking (viz., cognitively distorting). Table 9.1

Table 9.1 The Cognitive Profiles of Psychological Disorders

Disorder	Systematic bias
Depression	Negative view of self, experience, and future
Hypomanic	Positive view of self, experience, and future
Anxiety disorder	Physical or psychological threat—negative view of others, life, and the world
Panic disorder	Catastrophic misinterpretation of bodily or mental experiences—negative view of self
Phobia	Threat in specific, avoidable situations—negative view of life and the world
Paranoid state	Attribution of negative bias to others—negative view of others, life, and the world
Hysteria	Belief in motor or sensory abnormality—negative view of self
Obsession	Repetitive warning or doubting about safety—negative view of life and the world
Compulsion	Rituals to ward off doubts or threat—negative view of self, life, and the world
Suicidal behavior	Hopelessness—negative view of self
Anorexia nervosa	Fear of appearing fat (to self or others)—negative view of self or others
Hypochondriasis	Belief in serious medical disorder—negative view of life and the world

Source: Adapted from Beck and Weishaar (1989).

incorporates psychological disorders and corresponding systematic biases (according to Beck & Weishaar, 1989) or schema dynamics about view of self, world, and others.

Schema Dynamics and the Development of Personality Disorders

According to Benjamin and Karpiak (2002), one half of all clients coming for treatment have a diagnosable DSM personality disorder. However, a majority of manualized treatment protocols have focused on treating only psychological disorders (e.g., anxiety disorders, mood disorders) and ignoring the personality disorder, despite the fact that researchers have shown that there is a close association between the two. Why do many therapists appear to ignore or dismiss personality disorders? The reasons for this are varied. Some do it for theoretical reasons, believing either that DSM diagnoses are culturally insensitive or that diagnoses stigmatize clients (Coale, 1998). Other therapists may underreport personality disorders for financial reasons because such diagnoses are often not reimbursed by third-party payers (Koocher, 1998). Unfortunately, many other therapists underdiagnose personality disorders because they are often intimidating; therapists don't have the skills to treat such individuals, and they are so draining that the work seems unrewarding. Linear-thinking therapists generally attempt to treat clients by ignoring the personality disorder and focusing on the copresenting psychological disorder symptoms. They quickly find that therapeutic approaches that are effective for many psychological disorders are simply not efficacious with personality disorders (Benjamin & Karpiak, 2002; Young, Zangwill, & Behary, 2002). Perhaps this accounts for many of the treatment failures that beginning therapists encounter, as well as problems that some manualized treatment protocols have in replicating laboratory validations of their approaches.

Consider the definition of a personality disorder. According to the DSM-5 (American Psychiatric Association, 2013), all personality disorders share the following characteristics: "an enduring pattern of inner experience and behavior that deviates markedly from the expectations of the individual's culture and that is pervasive and inflexible . . . is stable over time and leads to distress or impairment" (p. 645). In other words, personality disorders are simply disorders that arise from one's schemas (See Table 9.2).

One critical feature of schema dynamics, that all personality disorders have in common, is that they are all unrealistic in nature, in the client's view of self, others, or the world. Horney (1945, 1950)

Table 9.2 Personality Disorders and Schema Characteristics

Axis II Personality Disorder	DSM-5 Description	Schema Dynamics
Paranoid Personality Disorder	A pervasive distrust and suspiciousness of others such that their motives are interpreted as malevolent.	*View of Others*: Negative and Unrealistic *View of World*: Negative and Unrealistic
Schizoid Personality Disorder	A pervasive pattern of detachment form social relationships and a restricted range of emotions in interpersonal settings.	*View of Self*: Negative and Unrealistic *View of Others*: Negative and Unrealistic
Schizotypal Personality Disorder	A pervasive pattern of social and interpersonal deficits marked by discomfort with, and reduced capacity for, close relationships as well as cognitive or perceptual distortions and eccentricities of behavior.	*View of Self*: Positive and Unrealistic *View of Others*: Negative and Unrealistic
Antisocial Personality Disorder	A pervasive patter of disregard for and violation of the rights of others occurring since age 15 years.	*View of Self*: Positive and Unrealistic *View of Others*: Negative and Unrealistic *View of World*: Negative and Unrealistic

Borderline Personality Disorder	A pervasive pattern of instability of interpersonal relationships, self-image, and affects, and marked impulsivity.	*View of Self*: Positive, Negative, and Unrealistic *View of Others*: Negative and Unrealistic *View of World*: Negative and Unrealistic
Histrionic Personality Disorder	A pervasive pattern of excessive emotionality and attention seeking.	*View of Self*: Negative and Unrealistic *View of Others*: Positive and Unrealistic
Narcissistic Personality Disorder	A pervasive patterns of grandiosity (in fantasy or behavior), need for admiration, and lack of empathy.	*View of Self*: Positive and Unrealistic *View of Others*: Negative and Unrealistic
Avoidant Personality Disorder	A pervasive pattern of social inhibition, feelings of inadequacy, and hypersensitivity to negative evaluation	*View of Self*: Negative and Unrealistic *View of Others*: Negative and Unrealistic
Dependent Personality Disorder	A pervasive and excessive need to be taken care of that leads to submissive and clinging behavior and fears of separation.	*View of Self*: Negative and Unrealistic *View of Others*: Positive and Unrealistic
Obsessive-Compulsive Personality Disorder	A pervasive pattern of preoccupation with orderliness, perfectionism, and mental and interpersonal control, at the expense of flexibility, openness, and efficiency.	*View of Self*: Positive and Unrealistic *View of Others*: Negative and Unrealistic *View of World*: Negative and Unrealistic

*Adapted from DSM-5 (APA, 2013)

suggested that individuals with personality disorders demonstrate dysfunctional schemas that are in some manner irrational, insatiable, impossible, inappropriate, intolerant, wanting things without effort, egocentric, vindictive, or compulsive (she referred to "overdriven attitudes," now known as schemas). Another critical feature that all schema dynamics that are personality disorders share is the rigidity or inflexibility of the particular schema dynamics. These features combined make it difficult for linear-thinking therapists to treat personality disorders; master practitioners, utilizing nonlinear thinking, do not get tripped up by these features and encounter less resistance by adapting therapy to account for it. Utilizing nonlinear thinking, they direct their attention toward the central organizing patterns of a client's problem (the schema, or view of self, others, and the world). The makeup of these elements gives the nonlinear-thinking therapist the ability to engage a client on a more meaningful level, as well as providing a better conceptualization of the peculiarities of the client's behavior. Clinical Case Exercise: Anxious and Dependent illustrates these points further.

Clinical Case Exercise: Anxious and Dependent

A well-educated, pleasant, happily married woman with a young child sought therapy because of overwhelming anxiety and an inability to comfortably leave her baby in the custody of others except for her husband and parents. She recognized this as aberrant but felt helpless to bring it under control. She reported her ton of anxiety as resulting from her baby's medical problems with numerous legitimate trips to hospital emergency rooms and a felt need for more than typical parental vigilance and new mother nervousness. Although medical authorities assured her that her baby would grow out of his condition, such reassurances had little ameliorating impact on a daily basis. She relied frequently and heavily on her parents in the event of any troublesome circumstances that she believed she simply could not deal with on her own—"I don't know what I would do without them!"

During the first session, she reported that she had "done a lot of thinking" and concluded that "as far back as high school," she could remember herself being consistently "excessively worried about something." In the process of collecting early-childhood and family-of-origin material, it was discovered that she had a very positive and endorsing family that was physically affectionate and supportive. At the same time, careful nonlinear listening to the woman's description of the family atmosphere revealed very subtle expressions of a nervous quality underlying the positive and loving picture. As the "baby" of her family, much older siblings could overwhelm and "beat up" on her as they would play roughhouse. Such encounters, although oftentimes fun, would also scare her and require her to call for help in need of "rescuing" by her parents or oldest sibling. Her mother and father's method of discipline included being "strict" with her, and "yelling" to gain "control" over rambunctious and energetic children. She also described her mother as somewhat nervous in nature, a person who did not easily relax. Then too, there were tornadoes to be frightened of and scary monsters she imagined that would prompt her to run for the cover of her parents' bedroom at night. In describing what her life was like in school, she casually related that teachers and authority figures in general were "intimidating." The net result of all of these nuanced descriptions revealed a pattern of thinking. There was a nervous edge to her experience of growing up as a child.

Nevertheless, she did well in school, had friends, and was well liked and successful in a beginning career before marriage. At the time of entering therapy, she was living in a healthy and successful marriage with a husband who was very "supportive and caring." Despite these positive factors, she still experienced the "ton of anxiety" over her child. She stated her goals for therapy as follows: "I'm looking for ways to think about things differently!"

In the case noted above, address the following questions:

1. What is the client's view of self? Realistic or unrealistic? Flexible or rigid? Positive or negative?
2. What is the client's view of life and the world? Realistic or unrealistic? Flexible or rigid? Positive or negative?
3. What is the client's view of others? Realistic or unrealistic? Flexible or rigid? Positive or negative?
4. What unique experiences in this person's life impacted her schema?
5. What messages did she pick up from her family of origin that may have impacted her schema?
6. How might her birth order or sibling relationships impact her schema?
7. How have these schema dynamics played a significant role in this woman's personality?
8. What personality disorder might this client have?
9. Does understanding this woman's schema dynamics make her chief complaint more understandable?
10. Can you translate the client's schema dynamics into a more useable, personal statement or statements—for example, "I am . . .", "Others are . . .", and "The world is . . ."

A nonlinear-thinking therapist realizes that schemas—even very problematic ones—have been reinforced and evolved over a lifetime (aided by self-fulfilling prophecies, family of origin, personal experiences, etc.) as a way of helping an individual navigate through life. They represent a client's attempt to solve the problem of "How am I going to manage my life without getting hurt or being immobilized by a fear of getting hurt, making a mistake, failing, losing, and so on?" This is how schemas become a roadmap providing guidance to an individual throughout life. It helps the individual to filter information and make sense of the world, organize an immense amount of information in need of processing, guide interactions with other people, and generally define who he or she is as a person. As mentioned in the last chapter, attitudes or behavioral responses adopted in schemas are adaptive, but when they are highly skewed or misapplied, this can lead to trouble. They can be difficult to alter. But, understanding, classifying, and interpreting schema dynamics in collaboration with a client in a consistent fashion can effectively help the client to address his or her concerns.

Linear Thinking, Listening, and Responding to Core Client Schemas

Recall that linear listening has two components: listening for content and information and listening for feeling. But schemas filter information and generate feelings. Thus, clients do not relate pure information or fact, but rather unconsciously screened, altered information—a map of reality. A prudent linear-thinking therapist is sensitive to listening for subtle clues about a client's schemas (i.e., view of self, others, and the world and life embedded in the facts of their story). When listening for content or information, therapists need to be mindful of specific questions to discover key elements of a client's schemas. What is the client saying about him- or herself, others, or the world? Are these statements generally positive or negative? Does the client seem rigid or inflexible about these statements? For example, clients often make statements such as "I can't ever seem to do anything right," "You can't be too careful around people," "*Every* time that I . . . I just can't ever seem to relax," and "It's a dog-eat-dog world." Each of these relatively straightforward statements suggests a negative view of self ("I can't . . ."), a negative view of others ("You can't be too careful around people"), or a negative view of the world ("It's a dog-eat-dog world").

Listening for feeling is another important linear source for identifying portions of a person's schema. As mentioned in Chapter 2, listening for feeling provides *shading* or nuanced information. Listening for feelings helps a therapist to refine an understanding of the elements of a client's schema. For example, if a client makes the statement "I just can't win!," but he or she gives a wry smile and a giggle (both tending to contradict what has been said), it may signify a more positive view of self (i.e., "I tried to get away with something and got caught with my hand in the cookie jar!"). On the other hand, a client looking sad and forlorn, with tears in her eyes, sighing deeply and saying, "I just can't win!" may be indicating a more negative view of self and life—someone who feels that life is unfair and perceives that she "always" gets the "short end of the stick." The verbal statements are identical ("I just can't win!") but qualified differently (i.e., one is more playful, and the other more painful). Clinical Exercise: Linear Listening for Schema presents a linear-listening activity designed to help define elements of a person's core schema.

Clinical Exercise: Linear Listening for Schema

Directions: Read each of the statements below and decide which of the elements of a person's schema (view of self, others, or the world or life) it reveals, and whether it is positive or negative.

1. "I don't know why I am so gullible, but I guess I never see the bad in people until it is too late!"
2. "Ugh! Men are such pigs! I mean it. They just are. I hate 'em!"
3. "I think that the problem is that people get too worked up about things. If people would just chill out more, things would work out for them."

4. "I try to keep a level head about most things, and I think that I do a good job of it; but sometimes I guess I lose my temper. Not often, but sometimes I just blow off steam."
5. "You know, we could all die tomorrow. A killer asteroid could hit, or they could drop the bomb, and it would all be over."
6. "I'm such a loser."

Variation: Create examples of statements that would translate the various elements of a person's schema (positive or negative view of self, others, or the world or life) into something more personally relevant to the client. Form pairs or small groups and identify schema elements underlying each of the above statements.

Counselors can use linear listening and responding to help figure out what can be useful in establishing reasonable hypotheses as to what a client's schema dynamics (view of self, others, and life and the world) are. For example, when a client's view of self is connected to the presenting problem or complaint, a therapist can present that hypothesis in a respectful way for consideration. For example, "It sounds to me like you see yourself as _____ (e.g., helpless or an innocent bystander)" or "Could it be that you see yourself basically as _____ (e.g., helpless or an innocent bystander)?" This is an extension of the translation mentioned in each of the view of self, others, and the world and life sections in Clinical Exercise: Linear Listening for Schema. Consider the 60-year-old widow cited in the clinical case examples in this chapter and Chapter 5. To respond to her effectively, it was necessary for the therapist to understand and appreciate her underlying self-schema. All of her complaints (e.g., wanting to stay in bed; being chronically annoyed, irritated, and critical; not wanting to visit relatives; being fed up; and chronically feeling unappreciated) needed to be taken into account to understand how they reinforced her negative view of self (i.e., "I feel less worthy than other people"). In turn, her irritability toward others allows her to act in ways that turn other people off. Such behavior garners negative feedback and leaves her feeling unappreciated, unsuccessful, and less than others. In addition, her decision not to visit relatives reinforces others' views of her as irascible. Sensing the plot of the client's story, the therapist communicated his ideas about her view of self via an image of the family ugly duckling. This characterization allowed for a better working alliance (i.e., "This therapist really understands how bad I feel about how I see myself!") and other effective interventions as well.[1] This is a good example of how basic skills (linear and nonlinear listening and responding) can be combined with advanced (Level II) skills (understanding a client's schema dynamics) to effectively work with a difficult client. We discuss how to use these in more detail next.

Nonlinear Thinking, Listening, and Responding to Core Client Schemas

We have emphasized that linear and nonlinear methods must be used together in order to be most effective with the client. This is especially true with understanding the influence of schema dynamics on a client's behavior. Sometimes, hypotheses that a therapist creates using linear listening (listening for content or feeling) can be confirmed or rejected by nonlinear listening. Straightforward client statements must be consistent and supported by other (often subtle) information. Nonlinear listening for subtle comments can expose faulty logic flowing from schemas, which provides information that supports hypotheses (or fails to). When this is fleshed out, a therapist can make more effective suggestions and interventions. In addition, nonlinear listening can often help a clinician to find the right image or theme for a client's story.

Rigid Schema Dynamics and Linear and Nonlinear Listening: Absolutes, Dichotomies, Extremes, Polarities, and Exclusionary Thinking

How rigidly a client holds to a set of beliefs reflects unrealistic schema dynamics and creates greater dysfunction (i.e., personality disorders). A nonlinear-thinking therapist listens for a combination of congruence, presence, and resistance when a client uses *conditional assumptions*. Listening for congruence (or incongruence) provides information about the strength of a belief or conviction. For example, a client states, "I would never stay married if my husband cheated!" But when an infidelity is revealed, she does not file for a divorce. Such incongruence could indicate that there are additional competing schemas involved (e.g., "Divorce is a sign of failure, and I must never fail.").

Likewise, listening for presence (e.g., nonverbal behaviors and tone of voice) adds to a therapist's understanding of how intensely someone feels about his beliefs, and how deeply conflicted someone is about how he thinks things should be and how they are. Consider the following: An individual believes himself to be indispensable to his office and has a positive but unrealistic view of self. When downsized, he cannot fathom being replaced. He may have difficulty finding a new job and place many (unreasonable) conditions on taking a new job, such as "I will apply for a job with them only if I don't have to travel." Declarations made in anger or frustration with corresponding body language give clues that the client is having trouble with his new reality. Resistant clients frequently avoid making a commitment to change by using conditional statements (e.g., "Yes, but . . ." or "I'll try . . ." statements). This is also generally indicative of conflicts between clients' core schemas and the realities they have to face.

Statements that include absolutes (always or never), dichotomies (this or that), extremes (the best or the worst), polarities (right versus wrong), and exclusionary thinking ("There is no way I could . . .") reveal rigidly held beliefs that typically flow from unrealistic schema dynamics. Perhaps the most common of these is the use of absolute words—such as *every, everyone, everything, all, always, never, no one, none,* and *nothing*. Clients use these terms to describe many experiences, describe the breadth and depth of their problems, and/or rationalize their behavior, despite the fact that they are rarely justified (Gula, 2002).

Yet, for a nonlinear-thinking therapist, such statements yield valuable clues about the client's schema dynamics. As described in Chapter 8, Seligman's (1990) concept of "explanatory style"[2] (i.e., view of self) is useful in this regard. Pessimistic individuals who give up easily see negative things as permanent and are prone to the use of terms such as *never* and *nothing* (e.g., "I can never get a break" or "Nothing ever goes my way"). They are also prone to seeing negative events as pervasive in their lives. Rather than perceiving unfortunate events (e.g., the breakup of a relationship) as indicative of specific circumstances (e.g., "Pete is a jerk!"), they tend to perceive such events in terms of universals (e.g., "All men are jerks!" or "I'll never find someone to marry").

Optimists tend to use qualifying words such as *sometimes* (e.g., "Sometimes, I get so discouraged that I just want to quit" or "Sometimes, there are days of being a parent that make me want to say I never heard of motherhood"). Optimists also tend to explain events to themselves in terms of permanent causes such as one's traits, one's abilities, and the use of the unrestricted qualifier *always* (e.g., "Lady Luck always smiles at me!"). Again, careful listening (linear and nonlinear) is critical for picking up on these important verbal clues about a client's schema dynamics.

Nonlinear listening is helpful in unraveling seemingly incongruous behaviors. Consider, for example, a client who comes to therapy complaining of being depressed and yet espouses an extreme philosophy of going for the "gusto" and "Eat, drink, and be merry." Her philosophy appears to be an expression of optimism and an enjoyment of life, but her complaint is one of being depressed and unhappy. Thus, such an individual may very well harbor an underlying philosophy that reflects the second half of the optimistic expression, "Eat, drink, etc.—for tomorrow we die!" Such a philosophy may very well be related to a pessimistic view of life that the client attempts to assuage by getting all the pleasure that she can because she knows it won't last.

Listening for congruence and for absence are powerful tools for the nonlinear-thinking therapist in understanding the schema dynamics behind statements a client makes. Clients can rarely justify statements such as "Nothing ever goes my way" when a therapist calls attention to them. A therapist can supportively ask, "Are you saying that *every* time you _____, there has never been a single instance in your life that has gone your way?" In addition, a therapist listening for absence searches for what it is the client is not saying or talking about.

Mature individuals hold more realistic views of themselves, others, and life and the world. They understand and accept that rigid dichotomies, absolutes, exclusionary thinking, and so on are simply not very functional in this less-than-perfect world. Nevertheless, human beings readily indulge in thinking such as "Either I get an 'A,' or I'm no good," "You're either for me or against me," and on and on. Client use of either-or thinking is simply not very functional in a world that is filled with shades of gray.

Elements of Formal Assessment in Understanding a Client's Schema Dynamics

Readiness for Change

As previously discussed, a client's readiness for and willingness to change (i.e., stages of change) are important components of any evaluation. Highly skewed, unrealistic, and rigidly held schemas are difficult to influence and directly affect a client's preparedness for change. These clients may get stuck in the precontemplation, contemplation, or preparing for action stage. Client motivation to change, however, is uniquely influenced by schema dynamics, and moving them from one stage to the next is heavily dependent on a therapist's understanding of the client's view of self, view of others, and view of life and world.

Client Resources

A therapist must tailor specific interventions in accord with a client's schema and resources. Effective therapy goes with the grain of a client's schemas, not against the grain. Clients' unrealistic and dysfunctional schemas place them at odds with others, their own ultimate best interests, or life circumstances. The contrariness of highly skewed schemas typically results in emotional discomfort as well as being dysfunctional in important areas of life. When clients encounter life circumstances that need to be addressed and will not recede (e.g., recall the clinical case example in Chapter 4, in which the client says that he's been arrested three times for DUI offenses), but that contradict schematized views of self, others, or the world (e.g., "I am not an alcoholic," "I do not have a problem," and "I am a responsible person"), then individuals can become immobilized. This can lead to a therapeutic impasse because dysfunctional elements of the client's schema (that are not useful in the current circumstances and are actually harmful) do not change. Rather than forcing the impasse and encountering resistance via a power struggle with a client, a nonlinear-thinking therapist searches for unused or overlooked resources and untapped empowerment to help a client reconcile such impasses. Such therapeutic focus can help identify the positive or useful elements of a client's schema (e.g., the man with three DUI arrests is dedicated to his job and family, or a young man with a lung transplant, who feels worn out and tired and doesn't want to do anything, is viewed as tough and resilient to have survived all that he has).

Themes

For the seven themes that are described in Chapter 5, there are corresponding schema dynamics that each theme suggests (see Table 9.3). Consider the client with a DUI. The theme is one of defensiveness. As a result, a clinician can assume that his schema dynamics include a positive and unrealistic view of self and a negative view of others or view of the world and life. In fact, when therapists discover these themes, they also are uncovering the plots to the client's story mentioned in Narrative

Table 9.3 Relationship between the Theme in a Client's Story and Schema Dynamics

Underlying Theme of Client Story	Schema Dynamics (Suggested)
1. Desperation	Positive or negative view of self; negative view of life and the world
2. Helplessness	Negative view of self
3. Hopelessness	Negative view of self, others, and life and the world
4. Defensiveness	Positive view of self; negative view of life and the world
5. Exhaustion	Negative view of self and life and the world
6. Despair	Negative view of others and/or life and the world
7. Double bind	Positive view of self; negative view of life and the world

Understanding of Client Core Schema, above. As another example, if a client has a theme of hopelessness (a chronic problem), then she probably has a negative view of self, others, and life and the world. Thus, the nonlinear-thinking therapist can (again) simultaneously combine beginning (Level I) and advanced (Level II) skills in order to help a client effectively.

Client Goals

Last, the role of goals in understanding schemas cannot be underestimated. Some individuals come to therapy with minor difficulties when compared with others who enter therapy with major long-standing personality difficulties. A client's goals for therapy (both stated and unstated), if originated by the therapist, must initially be congruent with the client's schema. Going back to the example from the clinical case example in Chapter 4 (about the DUI client), if the therapist's goal is to coerce the client into accepting that he has a problem, there will most likely be a premature termination. If, however, the therapist understands the client's view of self as "I don't have a problem," "I take care of my family," and "I am a responsible person," then the initial goal will be to help the client to not have a problem and to take care of his family. How to best accomplish this goal is a focus of exploration for the client and therapist. For this DUI client, this might take the form of presenting a challenge for the therapeutic relationship: "What do you think we might focus on to help you deal with this current dilemma and keep you taking care of your family?" The ultimate goal of moving the client toward greater readiness for change and better adaptive functioning, however, will have been preserved. Also, the therapeutic relationship is preserved and perhaps strengthened in the process.

Using the Therapeutic Relationship to Better Understand a Client's Schema Dynamics

Therapeutic Alliance

Understanding a client's schema (i.e., what and how a client thinks and feels—confirmed by the client) makes it easier to identify, empathize with, and address important client issues and particular dilemmas. When this occurs, a client understands that the therapist sees, hears, and feels his point of view: "My therapist 'gets' me, understands me and the spot I'm in. She's not critical or rejecting of me. She's not trying to get me to relinquish what it is that I believe and feel, nor is she demanding that I do something I'm ill-prepared to deal with or change." Such perceptions strengthen the working alliance and help a client to unravel the particular mystery of the problems for which he seeks relief.

Therapeutic Ruptures and Client Schemas

A client's schemas and skewed thinking can (and do) affect the therapeutic alliance, including how quickly it is established and its depth. In fact, client schemas are a potential basis for transference issues that have the potential to destabilize and rupture the therapeutic alliance. Recall from Chapter 7 the successful businessman in his early 50s who sought therapy to better understand how to respond to his angry wife. In treatment, the therapist grew increasingly more frustrated with the client, feeling that he was working harder than the client. Exemplifying how schemas can influence the therapeutic alliance (including transference and countertransference issues), the client's response to the therapist raising this issue was "As a child, I was told that children are to be seen and not heard. I gave my opinion only when I was asked for it—otherwise, I kept my mouth shut or paid the consequences!" Following this exchange, the client began taking a more active role in discussing issues that he needed to work on without being prompted by the therapist. Once a therapist understands a client's particular schema dynamics (negative view of self), and his actions are placed in a proper context, individual instances of *behavior* (e.g., seeming not to participate fully in therapy and not answering questions) are more understandable.

Utilizing Assessment of Client Schema Dynamics

To this point, we have shown how a nonlinear-thinking therapist utilizes skills in the Level I domains to gain an understanding of client schema dynamics. The following discussion is devoted to facilitating an understanding of how to identify and work with client schemas that can be revealed from a variety of sources. In particular, we introduce three nonlinear methods that master practitioners often use to assess client schema dynamics: the family of origin, sibling position, and early childhood recollections.

Using Family-of-Origin Dynamics to Understand Client Schema Dynamics

The influence of an individual's family of origin (however it is comprised) on the development of a client's schema cannot be underestimated. The family, as an individual's first exposure to life, the world, and others, has a pervasive influence on the development of schemas. For the most part, positive family experiences increase the likelihood that an individual will derive a somewhat positive outlook, and likewise, negative family experiences increase the likelihood of a somewhat negative outlook, although they don't guarantee it. Alas, positivity and negativity do not reveal the entire story. Children learn about values (i.e., what is important, not important, to be strived for, and to be avoided) from their parents (or surrogates), who convey (and reinforce) those values overtly and unconsciously. Thus, getting information about a client's family of origin is critical in understanding schema dynamics. Consider the following example from the case of Ashley.

Therapist:	"I see, so somewhere in all of this, you had what I like to call a 'Scarlett O'Hara' moment."
Ashley:	"What is that?"
Therapist:	"She is the lead character from the movie *Gone With The Wind.*"
Ashley:	"Oh, yeah. I have seen that before. Years ago."
Therapist:	"Okay, do you remember the scene where Scarlett O'Hara comes back to her home after the ravages of the Civil War, and there's no food; everyone is starving. At the climactic scene in the first half of the film, she runs out of the garden and digs up some rotted potatoes, and out of desperation, she eats them. She had gone from a wealthy and well-to-do Southern Belle, to being desperate and hungry. And crying, humiliated she shakes her fist at heaven and says 'As God as my witness, I will never go hungry again!' I think that everyone has their 'Scarlett O'Hara' moment in their lives where they are brought low and shake their fist at heaven and say 'As God as my witness, I will never ____, again.'"
Ashley:	"Yeah."
Therapist:	"And do you know what your 'blank' is?"

Ashley:	"I'll never be replaced again."
Therapist:	"I think you are right. And I think you have a 'go to' strategy to make sure that doesn't happen. Do you know what that is?"
Ashley:	"Having to be in control all the time?"
Therapist:	"Bingo. And, I think that your fear of messes, which drives you to clean everything up for everyone is a sign that you want help. But you are afraid to ask for it because you think they might get rid of you—replace you. So you adopt a 'go it alone' strategy. You try to do it all and then kick yourself when you can't live up to that. You wind up getting less of what you want, and more of what you don't want."
Ashley:	"I never thought of it like that before."
Therapist:	"And it is the same at home. It's the same pattern. You don't ask for help or togetherness, and instead you just do, well, everything. And while you don't get kicked out, you also don't feel like you are on the inside anywhere. You don't feel secure."
Ashley:	"No. I haven't felt that way, not for a long time. Maybe never, I don't know . . ."
Therapist:	"Kind of like you did as a girl?"
Ashley:	"Yeah, wishing someone would see me, see that I'm alone . . ."
Therapist:	"And that you need help?"
Ashley:	(reluctantly) "Yeah."

Take a few moments to reflect on the transcript above and answer the following questions:

1. Describe the client's schema dynamics (view of self, view of others, view of world).
2. Describe the client's central pattern.
3. Describe how her family-of-origin helped to shape this?
4. How has it affected her today?
5. How might a therapist use this to be effective with this client?

Sibling Position and the Development of Schemas

Understanding a client's birth order[3] is an important source of valuable information for master practitioners learning about client schemas. Different sibling positions predispose individuals to adopt certain roles, behavioral paths, attitudes, and so on rather than others. As an example, first-born children from different families are more likely to share common personality characteristics than a first-born and second-born from the same family. The adoption of different roles is guided by schemas that in significant ways are shaped by one's sibling position.

Kluger (2006) has described a recent burgeoning popular and scientific interest in understanding sibling position and birth order:

Within the scientific community, siblings have not been wholly ignored, but research has been limited mostly to discussions of birth order. Older sibs were said to be strivers; younger ones rebels; middle kids the lost souls. The stereotypes were broad, if not entirely untrue, and there the discussion mostly ended. But all that's changing. At research centers . . . investigators are launching a wealth of new studies into the sibling dynamic, looking at ways brothers and sisters steer one another into—or away from—risky behavior; how they form a protective buffer against family upheaval; how they educate one another about the opposite sex; how all siblings compete for family recognition and come to terms—or blows—over such impossibly charged issues as parental favoritism. (p. 1)

The clinical case example below demonstrates the influence of siblings on personality and schemas.

Clinical Case Example: An Unhappy Couple in Crisis

A woman and her significant other had moved in together with plans to marry. In their late 30s, each was intelligent, educated, verbal, and eager to have their relationship work because each had been previously unhappily married and divorced. Soon after purchasing a house together, the woman found herself increasingly unhappy but complaining little. After months of such unhappiness, Susan felt depressed and then erupted in emotional tirades against her suitor. Sensitive and responsive, Bob made efforts to amend his behavior to take her complaints into account. The complaints centered on his two young children, who were barely school-age. After brief individual therapy, Susan sought couples' counseling.

Bob's children split their time between living with their mother and living with their father. Susan readily admitted that Bob's children were likable, respectful, caring, well-mannered, and well-behaved, and in that regard, she had no complaints. In fact, she genuinely liked the children and felt that they liked her. If this was the case, what was the problem?

Susan had a difficult time in explaining what her complaint was other than saying that she did not "feel as though we are a family unit." She explained, "Bob doesn't take me into consideration in different ways and in different scenarios. When I explain what I mean, he doesn't get it, and we argue." In turn, Bob felt overwhelmed (i.e., "flooded") with the extent of Susan's anger and troubled by her apparent unresponsiveness to his efforts to address her concerns. Susan simply felt that Bob and his children didn't take her into account, didn't need her, and seemed to do things without consulting her. Even when consulted, she felt it was only temporary and that things would revert to "the old ways."

After the first few sessions of couples' therapy, Bob reported that they had reached a "crisis" and that they were at a serious breaking point in their relationship. During that crisis session, each revealed understandings from childhood that shed light on their current dilemma. In Susan's family of origin, her father was a severe substance abuser who was absent from the home much of the time. Although overt conflict seemed to be lacking, she perceived her parents as uninvolved with each other and basically unhappy. With numerous siblings, such conditions led to Susan's mother relying heavily upon her to get things done. She provided babysitting for her younger siblings, cooked, did the family laundry, and "had to make everything 'Okay' for them." Susan described herself as playing a "central role" in maintaining the family despite her father's alcoholism. She felt important (i.e., valued) in that role. Susan felt that she, her mother, and her siblings were "very connected and close and looked out for each other."

In listening to the depiction of her position in her family of origin, the therapist suggested that she seemed to have not only a significant role (i.e., a social place of value) but also a substantive, important, and central role. In contrast, her present circumstances led her to feel as though she not only did not have a substantive, central, and well-defined role but also had no role at all because of the highly functional way in which Bob and his children seemed to work together without conflict. Susan beamed at this explanation as being precisely what it was that she had been trying to convey to Bob without success. She didn't feel as though she had any "central" role in their system, and in fact, she felt excluded at times. Her unconscious view-of-self schema informed her as if to say, "The way things should be is that others rely on me, I am central and essential to the family, we are all close, we have fun together, and I have a well-defined role and am needed. That's how I derive my sense of feeling worthwhile. My present circumstances don't seem to give me that feeling. Bob and his children seem to do very well without significant input from me. I don't have a defined role of what (my schema unconsciously informs me) I'm supposed to be doing."

In Bob's depiction of his childhood, it was clear that although he was well-behaved and obedient, he also felt as though his alcoholic mother singled him out for special unjustified scrutiny, suspicion, and verbal abuse. Similarly, he felt under "attack" by Susan, who acted just like his mother, who was regularly and frequently inebriated, out of control, verbally abusive, and unpredictable, and often mean-spirited. When the therapist noted that Bob seemed to be saying that he felt Susan was unjustly scrutinizing and verbally abusing him just like he felt his mother had done, Bob's face flushed, and he acknowledged complete agreement. It was his view-of-others schema that informed him that he was being unjustly accused, verbally abused, and unfairly scrutinized, which was intolerable and unacceptable.

Master practitioners listen intensively for spontaneous client comments revealing information about the family of origin, its beliefs, the roles played, the values reinforced, feelings, and so on. Such client disclosures strongly suggest that schemas are operative in a client's current dilemma. Exploring such possibilities is encouraged—especially how a client viewed the particular family dynamics in question and how such dynamics relate to her current dilemma.

Early Childhood Recollections

A rich source of clinical understanding about client schemas and thinking can be found in a client's *early childhood recollections* (ECRs). But before discussing what can be learned from ECRs, it would be prudent to establish working definitions, describe subtle distinctions, and highlight new understandings about memory.

Cognitions in general are best described and understood as the process of thinking (i.e., a psychological activity), rather than by understanding them as things (i.e., concrete objects). Kandel, Schwartz, and Jessell (2000) addressed "memory" by subtly describing it as the process involved in acquiring, codifying, storing, and retrieving knowledge. The implication of this for clinicians is that memory and memories are not cast in stone. As Gonsalves and Paller (2000) and Shacter (1996) have indicated, memories do not provide a perfect rendering of what has transpired in a person's life. Rather, at retrieval, memories are constructed according to the particular methods that are used to retrieve them. Furthermore, Garry and Polaschek (2000) noted,

> The "autobiographical memories" that tell the story of our lives are always undergoing revision precisely because our sense of self is too. We are continually extracting new information from old experiences and filling in gaps in ways that serve some current demand. Consciously or not, we use imagination to reinvent our past, and with it, our present and future. (p. 6)

Because they are constructed, it is prudent to consider childhood memories as recollections—a regathering of the past rather than a tape recording of events. Hence, these recollections are subject to some editing by the client, and the conclusions drawn from them (schema dynamics) are modifiable as well.[4] Although research is limited, it suggests that ECRs have both linear and nonlinear dimensions that must be considered to maximize their usefulness and validity. Josselson (2000) noted,

> If early memories [EMs[5]] are indicative of an individual's present worldview or attitude toward life and offer insight into an individual's current ego organization, they should change in

parallel to developmental change in the individual. If, however, they represent "core" aspects of personality, they should remain stable over time. (pp. 464–465)

What research findings reveal is equally linear and nonlinear. Watkins (1992) reviewed 30 studies of early memories and concluded,

EMs are consistent with current interpersonal behavior . . . the EMs of psychiatric patients, when compared to normal controls, tend to be more negative in emotional tone, show more fear/anxiety themes, and reflect greater passivity or an external locus of control . . . the EMs of psychiatric patients show changes over the course of treatment, with EM content becoming more positive in nature as favorable life changes occur . . . the EMs of male delinquents and criminals, when compared with memories of control subjects, reflect more negative emotionality, injury or illness, rule breaking, victimization, and being alone in an unpleasant situation. (p. 259)

In other words, early recollections contain significant clues about a client's schema dynamics. Indeed, in a long-term study of stability and change in early memories, Josselson (2000) concluded,

Early memories seem to represent both stability and change within the individual in a form similar to musical development of theme and variation. As many writers have suggested, early memories mark unsolved issues that may be expressed, resolved, resurrected, or reexperienced in new guises at different periods of life. . . . Early memories operate like markers of individual destiny, offering expressive metaphors of core themes in personality that may not be as apparent in the welter of detail that a life story comprises. (pp. 477–478)

Collecting ECRs

Although there are a number of different ways to collect ECRs and we recommend that the reader seeks out some of the primary sources cited here, we present some guidelines for collecting ECRs here. Carlson, Watts, and Maniacci (2006) provide three guidelines for gathering early memories from before the age of 10:

First, the memory must be a single one-time event. Second, it must be visualized. Third, it must have two parts specifically articulated: (a) what was the most vivid part of the recollection and (b) how did the client feel during the recollection? (p. 116)

In general, anywhere from three to eight memories may be collected (Carlson, Watts, & Maniacci, 2006; Clark, 2002). From these, the clinician should be able to summarize the themes and dynamics of a person's view of themselves, others, and the world around them. In other words, their schema dynamics.

Clinical Case Example: ECRs That Go Bump in the Night!

An example may prove helpful in demonstrating the clinical usefulness of ECRs. The client presented earlier in the chapter (Clinical Case Exercise: Anxious and Dependent) reported the following ECR:

Client: "I was really scared in the middle of the night. I was seeing ghosts outside my room. I'd see shadows like dinosaurs. Then, when they went away, I would run into my parent's bedroom and crawl into bed with them."

Therapist: "What part of the memory is most vivid to you?"

Client: "Laying in my bed not knowing what to do—frozen."

Therapist: "How are you feeling about the memory?"

Client: "Scared! I remember thinking they—it—was going to get me."

The interpretation of the memory is straightforward: The client scares herself with frightening monsters of her own misperception and creation—she makes more of reality than is really there. There are other subtle implications from the memory, as the astute practitioner would discover. The client runs into her parents' bedroom to avail herself of the safety they provide. The possible meaning of this is that she relies on others for safety and reassurance in a life filled with scary things. This implies dependency on others to deal with some of life's scarier difficulties. The adroit practitioner will detect a particularly positive and important, albeit subtle, part of the memory as well: This is a very creative person. That is, in the context of her ECR, she uses her creativity to scare herself. Her creativity can also be called upon as a treatment resource to help her develop new ways to deal with anxiety-provoking life situations.

Given the research support that ECRs both are stable and change, the interpretation of memories in many respects is certainly as much nonlinear as it is linear. Several authors (Clark, 2002; Mosak & DiPietro, 2006) have provided guidance regarding the interpretation of ECRs from different theoretical frames of reference. ECR interpretation is certainly not formulaic and can be approached as part of a collaborative process between client and therapist. We offer the following suggestions regarding ECRs.

Rather than the factual basis of ECRs (i.e., something did or did not occur), it is the feelings about what is remembered that are critically important. In the final analysis, it is the feelings and emotions divulged by a client about what they remember that reflect what is important—the values. We have feelings and emotions about things that are important to us. Thus, it is the values behind the feelings that are important in determining the client's schema dynamics. The important consideration is the answer to the question "What was it about that memory that prompted you to feel that way?" Answers such as "It wasn't fair" betray schema dynamics in which fairness is prominent, and ones like "It wasn't right" point to schema dynamics in which rightness and wrongness are prominent personality values. "I was afraid that . . ." indicates a preoccupation with fearfulness, uncertainty, doubt, and vagueness—a need for guarantees and certainty in an uncertain world (on a schema level). In most instances, clients are unaware of the existence of such beliefs and the thinking that follows from them, let alone that they were formed during childhood with a child's limited capacity to understand events or put them into a greater context. Nevertheless, such unawareness does not prevent others from operating as full adults according to beliefs and thinking formulated and reinforced in childhood.

Clinical Exercise: Working with ECRs to Determine Schema Dynamics

Instructions: Consider the following two ECRs from the same client.

Memory Number 1: Client, Age 2 or 3

Client: "I remember my mother taking me to day care for infants. She had to go to work. It was the first day she took me to day care. I didn't want to go, and she left. I was there the whole day."

Therapist:	"What part of the memory stands out to you most clearly?"
Client:	"I remember the room with white walls. I was lying in a bed sitting on a stand."
Therapist:	"How are you feeling in the memory?"
Client:	"I felt awkward—my mother went away and had to go to work. I didn't appreciate that."
Therapist:	"What about that prompted you to feel that way?"
Client:	"I was scared that she left me. I didn't realize what was going to happen."

Memory Number 2: Client, Age 6

Client:	"In America, I remember one time my father was arguing with my mother, and he lost his temper. He picked up a drinking glass and threw it at my mother. He packed his things, and he left for a couple of days. He would provoke fights and make it seem like it's not his fault, like it was mother's fault."
Therapist:	"What part of the memory stands out to you most clearly?"
Client:	"Everyone was yelling, screaming at one another. Mother was crying. He broke the glass on her back. They weren't talking when he came back."
Therapist:	"How are you feeling in the memory?"
Client:	"I was very mad at him; I was small, but I wanted to call the police."
Therapist:	"What about that prompted you to feel that way?"
Client:	"The fact that I was playing with my toys, and he threw the glass, and it could have caused a lot worse damage—could have shattered in her eyes. It could have been a lot worse."

Questions

1. Briefly summarize the major schema theme in each memory.
2. What similarities, if any, can you detect in the two memories?
3. Can you differentiate between the specific contents of the memories and similar underlying commonalities?
4. What could be said about this client's view of self, life, and others?
5. Translate questions 1–4 into personally useful statements for the client.
6. What can you point to that supports your interpretation of the memories?
7. What complaints, preoccupations, concerns, and so on might be predicted about this client as a result of clinical clues derived from these memories?
8. What are likely diagnostic categories for this individual?
9. What leads you to this conclusion?

Our Nonlinear Brain: The Neurobiological Basis of ECRs

ECRs are a rich source of dynamic understanding about the clients who consult us, whether those recollections are systematically collected or arise spontaneously. Obviously, the brain is the specific body organ that stores memories and unconsciously retrieves and uses them in the service of the goals of the personality. The mystery of how ECRs become such a revealing part of personality is slowly being unraveled by cognitive neuroscience. Paradoxically, in order to understand ECRs, one must first understand fear.

LeDoux (1998) has advocated that the brain's fear system is a particularly good anchoring point for understanding the organization of other emotions in the brain. He gives three reasons for selecting fear in this way: (a) It is pervasive throughout humankind and the vertebrate kingdom, and yet paradoxically William James noted that humans are distinguished from other animals because of their ability to reduce conditions of fear under which they live; (b) whether it is anxiety, panic, phobias, posttraumatic stress disorder, or obsessive-compulsive disorder, fear plays an extensive role in psychopathology; and (c) fear is similarly expressed in humans and other animals.

To LeDoux's (1998) list of human fears, we would add an observation made by Adler (1956): the fear of failure that comes in an infinite variety of forms. Master practitioners are sensitive to the human fear of failure dynamic apparent in their clients, albeit disguised. Although apparently endemic to the human condition and sharing similar properties between individuals, fear of failure in its subtleties and nuances is unique to each individual.

The amygdala plays an essential role in fear mediation. LeDoux (1998) has called it the "hub in the wheel of fear" (p. 170). In turn, fear as a universal (i.e., all human beings are fearful of something, including failure) and a uniquely defined experience (i.e., each individual has different things, experiences, and so on, that he or she is fearful of, including different sorts of failure) is an emotional and physical survival emotion. Without it, we would not know to be afraid of things in life that can destroy us physically and hurt us emotionally. We learn to be fearful of specific things. LeDoux has suggested that through a process of classical conditioning that takes place in the brain of a child, human beings learn to associate certain experiences with certain fears or other emotions such as embarrassment. But there are "multiple memory systems" (p. 239).

It is the hippocampus of the limbic system and related cortical areas that are responsible for storing specific conscious memories, whereas "unconscious memories established by fear conditioning mechanisms" (p. 239) operate through an amygdala-based system. LeDoux (1998) concluded that:

> when stimuli that were present during the initial trauma are later encountered, each system can potentially retrieve its memories. In the case of the amygdala system, retrieval results in expression of bodily responses that prepare for danger, and in the case of the hippocampal system, conscious remembrances occur. (p. 239)

In their summaries of relevant research, Cappas, Andres-Hyman, and Davidson (2005) and Eichenbaum (2001) pointed out that once something is learned, the hippocampus begins to process that information, with consolidation of learning occurring over a period of years. The implication of this for clinicians to understand is that early childhood experiences (e.g., repeated physical abuse, neglect, pampering, anxiety-laden experiences, embarrassments, and being victimized by bullies) are processed by the hippocampus until consolidated as "old knowledge at which point it is organized in the neocortex" (Cappas et al., p. 376). We suggest that (a) a child creatively organizes such understandings into thinking templates (i.e., schemas); (b) a child automatically, unconsciously, and creatively concludes that her thinking template represents *truths* or operating principles through which she appraises experience and by which she acts; and (c) those core operating principles become the unique, defining, thinking principles of an individual personality.

A related issue pertains to the validity of a human memory and whether or not a recollected event did or did not factually occur. Experimental neuroscience data are growing that *false memories* can indeed be generated. With their particular experimental procedures using event-related potentials (ERPs), Gonsalves and Paller (2000) concluded that "people occasionally misattribute their memory of an imagined object to a memory of actually viewing a picture of that object. . . . We were thus able to use brain potentials to study neural processes related to the occurrence of false memories, both at encoding and at retrieval" (p. 1318).

It is not, however, whether something did or did not occur that is clinically relevant, as some theories question. Therapeutically, the important issue is the client's *belief* that something did occur. Although some clients may be preoccupied with the validity of a memory, for other clients Edelstein and Steele (1997) suggested that it really isn't whether recollected events took place that is presently harming a client but rather that "beliefs about them are harming you because you are following them now" (p. 209).

Given this analysis, spontaneous early childhood recollections divulged by a client in treatment can be particularly revealing and helpful. If correctly deciphered with the collaborative help of a client, such memories can reveal unconscious meanings, both cognitive and emotional, that clients have given to certain types of childhood situations when they occurred. The *paradigm* or blueprint laid down in the amygdala without specifics is sensitized to recognize similar threats in the adult environment so that the personality can take appropriate safeguarding actions. The hippocampus and related cortical structures make available a *specific* memory that a client recalls when he states, "There was this one time . . . I was about 4 years old. I remember . . ." The neocortex represents the template that an individual follows with as much loyalty as a personal religion, but it can be influenced by corrective experiences.

Clinically Working with a Client's Schema Dynamics

What are the underlying psychological processes for facilitating change? One of the earliest pioneers of schema theory was Swiss developmental psychologist Jean Piaget, who believed that children constructed schemas to help organize, classify, and understand the world (Myers, 2007).

According to Piaget, in order to be able to react to new life experiences, a person's schema naturally had to be flexible enough to change. Some changes merely take a new phenomenon and incorporate it within the structure of the existing schema (e.g., "I've never seen a soccer ball before, so I didn't know what it was; but I know it fits the 'rules' for a ball, so I will include it in my 'ball' schema"). *Assimilation* is the psychological process whereby new experiences are interpreted in terms of a current framework or schema (Myers, 2007).

Sometimes, however, an existing schema does not fully account for a phenomenon. These *rogue* phenomena require a person to either change her beliefs about how things should be (e.g., "Maybe all round things aren't balls?") or dismiss the event (e.g., "The orange object that smells like citrus is a 'ball,'" and "That oblong thing with laces that flies in the air just isn't a 'ball'! That's the way it has always been, and that's the way it will stay!"). Perhaps Sherlock Holmes, the greatest fictional detective ever, said it best when cautioning about clinging too hard to theories (schemas): "Insensibly one begins to twist facts to suit theories, instead of theories to suit facts" (Doyle, 1892/1986, p. 13). Instead, schemas that are no longer fully accurate must be adjusted to some degree to fit new experience (i.e., an "orange" or a "football"). *Accommodation* is the psychological process of adjusting schemas (Myers, 2007).

Assimilation, Accommodation, and Green Eggs and Ham

Understanding the differences between assimilation and accommodation is sometimes difficult because it is an abstract construct. However, a popular childhood story may help explain the difference and suggest how to change these schema dynamics. *Green Eggs and Ham* by Dr. Seuss gives us the perfect example. It tells the story of Sam I Am who is trying to get another character (who doesn't have a name) to eat green eggs and ham. The character staunchly refuses saying: "I do not like green eggs and ham. I do not like them Sam I Am!" In fact, one could say that he has a negative view of green eggs and ham. Sam I Am proceeds to convince the other character to *try* green eggs and ham and change his view of it. He tries to add different scenarios where he might try green eggs and ham ("Would you eat them on a boat? Would you eat them with a goat?"). This *adding* is an example of assimilation—new knowledge, in the form of different circumstances are added to existing schema. Unfortunately, the result is that now the other character has assimilated or added *more* places where he won't eat green eggs and ham! Hence, the character remains inflexible and rigid in his negative view of green eggs and ham. In other words, Sam I Am's strategy is not working, and he needs to have a more substantial change in order to get the character to try green eggs and ham.

Finally, after working with the other character (by following him all over the place), Sam I Am gets him to become a little more flexible by asking him to just *try* it (a new behavior). He does try it and declares that he *does* like green eggs and ham (based on his experience). In other words, his schematized view of green eggs and ham goes from negative to positive. It is a lasting change that causes him to reevaluate his whole view of green eggs and ham. This is an example of accommodation (changing the schema dynamics from rigid to flexible, and from negative to positive), and it dramatically and effectively gets the client to make long-term changes.

There are times when a client needs to assimilate new information or experiences into his schematized perceptions of the world. At other times, a client's schemas are not sufficient to cope with the world as it is, and behaviors that logically flow from it are responsible for developing impasses with changing life circumstances. As a result, accommodation or alteration of a client's existing schema dynamics is necessary in order to resolve disparities between what is and what exists in schemas. Sometimes presenting a verbal argument or a different point of view can do it. However, many times clients must try new behaviors, and from the experience reevaluate their schemas and accommodate (just like in *Green Eggs and Ham*). Recall the case presented earlier of Bob and Susan. In order to be able to live together peacefully, each would have had to assimilate new information (i.e., Bob: "My partner is not persecuting me") *and* accommodate their schemas (i.e., Susan: "I am not being rejected if I am not in the center of things; I am important and belong, although, at times, I play a peripheral role in the family"). Oftentimes, when individuals, couples, or families have to both assimilate and accommodate schema dynamics, therapeutic success can be elusive (hence, Susan and Bob's breakup in the end).

Linear Methods of Intervening with Client Schema: Facilitating Assimilation

Interventions that focus solely on the client's problem or deficit are indicative of linear thinking. There are times when the problem has to do with accepting a new reality, or assimilating new information into the client's existing schema, and hence linear approaches are reasonable. These usually take the form of specific skills training (e.g., assertiveness training, social skills training, time management, relaxation training, and self-hypnosis for stress management) that helps a client in developing a situational specific competence. If a client's stated purpose for counseling is to obtain assertiveness training, honoring such a request and providing such training represent a linear response to a linear request. But a therapist must also listen in a nonlinear manner to determine if there are more dynamic issues operating.

Cognitive therapists assist clients in identifying maladaptive thought processes (i.e., a negative/unrealistic view of self, others, and life and the world) and help them to develop more positive ways of thinking. They assess the pros and cons of the thoughts and beliefs that advance or hinder a client in relation to her goals and assist clients in challenging the believability of maladaptive thoughts (e.g., "Where is the evidence for this conclusion?," "Could there be another explanation of this observation?," and "If a friend told you this, what advice might you give them?"). Whether done in a conversational way or a more dramatic way, such therapeutic challenges are never presumptive and are always respectful of a client and the relationship.

Further linear methods of responding to a client's negative/unrealistic view of self include directly challenging his negative self-attributions. Therapist encouragement of the use of challenging would be represented by the rational-emotive therapy (RET) of Ellis (1962) and Ellis and Dryden (1987), who advocated catching oneself in the act of negativistic self-attributions and providing a "rational" argument to counter the expressed negative view of self. Consider the clinical case example below:

Clinical Case Example: Overly Sensitive

A successfully married career woman with an advanced degree came to therapy on a monthly basis, mostly for support after the death of her parents. In her family of origin, she was the caretaker for handicapped younger siblings who adored her. Indeed, parental feedback was extremely positive and emphasized how truly gifted and special she was. It did not take long to understand that her core positive view of self related to feeling, "I am special." Because of parental attitudes and behavior toward her, a parenthetical embellishment of her view of self seemed to be "I am a caretaker and special, and I expect others to see and treat me that way." Such a view of self, of course, would prompt her to feel very positive about herself.

She maintained a long-term complaint revolving around perceived slights at work, coupled with a sensitivity to how others treated her. For example, if she wasn't invited to a party, it became cause for extremely hurt feelings. If someone made a comment that pertained to her work, she tended to interpret such a comment as attacking her competence. She would defend her competence and add that the individual proffering the comment had no right to say such things.

During one of her monthly therapy sessions, she reported going to a wake for a distant relative who died quite tragically. At the wake, all the extended relatives seemed to be huddled around and preoccupied with a few members of the extended family who were extremely successful financially and who "everyone idolizes, and I wasn't one of them. Everything in my family is about achievement for everyone. That's my family; that's it! I walked out feeling sad and empty."

She then reported talking to a friend about her experience at a social gathering at the mansion of a prominent person in their community. Her friend reported similar feelings—"everyone" seems to cluster around the wealthy and beautiful people, who are the most influential and have the most status, and everyone else is like "chopped liver." She then made two especially important observations. The first was a rhetorical question: "Why is there a little person in me who is kicking and screaming that 'I'm important' (i.e., special)?" The second was her remark that "I'm getting over it."

Regarding her first question, it is quite obvious that her view of self is "I am important (or special, or worthwhile)," whereas her view of others suggests private thinking: "I want (i.e., expect) others to view me as important. When I'm not viewed in that way, there is 'a little person in me who is kicking and screaming' who *feels* 'I'm important.'"

About her latter comment, the therapist posed a question: "How did you manage to get over it?" She replied, "Time. It's a day-by-day thing in which you make small progress and don't let little things bother you. Putting things in perspective is another way of getting over it—I know that I'm important; it's just that at times, I don't particularly feel like it. I get over it by 'calming' myself down."

The woman's comments are especially powerful in several respects. They are very descriptive of how conscious change comes about—it is generally a gradual process of catching oneself, accomplished in small increments through attention and effort. In addition, in formulating her schema dynamics, she has fairly realistic views of herself, others, and the world.

Assimilation and First-Order Change

The value of skills training, like all approaches, lies in being able to apply the skills appropriately with clients in an appropriate context. Skills training generally does not address (or alter) the larger schema dynamics, it helps clients cope with life situations, and it helps them assimilate new information (skills) into existing schemas. This kind of symptom relief or surface change is called first-order change. According to noted family therapists Watzlawick, Weakland, and Fisch (1974), change can be either first-order or second-order. First-order change refers to alterations or variations in a system that leaves the fundamental organization of that system unchanged. It is superficial in nature, and the change may reduce a symptom or resolve surface issues. Examples of this include time management strategies or behavioral changes (i.e., diet, smoking, etc.). In terms of accommodation and assimilation, first-order change can be seen as the equivalent of assimilation. It works within the existing structures of the schema to create change (e.g., social skills training), but doesn't require the individual to change their outlook on the world. If the person is stable and healthy, then a simple problem-solving approach will be sufficient to put an end to the problem. Successful first order change should not be trivialized. Rather, it can be very helpful in alleviating suffering in some situations. But many times, clients interested in linear solutions report that they have tried that and have found such methods unsuccessful. Nonlinear listening reveals comments such as "I tried that, and it didn't work" as clinical clues that something more dynamic is operational. However, if the individual has deeper, underlying issues, then merely addressing the first-order change may temporarily halt a destructive behavior pattern, but it will not make a major impact on the individual that will last once therapy ends. At this point, change at the second-order level is necessary, and interventions that address larger schema dynamics are appropriate.

Nonlinear Methods of Intervening with Client Schema:
Facilitating Accommodation

In the television show *House, M.D.*, the lead character, Dr. Gregory House, is a misanthropic (but gifted) character who handles the most complex and mysterious medical cases. He and his team of doctors are often stymied by a patient's symptoms, whereby he utilizes metaphors to describe the behaviors of a patient's illness. This is meant to help him and his colleagues conceptualize and predict the course of the illness and arrive at a diagnosis. In one episode, a patient's systemic illness that attacks one organ system after another is metaphorically compared with a freight train speeding down the track from one station (or organ system, lungs, kidneys, etc.) to another. House and his colleagues struggle to stop it before it reaches the next destination and destroys another organ system, or before it reaches the terminal (i.e., death).

Metaphors are useful ways to describe and relate complicated client issues in a simple way (as with the example of *Green Eggs and Ham* or the Scarlett O'Hara moment above). They often entail the use of concise, descriptive events or phrases to draw parallels between the present (and complex) situation and the simple (and often commonly understood) phrase or story.[6] Instead, metaphors can help the therapist to describe the plot of the client's story or schema dynamics (see Kopp, 1995; Matthews & Langdell, 1989). A clinician might try to say to a client, "Hmmm, it appears that you have a negative and unrealistic view of the world that keeps getting you into trouble when you encounter new situations." Although accurate, such an appraisal might fail to impact a client in a personally meaningful way. A clinician could also employ a simple image[7] as a metaphor that would make the same point. For example, "You seem to consistently see the glass as either half empty or with a hole in it. Either way, it never seems to hold enough water, and you seem to feel as though you are going to get cheated or that anything good is just going to leak out the bottom of the glass." Such a metaphor has the potential to be more effective because, if accurate, it appeals to how the brain processes information—both cognitive and emotional aspects of a core schema.

The use of metaphor requires linear and nonlinear thinking, as well as accurate understanding of the salient components of a client's schema (view of self, others, and the world and life). It also requires therapists to be creative in devising a coherent and comprehensive image reflecting a client's schematized worldview—the individual's *template*. Sometimes, a client will be the one to provide a metaphor—"I feel like an emotional ping-pong ball!"—whereas at other times, it is the therapist who must. In that case, using linear and nonlinear listening (congruence, absence, inference, presence, and resistance) can provide essential information. Consider this example from the case of Mike:

Therapist: "Loss is hard at any age. And sometimes it feels better *not* to feel the pain, but it never makes the pain go away. So you do things that distract yourself—like you did in high school, but that didn't work. Now your father's death brings up this pain again, and you are lashing out at coworkers, and at your fiancée. You're hurt, you're hurting them, which, in turn, hurts you."

Mike: "Yeah, that's true. I never thought of it."

Therapist: "You are like the old story of the lion with the thorn in his paw. He was in pain, he roared about it that scared everyone, so no one helped him and he continued to be in pain, plus he felt betrayed because no one would ever help. That lion is you."

Mike: "I remember that story! Yeah, I always felt that the lion was misunderstood. I never thought I was the lion, till now."

Strategically, it is important to find a metaphor that encapsulates as many key aspects of a client's problem, worldview, sentiments, and the like as possible. Master practitioners are open-minded and receptive. Such a disposition is exceptionally useful in becoming sensitive to and absorbing themes from classical and contemporary literature, history, movies, books, media, music, TV, mythology, aspects of nature, and even elements of daily living (like the lion with a thorn in its paw).[8] In turn, such themes are useful in encapsulating key aspects of a client's problem, worldview, and so on. Clinical Exercise: Imagination and Metaphor provides an opportunity to practice the use of metaphor.

Clinical Exercise: Imagination and Metaphor

Directions: In order to bring into conscious awareness each individual's personal storehouse of imagery, stories, and creativity, we present the following exercise. Read each question below and answer as fully as possible.

1. Think of five movie characters. Derive a brief metaphor or image of them.
2. Think of five fairy tale stories or ancient myths. Derive a brief metaphor or image of them.
3. Think of the most peaceful place that you can. Derive a brief metaphor or image.
4. Think of the most disturbing place that you can. Derive a brief metaphor or image.

Next, form small groups and discuss the following:

A. The answer to each question.
B. What suggestions can group members make for improving the image or metaphor?
C. How quickly were you able to come up with the answers to each? Was it easy or difficult?
D. Discuss how some of the metaphors or images could be useful in helping to describe a client's schema dynamics. Discuss with the entire class.

This exercise will hopefully stimulate the art of creating metaphors and images to describe to clients.

In addition, paying close attention to a client's background, culture, family history, and employment can help. Matching a metaphor with characteristics from a client's background tends to enhance its effectiveness.

The most reliable indicator of how effective a metaphor is how well it *resonates* with a client (like a tuning fork; see Chapter 6). A good metaphor captures the client's imagination both *visually* and *verbally*. Metaphors that paint a vivid visual picture to illustrate a client's schema and verbal metaphors resonate like an auditory *catchphrase* that provides a client with a powerful way of remembering key concepts (such as the woman in the clinical case in Chapter 8 who found the phrase "Life makes me nervous" very helpful). Kinesthetic and tactile images are also possible. When these connections are made, the therapeutic alliance is strengthened as well. Consider this excerpt from the case of Ashley to see how a metaphor is used to help the client to take a different perspective on her behavior.

Therapist: "I can see that disturbed you (Ashley nods head yes slightly) but you see, while you think that you have organized things well, you really haven't."

Ashley: "What do you mean?"

Therapist: "Because *you* have to do all the work, and everybody else gets the reward. Let me ask, when something breaks or 'goes down' at the hospital, what happens?"

Ashley: "Well, there are backup systems."

Therapist: "Right, I assume backup power, backup data storage, and so on, right?"

Ashley: "Sure."

Therapist: "But in your office, do you have backup systems?"

Ashley: "Sure, for the computers and data . . ."

Therapist: "But there is one thing that doesn't have a backup . . ."

Ashley: "Me."

Therapist: "Yep. And what happens when you 'go down?' There is no backup. Who replaces you?"

Ashley: "No one right now, but they *could* replace me."

Therapist: "Is that what you are afraid of? That they'll replace you?"

Ashley: "Yeah, that's part of it."

Therapist: "And that is why you have to work harder than everybody else? Because you don't want to be cast aside, cast away?"

Ashley: (slowly) "Yeah . . ."

So the metaphor of a backup system and the lack of one (for her) allowed Ashley to be able to see how her behavior is not getting her what she wants out of her life. An important step in presenting a metaphor to the client is to verify that it is accurate and useful. This is typically accomplished when a client signifies this either verbally (e.g., by stating, "Wow! That is so right!") or viscerally (e.g., through recognition reflexes; see Chapter 2). Successful metaphors must make sense to clients and should provide additional insight about their schema. This introduces and invites clients to look at themselves from a different perspective. We present a clinical case example to illustrate this further.

Clinical Case Example: High-Powered Saleswoman

A successful single mother sought family counseling for her 12-year-old son, who was attending an exclusive private school and making B grades, which was unacceptable to the client. Her main complaint was "I am paying a fortune in tuition; I don't expect to get B minuses!" The client was herself an attractive, high-powered woman who was a successful advertising saleswoman for a major media outlet. She was highly self-motivated and concerned with being successful. This was clearly part of her motivation for therapy with her son and was part of her overall schema dynamics. She stated repeatedly that she did not want her son to become like his father (who she thought of as a loser because, although he was successful in his own right, he was not as driven as she was). In therapy, she was intense, often trying to dominate the conversation, and would become very defensive if the therapist might not agree with her. The therapist became aware of some countertransference feelings of irritation with the client.

In her childhood, the client strongly identified with her father, who was highly competitive, demanded perfection from his children, was frequently absent from her life, but was very successful. Her parents were divorced when she was 10.

The client was married in her early 20s after a brief courtship. Each of the spouses was successful by any objective measure, but when compared with her husband, she was slightly more successful. As this happened, she began to see her husband as "weak" and "lazy." This was augmented by the fact that he bought old homes, rehabilitated them, and then sold them at a profit. As a result, he did not have a "nine-to-five" job and often worked out of the family home. Tensions over such issues led to an eventual divorce when their only child, a son, was 5 years old. Although she took primary custody of her son, her ex-husband maintained a presence in her son's life. Following the divorce, the client had a series of relationships with men that did not last. She felt that the men she dated always seemed to "disappoint" her and couldn't meet her needs. For the most part, her son agreed but stated that there were some "cool" guys, adding, "Just like always, she would run them off." The client seemed embarrassed by this characterization and rebutted, "A lot of times, men find me too aggressive, and I frighten them off, when all I am trying to do is help them *improve* themselves."

Questions to Consider before Reading Further

1. How should the therapist deal with the countertransference feelings of irritation?
2. What are this client's basic schema dynamics (view of self, view of the world, and view of others)? How could these be translated into more personally useful statements (e.g., "I am . . . ," "Others are . . . ," and "The world is . . .")?
3. Are there any metaphors that come to mind that might be useful to describe to the client her particular schema dynamics how they might be helpful to her, and how they might be contributing to her problems in her life?

The therapist was aware of feelings of irritation that arose out of a sense of feeling dismissed by the client when he was working to help her. Such awareness proved to be useful in assessing the client's dynamics: She did not like having to ask for help (i.e., therapy), and she was reacting to feeling "one down" compared with the therapist. The therapist next drew connections between his experience of the client in the therapy (i.e., irritating and aggressive), the client's history (i.e., competitive and successful), and the current problem with her son (i.e., being too demanding and unrealistic). Given these factors, he surmised that she felt like she had to compete with the therapist. The common element between these relationships was her schema. In response, the therapist formulated the following: Her view of self is positive and unrealistic (based on her unbounded confidence in herself), and her view of others is negative and unrealistic (based on her history of relationships and how she was viewing her son's predicament and reacting to the therapist).

But what is the best way to present this to the client without risking a therapeutic rupture and premature termination? Relating to particularly difficult clients through the use of a metaphor can be very useful. In this case, the client provided an excellent metaphor for describing her schematic worldview. Although it was her ex-husband who did it for a living, the client boasted that she had also been investing in real estate on the side. Borrowing from the metaphor, the therapist told her that she seemed to treat people in her life like her real estate investments—find people who were in need of "rehabbing," invest a lot of her time and effort in them, and then "sell" them off better than they were (i.e., get rid of them before they could outdo her). The therapist explained that this is a profitable business strategy and a noble way to approach life, but there were three major flaws: (1) Her son was becoming a project, with his actions a reflection of his fear (and perhaps hers) that if he is successful, she would have to "sell" him off like everyone else; (2) she was so good at "fixing" people (via giving advice, telling people how they could improve, etc.) that it actually turned them off, which explained her sense of loneliness and lack of close friends; and (3) she was so good at being the "fixer" that she didn't know how to be the one needing care. This frequently led to neglecting her own needs and demanding that others meet them for her (i.e., her boyfriends and son). When these people were incapable of doing so, she would "cut her losses" and decide to either "gut" them completely (by tearing them down emotionally) or get rid of them fast.

In Chapter 6, we introduced the concept of two tuning forks—a metaphor—to describe how a client and therapist needed to be *in synch* (i.e., have a strong therapeutic alliance) in order for the therapy to be effective. A successful metaphor that describes a client's schema dynamics accomplishes this (e.g., "Gee, you really get what it is that I'm saying!"). In the example above, the dominant metaphor came from the client's life and activity (i.e., buying and renovating houses). It also served to express what she does in her relationships with other people, including her son. The boy may be fearful that if he is "too good," Mom might "sell him off"; but if he continues to be in need of "fixing up" (i.e., getting B grades), she might be forced to keep him around, even though she is unhappy with him. The metaphor allows a discussion of these issues in a nonthreatening way for either client, as well as a discussion with the therapist about how to address it (by either assimilation or accommodation). Last, metaphors provide client and therapist with a quick reference point for checking in on a client's progress (e.g., "Well I have met someone that I am dating, and I am not trying to do any refurbishing to him!").

Metaphor and Second-Order Change

Why do metaphors work? They work because they impact the client at the second-order level of change. Recall from the discussion above that second-order change refers to alterations that change the fundamental organization of the system. In helping the client to understand how their underlying schema functions and how it may be contributing to the problem, the client is encouraged to be more conscious of—and question—their underlying beliefs and assumptions about themselves, others, and the world, in other words, accommodation. It requires a level of commitment and readiness on the part of the client. In the example above, of the metaphor of the glass being half empty, once the client has a grasp of the meaning of the metaphor, he can chose to metaphorically plug the hole and begin to have a discussion about how the client can add water (i.e., make more positive choices, behavior changes, etc.). Second-order change is generally considered better than first-order change because it is structural and leads to more permanent solutions (Fraser & Solovey, 2007; Sperry et al., 2006).

In the example above of the woman and her son (the fix up metaphor), if the therapist took a linear approach and merely worked with the surface presenting concern (the son's grades) and tried to implement study skills to help boost the grades, but not work on the deeper relationship issues (which required an understanding of the mother's schema and the therapeutic use of a metaphor), then this would be an example of assimilation and first-order change (no change to the structure, rules, relationship, etc.). Second-order change, like accommodation, requires the individual to change the way they view and relate to themselves, others, or the world around them. It is a change in the rules that a person uses to construct the logic of their daily living, and the result of this logic is clearly noticeable and (usually) welcomed. Again, in the example above, the use of the metaphor allows the mother and son to discuss the impact of his maturity on their relationship, as well as give the client the ability to see how her behavior pushes people away from her. This is an example of accommodation or second-order change. As a result, metaphors are an important tool employed by nonlinear thinking, master therapists in effectively working with clients and their schematized worldview (i.e., what makes the client tick).

But Don't Take Our Word for It! Master Example

Consider how noted family therapist, Peggy Papp, works with a couple and uses metaphor to conceptualize their current situation and how they may be able to move past the current impasse (Alexander Street Press, 2012).

Peggy Papp: "Okay. Well, listen I was really impressed with your fantasies and, uh, I went out and thought about them for a few minutes and, uh, the thing that struck me was that you both saw her as a bird."

Husband: "Right."

Peggy Papp: "And, uh, you both saw him on the ground somehow, I mean, very, uh, uh, connected with the ground."

Wife: "Down to earth."

Peggy Papp: "And, um, since you have both said that, uh, you would like to change this pattern of missing each other we were thinking that, um, in order for you not to feel so responsible, and so burdened, so you know, weighted down with everything. What you would need to do would be to fly every now and then to learn to."

| Husband: | "Yeah, but when I flew and came back then I'm gonna have to straighten up everything when I come back, cuz' it'll be all disarrayed." |
| Peggy Papp: | "Well, not necessarily, you could learn to fly just a little bit and just kind of soar a little bit, and, uh, so it would be kind of nice. The thing that I was thinking that, uh, you would need to do in order to be more responsible, which you say, would be to yeah, come down to each more, and to be by his side." |

In the example above, Peggy Papp uses the metaphor of the bird flying to help both the husband and wife to visualize their problem in a different way. The metaphor also allows her to suggest a symbolic representation of a solution. Then the couple (and therapist) can discuss concrete ways to move from the metaphor that describes their present situation toward the new metaphor (solution). This kind of change is structural because it changes the way that each relates to the other one. They adjust their schema dynamics by becoming more flexible, which is an example of accommodation. It is also an example of second-order change, which is what most master practitioners aim for, and which produces lasting results (Fraser & Solovey, 2007).

Putting the Pieces of the Client's Story Together: The Formulation and Case Conceptualization

One of the signature characteristics of a master practitioner is the ability to assemble disparate pieces of a clinical puzzle (i.e., a client's complaint, behaviors, history, circumstances, ECRs, information about family of origin, etc.) into a cohesive understanding—a case conceptualization or case *formulation*. The formulation attempts to create a useful coherent narrative—a model—of why this person is here at this time and what kind of relief he or she seeks. Suggesting to a client what it is that he or she appears to be saying, how he or she appears to be thinking, and what he or she appears to be feeling in his narrative is a way of helping a client to make sense of his or her unique circumstances and the chaos that he or she often experiences. According to Sperry and Sperry (2012), "Case conceptualization is a method and clinical strategy for obtaining and organizing information about a client, understanding and explaining the clients situation and maladaptive patterns, guiding and focusing treatment, anticipating challenges, and roadblocks, and preparing for successful termination" (p. 4). Case conceptualizations include a diagnostic formulation, clinical formulation, and treatment formulation.

In Chapters 4 and 5, we discussed how assessment of the client's symptoms, diagnosis, strengths, resources, stage of change, and theme created the story of the client's problem. This is also called a *diagnostic formulation*. Persons (1989) suggested that formulations serve the purpose of sorting through a myriad of biopsychosocial assessment data and formulating a sense of the interconnectedness of relevant data. For purposes of the present text, the formulation is a brief, concise statement of understanding to a client regarding the source of self-generated suffering revealed in the complaint that led the client to therapy.

The next element of a case conceptualization is the *clinical formulation*. As we mentioned at the beginning of the chapter, if a diagnostic formulation is the story of the client's problem, the clinical formulation, which contains the client's background and history, and (most important) their schema dynamics (view of self, view of others, and view of the world). This individualizes the client's case formulation and connects the problem to the person (Sperry & Sperry, 2012). Such interconnectedness leads to developing a comprehensive treatment plan, often involving multidisciplinary practitioners—either on the treatment team or by other providers in the community. At the same time, however, the master practitioner is also resolutely mindful that a client's story has more to do with how a client interprets the "facts" of his or her story than the facts themselves.

Ultimately, a case conceptualization serves the necessary purpose of acting as a bridge between assessment data and a comprehensive treatment plan. Once the diagnostic and clinical formulations are created, the treatment plan or the story of the client's solution is created. This *treatment formulation* is the agreed upon course and map of how the client and therapist plan to make changes and help the client to improve. A client leaving therapy with a new and better perspective is very useful, calming, and reassuring. It can suggest, for example, that given the type of circumstances the client has described, his history and his makeup, anyone in similar circumstances would feel or behave similarly (see Sperry and Sperry, 2012 for a more thorough discussion of the creation of case conceptualization). Such a depiction of a client's dilemma is normalizing. For longer therapy, a formulation becomes the vehicle for the working-through process. Linear-thinking therapists may present the formulation in a very straightforward manner, whereas nonlinear-thinking therapists usually employ more creative ways to present case conceptualizations that increase the likelihood of a client engaging in therapy and successfully assimilating and/or accommodating his or her schema. The next few chapters discuss ways that the treatment formulation works with the client's emotional system and how to understand and resolve client ambivalence.

Information Box: Research Findings on Schemas

Tomorrow's practitioner must engage in treatment methodologies that are informed by research. The cognitive-behavioral therapy (CBT; i.e., using a variety of methods to help clients challenge their beliefs, assumptions, and schemas) movement has generated a substantial amount of empirical research demonstrating that therapy is effective in treating depression and anxiety. It has also been demonstrated to be as effective (in some cases) as psychopharmacology in the treatment of some forms of depression (Young, Beck, & Weinberger, 1993). At the same time, however, several authors have noted that cognitive-behavioral therapy has its limitations (e.g., Corey, 2005; Halford, Bernoth-Doolan, & Eadie, 2002; Young, 1990). Furthermore, several studies have reported attrition rates (clients who drop out of treatment) for CBT of 20% to 40% for depression and 0% to 50% for anxiety disorders (as cited in Halford et al., 2002). In addition, for those clients who make gains in treatment, nearly one half have a recurrence of depressive symptoms within 2 years (Gortner, Gollan, Dobson, & Jacobson, 1998). Curious about these findings, Young, an associate of Beck's, postulated that something deeper had to account for these treatment-resistant clients. He observed that these individuals frequently had "much more rigid cognitive structures; more chronic, often lifelong psychological problems; and more deeply entrenched, dysfunctional belief systems" (Kellogg & Young, 2006, p. 446). He began to explore the idea that schemas may hold the key for addressing these more difficult clients.

In point of fact, the emphasis on schemas in the psychotherapeutic literature has continued to grow since the 1980s. Many new approaches, particularly in the work of Johnson and Greenberg's (1985) emotion-focused therapy, Snyder's pluralistic approach (Snyder & Schneider, 2002), and Young's (1999) schema-focused therapy, ground themselves directly in concentrating on client schemas or indirectly by utilizing tenets of attachment theory. All of these authors, and others as well, have attested to the importance of understanding that what clients are thinking and recognizing patterns within their thinking are just as important as recognizing and understanding client behavior patterns.

Conclusion

A client's schemas give rise to affect—the emotions—that a client expresses. It is as if a client is saying, "I hold these beliefs, convictions, values, view of myself, the world, etc., and what I am now encountering in life threatens them. That provokes and fuels me to feel these emotions (i.e., anger, embarrassment, jealousy, depression, anxiety, etc.)—and that's what prompts me to come to therapy!" Encountering transient demands, threats, and challenges from the environment (i.e., others, life circumstances, or both) is part and parcel of what it is to be human; nevertheless, such life encounters are experienced as threatening, stressful, and irritating. Perceived demands and threats from the environment to rigidly held schema (e.g., confrontational interactions with others, overwhelming life circumstances, and extreme impasses) generate strong feelings, correspondingly strong emotional reactions, and impulses to action. More permanent such threats are experienced as intolerable and produce symptoms of anxiety, stress, depression, somatic complaints, insomnia, and so on. There is an inexorable relatedness and intimacy between cognitions and schemas and the emotions they generate. Hence, it is important to understand a client's schemas and his or her emotions as reciprocal partners. What are emotions? How do they specifically relate to schemas? How does a master practitioner deal with them in treatment? These and other questions are the subject to which we now turn our attention.

Notes

1. Upon feedback from a client, a therapist can ask how her client sees such a self-image affecting his behavior. As a follow-up, an inquiry can be made about how he might like his self-image to be.
2. One's explanatory style is highly reflective of an underlying core schema.
3. *Sibling position* rather than *birth order* is a better term because absolute birth order is not as clinically revealing as the term sibling position. Birth order simply refers to an ordinal ranking—who was born first, second, third, and so on, devoid of other meaningful information. Absolute birth order, however, does not reveal the entire story. As a simple example, it is one thing to be born into one's family as the youngest of four same-sex siblings who are far apart in age, and it is entirely another thing to be born as the fourth sibling and only boy—especially when the children are close in age and the parents desperately wanted a son. Because such an individual's arrival on this earth is a prized event and he is greatly loved and admired by all family members, it is quite likely to affect his personality development (and that of his siblings), perhaps by being spoiled by his mother and older sisters.
4. Many therapists observe the experience that over the course of successful therapy, a client's ECRs change. At times, recollected events become less threatening and more temporized. At other times, a client becomes more competent, with a greater sense of social connectedness in the re-recollected memory.
5. EM is the term Watkins (1992) used to refer to early childhood memories.
6. *Metaphor* is in actuality an umbrella term that incorporates the use of multiple levels of communication and includes such communications as the use of analogy, puns, jokes, and folk language.
7. We hypothesize that *images* are powerful nonlinear, right-brained media that represent how the brain processes a good deal of emotional information. See Pinker (1999).
8. Note that this proposed list of potential sources for metaphors is not considered exhaustive but rather suggestive. Furthermore, the most powerful source of metaphor is the creative capacity of the therapist.

10

The Domain of Addressing and Managing Clients' Emotional States
Basic Understandings

Introduction: *Good Will Hunting* and Emotions

Good Will Hunting (Van Sant, 1997) is an Academy Award–winning film about a brilliant young man (Will Hunting, portrayed by Matt Damon) who is unable to handle his emotions, despite his intellectual gifts. Unbelievably talented in mathematics and bestowed with a photographic memory, Will experienced horrible childhood physical abuse at the hands of his father and other foster parents. As a result, under the surface of an easygoing manner (and despite his intellect), he has a seething rage that explodes several times in the film and leads him into trouble with the law. In addition, he is unable to form close, meaningful relationships with people other than his small group of friends (including Ben Affleck) who seem to be going nowhere in life. Will works as a janitor at MIT and lives a somewhat aimless, beer-soaked, working-class life in South Boston, seemingly wasting his immense gift for complex, theoretical math.

While mopping the corridor outside of a major lecture hall at MIT, Will anonymously solves a math problem placed on the hallway chalkboard by a famous math professor as a challenge to the students in his class. When no one takes credit for having solved the problem, the professor places yet another more challenging problem on the board that Will again solves with unbelievable ease—this time he is caught solving the problem but escapes. After yet another encounter with the criminal justice system, Will finds himself in jail. By this time, the professor has tracked him down and spoken to the judge about Will's rare giftedness. The judge agrees to release Will under two conditions: He is to be subject to the professor's supervision, and he is to undergo psychotherapy.

The first two attempts to find a therapist for Will by the professor (who is also working out some issues relative to his fame as a mathematician) are abortive disasters. In fact, Will has fun using his intellect in mocking the entire therapeutic process. Of course, this is also a defense against having to deal with his complex, confusing, and painful emotions. His third encounter is with Dr. Sean McGuire, a psychologist played by Robin Williams. His performance is a powerful portrayal of a therapeutic relationship with an aggressive and apparently angry young man who does not want to be in therapy. But not even he is immune to being pushed by Will's crushing sarcastic intellect—Sean nearly chokes Will during a powerful emotional exchange in their first session.[1] This emotional explosion forces Sean to recognize that Will's intellectual talents, his provocation of others, and his explosive temper are all linked in a pattern. There are attempts to keep others at arm's length to avoid getting close to other people and avoid potentially being hurt by them. When Sean confronts Will about this, they slowly move forward and negotiate a powerful therapeutic alliance based on acceptance, trust, and mutual respect.

At the same time, Will's charming nonconformity is a magnet to Skylar, an upstanding (and orphaned) medical student portrayed by Minnie Driver, who provides Will with another challenge—managing his affection for her. He is powerfully attracted to her and, at the same time, is afraid of their closeness. As they become closer, she attempts to learn more about his past. When she notices his many scars and cigarette burns, he lashes out verbally at her and attempts to push her away. However, he is successful only to find out that, when she is gone, he truly wants to be with her. Through his relationship with Sean, he begins to understand his own reactions and the emotions that make him tick. Ultimately, he decides to take a risk and follow after the woman he loves to California, leaving the comfort of his familiar Boston home, friends, and going-nowhere life, although he has no guarantee that she will take him back and forgive him (the ultimate in being vulnerable to someone else).

But What Are Emotions?

Think about yourself right now. How are you feeling? Are you aware of any particular emotional feeling? Maybe you are fondly recalling the movie *Good Will Hunting* after reading the description of it above? Maybe you had an argument with someone before picking up this book? Or perhaps you really want to do something else, but you know you have to get through this chapter before a class? All of these situations, and a plethora of others, will produce some emotional reaction in you. It may be strong or mild, but emotions are a potent aspect of our lives. Emotional reactions can override our basic desires. For example, if a person is starving, but the food is rotten, the feeling of disgust will override the hunger drive. Or the seemingly all-powerful *will to live* can be overridden either by someone who is extremely depressed and suicidal, or by someone willing to endanger themselves to save someone else in an emergency. So emotions are powerful, but what *are* they?

For many scholars, it is believed that emotions serve the purpose of motivating a person into action, as well as to clearly communicate to other people what our intentions are. They have distinctive cognitive, psychological, neurological, and behavioral elements to them. However, a thorough and exhaustive definition of emotions would take up this entire book. Perhaps no other aspect of human existence has been given as much time and attention as emotions. We provide some brief guidance about emotions, borrowing from the work of Paul Ekman, a renowned researcher in the area of emotion. According to Ekman (2003), emotions have certain common defining characteristics. These include:

1. A feeling or set or sensations that a person is consciously aware.
2. Emotions can be brief (lasting a few seconds) or longer.
3. Emotions are about something that matters to the person.
4. Emotions result in an appraisal process that is automatic and reflect things in the environment that are important to the individual.
5. A person becomes aware of an emotion once the initial appraisal process is finished. Once aware, reappraisal can occur that includes conscious retrieval of memories, which can amplify or soothe the emotional reaction.
6. Emotional reactions have universal themes that reflect human evolutionary history, as well as cultural variations, which impact an individual experience of emotions.
7. "The desire to experience, or not experience an emotion motivates much of our behavior." (Ekman, 2003, p. 216)

Emotions are the fuel that powers behavior and changes in behavior. In clinical practice, however, emotions are only just beginning to reemerge as an area of significant focus. This has been partly due to the emphasis of cognitive and behavioral approaches that have been dominant for the last four decades. It has also been due to misunderstanding or misperceptions about emotions that many clinicians carry with them. Last, it may also be due to the fact that many clinicians feel uneasy with strong emotions or ill-equipped to deal with client emotions (Schwartz & Johnson, 2000; Sperry, Carlson, & Peluso 2006). Viewing emotions like this (and effectively removing from clinical practice) is like refusing to put gasoline in the car because it is flammable, and still expecting the car to drive. Although it will be very safe, it won't be very useful. The same is true for therapy. In the next two chapters, we present some linear and nonlinear approaches to understand and work with client emotions. In addition, we present some of the more modern approaches that have embraced emotion as a major focus of therapy. But first, we discuss some of the lingering misperceptions of emotion that clinicians may have.

Lingering Misperceptions of Emotions

Emotions Are Weak, Feminine, and to Be Feared

Emotions are often contrasted with intellect. Whereas intellect is stereotypically seen as calm, rational, and civilized, emotions are seen as wild, irrational, and uncontrollable. Paradoxically, at the same time, emotionality has been seen traditionally as something weak, childlike, and feminine (e.g., the 19th-century diagnosis of hysteria). Intellect is chauvinistically seen as the domain of rational, strong-minded men, whereas emotionality is seen as the domain of weepy, indecisive women in need of rescue. Thus, the emotions, and their expression, are often seen (by both men and women) as something to be feared or avoided—a form of weakness. The reality is that human emotions are often puzzling and demanding. But experiencing, understanding, and using the full range of emotions (both good and bad) are crucial to our survival as a species. They are essential to our ability to form relationships with others and necessary in order to lead a fulfilling life. According to Greenberg and Paivio (1997),

> Emotions provide a rich source of information about our reactions to situations. Emotions, or more accurately those constituents of emotions that may have been out of awareness, can be brought into awareness to enhance the way in which we evaluate our needs, desires, goals, and concerns. What is required, particularly in therapy, is an understanding of what emotions indicate to us about the way in which we are conducting our lives. (p. 4)

Catharsis of Emotion as Sufficient for Change

The idea of ridding one's system of emotions stems (in part) from the idea of *catharsis*, a Greek term meaning "to purge" or purify. It was used by Aristotle to describe a release from emotions such as fear and pity that might be evoked when watching a tragic play.[2] In early psychoanalysis (and subsequent systems of psychotherapy), it referred to the release and sense of relief that clients felt as a result of the expression of strong emotion previously repressed or suppressed. Although in some cases this might be true, when taken to its linear extreme (e.g., "Well, if some catharsis is good, a lot of catharsis will be really good!"), catharsis for its own sake can be misguided. Such misapplication of this principle led to dangerous abuses, particularly when therapists did not know how to place the emotional expressions into context. That is, therapists did not know how to help clients see how emotional states and expressions either fit with schema dynamics or offered a way or impetus to change their schematized views of self, others, and life and the world. Without such therapeutic guidance (via the therapeutic alliance), however, the connection between emotional expression and one's schematized worldview, clients are likely to feel tremendously vulnerable or (re)victimized by the experience. According to Yalom (1995), catharsis without insight is not helpful, and insight without catharsis is equally unhelpful: "We must experience something strongly, but we must also, through the faculty of reason, understand the implications of that emotional experience" (p. 28). In other words, it requires linear and nonlinear approaches.

In fact, there are sad examples of various once-fashionable approaches (and theorists) that attempted to work in a linear way on either cognitions or emotions while ignoring the other. Psychotherapy researchers such as Norcross, Koocher, and Garofalo (2006) have cautioned all clinicians against working on merely the affective domain because such one-sided efforts (e.g., abuses of primal scream therapy and the EST movement) are to the detriment of the client's welfare. Some of the damage inflicted on clients was due to poorly trained therapists using gimmicks or techniques that fail to consider emotions, emotional expression, and their true functions within the context of a broader understanding of human functioning and problem solving (Norcross & Wampold, 2011). Other damage to clients stems from the misguided notion that feeling strong emotions (that were often stifled or repressed) by a client is sufficient to produce change.[3] We discuss productive and effective ways to help clients understand, feel, and process therapeutic emotions in Chapter 11.

Emotions Are to Be Avoided, Contained, and Neutralized in Treatment

There is a theme inherent in the story of *Good Will Hunting* that is common in classical fiction. That theme concerns the protagonist, a successful and powerfully intellectual character who also has a beastly dark side of emotional turmoil. *Dr. Jekyll and Mr. Hyde* and *The Incredible Hulk* are but two popular examples of a character such as Will, a rare mathematical genius capable of an unbridled expression of emotions that can be overwhelming and uncomfortable. The implication is that intellect is rational and should be valued, whereas emotions are unpredictable and should be avoided.

Greenberg and Paivio (1997) and others (e.g., Nathanson, 1996; Plutchik, 2000; Schwartz & Johnson, 2000) noted that psychotherapists overwhelmingly tend to shy away from understanding both emotions and the information that they contain. They act as if emotions either do not exist or are something that must be dominated and controlled by reason. Many psychotherapists are taught cutting-edge theories with very effective methods of dealing with the cognitive aspects of a client's concerns (viz., automatic negative thoughts, discussed in Chapter 8; see Kirsch & Lynn, 1999). Unfortunately, overreliance on these methods tend to diminish the impact and role of emotions. Therapists taught such approaches that are often awkward and even inept with client discussions of feelings and expressions of powerful emotions. According to Plutchik, therapy conducted without a fundamental and thorough understanding of emotions is limited and often ineffective. Consistent with the theme expressed throughout this text, dominating and controlling emotions, or outright ignoring them as something unpleasant or disruptive to treatment, reflect extremely linear thinking.

Thus, the purpose of working with a client's emotions is to help him understand a given reaction (i.e., emotional expression) that is either: (1) out of the ordinary for a client, (2) not understood, or (3) out of a client's control. To do this effectively, a nonlinear-thinking therapist is obliged to reflect about and understand (1) a client's schema dynamics and (2) the function of and relationship between a client's emotional states, internal feelings, and experiences of those emotional states and their expression. We discuss these in detail, beginning with basic definitions.

Understanding and Differentiating: Expressions of Affect, Internal Feelings, Emotional States and Moods, Primary Emotions, Secondary Emotions, and Background Emotions

Expressions of affect, internal feelings, and emotional states (i.e., moods) can be as difficult to distinguish, describe, and make use of as they are to work with. Each is a distinct term, however, and each has a part to play in understanding a client's overall emotional experience of his or her life. In this section, we define each of these elements (i.e., expressions of affect, internal feelings, and emotional states or mood). We also discuss moderating and mediating influences on each (i.e., the appraisal process and schematized views) and conclude with a discussion of the difficulty in communication and translation of all these elements for clients, and how this becomes an important clinical issue deserving of attention. We begin by working backward—discussing emotional expressions that are observable by others.

Expressions of Affect

A person's *affect* is composed of a variety of internal (e.g., thoughts, memories, and reflections) and external (e.g., posture, facial expressions, body movements, and voice) expressions making up a person's emotional response. According to Othmer and Othmer (1989),

> Affect is the visible and audible manifestation of the patient's emotional response to outside and inside events, i.e., thoughts, ideas, evoked memories, reflections, and performance. It is expressed in posture, facial and body movements, and in tone of voice, vocalizations, and word selection. (p. 124; see also Othmer & Othmer, 1994)

In other words, expressions of affect are the more readily observable indicators of internal feeling states being described by a client. Thus, affect can be considered the end product of a person's experience of having an emotion. It represents the particular configuration in which an emotion in a particular person makes itself known at a particular time.

Expressions of affect are readily observable and detectable through linear and nonlinear listening and observing for congruence, absence, and inference via facial expressions, voice qualities (e.g., tone and pitch), and content of conversation. Such outward expressions signify that someone is experiencing—that is, something is going on inside an individual that he or she is not necessarily expressing in a linear manner. However, a challenge for clinicians is to be able to de-code the expression of affect to be able to accurately classify what the client is conveying. Understanding the universal signals or displays of emotion are an important first step that all clinicians should familiarize themselves with (see Ekman, 2003 or Ekman & Friesen, 1975, for a thorough review of the facial displays of emotions). Subtle or blatantly overt expressions of affect are the equivalent of clues that reveal a client's internal feeling states, but they must be examined, not assumed.

Internal Feelings

In their essence, feelings are sensations based upon what human senses (i.e., visual, auditory, tactile, gustatory, and olfactory are the five basic sensations) perceive that can be described as either pleasant or unpleasant in nature. In a landmark work still referenced today, Arnold (1960) described feelings in the language of everyday life as revealed by such expressions as "I feel cold." Everyday language also reveals expressions such as "I feel that I'm right!" To paraphrase Arnold, such expressions suggest that the speaker has reached a conclusion or decision that is correct, although he or she may not necessarily be able to prove it or describe the elements that led to that conclusion. Other expressions such as "I feel angry" are descriptions and statements of direct emotional experiences. Arnold succinctly summarized the complex topic of feelings as follows:

> If feeling is used to indicate awareness of some bodily or psychological state which I experience directly, that state itself can be felt as either pleasant or unpleasant. If it is neither, it will be reported as indifferent. In every case pleasantness and unpleasantness refer to the way in which this state is felt: how it feels to have a sensation or an emotion, to make a deliberate effort, or to engage in psychological or physical activity. (pp. 20–21)

In other words, when we experience an emotion whether we recognize it or not, we feel it. Through our consciousness, feelings are the vehicle by which emotions are experienced.[4] Clinically, listening acutely to the verbal expressions that clients use to describe what it is that they are feeling is critical to understanding what they are trying to tell us—it is information. Consider the following few client expressions of sensations they are experiencing to describe various emotions:

> "It's a heavy, heavy sensation in my chest that won't go away" to describe feeling the emotion of sadness.
> "I get a warm feeling—sort of a glow—throughout my body every time I'm with him" to describe feeling the emotion of infatuation.
> "My blood runs cold whenever I have to deal with that man" to describe feeling the emotion of intense fear.
> "I felt ill—sweaty, clammy, headachy—it's like I tried to scream and I couldn't. I gasped, like not enough air in my lungs" to describe feeling the emotion of intense anxiety.

To review, in the chain of human emotional experiences being described, expressions of affect (i.e., emotion) are the external manifestations of what is going on inside, and internal feelings are the elemental, sensory-based means by which we consciously experience emotions. The extent of the physical sensations can also tell the clinician something about the relative strength of emotion, from a vague nagging sensation to a pit in the stomach. Both pieces of information, the client's expressions of affect and the experience of internal feelings, helps the clinician to come to the more multifaceted and central element: emotional states.

Emotional States

The consensus among many theorists is that emotions explicitly serve two biological or evolutionary functions (Damasio, 1999; Ekman, 2003; Greenberg & Paivio, 1997; Plutchik, 2000). The primary biological function that the emotions serve is to produce biochemical and neural responses for a particular reaction to an event that stimulated the emotion. For example, emotions produce the appropriate physiological changes and reactions[5] necessary to flee, fight aggressively, make passionate love, withdraw, and so on. The second biological function that the emotions serve is to regulate specific internal physiological states so that an individual can be prepared for the specific reaction required. Damasio (1999) has put it this way:

> [T]he biological "purpose" of the emotions is clear, and emotions are not a dispensable luxury. Emotions are . . . part and parcel of the machinery with which organisms regulate survival . . . a fairly high-level component of the mechanisms of life regulation . . . sandwiched between the basic survival kit (e.g., regulation of metabolism; simple reflexes; motivations; biology of pain and pleasure) and the devices of high reason, but still very much a part of the hierarchy of life-regulation devices. . . . And as a result of powerful learning mechanisms such as conditioning, emotions of all shades eventually help connect homeostatic regulation and survival "values" to numerous events and objects in our autobiographical experience. Emotions are inseparable from the idea of reward or punishment, of pleasure or pain, of approach or withdrawal, of personal advantage and disadvantage. Inevitably, emotions are inseparable from the idea of good and evil. (pp. 54–55)

Damasio was essentially describing the interface between the realms of cognitive schemas and emotions. In fact, emotional reactions and expressions are inextricably tied to a person's schema dynamics (we discuss this later). Fundamentally, emotions serve human beings as survival mechanisms. The primitive survival mechanisms that Damasio referred to can be seen as those emotions of our primitive ancestors that signaled whether objects they perceived in their environment were something to be eaten or something that wished to eat them. The contemporary counterpart of survival mechanisms can be seen in the emotions brought about by the complexities of modern social living. Although we may not live in life-threatening situations on a daily basis like our ancestors did, we do face a dizzying array of complex social and emotional situations that can put a heavy burden on a person. As a result, there are several levels of emotional states that have been identified. Briefly these are: primary emotions, secondary emotions, and background emotions or mood. We discuss each below.

Primary Emotions

We referenced Ekman previously in this chapter and his landmark research on an understanding of human emotions (Ekman, 2003; Ekman & Friesen, 1975; Ekman et al., 1983). Among his major contributions was his discovery that, regardless of whether a person is from a primitive culture or a modern culture, there are commonly recognized, primary, universal, cross-culturally validated emotions. These are happiness, sadness, fear, anger, surprise, contempt, and disgust. By studying facial muscles, Ekman et al. (1983) found emotion-specific autonomic nervous system activity that not only differentiated positive emotions from negative emotions but also differentiated among the negative emotions. Cross-cultural universality suggests that there is a common neural architecture mediating emotional responses that are shared by all human beings.

According to Ekman (2003), each of these emotions have signals (some display of affect, usually on the face), physiology (internal feeling state), a trigger-theme (schema dynamic), and then likely actions (behavioral choices). For example, suppose you are at work and your boss comes in and (wrongfully) accuses you of stealing a laptop computer. You would likely feel surprised and angry. Your upper brow might raise up, your eyebrows crinkle together, and your mouth opens up (signals or display of affect). You might begin to feel a flushing sensation in your cheeks or a tensing in your body (physiology or internal feeling state), and you might begin to protest that you would never do something like that because you feel strongly that stealing is wrong, and the accusation is unjust (trigger-theme or schema dynamic). What comes next, however, may be the most interesting thing (behavioral choice or likely action). Some people might begin to argue passionately with the supervisor, whereas others may become very focused and find the evidence that proves their innocence. Another person may jump up and quit on the spot because of the insult, whereas still another person may begin to cry inconsolably because they fear that they won't be taken seriously or fairly when they profess their innocence. So although the same emotion may be triggered, the responses that different people have is where the real clinical work can begin.

Secondary Emotions

In addition to primary emotions that are universal, there are emotions that are not universally expressed or experienced (Ekman, 2003). Damasio (1999) proposed the term *secondary emotions* to describe embarrassment, jealousy, guilt, shame, and pride. Obviously, such emotions have somewhat of a social quality to them in that being embarrassed suggests discomfort in front of others, jealousy suggests covetousness toward others, and so on. In addition, many of the secondary emotions have different rules of display based on different cultures (see Contextually Cultural Box: Cultural Sensitivity, Diversity, and the Secondary Emotions). These do not have obvious signals or expressions of affect to them (especially the ones that a person tries to conceal like shame or jealousy). Today's survival mechanisms can be seen as those secondary emotions stimulated by perceived threats to self-esteem, the need to save face or maintain a sense of superiority, feelings of belonging, and so on.

Precisely what each individual interprets as a challenge or threat today is brought about by values, that is, what someone deems worthwhile as good or bad. According to Pinker (1999),

> Goals and values are one of the vocabularies in which we mentally couch our experiences. They cannot be built out of simpler concepts from our physical knowledge the way "momentum" can be built out of mass and velocity or "power" can be built out of energy. They are primitive or irreducible, and high-level concepts are defined in terms of them. (p. 315)

As discussed in Chapters 8 and 9, values that arise from schemas are unconsciously (i.e., unknowingly or primitively) held by an individual, and spontaneously give rise automatically and intuitively to emotions. As addressed in the "Our Nonlinear Brain" section of Chapter 9, whereas the amygdala appears to be the sentinel that contains information about what is threatening to an individual (i.e., his or her values and things held to be important), the emotions are its messengers, calling forth the appropriate response for maintaining the survival of the individual's personality (i.e., schema dynamics). As such, among their other properties, emotions are informative in nature (Greenberg, 2004). If attended to, sorted out, and interpreted well, they inform us of important values, beliefs, positions, etc. that we harbor, some of which may be nonnegotiable in nature. We emphasize that human beings have emotional reactions to those things in life that have meaning (i.e., value to us).

Contextually Cultural Box: Cultural Sensitivity, Diversity, and the Secondary Emotions

The secondary emotions having a social quality suggests the necessity for clinicians to take into account a client's cultural background in order to understand his or her emotional reactions. As Krauss (2006) has stated, "Culture is a transporter of value and meaning whether good or bad" (p. 2).

In turn, cultures differ widely in values and meanings. Thus, what might produce embarrassment in one culture might not be embarrassing in another, even though there may be an overlapping of circumstances that prompt embarrassment (Ekman, 2003). Certain values in one culture (e.g., arranged marriage, in which parents of the bride and groom select mates for their children) may produce extreme emotional reactions to the point of suicide in one of the betrothed, whereas in another culture an arranged marriage is not even remotely taken into consideration when thinking about or planning to get married.

Such considerations essentially require clinicians to be culturally sensitive. What precisely is cultural sensitivity? In the broadest sense, we propose that cultural sensitivity has at least three meanings. The first meaning refers to a clinician's specific knowledge base of the particular culture from which a client comes. Such knowledge disposes a clinician to be particularly responsive to issues for one client that might not be as relevant or might even be irrelevant for another client.

The second meaning of culturally sensitivity refers to differences between macro and micro issues. Macro sensitivities are differences in culture highlighted between the client's and clinician's backgrounds. A therapist must acknowledge such differences so that they are minimally influential in therapist decision making about interventions. Would this intervention be personally offensive in some manner and not interpreted according to the therapist's cultural norms? Such macro issues are large, are obvious, and speak for themselves. For example, a therapist trained at the doctoral level living a fairly affluent lifestyle cannot interpret psychological behaviors according to his or her cultural environment when working with impoverished immigrant clients living in a homeless shelter suffering from posttraumatic stress encountered in their war-torn country of origin. The micro issues are much more subtle, as suggested, for example, by a clinician with a Midwestern cultural background and values versus someone from the deep South or perhaps the West coast. A clinician sharing a similar micro background with a client still might have different values as expressed in one being a first-generation American and another being a fourth-generation American. Likewise, whereas individuals from the same country of origin may share many values, they may differ considerably regarding religious beliefs, issues of sin and guilt, and so on. Therapists' alertness to every client's unique background is a form of cultural sensitivity.

The third meaning of cultural sensitivity proposed is that reflected by master clinicians who are constantly alert to those influences from a particular client's background that possibly may affect why it is that a client believes and correspondingly feels the way he does about an issue. Such cultural sensitivity is seen as a subset of a clinician's general capacity to listen in a nonlinear manner for the possible meanings that clients attribute to circumstances and the feelings and emotions that are generated by those meanings.

As an example, we cite a case whose derivation is unknown. A well-educated, successful professional woman consulted a therapist reporting that she felt someone had placed a curse upon her. Originally from Haiti, she had not lived on the island for years. Nevertheless, the extent of her emotional reaction to the belief that a curse or spell had been placed upon her was profound—she was convinced that she would die if the curse was not removed! Linear thinking might prompt a clinician to regard the woman as paranoid, perhaps decompensating, and requiring psychotropic medications and psychotherapy. Nonlinear thinking suggests otherwise. Evaluating the woman's profound belief in the curse and the emotions it produced, the therapist helped the woman to locate a shaman from Haiti who lived in a part of the city with a large component of Haitian refugees. An appropriate spell to neutralize the curse she believed had been inflicted upon her by nefarious others promptly produced full and total symptom remission for the woman.

As Krauss (2006) has indicated, "Nature alone does not determine human actions nor fully circumscribe human behavior; culture is their managing director" (p. 1).

Background Emotions or Mood

Damasio (1999) also added a third category of emotions that he referred to as "background emotions" (p. 51), which for practical purposes can be considered a person's mood. Although not ordinarily considered in a discussion of emotions, the concept and label *background emotions* or mood, are of particular relevance to clinicians at all levels and require them to develop and refine the acute skills of linear and nonlinear observing and attending that we have described in Chapter 2. Othmer and Othmer (1989) defined *mood* as a "long term feeling state through which we filter all experiences" (p. 128).

Nonlinear listening to, observing, and attending to what a client is divulging about her emotional state serve as extremely valuable sources of information for clinicians. Damasio (1999) described background emotions as follows:

When we sense that a person is "tense" or "edgy," "discouraged" or "enthusiastic," "down" or "cheerful," without a single word having been spoken to translate any of those possible states, we are detecting background emotions. We detect background emotions by subtle details of body posture, speed and contour of movements, minimal changes in the amount and speed of eye movement, and in the degree of contraction of facial muscles. (p. 52)

Othmer and Othmer (1989) suggested that mood has five dimensions: quality, stability, reactivity, intensity, and duration. They suggested that perhaps the best way of understanding the *quality* of a mood is by relating it to a theme that permeates an individual's functioning. The seven themes outlined in Chapter 5 were built around a client's particular mood (e.g., themes of desperation, hopelessness, or sadness). The nonlinear-thinking clinician understands how such themes and their emotional accompaniments impact a client's internal feelings and affective expressions. As we discuss below, themes and their emotions and feelings relate to a client's schema dynamics. *Stability* refers to how lingering and steady a client's feelings are or, conversely, how unstable she may feel (e.g., up one minute and down the next). *Reactivity* refers to whether or not an individual's feelings respond to appropriate changes in the social environment. That is, does a client's mood perk up when he or she is shown attention, or does his or her mood remain down no matter whom it is that may be attempting to interact with her? *Intensity* of affect refers to the degree to which someone is experiencing particular feelings—in panic disorders, feelings experienced are described as intense, and likewise for someone who is high (i.e., manic). In contrast, schizophrenic clients are typically described as having a flat or shallow mood. The final quality of a mood that Othmer and Othmer (1989) described is *duration*—whether it is of short or long duration: "Dysphoria lasting hours or days is seen in personality disorders, sociopathy, alcoholism, and drug abuse, while depressive mood of affective disorder last two weeks or longer. The same is true for elated mood" (pp. 131–132).

The role of background emotions in our lives and especially in the lives of clients who consult us is important to understand. As suggested immediately above, understanding such background emotions and moods helps clinicians to discern differences between those emotionally acute crisis situations for which individuals consult therapists and those lingering and longer term emotional states with which some people live chronically almost as a way of life. Thus, a client might seek consultation for contextual issues (e.g., working long hours of necessity, the stress of raising children, feeling overwhelmed by medical problems, or fatigue) that generate strong emotions, both of which might be addressed via clinical interventions such as teaching a client self-hypnosis, meditation, or other relaxation techniques. Just as primary or secondary emotions are most often signals to a clinician that schema dynamics are at work, likewise background emotions of long duration can also reveal that schema dynamics are at work.

Indeed, background emotions seem especially to operate closely with a client's overall schema dynamics (positive or negative), which is discussed later in this chapter. Generally, a client's emotional state represents three essential elements in a person's life: the universal survival mechanisms of all human beings (primary emotions); information about the complex societal rules and values that either clarify or regulate the client's internal feelings and affective expressions (secondary emotions); and, last, information that is unique to the individual's views of self, others, and the world (background emotions). It should be clear by now that therapists who ignore or downplay a client's emotions (expressions, feelings, and states) are missing valuable clinical information.

Clinical Case Example: Chronic Low-Grade Depression

We reprint the case from Chapters 5 and 8 of a widow in her 60s with a long history of intermittent treatment. Recall that her presenting concern was that she has struggled with chronic depression her entire adult life. She furthermore described herself as "supersensitive," angry, chronically annoyed, and wanting to stay in bed although she forces herself to go to work. In reviewing her history, she felt criticized by her parents, who had high expectations but showed little demonstrable love, affection, and positive reinforcement (especially when compared with what she believed her siblings received). She also described her failure to thrive over the years (i.e., her depressive symptoms, chronic job dissatisfaction, few friends, etc.) as being due to the many years of deprivations and hardships in her family of origin.

Growing up in her family, she was presented with a set of standards that she believed was too high for her to reach. In addition, the little physical affection, warmth, or other demonstrations of love and affection she received from her family were too sparse to encourage efforts for her to even attempt to excel at anything, which added to a negative view of self (i.e., as someone not worthy of being loved). The essence of these experiences was "I am ordinary," "I am not (able to be) successful," or "My only claim to fame is to be critical, irascible, outspoken—that's who I am." In terms of her schema dynamics, she had a negative and unrealistic view of self. It was unrealistic because it was pervasive, and she was not able to see any of her positive attributes or accomplishments (e.g., she had a successful marriage, maintained steady albeit constantly changing employment, helped others less fortunate than herself, and engaged in volunteer community activities) as sufficient to warrant a self-view of "I'm okay—not perfect, but okay."

Questions

1. Describe the client's expressions of affect.
2. What internal feelings does the client appear to be struggling with?
3. How would you describe the client's emotional state?
4. What kind of emotions are present? Primary, secondary, or background?

Emotions, Mood, and Affect

As a helpful clinical suggestion, Othmer and Othmer (1989) distinguished clients' expressions of affect and their emotional states and mood according to four criteria:

1. The first criterion is that affect is more fleeting and shifting than mood, which can last for months and even years. Some clinicians equate affect to weather (which can change daily) and mood to climate (which remains relatively stable over time).
2. The second criterion is that emotions are reactive. That is, they are produced in response to internal stimuli (e.g., what someone is thinking about can produce a certain emotion) or external stimuli (e.g., a reaction to what someone encounters), whereas a mood state can change spontaneously.
3. The third criterion they proposed is that affect maintains the "foreground" of experience, whereas mood is the emotional "background" (Othmer & Othmer, 1989, p. 125).
4. Finally, Othmer and Othmer (1989) suggested that it is a practitioner who observes signs of affect, whereas a disturbed mood is typically reported by a client.

The point to listening (both linearly and nonlinearly) in order to recognize and understand what emotions a client is feeling is to convey that understanding to the client. As described in Chapters 2 and 3, by summarizing, paraphrasing, and reflecting back to a client an understanding of his or her feeling experience, a practitioner establishes and begins to solidify a fundamental requirement (i.e., the therapeutic relationship and alliance) for further therapeutic work.

Expressions of affect are the only part of the system that is visible to others. As noted earlier, as the amygdala (as well as other brain structures) generates a fundamental emotional state or states, it biochemically generates or stimulates appropriate feelings that, in turn, generate (direct or indirect) expressions of affect. It is important to note that this system can become disrupted because of the powerful, extremely fast, and automatic nature of emotions and the way the brain is wired to generate emotions. That is, clients can and do act out without being able to recognize their internal feelings (e.g., "I just snapped"), let alone the emotions generating those feelings. Clients can also have feelings without having an understanding of their emotional states or the reasons for feeling the way they do (e.g., having an upset stomach but not relating it to being anxious about something). It is an important therapeutic task to reconnect these elements of a client's emotional system. A client can then develop some awareness of how the components of the emotional system work and fit together to influence a behavior. Three other elements impact the emotional system, namely, the primary appraisal process, schema dynamics, and the secondary appraisal process. We discuss each of these elements below.

The Appraisal Process

Appraisal is a key component to understanding individual differences and emotions. Richard Lazarus (an early champion of appraisal) noted that emotions "involve appraisals of the environment and the individual's relationships with others and his or her attempts at coping with them" (quoted in Plutchik, 2000, p. 56). Just as with an appraisal of a house or a diamond ring that establishes its monetary value or worth, appraisals of people, the environment, and events in the environment are judgments involving personal value or worth. It is essential to reiterate that although we typically associate the term environment with our social surroundings, it may also pertain to our internal workings as well. For example, if a person receives bad news about his health and becomes frightened, and scans how he is feeling, he is basically appraising his internal environment. Thus, our emotional appraisals and scanning not only search our external environment but also alert us to our internal environment for signs of threat. In general, emotional appraisal is the automatic process by which a person assesses whether other person(s), an event, or the environment (1) poses a threat (physical, social, psychological, etc.) or (2) will help an individual meet his or her needs or achieve his or her goals. Again, Arnold (1960) has put it well:

> As soon as we appraise something as worth having in an immediate and intuitive way, we feel an attraction toward it. As soon as we intuitively judge that something is threatening, we feel repelled from it, we feel urged to avoid it. The intuitive appraisal of the situation initiates an action tendency that is felt as emotion, expressed in various bodily changes, and that eventually may lead to overt action. (p. 177)

In other words, Arnold is spelling out the relationship between the appraisal process, schema dynamics, affective expressions, feelings, and emotions. Correspondingly, appraisal has two components, primary and secondary.

Primary Appraisals and Assessment of Threats and Benefits

Primary appraisal is an evaluation of the environment or the events in the environment that individuals deal with in terms of whether these represent immediate or potential threats, or if there is a benefit to be gained (Plutchik, 2000; and see Arnold, 1960). Primary appraisals are intuitive and automatic, and take place very quickly, without the individual being aware of it. In essence, the appraisal system mediated by the brain's limbic system (and especially the amygdala) is the basis for

Gladwell's (2005) *Blink* or "thinking without thinking." Such rapid appraisals are possible because of the design of our central nervous system. The neural architecture of the brain (i.e., how the brain is constructed) contains a capacity for human beings to scan the environment for perceived threats quickly using sensory organs (sight, hearing, touch, etc.). If there is no appraisal of harm or benefit, no emotion is aroused (Arnold, 1960; Plutchik, 2000).

In evolutionary psychology terms, the automatic nature of primary appraisals is considered to be adaptive for the species, because it was not a good idea for our ancestors to be deliberating whether a hungry tiger was a threat! Threats to modern humans can be physically real (as in bodily harm), psychologically real (as in being verbally abused), or merely perceived (as in imagined menaces to a schema). As an example, an individual may be in physical danger if about to be struck by a car, whereas a psychological threat might be attending a staff meeting where an individual fears being unfairly and publicly criticized by a tyrannical boss. Each one will generally produce a change in one's emotional state, as well as a strong (negative) internal feeling. Examples of perceived threats might be conjuring up images of potentially getting into a car accident or images of being in the meeting. In each case, the brain evaluates threat primarily through the limbic system with the amygdala, a limbic structure playing an exceptionally critical role in that process (see Damasio, 1994, 1999; Ekman, 1992, 1995, 2003; Ekman et al., 1983; Goleman, 1995, 2006; LeDoux, 1998; Myers, 2007; Tolson, 2006).[6] If the primary appraisal produces some emotional change, then a secondary appraisal—involving structures of the brain responsible for judgment and personality (i.e., schema)—generally takes place (unless there is reason to act immediately, as when a person puts her hand on a hot stove or is facing down a tiger).

Secondary Appraisals and Responses to Threats

Secondary appraisals of the environment or events in the environment are those in which an individual decides how to best deal with what has been judged as either a threat or a benefit. Central to this is the idea of coping, which is the individual's response to manage and respond to the threat or benefit (Plutchik, 2000). Secondary appraisals involve judgments, but not necessarily conscious ones. This has led Damasio (1999) to comment that "the brain knows more than the conscious mind reveals" (p. 42). Such action tendencies, however, tend to operate in line with a person's schema dynamics and are more readily apparent (i.e., they result in observable behavior and expressions of affect).

But Don't Take Our Word for It! Master Example

In this example, master clinician Marsha Linehan, PhD (developer of dialectical behavioral therapy [DBT]) works with a woman who became angry about being treated unfairly at work (Alexander Street Press, 2012).

Marsha Linehan:	"Okay. So that's reasonable. How is it though that getting a schedule you didn't like, and it not being what you agreed to, how is it that you then got angry about that?"
Client:	"There's a little bit of history with the agency. Um, not getting um, things not working out the way we're told they're going to be."
Marsha Linehan:	"Okay."
Client:	"So. This isn't the first time this has happened."
Marsha Linehan:	"So in other words you have a history where you do things—you agree to things and then they give you things different from how you agreed to. So those thoughts come into your mind?"

Client:	"Oh yeah."
Marsha Linehan:	"So you—(yeah see I love that, "Oh yeah!" moment!)—So you saw this, you didn't like it, you said, 'it's not what we agreed to.' And then did it come into your mind: 'they're always doing this to me, or they've done this before, or they're doing it again?'"
Client:	"Yes!"

In the above example, the client made a primary appraisal that she was being unfairly treated, which triggered the emotional reaction of anger. In her secondary appraisal, she relied on her memories (history) of not having agreements kept to keep her anger going to the point where she reacted poorly and resorted to acting out at work.

Problem-Focused versus Emotion-Focused Coping

Relative to how best to deal with what has been appraised, according to Lazarus and Lazarus (1994), the two categories of coping are *problem-focused* coping and *emotion-focused* coping. Problem-focused coping is a way of dealing with problems or issues through action that changes or alters the event or environment (e.g., agreeing to do something if a good opportunity presents itself). Hence, problem-focused coping works primarily on the link between a person's internal feelings and his or her expressions of affect to motivate action. Emotion-focused coping, by contrast, is a style that primarily avoids the problem situation and instead attempts to change the emotion that is perceived (either by seeking out comfort and soothing, or by distracting and denial; Myers, 2007). As a result, this style of coping works by altering an individual's emotional state or by dampening his or her internal feelings. Returning to the brief examples of the approaching car and the painful meeting, a problem-focused coping style might result in the individual stepping on the brake or confronting the criticizing individual. An emotion-focused coping style would lead an individual to reduce the fear of being hit by a car and getting support or feedback from a trusted coworker about how to handle the criticism encountered.

Clinical Exercise: Identifying Client Emotions

Directions: Recall this exercise from Chapter 8. This time, read over each brief statement and answer the questions below.

1. A client enters therapy to address her fear of public speaking. She is interested in pursuing a career as an executive and knows that public speaking is an important part of attaining career goals. She also understands that this will entail receiving certain specific skills training that might make her uncomfortable.
2. A woman comes for a therapy session complaining of depression following a recent layoff from her job as an accountant. She states, "I'm good at what I do, but when I heard the rumors about layoffs, I knew it would happen to me. All my life, stuff like that seems to happen to me."
3. A man sought counseling because his family is concerned that he was becoming depressed. He is a highly intelligent, although aloof computer programmer who was working as a convenience store clerk because he was "waiting for the right job." The

therapist asked the client what he has done to find "the right job," and he replied, "I've e-mailed my résumé, but no one has called me. I figured I wasn't good enough."

4. A client tells his therapist that his wife sent him to counseling in order to deal with his anger problem. He resents that his wife thinks he has a problem: "It's not me. I know that I always give people a fair chance. Ask anyone who knows me, and they will tell you that I only get angry when the idiots around me do stupid things!"

Questions

1. What emotion does each client seem to be feeling?
2. For each client, is it a primary, secondary, or background emotion?
3. What do the clients' expressions of affect tell you about their emotions?
4. What might their primary appraisal be if confronted with a threat?
5. What coping style would they likely use: problem-focused or emotion-focused? What actions would they take?

Variation: Process together in a small group or with the whole class.

Knowing how the appraisal process works in individuals is an important part of understanding how emotions work. It is also one of the first areas that a therapist can help a client work on. First, a practitioner must understand how expressions of affect, internal feelings, and emotional states are linked, as well as understand how they can break down. Then a clinician must assess where a particular problem is taking place. After that, a therapist can utilize the appraisal process to direct a client's attention to what he or she is experiencing without distortion or alteration. This is part of what is commonly referred to as *awareness*. Simply put, awareness is the process of helping clients to understand how to connect with their own internal feelings, becoming alert to their expression of affect, and making connections to their emotional states. (We discuss specific therapeutic methods for doing this later in the chapter.) There is one more very important moderating structure in the emotional system that exerts a strong influence on both the appraisal process and emotions: schema dynamics.

The Relationship between Schemas, Appraisal, Emotions, and Behavior

We have described how the appraisal process can evoke or extinguish a person's emotional reaction, based on whether there is a perceived threat or benefit that warrants action (or coping). Precisely what each individual interprets as a challenge, a threat, or something desirable is determined by *values*—what someone deems as good or bad. As discussed in Chapter 8, values are embedded in schema and guide choices but are unconsciously (i.e., unknowingly) held by an individual. As unconscious entities, schemas give rise automatically and intuitively to emotions. We have emotions (i.e., emotional reactions) toward those things in life that have meaning (i.e., value to us). An early definition of emotions again came from Arnold's (1960) classic work:

[T]he felt tendency toward anything intuitively appraised as good (beneficial), or away from anything intuitively appraised as bad (harmful). This attraction or aversion is accompanied by a pattern of physiological changes organized toward approach or withdrawal. The patterns differ for different emotions. (p. 182)

The link between emotions and schema dynamics is nonlinear in nature. Many theorists and clinicians treat the two—(1) schemas and the beliefs that result from them, and (2) emotional states and the internal feelings or expressions of affect that result from schemas and beliefs—as discrete and separate entities. For the purposes of this text, we prefer to see them as two distinct domains with each having unique qualities that are integrally and systemically related. It is a clinician's challenge and responsibility to manage them together. To capture the essence of what we wish to convey, consider an ordinary electrical cord. The cord is a single entity, but it has two distinct wires, one black and one white. Although each has a particular function, they work seamlessly together to bring electrical current to an appliance. So it is with schemas and emotions.

Just as it was impossible in the Level I domain to connect with and engage a client without simultaneously working on the therapeutic relationship, it is also impossible to separate work on the cognitive or schema level from work on the emotional level. If a person has a generally positive schematized view of self, others, and life and the world (see Chapter 8), the person will be more likely to operate from a generally positive or optimistic emotional framework (i.e., background emotions/mood) and less likely to have prolonged bouts of negative emotional experiences. When the person does have any such bouts, they will generally be short. After the situation passes, the person will return to what is normal or baseline. In the same way, individuals who have generally negative schematized views of self, others, or the world are more likely to operate from a more negative emotional framework, and are likely to achieve brief experiences of positive emotions before returning to a more negative (or, at best, neutral) baseline. It also becomes quickly obvious that these schema dynamics (positive or negative) affect the appraisal process and the emotional action tendencies they generate. According to Greenberg and Paivio (1997):

> Emotions regulate mental functioning, organizing both thought and action. First they establish goal priorities and organize us for particular actions. . . . Second, emotions set the goals towards which cognitions and actions strive, making affect a crucial determiner of human conduct. . . . Someone who is sad and in need of comfort will find his or her perceptions and actions influenced in a number of ways. For example, one person will begin to move toward comfort; another will begin to think more and more sadness-enhancing thoughts such as "I'm all alone, no one cares" or will begin to retrieve sad memories and yearn for contact, comfort, and companionship. The first person who has enjoyed good attachments with significant others and so learned that comfort is possible, will eventually reach out and make contact with others. For those like the second person, above, who have learned that needs are not met, resignation, which is the poison of action, sets in. They quickly feel, "Its no use, I never get what I need" and give up. Here thought and action are unable to be mobilized in the service of goal attainment. Thus emotion sets the desired *end goal*; cognition and learning provides the *means* whereby the goal is met or not met. Emotions therefore are the guiding structures of our lives especially in our relations with others. Cognition thus sets out to solve the problem of how to reach the emotion-set goal of connecting, of getting comfort, or of separating. (p. 14)

Zaltman (2003) has described that values (which are held in schema dynamics) are oftentimes vaguely understood (if at all) and are difficult to articulate. However, when an individual appraises that there is a challenge or threat to a major schema dynamic, an emotional response is evoked (sometimes appropriately and sometimes not). These emotions give rise to corresponding attitudes, actions tendencies, or behavioral dispositions. Thus, if a given event or set of circumstances fits with a client's schematized worldview, he will be in a pleasant or good emotional state, or at least feel soothed (and not need to act or react). We reprint this example from the case of Ashley (originally in Chapter 2 under Listening for Congruence) as an example:

Ashley:	"Well, I'm here because I feel that I have recently hit my limit. I am at my wits end."
Therapist:	"That sounds serious, can you tell me a bit about what's going on?"
Ashley:	"I don't know where to begin. I have been married for almost 8 years. I have two children, aged 6 and 3 and I work for a local hospital here in town as a medical billing supervisor, which is very stressful in this economy."
Therapist:	"Wow! That *is* a lot to manage. How do you do it?"
Ashley:	"Well, that's the thing. We've won awards for our efficiency and productivity 10 out of the last 12 months this year. So the expectations on our department are huge. I have to be on top of everything. And if I'm not, it all comes crashing down."
Therapist:	"Can you give me a recent example of when you were not 'on top of things,' and they 'all came crashing down?'"
Ashley:	"Sure, that's kind of the reason that I came to see you. The other day I was home with my kids because school and day care were closed due to the holiday. The person who comes and cleans weekly couldn't come, and the house was especially messy (which I can't stand). I had to do some work via telecommuting . . . even though I had taken the day off. It was the end of the month, and if I didn't get a particular report done, there would've been thousands of dollars lost for the hospital. So I got the kids situated with a movie, then started to straighten out the house, but I kept feeling like I had to answer e-mails from work. I felt guilty that the kids were plopped in front of the TV, but I needed to get some work done. But before I could even get to that, I really had to clear the clutter (I can't work if there is clutter around!). Before I knew it, the morning had gone, it was lunchtime, and I was still in my pajamas. So as I got the kids' lunch together, I got a call from my assistant saying that the CEO was looking for me and needed to speak with me right away. I had an awful feeling that it was not good. At that very moment, my 3-year old spilled his entire lunch of Spaghetti-Os all over our new sofa (light beige, so it stained it nicely), and I lost it. I started crying and shrieking. I called my husband to come home, and I went to bed. I couldn't get out of bed the whole next day I had such a splitting headache. Thank God it was a Saturday and I didn't have to be at work."

In addition to listening for the incongruence, this time, it is possible for the reader to determine Ashley's schema dynamics (positive, unrealistic and rigid view of self, negative view of others) and how they intertwine with her emotional reaction when she was unable to do what she felt like she needed to do. As a result, when things didn't go as she had planned, it created a crisis and an extreme emotional reaction.

As Greenberg and Paivio (1997) noted above, emotions guide clients toward actions in ways congruent with their schema dynamics. Even if a client has a generally negative view of self, others, or life and the world, the client will at least feel neutral about the events (if appraisal is consistent with the schema). But if an appraisal of a given set of circumstances or events runs counter to a client's expectations (based on schema), the client is likely to feel threatened, develop negative emotional states, have negative internal feelings, and display negative affect (Ekman, 2003). In addition, clients with more unrealistic schematized worldviews are more likely to have emotional expressions that are in line with their schema dynamics (i.e., positive or negative) than the opposite. Typically, the more rigidly held they are (e.g., "I must . . . ," "It should . . . ," "I can *never* . . . ," "You *always* . . . ," or "Only if I can . . .") or the more outlandish (i.e., far removed from common sense) schemas are, the greater the potential for the mobilization of a strong emotional reaction to a perceived threat. This clinical case example may help to demonstrate the intimate connectedness between schema and emotion.

Clinical Case Example: Feelings, Emotions, and Schema

A middle-aged man appeared for his first therapy appointment that was arranged by his wife (with his consent). When the man appeared for his appointment, it was clear that he was significantly depressed. He reported that he had lost weight (seven to eight pounds within a 2-month period), could not sleep at night even with the aid of prescribed medications, and had been harboring suicidal thoughts. Although he was not psychotic and his reality testing was unimpaired, he reported that his thinking was very "negative." As he put it, "I'm a generally happy person—all my life. I've always been an optimistic and positive person. Now, I'm seeing everything negative. I ran into an incredibly difficult situation, and I'm not a happy person at all. I've reached lows that I didn't know were possible. My wife said, 'You're clearly depressed!' When she said it, I knew it was obviously true. She is my number one supporter."

The clinician asked the client what he meant when he said that he "reached lows that [he] didn't know were possible." That's when the client revealed the symptoms noted above. The client's suicidal ideation was the next issue clarified. He revealed that his wife and children were precious to him, and he realized that suicide would be a total abandonment of them. Once safety measures regarding the client's comments about suicide were in place, the next issue clarified concerned what it was that had changed in his life to bring about such a profound reaction. The client readily responded that the issue was an impending business failure.

Within the past year, he reported having engaged in a business transaction with several individuals, one of whom he now suspected of being "extremely dishonest." He acknowledged that he should have been more cautious regarding "due diligence." He further described how the impending business failure was making him more and more dysfunctional. Although he believed himself to be very competent, he wasn't able to perform well and manage his business. That led to a continued downward spiral with decreased feelings of confidence, more negativistic thinking and self-recrimination, and so on.

The clinician responded that such sad sets of circumstances were never pleasant and always harsh experiences, but not to suicidal proportions. In fact, he suggested that in this particular case, it appeared that something in the client's *cognitive template*[7] may have something to do with his extremely negative view of his circumstances and was prompting him to become more and more immobilized.

In response to this proposal, the man's posture changed significantly. His facial features brightened noticeably, and he responded with the following comment: "My 'template' gave me a purpose, and it was broken in this business. As a result, my goals and purpose didn't make a lot of sense. My mother and father divorced when I was 4 or 5 years old, and father left mother with a lot of money issues. Mother had a nervous breakdown with depression. My most vivid memory is of my mother crying on the stairs, asking how she is going to pay her bills."

He elaborated, "I've gone to the finest schools with the most competitive people you could possibly imagine. All during school, they would say that I'm the hardest working person that they know. Everything in my life has been driven by (a need for and pursuit of) economic security."

In the clinical case example, the client's failure to live up to his schematized values provoked strong emotional states (i.e., sadness and fear) and intense internal feelings (i.e., restlessness, hopelessness, and lack of energy), which were manifested in expressions of affect (i.e., crying, irritability, and a prolonged down mood). That understanding, along with the schema the client developed in early childhood, played a prominent role in his present circumstances and guided the therapist's intervention. Although oversimplified, the client harbors a conclusion (i.e., schema) that economic failure must be avoided at all costs because of the dire consequences noted with his mother under such circumstances. Correspondingly, he unconsciously arranged much of his life so as to make certain that he would not fall prey to the fate that befell his mother. Education, hard work, a scientific background, honesty, a good reputation, and so on all entered the mix of entities to pursue in life to insulate himself from the possibility of economic failure that so devastated his mother. In light of his present circumstances, his personality could not deal with the impending collapse and financial failure of his business. At the same time, the feelings of impending failure seemingly would not subside no matter how hard he worked. Like Ashley above, his defining view of self as a hard worker was being destroyed—he hadn't worked hard enough to avoid a business failure. The appraisal of threat to that schema produced profound fear, signaling that the personality was in danger. Those emotional reactions manifested themselves with his profound feelings of depression.

The Link between Common Negative Emotions and Psychological Disorders in Counseling

It is impossible to address the subject of emotions in one or two chapters. Discussing a general conceptual framework for emotions, their relationship to cognitions, methods of working with emotions in treatment, and providing a comprehensive overview of specific emotions are daunting. Earlier in this chapter, we described Ekman's six primary emotions. There are, however, literally thousands of gradations and combinations of emotions that human beings experience. As a result, we will not attempt to categorize or catalogue the entire range of human emotions. However, there is a relationship between emotions and psychological disorders. In fact, all psychological disorders have some emotional component to them. Ekman (2003) places the progression from a discrete emotion to an all-pervasive disorder on a continuum. For example, the emotion of excitement progresses to a euphoric mood, which then becomes a trait (think schema dynamics here) of optimist/risk taker and then finally the disorder of mania. We want to spend a little time discussing the progression of emotions to disorders that clients commonly present in therapy. They are the continua from fear to anxiety, from sadness to depression, and from anger to chronic impulsivity. We discuss the structural elements of each emotion (expressions of affect, internal feelings, and emotional states), as well as briefly discuss the relationship to schema dynamics and the impact on the appraisal process.

The Continuum from Fear to Anxiety

Even if you have never seen the film, almost everyone knows the theme from the movie *Jaws*. The first few strains of the low-pitched theme music followed by an ominous silence only to recur clearly convey the impression that something deadly and unseen lurks. Just like any horror film, the music and cinematography make the heart race and goose bumps percolate in a sympathetic terror with the actors on the screen. The reality is that fear is perhaps the most powerful emotion that human beings possess. According to Greenberg and Paivio (1997), its purpose is encoded in the survival of our species, as it helps to warn people that something potentially dangerous lurks. Fear helps to motivate a person to take flight from whatever the danger is, or to confront and change the fearful stimulus. Clients' expressions of affect may reveal a worried look, an easily triggered startle response, *skittishness,* and an unwillingness to take suggestions related to what is prompting the fear. As a person moves from the emotion of fear to a mood, individuals who are chronically fearful may seem to have an apprehensive mood or seem wary. Apprehension is anticipatory, that is, the dread of something to occur in the future. It keeps people on edge and at a state of alert. As this becomes more closely embedded with a person's schema dynamics (i.e., negative view of others), it becomes the *trait* of shyness. Shyness helps the individual not to feel fearful by forcing the person to withdraw from others, or from situations that make them fearful.

Finally, there is the *disorder* of anxiety. Individuals experiencing anxiety often operate with a belief that something bad may occur, and that they have to be prepared for it. Clients may describe their bodily sensations of fear or anxiety as cold, or that they feel distracted or antsy. Some people may manifest physical symptoms when they are feeling anxious or fearful (i.e., feeling sick to their stomach or having a headache). Such experiences of fear and anxiety put an individual in an emotional state in which they are on guard. If clients have unrealistic schema dynamics, however, they may be unable to distinguish what is a real threat from what amounts to scaring themselves for nefarious interpersonal purposes. We represent a case from Chapter 8 to illustrate.

Clinical Case Example: Chronic Worry and Anxiety

A well-educated, pleasant, happily married woman with a young child sought therapy because of overwhelming anxiety and an inability to comfortably leave her baby in the custody of others except for her husband and parents. She recognized this as aberrant but felt helpless to bring it under control. She reported her "ton of anxiety" as resulting from her baby's medical problems with numerous legitimate trips to hospital emergency rooms and felt a need for more than typical parental vigilance and new mother nervousness. Although medical authorities assured her that her baby would grow out of his condition, such reassurances had little ameliorating impact on a daily basis. She relied frequently and heavily on her parents in the event of any troublesome circumstances that she believed she simply could not deal with on her own—"I don't know what I would do without them!"

During the first session, she reported that she had "done a lot of thinking" and concluded that "as far back as high school," she could remember herself being consistently "excessively worried about something." In the process of collecting early-childhood and family-of-origin material, it was discovered that she had a very positive and endorsing family that was physically affectionate and supportive. At the same time, careful nonlinear listening to the woman's description of the family atmosphere revealed very subtle expressions of a nervous quality underlying the positive and loving picture. As the "baby" of her family, much older siblings could overwhelm and "beat up" on her as they would play roughhouse. Such encounters, although oftentimes fun, would also scare her and require her to call for help in need of "rescuing" by her parents or oldest sibling. Her mother and father's method of discipline included being "strict" with her, and "yelling" to gain "control" over rambunctious and energetic children. She also described her mother as somewhat nervous in nature, a person who did not easily relax. Then. too, there were tornadoes to be frightened of and scary monsters she imagined that would prompt her to run for the cover of her parents' bedroom at night. In describing what her life was like in school, she casually related that teachers and authority figures in general were "intimidating." The net result of all of these nuanced descriptions revealed a pattern of thinking. There was a "nervous edge" to her experience of growing up as a child.

Nevertheless, she did well in school, had friends, and was well-liked and successful in a beginning career before marriage. At the time of entering therapy, she was living in a healthy and successful marriage with a husband who was very "supportive and caring." Despite these positive factors, she still experienced the "ton of anxiety" over her child. She stated her goals for therapy as follows: "I'm looking for ways to think about things differently!"

Questions

1. What are the structural elements of this client's experience of anxiety (expressions of affect, internal feelings, and emotional state)?
2. How do her schema dynamics relate to her emotional experience of anxiety?
3. What part(s) of the continuum (emotion, mood, trait, disorder) do you see the fear manifest itself?
4. Speculate how this might impact her appraisal process (particularly related to her child) and what coping style she might choose.

The schema dynamics reflective of fear/anxiety consistently communicate to a person, "Watch out: I am in danger. Either I can't trust myself, others are a danger to me, or the world poses a threat to me (physically, emotionally, etc.). Life just makes me nervous." Another message that a state of anxiety communicates is "If I am not careful or on alert, then bad things will happen." The client in the clinical case example above anticipates that something troublesome and dangerous lurks and that it may get out of control, especially with her child. If a client is unrealistic in her view of self, others, or the world or life, then even if everything is going well, she will nevertheless continue to scan her environment for potential problems on the horizon—in effect, one can never rest assured. As a result, the primary appraisal of events is likely to amplify such a client's fear or anxiety, whereas the secondary appraisal will trigger a coping-style response that is not necessarily congruent with the circumstance. Regarding clinical interventions, linear confrontations (e.g., "So, there is never a time when it is good to trust someone you don't know well?") are typically ineffective. Often, clients experiencing anxiety disorders will have ready rationalizations for continuing to maintain their vigilance: anecdotal evidence to support their claims of a need for wariness, instances when they or others let their guard down and were taken advantage of, or others they have heard about who have encountered bad things. Hence, a nonlinear approach is necessary (see below).

Our Nonlinear Brain: Chronic Anxiety and Posttraumatic Stress Disorder

Although there are few absolutes in life other than death and taxes, it is an absolute that many of the problems human beings encounter are because of difficulty they have in regulating their emotions. In some individuals (e.g., those with posttraumatic stress disorder [PTSD] and generalized anxiety disorder [GAD]), emotions not only are difficult to regulate but also appear to have a life of their own. Research to unravel the mystery of emotions such as anxiety and fear has been based on both learning theory and brain functioning. For example, in reviewing contemporary learning theory perspectives on the etiology of anxiety, Mineka and Zinbarg (2006) have emphasized that "perceptions of uncontrollability and unpredictability play a role in the development and course of PTSD" (p. 19). Furthermore, the same authors contended that

people who have a history of uncontrollable and unpredictable life stress may be especially prone to developing GAD. Worry about possible bad outcomes or dangerous events, the central characteristic of GAD, seems to serve as a cognitive avoidance

response that is reinforced because it suppresses emotional and physiological responding. Because attempts to suppress or control worry may lead to more negative intrusive
thoughts, perceptions of uncontrollability over worry may develop, which is in turn
associated with greater anxiety, leading to a vicious cycle. (p. 20)

On the other hand, Joseph LeDoux (1998), the eminent neuroscientist, declared, "While
fear is a part of everyone's life, too much or inappropriate fear accounts for many common
psychiatric problems. . . . Fear is a core emotion in psychopathology" (p. 130). We would add
that due to humans' incessant striving from a felt minus to a felt plus, noted many years ago by
Adler (1956), fear of failure (in its innumerable forms) and fear of not belonging loom large in
the human psyche.

But what role does the brain play in mediating fear responses and in the regulation of fear?
LeDoux (1998) has called the amygdala a "hub in the wheel of fear" (p. 170). The amygdala is
part of the midbrain and the limbic system. Although even very low levels of cortical sensory
input can activate the amygdala, the hippocampus provides the emotional context. Goleman
(1995) has described the contributions of these two organs very aptly:

While the hippocampus remembers the dry facts, the amygdala retains the emotional fla-
vor that goes with those facts. If we try to pass a car on a two-lane highway and narrowly
miss having a head-on collision, the hippocampus retains the specifics of the incident,
like what stretch of road we were on, who was with us, what the other car looked like.
But it is the amygdala that ever after will send a surge of anxiety through us whenever we
try to pass a car in similar circumstances. As LeDoux put it to me, "The hippocampus is
crucial in recognizing a face as that of your cousin. But it is the amygdala that adds you
don't really like her." (p. 20)

It appears, then, that the amygdala can be overactive in some individuals, who become so
upset with emotional overload that they are unable to think very effectively and use rational
cognitive processes to inform, advise, and calm themselves. There is no mistaking it: Anxiety or
fear generated by the sentinel function of the amygdala affects performance. Collins, Schroeder,
and Nye (1989) studied the state and trait anxiety scores of 1,790 students training to be air
traffic controllers, a profession with extensive stress. Among the findings of the study were that
anxious students are more likely to fail and successful candidates demonstrate a higher amount
of tolerance for circumstances that might produce stress in others. Likewise for a wide variety
of academic performance, Seipp (1991) conducted a meta-analysis of 126 different studies on
academic performance that included over 36,000 subjects in total. In short, the study concluded that the more disposed a student was to worrying, the poorer was his or her academic
performance no matter what measure of performance was used, be it test grades, GPA, or
achievements (as cited by Goleman, 1995, pp. 83–84).

Other parts of the brain function as regulators for the emotions. Although the emotions can
overwhelm, they can also play a crucial part in making decisions as when the mind and clear
thinking appear to be saying one thing and the gut (i.e., amygdala) appears to be saying something
else. It is from the compromises affected by head and gut that wise decisions and clear thinking
arise (Goleman, 1995, p. 27). Gladwell (2005), in his widely popular book *Blink,* has referred to
decision making that apparently is done without conscious rational thought as "thinking without
thinking," a reference to the role that centers in the brain for emotions' play in daily life.

According to LeDoux (1998), fear responses are "programmed" into our genetic makeup for very good reasons—survival is at stake:

[C]onsiderable evidence shows that there is a genetic component to fear behavior . . . identical twins (even those reared in separate homes) are far more similar in fearfulness than fraternal twins. This . . . applies across many kinds of measurements, including tests of shyness, worry, fear of strangers, social introversion/extroversion, and others. Similarly, anxiety, phobic and obsessive compulsive disorders tend to run in families and to be more likely to occur in both identical than in both fraternal twins. (p. 136)

The good news is that even severe instances of trauma and the anxiety it can precipitate as a chronic condition (as represented by PTSD) can be better understood today with hope for its future cure. A study conducted by Rachel Yehuda, a psychologist and neurochemist at Yale University School of Medicine specializing in PTSD, reported on by Goleman (1992) was the first research to report "distinct biological changes" in Holocaust survivors with PTSD. That is, they demonstrated elevated norepinephrine, a well-known stress hormone. Likewise, similar elevated levels of norepinephrine have been discovered in Vietnam veterans plagued by PTSD. It is believed that many of the symptoms common to PTSD such as nightmares, flashbacks, insomnia, hypervigilance, and so on are due to a sympathetic nervous system that is too easily aroused. Nevertheless, Yehuda's research revealed that about one quarter of Holocaust survivors are free of PTSD symptoms. Addressing and correcting the condition of an overactive nervous system provides hope that such debilitating conditions as PTSD can be overcome.

The Continuum from Sadness to Depression

Sadness is the result of experiencing a form of loss or disappointment in life. This can range from the mundane (e.g., missing a train or not getting the last jelly doughnut) to the life altering (e.g., losing a job or getting a divorce) to the tragic (e.g., the death of a child). Sadness is triggered by an event (in the present or past) in which something did not turn out the way it was hoped, or where something important was lost. A more pervasive experience of sadness may lead to a blue mood where a person is down for a longer period of time. At the schema or trait level of the continuum, individuals who have a pervasive sadness are described as melancholic (and may have a negative view of self). However, as a disorder, depression can be related to prolonged episodes of melancholy, to the point that future events are predicted to be as disappointing as past or present events and circumstances. In addition, with a depressive disorder, the sadness that is experienced overwhelms most other feelings of emotion, and the individual is not able to feel pleasure in anything (which is called *anhedonia*). Such episodes can be mild, moderate, or severe, and reactions can last from weeks to decades.

Sadness, depression, and other points on the continuum have very similar, and limited, expressions of affect. Clients typically may cry when they feel sad or will have a very blunted (stoic) affect. They may seem downcast and are remarkable for what is absent (smiling, laughing, etc.). Some clients may mask depression with anger or other destructive behaviors (e.g., suicidal ideations or ruminations, or addiction) and must be thoroughly evaluated (see Chapter 11). In terms of internal feeling states, clients experiencing the continuum of sadness to depression have a wider range of feelings than their expressions of affect. Specifically, they may describe feelings as blue, down, and unhappy, and report a lack of energy or enthusiasm to do anything. Sometimes, depressed individuals will describe their internal feelings as dull, blank, and dark, or that there is no feeling at all. In these circumstances, a client's emotional state will be characterized as hopeless, defeated, and generally negative (Greenberg & Paivio, 1997). The clinical case example below revisits a case from Chapter 9.

Clinical Case Example: Disappointment and Sadness

A successfully married woman with an advanced degree came to therapy on a monthly basis, mostly for support. In her family of origin, she was the caretaker for handicapped younger siblings who were appreciative and even adoring of her. Indeed, parental feedback was extremely positive and emphasized how truly gifted and special she was. She maintained a long-term "complaint" that revolved around her "sensitivity" to how others treated her (e.g., perceived slights by coworkers or social snubs). For example, if she wasn't invited to a party, it became cause for extremely hurt feelings. If someone made a comment that pertained to her work, she tended to interpret such a comment as an attack on her competence. She elaborated that she was very competent, and the individual proffering the comment had no right to say such things.

During one of her monthly therapy sessions, she reported going to a wake for a somewhat distant relative who died quite tragically. She said that at the wake, all the extended relatives seemed to be huddled around and preoccupied with a few members of the extended family who were extremely successful financially. She noted, "Everyone idolizes (them), and I wasn't one of them. Everything in my family is about achievement for everyone. That's my family; that's it! I walked out feeling sad and empty."

Questions

1. What might be the structural elements of this client's experience of sadness or depression (expressions of affect, internal feelings, and emotional state)?
2. How do schema dynamics relate to her emotional experience of sadness or depression?
3. What part(s) of the continuum (emotion, mood, trait, disorder) do you see the sadness manifest itself?
4. Speculate how this might impact her appraisal processes, and what coping style she might choose.

Some individuals (e.g., with biochemical imbalances in the brain or lifelong bouts with depression) may have encoded (or accommodated) negative schemas (e.g., "I am unlovable," "I am worthless (or useless)," "Other people will only disappoint me, and I don't trust them," and "The world only wants to grind you into dust"). As a result, most of their secondary appraisals are likely to be emotion focused and motivate their assuming more defensive positions. They are more likely to withdraw from others for fear of further rejection, disappointment, loss, or alienation. Rasmussen and Dover (2006) have described the dynamics and "adaptive" aspect of depression:

In the face of recurrent or chronic battle, one option that is nearly always available is retreat. One can give up the challenge. However, it is important to note that no one happily retreats from a desired activity or goal [i.e., schema dynamics]. The more critical the victory is to the individual's sense of worth, dignity, and integrity [i.e., superiority], the greater the hesitancy to abandon the battle and the greater the pain associated with the retreat. When a person becomes hopeless and does not want to alter his or her goals but does not possess the skills necessary or does not want to do what is necessary to achieve those goals, then depression becomes adaptive. More explicitly, it may be more useful to do nothing when one perceives nothing useful to do, when the costs outweigh the benefits or a major roadblock has been encountered . . . [thus] depression is the emotion that removes a person from a battle that he or she is not going to win. (pp. 378–379)

Effective therapeutic interventions for such clients target the appraisal process and help the client to use more problem-focused coping strategies discussed earlier.

The Continuum from Anger to Chronic Impulsivity

Unlike fear or sadness, anger (although a primary emotion) is an emotion that always comes as a reaction to another emotion. Usually the anger is a reaction to fear, sadness, or pain, and it can be real or imaginary/anticipatory, physical, or emotional. For example, if someone reached over to your arm and hits it really hard, you would probably say (angrily): "Ouch! Stop it! What did you do that for?" But what was the first thing that you felt? It wasn't anger; it was the pain of getting hit. The anger came in response (a secondary appraisal) to the initial (real) feeling of pain. Take another example, if you are watching a child play outside, and the child begins to run out into a busy street to chase after a ball, you might grab the child's arm and/or yell (angrily) "Stop! Look where you are going!" Again, was anger the first emotion that you experienced? It was probably an intense fear about the child getting hit by a car as you saw it head into the street. In this case, the fear was imaginary or anticipatory because you were anticipating something awful happening. The anger was a way to try to prevent it (by yelling, grabbing the kid, or both).

The experience of the emotion of anger is relatively brief. In the first example, if the person looks horrified and apologetic and says "I am so sorry, but there was a bee and I thought it was going to sting you," then the anger begins to subside (again, because of the reappraisal of the situation). In the second example, if the child becomes frightened and cries hysterically or says "I'm so sorry," the anger may subside as you try to comfort them. However, as we move along the continuum anger as a mood becomes irritability. At the schema or trait level (particularly if it is rigidly applied), a person would be described as hostile (and probably has a negative view of others and a negative view of the world). Finally, at the end of the continuum, as a disorder, anger is experienced as chronic impulsivity or even intermittent explosive disorder.

According to Ekman (2003), anger is the most destructive of all emotions because it is the one that can lead to physical aggression or verbal responses that may be socially damaging. Contrary to popular belief, Tavris (1989) found that getting out or expressing anger doesn't make a person feel better, and it may even make matters worse. In addition, she found that suppressed anger, contrary to the Freudian belief, does not lead to depression or other medical conditions, provided that individuals feel that they have some measure of control—even if it is only control of their reactions.

But Don't Take Our Word for It! Master Example

In this example, master clinician Jon Carlson works with a husband who is having relationship difficulties. In this brief segment, Carlson discusses how the physiology of anger creates problems for the client trying to communicate with his wife when they are in conflict (Alexander Street Press, 2012).

Jon Carlson: "See, one of the things that I find happens, it sounds like what's going on with you, guys, is that you get into these situations and very quickly, they escalate. And I've learned that once your heart rate get above 96 beats a minute, you

Scott: "Yeah, I could see that."

Jon Carlson: "You know, you might even benefit from it too because it sounds like you've got a lot of the things and greetings that couples have when relationships go south. There are things like criticism ah, which, you know, that sounds like that's what was called contempt. You look at somebody in a negative way, sounds like that's there. Then you're each defending. You're defensive. You defend your right to do what you're doing even though that, you know, you defend your attitude and you defend your anger. And then there's this stonewall, you put up sometimes where you just won't talk. You remove yourself from one another. And those are the four things that really make a relationship go bad. And if you can learn how to pause, you can have some choices a little bit. So you can choose rather than defending. Maybe you can take a deep breath and you could say, 'So if I understand you right, you think we need to have the kids leave us alone so we can talk?' And he'll say, 'That's exactly right.' And you say, 'I agree with you. How should we handle it?' I think there's some real cooperation that you guys show at times when you keep your heart rates down."

Scott: "Yeah. Mine's so fast to go up though."

Jon Carlson: "Well, that's why I think you need some of this other training. You know, I don't think it's just gonna happen by talking. I think you really gonna have to do some work. You're gonna have to do some training."

The beginning of this excerpt (before Scott's first line) reads:

know what happens? All bets are off. When it happens, it becomes a fight or flight situation. And, and for you, it's getting defensive, you know. If, if we just put up our armaments and it's all over. So somehow we've got to get some way to teach you guys this, to soothe things a little bit, to keep things down a little bit. And if you had an agreed-upon strategy to use, that might really be helpful."

We have attempted to briefly discuss how the emotional system (appraisal, expressions of affect, internal feelings, and emotional states) applies to three of the most common emotions presented in therapy. In addition, we have discussed how these emotions are manifested along a continuum from emotion to mood to trait to disorder. In Chapter 11, more sophisticated techniques for working with these emotions is discussed. We now present an exercise in the application of the same analysis to other emotions.

Clinical Exercise: Deconstructing Emotions

Instructions: Choose one of the emotions in the list below.

- Anger
- Pain/hurt
- Shame/guilt
- Happiness

Record what you believe to be the following:

1. Structural characteristics (i.e., expressions of affect, feelings, and emotional state or mood)
2. Schema dynamics (i.e., view of self, others, and life and the world)

3. How the emotion is manifested along the different part(s) of the continuum (emotion, mood, trait, disorder)
4. How the emotion relates to the appraisal process (primary and secondary)
5. How each coping style (problem-focused or emotion-focused) is likely to be utilized by an individual experiencing the emotion

Variation: Form groups according to the emotion that was chosen. Share your answers with one another and create a group answer to the questions above. Then discuss as a class.

Conclusion

It is very important for clinicians to understand and help a client in interpreting expressions of affect, internal feelings, and emotional states. It is also important to help a client recognize and clarify whether the emotional states are primary, secondary, or background. If a client isn't aware of (or minimizes) internal feelings, then the affective expressions are likely to be incongruent with the client's emotional states. In addition, if a client is not fully aware of (or can't interpret) his or her feelings, the client may not be able to describe his or her particular emotional state. In turn, if clients cannot interpret their emotional states, they may be unable to fully explain or understand why they are acting in certain ways. Thus, when a therapist asks, "What seemed to prompt your feeling ____?," a client may answer, "I don't know." It is a therapist's role to help a client find ways to become aware of his or her affective expressions, internal feelings, and emotional states and what they mean. Non-linear thinking is essential in helping a client who is detached in some way from his or her emotional system, or is unaware of how his or her appraisal affects the way that the client feels about something and reacts toward it. In this chapter, we have tried to define each of these elements and how they are linked together.

We next discuss some of the most common emotions encountered in therapy and major issues in working with those emotions, followed by a discussion of linear and nonlinear therapeutic methods of working with client emotions.

Notes

1. The ethical issues regarding such behavior are discussed later in the book.
2. http://www.english.hawaii.edu/criticalink/aristotle/terms/catharsis.html.
3. This is why we strongly argue that therapists avoid becoming too enamored with gimmicks or techniques, but should rather develop their ability to understand how therapists think, especially regarding all of the domains of effective psychotherapy. Gimmicks or techniques are too easily adopted out of context.
4. Over a very long time, amongst specialists in the modern era (e.g., Arnold, 1960; Damasio, 1999; Goleman, 1995; Greenberg, 2004; LeDoux, 1998), there are many different orientations and philosophical issues that a complete grasp of feelings (and emotions) entails. Contemporary society and neuroscience research (see *The Economist*, 2007; Tolson, 2006) have developed a passionate and intriguing search for the relationship between mind and body, looking for an answer to the question of what ultimately determines consciousness. Central to this issue is an understanding of what it is that makes us aware of feelings, emotions, and a sense of self. Damasio (1994, 1999) appeared to strike the philosophical and neurobiological core of the issue of feelings and emotions with his analysis of the relationship between body, emotion, and consciousness. In essence, one of the conclusions he reached is that "the brain knows more than the conscious mind reveals" (Damasio, 1999, p. 42).
5. For example, to flee a situation in fear, it is necessary for the body to secrete adrenalin, increase heart rate and blood pressure, dilate the arteries to accommodate an increase in the flow of blood, and so on. A corresponding set of physiological reactions must occur for a variety of different emotional reactions, and those reactions must and do occur automatically. Upon alert from the amygdala, the thalamus and hypothalamus trigger the appropriate biochemical releases that a particular emotion calls for.

6. It should be noted that there are some neuroscientists who debate the centrality of the amygdala in this process, but most agree that as part of the limbic system, it is a key component in relaying sensory information to specific regions of the brain that are responsible for initiating the particular biochemical triggers appropriate for a particular emotion to be enacted.

7. The cognitive template was briefly described to the client as a series of beliefs, convictions, values, and so on concluded early in childhood (i.e., a schema) that, when challenged by life circumstances, can produce seemingly insoluble and overwhelming dilemmas.

11

The Domain of Addressing and Managing Clients' Emotional States

Managing Common Negative Emotions in Therapy

Introduction

Recall from Chapter 10 Ekman's (2003) quote: "The desire to experience, or not experience an emotion motivates much of our behavior" (p. 216). This is the essence of virtually all psychological problems—either trying to avoid something unpleasant or unwisely pursuing something pleasurable that is out of reach. Psychiatrist M. Scott Peck reflected this in his 1978 best-selling book *The Road Less Travelled*: "This tendency to avoid problems and the emotional suffering inherent in them is the primary basis of all human mental illness" (p. 17). Historically, clinicians including Freud, Adler, Horney, Fritz Perls, and even behaviorist B. F. Skinner agreed that problems (to one degree or another) occur when people try to *avoid* something painful or unpleasant. Sometimes they go to great lengths to do this. And although researchers and practitioners who employed cognitive and cognitive-behavioral approaches found that by changing a person's thinking—usually by logical persuasion, reality testing or by pointing out mistaken beliefs or cognitions—there were still large numbers of clients who would not change their behavior. In other words, despite the logic and reason of the clinician's position that what they were doing, or how they were thinking about their problem or circumstances, was wrong, clients would not give up their old (and problematic) way of doing things. In other words, how they felt about their behavior or point of view would overrule the logical or common-sense view that what they were doing was wrong.

For example, a client suffering with obsessive-compulsive disorder (commonly associated with anxiety) often knows that their obsessions are irrational (such as ritualized hand washing), but they cling to them. Again, the emotion (in this case, anxiety) overrides the logic that their hands are not really dirty. Therefore, simply knowing that something is irrational, or problematic, is not always sufficient to produce change. Relying solely on a logically reasoned argument to help a client work through long-held beliefs or behaviors is an obviously linear approach. The point to looking at, listening to, and understanding the deeper meaning (i.e., schema dynamics) of a client's emotions is to reflect and ultimately convey that understanding to a client. Indeed, according to Greenberg (2004),

> [P]eople need both capacities [i.e., emotions and conscious capacities/schema dynamics as well as what they have learned culturally].[1] . . . They need emotions to tell them, without thought, that something important to their well-being is occurring, and they need their

thinking capacities to work on the problems that emotions point out and that reason must solve. (pp. 29–30)

Greenberg noted that emotions inform the client and the counselor that something, which is important or of *perceived* value, is transpiring. Emotions provide emotional understandings and information rather than rational understandings of such things as psychological threats. Making the most use of information that the emotions provide, however, requires rational cognitive processes. Recalling the discussion in Chapter 10 on appraisal, Kiser, Piercy, and Lipchik (1993) described it thus: "Emotions are intuitive appraisals that initiate action tendencies . . . while corresponding cognitive processes [i.e., schema dynamics] determine whether or not impulses will be acted upon" (p. 235). So although emotions and cognitions may be distinct, they are not separate.

Nonlinear thinking is required to consider both the emotions as providing valued information and rational cognitive processing to evoke an understanding of what to do about it. In other words, each needs the other in a seamless relationship. In fact, according to Greenberg (2004) and others, in order to be maximally effective with clients, a practitioner must be able to work on both the cognitive and schema levels. The clinical case example below may help demonstrate the profound and sometimes confusing nature of the relationship between schema, behavior, and emotions.

Clinical Case Example: Schema, Emotions, and Symptoms

A woman in her 40s returned to therapy after a hiatus of several years. She and her husband had consulted the same therapist several years previously regarding a thoroughly unsatisfying marriage. At that time, the husband complained of never having loved his wife. The wife complained of her husband's 20-year history of marital infidelity, chronic lying, and deceit. Several years before, she had rescinded filing for divorce, and they resumed their unhappy and unsatisfying marriage. The current issue for which she was seeking consultation was the same as it had been before: Her husband was still philandering with a narcissistic air of entitlement and lying about it in a thoroughly unconvincing manner. But this time, his paramour was married with children, in the process of a divorce, and pregnant with his child. The wife once again filed for divorce, and they now lived in separate residences. In the meantime, her husband provided no support money for her and their children during their separation.

The client was an attractive woman—tall, slender, statuesque, athletic, and stylishly dressed with tasteful use of cosmetics. She revealed that in her social encounters with other men, it was clear that they found her attractive and would "come on" to her. She was equally clear and very firm in setting appropriate moral and psychological limits with other men, discouraged their advances, and engaged in no extramarital relationships—period. Her childhood history revealed that she was never given feedback for being a pretty girl but rather for being athletic. Hence, she acknowledged that she has never allowed herself to see herself as attractive.

Also during the course of their discussion, the woman disclosed that her husband appeared to be on the cusp of securing an important job for which he was well-qualified. In keeping with his other imperfections, he had been consistently financially irresponsible and had filed for bankruptcy a number of years ago although making an above-average living.

A Level II practitioner cannot help but ask, "Why would a woman want to stay in such an abusive relationship? What would motivate her?" Is it masochism? Dependency? Fear of being alone? The answer in this particular instance was not found in any of the above.

In pursuing an understanding of what it was that motivated her to remain in such a dysfunctional marriage for so long, she revealed a specific early childhood memory. In the essence of the memory, she recalled that as a child, she was in a race with cousins to see who could get to the door first. Although she won the race and was first to get to the door, she was pushed from behind and wound up breaking the glass in the door with her hand, for which she had to go to a hospital emergency room for stitches. Despite bleeding heavily, she reported being curious but unafraid at that time. Her reaction to this memory was "I was glad to get there first. I wasn't afraid to get stitches. I was happy I won. I wanted to be first."

The therapist suggested that perhaps an operative basic schema (template) was that she wanted to win—that is, be a winner. Getting divorced would make her a loser, and she had been willing to put up with all manner of pain, embarrassment, and humiliation vis-à-vis her husband's infidelity in order to maintain being married. No matter how many women her husband might have in his life, she would be the wife and hence first. The painful reality was that her husband would not fulfill her expectations—he always seemed to put his wants, impulses, and so on first. To her, staying married was the psychological equivalent of winning. In response to this, the woman began crying profusely. This emotional reaction was the equivalent of an important schema dynamic being revealed with all of its primitive and painful emotional accompaniments.

In the case above, there is a clear link between the client's conflicting feelings of hurt, outrage and sadness, and her view of herself as well as others. And although it might be tempting to work on just the cognitive, or schema level, clinicians need to work on the emotional level as well. This often requires nonlinear thinking that can be challenging to clinicians (especially novice ones). But working on the emotional level is producing some of the more dynamic and innovative approaches in the field today. In this chapter, we describe some of these. First, we discuss elements of listening and responding.

Using Other Domains in Dealing with Clients' Emotions

At this point, we turn our attention to using elements from other domains to assist in working with a client's emotions, particularly the nonlinear aspects that master therapists utilize.

Listening and Responding

Nonlinear listening for expressions of affect: A particularly important therapeutic task is nonlinear listening (as well as observing) for expressions of affect (emotion), no matter how subtle they may be. A less experienced Level I practitioner may be hesitant to ask a client about the tears welling up in his or her eyes for fear of prompting further client discomfort. However, it might just be the case that drawing the client's attention to his or her expressions of affect may be the most important experience for the client to express and understand. Recognizing that such moments contain the most potential opportunities for client growth is the mark of a master practitioner. We discuss some of these below.

Linear and nonlinear listening for and responding to incongruence: Clients are typically conflicted about what is at the core of their problem. Typically at the heart of a client's conflict are feelings of ambivalence (a topic of focus in Chapters 12 and 13). Because of this ambivalence, a client may demonstrate a certain incongruity or perhaps a disconnect between what he or she is saying and how he or she is saying it. Observing such disconnects and incongruities is important to the therapeutic process in that it affords an opportunity to explore and understand the ambivalence clients feel and begins to focus the client's attention on his or her emotional system. To accomplish such exploration, a therapist can make statements to a client such as "I notice that your heart doesn't seem to be in what you are saying," "You seem to be saying one thing and your body seems to be saying something else," "I notice that you appear to be hesitant in talking about . . . ," and "That was an awful big sigh that went along with what you were thinking at the moment." Such statements reveal a therapist's sensitivity to and awareness of the client's feelings of ambivalence about the situation.

Linear and nonlinear listening for absence of feelings: Frequently, a master practitioner will observe that a client does not appear to express feelings when it would be quite normal to do so, given the situation being described. Observing such behavior, therapists may ask themselves, "What are the feelings that are *not* being expressed? Why are they not being expressed? Are they too painful, too embarrassing, or too overwhelming?" In turn, such questions can be transformed into inquiries to the client: "I notice that you don't seem to express much feeling much about . . . ," "That sounded awful to me but I notice that . . . ," or "How do you keep going without being upset when . . . ?" Such questions are meant to give clients a safe environment and an opportunity to delve into what they are feeling but not expressing—a necessary step on the road to self-understanding and freedom from the tyranny of symptomatic behavior by reconnecting the elements of the client's emotional system.

Linear and nonlinear listening for inference: The feelings that a client expresses are connected to the values and value system to which the client adheres. Put another way, a client's expressions of affect, internal feelings, and emotional states are connected to his or her schema dynamics. When what a person believes and values is stimulated (i.e., positively or negatively through threat or what the client is attracted to), emotions are automatically triggered with corresponding feelings. Thus, helping clients recognize what they are feeling becomes a gateway to what they believe in their schemas. If a client didn't believe what it is that he or she believes, the client wouldn't feel the way he or she does. Feelings would not be aroused as a vigilant alarm that an individual is perceiving threat of some sort. Thus, linear thinking subtly suggests that emotions are an entity unto themselves—a human mystery. On the other hand, using nonlinear thinking, master practitioners can extrapolate and infer from a client's feelings that there are beliefs and convictions underlying those feelings.

Linear and nonlinear listening for presence: In essence, this entire chapter is about listening for the expression of client feelings. The most obvious, outward sign of these is the client's expression of affect. Overwhelming client feelings can and do begin to subside. When they do, it is often helpful to ask clients how that came about—is the client doing something differently that led to an attenuation or resolution of what the client had been feeling (e.g., "I could be wrong, but it appears to me that you had tears in your eyes just a moment ago when you were describing . . .")? An accompanying question is to inquire how he or she was able to accomplish such an attenuation or resolution of such strong feelings. The latter question is important because it highlights to the client how his or her own resources, resolve, actions, decisions, and so on were instrumental in his or her feelings subsiding—the client brings about the change with the therapist as the coach. It is naïve linear thinking that suggests that a therapist can take credit for therapeutic movement; it is nonlinear thinking that returns credit for bringing about change to the client.

The Therapeutic Relationship and Emotions

Master practitioners' listening for presence, absence, congruence, inference, and resistance plays a prominent role in dealing with client emotions. Responding to client expressions of emotion plays an equally prominent role. As Marci, Ham, Moran, and Orr (2007) have recently demonstrated, exactly how a therapist responds to client emotions is a significant variable in determining client perceptions of therapist empathy. A contemporary understanding of emotions informs us that they do not simply exist within a client; the therapist can conjointly experience what a client is experiencing—in fact, that is the essence of empathy (see Chapter 4).

Level II therapists, at this stage of development, have developed a much greater proficiency at attenuating any personal feelings of anxiety about their professional role. Obviously, achieving a greater sense of comfort in a therapy setting allows therapists to be less encumbered by internal processes that can easily detract from listening ever more acutely for feelings that a client is expressing directly or indirectly, or not expressing. When a therapist is relaxed, engaged, interested, hopeful, and empathic, a client can experience it.

Domain 5 Nonlinear Thinking Exercise—Hedonism and Epicurus

"You can live to be a hundred if you give up all the things that make you want to live to be a hundred."

—Woody Allen

"It is impossible to live a pleasant life without living wisely and well and justly. And it is impossible to live wisely and well and justly without living a pleasant life."

—Epicurus

Hedonism. The word evokes orgiastic pleasure of ancient Greek bacchanal wine festivals or a Mardi Gras parade in New Orleans. Founded by the Greek philosopher Epicurus, indeed, the definition of hedonism is the "pursuit of pleasure and the avoidance of pain" (Hayden & Picard, 2009, p. 146). In fact, the modern word hedonistic is synonymous with gluttony, luxury, and excess. So it would stand to reason that if someone wanted to be a hedonist, they should just do pleasurable things: eat, drink, and be merry. Indulging in sex, drugs, and rock 'n roll should also be the norm. In addition, people should avoid painful things. So, therefore, people should avoid work or other efforts or responsibilities that might be discomforting or difficult.

Stoicism is considered to be the opposite of hedonism. Think of the word *stoic*. To be called on is to be coldly logical (think Mr. Spock from *Star Trek*), unemotional (think Sheldon Cooper from *The Big Bang Theory*), and usually through the denial of pleasure. In fact, the philosophical school of stoicism was founded by the Greek philosopher Zeno, who felt that people should free themselves from passion (and all its disturbing emotional ups and downs) by following reason. The end goal of stoicism is to enable people to develop clear judgment and inner calm, thus having a pleasurable life.

However, hedonism and stoicism are not as opposite as people think. In fact, our modern interpretations are not what the originators of the philosophical schools intended. The philosophy indeed elevated pleasure and happiness as the most worthy pursuit, but specifically warned against fine food and frequent sex, for it could lead to dissatisfaction later. According to Epicurus "I spit on luxurious pleasures . . . not for their own sake, but because of the inconveniences that follow them" (as cited in Hayden & Picard, 2009). So, even though eating a piece of rich chocolate cake is pleasurable, and eating *half* the cake would be even more pleasurable, the hedonists would frown upon it because of the pain (tummy ache) that it would cause later. Instead, the goal was a long-term pleasure, marked by serenity and temperance, achieved through moderation rather than indulging. In fact, if you were to be a true hedonist, you would look like a stoic and not like a partygoer in the French Quarter at 3 a.m.!

Now what does this have to do with counseling? As we mentioned in the beginning of the chapter, people tend to want to avoid feelings, thoughts, or events that are unpleasant. Most people would say that they want to feel pleasure and lead a good, pleasurable life. And like the modern definition of hedonism, they want luxury and comfort while avoiding pain and effort. Philosopher John Stuart Mill (as cited in Hayden & Picard, 2009) wrote that people who are happy are ones who "have their mind fixed on some object other than their own happiness: on the happiness of others, on the improvement of mankind . . . something else they find happiness on the way" (p. 149). So the ironic, nonlinear aspect of this is that when people try to focus on their happiness, they become unhappy because they realize that they are not truly happy now, or if they are, their happiness will end soon (which then makes them unhappy). However, the nonlinear thought is that to have the pleasurable life, sometimes one must be more stoic, and rather than merely avoid pain, accept it and minimize its impact on their lives. This is the essence of many of the approaches that we discuss in this domain.

Emotion-Focused Therapy Using the Relationship between Emotions and Schema Dynamics

In Chapter 10, we described how schema dynamics introduced in Chapters 8 and 9 (i.e., view of self, view of others, and view of the world and life) played a role in the appraisal process. In addition, we described how it can be problematic for individuals who are not aware of the influences that their schema dynamics wield. We now revisit some of these ideas in order to show how therapists' use of nonlinear thinking can help clients connect the elements of their emotional system and help clients connect their emotional system to their schema dynamics, in order to reappraise their problematic circumstances. Specifically, we apply this to emotion-focused therapy (EFT), first developed for couples by Les Greenberg and Susan Johnson. Beginning in the late 1980s, they felt that emotion was being marginalized by many of the mainstream therapies and wanted to develop an approach that stressed "the primary significance of emotion and emotional communication" (Johnson & Best, 2003, p. 165). They anchored their approach in attachment theory, which holds that a person's constructs (called internal working models of self and others, or attachment style) for how to act and react are molded in early childhood relationships. In other words, EFT is based on a client's schema dynamics (attachment style) and works with their emotional system when problems arise (i.e., reactions). This is where the reconnecting process becomes essential, particularly in EFT.

EFT has three distinct stages that therapists move through relatively quickly (between 8 to 12 sessions (Johnson & Best, 2003). Stage one is cycle de-escalation, which is characterized by assessing the areas of conflict, identifying negative interaction cycles, accessing underlying emotional issues driving the interaction, and reframing the problem in light of larger attachment needs. Stage two is changing interactional patterns and includes promoting acceptance of each person's needs and facilitating the expression of emotions. Last, stage three is consolidation and integration where new solutions and cycles based on the understanding of the conflicts in light of the attachment (i.e., schema) needs and expression of emotions (Johnson & Denton, 2002; Sperry et al., 2006). We discuss some common methods of working with client emotions based on EFT below, including coaching, focusing, and reflecting.

EFT—Therapeutically Working with Emotions: Coaching the Therapist's Approach to Working Successfully with Emotions

As we mentioned at the beginning of this chapter, working with clients' emotions can be very difficult for many therapists, and some avoid actively engaging with client emotions because of their own issues, or their own lack of competence in this domain. In terms of EFT therapy, emotion is primary in organizing attachment behaviors and determining how self and other are experienced in intimate relationships: "Emotion guides and gives meaning to perception, motivates and cues behavior, and when expressed, communicates to others" (Johnson & Whiffen, 1999, p. 367). As a result, EFT therapists must privilege emotional communication and pay particular attention to the cycles of escalation and soothing of fear (Johnson & Best, 2003). In one form or another, many of the master practitioners in this domain—particularly Greenberg and Johnson—accomplish this by acting as an emotional coach. This is a fitting metaphor regarding emotional coaching when considering what a good coach[2] does. Coaches are important because they (1) collaborate with a client in strategizing to achieve specified goals, (2) confer responsibility for success upon the player (i.e., client), and (3) are supportive at moments that require calming, focusing, energizing, and so on. In EFT, this can be used at any of the three stages, although it is probably used most intently in stage one (cycle de-escalation).

Coaching is also an extremely useful metaphor for counselors to conceptualize what they can provide a client regarding emotional regulation. Within the context of the domain of establishing and maintaining a therapeutic relationship and the therapeutic alliance (see Chapter 7), appropriate coaching provides clients with greater potential opportunity for growth and better functioning. Coaches maintain clarity regarding the boundaries of the relationship and recognize that responsibility for success belongs to the player (i.e., the client), not the other way around.

Greenberg (2004) has defined two specific phases in the emotional-coaching process:

- *Arriving* (i.e., the process of helping a client come to a more informed awareness and acceptance of his or her feelings)
- *Leaving* (i.e., the process of deciding whether the particular place his or her feelings reveal is good or not good for him or her)

Arriving entails four steps: (1) identification of what a client is feeling; (2) welcoming and accepting of what one is feeling, as it is what it is; (3) labeling or putting into words and developing a vocabulary to describe what one is feeling; and (4) exploring a client's emotional experiences and determining what the core or primary feelings are (e.g., if a client expresses anger regarding someone, the therapeutic task is to determine if the anger betrays a feeling of being belittled, marginalized, etc.).

Leaving also entails four steps: (1) the process of assisting a client to assess if a primary feeling (or the core feeling being experienced) is healthy or unhealthy, and if it is the latter, it requires processing; (2) the process of identifying maladaptive destructive schema(s) (e.g., "I am worthless" or "Life sucks") connected to particular maladaptive emotion(s); (3) the process of gaining entrée to alternate adaptive emotions and needs (e.g., helping clients key in on what their needs, goals, and concerns are); and (4) the process of facilitating a client in transforming maladaptive emotions and beliefs that are destructive.

But Don't Take Our Word for It! Master Example

In this example of a transcript with a master practitioner, Susan Johnson (cocreator of EFT), works with a couple who are working through issues of being emotionally hostile to one another (Alexander Street Press, 2012).

Susan Johnson:	"'Let myself feel this longing, and for you to let me down, I couldn't stand that.' Is that what you're saying?"
Wife:	"Right I don't think I could be in the marriage anymore, to tell you the honest truth."
Susan Johnson:	"'I can't be hurt like that, I couldn't be hurt like that.'"
Wife:	"I can't be hurt like that, no. So that's why, no, I don't think I could stand it."

Susan Johnson:	"I hear you. [Addressing husband] What happens for you Earl when you hear your lady saying this?"
Husband:	"Uh that's difficult. Um, I think uh, I think I acted badly when we were in our very worst state, you know, would it be the first of the 'demon dialogues.'"
Susan Johnson:	"When you were attacking each other."
Husband:	"Yeah. And uh, I think that's in reflecting back on it, I was trying to push her away as quickly as I could to bring peace to the situation of the moment, which obviously did no good at all."
Susan Johnson:	"So you're saying to your lady, 'you help me' when she says this to you. You feel what? Sad, that she's saying this? Or you feel regret? You say to yourself, 'Gee, maybe she's got the right to be scared because I acted badly?' Is that how it goes?"
Husband:	"Well, yes, I think she's got the right to feel that way because I did act badly, and I do from time to time, and I think we both do, and it's distressing to me to think that it could be over, that she's reached the point where she can't take it any more [to wife] that you can't take it anymore. You know, that's certainly not what I want."
Wife:	"That's why it hurts so bad."

Clearly, a Level II clinician (in an emotional-coaching role) encourages a client to reflect on distressing feeling states and work through them via thoughtful, rational, and reflective processes in order to develop (1) a greater sense of understanding about the purpose of the emotion (i.e., what important information the emotion reveals about what a client values) and (2) a greater sense of mastery of the emotions (e.g., reconnecting the elements of the client's emotional system and developing a sense of understanding about the emotion[s]). In the case example above, Johnson was able to help the couple see the destructive nature of the attachment injury that the husband's behavior would cause to his wife. In turn, Johnson was able to help coach him to understand where her disappointment translated into arguments, rather than understanding how the display of emotion was damaging their relationship. Such understandings promote a client feeling less victimized and overwhelmed by his or her emotions as well as more in control of him- or herself. Facilitating such emotional reflection for clients through coaching, however, is not the entire object lesson regarding the process of examining feelings.

Recall that the goal of any effective therapist in working with clients' emotions is to help clients reconnect the three elements of their emotional system (expressions of affect, internal feelings, and emotional states), as well as connect with their schema dynamics in order to reappraise their situation and make different behavioral choices.

EFT—Therapeutically Working with Emotions: Focusing to Foster Recognition and Reflection of Emotions

As noted above, the process of differentiating positive and negative feelings and catching oneself in the process of having strong negative emotional moods can be daunting because of the very nature of the emotional process. In EFT, this type of intervention may be used in stage one (cycle de-escalation) or stage two (changing interactional patterns). The daunting aspect of dealing with feelings can result in a client feeling stuck and thus disconnected from his or her emotional states and internal feelings (Johnson, 1996). Gendlin (1978) developed a therapeutic process called focusing that was designed to help clients cope with this vague sense of being stuck, being uncomfortable, and not being able to move on (or what we would call being disconnected from internal feelings). His research demonstrated a crucial difference in successful versus unsuccessful therapy outcomes:

We found that it is not the therapist's technique—differences in methods of therapy seem to mean surprisingly little. Nor does difference lie in what the patients talk about. The difference is in how they talk . . . what the successful patients do inside themselves. (pp. 4–6)

Gendlin further demonstrated that this difference consisted of attending to a felt sense of sensations, feelings, and cognitions located in a client's body and that this was a teachable skill. This is very similar to Bitter's (2008) exercise (see Information Box: Assisting Clients to Recognize and Reflect on Emotional Processes), identified as the Inner Act. The first step is to recognize and get in touch with this vague feeling of being stuck and its affective expression (even if the expression is to do nothing). Then, it is important to begin to connect that expression with the internal feeling sensation of being stuck. Pursuing this allows the client to begin the process of reconnecting his or her internal feelings with emotional states and affective expressions.

Information Box: Assisting Clients to Recognize and Reflect on Emotional Processes

Throughout the history of psychotherapy, several prominent practitioners focused considerable attention on the emotions and emotional processing. Three such practitioners were noted: family therapist Virginia Satir (1964), and Erving and Miriam Polster (1974) from the Gestalt therapy school pioneered by Fritz Perls. Bitter (2008), a master practitioner who has studied with and was influenced by both Satir and the Polsters, effectively integrated their approaches. In understanding emotions, both Satir and the Gestalt schools emphasized present experience and directing a client's attention to experiencing the physical sensations (both the affective expressions and internal feelings) as a means of helping a client to connect to the emotional state and schema dynamics that underlie (and drive) affective expressions (behaviors). Bitter directly tied in the client's schema dynamics as well by utilizing a variation of the ECR (for early childhood recollection) techniques described in Chapter 9. We briefly describe the process below:

- A client describes in detail the issue that she wants to work on.
- The therapist asks the client to describe any feelings that she is aware of regarding the issue.
- Then the therapist asks about the client's internal feelings. Specifically, the therapist asks the client to create as many *sensory connections* as possible to the feeling in order to strengthen her recognition of the feeling, and also asks the following:
- Where is the feeling located on the client's body?
- Does the feeling have a particular shape?
- Does the feeling have a particular texture? Is it smooth, coarse, rough, sharp, or the like?
- Does the feeling have a particular temperature to it (hot, cold, etc.)?
- Once the client has a clear visual and verbal picture of the feeling, the therapist asks the client to recall the earliest memory she has of feeling this way. Clients generally associate the present concern to the early childhood memory as well as the emotional processing surrounding it and to a particular schema dynamic.
- The therapist will then help the client to recognize the impact of her emotions and invite her to reflect on the connections to help with the original presenting concern.

As described in the discussion of ECRs (Chapter 9), there is an important relationship between what someone is feeling in a recalled childhood memory and what about the circumstances that she described prompted her to feel that way. As Bitter (2008) pointed out in the information box, what prompts someone to feel a particular way betrays an important emotional schema that contains a value for a client. Otherwise, what value would there be in feeling that way? For example, if a client expresses uncertainty, vulnerability, anxiety, and fear in an ECR, obviously, the important value (i.e., schema) being expressed is safety. Correspondingly, the client is not expressing a sense of invincibility, bravado, and so on. Moreover, by extension, the client is indicating that the perceived vulnerability expressed in the memory (e.g., "I was so small, and it was so scary!") requires the person to be vigilant to perceived threats to safety. Of course, some things perceived as threats in adulthood will be unfounded or exaggerated, and the price paid for such misperception may be that of living in a state of chronic alertness and anxiety.

If the feeling being expressed in an ECR is outrage over something that was perceived at the time of the memory to be unfair, fairness (or the perceived lack of it) is perhaps a value being expressed in the schema behind the memory. But the emotional reactions generated may not necessarily come with an awareness of the connections to underlying schema dynamics. It is such emotional reactions that need to be regulated, and regulation begins with understanding.

But Don't Take Our Word for It! Master Example

In this example of a transcript with a master practitioner, Susan Johnson (cocreator of EFT), works with a couple who are working through issues of being emotionally hostile to one another (Alexander Street Press, 2012).

Susan Johnson: "... Take that elevator down, and then you go into that softer feeling that you might not ever let yourself even feel if you were being strong and silent, the image that comes up for you is a baby crying, yeah?"

Husband: "Um, that was just the analogy that I used. I think that looking at the literature and listening to the tapes, it was probably a fear of failure, you know?"

Susan Johnson: "Is that right? Fear of failure?"

Husband: "Not being good enough for this particular relationship."

Susan Johnson: "That's a huge one, isn't it?"

Husband: "Yeah."

Susan Johnson: "That's a hard feeling, yeah? To love somebody and really want to be with them, and somehow not know how to do it right?"

Husband: "Yes."

Susan Johnson: "Feel like, 'I don't know how to do it, and I'm never gonna make it here, I'm never going to be good enough, yeah?' That hurts."

Husband: "Intensely powerful."

It is also important to remember that in the basic list of universal emotions, the unpleasant emotions (i.e., anger, sadness, fear, and disgust) identified by Ekman and Friesen (1975) outnumbered the pleasant emotions (i.e., joy and surprise) by a ratio of 2:1. In fact, Shaver, Schwartz, Kirson, and O'Connor (1987) determined that individuals have three times as many terms to describe nuances in unpleasant emotions as they do to describe nuances in pleasant ones. These salient facts suggest that the basic brain architecture of human beings, in addition to its programming (i.e., early learning), is clearly inclined toward being sensitive to and aroused by threats to survival (i.e., both physical and psychological). As a result, many clients may not have the vocabulary to appropriately label their experiences (see the discussion of Greenberg's arriving and leaving, above). Recall from Chapter 3 Clinical Exercise: Increasing Your Feeling Vocabulary. In the exercise, you were asked to create synonyms for high-, medium-, and low-intensity words for each of the primary emotions. This exercise can also be helpful for clients to be able to begin to help them identify their internal feelings and connect them to their expressions of affect and emotional states.

EFT—*Therapeutically Working with Emotions: Revelation, Reflecting, and Focusing*

Revelation or reflection refers to an individual not only being aware of her feelings but also reflecting upon them. Greenberg (2004) has astutely observed that there are two types of awareness. One type of awareness is based in the here and now and reveals that an individual is aware of what he or she is feeling but otherwise lacks an informed understanding of what he or she is feeling. The second type of awareness that Greenberg referred to is a more thoughtful sort of awareness. In such a state, an individual is not only fully aware of what he or she is feeling but also able to assess whether or not he or she *wants* to feel that way. Once this information is reflected on by the client, the client can then decide what it is that he or she wants to do about this particular feeling state. In EFT, this might be done at stage two (changing interactional positions) or stage three (consolidation and integration). These awareness assessment processes are reflective and revealing in nature. Once again, Greenberg was helpful in summarizing this process:

> This state of being aware of one's conscious feeling of emotion allows one ultimately also to be aware of the lived past and the anticipated future and to make decisions about one's emotions in the present. One recognizes what one is feeling and considers whether one accepts one's response as appropriate. Developing and applying this capacity is an important aspect of emotional intelligence. (p. 30)

In practical terms, how does one go about encouraging a client to reflect on his or her feelings? Once again, the process is counterintuitive and nonlinear. As previously discussed, clients typically infer not wanting to feel in some particular way—they want to be rid of particular feelings, thus eliminating the discomfort attendant to such a feeling(s). The Level II practitioner may encourage a client to begin accepting the feeling, in effect as though the feeling was attempting to inform the client that something important is stirring. The next relatively simple step is to assess if it is drawing the client toward something or away from something—is it a friend or foe? Is the feeling healthy and adaptive, something a client should nurture and use its energy to move toward one's wants, or is it an unhealthy and maladaptive feeling, an obstacle to one's sense of well-being and goals and needing to be replaced (Greenberg, 2004)? One may also consider in this reflection phase suggestions from Gendlin (1978):

> What is the worst of this feeling? . . . What really is so bad about this? . . . What does it need? . . . What should happen? . . . Don't answer: wait for the feeling to stir and give you an answer. . . . What would it feel like if it was all O.K.? (p. 178)

Such reflection is cognitive in nature, although it refers to a process of regulating one's emotions (to be discussed below).

But Don't Take Our Word for It! Master Example

In this example of a transcript with a master practitioner, Susan Johnson (cocreator of EFT), works with a couple who are working through issues of being emotionally hostile to one another (Alexander Street Press, 2012).

Susan Johnson: "You said we are starting to, I am starting to realize that underneath this pattern that we would get caught in, where you know, you would move away

> and shut down and say 'I don't know what to say, so I'm not going to say any-
> thing,' and you'd get more anxious, more upset, you said 'I started to realize
> that really was like a baby crying.' Yeah."
>
> Husband: "Yes. Uh, and the reason I use that analogy is because, I just don't—I know
> for one that I didn't recognize what was going on. My family background is
> that you know, we were not a very close family unit, um, you know there was
> not a lot of love and tenderness shown around and being cast in a traditional
> male role, I thought, you know, 'you gotta be strong, you gotta do everything
> on your own, you gotta depend on yourself,' and you know when in doubt, I
> always just reach back into that mode to kind of just get me through."
>
> Susan Johnson: "Be strong, be silent, right."
>
> Husband: "And uh, looking at the literature, that was absolutely the worst thing I could
> have done, but I can almost honestly say that I didn't know there was a differ-
> ent way to be, not coming from a loving touching place."

Using Mindfulness to Help Clients Understand and Manage Emotions Therapeutically

Another counter-approach to the logic-based approach of cognitive-behavioral therapy (and for some and adjunct to it) came from Eastern meditative practices. Beginning in the 1970s—with some earlier precursors like Morita Therapy, Gestalt Therapy, and others—several practitioners began adapting popular practices like transcendental meditation, focused breathing, and yoga into therapeutic work (Rosch, 2007; Teasdale, 1999). These were used as techniques to try to teach clients to control their emotions when they felt out of control. However, it wasn't until practitioners began to make the ideas central to their theoretical approaches (rather than a mere technique) that a new approach to help-ing clients effectively manage their emotions came into practice. These approaches all draw from the central idea of *mindfulness* to inform their practice when working with client emotions. We begin with a brief description of mindfulness, and then discuss three approaches: mindfulness-based cognitive behavioral therapy, acceptance and commitment therapy, and dialectical behavioral therapy.

Definition of Mindfulness

Although mindfulness has it roots in Buddhist traditions, it has only been recently that a consensus clinical definition has been agreed to. In 2004, Bishop and his colleagues defined mindfulness in two components:

> The first component involves the self-regulation of attention so that it is maintained on imme-
> diate experience, thereby allowing for increased recognition of mental events in the present
> moment. The second component involves adopting a particular orientation toward one's expe-
> riences in the present moment, an orientation that is characterized by curiosity, openness, and
> acceptance. (Bishop et al., 2004, p. 232)

As a result, practitioners who work within a mindfulness-based approach remain focused on the pres-ent while also inviting the client to also become aware of their own experiences, without a need to distract or run away from it. Bishop et al. (2004) conclude that mindfulness is "a kind of non-elaborative, non-judgmental, present-centered awareness in which each thought, feeling, or sensation that arises in the attentional field is acknowledged and accepted as it is" (p. 232). Many Eastern mindfulness approaches help clients attain a level of emotional soothing by teaching some basic relaxation (and mindfulness) techniques. There are three essential elements in this process: (1) being in a relaxed state by focusing on one's breathing, (2) practicing *choiceless awareness* as distractions occur to the client (which they inevitably will), and (3) gently returning to the breathing and breath focus. This is the posture that a therapist takes toward her own feelings and that she models for the client to the client. Much like Greenberg's (2004) arriving phase in emotional coaching, mindfulness is the posture a therapist adopts in being with a client, and it is also the posture that a therapist encourages clients to adopt toward their own feelings (Benson & Proctor, 2003). This is the embodiment of being in tune, discussed in Chapter 6. Sometimes, client feelings can be so overwhelming, however, that it is difficult for a client to nonjudgmentally accept them without reacting to them. In such cases, a therapist can help a client to create some distance from his feelings by clearing a space for them: "You don't go into the problems. . . . [S]tand back just a little way. . . . [S]tand back a few feet from your problems. . . . [Y]ou can walk up and touch them if you like. . . . [Y]ou can pull back whenever they begin to get too threatening" (Gendlin, 1978, pp. 71–72). We discuss how this is reflected in various approaches to a client's emotional experience below.

Clinical Attitude and Disposition: Self-Soothing and Therapeutic Detachment

"The very winds whispered in soothing accents, and maternal Nature bade me weep no more."
—Mary Wollstonecraft Shelley

"The language of excitement is at best picturesque merely. You must be calm before you can utter oracles."

—Henry David Thoreau

Working with clients in therapy is not only a mentally challenging endeavor, it is also emotionally taxing for the therapist. In previous chapters we have discussed mirror neurons and emotional tuning forks to describe the process of being in synch with the client. And although these are important tools for clinicians, there can be a downside as well. When clients show strong emotions—sadness, fear, anger—it can often cause a reaction in the therapist. A very angry client may cause the therapist to feel defensive (if the anger is directed at them) or frustrated (if the anger is unproductive and the client is unable to calm down). An anguished client may produce intense feelings of sadness and loss in a therapist, and an anxious client may produce feelings of frustration or mild anxiety in the therapist. The source of these feelings—for the clinician—may simply be sympathetic activation (i.e., emotional tuning forks), or it may arise out of the client's own past (see the discussion on countertransference in Chapter 5). Or these feelings may come from the clinician's fear about his or her own competence as a therapist.

Many times clinicians don't know what to do or how to help someone who is showing strong emotions. They may feel overwhelmed and, as a result, try to subtly discourage clients from becoming too emotional, out of a fear of not being able to help the client. This sends a message to a client that it is not okay to show strong emotions in sessions. Clinicians may move too fast away from emotionally charged issues and switch to a safer topic that won't arouse strong feelings. This way they can feel more in control and less overwhelmed. Sometimes this is a useful strategy when the client is so overwhelmed that the emotion just gets in the way, but if it is done because the clinician is overwhelmed, then it is a problem. Unfortunately, this emotional intolerance by clinicians robs them of one of the most important sources of motivation for change in the client. At the same time, clients are sensitive to their counselors or therapists failing to react (i.e., acknowledging, joining with, and responding to clients' emotions) or reacting poorly to their emotional expressions because of countertransference or anxiety issues associated with their role as counselor. Piercy, Lipchik, and Kiser (2000) and Schwartz and Johnson (2000) noted that a client's sensitivity to such inabilities leads to feelings that the therapist is not in synch with the client. This creates potential for a therapeutic rupture and the beginning of disengagement from the therapy process, which can likely result in premature termination (as discussed in Chapter 7).

So how do clinicians successfully manage their reactions in the face of strong client emotions? They must do it nonlinearly. In other words, in order to keep it from becoming problematic or overwhelming, master clinicians learn how to both feel the emotions that are present in the room (whether it is their own or the client's), while at the same time keep themselves relaxed and soothed. In this domain, we present some techniques borrowed from the mindfulness schools of thought. These approaches value the experience of emotions but don't allow them to overwhelm the therapist or the therapy. In family therapy, Augustus Napier and Carl Whitaker used the metaphor of a *crucible* to describe the purpose of (family) therapy, as well as the stance of the therapist. From this perspective, the therapist must remain emotionally nonreactive, so that whatever powerful emotions the clients bring into the session can be reflected back on them (just as high heat is reflected back into the metals or chemicals in actual crucibles) in order to produce a structural (i.e., second-order) change in the clients (Napier & Whitiker, 1978). If the therapist becomes reactive (angry, scared, sad) and gets too emotionally involved, then his or her ability to remain detached or objective disappears. When this happens, it can change the client's experience in therapy and (usually) negatively impacts the effectiveness of it. This is the essence of therapeutic detachment.

Master clinicians develop a number of ways to be both connected emotionally and detached therapeutically. They can balance using their emotional tuning forks and mirror neurons, while at the same time remain reflective and attentive to clients. Skovholt and Jennings (2004) found that master therapists distinguish themselves in this domain by demonstrating an ability to attend to and effectively work with clients' emotions and emotional states, while simultaneously paying attention to their own emotional states. As the work of Jackson et al. (2006) have demonstrated, there are similar brain processes operating when we are in pain and when we are empathizing with others' pain. But although these neural processes overlap, they are not identical. That allows therapists to not only be empathic but also remain objective and maintain appropriate professional boundaries. Nonlinear understandings of emotions aroused within a therapist are viewed as a valued source of knowledge that provides information regarding potentially important issues (see Chapters 6 and 7). For example, the astute Level II clinician asks, "Are the feelings I'm experiencing being stimulated by issues that I have? If so, do they represent unresolved concerns that I have about certain sensitive areas of my life? Or are these feelings being aroused within me because of some sort of provocative behavior in the client?" When their own inappropriate emotional issues enter the therapeutic alliance (viz., inappropriate countertransference), many Level I practitioners become somewhat befuddled, making it impossible for them to manage clients' emotions effectively. This is the idea behind therapeutic detachment and self-soothing. In order to remain nonreactive in the face of client emotions, the therapist must use many of the same soothing techniques that they teach clients (like focused breathing, progressive relaxation, mental visualization, etc.), and they avoid the trap of either emotionally distancing (or "checking out") or becoming too emotionally engrossed in the client's problems. Both traps essentially doom the therapy. As you review some of the master clinician vignettes or videos, observe how they are able to keep themselves emotionally soothed, while remaining both wholly engaged with the client, and at the same time, somewhat therapeutically detached. Clearly it is a nonlinear feat.

Mindfulness-Based Cognitive Therapy—Basic Mindfulness and Getting Emotional Distance

Mindfulness-based cognitive-behavioral therapy (MBCT) was designed to help clients who suffered with repeated bouts of major depressive disorder. In addition to traditional cognitive-behavioral methods of cognitive restructuring and disputing, MBCT added components of mindfulness (like meditation or focusing on awareness) as an additional method for interrupting automatic negative thoughts when a downward cycle began, which could trigger a full-blown depressive episode. Instead, the mindfulness techniques worked to get the client not to focus on reacting to their perceptions but to notice them and let them pass (Manicavasgar, Parker, & Perich, 2011). According to research conducted by Ma and Teasdale (2004), this approach was able to reduce the relapse of people with chronic depression by one half.

But Don't Take Our Word for It! Master Example

In this example, we present master cognitive-behavioral therapist Michael Yapko, who uses a focusing technique to help the client experience his previously uncontrollable temper and negative affect (Alexander Street Press, 2012).

Michael Yapko: "... The idea of focusing to you, alright? If you're comfortable with the way that you're sitting that's fine, what I suggest that you do is that you let your eyes close, take a few deep breaths, and just orient yourself for a couple of minutes to the notion of absorbing yourself in a different way of thinking about your own experience. Now you probably haven't thought about this before, but when you get absorbed in the past, the negative feelings of the things that have gone on, you can get so absorbed in it that you don't really see other ways of thinking, other ways of feeling. But one of the things that is potentially valuable about taking a few minutes to just sit quietly the way you are now, is that it gives you the freedom to explore other parts of yourself. You know you are much, much more than your past, Mike. And that phrase of being much more than your past is going to surface at different times, and different places. But when I encourage you to start thinking about yourself and your experience, and to go exploring within yourself, there are strengths that you have that you use to cope, that you've used to build a different life for yourself, being married, having your own family. Things that you have clearly left behind.".

Client: (has eyes closed, is in a meditative state)

Michael Yapko: "Feel. Now certainly you know that your mind is generating lots of different things. Audio clips and video clips from different life experiences. But it is so interesting when you're in a more comfortable state of mind to realize that those are things that can just drift past and not really stick to you. Things that can just float by that you never latch on to, or give time to."

Using Elements of Acceptance and Commitment Therapy to Therapeutically Work with Emotions

Acceptance and commitment therapy (ACT), developed by Steven C. Hayes and his colleagues in the 1980s and 1990s was one of the first approaches to place mindfulness as part of its core constructs. They began with the idea that pathology is due to psychological inflexibility. According to Hayes, Luoma, Bond, Masuda, and Lillis (2006), individuals who experience psychological problems have a lack of values or clarity; are avoidant of certain unpleasant experience or emotions; tend to be impulsive; and are fused with their dominant thoughts of a concept of the past that they are damaged and that the future is certain (and usually bad). However, instead of trying to teach people to just control their thoughts, feelings, and behaviors (as most cognitive-behavioral approaches do), ACT teaches clients to increase their psychological flexibility (not unlike accommodation of schema dynamics, described in Chapter 9) by noticing, accepting, and embracing their internal thoughts and feelings. These are viewed as "positive psychological skills, not merely a method of avoiding psychopathology" (Hayes et al., 2006, p. 8). There are six core clinical principles that ACT clinicians utilize which include: acceptance, cognitive diffusion, contact with the present moment, viewing the self as context, values, and committed action. We discus these below.

Acceptance

In ACT, *acceptance* is taught as an alternative to experiential avoidance. "Acceptance involves the active and aware embrace of those private events occasioned by one's history without unnecessary attempts to change their frequency or form, especially when doing so would cause psychological harm" (Hayes et al., 2006, p. 8). Such individuals are in synch with their emotional feelings and are accepting of what they are feeling, regardless of whether it is positive or negative (Mayer & Stevens, 1993). For example, anxious clients are taught to feel anxiety, as a feeling, fully and without defense. In other words, thoughts are allowed to come and go without struggling with them.

But Don't Take Our Word for It! Master Example

In this example of a transcript with a master practitioner, Steven Hayes (cocreator of ACT), works with a client who is working through issues of accepting her needs and problematic social behaviors (Alexander Street Press, 2012).

Steven Hayes: "Now what I want you to do is see if you can get in touch with the amount of pain that she's in, and judgment that she's carrying. Wanting safety and not getting it. Getting criticism from mom. And not even in a sense stepping up to honoring that violation that happened to her or acknowledging it. Is there something she wants from you that you can give her? You've got her here [holds air]. What does she want?"

Client: "To feel loved."

Steven Hayes: "Okay. Do you love her?"

Client: "Maybe. I don't know. I mean. I'm annoyed at her a little bit."

Steven Hayes: "Alright, she's coming back off your lap."

Client: (laughs, speaking to air) "Sorry!"

Steven Hayes: "Now go in there. Don't answer this quickly but go inside this resistance. There's a place that you're sort of withholding, it's conditional? Yeah? With her? And I want you to open up to that, and see if there's some possibilities other than just getting stuck just there."

In the example above, Hayes is able to use acceptance to allow the client to be honest with herself about her complicated feelings about the younger version of herself. This is one of the most important ACT core principles, as it allows the client to take a different perspective on their emotional states.

Cognitive Diffusion

According to Mayer and Stevens (1993), individuals who habitually feel overwhelmed or swamped by their emotions and somewhat "helpless to escape them, as though their moods have taken charge" (p. 48), are "engulfed." Correspondingly, such individuals are not very aware of their feeling states, cannot easily identify their feelings, and don't feel that they can influence or control their emotions.

It is as though they are chronically stressed by a feeling of being overwhelmed and emotionally out of control but without being aware of it. Indeed, many clients come to therapy with this style. In ACT, the core principle of cognitive diffusion is used to counteract this engulfed style of emotional reaction. According to Hayes et al. (2006):

> Cognitive diffusion techniques attempt to alter the undesirable functions of thoughts and other private events, rather than trying to alter their form, frequency or situational sensitivity. Said another way, ACT attempts to change the way one interacts with or relates to thoughts by creating contexts in which their unhelpful functions are diminished." (p. 9)

This could mean just observing: "I am thinking that I am no-good," which would weaken the strength of the particular thought or feeling that made the client feel bad about him- or herself.

But Don't Take Our Word for It! Master Example

In this example of a transcript with a master practitioner, Steven Hayes (cocreator of ACT), works with a client who is working through issues of accepting her needs and problematic social behaviors (Alexander Street Press, 2012).

Steven Hayes: ". . . Get close to. Is your painful part, your lonely part, the pain of that judgment, your enemy? Or does it tell you something about what you want?"

Client: (nods) "Yeah, I mean yeah, it does. It tells me how much I want to be close to somebody. And how much I really want a relationship to work."

Steven Hayes: "Okay. Now if you have that, what's out in the future, and pull it into the present so it isn't just 'I want to have a good relationship,' but it's something more like 'I want to step toward that kind of connection that I know something about, and it hurts when it's not there.' What are you going to have to carry . . . I asked you if we had that pain on one side, what was on the other side? Okay? Suppose these are two flip sides of the same thing? Suppose that sweet spot, and the pain of loneliness, judgment, lack of safety, lack of creating a place, of the adults creating a place for you. What if that sweet spot and that pain are two sides of the same coin? Suppose I give it to you, and I say 'Here's this thing, and you can get rid of it.' You can hide the loneliness and the pain, but you're going to have to throw away both sides. I'm sorry, but you've got to throw away this sweet spot too. You can't care about that."

Client: "I don't think that's possible."

Steven Hayes: "Well you kind of in a way have been doing it, you know? You've been trying to throw it away, and then get mad that this other side gets thrown too."

Client: "Right."

So in the session excerpt above, Hayes works with the client to see that there is another way of looking at her painful memories and feelings. In ACT, cognitive diffusion is a nonlinear method for teaching clients to learn how to change how they experience their thoughts, images, emotions, and memories in a way that is less hurtful for them.

Contact with the Present Moment

Contact with the present moment is characterized by developing an awareness of the here and now, experienced with openness, interest, and receptiveness. According to Hayes et al. (2006) "the goal is to have clients experience the world more directly so that their behavior is more flexible and thus their actions more consistent with the values that they hold" (p. 9). This is accomplished by showing the client that she has more ability to exert control over her behavior. Much like the narrative therapy practitioners (see Chapter 13), by using language more as a tool to note and describe events, clients find that they are not emotional hostages to their previous beliefs or ideas, but rather authors of their own reactions and feelings.

But Don't Take Our Word for It! Master Example

In this example of a transcript with a master practitioner, Steven Hayes (cocreator of ACT), works with a client who is working through issues of accepting her needs and problematic social behaviors (Alexander Street Press, 2012).

Steven Hayes: "Reach out, and touch folks. Take some time to sort of go in there and get in touch with that, okay? If we were to give it a word, give me a couple words as to the core of it. Take a moment to actually see if you can actually find it?"

Client: "Lonely. Anxious. Just pain."

Steven Hayes: "Okay. What I want you to do is sort of take that pain and just flip it over. Tell me what you care about such that it would be so painful? Like what would you have to not care about for that not to hurt?"

Client: "People."

Steven Hayes: "Okay."

So in this excerpt, Hayes shows the client that she can be present in the moment with an uncomfortable feeling without avoiding it, as well as get her to be aware of what the cost is for her to avoid the feeling (i.e., contact with people, which is what she wants in the first place).

Observing the Self as Context

Observing the self as context demonstrates a significant sophistication in recognizing emotions. It means accessing a transcendent sense of self, which is unchanging compared with emotional states, which shift depending on the circumstances. Associated with awareness of their emotional states, those possessing this style tend to be autonomous, have an acute sense of their boundaries, and in general enjoy good psychological flexibility. Bad emotional moods don't occupy them for long because they tend to let them pass without ruminating or obsessing about them (Goleman, 1995; Hayes et al., 2006; Mayer & Stevens, 1993). According to Hayes et al. (2006) self as context:

> is important in part because from this standpoint, one can be aware of one's own flow of experiences without attachment to them or an investment in which particular experiences occur: thus defusion and acceptance is fostered. Self as context is fostered in ACT by mindfulness exercises, metaphors, and experiential processes. (p. 9)

Values

In ACT, psychological inflexibility is a possibility because a person is not clear on what their values are and how to achieve them in life. According to Hayes et al. (2006): "Values are chosen qualities of purposive action that can never be obtained as an object but can be instantiated [exemplified] moment by moment: (p. 9). ACT uses a variety of exercises that undercut verbal processes (e.g., "I *should* value . . ." or "A good person would value . . ." or "My mother wants me to value . . .") that might lead a person to make choices based on avoidance, social compliance, or fusion rather than from their own values. Here nonlinear listening for congruence, inference, or absence would be important. This is an example of understanding and clarifying a person's schema dynamics (view of self, view of others, and view of world) in order to make them more positive, realistic, and flexible, rather than negative, unrealistic, and rigid. According to Hayes et al. (2006), this is what leads a person to having a more dynamic, values-consistent life.

Committed Action

In ACT, the goal is to be able to act (no pun intended) in a way that is consistent with one's values (i.e., schema dynamics). When this occurs, then the emotions that come with disappointment because of things that are beyond a person's control (like random events in life or choices that other people make) do not create devastatingly negative consequences for the client. According to Hayes et al. (2006):

> ACT encourages the development of larger and larger patterns of effective action linked to chosen values ... ACT looks very much like traditional behavior therapy, and almost any behaviorally coherent behavior change method can be fitted into an ACT protocol, including exposure, skills acquisition, shaping methods, goal setting, and the like. Unlike values, which are constantly instantiated but never achieved as an object, concrete goals that are values consistent can be achieved, and ACT protocols almost always involve therapy work and homework linked to short, medium, and long-term behavior change goals. Behavior change efforts in turn lead to contact with psychological barriers that are addressed through other ACT processes (acceptance, diffusion, and so on). (pp. 9–10)

Using Elements of Dialectical Behavioral Therapy to Therapeutically Work with Emotions

Another approach that has been developed with mindfulness as a core element to help clients understand and manage their emotions is dialectical behavioral therapy (DBT). Developed by Marsha Linehan and her colleagues in the 1990s as a treatment for clients with borderline personality disorder (BPD), who were not being helped by more traditional (cognitive-behavioral) therapeutic approaches, due primarily to the extreme emotionality that clients with BPD tend to have (Linehan, 1993; Linehan & Dimeff, 2001). According to Lynch, Chapman, Rosenthal, Kuo, and Linehan (2006):

> In treating chronically suicidal patients who have BPD, Marsha Linehan discovered an important shortcoming in standard cognitive and behavioral treatments: They focused almost exclusively on helping patients *change* their thoughts, feelings, and behaviors. A treatment solely focused on change often was not palatable to these patients, who often felt invalidated and criticized and dropped out of treatment. On the flip side, a treatment focused entirely on acceptance invalidated the seriousness of the patients' suffering and the urgent need to produce change. As a result, Dr. Linehan anchored DBT in a dialectical philosophy that encourages the balance and synthesis of both acceptance and change. (p. 461)

In order to accomplish this, DBT has four modules: mindfulness, distress tolerance, emotion regulation, and interpersonal effectiveness (Linehan, 1993). These are generally taught in both individual and group therapy as part of comprehensive treatment with DBT, which has been shown to have demonstrable effects (see Linehan & Dimeff, 2001; Lynch et al., 2006 for details). We discuss several elements of the modules as they relate to working with client emotions below.

Mindfulness

As mentioned above, mindfulness is one of the core concepts of DBT. It is the foundation for the other skills taught to clients in DBT, because it helps them tolerate and accept their emotions when they are faced with upsetting situations. As with other mindfulness approaches, in DBT it is the capacity to nonjudgmentally attend to the present moment and experience one's emotions and senses fully, without distortion (Linehan, 1993).

As part of the training of mindfulness, clients are taught two sets of skills. They are called *what* skills and *how* skills. The what skills include teaching clients to *observe* (nonjudgmentally) what is going on in a given circumstance); *describe* (explain simply what has been observed); and *participate* (becoming fully focused and involved in the events around them). The how skills give instruction about *nonjudgmentally* (describing the facts and not thinking about what's good or bad, fair or unfair, which helps to get the point across in an effective manner to someone else); *one-mindfully* (maintaining focus without becoming distracted by the emotional reactions that may be occurring); and *effectively* (doing what works and avoiding what does not). The primary purpose of these skills is to help a client determine if the powerful emotions that the client recognizes and is experiencing are adaptive or not. Mindfulness focuses the client's attention on his or her emotional states (primary emotions, secondary emotions, and background mood) as a way to help reconnect the client to internal feelings, as well as to schema dynamics. Obviously, if emotions are adaptive, they are endorsed and supported as authentic. If they are not adaptive, intense negative emotions must be subjected to a process of scrutiny. The first step in such scrutiny is to facilitate a sense of calm.

Distress Tolerance

Distress tolerance skills go hand-in-hand with DBT mindfulness skills. Briefly, distress tolerance is the ability to accept, in a nonevaluative and nonjudgmental fashion, both oneself and the current situation. Acceptance and tolerance are not signs of approval or rejection but acknowledge the reality of a situation as it is. The goal is to become capable of calmly recognizing negative situations and their impact, rather than becoming overwhelmed or hiding from them. Dialectical behavior therapy emphasizes learning to bear pain skillfully and making wise decisions about whether and how to take action, rather than falling into the intense, and often destructive emotional reactions that are a part of BPD (Linehan, 1993).

The first distress tolerance skill that is taught is distraction. Clients are taught to recognize the unpleasant situation or reaction, and then distract their attention temporarily, rather than act out. DBT therapists use the acronym ACCEPTS for the specific strategies used which stands for:

- Activities—Use positive activities that you enjoy.
- Contribute—Help out others or your community.
- Comparisons—Compare yourself either with people that are less fortunate or to how you used to be when you were in a worse state.
- Emotions (other)—Cause yourself to feel something different by provoking your sense of humor or happiness with corresponding activities.
- Push away—Put your situation on the back-burner for a while. Put something else temporarily first in your mind.
- Thoughts (other)—Force your mind to think about something else.
- Sensations (other)—Do something that has an intense feeling other than what you are feeling, like a cold shower or a spicy candy (taken from Linehan, 1993).

Another distress tolerance technique that DBT therapists teach is self-soothing. Although not limited to DBT, self soothing is a powerful tool to teach clients who have difficulty with strong emotions. Indeed, Frija (1986), Goleman (1995), Gross (1999), and Greenberg (2004) have all advocated soothing or emotional regulation, as being essential to emotional competence. This is a skill in which one behaves in a comforting, nurturing, kind, and gentle way to oneself. The process of learning self-soothing begins in childhood and is clearly facilitated by good parenting.

If self-soothing has not been learned in childhood (and incorporated into one's emotional system and schema dynamics), it can be challenging to learn as an adult. In a linear way, soothing can be seen to stem from the nurturing and intimate nature of the relationship between mother and child. With an ideal set of conditions, an infant who is upset and in distress because of the pain of hunger, being startled, and so on is highly amenable to the soothing nature of his mother's (or mother surrogate's) sight, voice tone, and touch. Likewise, an older child learns that her mother (or father) can provide the necessary soothing to assure her safety. It is axiomatic that a felt sense of safety in a child is essential for feeling comfortable in venturing out in the world.

In adult life, human beings learn that a spouse, significant other, relatives, friends, or even trusted coworkers are important sources of emotional support and soothing under a myriad of difficult circumstances that life can conjure. Although all of these are necessary and wonderful sources of comfort in a world and life that can be harsh, emotional competence demands more. It also requires self-soothing. However, the processes of allowing others to sooth and self-sooth require appropriate reappraisals and being aware of one's schema dynamics.

The objective of self-soothing is for an individual to provide feelings of emotional comfort to him- or herself as an antidote to a wide spectrum of negative thoughts, urges, and feelings. This is accomplished through a variety of methods such as promoting a dialogue with the self, treating the self well, and engaging in a healthy feeling experience. When an individual focuses on engaging in pleasant, nonharmful experiences (e.g., a warm bath, listening to one's favorite relaxing music, or engaging nature through a walk), this allows for a disengagement from emotions that for the moment are sensed as overwhelming. Such disengagement allows an individual a respite from the intensity of negative emotions and simultaneously demonstrates to a client in a nonlinear way that he or she has the capacity to exercise control over his or her emotional life.

Clinical Exercise: Therapeutic Methods for Self-Soothing

Directions: Think about and write down five self-soothing behaviors, activities, or rituals. Then think of five additional ways that you could recommend to a client.

Variation: Form groups and create a list of self-soothing behaviors, activities, or rituals to share with the class or group.

But Don't Take Our Word for It! Master Example

In this example, master clinician Marsha Linehan, PhD (developer of DBT) works with a woman who became angry about being treated unfairly at work (Alexander Street Press, 2012).

Marsha Linehan: "But, nonetheless, right at the moment, your current lack of skills it seems like what we have to insert is the thought in your mind that says 'I won't like mine'?"

Client: "If I wasn't that way with people . . ."

Marsha Linehan: "Alright so your self-respect is on the line."

Client: "Right."

Marsha Linehan: "Okay. So then. We're going to have to switch what you're saying to yourself. Because telling yourself that you'll be more effective when you use skills than not may not actually be true to some people. Least not at your current

> level of skills. I have to tell you though, I think you can get skilled enough where skill will work better than anger most of the time. Nonetheless, right at this moment, your current level of skills it seems like what we have to insert is the thought in your mind that says, 'I won't like myself if I do this.' Because that's the really reason you want to change, right?"
>
> Client: "Mmhmm."

A key to learning self-soothing in the face of persistent negative emotions is nonlinear thinking. Equally ironic, it involves, as a first step, embracing whatever it is one is feeling (i.e., mindfulness). Clearly, this is counterintuitive because most individuals just want to be rid of negative emotions (e.g., "I don't want to feel this way!"). Nevertheless, a client must learn at first to tolerate and own what emotions he or she is feeling and embrace them before he or she can learn from them, neutralize them, or bring about their metamorphosis.

Finally, the therapeutic alliance can be seen as a primary source of soothing. With a therapist in the client's corner and providing a safe place, it becomes possible for the process of healing to begin. Although few may see it as a source of soothing, the therapeutic alliance should be that place in life in which a client feels it is safe to be exposed, vulnerable, honest with oneself, and accepted just as he or she is—unconditionally. Such unconditional acceptance, as described by Rogers (1957) many years ago, is nothing short of soothing. Related to this in DBT is the principle of practicing radical acceptance. This is a distress tolerance philosophy whereby the client lets go of their need to fight with reality and instead accept the situation for what it is, even if it is flawed, incomplete, or negative (Linehan, 1993).

Emotion Regulation

The purpose of emotion regulation is to help a client to recognize, identify, and reflect upon his or her emotions to establish the beginnings of a rational process—a more conscious and reflective reappraisal—of circumstances, if alternative interpretations of those circumstances are plausible, if alternative reactions are possible, and so on. It is, in effect, a working through and integration of the elements in the emotional system (i.e., affective expression, internal feelings, and emotional state) with the schema dynamics. We caution the reader not to mistake the term rational process with the idea that cognitive processes (thoughts, cognitions, beliefs, or logic) are superior to emotions and can be used to control emotions. This has been a bias in the counseling and helping professions that has led to the view of emotions as second-class citizens (i.e., weak and feminine, or something to be feared). Moreover, helping a client to develop such rational processes facilitates an increased sense of competence in dealing with emotions in the present and on an ongoing basis. Establishing such rational processes ultimately facilitates clients' understanding of the particular schema dynamics that may be responsible for generating the particular emotion(s) they are experiencing by reconnecting the emotional system. Such processes at times produce an "I never thought of that" reaction, along with strong affective expressions (e.g., powerful abreactive crying or a wry smile).

Rational processes can and do lead to regulation of emotions—that is, understanding and dealing more appropriately and effectively with emotions and emotional reactions. In fact, using one's cognitive powers of attention, recognition, and thoughtful reflection begins the process not only of regulating emotions but also of actually using them for one's benefit (i.e., to see emotions as informative in nature) rather than seeing them as powerful autonomous entities that overwhelm and victimize. Examples of such recognition include comments such as "I was really embarrassed because . . . ," "Confrontation doesn't bring out a very good side of me," "I know I'm awkward at that because my sister was so good at it," "I'm uncomfortable with being late—it reflects poorly on me to others," and "This situation makes me somewhat anxious because . . ." Greenberg (2004) has summarized this very well:

> They (i.e., clients) need emotions to tell them, without thought, that something important to their well-being is occurring, and they need their thinking capacities to work on the problems that emotions point out and that reason must resolve. (pp. 29–30)

Thus, everyone needs their emotional capacities and processes to enlighten them about issues of importance, as well as their rational cognitive processes to make sense out of the emotional information provided.

But Don't Take Our Word for It! Master Example

In this example, master clinician Marsha Linehan, PhD (developer of DBT) works with a woman who became angry about being treated unfairly at work (Alexander Street Press, 2012).

Marsha Linehan: "That's what it sounds like, it sounds like in fact, anger might be getting reinforced in this situation."

Client: "Because I get heard if I get louder."

Marsha Linehan: "Yeah that's my guess, that it actually is an effective response. In the sense that it gets you heard. So let's look at this then. So, okay so now you're angry. How many minutes was it before you called your boss?"

Client: "It was about like I said about a half an hour."

Marsha Linehan: "Okay so what happened in this whole half an hour?"

Client: "I was trying to tell myself, okay wait, talk to her, okay no . . ."

Marsha Linehan: "Okay, so you tried to regulate. That's fine, okay that's very good. Okay so your anger went up and you actually tried to regulate. Oh, so let's look at what you tried and see why it didn't work. So what did you try first?"

Client: "Tried just telling myself well, the main concern was no days off for several months."

Marsha Linehan: "Yeah."

Client: "So I tried to tell myself, 'Well, it's only a couple of months.' You can do this, this is the end, you're at the end of the program, you can do this, and tried to . . .'"

Marsha Linehan: "So you tried to get yourself to actually not care."

Client: "Right."

Marsha Linehan: "Okay so, anger is often a response to having goals or what you want, interfered with, blocked, so this was, this would be thought of as justified shame in the sense of it's a usual or normative shame. Or not shame, sorry, anger. Okay, however, so what you tried to do was get rid of the trigger. You tried to say 'No, it's really not blocking anything and I really can handle this,' except, so that's a pretty good strategy, so why didn't it work?"

In DBT, specific skills for emotion regulation include:

- Identify and label emotions
- Identify obstacles to changing emotions
- Reduce vulnerability to emotion mind

- Increase positive emotional events
- Increase mindfulness to current emotions
- Take opposite action
- Apply distress tolerance techniques (Linehan, 1993)

Another acronym, that targets ineffective health habits, which can inhibit a person's ability to effectively regulate their emotions is PLEASE MASTER. The PLEASE part outlines common problematic physical conditions (and their remedies):

PhysicaL illness (treat)—If you are sick or injured, get proper treatment for it.
Eating (balanced)—Make sure you eat a proper healthy diet and eat in moderation.
Avoid mood-altering drugs—Do not take nonprescribed medication or illegal drugs. They are very harmful to your body and can make your mood unpredictable.
Sleep (balanced)—Do not sleep too much or too little. Eight hours of sleep is recommended per night for the average adult.
Exercise—Make sure you get an effective amount of exercise, as this will both improve body image and release endorphins, making you happier (from Linehan, 1993).

Whereas the MASTER part is a reminder for the client to do one thing (skill) each day that builds mastery of emotional competence and control.

Interpersonal Effectiveness

Remember that the goal of working with a client's emotional system is to help clients connect the three elements of their emotional system along with their schema dynamics in order to reappraise their circumstances. This allows the client to make the best behavioral choices for themselves. In DBT, the module of interpersonal effectiveness is the choice of behaviors that the client makes based on the previous three modules (mindfulness, distress tolerance, and emotion regulation). The skills advocated in this DBT module are very similar to assertiveness skills classes and other interpersonal problem-solving (behavioral) approaches that help individuals to appropriately advocate for what they need (Linehan, 1993; Lynch et al., 2006).

The interpersonal effectiveness module in DBT focuses on teaching skills to handle situations where the client has to make a request that someone does something or request change, or to say no to someone else and resist change that someone is attempting to make. The focus of the skills that are taught are to help insure that the client's goals for a particular situation will be met, whereas at the same time not damaging either the relationship or the person's self-respect. Three acronyms encapsulate the skill sets that are taught to increase interpersonal effectiveness. They are DEARMAN, GIVE, and FAST.

First, DEARMAN is an acronym to help clients remember the steps they need to get what they want when making a request of another person. They are:

Describe your situation.
Express why this is an issue and how you feel about it.
Assert yourself by asking clearly for what you want.
Reinforce your position by offering a positive consequence if you were to get what you want.
Mindful of the situation by focusing on what you want and ignore distractions.
Appear confident even if you don't feel confident.
Negotiate with a hesitant person and come to a comfortable compromise on your request (from Linehan, 1993).

GIVE is the next skill set that focuses on maintaining relationships when making requests. It stands for *gentle* (using appropriate language, being courteous, and nonjudgmental), *interested* (asking questions, etc.), *validate* (communicating verbally and nonverbally that you are engaged with the other person), and *easy manner* (being calm, using humor, etc.). Finally, FAST is a set of skills that help the client to keep their self-respect when engaging interpersonally with another person (and is used in combination with the other two skill sets). It stands for *fair* (to one's self and others), *apologies* (don't apologize more than once for something or for something that was effective), *stick* to your values (don't allow others to manipulate you to do something that goes against your values), and *truthful* (lies will only damage relationships and self-respect).

But Don't Take Our Word for It! Master Example

In this example, master clinician Marsha Linehan, PhD (developer of DBT) works with a woman who became angry about being treated unfairly at work (Alexander Street Press, 2012).

Marsha Linehan: "You're in a lot of trouble if that's true. You're in a world of trouble. If only anger works in your agency."

Client: "Yeah."

Marsha Linehan: "Okay. But if only, and a lot of people are in that situation where the only thing that works is angry behavior. But the trick to angry behavior is then to do it skillfully. In other words to be in control of angry behavior. Acting angry in other words can be useful, but it's usually more useful if you can act angry and you're not angry."

Client: (client laughs) "And you can think more."

Marsha Linehan: "You can be more strategic, yeah."

In this approach, therapeutic focus is on changing the uncomfortable emotions as an immediate priority of treatment and attending to cognitions and schemas later, if necessary, after a measure of relief has been gained. If negative emotions can be troubling to deal with, they can also be powerful resources put to good use. Changing emotion with emotion uses the power of another emotion to neutralize or transform a maladaptive emotion. It is active and promotes self-efficacy—through reconnecting the emotional system and allowing for a reappraisal of the client's situation. It moves preoccupation with the negative emotion that is center stage to a different part of the theatre that is human consciousness. Essentially, this replaces the destructive emotional cycle with healthier and equally powerful emotions, and achieves the goal of interpersonal effectiveness.

Conclusion

In having a richer appreciation of emotions and their manifestations, meanings, functions, and ability to convey useful information, a Level II practitioner can begin to understand more about what Sroufe and Waters (1977) meant by stating that there are "no more important communications between one human being and another than those expressed emotionally" (p. 197). It is the emotional communication between client and therapist that transforms a professional relationship from one that is somewhat distant, mechanical, officious, and artificial into the vibrant human partnership described in Chapters 6 and 7 as the therapeutic relationship and the therapeutic alliance. This does not mean that appropriate boundaries and professional behaviors are not maintained. Quite the contrary, a therapist emotionally in tune with a client—one human being relating to another in as fundamental a manner as can be—can simultaneously convey the rapport, empathy, and support required for solid therapeutic work to be accomplished and maintain appropriate objectivity and boundaries. Such an understanding of emotions greatly facilitates the transition of therapeutic work from being conducted at Level I to being conducted at Level II. As previously described, at Level I, anxiety and the struggle to do things right often dominate; at Level II, clinicians are more relaxed, more authentically themselves, and emotionally in tune with clients.

In this chapter, we have presented the complex issue of human emotions, including a model for understanding the different behaviors that clinicians see in a counseling session. In addition, we have discussed the link between the emotional system, the appraisal process, and a client's schema dynamics. In all, the domain of understanding and working with a client's emotional system has both linear and nonlinear aspects. Finally, we presented both linear and nonlinear therapeutic interventions to help clients recognize, reflect, and regulate their emotional reactions. We next turn to instances in which there can be numerous emotions present. Such complexities create feelings of ambivalence—an emotional reaction that can immobilize a client and the therapeutic process if not attended to skillfully.

Notes

1. Comment in brackets has been summarized from Greenberg.
2. In addition to the metaphor, there is the subclinical field of executive (or life) coaching that has become very popular.

12

The Domain of Addressing and Resolving Ambivalence
Understanding and Identifying Client Ambivalence

Introduction: Odysseus's Dilemma

While the modern practice of psychotherapy has been around for slightly more than a century, the problems that human beings have faced are timeless and universal. One such epic tale of struggle that parallels the plight of so many clients is Homer's *Odyssey*. In it, Odysseus, a Greek hero of many battles in the Trojan War, must face a number of trials set forth by the jealous gods before he can return to his home.[1] One of the most poignant trials that Odysseus had to face was that of sailing past the mystical Sirens.

Enchanting creatures, the Sirens were part woman and part bird, but with voices that were literally and potently hypnotic. Their singing would call sailors to seek them out and sail in their direction, only to steer their boats onto the rocks where they would languish until they died. Odysseus was a powerful hero in the war and wanted to be the only human being to hear the Sirens singing without being destroyed in the process. At the same time, he and his crew had fought long and hard in the Trojan War and wanted to go home. Circe, a sorceress and lover of Odysseus, outlined the dimensions of Odysseus' challenge, telling him,

> First you will come to the Sirens, who bewitch every one who comes near them. If any man draws near in his innocence and listens to their voice, he never sees home again, never again will wife and little children run to greet him with joy. (Homer, 1958, 12: 40–44)

The problem is now clear: If he does what he wants and listens to the Sirens' singing, he will be drawn to them like all of the other voyagers and be destroyed, yet if he sails straight on through to safety, he will not have heard their song. This is his dilemma, and although the subject of Odysseus' dilemma is obviously unlike dilemmas faced by clients today, at the same time his dilemma is very much like those of so many other troubled human beings: He wants to have his cake and eat it too. That is, by being the only human being to hear the Sirens singing without being destroyed—a prestigious accomplishment—Odysseus would become quite unique in the annals of history! His ego is clearly at stake! In essence, his desires to be the only human being to accomplish the feat of hearing the Sirens sing and sail safely past them carry with them a very powerful positive emotional valence. It is as though he is reflecting a view of self that says, "I want to be known as someone very special because I believe that I am special." But to accomplish that, he has to encounter danger and his probable death. On the other hand, if he preserves his safety and returns home—a very appealing alternative, considering that he has been away for a long time and fought a war along the way—he will not have heard them singing.[2] In this classical, millennia-old tale, Homer conveys the fact that he understood the connection between values, beliefs, and desires, as well as the feelings they generate. Odysseus could choose safety and return home (i.e., an obvious positive value), or he could choose a course of action that would be unique in the annals of history (i.e., an extremely appealing alternative for a Greek hero). In fact, he wants both. In essence, that represents the ambivalence of a double bind: Wanting to have our cake and eating it too.

To further drive home the point, Homer again addressed a similar dynamic clothed in new circumstances. Odysseus confronts another perilous dilemma while homeward bound: He wants something that is virtually impossible to attain without peril. Circe advised that in another task, after passing the island of the Sirens, Odysseus must sail through a passage between two overhanging rocks. She says, "When you have got clear of them (i.e., the Sirens), there is a choice of two courses, and I will not lay down for you which to take; use your own judgment. I will just say what they are" (Homer, 1958, 12: 68–72).

Each of the two courses that Circe highlights is ominous: No one has ever safely passed through one of the routes,[3] and the other course she outlined for Odysseus is equally forbidding and has two ominous and deadly cliffs. Circe informs him that one of the cliffs is inhabited by the evil monster Scylla, who has six heads: "No seamen can boast that they have escaped scot-free from her: She grabs a poor wretch with each head out of the ship as it sails along" (Homer, 1958, 12: 120–124). Upon the other cliff dwells Charybdis, a monster in the form of a mighty whirlpool that sucks down any ship that goes past: "Three times a day she spouts it out, three times a day she swallows it down: She is a terror—don't you be there when she swallows! No one could save you from destruction[,] not Earth-shaker [Poseidon, the sea god] himself" (Homer, 1958, 12: 129–135). Although he wants to avoid peril, he must choose a path even though each has a very heavy price associated with it.[4] Hence, it is the source of the modern-day expression that someone is "stuck between a rock and a hard place."

Regarding being stuck between a rock and a hard place, if the woeful tale of Odysseus and his crew is too remote for you, consider this clinical case example:

Clinical Case Example: Stuck in a Loveless Marriage—or Perhaps Not!

Quinella, a 60-year-old teacher, sought treatment because of her feeling "stuck" in a loveless marriage of 35 years. Having tried marriage counseling with little apparent positive results, she came for treatment and stated her dilemma in the first session: Quinella felt as though she was very far down the list of her husband's priorities. In order of priority, she believed that her husband's first priority was a 2-year-old grandson, their first and only grandchild who resembled her husband. The second priority seemed to be his younger sister, his favorite sibling, who was terminally ill with cancer. Her husband's third priority seemed to be his job, which he relished because of how much he was admired, respected, and valued for his expertise. Quinella announced her belief that her husband's fourth priority was a group of friends with whom he met on a regular basis. Finally, due to their strained method of relating to one another over a period of years, she believed her husband's fifth priority was "Quinella." This prompted her to feel that there was very little incentive for her to remain in the marriage. She was quick to add, however, that "on the other hand," her husband was a good person, they had three wonderful children, looking forward to retirement as a single person had very serious financial consequences for her, and the prospects of being alone and getting older were not particularly appealing. Her vacillating back and forth was disturbing and depressing, and left her feeling hopelessly deadlocked within herself. Quinella is truly left feeling as though she is stuck between a rock and a hard place: To stay in the marriage means to continue feeling like she is at the bottom of her husband's priorities with no sex life, for practical purposes no affection expressed between them, little attention or affirmation expressed toward her, and so on. To leave the marriage means facing the prospects of being alone as she approaches retirement, her financial status will be precarious, and she will feel like a failure. As Quinella put it, "I'm not a happy camper!"

She expressed her dilemma as follows:

Quinella:	"He (her husband) claims I'm always angry and defensive . . . he's probably right. I feel like the last one on his list . . . how am I supposed to feel given such a low priority?"
Therapist:	"Sort of like the last kid picked when teams are being chosen. That's not an upper."
Quinella:	"Exactly! We went for therapy before . . . I thought it would get better if we got some tools and assignments to work things out and improve communication between us but it didn't."
Therapist:	"That's really a let down."
Quinella:	"Yeah . . . you know just two weeks ago, our pastor died very suddenly. He was a very charismatic man, close to the youth community, very committed . . . we both liked him. I thought to myself life is too short; I need to make a decision, and yet I've gone both ways with the decision, back and forth. I just don't know if I love him enough to stay with him. He's a good person, decent. When I'm away to visit my family, I think, 'We can make it.' But, then when we're together, we tend to be silent or negative with each other. That's no way to live. The year we were separated, and I lived in an apartment working full time I was really happy. I occasionally go by that apartment and look at it fondly. Then there's the potential loneliness, the finances, and whether or not I could make it on my own. The really big question is: No matter what decision I make, one year from now I'll be wondering if I made the right decision."
Therapist:	"Well, there is a lot at stake . . . and you seem to be saying, 'I need to make a decision.' But keep in mind, whatever decision you make, it will be based on the information that you have available at the time. The rest is a leap of faith."
Quinella:	"Yes, you're right. In the final analysis, I just don't know if I have the energy for it . . . the marriage . . . the spirit isn't there to work it out. The responsibility, accountability in me says, 'It will get better,' but like I said, the spirit and the energy just isn't there."
Therapist:	"You really are dispirited and want to call it quits, but the responsible person in you says, 'You can't just leave after all these years.'"
Quinella:	"That's it exactly!"
Therapist:	"Do you know how your husband feels about the state of things between the two of you . . . no positive communication, no affection, last one on his list of priorities."
Quinella:	"Actually, no I haven't talked to him about it. As I said, we hardly speak to each other."
Therapist:	"Could I make a suggestion?"
Quinella:	"Absolutely!"
Therapist:	"At a particular time when things are civil, cordial between the two of you, perhaps you could let him know about how unhappy you are and ask him how he feels about things and whether or not the two of you should give it one more try or call it a day. At least you'll have more information, and that can help you to land on one side of the fence or the other."

Needless to say facing such perceived ominous personal circumstances and real consequences, to whatever decision is made, clients clearly experience feelings of emotional discomfort and immobilization.

Also needless to say, with Quinella facing the perceived ominous personal circumstances and real consequences, to whatever decision she makes, she is clearly experiencing feelings of what to do, emotional discomfort, and immobilization. Like Odysseus, Quinella wants to avoid both the rock and the hard place. This is simply not realistic, however. The realities of life continue to impose themselves, and she is faced with the necessity to make a decision this way or that way and go forward with her life. She wants relief from feeling stuck. This precipitates feeling pulled in two directions at the same time, and feeling immobilized and unable to make a commitment.[5] Clinically, what Odysseus and Quinella were experiencing, practitioners label as ambivalence.

Ambivalence is an inherent, universally-found emotion in human problem solving, and problems both big and small can stimulate it. It is doubtful that anyone reading this text has been exempt from feeling the impact of ambivalence. To advance their level of sophistication and ability to help and influence clients who consult them, therapists must (1) learn first about the nature of ambivalence; then (2) understand how to recognize it in all its subtleties; and, finally, (3) learn how to therapeutically respond to it. Master practitioners are skilled at all three of these tasks. As previously discussed, Level I and Level II practitioners, prone to linear thinking, often see a client's feelings of ambivalence as an obstacle to treatment (or resistance, see Chapter 7). Such practitioners are also prone to experiencing client ambivalence as a judgment of or a poor reflection on their ability to be an effective therapist, thereby undermining professional confidence.

The reality is that clients' expressions of ambivalence are a natural part of the change process. A client's expressions of ambivalence are also likely to be reflected in feelings about therapy and the therapeutic process because (1) these are potentially threatening to the client's customary ways of thinking and operating, and (2) the client can feel coerced (i.e., psychological reactance, see Chapter 7) by the therapeutic situation into choosing one or the other of two distasteful options. A nonlinear-thinking therapist also understands that most clients, to some degree, want to have their cake and eat it too, feel pulled in two directions at the same time (between the process of change and the fear of change), and ultimately find themselves stuck between a rock and a hard place. In actuality, these three commonplace expressions represent the essence of the domain that is explored in this chapter. But how is it that human beings develop ambivalence?

Understanding Clinical Ambivalence

Definition

The term *ambivalence* was originally coined in 1911 by Eugene Bleuler, who is perhaps best known for suggesting the term *schizophrenia* as a substitute for what had been called dementia praecox. A contemporary of Freud, he used the term ambivalence to describe one of the symptoms of schizophrenia. Although Bleuler (1950) described ambivalence as being of different types (i.e., emotional, intellectual, and volitional), today it appears to be used more as a general term reflecting coexisting but antithetical emotions, attitudes, beliefs, or desires toward a given set of circumstances or a given object (e.g., a person; see Hinsie & Campbell, 1970). The prefix *ambi* is Latin, meaning "both" or "in two ways." The word *valence* comes from Latin and means having strength or a powerful attraction, or the degree of attractiveness of a goal (Merriam-Webster's, 2006).

For present clinical purposes, we refer to ambivalence as a client's experience of being stuck between a rock and a hard place because clients want to have their cake and eat it too. This poetic definition comes both from clinical experiences with clients as well as from the etymological origins of the word. Thus, in a clinical context, ambivalence refers to a person being pulled in two directions, alternately attracted to or repulsed by both sides (i.e., valences) of alternative choices inherent in a given set of life circumstances that ultimately become described as a problem. Intrinsic in a client's experience of ambivalence is a desire to maintain the status quo (typically reflective of schema dynamics—view of self, view of others, and view of the world and life) versus the need to adapt to demanding life circumstances that are typically perceived as threatening because they call for some sort of change. This is especially true when a client has to make a decision or solve a problem. Ultimately, it is a client's schemas that interfere with making decisions and constructively solving problems.

Erickson and Rossi (1980) described it thusly: "Psychological problems develop when people do not permit the naturally changing circumstances of life to interrupt their old and no longer useful patterns of association and experience [i.e., schema] so that new solutions and attitudes may emerge" (p. 71). Mozdzierz, Greenblatt, and Thatcher (1985) have described the role of schemas and the reasoning that flows from this role as follows:

> When the demands of life require a solution different from one's long-held ways of thinking (private logic), the individual is caught in a double bind: The solution does not fit the puzzle. Yet the individual cannot discard the solution since it is sensed as a part of oneself and would represent, in effect, a disavowal, repudiation, and rejection of self. (p. 456)

Decision making has become the focus of a great deal of attention in the research literature. The role of schema dynamics has become quite prominent among the many salient variables that have been identified to help explain how human beings come to decisions. Ajzen (1996) has described the role of schemas in this way:

> Even if biased, the various cognitive and motivational processes [i.e., schemas] that have been identified lead to the formation of beliefs about the alternative courses of action, about their advantages and disadvantages, about the resources they require, about the expectations of other people, and so forth. Although subjective and not necessarily accurate, these beliefs guide the decisions people make, and it is by examining the beliefs people hold that we can gain an understanding of decision making in real-life situations. (p. 316)

Thus, ambivalence results when a client is faced with life circumstances requiring a choice in which either or both of the perceived options run counter to the schematized view of self, others, or life or the world. On the one hand, clients' dilemmas represent their beliefs and experience of what they want (or don't want). On the other hand, they are confronted with what their life situation demands, which is incompatible with what they want (or don't want).

The therapist's job is to use the therapeutic alliance, described in Chapter 5, to support the client as they work through the issues at hand, help clients explore the pluses and minuses of their alternatives in a safe and trusted environment, and help clients develop the courage to face their trial. Part of the working-through process involves guiding the client to become aware of and understand the powerful influences that unconscious values, beliefs, and attitudes have on them and the anxiety that is generated when those beliefs are threatened. In the light of such threats, clients can demonstrate great resistance (or reactance) to any demand that they need to select an alternative and change the status quo, even when they accept that it is necessary. Therefore, it is important for the clinician to adapt their approach depending on the client's reactance level (see Domain 3) and help them to become more flexible and less rigid about these beliefs (Domain 4). For example, a client may come to counseling to control his temper because his bursts of anger have caused him difficulties with his wife or boss. He does not particularly want to come for treatment, but does so to avoid negative consequence (losing his job or spouse). The reality may be that he does not feel that it is a problem that requires help, because his temper usually allows him to get his way. As a result, he is most likely to be in the precontemplation or contemplation stage of change. After all, human beings have great loyalty to their unconscious values, beliefs, and attitudes and attribute many successes (and avoidance of failures) to them. In essence, clients are threatened with giving up a winning formula. But in the example above, if the husband doesn't give up his winning formula, he will lose his wife and family, which makes it no longer a winning formula. Hence, he is ambivalent.

Clients may describe this phenomenon in a number of ways, such as an internal conflict, wanting to versus not wanting to, fear of doing something in their lives, "my head says one thing and my gut says something else," "wanting my cake and eating it too," and being "caught between a rock and a hard place." Briefly stated, a client has at least two distinct alternatives (valences poles or sides of the dilemma) from which the client must choose. Each available alternative has advantages and disadvantages for the client that are based on his or her beliefs and desires about the issues in question. Choosing may be very anxiety producing. Once a therapist understands the meaning a client attributes to the various perceived options (from the client's point of view), it becomes clearer why it is that a client feels stuck. This is important because clients' understanding of the reasons for their powerful feelings of ambivalence is most often vague and leads to impasses in therapy. Such vague understanding is thoroughly in keeping with the unconscious (i.e., "I want to have my cake and eat it too") dimensions of ambivalence.

Clinical Exercise: Dilemmas

Practical examples of personal dilemmas abound: to get married or not; needing to choose one man or another; needing to choose one woman or another; going to college but not wanting to work hard at one's studies and/or facing failure; completing a degree or not; applying for a promotion and risk not being chosen; wanting more money in a job but not wanting to take on more responsibility; the decision to start a family or forgo children in marriage; having an abortion or giving birth; keeping a child born out of wedlock or giving it up for adoption; and so on.

Directions

1. After reading the personal dilemmas above, generate five additional dilemmas that people commonly face in life and record them.
2. Share them with the class to create a list.
3. Discuss what it is that causes life choices and circumstances to develop into these dilemmas.
4. Flesh out how these circumstances represent a person feeling pulled in two directions at the same time and wanting to have her cake and eat it too, while being stuck between a rock and a hard place.
5. Do you notice any patterns (i.e., repetitions) that are commonly repeated among the various circumstances listed?
6. How might you describe the patterns, if any, that you have identified?

Types of Ambivalence

Kurt Lewin (1935, 1938) is credited with having drawn scientific attention to the need to resolve conflicts generated from competing forces of attraction and repulsion when human beings need to make complex decisions. An individual experiences forces that render the individual unable to make a decision as a conflict. Individuals become therapy clients when the competing forces of attraction and repulsion become immobilizing, and life circumstances are demanding a decision. (See Information Box: Examples of Each Type of Conflict, for examples.)

Lewin's concept of conflict is classical and can be useful to clinicians in recognizing double binds and their associated ambivalences (a client theme originally described in Chapter 5). He identified four types of conflict: approach–approach, avoidance–avoidance, approach–avoidance, and double approach–avoidance. An *approach–approach* conflict represents a choice between two alternatives that both have positive valences or poles that are attractive, and the person must find a way to choose the best option. Typically, a person fears making a choice and regretting the choice he or she made because it did not include all of the positive elements that the client desired. This is often called *buyer's remorse*. In an *avoidance–avoidance* conflict, the choice is between two options that have negative valences (i.e., are not attractive). A simple example of this might be having to choose between getting an immunization shot in the arm or a shot in the leg—both are going to be painful. Many times, clients will delay taking action because taking no action is seemingly less painful than taking action (although it might not be for the long-term benefit). The third conflict identified by Lewin was *approach–avoidance,* in which both options that a person must choose from have both positive and negative valences. Individuals feel compelled to make a choice between options that simultaneously attract them (which brings a fear of regret) and repulse them (which leads to a desire not to act), or to do nothing and stay the same. Finally, there is *double approach–avoidance,* in which both options that a person must choose from have both positive and negative valences. This is a double whammy because individuals must make a choice between two options that simultaneously attract them and repulse them (in Chapter 5, this was introduced as a Double Bind, which we revisit later in this chapter). An example of this is a cheating spouse, who must choose whether to stay with their spouse (who is familiar and safe, but feels hurt by the betrayal from the infidelity) and the lover (who is exciting, but who is also a reminder of the unfaithfulness and guilt over leaving the spouse). These individuals seem to vacillate the longest.

Individuals become immobilized and often enter therapy when the competing forces of attraction and repulsion are experienced as intolerable in the face of life circumstances that demand a decision.

Information Box: Examples of Each Type of Conflict

Approach—Approach Conflict

A client enters therapy and states that she has a choice of two jobs. Each pays approximately the same, and both are attractive to her. She worries about making the wrong choice.

Avoidance—Avoidance Conflict

A client in counseling complains of having a difficult decision to make: whether or not to put his elderly mother, who is suffering from Alzheimer's disease, in a nursing home, or have her move in with him and he becomes her primary caretaker.

Approach—Avoidance Conflict

A client states that it is her life's ambition to attend medical school and fulfill her dream of becoming a doctor. At the same time, she expresses fears of what she will do if she fails to gain entrance to medical school. Correspondingly, she continues to postpone taking the Medical College Admission Test.

Double Approach—Avoidance Conflict

John was married to Michelle and best friends with Danny. They all worked together as partners in a small but successful company. As a result of some late nights working closely to each other, Michelle and Danny began a flirtation, which soon became a mutual interest in each other. Danny feels great conflict between the options of pursuing Michelle and not pursuing Michelle.

Exercise

On a separate sheet of paper, define the poles in each of the conflicts above.

- What is the attraction (approach pole or positives)?
- What is the repulsion (avoidance pole or negatives), if applicable?
- Speculate about what kind of behaviors the client may use to signal his or her conflict or ambivalence.

Variation: Develop examples for each of the four types of conflicts given above. Share with classmates in dyads or small groups, and challenge them to define each of the poles of the dilemma.

What Ambivalent Rats Can Tell Us about Human Behavior?

In the 1950s, two researchers, Miller and Dollard, took Lewin's ideas and empirically tested them with rats. The reader might wonder, what does 6-decade-old rat research have to do with the practice of psychotherapy today? The answer is that their work does shed light on what people do when confronting many of these difficult decisions. They placed rats in long boxes that could have food at either end (positive valence) or deliver a foot shock to the rat at either end (negative valence). They found that in the approach–approach situation (i.e., food at both ends and no shocks), rats placed in the box would vacillate, but as soon as they got closer to one end (i.e., randomly, by coincidence, or by convenience), they started moving toward that end and never looked back. In the avoidance–avoidance situation, rats had shocks at both ends (but no food). Under those circumstances, the rats tended to just vacillate between the two ends without committing to one side or the other. In the approach–avoidance situation, the food and shocks were on the same side; the rats would move toward the goal (food) until they received the shock. Then they would back off and vacillate. Last, in the double approach–avoidance, the rats would vacillate (like in avoidance–avoidance), until they would get exhausted and try to escape somehow from the (closed) box (see Dollard & Miller, 1950).

What happens if an individual faced with a decision like Dollard and Miller's (1950) rats cannot comfortably come to make a choice? Ajzen (1996) has described it as follows:

Consistent with the cognitive miser view, people are assumed to maintain the status quo and avoid the stress associated with decisional conflict unless circumstances demand a change of behavior. Little conflict is generated if an acceptable alternative is readily available, but if it is not, the resulting stress can produce *defensive avoidance*: procrastinating, shifting responsibility for the decision to others, exaggerating the desirability of the status quo. . . . Alternatively, the person may be stricken with panic, a state called *hyper-vigilance*, with a paralyzing effect on action. (p. 310)

In many ways, these observations help to explain many of the behaviors of ambivalent clients. Their behavior may look like they are immobilized, endlessly vacillating, or trying to escape or avoid; or if they do make a decision, it may be due to random chance. That is the time an individual may seek help.

Clinical Case Example: Ambivalence and Life or Death

A married woman in her mid-50s with grown children was referred for psychological evaluation and possible therapy because of her adjustment to a severely damaged heart muscle. She had developed dilated cardiomyopathy (i.e., an enlarged heart), a condition in which the heart muscle's pumping efficiency has decreased severely. This means that it gradually becomes more and more ineffectual at perfusing other vital body organs with oxygenated blood. At that time, because those other vital organs (i.e., the liver, kidney, lungs, and brain) begin to fail, the patient develops what is called multi-organ system failure. After thorough medical evaluation, her cardiologists determined that the only treatment available to save this woman's life was cardiac transplant.

Medically, the woman was a good candidate for transplant. A discussion of her possible need for transplant had arisen with her doctors several years before, so the idea was not new to her. As her health deteriorated in keeping with the gradual decline in her cardiac functioning, she did not seem to want to discuss being listed[6] for transplant with her doctors. According to the referring cardiologist, for this woman, time was running out.

During a discussion with the psychologist performing the evaluation, the question came up as to what her thoughts and feelings about transplant were. She replied, "It's not that I'm against transplant. It's just that I've heard things about it such as there can be complications and problems after surgery—it can be dangerous." She was neither refusing to obtain transplant nor consenting to seek such treatment. The treatment team and her physicians did not know how to proceed given the woman's ambivalence, but they knew that without transplant she would die soon. This dire prediction is about as certain as any that modern medicine can make.

The woman's dilemma is rather straightforward but fraught with life-and-death alternatives and consequences. On the one hand, she clearly needs transplant, or she will die prematurely. On the other hand, the information she has gathered about transplant and her interpretation of it have led her to conclude that it is equally dangerous. Although her present health is poor, she is alive and functioning, albeit with great limitations on her physical activity. Such functioning and denial of the urgency of her circumstances may be blinding her to the true risks of opting to forgo transplant versus taking her chances with a new heart.[7]

The woman in this example appears to be in a double approach–avoidance scenario. On the one hand (or pole), if she chooses to be listed for transplant, she could face complications (e.g., not surviving surgery, organ rejection, or a post-transplant life of unending multiple medical complications). On the other hand, if she chooses not to be listed, she would maintain her current life status (i.e., alive and not rejecting a new organ), but her medical condition (i.e., enlarged heart) and quality of life (i.e., severe physical limitations) will continue to deteriorate until she dies. Too often, clients in such circumstances are characterized as being in a state of denial. Of course, when clients decide not to make a decision regarding the choices that they have, they are actually deciding. But, as such, they relinquish control of their life and are deciding to leave outcomes to chance, letting fate work things out (i.e., random chance). In this clinical case example, as a result of the woman's constant equivocation, her behavior appeared to transplant team members as constant stalling (immobilization) and deliberating (vacillating) about change or making a decision, denial about how seriously ill she really was, or some form of distancing or dissociation from the reality of the problem situation (escape). Although the choice may seem simple and straightforward, until they are actually in such circumstances, no one knows the immobilization that can result from life-or-death decisions. For practical purposes, this woman was being pulled in two directions (i.e., having the transplant but being exposed to the risks of surgery and those of transplant as well, or remaining in poor and declining health most likely leading to death), feeling stuck between a rock and a hard place (i.e., each choice is fraught with risk), and wanting to have her cake and eat it too (i.e., being in poor health but alive without subjecting herself to the dangers of transplant surgery). Neither alternative is perceived as pleasant or appealing. The treatment team faced the pressure of time to make a decision and list the woman for transplant in time to provide an opportunity to save her life or use palliative measures until she dies. But whenever the subject would arise, she would waver with ambivalence. It is important to note that not all clients have such life-threatening, dire circumstances, but their dilemmas are usually just as debilitating for them.

But Don't Take Our Word for It! Master Example

In this example of a transcript with a master practitioner, William Glasser (creator of Reality Therapy), works with a woman who is deciding about whether to commit to a relationship or not (Alexander Street Press, 2012).

William Glasser: "Human beings have a variety of needs, that's one of the things that I teach, and one of the needs is freedom. Do you think that your need for freedom is kind of something that's important to you?"

Ann Mary: "Absolutely."

William Glasser: "Hmm . . . hmm. It sounds that way to me that everything you've talked about is it, I mean, that song, 'Don't fence me in,' and you remember . . ."

Ann Mary: "Yeah!"

William Glasser: "You look like the kind of person that doesn't want to be fenced in and . . . and Chicago doesn't fence, and this is kind of a big place and you go here and there."

Ann Mary: "But I don't you know I don't know, he's . . . he's a wonderful guy, and he is great to me, and I just don't understand why I'm so hesitant."

William Glasser: "Well I think, you've explained I guess about this as clear as you can on why you're so hesitant. Its one thing to see him every other weekend or every weekend and so another thing, when you're with him a lot of the time, I said, in this summer you were with him for about a month or something, how long were you with him down there?"

Ann Mary: "About three weeks."

William Glasser: "Three weeks and . . . and that was in the beginning of the relationship too."

Ann Mary: "Right."

William Glasser: "And that's when things were sexually hot and all that kind of stuff?"

Ann Mary: "Yeah, everything was 'love and sunshine.' So, I don't know. And then I feel bad if it doesn't work out, and it's like I'm kind of in a lose-lose situation here, you know? If I do end it, I will lose it; if I do marry him and I hate it, I lose, you know? So I don't know."

William Glasser: "Had you ever had a win-win situation in your relationship?"

Ann Mary: "No. I've never had one of those either, so . . . No, I really wouldn't know, you know?"

William Glasser: "This is as far as the personal treatment of this man by you; this is about as good as you've had? Is this what you'd say?"

Ann Mary: "Oh, yeah, absolutely."

Our Nonlinear Brain: Ambivalence

Ambivalence is a complex human emotional state. As a result, it is also a complex neuro-biological state. It activates multiple regions of the brain associated with cognitive tasks (like decision making) as well as areas related to the experience of positive and negative affect. As Goldberg (2001) has said,

> it is the executive brain in the form of the frontal lobes and prefrontal cortex that plays a central role in forming goals and objectives and then in devising plans of action required to attain these goals. It selects the cognitive skills required to implement the plans, coordinates these skills, and applies them in a correct order. (p. 24)

It is clear that the frontal lobe takes us where we want to go in life. It is the executive that carries out our plans. And yet, clients report feeling helpless, feeling powerless to change, being out of control, and being unable to help myself. They experience ambivalence as a moral dilemma, where they are not able to execute goals, plans, ambitions, and so on. What accounts for this?

Recent research by Greene, Nystrom, Engell, Darley, and Cohen (2004) has provided data that such moral dilemmas are likely mediated by different brain structures. Executive functions mediated by the dorsolateral prefrontal cortex provide the rational answers as to what the right thing to do is (from a utilitarian perspective of the most good for the most people), whereas the emotional thing to do (i.e., something we want or want to avoid) appears to be mediated by the limbic system. The anterior cingulate cortex (ACC) appears to be a limbic system-associated area of the brain that elicits prefrontal cortex (PFC) activity in resolving such conflicts.

Until recently, studies have focused on these cognitive tasks when studying ambivalence, but new research has found that it is a much more complex neurobiological phenomenon, with interesting implications for clinicians. Nohlen, van Harreveld, Rottveel, Lelieveld, and Crone (2013) used fMRI to study subjects in an ambivalence-provoking situation. They looked at regions of the brain that are associated with cognitive tasks (ACC), regions of the brain associated with emotional responses (limbic system), as well as areas of the brain associated with the social brain network (medial pre-frontal cortex, posterior cingulate cortex (PCC), temporo-parietal junction (TPJ), and the insula region). The social-brain network is a relatively new discovery in neuroscience that is intriguing researchers as it is associated with how a person interacts with others in a social context, takes on multiple perspectives, and is influenced by other people.

Nohlen et al. (2013) found that the human brain *is* different in ambivalence producing situations compared with univalent decision making (i.e., a yes/no clear option decision). There is greater activation in the lateral PFC and ACC regions compared with nonambivalent situations. This confirms the contribution of the prefrontal cortex in decision-making situations. In addition, they found that ambivalence is more sensitive to fluctuations in negative affect (but not positive), and that being confronted with an ambivalence-producing decision leads to greater negative affect. This also seems to affirm the current thinking of the inefficacy of confrontation (see Chapter 13).

However, Nohlen et al. (2013) also found some interesting relationships between activation of the social-brain network (including the TPJ, PCC, and insula regions) and ambivalence. First, they found that activation of these areas was related to being preoccupied with making the wrong choice or having negative consequences of this choice. They also found that activity in the social brain network could also help to reduce ambivalent experiences, by projecting into another time or place. In addition, activation of this region also played a role in taking in another person's perspective and relating to other interpretations of the current scenario.

These findings have a direct implication for therapy if the clinician can help the client to activate the social-brain network and adopt another perspective on their current ambivalence-producing struggle. In addition, helping the client to reduce the impact of the negative affect, while at the same time addressing the consequences of the decision within a larger social (i.e., "How will this affect others") or temporal (i.e., "So, five years from now, when you look back on this decision, how will it look to you?") context can engage the client's thinking and decision making process in a way that can resolve their ambivalence, rather than getting stuck in it. We discuss some ways of doing this in Chapter 13.

Linear and Nonlinear Views of Ambivalence

With linear thinking, ambivalence can be misinterpreted as a lack of commitment to the change process, dissembling (i.e., changing one's story), uncooperativeness, and the like. Indeed, some Level I or even Level II therapists may misinterpret ambivalent behaviors as resistance and attempt to pathologize the client (e.g., as oppositional-defiant). Even more misguided, ambivalences can be misinterpreted as behaviors that must be overpowered by such interpretations such as "You don't seem to be interested in treatment," "You don't seem to want to change," or "You don't seem to want to get better." Such therapeutic comments are counterproductive, corrosive to the therapeutic alliance, and born of frustration (see Chapter 7). Or consider this bad example:

Client:	"I just don't know what to do. I think that I should marry Fred, but I love John."
Therapist:	"You should marry Fred."
Client:	"But I want John."
Therapist:	"Marry Fred."
Client:	"But—!"
Therapist:	"Get off the fence! You want to be alone all of your life? You've been here for five years saying you want a man. I say marry Fred!"

A nonlinear view of ambivalence is to understand that it is *part* of what can be expected in the change process and not an aberration (or sabotaging) of the treatment process. Miller and Rollnick (2002) put it succinctly thus:

It is easy to misinterpret such ambivalent conflict as pathological—to conclude that there is something wrong with the person's motivation, judgment, knowledge base, or mental state. A sensible conclusion from this line of reasoning is that the person needs to be educated about and persuaded to take the proper course of action [linear thinking] . . . we regard ambivalence to be a natural phase in the process of change. It is when people get stuck in ambivalence that problems can persist and intensify. Ambivalence is a reasonable place to visit, but you wouldn't want to live there [nonlinear thinking]. (p. 14)

Although there is an advantage to the discomfort that a client feels when he or she is stuck in ambivalence (e.g., not having to let go of either of two attractive alternatives, or not having to choose between two equally unpleasant alternatives), working through the ambivalence can come at a cost as well. Among other things, it can mean such things as

- giving up something enjoyable (e.g., alcohol, fatty foods, cocaine, or promiscuous sex);
- facing circumstances that are personally demanding (e.g., having to exercise, watching what one eats, doing the right thing, finishing a degree, or applying to graduate school);
- facing circumstances that are uncertain and, in extreme situations, even life threatening;
- accepting responsibilities that one would rather avoid;
- facing possible failure, loss of prestige, harsh realities, or the like;
- modifying deeply held beliefs that are core to one's personality; and
- being viewed by others in a negative light.

Consider this better example of therapeutically responding to client ambivalence below:

Therapist: "It sounds like you have quite a dilemma. You are unsure about marrying Fred."
Client: "I didn't say I don't love him, I could be happy with him and build a life with him."
Therapist: "But on the other hand, you have these feelings for John."
Client: "Ri—ight."
Therapist: "Which have come on suddenly. So maybe these feelings are real and maybe they are not."
Client: (defensively) "What makes you think that they are not real?"
Therapist: "Well, unless I'm wrong, they seem to have come at a critical moment as you are having to make a choice about committing to Fred. And I know that marriage is a commitment you don't take lightly. So it might be a good thing to think it through."
Client: "I just don't know what to do."
Therapist: "It is a decision that only you can make. It seems to be a decision between fear of making a lifelong commitment to one person, and fear of making a mistake."
Client: "I'm just so confused, I don't know what to do!"
Therapist: "Well, not making a decision is making a choice. You will have to decide if that is best for you. It all really depends on what you want for your life and what you are willing to live with."

Domain 6 Nonlinear Thinking Exercise—Buridan's Donkey and Bridge

For the nonlinear thinking exercise for this domain, we present two thought experiments from the 13th century, courtesy of Jean Buridan. He believed that people cannot act without intellect, and that when faced with a choice, a person will always choose what they think is the better option. This sounds reasonable, but there is a catch.

In his classic thought experiment, he proposes that a donkey has the choice of two equal bales of hay spaced the same distance apart from the donkey. They are alike in every way (smell, appeal, etc.). The donkey, although hungry, cannot choose between the two (because neither option is better than the other), and as a result, dies of starvation (an extreme approach-approach dilemma). This is, of course, absurd because the donkey's self preservation instinct would kick in, and he would invariably eat one of the bales of hay. But when we think of this scenario in light of an individual's ambivalence, it begins to take on a different meaning. In this situation, we might see that the donkey would endlessly vacillate between which hay bale to choose. We could see that he acts paralyzed because he cannot make a choice, and finally lets fate decide (by starving to death), thus ultimately escaping the dilemma! Buridan's point, and the nonlinear element here, is that by trying to make the best choice (a beneficial strategy), people often make no choice (a bad strategy) when a "second best" choice would be better. This is what happens with clients facing ambivalence to change. For fear of making a bad choice, or because they only want the best choice, they will often make no choice, which means that they settle for the worst choice. In order to help the client resolve their ambivalence, master clinicians often have to help the client see that this fear—the same one that keeps the donkey from making a choice—is the same fear that is paralyzing them (or causing them to vacillate, try to escape, or let fate decide).

Buridan also proposed the following dilemma, which shows the same philosophy. See if you can figure out the best answer: Socrates wishes to cross a river using a bridge. Plato, who is the bridge keeper, says to him: "If your next statement is true, I will let you cross. But if it is false, then I will throw you into the water." Socrates thinks for a moment, then says mischievously: "You will throw me into the water." Buridan asks the question, "Can Plato do what he promised? What would the best action be?" Think it through (or discuss it) and discuss the answers to Buridan's questions. Then, consider how this is an example of a dilemma that produces ambivalence. (Answer is at the end of the chapter.)

Yes, working through a client's ambivalence can be arduous, painful, time-consuming, and demanding on the client. A Level II therapist (particularly a nonlinear-thinking one) has the maturity to focus his or her efforts more fully on clients' concerns and is more comfortable in realistically being able to differentiate client behavior from his or her own performance or abilities. Skillful Level II clinicians utilize the knowledge of all three Level I domains (see Chapters 2–7), and the other two Level II domains (Chapters 8–11) to be able to help the client to resolve ambivalence. We now point our attention to describing how master practitioners recognize and work with client ambivalence.

Listening for and Recognizing Ambivalence

In Chapter 2 (and throughout the book), we have presented linear and nonlinear approaches to listening as major elements in the domain of communicating and engaging with clients. The same nonlinear listening can be used to detect client ambivalence and is often the first step in successfully resolving it. Nonlinear listening for expressions of ambivalence is particularly important because clients are often unlikely to state that they are ambivalent. This is in keeping with Pinker's (2007) observations that people don't necessarily say what they mean. Instead, a therapist must listen for clues in a client's verbalizations that suggest that he or she is ambivalent about change or therapy itself. Listening for congruence, absence, inference, presence, and resistance are all important in this process. For example, a client making statements that are incongruous with accompanying behaviors (e.g., voice intonation and facial expression) or incongruous with how he or she expresses themselves emotionally can be signs of ambivalence. We discuss nonlinear-listening skills and linguistic patterns as a means of detecting client ambivalence.

Listening for Congruence

A client can reveal ambivalences through direct expression of equivocation, a statement that is not literally false but that cleverly avoids an unpleasant truth (*American Heritage Dictionary of the English Language*, 2000). Equivocation reveals that one side and then another side of the ambivalent polarities have their pitfalls and unpleasant truths; it can also reveal that a client wants the perceived advantages of one option but does not want to relinquish the perceived advantages of another incompatible option. Listening for congruence or, more specifically, incongruence in a client's story can help to reveal the equivocation. This can alert a clinician that a client is feeling ambivalent about the situation or issue at hand.

Listening for Absence

Many times, a client's ambivalence manifests itself as behavior that effectively detours around a given problem. Detouring refers to diverting attention to less significant concerns along with devoting extraordinary amounts of time, energy, and resources to them (e.g., see land mines, rabbit holes, and red herrings from Chapter 2). For example, a client may enter therapy because of experiencing recurring intrusive thoughts, but instead of discussing those thoughts, when they occur, under what circumstances, and so on, he engages in stories about him and his wife's sexual escapades. Such diversions may have the effect of temporarily minimizing one of the poles, which either allows a client to escape the dilemma or lets fate decide what choice should be made. Listening for absence allows a therapist to pick up on the minimized pole and helps bring the full picture into focus for the client (this is discussed further below).

Listening for Inference

Formally, the word if is a part of speech called a conjunction, meaning that it brings two things together. In terms of ambivalence, the client is bringing together the two poles of the dilemma. When clients express a linguistic pattern that states, "If only . . ." (something would occur, stop, go away, or the like), then this entire problem would go away. For example, a client may use feelings of depression as a way to slow down (or hesitate) any change from occurring. She may say, "Oh, if only I didn't get so depressed, I would have the energy to make the changes you suggest, and I could be a better wife (mother, worker, etc.)." Typically, it is other people, the world, or life that a client is demanding to be altered (e.g., things shouldn't be so hard to accomplish) and not her central values (e.g., wanting ambition fulfilled but not wanting to learn what is necessary to fulfill it). The inference, or wish, that is contained in the "If . . . then" statement reveals a client's schema or core beliefs: "If only others would change or the world would go away, then I could be happy—then I wouldn't be in this bind that I feel." The conjunction implicitly brings together both poles of a dilemma: Clients want to stay the same while life is demanding a change—hence, they want to have their cake and eat it too.

Listening for Presence

Clients who are ambivalent may demonstrate their feelings through their nonverbal behaviors. A client's emotional arousal and emotional reactions to discussing a particular topic will often reveal ambivalence. Although they may say one thing, their body language tells a different story. When clinicians listen for presence, they listen for the conflicts and dilemmas that are paralyzing the client. These can be brought to the client's attention by developing discrepancies, externalizing the problem, or looking for exceptions (these are all discussed in Chapter 13).

Listening for Resistance

In Chapter 2, we described "Yes, but . . ." as a common indicator of resistance (and now ambivalence). Just like the term *if*, linguistically the word *but* is a conjunction and connects the two poles of the dilemma. The word but, however, usually means that the second choice negates the first, even if they are both in the same sentence. Such masked equivocation is clearly an expression of ambivalence and a reluctance to be held to one alternative or another. Either alternative (or pole) may be perceived as impinging on a core client value or belief (i.e., schema dynamic), regardless of the life circumstances. As a brief example, consider a client entering therapy who states that he wishes to lose weight. When, however, the therapist suggests a plan that includes an exercise routine, the client responds initially by agreeing and then immediately talking about his lack of time, his discomfort with going to gyms, his aesthetic displeasure in sweating, the distance to travel to a gym, and so on, effectively negating the suggestion. Many client behaviors that hinder the pursuit of important (or obvious) therapeutic goals because the clients do not complete homework tasks or instead make meager commitments to challenges (e.g., "I'll try . . ." from Chapter 2) are manifestations of ambivalence. A therapist must listen for resistance, understand the poles of the dilemma that are essential to the experience of ambivalence, grasp the underlying schema dynamics, and intervene to keep a client focused on the therapeutic task at hand. Consider the following example.

But Don't Take Our Word for It! Master Example

In this example, master clinician Leigh McCullough works with a woman who is in an abusive relationship. In this brief segment, the client expresses her ambivalence about getting a divorce (Alexander Street Press, 2012).

Leigh McCullough:	"Right, right. I guess what I was thinking is, um, again you keep saying: 'If I could just not provoke him.'"
Marcy:	"Just until I get enough saved up to leave him. You know, and just for us to have an understanding that we're not, we don't belong together. And I just wish he would understand that we don't belong together 'cuz we really don't."
Leigh McCullough:	"Why is it that you, you need him to understand? Why do you think he will understand?"
Marcy:	(crosstalk) "'Cuz it, 'cuz I want it to be a mutual divorce. I don't want to fight over nothing. I just . . ."
Leigh McCullough:	"I see."
Marcy:	"I'm tired of fighting."
Leigh McCullough:	"It's not some magical thinking. You've got a man who is punching you in the face . . ."
Marcy:	"Yeah, I know. Wishful thinking, yeah."
Leigh McCullough:	"It's magical thinking that there's gonna be some 'reasonable' divorce here. You're, you're wishing for something that's clearly not going to happen."

In addition to these nonlinear-listening skills, the assessment skills described in Chapters 4 and 5 are vital in helping to detect ambivalences that a client is living with but can't necessarily articulate very well. It is essential to remember that, for a variety of reasons (e.g., anxiety about coming for treatment, confusion, emotional turbulence, and uncertainty about what the therapist's reaction to their problem will be), clients frequently don't know where to begin and don't necessarily provide a coherent history and logical narrative of their problem(s) and efforts to solve them. Clients often are somewhat oblique in how they go about telling their story and reason for seeking help. Both linear- and nonlinear-listening skills are vitally important in this regard because it is not necessarily very often that a client will directly articulate a dilemma as a double bind. That is why master practitioners find it useful in asking such questions as "What is it that prompted you to seek counseling at this particular time? Why not 6 weeks ago or 6 months ago? What has changed in your life?" This line of inquiry is important; it helps a therapist to identify particular events that have tipped the balance of equanimity and are part of the creation of the client's double-bind equation. In addition, understanding the theme of the client's story (also from Chapter 5) can also provide a therapist with some important clues about the role that ambivalence will play in the therapeutic process (e.g., themes of desperation, hopelessness, and helplessness).

Stages of Change and Ambivalence

In Chapter 4, we introduced the stages of change model as part of the domain of assessing clients' needs and accessing resources and goals for treatment. The stages of change model suggests that not all clients come for treatment with the same preparedness or motivation to change. Likewise, nonlinear thinking suggests that clients also have differing levels of ambivalence. For example, precontemplators (i.e., resistant, rebellious, resigned, and reluctant) are likely to demonstrate ambivalence with certain characteristics. Behaviorally, their ambivalence may resemble Chamberlain et al.'s (1984; as cited in Miller & Rollnick, 2002) four categories of disruptive client behavior (i.e., arguing, interrupting, negating, or ignoring—see Chapter 7). Usually, this is a reflection of the fact that precontemplators are caught between the two poles of having to come to therapy (e.g., being forced by the court, one's family, or an employer) and not wanting to come to therapy at all. The ambivalence comes as a result of their trying to avoid the unpleasant consequence of not coming or not making some attempt (halfheartedly) at changing. Consider the following example.

A client enters individual therapy after staying out all night drinking with his buddies—the fifth time in the past year that he has done this. His fiancée believes that this is a problem and threatens to break off their engagement if he does not seek help. He doesn't want to lose her and feels badly about his behavior, but he also enjoys his drinking activities with his buddies. He reluctantly comes to therapy. He really doesn't believe that he has a problem, however, and refuses to engage in the therapeutic process. Clearly, he is ambivalent: He comes for treatment, although he doesn't want to and won't make any changes, just to avoid a worse consequence. Such clients have some motivation (e.g., they feel that they are demonstrating motivation by keeping their appointment).

Those clients in a contemplation mode of treatment are more likely to be acutely ambivalent. They recognize their dilemma (e.g., that what they are doing is bad for them), and yet they perceive something of value in maintaining the status quo. The typical methods of coping with ambivalence in this stage of change are reminiscent of Lewin's (1935, 1938) and Dollard and Miller's (1950) descriptions of behavior when facing a dilemma: letting random chance decide, vacillation, paralysis, and escape. Obviously, such coping strategies impede the change process.

Even clients in the preparing for action stage express ambivalence. The trap of endlessly preparing to make some change and believing that action is actually taking place is an example of the underlying struggle of wanting to have one's cake and eat it too. To the nonlinear-thinking therapist, endless preparation for change reveals a client's vacillation as ambivalence. We discuss specific strategies and methods for working through ambivalence later in this chapter.

What about the Therapeutic Relationship?

The next domain we should discuss is the therapeutic relationship and the therapeutic alliance and ambivalence. However, we are going to be nonlinear about it and not devote a lot of space to that here! The reality is that preserving the therapeutic relationship and the therapeutic alliance is critical in helping a client work through ambivalence. We discuss this in great detail in Chapter 13, so we forego this topic until then.

Schema Dynamics and Ambivalence

Because schema dynamics are inextricably linked to the experience of ambivalence and we have, and will continue, to discuss, we will not go into much detail here, either. However, it does bear repeating that often the source of ambivalence is the mismatch between the client's schema dynamics (view of self, view of others, view of the world) and the demands of life. Therefore, knowing a client's particular schema dynamic and understanding their role in the experience of ambivalence is crucial for helping a client work through it.

Emotions and Emotional Reactions

If understood, a client's expression of emotions can frequently reveal ambivalences of sufficient magnitude to warrant attention. What a clinician is listening for is the emotional impact that a client's alternatives have. It is a client's emotional arousal, emotions, and emotional reactions to the discussion of a particular topic that will often reveal immobilizing ambivalence and the prompting of symptom development. As mentioned above, an individual is placed in a double bind when life in its infinite variety presents circumstances that must be addressed but require behavior in conflict with core values. It is exactly those things that people value that they have feelings about. Emotions (e.g., anger, resentment, and frustration) are aroused because the client appraises the situation to be threatening to his or her beliefs or schema dynamics. Symptoms are experienced (e.g., depression, anxiety, insomnia, and bulimia) as a result of ineffective and maladaptive coping strategies to these situations that cause feelings of ambivalence.

Clinical Case Example: Ambivalence Expressed via Symptoms

A bright, college-aged client was in treatment on an episodic basis due to school commitments during the academic year and work commitments during the summer hiatus. Nevertheless, she worked steadily at her initial presenting problem—bulimia. Over a 2-year period, she came for a total of 18 therapy visits. As she seemed to decrease the frequency of her episodes of bulimia, the therapist reinforced the idea that her symptom was an expression of her attempts to problem-solve. To complicate matters, as her bulimia would occasionally wane, she found herself inexplicably taking a razor blade and making very small surface cuts in the skin on her arm. With concern about their very serious and potentially lethal consequences, the therapist followed up on what those symptoms might be about. The young woman indicated that she had no intention of harming herself and had no thoughts of suicide either before or after engaging in such behavior. She was certain that it was another manifestation of an attempt to problem-solve, as had been discussed in therapy previously. Appropriate safeguards for potential suicide were taken to both the client and the therapist's satisfaction. In addition, her bulimia had never progressed to a point of substantial weight loss.

In working through her problem, it was clear that she perceived herself as a good girl (i.e., a core schema reflecting view of self) who found it difficult to express negative feelings or dissatisfactions for fear of offending others, thus threatening her sense of identity as a good girl. This was especially the case with family members. Her mother in particular was someone whom she described as controlling and difficult for her to talk to at times. This appeared to be a characteristic manner in which her mother related to the world—having things the way she wanted, including her children. But as the young woman improved and progressed in confidence, the focus of therapy was more and more directed toward her recognizing feelings and constructively telling her mother and others how she felt.

During the 18th visit, the therapist asked about how she was doing with her symptoms. She indicated that it was now over 6 months since she had vomited or cut herself. She explained, "I've kicked all the bad habits. . . . If I'm not 'throwing it up'[8] and not throwing it away, I have to 'sit on it.' . . . Mother would be coming at me in an accusing way with a rude tone, and I used to throw it back at her[9] . . . (as if to say) who can hurt the other person more." The difference now seemed to be that she had begun to identify what she was feeling and was expressing it more and more appropriately, withdrawing from hostile confrontations from her mother until she was more approachable and listening to what her mother had to say, all of which were compatible with goals of therapy—finding other ways of dealing with her feelings besides bulimia and cutting herself while still considering herself to be a good girl.

Questions

1. What are the significant values (i.e., view of self, others, and life and the world) to which this woman adheres?
2. How do her symptoms (i.e., bulimia and cutting) allow her to have her cake and eat it too?
3. As briefly as possible, describe the double bind she faced.
4. How do feelings reveal the existence of ambivalence in this particular case?
5. What environmental impact could her symptoms be seen to have?

Clinical Attitude and Disposition: Mindfulness

"Nothing is worth more than this day."

—Goethe

"I do not want to foresee the future. I am concerned with taking care of the present. God has given me no control over the moment following."

—Mahatma Gandhi

Over the past five domains, we have presented separate clinician attitudes or dispositions that we think, cumulatively, make up a master practitioner who is fully capable to use linear and nonlinear thinking to best help a client. We feel that when you look at masters at work, you should be able to see evidence of curiosity, collaboration, optimism and hope, pattern recognition, and self-soothing, clearly. Although we add one more of these to that list in this domain, it is important that none of these dispositions should be considered without a consideration of all the preceding dispositions. In Domain 6, we add mindfulness to the list of therapist attitudes or dispositions. Now, in Chapter 11 we discussed several mindfulness-based approaches in the context of dealing with client emotions and emotional responses. Recall that mindfulness is defined as "a kind of nonelaborative, nonjudgmental, present-centered awareness in which each thought, feeling, or sensation that arises in the attentional field is acknowledged and accepted as it is" (Bishop et al., 2004, p. 232). However, for the therapist to be mindful, they have to be in a place of peace—cognitively and emotionally—which is why self-soothing (Domain 5) should be considered a precursor to mindfulness (Domain 6). It allows for the nonjudgmental attitude of events (like a client's thoughts, feelings, or behaviors) to occur when a client is actively engaged in their ambivalence, while simultaneously preserving the therapeutic relationship. However, mindfulness without the previous attitudes or dispositions is not enough to be successful in helping clients manage and resolve their ambivalence. But what does it mean for the therapist to be mindful?

Level I therapists who tend to focus more on their own anxieties are less able to see beyond surface behaviors and less able to appreciate the true nature of ambivalence. By contrast, a Level II therapist is clearly more focused on client behavior than his or her own. As such, he or she is in a better position to be able to discern and understand the client's behavior in terms of the underlying ambivalence (i.e., a type of conflict or dilemma). This is what it means to be mindful. Aided by nonlinear thinking, such a focus is more likely to result in moving the therapeutic process forward to a successful conclusion. Given the dynamic importance of ambivalence in the change process and its integral connection to emotions generated by threats to schemas, nonlinear thinking is required to manage a client's ambivalence. Mindfulness on the part of the clinician helps the client to resolve it. Nonlinear thinking is also critical to the therapist being mindful.

Another reason why master practitioners are mindful has to do with self-care and the potential for clinicians to get sucked into the client's ambivalence, particularly the desire to fix the problem. Rather than being immune from having problematic encounters with life and living, practitioners are human beings. This subject is unfortunately avoided in the psychotherapy literature except in discussion of therapist burnout (e.g., see Kottler, 1993). Correspondingly, therapists are subject to the same frustrations, ups and downs of everyday living, and emotional reactions to situations, circumstances, and people as the clients they serve. The all-too-evident truth is that practitioners at any level are not robots. As such, from time to time, even journeymen practitioners can find themselves frustrated, feeling incompetent, and even exasperated in response to clients apparently not making any movement toward resolution of ambivalences. Such responses can be perceived by therapists' personalities as threats to their view of self (e.g., "I'm not as good at my profession as I should be" or "I'm really not as good as a therapist as I think I am"). Should that develop, a therapist's use of confrontation (i.e., a learned therapeutic intervention) unfortunately becomes subject to being tainted with defensiveness no matter how slight or subtle. Mindfulness reminds the therapist to be disconnected or removed from such messages of rejection. By resisting this temptation to be correct, the mindful therapist can reflect the client's ambivalent struggle back to them and rather than take a side, help the client resolve their own ambivalence and take the side that is best for them. In the master videos (or transcripts) that follow, look for evidence of this mindful stance. Think about how you might adopt it in your own practice.

Behavioral Manifestations of Ambivalence

Ambivalence is a human behavior that has been documented throughout human civilization. Earlier in the chapter, we utilized the literature of ancient Greece to capture the heart of ambivalence (feeling pulled in two different directions at once, being stuck between a rock and a hard place, and wanting to have one's cake and eat it too). In the first-century CE writings of St. Paul, he poetically outlined the experience of struggling with ambivalence:

I don't understand myself at all. I really want to do what is right, but I can't. I do what I don't want to do—what I hate. I know perfectly well that what I am doing is wrong, and my bad conscience proves that I agree with these laws that I am breaking. . . . No matter which way I turn, I can't make myself do right. I want to, but I can't. When I want to do good, I don't; and when I try not to do wrong, I do it anyway . . . there is something else deep within me, in my lower nature, that is at war with my mind, and wins the fight, and makes me a slave. . . . Oh, what a terrible predicament I am in! Who will free me from my slavery to this deadly lower nature? (*The Living Gospel*, Romans 7:15–24)

St. Paul's words could have come from the lips of many clients coming to any contemporary practitioner's office. Clients don't understand themselves and their behavior. They oftentimes know what they are doing is ill-fated and bad for them but can't make themselves change. Those feelings and the words that typify them (i.e., "What a terrible predicament I am in . . .") describe people as feeling helpless to become calmer, feel less depressed, eat according to their diet, maintain sobriety, stop yelling at the kids, get along with their spouse, fall asleep naturally, and so on. St. Paul describes all of those things that he doesn't want to do. Without too much extrapolation, when St. Paul states that "something else deep within me, in my lower nature . . . is at war with my [conscious] mind, and wins the fight," he sounds like all troubled human beings who feel trapped by such apparent polarities (e.g., what someone wants to do, knows they should do or doesn't want to do, and knows they shouldn't do it) and yet powerless to change. Immobilization, fretting, anxiety, depression, confusion, and the like (i.e., the development of symptoms) become the expression of the fact that an individual is being squeezed between these polarities. The contemporary client is as confused as St. Paul was by the fact that he cannot make himself do what he knows is the right thing. Modern psychotherapy research and literature have identified a number of psychological means by which practitioners can recognize client manifestations of ambivalence. They include the flight into illness or flight into health, secondary gain, and double binds. When viewed nonlinearly, the reality is that these behaviors actually begin to make sense. We detail these below.

Flight into Illness and Flight into Health

As discussed in Chapter 4, a prudent clinician must exercise caution when assessing psychological symptoms. Such symptoms can overlap with signs of a physical illness. Thus, the possibility of a client having an organic illness must always be balanced with people's propensity to use illnesses as excuses. This is especially true if they feel that such complaints are likely to gain sympathy and concern from significant others in their life circumstances or provide some other advantage. This is analogous to a child who has not done his homework and does not want to go to school to face the music. He might complain to an overanxious mother of having a stomachache, who then lets him stay at home sick. Although he is excused from facing the consequences in school, he does pay a price by being confined to a bed and not being able to play outside.

Of course, the symptoms most frequently encountered by clinicians are some variation of anxiety and depression. But it cannot be emphasized sufficiently that symptoms can also be generated by somatic conditions (e.g., a heart condition). In turn, a rule of thumb for the prudent practitioner is that somatic complaints by a client must always be taken as possibly having a true physiological origin. As such, they must be evaluated by a physician until a client and his or her physician believe that there is no physiological basis for the person's somatic complaint(s). In effect, one of the consequences that ambivalence can have is to prompt behavior known as a flight into illness or a flight into disease. A psychoanalytic term in origin, it represents the following: "flight away from a threatening reality by means of the conversion symptoms describes the paranosic or primary gain of the illness" (Hinsie & Campbell, 1970, p. 304). Under the influence of strongly felt and unrelenting ambivalence, a flight into illness can represent a client's maladaptive attempt to solve the dilemma—as illustrated with the client above, who solves his dilemma caused by not having done his homework by pretending to be sick. The illness or disease and its accompanying symptoms essentially excuse or absolve an individual from having to address those life circumstances that demand attention and will not relent. Simultaneously, the self-esteem of the individual is preserved. It is as though a client is addressing the significant individuals and life circumstances that he believes to hold him accountable and says, "I would have attended to this but for my illness!" After all, who can find fault with someone who is sick? In fact, Adler (1959, 1956; Mosak & Shulman, 1967), taking a different view from that of Freud about the nature of symptomatic behavior, came to understand symptoms as having a purpose, namely, to preserve self-esteem and/or to excuse. This clinical case example may prove useful in illustrating this.

Clinical Case Example: Flight into Illness

Upon the advice of his family doctor, a middle-aged man with excellent job performance and more than 15 years at the same company sought treatment for a virulent depression. He reported a number of significant losses in the past 2 years (i.e., a very sad if not quarrelsome divorce, the loss of both parents, and the permanent disability of a sibling). His major complaint at the outset of treatment, however, concerned his depression over an unrelenting work environment with a boss who seemed to care nothing for people but rather only about getting the job done regardless of safety issues for his employees. That was a view with which the client disagreed. He had felt abused by this boss much as he had been physically and verbally abused by his stepfather. But in addition, he complained of a variety of other vague physical symptoms (e.g., headaches and episodes of confusion).

Upon the advice of the psychiatrist prescribing his medications, the client went on extended but paid sick leave. As his time on sick leave lengthened, he complained of periodic unrelenting headaches, lightheadedness, blurred vision, and bouts of confusion (e.g., on a trip with his girlfriend to see relatives, he woke up in a hotel room and was unclear about where he was and how he got there). In addition, he had sleep apnea and was obese and diabetic. Under such circumstances, his physician rightly ordered specific tests for his apnea, blood work, and an electroencephalogram and computerized tomography scan of the man's head to rule out such things as a possible space-occupying lesion and seizure disorders. In addition, a spinal tap was being contemplated to rule out still other possible organic causes for the man's varied physical complaints. Human beings don't necessarily come to see counselors, therapists, and others in the helping professions in pristine physical condition, and their complaints may be organic in nature.

Vague complaints of fatigue, chest pains, headaches, numbness and tingling in one's extremities, and so forth may very well have a physiological basis. Although they may also be psychological effects of wanting one's cake and eating it too, the prudent clinician does not make such an assumption. But upon receiving his disability compensation, the client was able to maintain his financial responsibilities to his family and was able to preserve his self-esteem as a responsible person. He applied for temporary disability and then permanent disability.

Questions

1. What are the poles of the ambivalence in this case?
2. What is or are the benefit(s) to the client of the vague physical complaints for which no organic explanation could be found?
3. What is or are the detrimental negative valence(s) of the client being ill?
4. What kind of nonlinear listening might be helpful in uncovering the client's ambivalence?
5. Looking back, what should the clinician have done within the therapeutic relationship to increase the likelihood that the client would have come back for a second session?

Unfortunately, the success of the symptoms at excusing oneself and escaping a more direct resolution of one's ambivalence extorts a heavy price. In this clinical case example above (the obese, diabetic, depressed man with varied other complaints), the client must now present himself as someone who is disabled. Use of nonlinear listening is a critical method for recognizing ambivalence when it manifests itself through a flight into illness. In particular, listening for congruence, absence, presence, and resistance can help unravel the constructed illness and the poles of the client's ambivalence.

A flight into health (the reverse of a flight into illness) is another potential consequence of ambivalence. It is defined as "a relinquishing of symptoms that occurs not because the patient has resolved his neurosis, but rather as a defense against further probing by the analyst into painful, unconscious material" (Hinsie & Campbell, 1970, p. 304). As defined, the flight into health can be an expression of a client's additional ambivalence about (1) being in therapy or (2) having to address the issues underlying his problems as a result of therapy. Such ambivalence can appear precipitously, with a symptom or problem temporarily getting better without a client really making any changes. This behavior is similar to that demonstrated by precontemplators. A flight into health alleviates further need for therapy, and a client is allowed to keep doing the things that were harmful in the first place, avoid the pain of addressing the problem, or both. This clinical case example may prove helpful.

Clinical Case Example: Obsessive Thoughts

During an initial interview, a client reported that he has obsessive, intrusive thoughts while driving. Those thoughts suggest to him that he has hit someone. Even though he knows that is not the case, he feels compelled to stop every few blocks, get out of his car in order to check for evidence of a collision, and convince himself that he has not hit anyone. Asking somewhat routine questions, the therapist asks about the client's past, to which he gives vague answers. At the end of the session, the therapist suggests that given the current information about the problem as stated, it might be prudent to explore more information about his family of origin.

Before the next scheduled session, the client calls to tell the therapist that he has not experienced the thoughts, and that he no longer needs therapy. Although it is impossible to say definitively whether he was cured, the chances are that the client was feeling ambivalent about addressing issues related to his family of origin. Instead, the client developed a solution that allows him to avoid discussing such issues: He took a flight into health. The flight into health allows the client to avoid the threat (whatever it might be) of discussing his family of origin.

Questions

1. What are the poles of the ambivalence in this case?
2. What are the benefits to the client of being healthy?
3. What are the liabilities to the client of being healthy?
4. What kind of nonlinear listening might be helpful in uncovering the client's ambivalence?

The behavior of the client in this clinical case example is a form of maladaptive problem solving. It is maladaptive because such solutions resolve the immediate problem (i.e., the client escaped potentially having to discuss or confront something that he viewed as threatening), but the client's solution leaves him with his original problem (albeit temporarily in abeyance). The more likely reality is that in such instances, the respite is temporary, the problem doesn't change, and the person continues to suffer. What is abundantly clear is that the client is not prepared to engage therapy with the resolute perception (see Hanna, 2001) needed for a successful outcome.

The flight into illness and the flight into health are both good examples of client nonlinear thinking. That is, the flights are behaviors motivated by privately logical thinking and not common sense. Flights are privately logical because they are based on skewed schemas and not based on common sense. Such reasoning motivates and allows a client to escape a threatening situation while the underlying issues remain unaddressed.

Commonsense problem solving is direct and addresses an issue in a straightforward way. In the clinical case example about the individual who does not return to therapy, common sense suggests that when the therapist brings up the issue of family of origin, the client would likely say that talking about the family of origin is something that makes the client feel anxious and is something that he or she doesn't want to talk about. That would be important information for the therapist. The master practitioner hearing such important information would endorse the client's courage in acknowledging the difficulty in discussing the family of origin, pay careful attention to that topic, and afford the client an opportunity to revisit it when the timing was appropriate (e.g., when the client is more comfortable in therapy and makes an oblique reference to family).

Secondary Gain

On the surface, both a flight into health and a flight into illness are useful to a client. They have a primary gain. That is, the client derives a direct and immediate benefit from the effects of his or her behavior. The client is able to escape a threat because of health or illness. In addition to a client deriving a direct and immediate benefit from a flight, the client can also derive a more subtle gain that is called a *secondary gain*. Secondary gains represent interpersonal or social advantages or actual financial compensations that are derived indirectly from symptomatic behavior. This is one reason why it is essential for nonlinear-thinking therapists to pay attention to the issue of ambivalence and the way it might be expressed in therapy: Client behaviors have potential hidden benefits (i.e., secondary gains) associated with behaviors that are difficult to relinquish (Rogers & Reinhardt, 1998).

Although not always evident, secondary gains are frequently very powerful reinforcers and motivators for behavior. An example can be found in the obese, insulin-dependent, diabetic client mentioned in the Flight into Illness example. As a result of his condition, he continues to collect most of his salary, even though his depression and vague physical complaints have no physiological basis. Another more brutal example would be that of a man physically abusing his wife. Such behavior gives the perpetrator a sense of power and control over his spouse by intimidation and coercion. When such an individual is asked to change (and even when he too espouses wanting to change), his resulting ambivalence is understandable. On the one hand, he doesn't want to be a wife beater, but on the other hand, he doesn't want to give up the control of his partner. This is one reason why it is essential for nonlinear-thinking therapists to pay attention to the issue of ambivalence and the way it might be expressed in therapy: Client behaviors have potential hidden benefits (i.e., secondary gains) associated with behaviors that are difficult to relinquish (Rogers & Reinhardt, 1998). Although clients can never be accused of simply wanting to achieve secondary gains (e.g., compensation in the form of a settlement from a lawsuit, being excused from having to work, or being excused from responsibilities because of illness), the possibilities of such gains must be taken into account in one's formulation of the problem (see Chapter 9).

The concept of secondary gain has been discussed by both psychodynamic as well as behavioral schools of therapy and has become a commonly accepted concept in understanding some client behavior. For psychodynamically oriented theorists, secondary gain is motivated by the protection from trauma that it affords the psyche. According to Rogers and Reinhardt (1998), "Incapacitation largely exempts an individual from social expectations and subsequent failures. Adoption of a sick role provides a socially acceptable escape from threatening circumstances and personal inadequacies" (p. 58).

On the other hand, behaviorally oriented theorists ascribe the motivation behind secondary gains to be the avoidance of negative or painful stimuli. That is, when individuals are placed in circumstances that produce pain or fear and discover behavior (e.g., becoming sick, or being docile and meek) that reduces the pain or fear, it becomes reinforced. Such reinforced behavior is adopted and becomes learned behavior. For example, recall the discussion of nonlinear thinking from Chapter 1 about the client who kept obsessing about his wife. The linear and primary gain for this behavior was that the client was hurt and upset over the breakup, and not able to get over it (self-protecting). The more threatening fear, however, was the need to start dating again and possibly being rejected and hurt. In order to reduce this fear, he found that obsessing about his ex-wife spared him from the potential pain of those circumstances, and thus obsessive behavior became self-reinforcing and represents a secondary gain (Rogers & Reinhardt, 1998). This is a classic example of ambivalence: A client feels like he is being pulled in both directions (i.e., "I should give her up, but I don't want to") while wanting to have his cake and eat it too (i.e., "I can still have her in my thoughts, even though I don't have her in reality"), and ultimately finding himself stuck between a rock and a hard place (i.e., "This really hurts because it reminds me that I really don't have her, but it's just as bad as having to start all over and be rejected with nothing").

Regardless of the proposed explanation for a secondary gain (psychodynamic or behavioral),[10] nonlinear-thinking processes are at the heart of understanding a client's development of the behavior. That is, the ostensible reason for a problem may not bear correspondence to the underlying reason. Rather, there are hidden (i.e., privately logical, nonlinear) motivations for behaviors that make sense or serve a purpose for a particular individual that may not be readily apparent.

But Don't Take Our Word for It! Master Example

In this example, master clinician Jon Carlson works with a couple who are having relationship difficulties. In this brief segment, the couple discusses an ongoing area of conflict. Carlson introduces the idea of another motivation for the conflict (Alexander Street Press, 2012).

Scott:	"She gets irritated that she has to do this all of the time. 'Why, why does your bedroom gotta be such a mess? You know, you're not gonna put that there, you're not going to put . . .'" (crosstalk)
Jon Carlson:	"Okay. But how does that become your problem?"
Scott:	"We don't have ah, ah." (crosstalk)
Jon Carlson:	"Ah, don't have time?" (inaudible) (crosstalk)
Scott:	"Yeah, we don't have time."
Jon Carlson:	"Okay."
Scott:	"Because she's, she's always got to be cleaning up. Now, I don't think she will admit to you, I don't have a problem helping her."
Jon Carlson:	"And I have a hunch though, let's just put that on advance right now. And I think you're making a good suggestion. But my guess is that maybe sometimes people do things when relationships are going bad, so they can avoid one another. So as long as I'm busy picking things up, then I don't have to be with one another. Just, just hold that as a possibility and then as you guys start to do some of these other more positive things, let's just see if that doesn't take care of itself. Just a hunch. That's the hunch I have."
Scott:	"Good enough."

Nonlinear listening (especially congruence, absence, and inference) can be very useful in discovering underlying ambivalence. This is especially so when there are schema-driven reasons for the secondary gain (e.g., unconsciously harboring thoughts such as "Everyone is in it for themselves," "I am lovable when I am vulnerable," or "I'm *entitled* to this insurance settlement money even though I'm not that disabled"). Three types of behaviors can be generated by the ambivalence, but they are all expressions of being pulled in both directions, while wanting to have one's cake and eat it too, but ultimately finding oneself stuck between a rock and a hard place. We discuss in this chapter how each of these reveals the nonlinear nature of client thinking.

Double Binds (Revisited)

In the movie *2001: A Space Odyssey* a mission to the planet Jupiter goes horribly wrong when the on-board computer, the HAL 9000 ("HAL" as he is called) suddenly, and without explanation, begins to malfunction. At one point early in the film, HAL proclaims: "No 9000 computer has ever made a mistake or distorted information. We are all, by any practical definition of the words, foolproof and incapable of error." This is hard-wired into his systems; it is the equivalent of his schema dynamics. However, unbeknownst to the crew, HAL was also programmed by the government not to reveal the secret nature of its mission (i.e., his demands of life). This puts HAL into a dilemma. How can he fulfill his basic programming (not to distort information) and fulfill his contradictory programming (not to tell the crew the real details of the mission) at the same time, since they are inconsistent with one another? It puts him into an impossible situation, and he comes up with a unique (and coldly diabolical) solution: kill the crew. HAL reasons that if there is no crew to ask questions about the mission, he will not have to distort any information, and he can keep the mission a secret. It helps him to get out of his dilemma, but at a terrible cost. However, the same underlying dynamic, a double bind and the ambivalence that flows from it, are common in all therapy settings.

Back in Chapter 5, we discussed the Theme of Fear and Confusion: Double Binds; however, in this chapter, we want to present a fuller description of double binds, especially as they fit with the discussion of ambivalence (i.e., double-approach avoidance dilemma). First described by Gregory Bateson and his colleagues, double binds have the following common elements (Gibney, 2006). First, the double bind requires two or more people, with one person being the victim or recipient of the double bind. The other person (or persons) are the recipient's superiors (meaning that they have some power, influence, or are respected), such as parents or supervisors. Second, the experience of the double bind is repeated or a reoccurring theme in the client's life. As a result, attempts to solve the dilemma in one instance (first-order change, see first domain) are not going to successfully resolve the double bind. Next, a series of injunctions or directives are placed on the recipient by the superiors. They are:

1. A primary injunction in one of three formats:
   a. "Do (some behavior), or I will punish you";
   b. "Do not do (some behavior), or I will punish you."
   c. (or both a and b)

The punishment may include the withdrawing of love, the expression of hate and anger, or abandonment. This induces the fear element.

2. A secondary injunction is imposed on the recipient, which conflicts with the first at a higher or more abstract level. For example: "Do not notice the contradiction between my claim to be a loving parent and my willingness to withdraw my love from you." And "Do not notice nor comment on the unfairness of this situation." "Do not question my love (even though I threatened to take it away in the first injunction)." "You must do X, but only do it because you want to." It is unnecessary for this injunction to be expressed verbally. This induces the confusion element.
3. If necessary, a tertiary injunction is imposed on the victim to prevent them from escaping the dilemma. These can include reversals (e.g., promises to be better; threats of harm to the recipient, the superior, or some one else the victim cares about).

Thus, the essence of a double bind is two conflicting demands, each on a different logical level, neither of which can be ignored or escaped. For a double bind to be effective, the victim must be unable to confront or resolve the conflict between the demand placed by the primary injunction and that of the secondary injunction. This is where the fear and confusion induces ambivalence (Gibney, 2006). The recipient feels that "Even if I want to get out, I can't without something bad happening." This leaves the victim torn both ways, so that whichever demand they try to meet, the other demand cannot be met. This was the case with HAL being unable to resolve his impossible dilemma between his primary injunction (no distortion of information), his secondary injunction (you must not reveal any information about the secret nature of the mission), and finally his tertiary injunction (this mission is vital to national interests and must succeed).

The important thing to remember is that client's schema dynamics may also play a role in double binds. Often schema-dynamics form the secondary injunction. For example, a person may be faced with a situation where they have to discipline their child from acting out in school. So the primary injunction is teach your children a lesson or else they will keep getting in trouble in school. But the parent wants desperately to be a cool parent, or a friend to their child. This may be because they had a bad relationship with a harsh parent who was punitive to them. So their schema dynamics include not being a punishing parent like their parents were to them (this becomes the secondary injunction). Finally, the child may say: "Hey the teacher was out to get me, she doesn't like me, all she does is yell at us. I know that I would do better if I had another teacher. You wouldn't punish me for something I didn't have control over, would you?" As a result, this puts the parent in a double bind. Do they discipline the child or not? It is likely that they will either vacillate endlessly, become paralyzed, let fate decide, or try to escape the problem altogether. Now it is important to note that not every instance of ambivalence comes from a double bind (or double approach-avoidance dilemma). In many of the cases presented above, the clients are not in double binds. However, in a few of the clinical exercises (like the case of Quinella at the beginning of this chapter), and in some of the Don't Take Our Word for It boxes in this chapter and others, there are examples of double binds. Review the clinical exercise for practice.

Clinical Exercise: Hidden Double Binds

As a summary clinical exercise, consider reviewing the clinical case example in Chapter 3 called Impulsivity, Panic, and a Need to Know Why and the clinical case example in Chapter 5 called The Aftermath of an Affair, and identify the double bind that the woman is in and the ambivalences that the woman expresses. Look for examples of the primary, secondary, (and if appropriate) tertiary injunctions that keep them trapped in the double bind.

Variation: Go through other chapter clinical examples and identify instances of double binds.

Vague client expressions of stress also reveal ambivalences and can be a sign that the person is caught in a double bind. Recall from Chapters 10 and 11 that stress is caused by stressors, those elements in the environment that an individual perceives (via the appraisal process) as threatening and for which they have not devised an effective means of coping. Stressful situations can easily reveal double binds and their inherent ambivalences by carefully analyzing a person's particular environmental circumstances (e.g., changes and/or demands in relationships, work, or commitments). These stressors are usually the injunctions (primary, secondary, or tertiary) that are listed above. As a brief example, a client might come to therapy asking for help with time management skills, particularly because the client always seems to wait until the last minute to get things done (primary injunction). Such behavior disrupts the client's life, stresses him or her, and eventually upsets the client's family or others in his or her social environment (secondary injunction). After accumulating basic information, if a therapist begins to make some tentative suggestions regarding being more organized (e.g., setting reasonable goals and getting a day timer), and almost immediately the client begins to protest that he or she never seems able to do those things, the inferred message that the client is sending is that he or she would like to be more organized without having to make any real changes to his or her life (e.g., without having to exert any effort or assume responsibility). Listening for the inferred meaning of stress, the sources or origins of the stressor, and what the client would like to do with it can help to uncover the underlying double bind and resulting ambivalence.

We conclude this brief discussion of double binds by noting that clients are ambivalent about issues that are troubling them, and ironically, they are ambivalent about getting the help that they need to resolve the problem for which they have sought treatment. As a result, clients express their hesitancy to therapy itself in the form of noncompliance with the therapist, because sometimes therapy itself is a process that naturally produces a double bind. At times, therapy produces the feeling of being pulled in two directions (i.e., "I want to change, but I don't want to be forced to change") while wanting to have one's cake and eat it too (i.e., "I know that I need outside help to change, but I don't want to give up control"), and ultimately finding oneself stuck between a rock and a hard place (i.e., "I can't stay the same, but I'm not sure I want to change"). Understanding such ironies is part of the challenge and excitement of becoming a therapist. In fact, master practitioners use this to create positive double binds that take the injunctions in the original double bind, deconstruct them, and move the client from the lose-lose proposition of the double bind, to a win-win in the therapeutic positive double bind (Gibney, 2006). This requires nonlinear thinking, and it is the focus of the next chapter, as well as the advanced text.

Take Aways for Practitioners

- Ambivalence is a universal experience of human beings as they navigate life encounters and are called upon to make choices that they are unwilling to make.
- Not being able to make up one's mind regarding what to do, being caught between having to give up one desirable alternative if another is chosen, and being caught between two undesirable alternatives are all manifestations of human ambivalence. Human beings frequently feel caught between a rock and a hard place, and they want their cake and eat it too.
- Ambivalence is a part of the normal processes that occur in treatment.
- Ambivalences are most often embedded in a client's narrative, and sometimes because of the way in which human beings communicate, those ambivalences can be quite subtle. Values to which a client adheres are the substratum upon which ambivalences are formed.
- Nonlinear listening is an exceptionally useful tool for detecting a client experiencing ambivalence.
- There are numerous ways in which manifestations of ambivalence can be demonstrated including expressions of language, demonstration of emotions, and emotional reactions to therapeutic processes.
- At times, a client deriving secondary gains from maintaining the status quo when action is required makes it difficult for movement to occur in treatment despite their protestations to the contrary.
- Understanding the nature of double binds and using the elements of them to help clients to resolve their ambivalences is a major part of the work of therapy for many clients.

Conclusion

Even if clients come to therapy and insist that they are ready to make changes, when it comes time to face the music, they may not feel or be prepared to do so and hence feel very vulnerable. They may engage in many types of behaviors (described above) that can have a negative effect on the therapeutic process. It is incumbent on a therapist to see such behaviors as normative to the therapeutic process and then bring those feelings (and the values, beliefs, and attitudes responsible for them) as clearly as possible into clients' awareness at a pace they can tolerate without being overwhelmed, and help them to resolve those feelings. Erickson (1977) stated,

> The patient does not come to you just because you are a therapist. The patient comes to be protected or helped in some regard. But the personality is very vital to the person, and he doesn't want you to do too much, he does not want you to do it too suddenly. You've got to do it slowly . . . gradually . . . in the order in which he can assimilate it . . . you approach everything as slowly and as rapidly as the patient can endure the material. . . . The patient doesn't consciously know what the problems are, no matter how good a story he tells you, because that's a conscious story. (pp. 20–21)

Erickson is cautioning therapists to understand that clients are stuck between a rock and a hard place—that they want to change, and simultaneously want things to stay the same and want to be protected. Therein lies the challenge to becoming a master practitioner: helping to identify and understand a client's ambivalence, bringing it into the client's awareness, and keeping it in the focus of the therapy while at the same time not overwhelming the client, who is in therapy because he or she is not necessarily prepared to address the life circumstances that are immobilizing.

When a client is faced with the choice of whether or not to move forward in therapy and feels pulled in two directions at the same time, a therapist must reassuringly guide the client through sometimes paralyzing feelings. In Chapters 6 and 7, we presented research that overwhelmingly supports the importance of the therapeutic relationship and therapeutic alliance as the foundation from which change can occur. As discussed earlier in this chapter, clients who are not willing to tolerate their anxiety are more likely to fly into health (or illness), or they are liable to vacillate and become paralyzed for fear of making a wrong decision. They may resemble precontemplators or contemplators who seemingly don't want to change. But such clients may be attempting to protect themselves from feeling overwhelmed about the potential consequences of making changes. As always, the efficacy of all therapeutic transactions, including managing a client's ambivalence, is contingent upon maintaining the therapeutic alliance.

A nonlinear-thinking master practitioner is more likely to sense a client's feelings of ambivalence, and he or she (1) expects it as a natural part of the therapeutic process and (2) understands that a client's behavior might be a method of protection from threat (e.g., the therapist or change itself). If therapists are able to discern these nonlinear thought processes and utilize their alliance and rupture skills (i.e., vibrating with a client's feelings like a tuning fork; see Chapter 6), they may be able to see past a client's flights, gains, resistance, or reactance, and understand its true meaning: an expression of client ambivalence. Seen as such, it is easier to engage a client than by seeing the client's behavior as uncooperativeness or a power struggle. Understanding the manifestations of ambivalence and their impact on clients and the change and therapeutic processes are only half the battle. We now turn our attention to the practitioner's role in helping clients to resolve their ambivalence.

Answer to Buridan's Bridge

Can Plato do what he promised? The answer is no. He cannot. He cannot throw Socrates into the water, because if Plato does, then what Socrates said ("You will throw me into the water") was the truth. However, he cannot let Socrates cross the bridge because if he does, then Socrates' statement was false—which means that Plato should throw him into the water. Therefore, Plato is stuck with a real dilemma. What is his best choice?

Notes

1. The journey home was a metaphor that Homer used to convey man's search for freedom from suffering.
2. In case you were interested to know what happened to Odysseus: Circe helps him to resolve the double bind he is in by instructing Odysseus to have his crew tie him to the mast while they row through to safety with their ears plugged with wax. He listened to Circe and did just this. Odysseus was able to hear the Sirens' song and sail safely toward home—although the story doesn't end there.
3. Except for Jason, but he wasn't able to do it without the intervention of one of the gods.
4. Odysseus chose to avoid Charybdis, but doing so was at the expense of losing six sailors to Scylla's multiple maws (i.e., mouths with voracious appetites).
5. Note on Quinella: While on the way to the airport for a class reunion out of state, Quinella called her husband and told him how she was feeling. She asked him how he was feeling about their marriage. Sincerely moved by her question, he began to cry and asked her to please not leave. She chose not to leave, and they have assumed a more satisfying marriage. Understandably, Quinella indicated that she no longer felt the need to come for treatment; the therapist agreed.
6. Being listed refers to a list of candidates according to priority as determined by criteria developed by the United Network for Organ Sharing.
7. The treatment team faced the pressure of time to make a decision and list the woman for transplant in time to provide an opportunity to save her life or treat her palliatively. But whenever the subject would arise, she would clearly waver with ambivalence between alternatives, as described above. The woman eventually acquiesced to the pleading of her husband and children, consented to transplant, was eventually transplanted, and is still alive as of this writing.
8. A clearly symbolic reference to her throwing up (i.e., vomiting), which the therapist asked her to repeat. Upon repeating what it was that she said and hearing her own words, she began to smile and laugh at having caught herself in a moment of true understanding.
9. Perhaps another oblique and unconscious reference to her vomiting.
10. Rogers and Reinhardt (1998) have a third explanatory approach for secondary gain: the forensic approach. This looks for the potential legal or monetary reward as the motivation (or secondary gain) for problem behavior (particularly in the absence of physical evidence of a problem). This is frequently seen in cases of bogus workman's compensation claims, fraudulent disability clams, issues of competency to stand trial, and other legal or quasi-legal proceedings.

13

The Domain of Addressing and Resolving Ambivalence

Working with and Resolving Client Ambivalence

Introduction: The Kobayashi Maru

At the end of the last chapter, we presented a discussion of double binds. As part of that, we used the illustration of HAL from the movie *2001: A Space Odyssey,* and the difficulty that he had when confronted with a double bind. We want to start this chapter with another illustration from a science fiction movie from the *Final Frontier.*

In the 2009 movie *Star Trek,* which chronicles the legendary characters in their early years at the Academy, James T. Kirk must face a test: The Kobayshi Maru. It is a simulation test that no one passes because it is a "no win" scenario. In the test, a space ship (the aforementioned Kobayshi Maru) puts out a distress call that it is stranded in the Neutral Zone, which is a boundary set up with the Klingons to avoid all-out war. If a space ship crosses into the Neutral Zone without authorization, it is considered an act of aggression and a declaration of war. However, the ship and all of its crew are in danger of being killed as its engines are about to explode, destroying the ship. So what is a Captain to do? Does he or she violate the Neutral Zone to rescue the crew and risk their ship and crew as well as all-out war, or do they stay on the safe side and let the ship and its crew die? Of course, once the ship crosses into the Neutral Zone, the Klingons are there to meet them and proceed to overwhelm and destroy their ship in the simulation. In other words, *there is no way to win.*

In the movie, the audience is told that Kirk has taken the test twice and was beaten both times. When he proposes to take the test a third time, his friends think that he is crazy. Kirk, however, is determined saying, "I don't believe in the 'no-win' scenario." Once in the simulation, the events occur as they have before (ship in distress, entering the Neutral Zone, attacked by Klingons), but then there is a power outage, and when the simulation returns, suddenly Kirk is able to defeat the Klingons and rescue the survivors. Kirk (having sabotaged the computer program) is accused of cheating. Kirk defends himself by saying that the *test* is a "cheat" because it does not allow for a solution. Instead, he changed the conditions of the test to create a way out of the no-win scenario. In fact, Kirk is awarded commendation for his clever (and we'd say *nonlinear*) thinking.

In many ways, the Kobayashi Maru test is emblematic of ambivalence. For our clients, it feels like a no-win scenario. There are often double binds that keep the client bogged down with no good options. Master clinicians know that often times this is because the constraints that the client is in prevent the client from seeing that there are alternatives. What is needed in order to help the client overcome or resolve their ambivalence is some clever thinking that changes the conditions of the situation. In this chapter, we present some linear and nonlinear strategies and interventions to manage and resolve client's ambivalence.

Linear Strategies and Interventions to Manage and Resolve Client Ambivalence

The Level I and Level II domains work in tandem to facilitate change. It is the Level I domains that are important for setting the basic framework for counseling and establishing the therapeutic alliance. The alliance is essential for creating the context and environment for resolving client ambivalence. In turn, it is the Level II domains pertaining to schemas and emotional reactions that are at the very heart of understanding, addressing, and resolving ambivalence and making lasting change in the client. Most conflicts that clients experience are the result of incongruity between their schema dynamics (i.e., view of self, others, or the world or life) and the reality of the circumstances that they face (which, again, requires both Level 1 and Level 2 domains). We wish to present some linear strategies (confronting, creating awareness, and using pacing) to address client ambivalence.

Resolving Ambivalence: Holding a Mirror up to a Client

No matter what approach (linear or nonlinear), the underlying goal in this domain—and perhaps the most important task that a counselor must perform—is to help clients resolve their ambivalence. Confronting is a process of directing someone's attention to something that he or she potentially avoids looking at (either deliberately or unconsciously). The qualifier potentially is used because therapists of necessity have limited certainty about being accurate in their ability to know exactly what it is that a client may be avoiding. Confronting is often thought of as holding up a mirror to a client and asking him or her to look at or bring to light something that the client appears to be avoiding. According to Hanna (2001),

> Confronting is the function of actively observing and closely scrutinizing a problem, issue, thought, behavior, emotion, person, situation, or relationship. The person uses his or her attention and powers of viewing to look into, through, and even beyond a problem or issue . . . In terms of the actual change process, confronting involves an intentional, sustained, and deliberate directing of attention or awareness toward anything that is painful, intimidating, or stultifying. It involves continuing to examine or investigate—digging in one's heels—in spite of fear, confusion, or the tendency toward avoiding or acting out. Almost anything at all can be confronted: mental images, memories, emotional pain, behaviors of all varieties, thoughts, thought patterns, beliefs, persons, places, objects, and relationships. (p. 71)

At Level I and at times Level II, perhaps the biggest concern about the use of confronting is practitioners' misunderstanding of its true therapeutic meaning and intent. To begin with, confronting is mistaken for confrontation. Synonyms for confrontation are words such as quarrel, argument, "war of words", and conflict. Unfortunately, all of these synonyms suggest pejorative and aggressive images of being "in your face!" Any therapist behavior that implies being confrontational (i.e., deliberately or unintentionally hostile in nature) is decidedly counterproductive, ill-advised, and likely born of ill-conceived therapist motivations (e.g., frustration or anger) or misguided intentions (see Chapter 7). The purpose of being confrontational is most likely to prevail over a client (e.g., insisting to be right) regarding an issue under discussion. This has been shown to be counterproductive for any therapeutic endeavor (Horvath & Bedi, 2002; Norcross & Wampold, 2011). Such therapist behavior places a client in a one-down position—a place from which it is difficult to move forward. Thus, extreme caution is urged regarding practitioners' understanding and use of confronting.

Clients must feel that their therapist is aligned with them before they will engage in a dialogue about change. This means that a therapist must walk a delicate tightrope between understanding a client's perspective and supporting the status quo of destructive behaviors. This understanding leads to acceptance of the client (at whatever the stage of change) and a sense of safety for the client, which, in turn, facilitates an exploration of ambivalence. Even when a therapist must confront or redirect a client's attention back to the therapeutic tasks at hand, the strength of the therapeutic alliance, empathy, and support expressed will often balance discomfort that a client may be feeling due to his or her ambivalence. It is the therapist who must guide the client through the sometimes immobilizing ambivalence. But clients must be prepared to work through their ambivalence, and in order to do so, they must be able to trust the therapeutic relationship. Thus, it is reiterated that the most fruitful way to understand confronting is by keeping the focus of therapeutic attention on clients' problems, their symptoms that result from their dealing with their problems, and the ambivalence(s) that clients have concerning the problems. Consider this exchange from the case of Mike:

Therapist:	"So let me go back to something you said earlier. You said your fiancée also felt that coming here would be good. Why is that? What does she want you to get out of coming here?"
Mike:	"Well, she complains that I am stubborn and that my temper can be explosive, and sometimes she gets the brunt of it, you know? She thinks that I need to learn to control it."
Therapist:	"Let me guess, this happens when she won't listen to you?"
Mike:	"Uh-huh."
Therapist:	"Kind of like your coworker?"
Mike:	"Yeah."
Therapist:	"So there is a pattern here. You are following your father's philosophy? And sometimes it gets you into trouble with the people in your life?"
Mike:	(getting defensive) "Uh-huh."
Therapist:	"Well, let me ask you, we are not dumb creatures. We don't adopt strategies or a philosophy that won't work for us. We do things that help us to be successful. So tell me how this philosophy is helpful or useful to you?"
Mike:	"What? Losing my temper? Being stubborn?"
Therapist:	"Yes."
Mike:	"Hmmm. It doesn't seem to help me. Most people avoid me, it pushes people away."
Therapist:	"So it does help you by keeping you from having to deal with other people?"
Mike:	"Yeah."
Therapist:	"And that is good when you want to avoid some people (Mike nods head yes), but it also spills over to people that you care about, like your fiancée?"
Mike:	"Yeah, I guess it does."
Therapist:	"Is that something that you would like to change?"
Mike:	"Yeah. I don't want to push her away!"

To illustrate, care must be taken regarding the difference between confronting and being confrontational. In the example above, the therapist works with the client's ambivalence, but also uses the therapeutic relationship to demonstrate understanding of the situation, while simultaneously confronting the perception of his or her behavior, all without being confrontational. Miller, Benefield, and Tonigan (1993) found that:

Specific and observed therapist behaviors commonly associated with the term *confrontational* were found to predict poorer outcomes for problem drinkers. These findings are consistent with earlier reports that a directive-confrontational style evokes client resistance (Patterson &

Forgatch, 1985) and is associated with unfavorable outcomes in treating alcohol problems (Miller et al., 1980; Valle, 1981). Indeed, the level of client resistance evoked during a treatment session appeared to be negatively related to long-term treatment success. (p. 460)

In their study of the influence of different therapist styles on client drinking, Miller et al. (1993) also noted, "Therapist styles did not differ in overall impact on drinking, but a single therapist behavior was predictive ($r = 0.65$) of 1-year outcome such that the more the therapist confronted, the more the client drank" (p. 455). Seeming to contradict these findings, Hanna (2001) noted that almost all modalities of psychotherapy confront clients in some way. Orlinsky, Grave, and Parks (1994) found that focusing directly on the problem in therapy was related to positive outcomes in 64% of the findings they investigated. Are these finding contradictory? The answer is "No." Miller et al. (1993) appeared to have the most cogent rationale for understanding this subtle but exceptionally important issue:

Confrontation and empathy are not, we believe, inherently incompatible. In its etymology, confrontation literally means "to bring face to face," which does not necessarily mean going head to head. To confront is to help another person face the facts. In this sense, confrontation is a *goal* rather than a therapeutic procedure (Miller & Rollnick, 1991). What constitutes the most effective means for accomplishing this goal remains an open question. (p. 460)

The key to understanding how to keep a client focused on his or her ambivalences regarding the choices he or she faces without alienating him or her is empathy and understanding that confrontation is a goal rather than a method or technique. We present this clinical case example to illustrate.

Clinical Case Example: Facing (Confronting) Ambivalence

A female client in her late 20s entered therapy because she had been having panic attacks and was beginning to have difficulty leaving her home (agoraphobia). During her initial visits, she explains that she is living with her boyfriend of 4 years, and that she loves him very much and doesn't want to jeopardize their relationship. They met at a club, and much of their dating life has revolved around the "club scene" (i.e., music, drinking, dancing, and late nights). About a year ago, the client began to feel tired of the same old "scene." She mentioned to her boyfriend that she wanted to do other things besides the "clubs." She reported to her therapist that her boyfriend said, "I couldn't be with someone who isn't into this scene. That is one of the things that I love most about you. Besides, you know that I don't want to be tied down."

About 6 months later, she had her first panic attack in a club while there with her boyfriend. Subsequently, she has had three other panic attacks. Each time she experienced such an episode, she reported that her boyfriend was supportive—but she expresses fears that he is beginning to think that her panic attacks are becoming "old."

Exercise

1. What kind of dilemma (i.e., conflict—e.g., approach-approach) would you describe this as?
2. How would you describe the poles of the dilemma?
3. How did the client's ambivalence manifest itself? As far as can be determined, what are the client's schema dynamics?
4. How would a therapist directly confront her about this (without being confrontational)?

In the case above, the client's dilemma appears to be that, on the one hand, she no longer wants to participate in the club scene; but on the other hand, if she quits the club scene, she risks losing her boyfriend, who has made it clear where he stands on the issue. The panic attacks have a secondary gain (see Chapter 12) for the client: They allow her to have her cake (i.e., she doesn't have to risk losing her boyfriend over the issue of not wanting to go to the club) and eat it too (i.e., she doesn't have to go to the club because her ostensibly involuntary panic attacks excuse her from responsibility for going). At the same time, however, she knows that this is not going to be helpful for her relationship in the long run, which becomes a motivating factor for her to address it in therapy. Her fear of losing her boyfriend can trigger feelings of ambivalence, which in this case are manifested by panic attacks. The therapist must be persistent in keeping a client's focus on the issue at hand and not becoming sidetracked.[1] In other words, in order to overcome ambivalence, a client must develop resolute (i.e., determined) focus. Such determined focus must take place within the bounds of a safe therapeutic relationship that can effectively hold or contain a client's emotional processes while confronting the painful aspects of the client's life despite the pain. According to Prochaska (1999), it is important for therapists to move clients from precontemplation to at least the preparation for action stage within the first three sessions, or else they are more likely to prematurely terminate from therapy. Although this may or may not be reasonable in all cases, it is worth considering. Thus, a client needs to be made aware of his or her problem and—connected to that—understand the necessity of facing it and working through his or her ambivalence. That increases the client's chances of being successful in therapy.

Awareness, Ambivalence, and Effective Treatment

Clients who are willing to experience this anxiety (or ambivalence) are ready to face the emotional turmoil and pain that accompanies decision making. They either recognize the long-term benefit of experiencing discomfort, fears, and so on, or see the futility of endlessly utilizing behaviors that avoid difficulties in their life. In fact, Orlinsky et al. (1994) found that being open to experiencing anxiety is highly predictive of successful outcome. Individuals willing to experience anxiety are generally more honest with themselves about the severity of their problem (i.e., "own the problem"), likely to be in the preparation for action or action stage of change, and hold a belief that some sacrifice (e.g., experiencing anxiety or ambivalence) is required in order to be successful, especially with change (Hanna, 2001).

Clinical Case Example: A Client Willing to Experience Anxiety

Recall from Chapter 5 the case of the pregnant woman who is afraid of needles (in the section entitled Theme of Helplessness: The Symptom Is Out of Control). When asked what she would like to realistically accomplish through treatment, she indicated that she would like to get through her labor, have a healthy child, and not hurt her baby. She also specifically stated, "It's not to have hypnosis give me a quick fix! My goal is not just to get blood samples or vaccinations!" Rather, she revealed that she would like to "go through the delivery like an adult!" As a result, she is ready to face the unpleasantness of her particular anxiety so that she can achieve her goals—growing up and acting as an adult. This is an individual who understands that she is going to experience the pain of childbirth, but she mitigates it by reminding herself of the reason that she is in therapy. As the philosopher Friedrich Nietzsche (1968) wrote, "He who has a *why*, can endure any *how*."

As in the previous case, the mother-to-be must be aware of what her underlying fears are in order to face the unpleasantness of her situation and the anxiety it produces. In other words, clients have to (1) be *aware* of their problem (not deny it, run away from it, etc.), (2) understand what kind of problem they have, and (3) have a meta-awareness about the fact that they are ambivalent about changing their behavior so that they confront themselves eventually. In this case, the woman recognizes that she has a problem, and by coming to therapy, she faces her fear and anxiety. In addition, she recognizes that a quick fix (i.e., hypnosis) is available, but not the solution. Hanna (2001) described this process:

> Awareness has to do with a client's recognition of or clarity of perception about a problem. It is the function that brings a mental, emotional, or environmental issue in from the edge of consciousness and into focused detail. In general, awareness is the identification or pinpointing of issues or relationships that are in need of addressing as part of the therapeutic process and its tasks. (p. 62)

In other words, a client's awareness allows therapy to continue and progress even when the client begins to display ambivalence. Consider this exchange from the case of Ashley:

Therapist: "What do you mean when you say a mess? Just a moment ago, you said that you have won awards for efficiency and productivity. How do those two reconcile?"

Ashley: "That's usually because I pick up the slack and make sure everything gets done."

Therapist: "Even though it is not your job?"

Ashley: "Yes."

Therapist: "So tell me what you mean when you say that it is a mess?"

Ashley: "Well, my coworkers don't take their jobs seriously. They are sloppy with their paperwork. When this happens, bills don't get submitted correctly, and we don't get paid. This puts the hospital in jeopardy! No one seems to care, so I usually have to go and correct all of their mistakes before we submit the claims."

Therapist: "I am confused, why don't you send it back to them."

Ashley: "Because it would delay payment."

Therapist: "And if you just let the errors go through as is?"

Ashley: "It would get denied and that's a whole other set of procedures and paperwork to correct. So it is just easier if I correct it before it gets submitted. That way I save myself the work of doing the corrections and the headache of hearing from the CEO that the billing department is inefficient and hopeless."

Therapist: "Okay, so you do all this work up front (other people's work), so you don't have to do it later, but it comes at a cost."

Ashley: "Yeah!"

Therapist: "Yeah, your coworkers never have to take responsibility, you take all the responsibility and they get the reward?"

Ashley: "Yeah, I never thought of it like that, but you're right."

Awareness includes knowledge of schema dynamics and how they are related to the ambivalence. Such awareness allows a therapist to point out how client behavior relates to his or her ambivalence in a way that will bring the client's focus back on the issue at hand—or the client's reason for therapy in general. In the example with Ashley, the therapist brought the idea of the underlying unfairness of his or her schematized belief that he or she has to do everyone's work into awareness. This allows the client to begin to see the problem differently and possibly do something to change it.

Conversely, clients who are not aware resemble the precontemplators (i.e., reluctant, rebellious, resigned, or rationalizing) or contemplators described in Chapter 4, and they behave like the ambivalent clients described above (e.g., vacillating, attempting to escape, and utilizing safeguards). They may be characterized by being vague, noncommittal, back and forth, and even oblivious to their surroundings or condition (often saying, "I don't know . . ." or "I guess . . ."). They may be meek and kind but clueless, or they may be bellicose and blame others outside of themselves for their problems (e.g., "It is all my parent's fault") or act passive and feel helpless ("There's nothing I can do"). Such clients can be very frustrating and even tempt therapists to give up on them. The use of metaphors described in Chapter 9 can be especially useful in keeping a client's focus on the issue at hand, especially when the client is trying to escape, becomes paralyzed, vacillates, or lets fate decide. This is, however, merely a symptom of underlying ambivalence about making a change and a way for them to demonstrate to the therapist how much they want to have their cake and eat it too, feel pulled in two directions at the same time, and are ultimately stuck between a rock and a hard place.

Pacing, Reactance, and Nonlinear Thinking

The confronting that "maintains and sustains attention in spite of the impulse to avoid, give into confusion, or act out" advocated by Hanna (2001, p. 74) must be balanced by Erickson's (1977) admonition, "The patient comes to be protected or helped in some regard" (p. 20). Indeed, Hanna (2001) also urged caution regarding clients who are not prepared to encounter the level of self-examination required in a therapist's confronting. He indicated that such clients are generally in an earlier stage of change, highly ambivalent about therapy, and probably engaging in safeguarding behaviors. For them, Hanna (2001) advised therapists to exercise caution:

> Forcing a person to confront too much, too soon, is traumatic by definition. Bringing a client to contact painful phenomena must be done with care and attention to the person's level of tolerance. Overwhelming a client with mental, emotional, or environmental material that is too much to confront will not only bring about early termination, it will cause harm. Thus, exposure to sensitive memories, feelings, or beliefs should be done gradually so the client will be successful and not view therapy as a source of failure and pain. (p. 241)

There are two important factors that must be honored simultaneously: (1) pursuing the objectives of the therapy, even though it can be uncomfortable, frightening, or even painful and (2) doing so at a pace that a client can tolerate. If only one is done and not the other, the result will be therapy that is either too aggressive, overwhelming, and/or hostile, or too timid. This will likely arouse the client's natural reactance (see Chapter 7). Hence, confronting cannot be done unless the therapist is also operating with a friendly tone within all of the domains previously discussed (i.e., engagement, assessment, and maintaining the therapeutic alliance). The linear-thinking practitioner will find this more troublesome, both conceptually and clinically, than the nonlinear-thinking practitioner. When it is done with relationship considerations in mind, however, a client is more likely to be receptive to what a therapist has to present (even though it may be uncomfortable) rather than reject it outright because it is too threatening. We present several additional, nonlinear methods for managing ambivalence below that take these two principles into consideration.

Nonlinear Approaches: Using Solution-Focused and Narrative Therapy Methods to Help Manage and Resolve Ambivalence

Many times, clients will demonstrate their ambivalence by discussing the chronic nature of their problem or the failure of attempts that they have made to fix it (see Theme of Desperation: "I Have a Problem That I Need to Work On!" or Theme of Hopelessness: "I Have a Chronic Problem" from Chapter 5). Nonlinear listening for absence would detect that most often, there is little mention of anything positive in the client's story, whereas nonlinear listening for resistance would detect the "Yes, but . . ." nature of any attempts at intervention on the counselor's part (e.g., "Have you tried . . . ?" and "Oh yes, I tried that already, but it didn't work"). Such impasses can often leave linear-thinking therapists feeling frustrated by a client's lack of cooperation. A way to have the client actively engage in trying to resolve his or her ambivalence was developed by de Shazer (1985; de Shazer, Dolan, & Korman, 2007) and expanded by Berg (1994; Berg & Szabo, 2005). It evolved as a direct response to the problem-obsessed and problem-focused nature of psychotherapy—as if understanding the problem alone will somehow yield its solution. As its name implies, solution-focused therapy centers its attention on solutions rather than problems. Toward that end, solution-focused therapists rely on the power of a client's subjective perspective and operate with the assumption that clients are merely stuck (i.e., struggling with their ambivalence) rather than sick and that they have the capacity to orient toward wellness by choosing better solutions than they have done so in the past (Hoyt, 2002).

In solution-focused therapy, problems are approached in a nonlinear way. That is, a client's problem or concern is seen as a client's attempt at a solution that once worked, but is not working any longer. In terms of working through the ambivalence, the therapist focuses the client's attention on times when he or she has been successful, and not when he or she was ambivalent. Consider the following clinical case example.

Clinical Case Example: Call for Attention

A young man who discovered and acknowledged his homosexual identity during high school found himself in therapy shortly after graduating from high school in order to deal with overwhelming feelings of depression and suicidal thoughts. As an adolescent, after convincingly discovering and owning his sexual orientation, he suffered unimaginable taunting, derision, and threats of violence at the hands of thoughtless other male high school students. Nevertheless, he felt "liberated" from being in the "closet," and as a point of fact, he seemed to revel in the attention that he garnered, albeit negative in nature.

Feeling ignored by his father, he lived in the shadow of an older sibling who followed and fulfilled parental expectations and appeared to be the apple of the father's eye. Again, it was the father's attention that the client seemed to crave. With his older sibling excelling in school, the client found poor school performance to be an effective way of garnering family attention, but again it was negative in nature. In his interpersonal style, the client craved excitement and used outrageous, histrionic, mischievous, and somewhat flamboyant behaviors to garner the attention and excitement that he craved. Without a college career, and with few marketable skills and his adolescence behind him, he found himself going through a succession of jobs, drinking, smoking, and keeping late hours with friends, but without any real direction in life. Jobs that seemed to have potential lasted a few weeks.

His antidepressant medications seemed to have little effect on his mood, and subsequently he was hospitalized on three occasions for suicidal ideation after episodes of drinking. His suicidal thoughts were described in outlandish terms and received legitimate expressions of concern from his friends. He discovered in therapy that his view of self ("I only feel worthwhile if life is exciting and I am the center of attention") was leading him to garner attention but only in self-destructive and nonproductive ways. The therapeutic task was to determine how it was that he would be able to get attention and excitement in his life in new ways—other than those that have been so destructive. Although seeking excitement and acting flamboyant, histrionic, and overreacting to life's everyday circumstances had once been effective in garnering attention, such behaviors were now only resulting in largely negative consequences.

From a solution-focused perspective:

1. If you were to choose a solution-focused approach to intervening with this client, what questions would you present to him?
2. What is the basis for your choosing those particular questions?
3. How would you go about differentiating this client expressing suicidal thoughts that are motivated by a need for excitement and attention and those that may result in his acting on such thoughts?
4. What is the client's dilemma (approach–approach, avoidant–avoidant, etc.)?
5. What are the poles of the dilemma?
6. What are the relevant schema dynamics in this client example (view of self, etc.)?

Solution-focused therapy is an exploration of how a behavior (solution) used to be functional for a client and what could now be done either to make the solution functional again or to substitute a new solution that will be less problematic. This is accomplished by discovering exceptions to the problem (e.g., "Tell me when the problem is not a problem"). Exceptions to the problem refer to those times when a client's goal is already happening at least a little, or when the problem is not happening as much. In other words, the therapist asks the client to find a time when the client was able to resolve his or her ambivalence, or when it did not exist. In these exceptions to the problem, the focus is why and how these exceptions were able to take place. The line of inquiry that a therapist pursues concerns what was different about what a client was doing, thinking, saying, feeling, or relating. When a client is imagining a future of what life would be like without the problem and when the client is looking at what was different during these exceptions to the problem, a therapist is engaging the client in solution talk rather than problem talk—hence, the dialogue is solution-focused and not problem-focused. This focus can be utilized to help resolve a client's ambivalence by gently challenging his or her rigid, unrealistic schematized views (i.e., "I always . . ." or "I never . . ."). When exceptions are generated, a therapist can probe for what the client did differently. This allows for one of two things to happen: (1) A client can explore specific instances in which an outcome was different, which is a potential roadmap out of the current dilemma; or (2) a client may begin seeing him- or herself in a new light (i.e., accommodating the schemas).

The Miracle Question

If a client cannot identify exceptions to the problem, a solution-focused therapist may use a technique called asking the miracle question. In this technique, the therapist asks a client to imagine what life would be like if a miracle happened during the night and the client awoke to find that the problem no longer existed. This approach is very useful when the ambivalence is manifested as a flight into illness or flight into health, or if there is a secondary gain involved (see Chapter 12). The client can begin to imagine a new alternate reality without the problem, which can be beneficial, or they reveal the hidden, underlying issue that is preventing them from moving forward. The next task is to ask the client what small part of this the client might begin implementing, acting as if the miracle occurred; and if these exceptions are effective, a client is encouraged to do more of them (Walter & Pellar, 1992). A variation of this is to ask, "Suppose a miracle occurred overnight and the problem would be gone. How would you know? What would be different in your life?" Again, as with exceptions to the problem, the miracle question is related to a client's schema; it can be helpful in resolving ambivalence by exploring similar roadmaps or by expanding a person's views (schema accommodation).

But Don't Take Our Word for It! Master Example

In this example of a transcript with a master practitioner, Matthew Selekman (creator of collaborative strengths-based therapy), as he works with a mother and her teenage daughter (Tiffany) about the conflict in their home (Alexander Street Press, 2012).

Matthew Selekman:	"Well, let me ask you guys a fun question. Let's say tonight you go home, and while you're sound asleep, a miracle happens, and this problem is completely solved. It's no longer an issue, this anger and this bitterness and out-of-control stuff. Um, and, and things have changed the way you want them to. What would be in each of your miracle pictures the next day when you wake up?"
Tiffany:	"I don't know. I wouldn't. I don't know. It would be weird because it wouldn't be the same as it always is, and so I wouldn't know what I would want 'cuz I can't react well to peace. It just doesn't work right with me."
Matthew Selekman:	"You're not used to it."
Tiffany:	"No."

So in this brief exchange, Selekman is able to get the daughter, Tiffany, to reveal elements of her ambivalence that while she would like things at home to change (and be peaceful), it would be difficult (i.e., weird) because she wouldn't know how to react. At this point, a therapist can begin to work on both sides of the ambivalence.

Scaling Questions

Many times, follow-up questions are used to clarify exactly how the old solution negatively impacts a client and how to begin to create new solutions (de Shazer, 1991; Hoyt, 2002). One such follow-up inquiry is a scaling question (e.g., "On a scale of 1 to 10 . . .") to measure the relative strength of the problem to the client. As a method for resolving ambivalence, scaling each of the poles of the dilemma gives a numeric weight to each of the sides and can help tip the balance one way or another. Again, we continue with Matthew Selekman.

But Don't Take Our Word for It! Master Example

Matthew Selekman:	"Just play around with, just an estimate. Where, where would you have seen things, let's say, in the past, a month or two. On that scale, ten is the best, one is the pits."
Kathy:	"I'd say about a four."
Matthew Selekman:	"About four? Okay. How about now?"
Kathy:	"Maybe a five, but that's only because my husband's laid off from work and because he's acting differently because he's, he's not under the stress of work."
Matthew Selekman:	"Okay."
Tiffany:	"And he wants to sleep in the same room, too. He doesn't wanna sleep on the couch."
Kathy:	"Right. That's what I'm saying."

Matthew Selekman:	"Sleep in the same room with you."
Kathy:	"Yeah."
Matthew Selekman:	"Okay."
Kathy:	"It's bad enough that he's laid off from work, you know what I mean?"
Matthew Selekman:	"Sure."
Kathy:	"So, uh, he's just, he's been doing, he's been trying a lot harder."
Matthew Selekman:	"Okay. And you think that's been really helpful to Tiffany?"
Kathy:	"Yes."
Matthew Selekman:	"Okay."
Kathy:	"Right."
Tiffany:	"'Cuz he's like our dad now. Before he was just like a prison guard or something. 'Oh boy, I get to go home and get yelled at.'"
Matthew Selekman:	"Have you, have you let him know that?"

In this exchange, Selekman uses the scaling question to have the clients discuss a small improvement in a way that can create more improvements in the family.

Clinical Exercise: Revisiting Solutions

Return to a previous clinical case example dealing with ambivalence in Chapter 12 as well as in this chapter to look for ways that a therapist could begin to use a solution-focused approach (e.g., looking for exceptions, asking the miracle question, or asking a scaling question) with that client. Share your ideas with a small group or with the entire class.

Externalizing the Problem

Too often, a client's expression of ambivalence is an internal one. The client goes back and forth in his or her own mind, until the client feels trapped. Language becomes the method by which this ambivalent (distorted) thinking becomes entrenched or enshrined (e.g., "I am bipolar"), with individuals becoming bound up by their (problem-focused) language. Likewise, relanguaging a problem (or restorying) is one of the chief methods for helping clients resolve their problems and their ambivalence. Therapists using narrative therapy[2] adopt a "not-knowing" stance, which places them in an equal (or even inferior) position to a client and allows a therapist the privilege of listening over questioning. Clearly, this is a nonlinear approach to therapy as well as addressing ambivalence.

One of the more unique and revolutionary elements of narrative therapy is externalizing the problem. When narrative therapists place the problem outside of a client (or couple, family, etc.), an individual becomes free to stop fighting against him- or herself or, in the case of a couple, fighting against each other, which can prolong ambivalence. Such fighting creates a useless cycle of shame, blame, and denial. Instead, a client (i.e., an individual, couple, or family) can join together to fight against the problem. A couple can gain a greater sense of control by labeling what the problem is (an extension of externalizing) or can begin to exert a measure of influence over it by setting some boundaries on the problem's influence. For example, instead of a person being diagnosed with depression and having his identity bound up in the illness, depression is conceived of as an entity outside of the individual. The entity is then something for the individual and others (e.g., spouse, partner, friends, and/or family) to combat. This frees the individual to look for unseen, unused, or untapped resources (see Chapter 4), rather than being victimized by the illness. In turn, a client can rewrite, or restory, the narrative from one of weakness to one of strength. As discussed in Chapter 8, this story or narrative reflects a client's schematized views, but externalizing the problem allows the client to make either first-order (i.e., surface) changes (assimilation) to the schemas or more substantial second-order changes (i.e., accommodation). In essence, a client creates a new story in which the client is more important than the problem (Carr, 1998; Freedman & Combs, 2002; Sperry et al., 2006; White & Epston, 1990). This in turn helps to resolve ambivalence by taking the problem from inside the client to outside the client.

But Don't Take Our Word for It! Master Example

In this example of a transcript with a master practitioner, G. Alan Marlatt works with a client wrestling with heroin addiction (Allyn & Bacon, 2000a).

Dr. G. Alan Marlatt: "Does it ah, seem like a friend in a way, heroin?"

Danny: "Uh hmm, somewhat. Somewhat."

Dr. G. Alan Marlatt: "Of what, what kind of a friend?"

Danny: "I'm saying like, you know, you know, like, like when it hits you, you know, it's like it's, you know how when you, you know, had a real close buddy or something."

Dr. G. Alan Marlatt: "Yeah."

Danny: "And, or it's like when you get back into it, it's like the heroin in your body and, and in the body like, like, like two friends that's been drifted away from each other and now they met back up again, you know."

Dr. G. Alan Marlatt: "Like a big reunion or something."

Danny: "Yeah."

Dr. G. Alan Marlatt: "Yeah."

Danny: "Uh hmm."

Dr. G. Alan Marlatt: "So your body likes the way it feels when it's with it?"

Danny: "Somewhat. Yeah."

Dr. G. Alan Marlatt: "But not totally?"

Danny: "Not totally."

Dr. G. Alan Marlatt: "What's, what's not right with this?"

Danny: "You know, because, you know, your body knows the control that this drug can have over it."

Dr. G. Alan Marlatt: "Yeah."

Danny: "You know what I'm saying? Yeah. And the way it, you know, it makes you feel, you know, when the problem that you're going to have when, like when that friend ain't there, you know."

Dr. G. Alan Marlatt: "Yeah. What are you gonna do when the friend ain't there?"

Danny: "Yeah, then you're in trouble, see."

Dr. G. Alan Marlatt: "Yeah. Is there any replacement? Anything that would, like in the, when you were married, it was more important to stay with her than to take the drug, right?"

Danny:	"Uh hmm."
Dr. G. Alan Marlatt:	"What about now, nowadays?"
Danny:	"Ah, what you mean by that?"
Dr. G. Alan Marlatt:	"What would be more important than taking the drug?"
Danny:	"My life."
Dr. G. Alan Marlatt:	"Your life."
Danny:	"Like in my life, what would be more important? My kids."
Dr. G. Alan Marlatt:	"Your kids."
Danny:	"Yeah. It's the most important thing in my life now, you know. Even though, you know, I'm back messing with the heroin, but . . . I would leave it alone for them."

In the above example, Marlatt takes the issue of heroin addiction and externalizes it for the client (suggesting that it is a friend). He then begins to get the client to envision what he might do when the friend goes away as well as what might be more important than the friend (i.e., his children). In this way, the therapist using nonlinear thinking gets the client to change their way of thinking or relating to the problem as an internal issue to relating to it as an external one. This clinical case example may prove helpful.

Clinical Case Example: A Marital Couple

A young, highly successful, accomplished, and attractive couple sought marital counseling due to emotional distance that had grown between them for a variety of reasons. Both earned six-figure salaries, both had graduate degrees, and both had exceptionally bright future career prospects. They had made progress in understanding the basis for their emotional distance from one another and sufficiently working through certain crises.

During their fifth session of therapy, which had been spread over the course of approximately 2 months, the discussion turned to how their work schedules, career paths, and future choices concerning careers affect their marriage. The woman bemoaned the fact that she was tired of seeing others taking credit for projects she had designed and seen to completion and being promoted as a result of her efforts. Very tearfully, she lamented the fact that she was very nearly within grasp of being given a promotion that would clearly mean recognition, success, and her future career path. As the oldest child in her family of origin, she felt she had been achievement-, career-, and success-oriented since early childhood, thus reflecting strong family values of what constitutes self-worth.

At the same time, she began to sob that she knew that her children desperately needed her at home at this critical preschool time in their lives. Although she could change her employment status with her current company to part-time, she knew that it would be the death knell for a strong upward career move and the promotion, recognition, and status she covets. She also recognized that if she devoted more time and attention to her children, who need her at home, she could return to full-time employment in the future and resume her achievement orientation. But she also believes that by then, she would be an "also-ran" in the company thicket of high achievers.

Questions to Consider
1. What are the client's schema dynamics?
2. What are the poles of the client's dilemma? What kind of dilemma is presented here (e.g., approach avoidance)?
3. How does the client's language construct and maintain the problem?
4. How could she relanguage or restory the problem to be externalized?
5. How would externalizing the problem help relieve the ambivalence?
6. What could the counselor do to help externalize this problem?

What is the wife in this clinical case example to do? Should she forgo what she believes that she has been groomed and trained for all of her life in order to care for her children, who need her? Or should she sacrifice the needs of her children and continue with a career path that she truly enjoys? The pendulum of her schema dynamics sways her in one direction, whereas the circumstances of her life sway her in another. Therein lays the ambivalence that torments her. She would like to be able to both have her cake and eat it too. That is, she would like to continue with her career path and care for young children who she knows need her, but she perceives these two alternatives as being largely incompatible. She feels that she cannot have it both ways and must make a choice, and it is a painful choice to make, with no one able to give her the right answer. Her husband is supportive but knows he must leave the decision to her. The therapist urged careful balancing and consideration of the two alternatives that confronted her. Because of other subtle comments the woman made, the therapist suggested that some of her tears appeared to be the result of letting go of at least some of her career aspirations—not only a sign that she was mourning their loss but also a healthy sign that she was beginning to get on with her life (i.e., listening and responding to presence). As the oldest child in her immigrant family of origin, she values success, achievement, and all its accouterments (e.g., status, money, and overcoming the disadvantages of being an immigrant). When she developed those values, however, she had not been married or had any children. Having children became a value that ultimately came into conflict with career success as a value. But that does not mean that career success and all that it signifies to her as a long-held value will simply evaporate in the cognitive schema she has held dear and worked very hard to fulfill for many years. By externalizing the client's issue or symptom (in this case, her career ambitions), however, the therapist can help the client work through the ambivalence and make a choice, or be able to restory the ambivalence and incorporate it into her life choices.

To be able to utilize these narrative practices, a therapist is required to prize listening and understanding first and questioning second (i.e., nonlinear listening). Questions should be used only to help couples to see that the narratives of their lives and relationship are actively constructed rather than passively recounted and given. Therapists who begin to use a narrative approach are

> interested in collaborating with people to change their lives through enriching the narratives they and others tell concerning their lives. . . . It seems that through these alternative stories, people can live out new identities, new possibilities for relationships, and new futures. (Freedman & Combs, 2002, p. 308)

In other words, they adopt the master practitioner attitude or dispositions (curiosity, collaboration, optimism and hope, pattern recognition, self-soothing, and mindfulness), and are invested in maintaining a robust therapeutic alliance with a client. These practitioners realize that it is a primary method for helping to resolve ambivalence and begin a conversation that elicits change talk. In the next section of this chapter, we introduce the basics of motivational interviewing—a robust, nonlinear approach to dealing specifically with client ambivalence.

Nonlinear Approaches: Using Motivational Interviewing to Help Manage and Resolve Ambivalence

In Chapter 4, we presented research on moving clients from one stage of change to the next. In concert with helping clients to move along the change process, Miller & Rollnick (2012) developed a clinical model called *motivational interviewing* or sometimes called *motivational enhancement therapy,* whose central tenet involves addressing clients' ambivalence and helping them to resolve it. According to Miller and Rollnick (2012), motivational interviewing is defined as "a collaborative conversation style for strengthening a person's motivation and commitment to change" (p. 12).

Empirical support for the efficacy of motivational interviewing also comes from recent empirical research. For example, Burke, Arkowitz, and Menchola (2003); Miller et al. (1993); and Miller and Rollnick (2012) have suggested that motivational interviewing-based interventions are indeed clinically effective and potent in addressing problem drinking, behavior that is difficult to change. As Tashiro and Mortensen (2006) pointed out,

> Meta-analyses have found motivational interviewing for substance abuse to be as efficacious as other treatment modalities but that a lower dose of treatment is required (three fewer sessions) than with typical treatments. (p. 962)

Although the stages of change model (see Chapter 4) identifies where along the continuum of change a particular client may be, motivational interviewing, in essence, provides a nonlinear way of thinking about ambivalence. It facilitates psychological movement regarding ambivalence from any one stage of change to the next stage by working with a client's natural propensities for growth, competence, changing, and protectively staying the same. Central to motivational interviewing is the nonlinear understanding that clients paradoxically express a desire to change and simultaneously resist change and seek to maintain the status quo. This is because change (potentially) disrupts a client's schematized view of self, others, or life or the world, which can precipitate feelings of failure, shame, embarrassment, loss of prestige, and the like.

OARS: Basic Motivational Interviewing Methods

According to Miller and Rollnick (2012), clinicians using motivational interviewing are encouraged to use four basic methods when interviewing a client—particularly in the beginning. Using the acronym OARS, these methods include: open-ended questions, affirmations, reflective listening, and summaries. Each of these are useful in gathering information about the client ambivalence without arousing resistance or reactance in the client. We discuss each, briefly.

Asking *open-ended questions* are questions that require clients to elaborate on their stories. They are different from closed-ended questions that the client can answer with one word (like yes or no). Some examples include: "Tell me more about your job?" or "How would you like for your life to be different?" Next are *affirmations,* which communicate to the client that the therapist understands the difficulty that the client might be having, as well as complimenting them on changes that they have tried. Examples of this include "I can see that it's important for you to be a good mother" and "I appreciate that you want to make things different." The next method is *listening reflectively.* In this text, this includes all of the linear and nonlinear methods of listening (and responding). Finally there is *summarizing.* This is a method that helps the client know that the therapist has understood (or misunderstood) what they are saying. It is also a way to transition from one topic to the next (i.e., from the past where the problem is, to the future where the solution is). It also helps with goal setting and structuring the session time (Miller & Rollnick, 2012).

But Don't Take Our Word for It! Master Example

In this example of a transcript with a master practitioner, G. Alan Marlatt works with a client wrestling with heroin addiction (Allyn & Bacon, 2000a).

Dr. G. Alan Marlatt:	"Uh hmm, so, you're, it sounds like you're of two minds about this; part of you wants to go, but part of you doesn't, right?"
Danny:	"No, I want to, I want to. I just, you know, I just haven't really took the steps yet but, uhm."
Dr. G. Alan Marlatt:	"Right. But if we, if you were to start thinking about, you know, taking some small steps toward that, right? Does that seem possible?"
Danny:	"Yeah."
Dr. G. Alan Marlatt:	"Oh, what could you, what would be the first thing that you could do?"
Danny:	"The first thing to do is run and get signed up. That would be the first step."
Dr. G. Alan Marlatt:	"Sign up?"
Danny:	"Yeah, and then go from there, you know."
Dr. G. Alan Marlatt:	"So, you'd just come, go to one of your friends and say, 'I wanna sign up.'"

In the example above, Alan Marlatt uses several of the OARS responses to help the client clarify the ambivalence and begin to take steps to make changes in his behavior (were you able to detect them?). Of course, many of these should sound like elements from all of the Level 1 domains (connecting and engaging, assessment, and building the therapeutic relationship). However, it is when they are applied to client ambivalence that their full potential to help clients is realized. Next, we discuss how the motivational interviewing use of reflection and responses beyond reflection helps clinicians address and resolve ambivalence.

Using Reflection and Responses beyond Reflection to Address Ambivalence

Miller and Rollnick (2012) outlined several strategies for addressing and resolving ambivalence, loosely classified as *reflective responses* and *beyond reflective responses* (see Information Box: Strategies for Resolving Ambivalence). Reflective responses are similar to the linear listening and responding approaches outlined in Chapters 2 and 3 in which a therapist simply paraphrases and reflects back a client's feeling, sentiments, attitudes, and so on. In this way, a therapist is able to help a client thoroughly explore each side of his or her ambivalence. It is a method that requires patience and subtlety rather than mimicry. One of the reflective responses, called *amplified reflection,* may include some interpretation or logical extension of a client's argument (at times rendered to the point of hyperbole). For example, a client complains of having an overwhelming, chronic back pain that keeps him returning to work, but refuses to adhere to his physician's recommendation to go to physical therapy. By use of logical extension of the dilemma, a therapist can explore all of the ways that a client's life will be impacted when he is no longer able to get out of bed due to the pain (e.g., "So, your back condition *may* take a turn for the worse if you aggravate it, and then there would *really* be a price to pay—you might have to have back surgery, and that can really be treacherous!"). The caution here is that any amplified reflection should be done without sarcasm, otherwise it may embarrass or make the client react poorly.

Another of the reflective responses is called *double-sided reflection,* in which a therapist simultaneously affirms both sides of a client's ambivalence. This usually takes the form of "On the one hand . . . on the other hand . . . " For example, a clinician may say "On the one hand, I can see how it would be fulfilling to pursue your dreams of acting; after all, how many times do we get to go through life? On the other hand, I can also see how having a steady job and a regular paycheck would calm your fears of having to rely on your parents to support you." At times, a client may simply be fatigued by the endless back-and-forth and resolve his or her ambivalence by making a decision (which ends the processing). Consider this brief exchange from the case of Mike:

Therapist: "Okay, so on the one hand, your anger gets you what you want—people give in and do what you want. Kind of like your father. But on the other hand, the cost for this is either you get into trouble, could lose your job, or worse: you turn on your fiancée, push her away, and lose her."

Mike: "Yeah, I dunno, I just don't want to look 'weak' in front of people. I don't want people to think they can walk all over me."

These are powerful methods for discovering the important issues that are keeping the client trapped in their ambivalence (e.g., "I just don't want to look 'weak'"), which can then become a focus of therapy. This can also move a client from an earlier stage of change (i.e., precontemplation or contemplation) to a more advanced stage of change in a way that preserves the therapeutic alliance.

Information Box: Strategies for Resolving Ambivalence

Reflective responses (linear)

- Simple reflection
- Amplified reflection
- Double-sided reflection

Other responses beyond reflection (nonlinear)

- Shifting focus
- Reframing
- Agreeing with a twist
- Emphasizing personal choice and control
- Coming alongside

Source: Adapted from Miller and Rollnick (2002).

Another response to client ambivalence, called *beyond reflection,* appears to have many elements in common with principles of nonlinear thinking, as well as similarities to the nonlinear responding outlined in Chapter 3 and elsewhere in this text. These include shifting focus, reframing, agreeing with a twist, emphasizing personal choice and control, and coming alongside. *Shifting focus* refers to parrying or evading a troublesome subject posed by a client, usually to arouse resistance and defensiveness, and derail the therapeutic process (i.e., safeguarding). For example, a teenage client may say, "You're just going to judge me by my appearance and say that I need to listen to my parents, and do what they say." If a therapist tries to deal with this subject confrontationally, he will either get into a power struggle (e.g., "Your parents want what is best for you") or try too hard to ally with the client. Shifting focus sidesteps the ambivalence in the hope of engaging the client in therapy (e.g., "Well, maybe they are right, and maybe you are right, but I know that I don't know nearly enough about your situation to make that determination"). At this point, the client can decide to explore each side of the conflict (e.g., "I want to do it my way, which will hurt my parents," versus "If I listen to them, I sacrifice my individuality"). The nonlinear methods of listening and responding (e.g., for congruence, absence, inference, presence, and resistance) are useful here as well.

Agreeing with a twist is accomplished when a therapist reflects back what the client says with agreement, but also adds a new frame of reference to it. Consider, for example, that a client is seeing a therapist for depression, but doesn't feel much hope for a recovery from her symptoms: "I've been down this road before, Doc. I may feel better for a while, but it always comes back." Agreeing with a twist, a therapist may respond by saying, "Recurrence is a common feature in people who suffer from your condition, and while one episode may feel like one too many, there are also long periods when your mood seems to be very stable and you can be productive." In other words, the therapist validates that although the client has a right to be concerned, she would be squandering a good opportunity if she didn't make use of her time when she was not sick.

Emphasizing personal choice and control is a way to deflect client criticism and reactance by asserting the belief that it is the client who ultimately has the say-so in determining the course of therapy—and his or her life. For example, a client may feel that she is being pressured by her therapist to make a decision and lash out, "I have five kids that I have to look out for. If I leave my husband, who is going to feed them, and clothe them? I'd need to get a job and then pay for day care." The agreement with a twist may sound like "Having a large family is a great financial strain, and going out on your own is an enormous personal strain. Perhaps staying in an unsatisfactory and abusive relationship may be the best option open to you right now." Again, many of the nonlinear methods of listening and responding discussed above and in Chapters 2 and 3 are helpful in these situations to move the client along the stages of change.[3]

But Don't Take Our Word for It! Master Example

In this example of a transcript with a master practitioner, William R. Miller (cocreator of motivational interviewing) works with a client wrestling with a substance abuse addiction (Allyn & Bacon, 2000b).

Mike:	"Well, I mean, whether you think, I'm, I'm, I'm thinking basically that the, that the thing I could best do is, is just start running again and just start, ah, really substituting habits. I don't think, ah, I think, substitution of habit make a habit so counterproductive or kinda, kinda contradictory, I should say, maybe, ah." (crosstalk)
William Miller:	"Not worth it."
Mike:	"Yeah, which you just replace one habit with another habit ah, rather than just try to get rid of one habit. I think it kinda comes up to a vacuum state. Now, what do I do? I gotta rid of this habit. Now what do I replace it with, you know? So."
William Miller:	"Well, and you're, you're clearly telling me that's what works for you."
Mike:	"Yeah."
William Miller:	"Uh hmm. Well, and, and, it sounds like you wanna have an active life in a way, not drinking. It's doing, it's not doing something. It's doing nothing, yeah."

Mike:	"Yeah. It's doing nothing."
William Miller:	"So for you, the question is 'What am I gonna be doing? Well, how do I spend my time?'"
Mike:	"Yeah."

Clinical Exercise: Nonlinear Listening and Motivational Interviewing Interventions to Help Resolve Ambivalence

Instructions: Read each of the following case vignettes and develop reflective (i.e., linear) or beyond reflective (i.e., nonlinear) responses that best describe the client's behavior.

1. A client comes to therapy following an argument with his wife that became physical. As a result, the police became involved, and the client was required to come to therapy. Although you invite the client to talk about the incident, he devotes much of the time in therapy to talking about how unfair the criminal justice system is and how "all that the cops and judges want is my money."

2. A client enters therapy and describes how she had been to several therapists but hasn't found the right one yet. She tells you that she has heard great things about you and that in just the brief time that you have been together, she really feels that you will be the one to help her solve her problems.

3. A client comes to therapy and states that he no longer feels any joy from life. When asked about his background, he states that it was "normal," but later proceeds to describe how his mother had to be hospitalized following the accidental drowning of his younger brother when he was 6 years old. Following your empathetic expression of the magnitude of the loss for the family, the client's only remark was to say, "Yeah, mom took it kind of bad."

4. A couple comes into therapy because the wife is diagnosed with major depression and has been hospitalized twice for it. The husband made the appointment with the therapist and begins the session by saying, "My wife's condition makes it hard to do anything. I have to do a lot around the house, especially when the depression gets bad, but I don't mind as long as she gets well." As the wife begins to tell her story, the husband either attempts to "correct" her or shakes his head to indicate "no" when she makes statements about her illness.

5. A client comes for his second therapy session following what you believed to be a successful first session. The client's presenting concern was anxiety, especially around his supervisor at an accounting firm. At the end of the initial session, you and the client agreed to some specific homework tasks that included speaking up at a staff meeting, setting up an appointment to speak with the supervisor, and inquiring if a female coworker who he has been interested in is dating anyone. When he returns, he says that he didn't accomplish any of the tasks because "the meeting went too long, the secretary was never at her desk to make the appointment, and I just didn't get around to it" (i.e., asking about the coworker).

6. A client comes to session for help in dealing with her 6-year-old son, whom she describes as "uncontrollable." The client discusses how she punishes the child and physically disciplines him by spanking, but it doesn't work. You suggest using logical consequences with the child, and time-out procedures instead of spanking. In response, the client says, "Oh, I don't think that will work," but agrees to try it. At the next session, the client reports that she tried using a time-out, but that the child didn't behave, and that she "had" to use physical discipline.

Questions

1. Describe the poles of the dilemmas that each client is facing.
2. What kinds of nonlinear listening would be used to best understand the client's ambivalence?
3. Consider how you might use OARS methods in working with these cases?
4. Choose one of the motivational interviewing methods of responding to the ambivalence presented above that would help the client best work through the ambivalence (amplified reflection, double-sided reflection, shifting focus, reframing, or agreeing with a twist).

Variation: Form small groups and discuss your answers to the questions. Which approaches were chosen? Was there agreement on which approaches might work better than others? Then discuss with the entire group.

Rolling with the Resistance

Motivational interviewing has its origins in the treatment of substance abuse. For many substance abuse counselors, confronting an addict (i.e., confrontation as in your face) has been an important traditional step toward breaking through clients' denial. In addition, such confrontation has been viewed as an indispensable prerequisite to fully engaging clients in treatment and recovery. Thus, when Miller and Rollnick (2012) originally proposed that the best way to deal with resistance was not to fight it, but to roll with it, a considerable controversy was born. However, they made a convincing argument for their unconventional approach:

Reluctance and ambivalence are not opposed but are acknowledged to be natural and understandable. The counselor does not impose new views or goals; rather, the person is invited to consider new information and is offered new perspectives. "Take what you like and leave the rest" is the permissive kind of advice that pervades this approach. It is an approach that is hard to fight against. (Miller & Rollnick, 2012, p. 40)

They described resistance and ambivalence about change as two sides of the same coin (a decidedly nonlinear approach). When a client is discussing the need for change, why something is the right thing for her to do, or the like, she is embracing change talk (i.e., dialogue that leads to change and is one side of the resistance coin). On the other hand, clients will also advocate for not changing or engage in resistance and counterchange talk, which essentially preserves the status quo. The clinician's primary task is to decrease a client's level of resistance and keep resistance low. In doing so, a therapist can develop discrepancies more clearly, and clients can engage in more change talk and ultimately resolve their ambivalence about the problem.

But Don't Take Our Word for It! Master Example

In this example of a transcript with a master practitioner, G. Alan Marlatt works with a client wrestling with heroin addiction (Allyn & Bacon, 2000a).

Dr. G. Alan Marlatt: "What's to, what's keeping you from doing that first step, do you think?"
Danny: "I don't know. I don't know, really nothing. You know, well, somebody else, sometimes when I, when I wake up in the morning, you know, the

	way I be feeling, you know, I got to, the first thing I have to do is go out there and try to, you know, try to get something to get me, get me right first, you know before I can do anything."
Dr. G. Alan Marlatt:	"Before you can do anything indeed."
Danny:	"Yeah. 'Cuz see like, just like, it's just something that you've got to have every day."
Dr. G. Alan Marlatt:	"Right."
Danny:	"You know, and you've got to have it like as soon as you wake up but if you don't, you know, then, ah, you messed up. You know, your whole body functions and everything is just like, you know, is just messed up."
Dr. G. Alan Marlatt:	"So, you need that morning fix to just feel normal?"
Danny:	"Uh-huh."
Dr. G. Alan Marlatt:	"But if you felt normal, then you'd be more likely to go and sign up?"
Danny:	"Yeah."

Motivational-interviewing theorists see resistance as developing frequently as a result of a client perceiving an infringement on his or her personal freedom (i.e., reactance) by a therapist engaging in confrontational interventions rather than in a collaborative process. Rather than viewing it as a static trait that belongs to a client, motivational interviewing views resistance as a dynamic process that can ebb and flow between client and therapist. Change occurs at lower levels of resistance; thus, therapists must keep resistance low—a fact that Norcross and Wampold (2011) and Beutler et al. (2011) found to be demonstrably effective methods of adapting the therapeutic relationship (see Chapter 7). Resistance is not something a client has or doesn't have; it is more useful to view it as a continuum that is always moving back and forth between resolution and doubt—just like the dilemmas (e.g., approach-avoidance) outlined in Chapter 12. Nonlinear-thinking clinicians who roll with the resistance recognize that anyone who continues to be stuck in this state of flux feels awful. As a result, a client may search for someone (e.g., a spouse, friend, coworker, or therapist) to take one side of the client's ambivalence for him or her (and *from* him or her), so the client can argue for the other side and seemingly make a decision. Of course, the side that a client usually takes is the side that says, "Keep doing what you are doing; don't change." Thus, rolling with the resistance (a nonlinear paradoxical way of thinking) frustrates that strategy by avoiding the trap of taking a side and instead moving a client to keep vacillating in his or her ambivalence until the client is ready to act. Consider the following example with a master practitioner:

But Don't Take Our Word for It! Master Example

In this example of a transcript with a master practitioner, William Glasser (creator of Reality Therapy), works with a woman who is deciding about whether to commit to a relationship or not (Alexander Street Press, 2012).

Ann Mary:	"I'm deciding do I really like this independence thing or is a just a reason that I'm giving everybody for not wanting you know to make that commitment."
William Glasser:	"Well it's, you know it's not as if anyone can tell you that. But there is a reason. I mean, here the guy's kids are grown up and not dependent on him . . . Does he make a fairly good living?"

Ann Mary:	"We'll see, that's what bothers me, I don't know because it's like, he's from the South and up in the Midwest here we're very fast paced and bigger, and so on. I think he makes an okay living, but he doesn't really say. And his work ethic is totally different than mine, or my family, and I worry about that."
William Glasser:	"That's the difference. Yeah, just kind of like a, 'live today and let tomorrow take care of itself' kind of a thing."
Ann Mary:	"Yeah, like how 'its only money,' you know? And up here it's you know, you have to hustle and down there I don't know if it's they're just you know …"
William Glasser:	"Well, I don't know, I can't judge the south with the north, but I mean his work ethic, which means some of the ways he approaches life, if he's not a, he is in his 40s already now."
Ann Mary:	"Right."
William Glasser:	"I mean, it's not like he's going to change a great deal at this stage of the game."

Oftentimes, however, the feelings of ambivalence are strong, and it calls for a therapist to utilize different approaches (or to employ knowledge of different domains) that are tailored to a client's specific needs. In fact, according to Miller and Rollnick (2012), resistance is often the first signal for a therapist to take a different approach with a client. Such is the point in time that a clinician may find it useful to develop discrepancies.

Developing Discrepancies

As previously noted, some clients present themselves for treatment on an involuntary or mandated referral basis. Other clients enter treatment when their circumstances have become intolerable. Many times, such clients will attempt to distort realities and reflect little or no desire to see things as they actually are (e.g., "This whole DUI thing has been blown way out of proportion. I mean, sure drinking and driving is bad, but I didn't have that much to drink. It was bad timing that I got stopped"). Many times, they would also prefer to express feelings about the way they would like things to be (e.g., "I wish this whole thing would just go away instead of me having to deal with lawyers, the court, and alcoholism counseling. This is costing me a lot of time and money over something that has all been a big mistake"). The blurring and/or denial are manifestations of ambivalence being expressed in order to justify the status quo.

As described above, in light of such client protestations, a nonlinear-thinking therapist's first approach is to roll with the resistance. That is, allow the client to have his or her say and do not contradict the client. The next, more active step is to develop discrepancies. *Developing discrepancies* refers to expanding upon inconsistencies between circumstances as they are and the way a client proclaims that he or she would like them to be. The Columbo Approach (see Chapter 4) can be very useful in developing discrepancies in a nonthreatening way.

According to Miller and Rollnick (2012), a client who is blurring or distorting reality and not seeing any difficulty with his or her behavior should be a clinical opportunity for the therapist to give voice to the arguments for change, not just against it. For example, a therapist might respond to the fictional DUI client's protests about being arrested for a DUI by saying, "You seem really upset by this mess of having to deal with a lawyer, a court date, maybe losing your driver's license, going for alcoholism counseling, spending a bundle of cash for all of this, and so forth. I don't know if you have a drinking problem or not, but if you did have a drinking problem, how might that affect your life?

What do you think it would mean to you?" From a nonlinear perspective, therapists are required to point out the fact that the present state of affairs is very different from how a client wants them to be. At the same time, a therapist must not appear to be an advocate for any particular position. By utilizing his or her communication skills (both linear and nonlinear listening and responding), a therapist can draw very clear distinctions between the two poles of a client's conflict and reduce the comfort that a client may derive from blurring. This is akin to holding the client's feet to the fire. Unlike confronting, merely having a therapist not advocating for one side of a client's ambivalence or the other puts a client in a less threatening position.

But Don't Take Our Word for It! Master Example

In this example of a transcript with a master practitioner, William R. Miller (cocreator of motivational interviewing) works with a client wrestling with a substance abuse addiction (Allyn & Bacon, 2000b).

William Miller: "But with alcohol you're kinda getting a point where, 'No, this isn't worth it anymore.'"

Mike: "Yeah. Yeah. But it's not because anyone is telling me for the outside. It's not because I'm being forced to do that. It's just because I got to wake up in the morning, and I know how I feel, and I think what happened before I used to drink, drink, drink all the time, and I was, I was, I was always drinking, then I, then I stopped. Then I thought of how good I felt."

William Miller: "Uh hmm."

Mike: "Okay? Now, I have a compare and contrast. Whereas before, I never had a compare and contrast."

William Miller: "Now you know."

Mike: "Now you know. Yeah, now you know. 'Hey, wait. Wasn't it a lot better; I was more clear-headed than when I was,' you know."

William Miller: "Uh hmm."

Mike: "So and, ah, ah, to me, then, then it does become a problem, because now you, at least you have something you can relate to. You can say, 'This is, this is how I am without it, this is how I am with it. This is my performance without it, this is my performance with it.' You know?"

William Miller: "It's only when it's a problem for you, really, that it matters."

Mike: "Right. Alright."

William Miller: "If somebody else is telling you."

Mike: "Yeah, it doesn't work"

Sometimes, simply bringing a discrepancy to the surface is enough to motivate a client to begin embracing the desire to change. The likelihood of this occurring is greatly enhanced when a client perceives his or her behavior to be incongruous with important personal values or goals. As a brief example, a client who had deeply disappointed his family by his errant ways commented in therapy that his epiphany occurred when he saw the depth of the "pain and hurt" his wife and children were experiencing as a result of his behavior. Having come from a dysfunctional family of origin, he had vowed as a young man never to inflict upon his own family what his family of origin and especially his father had inflicted upon him. Yet here he was, having hurt the ones he loved the most. Consider this somewhat similar example with Steven Andreas:

But Don't Take Our Word for It! Master Example

Consider this example from master practitioner, Steven Andreas (creator of neurolinguistic programming) and how he responds to Melissa's inference (Alexander Street Press, 2012).

Melissa:	"It's that revenge thing."
Steven Andreas:	"Okay!"
Melissa:	"But then there's part of me that wants to let it go."
Steven Andreas:	"Okay! Now what would revenge do for you?"
Melissa:	"Make me feel better."
Steven Andreas:	"That'd make you feel better. I'd like you to feel better. I don't think revenge is the best way to do it, it's a way. Now, tell me . . . tell me this. Close your eyes and go into wild revenge fantasies, what would you do if you have . . . if you were totally omnipotent and you had all the power in the world and you could take revenge on this guy and be into a bloody pop or whatever. How would that make you feel?"
Melissa:	"Like I won."
Steven Andreas:	"Okay! So, would you feel stronger?"
Melissa:	"No, I'd still feel equal."
Steven Andreas:	"Equal! So you feel unequal now?"
Melissa:	"I want him to feel the hurt that I felt."
Steven Andreas:	"Yeah! And that would make you feel equal?"
Melissa:	"Hmm . . . hmm . . ."

At other times, discrepancies result when the cost of clients' behavior is brought into stark relief, and they must acknowledge that the personal and psychological expense of the problem behavior is not worth the cost. In the example above, Andreas gently keeps Melissa focused on what her need for revenge would get her (equality) and why forgiveness is so hard (it would leave her feeling unequal). In the end, however, she is also gently reminded to think about whether it would be worth it. Two motivational interviewing exercises commonly useful in developing discrepancies to facilitate client discussion of their ambivalence are *values clarification* and *weighing the cost of behavior*. Such an exercise allows a therapist to develop discrepancies more sharply in the hope that it "overrides the inertia of the *status quo*" (Miller & Rollnick, 2002, p. 39). For example, in the clinical case example in Chapter 10 in which a wife was wrestling with her feelings of rage at her husband's infidelity, the therapist might point out that, on the one hand, the client valued her commitment to marriage; whereas on the other, she valued integrity. She acutely feels the dimensions of the dilemma she is in: If she continues to be hurt, angry, and upset and decides upon divorce, she will be a loser; on the other hand, if she stays with her husband, she is constantly reminded that he chose to be intimate with someone else over her, which also defines her as a loser (i.e., a second choice). By clarifying and labeling the client's values, as well as the cost of continuing versus the cost of not continuing the behavior, the therapist provides a framework for the client to make a decision (about the ambivalence).

It takes a master practitioner to uncover such dynamics and present them without stimulating additional anxiety or imposing a sense of coercion on a client that is likely to prompt reactance or safeguarding behaviors. Consider this clinical case example.

Clinical Case Example: In a Quandary

Jane is in a quandary. Cumulatively, she has many stressors in her life, particularly with work. Despite the fact that there were several coworkers who were senior to her, she was promoted to project director over her area. On some level, she was proud of the title and the authority to manage. On the other hand, she did not like having to confront her coworkers, nor did she like dealing with some of the day-to-day operations (along with the occasional crises) that drained her of time and energy. Nevertheless, Jane has felt a strong sense of duty since she committed to the position. But she has felt that it has taken her away from other parts of her job that give her greater satisfaction. After a year of doing this and making some progress, Jane started to feel tired and unappreciated at work. Her sense of duty and commitment drove her to continue in her position, but she began to resent it more and more.

Finally, a senior coworker, someone who Jane trusted and confided in, confronted her about her performance. She cautioned Jane that she was in danger of burning out, and it was starting to show. She was greatly embarrassed by the feedback and reluctant to admit it, although she felt her colleague's comments were accurate. At the same time, the colleague offered to take on Jane's duties for her. Despite her trust in and relationship with the colleague, Jane suspected her motives (i.e., the job entailed better pay, more flexibly in work assignment, etc.), although the colleague denied it.

Questions

1. What are the poles of the dilemma that the client is facing?
2. Speculate on what the client's schema dynamics (particularly view of self and view of others) might be and how they are contributing to the client's ambivalence.
3. In what sort of dilemma does the client find herself (e.g., approach-approach)?
4. How might a linear-thinking therapist handle the client's behavior?
5. How might a nonlinear-thinking therapist develop discrepancies in this example?

Jane's dilemma is clear: On one hand, she would like to enjoy the perks of her job, but she dislikes the hassles it poses for her. On the other hand, she finds the idea of freedom from the burden of this job very appealing. At the same time, the thought of shirking her duty was very unappealing to her—it wouldn't leave her feeling very good about herself. Thus emerges her feeling ambivalent about what choice to make. She felt that she was being pulled in two directions (i.e., give up the job or remain in the uncomfortable position), feeling stuck between a rock and a hard place (i.e., there is no good alternative), and wanting to have her cake and eat it too (i.e., have the perks of the title and the power to make decisions, but also be free of hassles). As a result, her behavior may look like endless stalling and deliberating (i.e., vacillating) about change or some form of distancing or dissociation from the reality of the problem situation (i.e., escape).

Developing discrepancies serves the purpose of providing motivation for a client to make a decision by making certain that a client's ambivalence remains the focus of therapeutic attention. This is done by extrapolating the consequences of the client's action or lack of action. In the example with Jane, if she does not have the courage to make a choice about her situation, she would either do nothing and eventually be removed from the position, which would be embarrassing, but at least she wouldn't have been the one to make the decision. The therapist would respectfully draw this distinction and remind the client that the choice is ultimately hers. Too often, when clients decide not to face the conflict that they are in, they give up control of their life, and leave things to chance and let fate work it out for them (e.g., develop a physical, stress-based illness). Put simply, they are merely reacting to being pulled in both directions while wanting to have their cake and eat it too, and so on.

Clinical Exercise: Developing Discrepancies

Return to a previous clinical case example in Chapter 12 and/or this chapter that dealt with ambivalence, and think about how a therapist could begin to develop discrepancies with that client. Share your ideas with a small group or with the entire class.

Listening for and Eliciting Change Talk

One way that therapists begin to make progress in helping clients to resolve ambivalence is through the development of change talk (see Miller & Rollnick, 2012; Watzlawick, 1978). This is particularly important in motivational interviewing. According to Miller and Rollnick, change talk reflects movement of the person toward change, whereas resistance represents and predicts movement away from change. Although the initial stages of therapy focus on building motivation for change utilizing principles outlined above, the working-through phase of therapy focuses on instituting and stimulating change. This can be seen as the movement of a client from a precontemplation or contemplation stage toward a preparation for action and even an action stage of change. From our perspective, in order to elicit such change talk, therapists must be able to listen and respond nonlinearly (i.e., congruence, absence, inference, presence, and resistance, as outlined in Chapter 3). Likewise, non-linear listening and responding can also help a clinician to reflect back to a client when he or she is beginning to use change talk, make positive decisions, or work through his or her ambivalence. For example, if a client has habitually come to therapy talking about how difficult it is to manage her daughter and instead comes to therapy and discusses her daughter's positive traits, listening for absence can help the therapist to identify her positive movement via the change talk. Change talk is also similar to solution-focused speech (in solution-focused therapy) and externalizing (in narrative therapy). Ultimately, change talk indicates that the client is in the processes of considering second-order change or change in the schema level of the client's awareness. Thus, it is important for clinicians to listen for and be aware of a client's change talk, which falls into one of four general categories:

1. *Disadvantages of the status quo*: Dialogue that highlights the disadvantages of the status quo signals that a client has begun to realize that the way things are is presently no longer acceptable or desirable (i.e., moving from precontemplation to contemplation). For example, a client with a history of substance abuse who has consistently perceived his drug usage as "partying" or "recreational" begins to have real consequences for his behavior (loss of job, family, etc.). A client realizes, "This is more of an issue in my life than I thought. . . . I never realized how much this affected my family." At times, therapists can elicit disadvantages by asking questions such as "What worries you about your situation?" and "How has this prevented you from doing what you want?" Listening for congruence, inference, as well as resistance is important for identifying this type of change talk. Looking for exceptions and developing discrepancies are useful additional strategies for eliciting disadvantages as well.

2. *Advantages of change*: Dialogue that highlights the advantages of change signals that a client has begun to consider how life might look different (better) if a change took place (i.e., moving from the precontemplation to contemplation stage). For example, a wife in a

marriage with incidents of repeated domestic violence may begin to dream (visualize) what it would be like to live a life without fear. A client realizes, "Hmmm, without (the particular problem) I'd be able to . . ." or simply "I would feel so much more relaxed, and I'd be able to do so much more." In addition, sometimes therapists can elicit this by asking questions such as "How would you like things to be different . . ." (i.e., the "miracle question"). Listening for congruence, absence, and presence can also be important for identifying this type of change talk.

3. *Optimism for change*: Dialogue that highlights a client's sense of optimism signals that a client has begun to accept that change is possible (i.e., moving from the contemplation to preparation for action stage). For example, the substance-abusing client above, after some initial work on his motivation for change, may begin to feel a measure of confidence in his ability to bring about change (self-efficacy). The client states, "I did (make a positive change) before. . . . I think I could again if I put my mind to it." In addition, therapists can support such optimism by asking questions such as "Who could offer you support (to make this change)?," "When in the past have you made a change like this?," and "What was helpful to you?" Listening for congruence, absence, and presence can also be important for identifying optimism for change talk.

4. *Intention to change*: Clients' expressions of their intention to change are signals that they have made a decision to implement change and no longer see advantages to their previous behavior (i.e., moving from the contemplation to preparation for action stage). An expression of intention to change is a sign that significant ambivalence may have been resolved.[4] For example, a client in a violent relationship may recognize that her husband is not going to stop his behavior and decides that she must leave in order to protect herself and her children. Such a client may realize, "I think it is time. . . . I don't want this for my family anymore. . . . I have to do something." In addition, therapists can stimulate intentions and resolve by asking questions such as "What do you intend to do?" or "Let's not be concerned about how you might accomplish this for now and instead focus on how you want things to be!" Listening for congruence, absence, presence, and inference are also important for recognizing this type of change talk. Again, looking for exceptions and developing discrepancies are useful strategies for eliciting this type of change talk.

Consider this brief example from a master practitioner:

But Don't Take Our Word for It! Master Example

Consider this example from master practitioner Michael Yapko and how he elicits change talk for Mike, a person with chronic self-esteem problems (Alexander Street Press, 2012).

Mike: "I also realized that I can be whoever I wanna be. Or do whatever I wanna do, you know. Um."

Michael Yapko: "There will always be people who tell you can't."

Mike: "Yeah."

Michael Yapko: "What're you gonna do?"

Mike: "Well, what I realized, or, had thought about was when I was talkin' about different abilities and things like, I'm capable of making things happen on my own. And I've used that throughout my life but never took the time to think about it."

In this brief example, it is clear to see that Mike reflects on the advantages of change, optimism for change, and intention to change. This is a good example of the type of change talk that comes at the end of successfully resolving client ambivalence that motivational interviewing aims to do. Now, try the following exercise to see how you might elicit change talk.

Clinical Exercise: Change Talk

Instructions: Read each of the statements and answer the questions below.

1. A client comes to therapy and complains that he no longer feels any pleasure from his life. As a result of therapy, he comes to understand that his career is "draining" him, despite the fact that he is successful at it. He has spent a great deal of time going "back and forth" on making a career change, weighing the positives and negatives of each. Finally, during one session he excitedly talks about the possibilities that a new career would bring and how energized he was feeling about what was in store.

2. A client has been in therapy to address panic attacks. His attacks frequently disrupt his family and work life, requiring the people around him to drop everything and care for him. Although he has made progress in therapy, it has been strongly recommended that anti-anxiety medication would be most effective for his type of anxiety. The client has actively resisted this, stating, "I don't want to have to be dependent on medication to feel normal." But after a particularly debilitating panic attack, the client began asking about medication, saying, "I just can't do this to my family and friends anymore."

3. A client with a history of substance abuse comes to therapy as a condition of probation. Although she knows that it can be helpful to her and that her abuse is problematic, she also finds it difficult to give up her habit. The therapist gives her a homework assignment of tallying up the cost (in both time and money) of her abuse. The client came back, stating, "I seriously underestimated how much of my life this was consuming. It is really taking over, isn't it?"

4. A client has been dealing with issues of guilt surrounding the death of her mother over a year ago. She was her mother's primary caregiver and has found her death difficult to come to terms with—despite her mother's long-known terminal illness. As a result, she has frozen her life (including her home) to keep things as they were the day her mother died. Her husband has found this difficult and strongly suggested that she "get some help." After several sessions of therapy, where the client began to grieve her mother's loss, the client came in and began to talk about what she could do with her life now that she had extra time on her hands.

Questions

1. What is the dilemma that is presented in each of the scenarios?
2. What kind of nonlinear listening would you use in each?
3. Which of the strategies presented above for handling ambivalence might be useful in these situations?
4. What kind of change talk is the client in each scenario beginning to use?

Successful Resolution of Ambivalence

Clients come to therapy feeling ambivalent. Miller and Rollnick (2012) suggest signs that a client has successfully resolved his or her ambivalence and is ready to begin implementing changes:

1. Decreased resistance
2. Decreased discussion about the problem
3. Resolve
4. Change talk
5. Questions about change
6. Envisioning
7. Experimenting with new behavior

They cautioned, however, "It is quite tempting to assume that once the client is showing signs of readiness for change . . . the decision has been made and it is all downhill from there on" (Miller & Rollnick, 2012, pp. 128–129).

What is known about the change process is that the most lasting change comes about slowly and that even when a person has made a choice, feelings of ambivalence may still linger. If therapists are successful in helping a client to resolve his or her ambivalence, the client can begin on a path to change. Yet these first steps are tentative, and a client may not be fully committed to them. It is like starting a fire in a fireplace—although a spark may ignite a flame, it is the therapist who can contribute to the fire by adding a warm glow—or let it die out. Although it is a client's responsibility to continue the change, the therapist must encourage client efforts toward change. At the end of it all, there is no one best approach to resolving ambivalence; such thinking would be decidedly linear. There is a wide variety of choices within this domain that, when artfully employed, represent the best in nonlinear thinking regarding facilitating a client to resolve his or her ambivalence and advancing the therapy toward a successful outcome.

Take Aways for Practitioners

- Confronting a client with his or her ambivalence is not to be confused with confrontation and being in someone's face regarding his or her behavior. The former is reflected in bringing the client's attention to the ambivalences by holding a mirror to them so that they may see the dilemma and the difficulties that it poses.
- Among the linear responses to helping a client resolve ambivalence are simply reflecting a client's dilemma, perhaps amplifying it, or articulating an understanding of both sides of the client's dilemma.
- Shifting a client's focus, reframing, agreeing with a client, and emphasizing personal choice and control are among the nonlinear responses to helping a client resolve his or her ambivalences.
- Finding exceptions to a problem and solution focus can be of help in resolving ambivalence. Likewise, finding exceptions to a problem can also be of help in resolving a client's ambivalence regarding an issue.
- Motivational interviewing offers several effective strategies for helping clients to resolve the ambivalences regarding the dilemmas that a client might be facing. These strategies include both linear and nonlinear responses to a client's feelings of ambivalence.

Conclusion

Clients may come to therapy feeling ambivalent, or being pulled in two directions, while wanting to have their cake and eat it too and ultimately finding themselves stuck between a rock and a hard place. Master clinicians understand that this requires linear and nonlinear thinking in order to help the client address and then resolve the ambivalence. Often times resolving the ambivalence is all that the client needs, whereas other times the ambivalence is the start of the real clinical work that the client needs. Either way, resolving ambivalence requires a curious, collaborative, optimistic, pattern-recognizing, self-soothing, and mindful therapist who can connect and engage the client, fully assess the client, establish a therapeutic relationship, and understand both the client's schema dynamics and emotional system. In short, it requires knowledge of all of the previous domains, along with a thorough knowledge of this domain. In the next and final chapter of this book, we review the domains and their takeaways, discuss the ethical practice of psychotherapy, and preview the seventh and final domain (which is covered in the advanced text).

Notes

1. Hanna (2001; Hanna & Puhakka, 1991) defined this process as "resolute perception." Resolute perception is a process whereby a client, with the help of the therapist, makes a decision to become single-minded in facing whatever mistaken beliefs, poor choices, or maladaptive behavior sequences that are allowing problem behavior to continue.
2. Narrative therapy was first described by Michael White and David Epston (1990, 1992). It draws on the philosophy and writing of Michel Foucault and his critical analysis of the interplay of language, knowledge, and power on society's marginalized individuals (e.g., the others, sick, insane, or criminal).
3. Note: *Coming alongside* is a type of intervention called a paradox that is discussed in much more detail in our advanced text.
4. However, this does not necessarily mean that the change is certain. Recall from Chapter 4 that many clients can be stuck in the preparation for action stage with the false belief that they are making changes. It is significant in terms of client adherence to treatment.

14
Summary and the Disengagement/ Engagement Hypothesis

Nonlinear Thinking and the Domains of Competence Revisited

Learning how to think like a therapist (i.e., the process of formulating a case conceptualization; understanding double binds in which a client may find him- or herself in; realizing the purpose being served by certain symptomatic behavior; and devising a coherent plan about how to proceed that encompasses the relevant clinical findings and social circumstances of the person) is vastly different from telling someone what to think. Such how thinking maximizes therapist flexibility in dealing with the infinite variety that clients and their circumstances bring to the treatment setting. Teaching what to think would involve, for example, insisting that others learn a particular orientation (e.g., Freudian, Adlerian, or Jungian) framework and working only from that framework no matter what the problem or complaint of the client might be. Traditionally, clinicians in training are exposed to a particular theory of personality, a theory of therapy, specific protocols on how to treat particular conditions (e.g., anxiety, obsessive-compulsive disorder, or depression), or a set of microlevel skills that they then adopt as an operational model. The amazing thing is that the research literature demonstrates that the particular theory or model of therapy (e.g., object relations, Adlerian, or Jungian) makes absolutely no difference in treatment outcome (see Duncan, Hubble, & Miller, 2000; Hubble, Duncan, & Miller, 1999; Lambert & Barley, 2002; Miller et al., 1997a; Norcross, 2002b; Walt, 2005). In fact, research from more than half a century ago (i.e., Fiedler, 1950) revealed that experts with different theoretical orientations are much more similar than different in what they actually do with clients. Duncan (2010) has summarized this issue quite cogently:

> Given a therapist who has an effective personality and who consistently adheres in his treatment to a system of concepts which he has mastered and which is in one significant way or another adapted to the problems of the sick personality, then it is of comparatively little consequence what particular method that therapist uses. It is . . . necessary to admit the more elementary consideration that in certain types of mental disturbances certain kinds of therapy are indicated as compared with certain others . . . the following considerations . . . apply in common to avowedly diverse methods of psychotherapy: (1) the operation of implicit, universalized factors, such as catharsis, and the as yet undefined effect of the personality of the good therapist; (2) the formal consistency of the therapeutic ideology as a basis for reintegration; (3) the alternative formulation of psychological events and the interdependence of personality organization as concepts which reduce the effectual importance of mooted differences between one form of psychotherapy and another. (pp. 12–13)

We have asserted that to learn about therapist nonlinear thinking, in combination with the factors that are known to increase a therapist's general effectiveness, from the earliest point of development seems to be the most appropriate way to train clinicians. In this text, we have attempted to do just that, by describing clinician attitudes or dispositions that accompanied each of the domains covered in the text. The attitudes included curiosity, collaboration, optimism and hope, pattern recognition, self-soothing, and mindfulness. Each of these combined creates a therapist who has the type of disposition that master practitioners have that makes them especially effective.

This text has also emphasized the use of nonlinear thinking as the method that master practitioners use to develop an understanding of how clients see their problems, what they mean by what they are saying and doing, and how to respond to clients' concerns. Nonlinear thinking is thus a natural way in which human beings process information, and it is what master practitioners utilize to effectively help clients. We have attempted to tap into your natural nonlinear thinking through the use of nonlinear-thinking exercises. These included exploring the quirks of language, considering Galileo's paradox, contending with the prisoner's dilemma, the gambler's fallacy, how hedonism is not what it seems, and Buridan's donkey and bridge. These thought experiments and word puzzles were designed to provide examples that illustrate what we mean by nonlinear thinking, as well as to stimulate some nonlinear thinking as well.

This book has also drawn from the research on common therapeutic factors (or what we called domains of convergence) as an important starting point in training new clinicians. Wampold (2010) put it thus: "A model that emphasizes the common factors predicts that, with some qualifications all cogent treatments, embraced by therapists and client competently delivered to a client motivated to engage in the process are equally effective" (p. 56). These factors are the basic ingredients that consistently appear to be identified in the literature as vital to all effective therapy, regardless of a practitioner's theoretical orientation. We know from the research that therapists who exhibit more positive behaviors—warmth, understanding, and affirmation—and fewer negative behaviors—belittling, neglecting, ignoring, and attacking—were consistent predictors of positive outcome. According to Norcross and Lambert (2011):

> How to improve psychotherapy outcome? Follow the evidence; follow what contributes to psychotherapy outcome. Begin by leveraging the patient's resources and self-healing capacities; emphasize the therapy relationship and so-called therapeutic factors; employ research-supported treatment methods; select interpersonally skilled and clinically motivated practitioners; and adapt all of them to the patient's characteristics, personality and worldviews. This, not simply matching a treatment method to a particular disorder, will maximize success (Norcross & Lambert, 2011, p. 13).

In this text, we have done this by showing how each of the domains have been used by masters (via the But Don't Take Our Word for It boxes), as well as the research evidence for the efficacy in therapeutic outcomes. As a review of some of the ingredients required to think like a master practitioner in a nonlinear way, we present Information Box: Nonlinear Thinking and the Domains of Competence, as a summary of nonlinear thinking reflected in all of the domains.

Information Box: Nonlinear Thinking and the Domains of Competence

Nonlinear thinking facilitates disengagement because it reflects the following:

Introduction and Chapter 1

- Unlike linear thinking, nonlinear thinking does not resemble a straightforward, characteristic, one-dimensional, logical approach to human problem solving.

- Nonlinear thinking turns things upside down and inside out, departs from the linear way of thinking about things in the physical universe, and requires appraisal/interpretation.
- Deliberate practice is the chief method to develop mastery in any field, including psychotherapy. As a result, this text included multiple opportunities to work with the elements being presented.

Chapters 2 and 3

- Listening not only with one's ears but also with one's eyes, feelings, and intuitions and a generally open mind.
- Hearing things that aren't spoken or are conspicuous by their absence.
- Understanding the significance of discrepancies between what is said and how it is said.
- Developing the capacity for understanding the potential implied meaning of messages.
- Seeing beyond what is present to what is absent, as a result of therapist curiosity being piqued by what a client isn't saying or discussing.

Chapters 4 and 5

- Understanding that not all clients seek treatment with the same motivation or readiness for change.
- Recognizing and endorsing the value of client strengths and resources, and utilizing creative methods for including them in the therapeutic dialogue.
- Integrating both a client's problem or symptoms and the client's strengths or resources into a multidimensional picture of the client and a plan for his or her treatment.

Chapters 6 and 7

- Facilitating rapport and empathy to develop a therapeutic alliance. Practitioners do not respond to peculiar or abnormal client behaviors in ways that others might ordinarily do. Behaviors that keep people at bay or alienate others can be seen as assets.
- Mirroring the client's exceptionally idiosyncratic nonlinear thinking as a vehicle for achieving therapeutic progress (like a tuning fork).
- Utilizing the best available research findings (i.e., APA Second Task Force, Norcross (2011) to inform therapy).

Chapters 8 and 9

- Understanding the client's worldview or schema is what makes it possible to make sense of a client's behavior.
- Directing client attention toward the central organizing patterns of their problem (the schema, or view of self, others, and life and the world) of which the client may not be aware.
- Understanding that schemas—even very problematic ones—have evolved over a lifetime of reinforcing experiences (aided by self-fulfilling prophecies) as a way of helping an individual navigate through life—sometimes successfully and sometimes problematically.
- Using assimilation and accommodation to help alter schema dynamics on either the first-order or second-order level of change.

Chapters 10 and 11

- Extrapolating and inferring from a client's affective expressions, internal feelings, and underlying emotional states.

- Utilizing client emotions as information and an opportunity to empathize with a client and help a client to understand that emotions inform.
- Demonstrating to a client in a nonlinear way (via mindfulness approaches) that the client has the capacity to exercise control regarding his or her emotional life.

Chapters 12 and 13

- Understanding that most clients, to some degree, want to have their cake and eat it too, feel pulled in two directions at the same time, and ultimately find themselves stuck between a rock and a hard place.
- Understanding that ambivalence is a method of protection from threat (e.g., the therapist or change itself) and thus a part of what can be expected in the change process; resistance to change and ambivalence are not aberrations of the treatment process but a typical part of the therapeutic process.

So What Is the Point to All This?

There is a comedy skit from the show *MadTV* featuring Bob Newhart as a therapist that can help to illustrate this question (easily accessible by searching "Bob Newhart Stop It" on YouTube). In it, he is meeting a female client for the first time. He explains his unusual "billing practices" by saying: "Just have a seat and let me tell you a bit about our billing. I charge five dollars for the first five minutes and then absolutely nothing after that. How does that sound?" She thinks it is "too good to be true," and he adds "Well, I can almost guarantee you that our session won't last the full five minutes. Now, we don't do any insurance billing, so you would either have to pay in cash or by check. And I don't make change." Then he asks her to tell him about her problem. She proceeds to tell him that she has a specific phobia of being buried alive in a box, which paralyzes her to the point where she doesn't want to be in elevators, or anything remotely "boxy." The therapist astutely assesses that she is claustrophobic and calmly says, "Katherine. I'm going to say two words to you right now. I want you to listen to them very, very carefully. Then I want you to take them out of the office with you and incorporate them into your life." Then he sits upright in his chair and yells at her "Stop it!" The client is shocked and says, "What do you mean?" The therapist responds, "You know, it's funny, I say two simple words, and I cannot tell you the amount of people who say exactly the same thing you are saying. I mean, you know, this is not Yiddish, Katherine. This is English. Stop it!" For the remainder of the skit, he berates her as being a "kook," and his solution to all of her problems (e.g., "I have a difficult time in relationships with men") is to yell at her and say: "Stop it!" And although this is not a good example of an effective, nonlinear-thinking therapist, it does (humorously) get at the heart of one of the two main purposes of therapy.

Wondering what is the point of counseling after reading the last 13 chapters of this book may seem ridiculous, but there is a serious question to consider. After you have connected and engaged with a client; assessed their symptoms, strengths, and stage of change; established a therapeutic relationship; deciphered their schema dynamics; managed their emotional expressions; and helped them to resolve their ambivalence, the question remains: What is it all for? *What* is it that we want these clients to do? What is it that these clients want us to do for them? Ultimately, we have come to understand the work of therapy or counseling as being a way to guide clients so that they can achieve changes that result in resolving their problem, conflict, dilemma, and so on, and lead more functional and satisfying lives. Typically, this requires two reciprocal developments: (1) clients must diminish/stop—or disengage from—old, maladaptive patterns of association, thoughts, and behaviors—but stopping a behavior, thought, or feeling represents a linear mode of thinking about change, and (2) clients must engage in or embrace different, more positive responses to the inevitable demands and changes of life; more adaptive behaviors, activities, pursuits, relationships, and so on; more thoughtful/effortful consideration of things as they are in the here and now (rather than as similar to past unfavorable events, circumstances, experiences, etc.) or as we would like them to be; and less emotionally directed responses to our unsatisfying, disappointing, and so on encounters with life.

The Disengagement/Engagement Hypothesis

At the expense of overstating the purpose of treatment, we suggest that the most encompassing goal for treatment in generic terms is *disengagement*. What is disengagement and what leads us to conclude that it is the goal for clients in treatment regardless of the presenting problem? Recall from Chapters 12 and 13 the four most common behavioral responses to ambivalence are to vacillate endlessly, become immobilized, let fate decide, or try to escape. Often these behavioral responses manifest themselves in very different ways that are unique to each individual, but are almost always related to the client's symptoms or presenting concerns. Thus, disengagement usually means that a client needs to stop one of the four responses. We conclude that it is disengagement that is at the heart of the change process, as well as its ultimate goal. It is the means of helping clients to discontinue struggling (i.e., remove from preoccupation and stop fighting) with their problem and the inappropriate/ineffective solutions that have evolved or that they have been using to cope (generally manifested as a form of ambivalence; see Chapters 12 and 13). We begin our discussion with a consideration of broad categories that can facilitate client disengagement from the maladaptive.

Disengagement through Linear and Nonlinear Understanding

Disengagement is facilitated by clarifying the meaning of what a client is saying. The purpose of such clarification is to develop a common understanding of what a client is saying, which is essential to the therapeutic encounter. Linear and nonlinear listening and responding can be helpful in facilitating disengagement. As we have discussed throughout this text, although clients may be saying one thing, they may be engaging in behavior that is entirely different. Understanding the discrepancies (i.e., listening for incongruence) between meanings is an essential step in the disengagement process. When those discrepancies are resolved, a client has moved in the direction of letting go of and beginning the process of engagement in healthier, more pro-social, and productive means of coping. In addition, working within several of the other domains can help facilitate disengagement. For example, using assessment to define the problem clearly, understand the client's stage of change, and knowing the theme of the client's story sometimes can be enough for the client to reflect on and stop or disengage from a problem behavior.

The take away implications for practitioners regarding linear and nonlinear understanding are:

- It is necessary to listen at two different levels of meaning and understanding: The linear/literal level and the nonlinear level of implied meaning embedded not only in words but behaviors.
- It is a common and reasonable expectation that practitioners respond to what their clients are saying, feeling, and doing.
- It is important for practitioners to thoughtfully formulate nonlinear responses to their clients' concerns and preoccupations. Such nonlinear responding is useful in clarifying, focusing on troublesome issues, resolving concerns, and so on.

Disengagement Facilitated through the Therapeutic Relationship and Therapeutic Alliance
As we described in Chapters 6 and 7, when all of the research about the effectiveness of the therapy experience is distilled down to manageable and useful information, the strength of the therapeutic relationship provides the basis for much of client satisfaction with the outcome of treatment. The therapeutic relationship provides the foundation for disengagement from maladaptive patterns of adjustment. Because practitioners do not respond to clients in the same way that others do, clients have the opportunity to make changes and try new behaviors. The safety and security afforded by the therapeutic alliance provides human support and acceptance. That support and acceptance become essential to working through mistaken beliefs, unrealistic fears, irrational anxieties, and so on that haunt individuals in their quest to have a happier, more functional, more satisfying life. The therapist's empathy, support, and acceptance also form the basis upon which clients can increase their positive risk taking in the world at large and in interacting with others. Among the most important qualities as Elliott et al. (2011), Rogers (1951, 1957), and others have noted is empathy. Empathy is neither unidimensional nor to be confused with sympathy. As Elliot et al. (2011) have suggested, it is complex and composed not only of a compassionate attitude for and staying attuned with a client on a moment-to-moment basis but also as experiencing the person's world through their eyes and resonating with what a client is experiencing.

> Take away implications regarding the therapeutic relationship for disengagement: For novices aspiring to master practitioner status in the future, it is important to remember these factors about the therapeutic relationship in facilitating clients' disengagement from the maladaptive/symptomatic:
>
> - Value the therapeutic relationship and the therapeutic alliance.
> - The therapeutic relationship instills hope that things can improve in some dimension for the client and that they are not alone.
> - Breaches to the therapeutic relationship and the therapeutic alliance must be repaired.
> - Soliciting and incorporating client feedback about how to improve the relationship and where/how the therapy is going is an effective, essential, and nonnegotiable aspect of the disengagement process.

Disengagement through Externalization of the Symptom
You will recall that in Chapter 13 we discussed the process of resolving client's ambivalences regarding the dilemmas that they face. All practitioners are thoroughly familiar with clients who use extraordinarily discouraging language to describe and self-identify themselves such as, "I'm bipolar . . . I've been a depressive all my life . . . I can't get rid of this anxiety . . . I'm a failure . . ." These statements are made declaratively intertwining one's identity with one's illness, diagnosis, symptoms, and so on. Over time, both a client and their loved ones begin acting and treating the client's illness, diagnosis, and so forth, like it is a part of their DNA that has fused itself to the identity of the client with incredible properties of adherence. Perhaps the characteristic most often that clients ascribe to themselves is, "I'm a failure!" When analyzed carefully, such a statement directly implies that the client has never been successful at anything. Consider how astounding the implications of such an assessment can be on one's view of self and correspondingly one's hopes for the future. How can anyone who deems him- or herself a failure ever hope to have any success whatsoever?

A powerful method of facilitating a client's disengagement from their maladaptive behavior is to support a client on the one hand, while simultaneously addressing the fact that there is a difference between their engaging in depressive thoughts, misdeed, or poor adaptive behaviors and being "a depressive . . . a neurotic . . . a failure . . . , and so on." The same holds true for any negative quality, symptom, diagnosis, or illness that a client might espouse. In many respects, what is being advocated is reminiscent of dealing with a child's misbehavior. In that regard, it is important to encourage parents to separate the deed from the doer. Making the symptom, illness, and so on something external to the client frees resources to engage and embrace in healthier pursuits. Encouraging differences between who and what, the client is no longer a victim of something felt as malevolent that has become synonymous with the client: "I am my symptoms."

But Don't Take Our Word for It! Master Example

Consider this example from master practitioner, Steven Andreas (creator of neurolinguistic programming) and how he responds to Melissa's internal placement of her habit.

Steven Andreas:	". . . something like that?"
Melissa:	"Hmm . . . hmm . . ."
Steven Andreas:	"Tell me what I need to do; you feel calm and so on and find your way through the system? Would that be okay?"
Melissa:	"But that's gonna be hard, yeah, but . . ."
Steven Andreas:	"You think it's gonna be harder than blowing up and getting angry?"
Melissa:	"No, it's gonna be hard to stop myself from blowing up and . . ."
Steven Andreas:	"Okay! And what would make it hard?"
Melissa:	"Because it's this habit, this is formed."
Steven Andreas:	"Well, what we can do here is build your new habit."
Melissa:	"Okay!"
Steven Andreas:	"And it'll run off just the way you want it, just as repetitive way and just as 100% as the habit you've already got, will that be alright with you?"
Melissa:	"Yeah!"
Steven Andreas:	(inaudible) "Doing it?"
Melissa:	"Yeah!"

Take away implications regarding externalization of the symptom for disengagement: For novices aspiring to master practitioner status in the future, it is important to remember these factors about externalization of the symptom in facilitating clients' disengagement from the maladaptive/symptomatic:

- A client having symptoms or a diagnosis is not one in the same thing as the client.
- Specific use of language can help a client to separate him- or herself from whatever it is that has become part of his or her identity.
- Separating a client from their illness, symptoms, and so on is not the same thing as excusing them from behaviors for which they are responsible. Accepting responsibility for one's life can represent a significant advance in the process of any recovery.

Disengagement through Focusing Outward versus Focusing Inward
There is probably no more universal characteristic of maladaptive adjustment and mental illness than self preoccupation or an internal focus. Such inward focus can also be used quite constructively as in open and honest self-reflection, meditation, and self-encouragement and self-hypnosis. But when the concentrated essence of inward focus distorts, deletes important facts, becomes negativistic, anxious, depressive, self-critical, fatalistic, catastrophic, and is continually critical, then the outcome is almost guaranteed: The human spirit will be dragged down into dysfunctionality of varying proportions.

As discussed in Chapters 8–11 on schema dynamics and emotion, there are many specific ways in which human beings become preoccupied with and manifest dysfunctional thoughts and emotions. In many respects, it is as though such thoughts and emotions function like a high definition Blue Ray DVD slipped into the conscious-thought drive of the mind and then played endlessly on automatic pilot. The mind plays such thoughts over and over and over, seemingly without any end.

The disengagement antidote for such internal focusing is linear in nature, namely, to assist a client in becoming more aware of the differences between internal and external focus and to help in developing more of an external focus. This is typically accomplished by encouraging a client (e.g., providing an assignment) to engage in some activity—whether it is something simple like going for a walk, counting to ten, accomplishing some small task, postponing the inward focus until a later time in the day, and so on. Such straight-forward assignments can be the starting point for developing a healthier outlook on one's problems.

But Don't Take Our Word for It! Master Example

Consider this example from master cognitive-behavioral therapist, Judith Beck and how she responds to Latrice's decision making to help her disengage (Alexander Street Press, 2012).

Latrice: "I feel confident in the decision of me wanting to move first when I share with every-, with my mother and my sisters and everybody. And then it's like all the pains come in."

Judith Beck: "I see, right. And some people agree with you, and some people don't agree with you."

Latrice: "Right. They agree that I should move, but they agree that I should get a car first, and I don't think it's as important. Even though they do, they think that . . ."

Judith Beck: "Yeah."

Latrice: "I need to have a way to get around. But I think that I really need to have somewhere to live."

Judith Beck: "Well it certainly sounds sensible to me. Sometimes when you have to make a decision, it's helpful to look at, what are the advantages of say moving first, and what would be the disadvantages of moving first. And then you can also look at what are the, um, advantages of getting a car first, and the disadvantages of getting a car first. And I think if you do that, you probably are right about moving first, since you seem to feel it pretty strongly in your gut, but I think if you put it down on paper, it may then help you to answer your family members who are saying, 'No you should do something different.'"

Latrice: "Okay, okay."

Judith Beck: "Does that sound sensible to you?"

Latrice: "Yes. It does."

Judith Beck: "What would be some of the advantages of moving first?"

Take away implications for disengagement regarding internal versus external focus:

- Practitioners are well-advised to note that internal focus, although unavoidable, on a long-term basis leads to looking for what is wrong, ineffectual, needs to be fixed, and so on.
- Assisting a client in developing more of an external focus is useful in breaking the spell that unnoticed internal focusing can have on the functioning of the personality.

- It is important for practitioners to understand the differences between earnest self-reflection, self-examination, thinking through, objective consideration of choices, and so on with sincere circumspection and unproductive self-absorption and internal focus. The former is growth enhancing with a sense of self-direction; the latter is an energy absorbing, self-defeating exercise in futility.

Engagement, Nonlinear Thinking, and Second-Order Change:
Effective Means and Effective Ends

In Chapters 9 and 13 (as well as others), we discussed first- and second-order change. First-order change is a change at the symptom level. As we have mentioned, first-order change is generally linear in nature. However, it should be obvious that disengagement also works on a first-order symptom change level. Based on Whitehead and Russell's (1910–1913) theory of logical types, Watzlawick, Weakland, and Fisch (1974) described first-order change as representing direct attempts to coerce change on the same level of reality (i.e., within the same logical type or class). Examples would be arguing with a spouse and demanding that he changes his behavior, insisting that a loved one stop drinking, managing anxiety by avoiding potentially threatening situations, wrestling with depressed feelings in an effort to make them go away, and the like. Such change efforts are first order because they represent the same level of reality and the same logical type or same class of behaviors. Practically speaking, first-order changes are those things that clients have been trying as solutions to their problems. They represent linear thinking and are mostly ineffective in bringing about the sort of long-term changes that people desire.

Recently, Fraser and Solovey (2007) analyzed the relevant literature on therapy and its effectiveness, and found that second-order change was the common element in all effective psychotherapies. In other words, they concluded that both the practices of master practitioners and *empirically supported therapies* (i.e., EBPPs for evidence-based psychological practices) are effective because their interventions occur at a second-order level of change. Theoretically and practically, it begins to reconcile the debate between those advocating for EBPPs and those advocating for a strong therapeutic relationship (along with other factors) as the basis for effective treatment.

In other words, in order to be effective at the second-order level of change, therapists must (1) understand that linear solutions are often just the first step in truly understanding a client's problem; (2) intervene in a fundamentally nonlinear manner (one that is seemingly absurd to the client); (3) realize that it is necessary for an individual to face and resolve the ambivalence that he or she is feeling now, rather than focus on past hurts, distant causes, or future fears; and (4) help create accommodations to an individual's schema by altering his or her perspective (i.e., changing the context and prompting a reappraisal of circumstances) regarding the problem. Based on this, we conclude that how therapists facilitate genuine client second-order change is through nonlinear approaches. Broadly speaking, this is what we call the process of engagement.

Engagement

There are many avenues that therapists use to help clients disengage/engage, depending upon the client and their circumstances. Many therapists focus their therapeutic efforts on clients disengaging from their problematic behavior by attempting to arrest or stop a particular client behavior; that is to get a client to do something or stop something (i.e., force something on) on a client that they may be ill-prepared to embrace. Rather than attempting to get a client to do anything, a practitioner facilitates the conditions under which a client can come to healthier conclusions. A practitioner does this by adjusting his or her responses to a client from linear to nonlinear and moving from disengagement of old behaviors to engagement in new behaviors.

Just as practitioners use a variety of methods to facilitate clients' disengagement from self-defeating, maladaptive behaviors, thoughts, and emotions, simultaneously they likewise use a variety of avenues to facilitate clients to engage with life in more constructive ways. In many ways, the processes of engagement will seem intuitively obvious, and yet many times in clinical education, such processes will be overlooked. It is important for practitioners to train themselves to constantly look for signs of improvement, even very tiny signs, and to capitalize on those signs. It is equally important for practitioners to monitor and gauge a client's readiness for engagement and at times to caution a client to move more slowly toward constructive behaviors, attitudes, thoughts, and so on. Finally, it is essential for practitioners to remember that it is the uniqueness of each individual's personality, circumstances, strengths, resources, circumstances, culture development, behaviors, and so on that must be taken into account regarding the positivity of their therapeutic movement. That brings us to the more specific question of what is engagement.

Definition of Engagement

Engagement represents the movement of a client/patient toward more constructive means of dealing with the life circumstances for which they sought treatment and which involves risk-taking without guarantees of immunity from perceived failure and damage to self-esteem. Obviously, the key words in the definition above are movement, constructive, and risk-taking. A client's movement can be construed as their progress, growth, and development psychologically, behaviorally, emotionally, attitudinally, and so on. However, constructive dealing with life circumstances, oneself, and so on is seen as a relative term. That is, what may not seem particularly positive for one client may be very positive for another; small improvements for one client might represent substantial improvement for another.

Engagement can also signify a reconnection with the requirements or demands of life (i.e., a work life, interpersonal life, intimate life, etc.) as a client resolves his or her ambivalence and sheds what has kept his or her life on hold. Just as disengagement was related to the four common behavioral responses to ambivalence, engagement can only happen when the client truly understands and resolves his or her ambivalence. Furthermore, it can signify a healthy recovery from the set-backs to which any human being is vulnerable to (i.e., death of a loved one, divorce, devastation of natural disasters, engulfment by debilitating and or life-threatening illness, etc.). That is, to live more so without the threat of constantly reliving traumatic experiences. For those individuals with chronic personality disorders, engagement can represent an attenuation of maladaptive modes of adjustment but not necessarily an elimination of them. Adopting a more mindful, calmer, less preoccupied, or less emotionally volatile attitude are all possible regarding such clients within the scope of the concept of engagement.

If there is a key to the engagement hypothesis, it would be timing. If practitioners must be constantly vigilant as to constructive movement that clients are making, they must be equally vigilant for a client's readiness to embrace changes on an ongoing basis no matter how small. It is not infrequent that clients will realize that more constructive movement implies greater responsibility; that can be anxiety producing to say the least. In such instances, the therapeutic relationship, encouragement, and perhaps even counterintuitive thinking of suggesting that a client slow down are all means of helping a client to cope with making progress.

Encouraging Engagement through Specific Therapeutic Goals

Establishing of goals at the outset of treatment provides the therapeutic encounter with guidance—what is to be the focal point for the therapy sessions. Client and practitioner must be ever mindful of that focal point and how digressions taken from it serve the purpose of the overall treatment goal(s). Engagement is clearly facilitated by making certain that goals are as specific as possible. Typically such goals could be described as visualizable and concrete as possible. For example, can the client see him- or herself engaged in new behaviors, specifically different responses, being calmer, having a greater sense of control over overwhelming affect, conveying his or her needs more directly to a spouse, and so on.

Establishing specific goals can be simple or very difficult. It is for certain that it must be done collaboratively. The question "How would you know that you were better?" can facilitate that process. All too often, however, clients respond to such a question with the response, "I'd feel better ... I'd be happier . . . I'd feel more relaxed . . . " Any of these responses would, of course, be accurate because a client is feeling better, is happier, and so on. It is useful to clarify such nebulous but improved feelings by asking, "If I could see you on a video, how would I recognize that you are indeed better? What would you be doing that I could see on a video of you?" Those images are the concrete goals toward which the therapeutic enterprise aspires.

Establishing specific goals must also pass the test of reality. Reality checking must be applied as to how realistic a client's goals are. In many ways, reality checking can be defined as the reasonableness of a goal. This becomes a very delicate task. Long-term goals must be distinguished from short-term goals. Aspirational goals must be carefully considered for the probability of success without dampening a client's enthusiasm and ambition. Although reality can be a cruel task master, human determination, creativity, hard work, and just plain dumb luck can coalesce to not only tame reality but crush it. That can apply in a certain percentage of the cases but in another percentage of cases, reality will exact its toll and impose itself. It is the practitioner's role to explore the realistic and reasonableness aspects of what a client aspires to without dampening and/or devastating the human spirit.

Making Progress Not Seeking Perfection

Working toward therapeutic goals and achieving them is certainly not a uniform process. In most instances, it is represented by small incremental steps, small but palpable set-backs, reinstitution of fears, and then regrouping and moving forward. In some instances, success is represented by a straight-forward process. In such instances, the client uses the therapy experience to put him- or herself through the final steps necessary to implement actions. Perhaps it is the support of the practitioner or perhaps their guidance. In such instances, it is best to not impede the client's progress.

More typically, clients in treatment are able to calm down and can think more clearly and reasonably. In such circumstances, goals can be achieved by a series of successive approximations. That is, a client gets closer and closer to behaviors, thoughts, emotions, and so on in small steps that the therapist can point out and ask the client about. The therapist can also point out the advisability of taking steps in a hierarchical manner to prevent a client from getting ahead of him- or herself. Such undertakings increase the probability of achieving therapeutic goals.

Engagement through Affirmation and Reaffirmation of Assets and Resources

Although it may not seem like it, everyone has assets and resources. In Chapters 4 and 5, we described how assets and resources can be employed to help clients. Assets can be physical (i.e., strength, beauty, monetary, etc.), social (i.e., family, friends, coworkers, neighbors, etc.), and psychological. Psychological assets can be such traits as a knack for survival despite the cruelties and hardships imposed by life, determination, ability to self-protect, a never say die attitude, and so on. Social/interpersonal support systems are especially important assets. The people caring about a client and the people that a client cares for are important for the process of recovery. Likewise, many people identify with their job/career and find it a source of comfort that they are able to do perhaps what few others can do so well.

But Don't Take Our Word for It! Master Example

In this transcript, master clinician and author Bradford Keeney is interviewing a female client who is struggling with her relationship with her husband. In this brief exchange, he begins to uncover some ways to begin to engage in new behaviors toward her husband (Alexander Street Press, 2012).

Bradford Keeney: "Did you play practical tricks, did you go to trick shops in the past and get things like that or . . . or is that said something you did not explore."

Client:	"I have done little things like that where I've hidden things from him, make him go on a maze to find things."
Bradford Keeney:	"Really?"
Client:	"He has (inaudible) me too though, like Christmas presents are always hidden somewhere with little notes that I have to collect them to figure out."
Bradford Keeney:	"That's fantastic, that's fantastic. So you all have a lot of knowledge that other couples would benefit upon it."
Client:	I guess so."
Bradford Keeney:	"You can figure out this mothering and wake business to get past that."
Client:	"If we can get past all that."
Bradford Keeney:	"Yeah. Yeah that's fascinating. It's like treasure hunts."
Client:	"Yeah, treasure hunts."
Bradford Keeney:	"Oh that's excellent. So you willing to announce that the shock is back?"
Client:	"Yes, I probably could do that. Yes."

Engagement through Mindfulness/Self-Encouragement/Self-Soothing

As we mentioned in Chapter 11, the process of mindfulness is important to help clients work with their emotions. In addition, in Chapter 12 we presented mindfulness as a crucial clinical disposition for the therapist. It is important for practitioners to be mindful of the fact that clients live their lives mainly outside of the safety and security of the consultation room and therapeutic alliance. That's why it is so important to provide "homework" for clients in between therapy sessions. Likewise, it is important for clients to be mindful of the need to engage in positive self-talk and to learn that each individual can be a comfort to him- or herself. If we human beings have the ability to give ourselves negative self-talk messages, it stands to reason that we have the capacity to give ourselves positive self-talk messages. We get to choose which sort of message we want to give ourselves and accept. If negative self-talk can cause such havoc in an individual's life, self-encouragement, positive self-talk, "I can do it," "calm down," and so on, can be used to address perceived setbacks/failures. Therefore, helping the client to adopt a more mindful mindset can help them take a more balanced perspective on their experiences.

But Don't Take Our Word for It! Master Example

In this transcript, master reality therapist and author Robert Wubbolding discusses with a client how to disengage and engage in new behaviors (Allyn & Bacon, 2000c).

Robert Wubbolding:	"You know, see, I have a little motto, if something works, do more of it."
John:	"Yeah. That's ah." (crosstalk)
Robert Wubbolding:	"If something doesn't help, do less of it."
John:	"I like that."
Robert Wubbolding:	"It's the essence of the kinda counseling, the work that I do."
John:	"Okay. I think what I've done is kinda like knocking my head against the wall and trying to make something work."
Robert Wubbolding:	"Yeah. And maybe stop worrying about dealing with this thing."
John:	"How do I do that?"
Robert Wubbolding:	"By doing more of what does work."

John:	"Okay."
Robert Wubbolding:	"That's why I said, if you were good at denial, we'd be trying to help you deal with that, but you're not good at denial. You're, you're good at taking it on board. So, maybe, maybe the opposite is better for you, is to, to, to do some things that would distract you. I mean, that's something against you."
John:	"You know very much, though."

In our advanced text, we describe, in more detail, how master practitioners work to help clients disengage from old behaviors and engage in new behaviors. We present a specific application of nonlinear thinking with all the domains in order to achieve lasting, second-order change. These sophisticated clinical processes are clearly indicative of how master practitioners work. Although many practitioners are able to be very successful stopping with the domains that we have presented here, we feel that there are several final secrets that have not yet been revealed!

The Final Secret: Deliberate Practice and Back to the Sorcerer's Apprentice

We started this text with the aim of presenting nonlinear thinking as a major means of conceptualizing and understanding what it is that master practitioners pay attention to (i.e., the seven domains of competence) to achieve the results that they do. As mentioned earlier, because of space limitations, the topic of specific paradoxical interventions has been expanded and moved to our advanced volume due to space and time considerations. Although it was once confined to mystical and mythic realms, and given only brief consideration in the literature, we have aspired to delineate the secrets of nonlinear thinking and the domains in which it is expressed in clinical practice. If our efforts have not fully explained how to become proficient in using the concept of nonlinear thinking, it is hoped that at least we have provided a roadmap to understanding it.

To begin with, we used the story of the sorcerer's apprentice to explain most people's experience of the master therapist. The key, we asserted, was that novice therapists, like the sorcerer's apprentice, may know how to act like their respective masters but did not know how to think like them. This brings us full circle back to Mickey Mouse as the sorcerer's apprentice. He, like many beginning counselors, wants to have the power that he sees that masters have and tries to seize it by mimicking the actions of the master.

In today's society, with a resurgence in secret societies or ancient wisdom (consider the success of the novel *The Da Vinci Code*; Brown, 2003), it is easy to see how master therapists using nonlinear thinking may look as though they possess some mystical knowledge. And in some respects they do. That is, they understand some of the most basic, fundamental elements of human thought and behavior from the efficacy of establishing a therapeutic relationship to the revelations that neuroscience and behavioral economics research have revealed about how human cognition operates. However, it has also been our contention that this knowledge is not the sole possession of these masters, and that this knowledge can be taught to and understood by a majority of individuals (rather than a select few). We have attempted to break down, as best possible, the nonlinear processes of treatment, as well as the processes underlying these strategies. Furthermore, we have tried to show how these underlying processes mirror clients' private nonlinear thinking and create a working alliance with them, which tends to minimize the probabilities of any inherent resistance.

However, now that you have finished this book, taken this journey, and discovered the mystery behind the thinking of the most effective clinicians, there are two final secrets of the masters to share with you: You must go back to the beginning. As you will recall from Chapter 1, Skovholt and

Jennings (2004) found that master practitioners were distinguished by their desires to keep learning and to continue to pursue knowledge (both in and out of the counseling field). Skovholt and Jennings (2004) observe that master therapists kept up their sense of curiosity and never felt that they had attained mastery. As a result, they pursued every counseling interaction with a sense of newness and wonder. George Leonard (1992), in his book *Mastery,* found that masters find enjoyment in doing the most basic skills of a given discipline, not in the accomplishment or achievement of some goal. He stated that masters enjoy "practice," whereas individuals who merely "dabble" want to be profi-cient without the practice.

The people we know as masters don't devote themselves to their particular skill just to get better at it. The truth is, they love to practice—and because of it they do get better. And then, to complete the circle, the better they get, the more they enjoy performing the basic moves over and over again. (Leonard, 1992, p. 75)

In essence, although they were masters themselves, these practitioners become apprentices again. This time, however, they do not learn from great masters, but instead from clients, students, super-visees, and the practice of the therapeutic process itself. It would be as if Mickey Mouse, instead of becoming afraid of the multiplying brooms and flooding waters, approached the chaos with won-der and excitement about what he would find out about the experience. Indeed, that is a nonlinear thought!

The second final secret is that there is more to learn. Fear not, the masters know that there will always be new things to learn. The more that we refer to concerns not only our advanced volume but a life-long process of learning. In the advanced volume, we devote considerable attention to describ-ing specific paradoxical interventions as a seventh domain demonstrated universally by all master practitioners whether they specifically recognize it or not. We also dedicate attention to the use of humor in treatment and its relationship to nonlinear thinking. It is a powerful means of responding to clients in an encouraging way.

In the final analysis, however, interventions that master therapists use are not magical or whimsi-cal, but rather the careful application of solid researched principles of counseling and psychotherapy (i.e., domains) combined with a firm understanding of the processes of nonlinear thinking. The reality is that the true master adopts a way of thinking about the practice of psychotherapy that is less interested in power and is more interested in helping clients see through their pain and out of their trapped circumstances, to a better vision of their lives. Striving to bring out the best in others and oneself is perhaps the best description of mastery. So we invite you to take that next step—the advanced volume. Wherever you are in your development (Level I, Level II, or Level III), you can go back to the beginning of this book and reread the chapters as a reference. We believe that the information that is contained within will have different meanings to each person if he or she reads it a second or third time. We also believe that as people develop as therapists and come back to this material, they will see and understand things differently that they can apply in their work, and per-haps to their lives. It is a powerful thought, but as we have attempted to show, thinking is what the magic and healing of psychotherapy is all about.

References

Adams, N., & Grieder, D. M. (2005). *Treatment planning for person-centered care: The road to mental health and addiction recovery.* Burlington, MA: Elsevier.

Adler, A. (1927). *Understanding human nature.* New York, NY: Greenberg.

Adler, A. (1929). *The science of living.* New York, NY: Greenberg.

Adler, A. (1956). *The individual psychology of Alfred Adler.* New York, NY: Basic Books.

Adler, A. (1959). *The practice and theory of individual psychology.* Totowa, NJ: Littlefield, Adams. (Originally published in 1920.)

Ajzen, I. (1996). The social psychology of decision making. In E. T. Higgins & A. W. Kruglanski (Eds.), *Social psychology: Handbook of basic principles.* New York, NY: Guilford Press.

Alexander Street Press (Producer). (2012). *Principles of counseling and psychotherapy: The essential domains and non-linear thinking of master practitioners* [motion picture]. Available from Alexandria, VA: Alexander Street Press.

Alighieri, D. (1805). *The Divine Comedy of Dante Alighieri* (H. F. Cary, Trans.). Retrieved September 30, 2008, from http://www.divinecomedy.org (Originally written in 1321)

Allport, G. (1960). *Personality and social encounter.* Boston, MA: Beacon.

Allyn & Bacon (Producer). (2000a). "Harm reduction therapy for addictions," *Brief therapy for addictions 4* [motion picture]. Available from Alexandria, VA: Alexander Street Press.

Allyn & Bacon (Producer). (2000b). "Motivational interviewing," *Brief therapy for addictions 6* [motion picture]. Available from Alexandria, VA: Alexander Street Press.

Allyn & Bacon (Producer). (2000c). "Reality therapy for addictions," *Brief therapy for addictions 7* [motion picture]. Available from Alexandria, VA: Alexander Street Press.

Allyn & Bacon (Producer). (2000d). "Stages of change for addictions," *Brief therapy for addictions 10* [motion picture]. Available from Alexandria, VA: Alexander Street Press.

Allyn & Bacon (Producer). (2000e). "Client-Directed Interaction: Adjusting the Therapy, Not the Person," *Brief therapy Inside Out 5* [motion picture]. Available from Alexandria, VA: Alexander Street Press.

American heritage dictionary of the English language. (2000). 4th ed. New York, NY: Houghton Mifflin.

American Psychiatric Association. (2013). *Diagnostic and statistical manual of mental disorders* (*DSM-5;* 5th ed., text rev.). Washington, DC: Author.

American Psychological Association. (1998). *Communicating the value of psychology to the public.* Washington, DC: Author.

Arnold, M. (1960). *Emotions and personality* (Vols. 1 & 2). New York, NY: Columbia University Press.

Asay, T. P., & Lambert, M. J. (1999). The empirical case for the common factors in therapy: Quantitative findings. In M. A. Hubble, B. L. Duncan, & S. D. Miller (Eds.), *The heart and soul of change: What works in therapy* (pp. 23–55). Washington, DC: American Psychological Association.

Augustine. (1909–1914). Confessions (E. B. Pusey, Trans.). New York: Collier. Retrieved September 30, 2008. from http://ccat.sas.upenn.edu/jod/Englishconfessions.html (Originally written in 397 CE)

Bachelor, A. (1988). How clients perceive therapist empathy: A content analysis of "received" empathy. *Psychotherapy: Theory, Research and Practice, 25,* 227–240.

Baird, K. (2006). The ethical dilemmas involved in going from individual therapy to couples therapy (or the other way around) with the same client(s). *Illinois Psychologist: Newsletter of the Illinois Psychological Association, 43,* 11–30.

Bandler, R., & Grinder, J. (1975). *The structure of magic* (Vol. 1). Palo Alto, CA: Science and Behavior Books.

Barber, J. P., Connolly, M. B., Crits-Christoph, P., Gladis, L., & Siqueland, L. (2000). Alliance predicts patients' outcomes beyond in-treatment change in symptoms. *Journal of Consulting and Clinical Psychology, 68,* 1027–1032.

Beck, A. T., & Weishaar, M. (1989). Cognitive therapy. In A. Freeman, K. M. Simon, L. E. Beutler, & H. Arkowitz (Eds.), *Comprehensive handbook of cognitive therapy.* New York, NY: Plenum.

Beck, A. T., & Weishaar, M. (2005). Cognitive therapy. In R. J. Corsini & D. Wedding (Eds.), *Current psychotherapies* (7th ed., instr. ed., pp. 238–268). Belmont, CA: Thomson Brooks/Cole.

Benjamin, L. S., & Karpiak, C. P. (2002). Personality disorders. In J. C. Norcross (Ed.), *Psychotherapy relationships that work: Therapist contributions and responsiveness to patients* (pp. 423–438). New York, NY: Oxford University Press.

Benson, H., & Proctor, W. (2003). *The breakout principle.* New York, NY: Scribner.

Berg, I. K. (1994). *Family based services: A solution-focused approach.* New York, NY: Norton.

Berg, I. K., & Szabo, P. (2005). *Brief coaching for lasting solutions.* New York, NY: Norton.

Berne, E. (1964). *Games people play.* New York, NY: Grove.

Berne, E. (1966). *Principles of Group Treatment.* Oxford, UK: Oxford University Press.

Beutler, L. E., Harwood, M. T., Michelson, A., Song, X., & Holman, J. (2011). Reactance/resistance level. In J. C. Norcross (Ed.), *Psychotherapy relationships that work: Evidence-based responsiveness* (2nd ed., pp. 261–278). New York, NY: Oxford University Press.

Beutler, L. E., Moleiro, C. M., & Talebi, H. (2002). Resistance. In J. C. Norcross (Ed.), *Psychotherapy relationships that work: Therapist contributions and responsiveness to patient needs.* New York, NY: Oxford University Press.

Bien, T. (2004). Quantum change and psychotherapy. *Journal of Clinical Psychology/In Session, 60,* 493–501.

Bishop, S. R., Lau, M., Shapiro, S., Carlson, L., Anderson, N. D., Carmody, J., . . . Devins, G. (2004). Mindfulness: A proposed operational definition. *Clinical Psychology: Science & Practice, 11*(3), 230–241.

Bitter, J. R. (2008). *Theory and practice of family therapy and counseling.* Pacific Grove, CA: Brooks/Cole.

Bleuler, E. (1950). *Dimentia Praecos: Or, The group of schizophrenias.* New York, NY: International Universities Press.

Bohart, A. C., & Tallman, K. (1999). *How clients make therapy work: The process of active self-healing.* Washington, DC: American Psychological Association.

Bordin, E. S. (1979). The generalizability of the psychoanalytic concept of the working alliance. *Psychotherapy: Theory, Research and Practice, 16,* 252–260.

Bowlby, J. (1969). Disruption of affectional bonds and its effects on behavior. *Canada's Mental Health Supplement, 59,* 12.

Bowlby, J. (1988). *A secure base: Parent-child attachment and healthy human development.* New York, NY: Basic Books.

Brogan, M. M., Prochaska, J. O., & Prochaska, J. M. (1999). Predicting termination and continuation status in psychotherapy using the transtheoretical model. *Psychotherapy: Theory, Research, Practice, Training, 36,* 105–113.

Brown, D. (2003). *The Da Vinci code.* New York, NY: Doubleday.

Brown, J., Dreis, S., & Nace, D. K. (1999). What really makes a difference in psychotherapy outcome? Why does managed care want to know? In M. A. Hubble, B. L. Duncan, & S. D. Miller (Eds.), *The heart and soul of change: What works in therapy* (pp. 389–406). Washington, DC: American Psychological Association.

Burke, B. L., Arkowitz, H., & Menchola, M. (2003). The efficacy of motivational interviewing: A meta-analysis of controlled clinical trials. *Journal of Consulting and Clinical Psychology, 71,* 843–861.

Cappas, N. M., Andres-Hyman, R., & Davidson, L. (2005). What psychotherapists can begin to learn from neuroscience: Seven principles of a brain-based psychotherapy. *Psychotherapy: Theory, Research, Practice, Training, 42*(3), 374–383.

Carkhuff, R. D. (2009). *The art of helping* (9th ed.). New York, NY: Human Resources Development Press.

Carlson, J., Watts, R. E., & Maniacci, M. (2006). *Adlerian therapy: Theory and practice.* Washington, DC: American Psychological Association.

Carr, A. (1998). Michael White's narrative therapy. *Contemporary Family Therapy: An International Journal, 20*(4), 485–503.

Carr, L., Iacoboni, M., Dubeau, M., Maziotta, J. C., & Lenzi, G. L. (2003). Neural mechanisms of empathy in humans. *Proceedings of the National Academy of Science, USA, 100,* 5497–5502.

Castonguay, L. G., Goldfried, M. R., Wiser, S. L., Raue, P. J., & Hayes, A. M. (1996). Empirically supported treatments: Implications for training. *Journal of Consulting and Clinical Psychology, 64,* 497–504.

Centorrino, F., Hernán, M. A., Drago-Ferrante, G., Rendall, M., Apicella, A., Längar, G., & Baldessarini, R. J. (2001). Factors associated with noncompliance with psychiatric outpatient visits. *Psychiatric Services, 52*(3), 378–380.

Chamberlain, P., Patterson, G. R., Reid, J. B., Kavanaugh, K., & Forgatch, M. S. (1984). Observation of client resistance. *Behavior Therapy, 15,* 144–155.

Cheek, D. B., & Le Cron, L. M. (1968). *Clinical hypnotherapy.* New York, NY: Grune & Stratton.

Chi, M. T. H. (2006). Laboratory methods for assessing experts' and novices' knowledge. In K. A. Ericsson, N. Charness, P. J. Feltovich, & R. R. Hoffman (Eds.), *The Cambridge handbook of expertise and expert performance* (pp. 167–184). New York, NY: Cambridge University Press.

Clark, A. J. (2002). *Early recollections: Theory & practice in counseling and psychotherapy.* New York, NY: Brunner-Routledge.

Coale, H. W. (1998). *The vulnerable therapist: Practicing psychotherapy in an age of anxiety.* New York, NY: Haworth.

Collins, W. E., Schroeder, D. J., & Nye, L. G. (1989). *Relationships of anxiety scores to academy and field training performance of air traffic control specialists* (FAA Office of Aviation Medicine Reports). Washington, DC: Office of Aviation Medicine.

Constantino, M. J., Glass, C. R., Arnkoff, D. B., Ametrano, R. M., & Smith, J. Z. (2011). Expectations. In J. C. Norcross (Ed.), *Psychotherapy relationships that work: Evidence-based responsiveness* (2nd ed., pp. 301–315). New York, NY: Oxford University Press.

Corey, G. (2005). *Theory and practice of counseling and psychotherapy* (7th ed.). Pacific Grove, CA: Brooks/Cole.

Coutinho, J., Ribeiro, E., Hill, C., & Safran, J. (2011). Therapists' and clients' experiences of alliance ruptures: A qualitative study. *Psychotherapy Research, 21*(5), 525–540.

Crits-Christoph, P., & Gibbons, M. C. (2002). Relational interpretations. In J. C. Norcross (Ed.), *Psychotherapy relationships that work: Therapist contributions and responsiveness to patients* (pp. 285–300). New York, NY: Oxford University Press.

Cummings, N. A. (1986). The dismantling of our health system: Strategies for the survival of psychological practice. *American Psychologist, 41,* 426–431.

Cummings, N. A. (1999). Medical cost offset, meta-analysis, and implications for future research and practice. *Clinical Psychology: Science and Practice, 6*(2), 221–224.

Cummings, N. A., & Follette, W. T. (1968). Psychiatric services and medical utilization in a prepaid health plan setting. *Medical Care, 6*(1), 31–41.

Damasio, A. (1994). *Descartes' error: Emotion, reason, and the human brain.* New York, NY: Penguin.

Damasio, A. (1999). *The feeling of what happens: Body and emotions in the making of consciousness.* New York, NY: Harvest Book, Harcourt.

de Bono, E. (1994). *De Bono's thinking course.* New York, NY: Facts on File.

Delphin, M. E., & Rowe, M. (2008). Continuing education in cultural competence for community mental health practitioners. *Professional Psychology: Research and Practice, 39,* 182–191.

de Shazer, S. (1985). *Keys to solutions in brief therapy.* New York, NY: Norton.

de Shazer, S. (1991). *Putting differences to work.* New York, NY: Norton.

de Shazer, S., Dolan, Y. M., & Korman, H. (2007). *More than miracles: The state of the art of solution-focused brief therapy.* New York, NY: Haworth.

DiAngelis, T. (2008). When do meds make the difference? *Monitor on Psychology, 39,* 48–51.

DiAngelis, T. (2010). Closing the gap between practice and research. *Monitor on Psychology, 41*(6), 42.

DiClemente, C. C., & Hughes, S. O. (1990). Stages of change profiles in outpatient alcoholism treatment. *Journal of Substance Abuse, 2,* 217–235.

DiClemente, C. C., & Velasquez, M. M. (2002). Motivational interviewing and the stages of change. In W. R. Miller & S. Rollnick (Eds.), *Motivational interviewing: Preparing people for change* (2nd ed.). New York, NY: Guilford Press.

Doctors Without Borders. (n.d.). *About us.* Retrieved from http://www.doctorswithoutborders.org/aboutus/index.cfm.

Dollard, J., & Miller, N. E. (1950). *Personality and psychotherapy: An analysis in terms of learning, thinking, and culture.* New York, NY: McGraw-Hill.

Doyle, A. C. (1892/1986). *Sherlock Holmes: The complete novels and stories.* New York, NY: Bantam.

Dreikurs, R. (1973). Private logic. In H. Mosak (Ed.), *Alfred Adler: His influences on psychology today* (pp. 19–32). Park Ridge, NJ: Noyes.

Dreikurs, R., Grunwald, B. B., & Pepper, F. C. (1982). *Maintaining sanity in the classroom.* New York, NY: Harper & Row.

Duncan, B. L. (2010). Prologue: Saul Rosenzweig: The founder of common factors. In B. L. Duncan, S. D. Miller, B. E. Wampold, & M. A. Hubble (Eds.), *The heart and soul of change: Delivering what works in therapy* (2nd ed., pp. i–xxii). Washington, DC: American Psychological Association.

Duncan, B. L., Hubble, M. A., & Miller, S. D. (2000). *The heroic client.* San Francisco, CA: Jossey-Bass.

Duncan, B. L., Miller, S. D., & Sparks, J. A. (2004). *The heroic client: A revolutionary way to improve effectiveness through client-directed, outcome-informed therapy* (Rev. ed.). San Francisco, CA: Jossey-Bass.

Duncan, B. L., Miller, S. D., Wampold, B. E., & Hubble, M. A. (2010). *The heart and soul of change: Delivering what works in therapy* (2nd ed.). Washington, DC: American Psychological Association.

The Economist. (2006, November 25). The invisible scars, p. 41.

The Economist. (2007, December 23). I think, therefore I am, I think: Consciousness awaits its Einstein, pp. 11–12.

Edelstein, M. R., & Steele, D. R. (1997). *Three minute therapy: Change your thinking, change your life.* Aurora, CO: Glenbridge.

Egan, G. (2009). *The skilled helper: A systematic approach to effective helping* (9th ed.). Pacific Grove, CA: Brooks/Cole.

Eichenbaum, H. (2001). The long and winding road to memory consolidation. *Nature Neuroscience, 4,* 1057–1058.

Ekman, P. (1992). Facial expressions of emotions: New findings, new questions. *Psychological Science, 3,* 34–38.

Ekman, P. (1995). *Telling lies: Clues to deceit in the marketplace, politics, and marriage.* New York, NY: Norton.

Ekman, P. (2003). *Emotions revealed.* New York, NY: Norton.

Ekman, P., & Friesen, W. V. (1975). *Unmasking the face: A guide to recognizing emotions from facial clues.* Oxford, England: Prentice-Hall.

Ekman, P., Levenson, R. W., & Friesen, W. V. (1983). Autonomic nervous system activity distinguishes among emotions. *Science, 221,* 1208–1210.

Elliott, R., Bohart, A. C., Watson, J. C., & Greenberg, L. S. (2011). Empathy. In J. C. Norcross (Ed.), *Psychotherapy relationships that work: Evidence-based responsiveness* (2nd ed., pp. 132–152). New York, NY: Oxford University Press.

Ellis, A. (1955). New approaches to psychotherapy techniques. *Journal of Clinical Psychology Monograph Supplement, 2.*

Ellis, A. (1962). *Reason and emotion in psychotherapy.* New York, NY: Lyle Stuart.

Ellis, A., & Dryden, W. (1987). *The practice of rational-emotive therapy.* New York, NY: Springer.

Emerick, J. J. (1997). *Be the person you want to be: Harness the power of neuro-linguistic programming to reach your potential.* Rocklin, CA: Prima.

Erickson, M. (1977). Hypnotic approaches to therapy. *American Journal of Clinical Hypnosis, 20,* 20–35.

Erickson, M., & Rossi, E. (1980). *Hypnotherapy: An exploratory casebook.* New York, NY: Irvington.

Ericsson, K. A. (2006). An introduction to Cambridge handbook of expertise and expert performance: Its development, organization, and content. In K. A. Ericsson, N. Charness, P. J. Feltovich, & R. R. Hoffman (Eds.), *The Cambridge handbook of expertise and expert performance* (pp. 3–19). New York, NY: Cambridge University Press.

Farber, B. A., & Doolin, E. M. (2011). Positive regard. In J. C. Norcross (Ed.), *Psychotherapy relationships that work: Evidence-based responsiveness* (2nd ed., pp. 168–186). New York, NY: Oxford University Press.

Feltovich, P. J., Prietula, M. J., & Ericsson, K. A. (2006). Studies of expertise from psychological perspectives. In K. A. Ericsson, N. Charness, P. J. Feltovich, & R. R. Hoffman (Eds.), *The Cambridge handbook of expertise and expert performance* (pp. 21–30). New York, NY: Cambridge University Press.

Fiedler, F. E. (1950). A comparison of therapeutic relationships in psychoanalytic, non-directive and Adlerian therapy. *Journal of Consulting Psychology, 14,* 436–445.

Fisch, R., Weakland, J. H., & Segal, L. (1982). *The tactics of change: Doing therapy briefly.* San Francisco, CA: Jossey-Bass.

Frank, J. D. (1961). *Persuasion and healing.* Baltimore, MD: Johns Hopkins University Press.

Frank, J. D., & Frank, J. B. (1991). *Persuasion and healing: A comparative study of psychotherapy* (3rd ed.). Baltimore, MD: Johns Hopkins University Press.

Frankl, V. (1963). *Man's search for meaning.* New York, NY: Washington Square Press, Simon & Schuster.

Fraser, J. S., & Solovey, A. D. (2007). *Second-order change in psychotherapy: The golden thread that unifies effective treatments.* Washington, DC: American Psychological Association.

Freedman, J. H., & Combs, G. (2002). Narrative couple therapy. In A. S. Gurman & N. S. Jacobson (Eds.), *Clinical handbook of couple therapy* (3rd ed., pp. 308–334). New York, NY: Guilford Press.

Frija, N. H. (1986). *The emotions.* Cambridge, England: Cambridge University Press.

Garry, M., & Polaschek, D. (2000). Imagination and memory. *Current Directions in Psychological Science, 9*(1), 6–10.

Gelso, C. J. (2011). *The real relationship in psychotherapy.* Washington, DC: American Psychological Association.

Gelso, C. J., & Carter, J. A. (1985). The relationship in counseling and psychotherapy: Components, consequences, and theoretical antecedents. *The Counseling Psychologist, 13,* 155–243.

Gelso, C. J., & Carter, J. A. (1994). Components of the psychotherapy relationship: Their interaction and unfolding during treatment. *Journal of Counseling Psychology, 41,* 296–306.

Gelso, C. J., & Hayes, J. A. (2002). The management of countertransference. In J. C. Norcross (Ed.), *Psychotherapy relationships that work: Therapist contributions and responsiveness to patients* (pp. 267–283). New York, NY: Oxford University Press.

Gendlin, E. (1978). *Focusing.* New York, NY: Everest House.

Gibney, P. (2006). The double bind theory: Still crazy-making after all these years. *Psychotherapy in Australia, 12*(3), 48–55.

Gibson, L. (2006, April). Mirrored emotion. *University of Chicago Magazine,* pp. 34–39.

Gill, R. E. (2005, September/October). Evidence based psychology gets APA Council approval. *The National Psychologist, 14,* 4.

Gladwell, M. (2005). *Blink: The power of thinking without thinking.* New York, NY: Little Brown.

Goldberg, E. (2001). *The executive brain: Frontal lobes and the civilized mind.* Oxford, England: Oxford University Press.

Goldberg, E. (2005). *The wisdom paradox: How your mind can grow stronger as your brain grows older.* New York, NY: Penguin.

Goldfried, M. R. (1989). Foreword. In A. Freeman, K. M. Simon, L. E. Beutler, & H. Arkowitz (Eds.), *Comprehensive handbook of cognitive therapy.* New York, NY: Plenum.

Goleman, D. (1992, October 6). Holocaust survivors had skills to prosper. *New York Times,* Sec. C, p. 1.

Goleman, D. (1995). *Emotional intelligence: Why it can matter more than IQ.* New York, NY: Bantam.

Goleman, D. (2006). *Social intelligence: The new science of human relations.* New York, NY: Bantam.

Gonsalves, B., & Paller, K. A. (2000). Neural events that underlie remembering something that never happened. *Nature Neuroscience, 3,* 1316–1321.

Gonzalez, H. M., Vega, W. A., Williams, D. R., Wassim Tarrif, W., West, B. T., & Neighbors, H. W. (2010). Depression care in the United States: Too little for too few. *Archives of General Psychiatry, 67,* 37–46.

Gortner, E. T., Gollan, J. K., Dobson, K. S., & Jacobson, N. S. (1998). Cognitive-behavioral treatment for depression: Relapse prevention. *Journal of Consulting and Clinical Psychology, 66*(2), 377–384.

Gottman, J. M. (1993). *What predicts divorce: The relationship between marital processes and marital outcomes.* Hillsdale, NJ: Erlbaum.

Gottman, J. M. (1995). *Why marriages succeed or fail: And how you can make yours last.* New York, NY: Fireside.

Gottman, J. M., & DeClair, J. (1997). *The heart of parenting: How to raise an emotionally intelligent child.* New York, NY: Simon & Schuster.

Gottman, J. M., & Silver, N. (1999). *The seven principles for making marriage work.* New York, NY: Three Rivers.

Greenberg, L. S. (2004). *Emotion-focused therapy: Coaching clients to work through their feelings.* Washington, DC: American Psychological Association.

Greenberg, L. S., & Johnson, S. M. (1986) Emotionally focused couples therapy: An integrated affective systemic approach. In N. S. Jacobson & A. S. Gurman (Eds.), *The Clinical Handbook of Marital Therapy,* pp. 253–276. New York, NY: Guilford Press.

Greenberg, L. S., & Paivio, S. C. (1997). *Working with the emotions in psychotherapy.* New York, NY: Guilford Press.

Greene, D. G., Nystrom, L. E., Engell, A. D., Darley, J. B., & Cohen, J. D. (2004). The neural basis of cognitive conflict and control in moral judgment. *Neuron, 44,* 389–400.

Gross, J. J. (1999). Emotion and emotion regulation. In L. A. Pervin & O. P. John (Eds.), *Handbook of personality theory and research* (pp. 525–552). New York, NY: Guilford Press.

Gula, R. J. (2002). *Non-sense: A handbook of logical fallacies.* Mount Jackson, VA: Axios.

Haley, J. (1963). *Strategies of psychotherapy.* New York, NY: Grune and Stratton.

Haley, J. (1996). *Learning and teaching therapy.* New York, NY: Guilford Press.

Halford, W. K., Bernoth-Doolan, S., & Eadie, K. (2002). Schemata as moderators of clinical effectiveness of a comprehensive cognitive behavioral program for patients with depression or anxiety disorders. *Behavior Modification, 26*(5), 571–593.

Hammond, D. C. (1984). Myths about Erickson and Ericksonian hypnosis. *American Journal of Clinical Hypnosis, 26,* 236–245.

Hanna, F. J. (2001). *Therapy with difficult clients: Using the precursors model to awaken change.* Washington, DC: American Psychological Association.

Hanna, F. J., & Puhakka, K. (1991). When psychotherapy works: Pinpointing an element of change. *Psychotherapy, 28,* 598–607.

Hansen, J. (2002). Postmodern implications for theoretical integration of counseling approaches. *Journal of Counseling and Development, 80,* 315–321.

Hayden, G., & Picard, M. (2009). *This book does not exist: Adventures in the paradoxical.* New York, NY: Fall River Press.

Hayes, J. A., Gelso, C. J., & Humel, A. M. (2011). Managing countertransference. In J. C. Norcross (Ed.), *Psychotherapy relationships that work: Evidence-based responsiveness* (2nd ed., pp. 239–258). New York, NY: Oxford University Press.

Hayes, J. A., McCracken, J. E., McClanahan, M. K., Hill, C. E., Harp, J. S., & Carozzoni, P. (1998). Therapist perspectives on countertransference: Qualitative data in search of a theory. *Journal of Counseling Psychology, 45*(4), pp. 468–482.

Hayes, S. C., Luoma, J. B., Bond, F. W., Masuda, A., & Lillis, J. (2006). Acceptance and commitment therapy: Model, processes and outcomes. *Behaviour Research and Therapy 44*(1): 1–25. doi:10.1016/j.brat.2005.06.006. PMID 16300724.

Henry, W. P., Strupp, H. H., Butler, S. F., Schacht, T. E., & Binder, J. L. (1993). Effects of training in time-limited dynamic psychotherapy: Changes in therapist behavior. *Journal of Consulting and Clinical Psychology, 61,* 434–440.

Hill, G. R. (2004, April 13). *Emotion-focused therapy and the treatment of trauma.* Workshop sponsored by the Academy of Treatment Addictions Professionals, Springfield, Illinois.

Hinsie, L. E., & Campbell, R. J. (1970). *Psychiatric dictionary* (4th ed.). New York, NY: Oxford University Press.

Hirstein, W., Iversen, P., & Ramachandran, V. S. (2001). Autonomic responses of autistic children to people and objects. *Proceedings of the Royal Society of London, 268,* 1883–1888.

Hobson, J. A., & Leonard, J. A. (2001). *Out of its mind: Psychiatry in crisis: A call for reform.* Boulder, CO: Perseus.

Homer. (1958). *The odyssey: The story of Ulysses* (W. H. D. Rouse, Trans.). New York, NY: Mentor.

Horn, J., & Masanuga, H. (2006). A merging theory of expertise and intelligence. In K. A. Ericsson, N. Charness, P. J. Feltovich, & R. R. Hoffman (Eds.), *The Cambridge handbook of expertise and expert performance* (pp. 21–30). New York, NY: Cambridge University Press.

Horney, K. (1945). *Our inner conflicts.* New York, NY: Grune & Stratton.

Horney, K. (1950). *Neurosis and human growth: The struggle toward self-realization.* New York, NY: Norton.

Horvath, A. O. (2001). The alliance. *Psychotherapy: Theory, Research, Practice, Training, 38,* 365–372.

Horvath, A. O. (2006). The alliance in context: Accomplishments, challenges, and future directions. *Psychotherapy: Theory, Research, Practice, Training, 43,* 258–263.

Horvath, A. O., & Bedi, R. P. (2002). The alliance. In J. C. Norcross (Ed.), *Psychotherapy relationships that work: Therapist contributions and responsiveness to patient needs.* New York, NY: Oxford University Press.

Horvath, A. O., Del Re, A. C., Flückiger, C., & Symonds, D. (2011). Alliance in individual psychotherapy. *Psychotherapy, 48*(1), 9–16.

Hoyt, M. F. (2002). Solution-focused couple therapy. In A. S. Gurman & N. S. Jacobson (Eds.), *Clinical handbook of couple therapy* (3rd ed., pp. 335–369). New York, NY: Guilford Press.

Hoyt, M. F., & Berg, I. K. (1998). Solution-focused couple therapy: Helping clients construct self-fulfilling realities. In M. F. Hoyt (Ed.), *The handbook of constructive therapies: Innovative approaches from leading practitioners* (pp. 314–340). San Francisco, CA: Jossey-Bass.

Hubble, M. A., Duncan, B. L., & Miller, S. D. (1999). Directing attention to what works. In M. A. Hubble, B. L. Duncan, & S. D. Miller (Eds.), *The heart and soul of change: What works in therapy* (pp. 407–448). Washington, DC: American Psychological Association.

Hubble, M. A., Duncan, B. L., Miller, S. D., & Wampold, M. A. (2010). Introduction. In B. L. Duncan, S. D. Miller, B. E. Wampold, & M. A. Hubble (Eds.), *The heart and soul of change: What works in therapy* (2nd ed., pp. 23–46). Washington, DC: American Psychological Association.

Hunsley, J. (2007a). Addressing key challenges in evidence-based practice in psychology. *Professional Psychology: Research and Practice, 38,* 113–121.

Iacoboni, M. (2009). Imitation, empathy, and mirror neurons. *Annual Review of Psychology, 60,* 653–670.

Jackson, P. L., Brunet, E., Meltzoff, A. N., & Decety, J. (2006). Empathy examined through the neural mechanisms involved in imagining how I feel versus how you feel pain. *Neuropsychologia, 44,* 752–761.

Jackson, P. L., Meltzoff, A. N., & Decety, J. (2005). How do we perceive the pain of others: A window into the neural processes involved in empathy. *NeuroImage, 24,* 771–779.

Jennings, L., Skovholt, T., Goh, M., & Lian, P. (2013). Master therapists: Exploitations of expertise. In M. Ronnestad & T. Skovholt (Eds.), *The developing practitioner: Growth and stagnation of therapists and counselors* (pp. 213–246). New York, NY: Routledge.

Johnson, L. D. (1995). *Psychotherapy in the age of accountability.* New York, NY: Norton.

Johnson, S. M. (1996). *The practice of emotionally focused marital therapy: Creating connection.* New York, NY: Guilford.

Johnson, S. M., & Best, M. (2003). A systemic approach to restructuring adult attachment: The EFT model of couples therapy. In P. Erdman & T. Caffery (Ed.), *Attachment and family systems: Conceptual, empirical, and therapeutic relatedness* (pp. 165–189). New York, NY: Brunner-Routledge.

Johnson, S. M., & Denton, W. (2002). Emotionally focused couple therapy: Creating secure connections. In A. S. Gurman & N. S. Jacobson (Eds.), *Clinical handbook of couple therapy* (3rd ed., pp. 221–250). New York, NY: Guilford.

Johnson, S. M., & Greenberg, L. S. (1985). Differential effects of experiential and problem solving interventions in resolving marital conflict. *Journal of Consulting and Clinical Psychology, 53,* 175–184.

Josselson, R. (2000). Stability and change in early memories over 22 years: Themes, variations, and cadenzas. *Bulletin of the Menninger Clinic, 64,* 462–481.

Kandel, E. R., Schwartz, J. H., & Jessell, T. M. (2000). *Principles of neural science.* New York, NY: McGraw-Hill.

Kashdan, T. B., & Steger, M. F. (2007). Curiosity and pathways to well-being and meaning in life: Traits, states, and everyday behaviors. *Motivation and Emotion, 31*(3), 159–173.

Kay, C. (2000). *A survivor's perspective: Understanding therapy exploitation: Resources to help you through your recovery from exploitation and negligence by your therapist.* Retrieved from http://www.advocateweb.org/hope/bibliographykc/selfdisclosure.asp.

Kazdin, A. E. (2008). Evidence-based treatment and practice: New opportunities to bridge clinical research and practice, enhance the knowledge base, and improve patient care. *American Psychologist, 63,* 146–159.

Kazdin, A. E., & Rabbitt, S. M. (2013). Novel models for delivering mental health services and reducing the burdens of mental illness. *Clinical Psychological Science, 1*(2), 170–191.

Kellogg, S. H., & Young, J. E. (2006). Schema therapy for borderline personality disorder. *Journal of Clinical Psychology, 62*(4), 445–458.

Kelly, G. (1955). *The psychology of personal constructs* (Vols. 1–2). New York, NY: Norton.

Kessler, R. C., Aguilar-Gaxiola, S., Alonso, J., Chatterji, S., Lee, S., Ormel, J., . . . Wang, P. S. (2009). The global burden of mental disorders: An update from the WHO World Mental Health (WMH) Surveys, *Epidemiologia e Psichiatria Sociale, 18,* 22–33.

Keysers, C., & Gazzola, V. (2010). Social neuroscience: Mirror neurons recorded in humans. *Current Biology, 20*(8), 353–354.

King, L. A., & Burton, C. M. (2003). The hazards of goal pursuit. In E. C. Chang & L. J. Sanna (Eds.), *Virtue, vice, and personality: The complexity of behavior* (pp. 53–69). Washington, DC: American Psychological Association.

Kirsch, I., & Lynn, S. J. (1999). Automaticity in clinical psychology. *American Psychologist, 54,* 504–515.

Kiser, D. J., Piercy, F. P., & Lipchik, E. (1993). The integration of emotions in solution-focused therapy. *Journal of Marital and Family Therapy, 19,* 233–242.

Kluger, J. (2006, July 2). *The science of siblings.* Retrieved from http://www.time.com/time/magazine/article/0,9171,1209949,00.html.

Kolden, G. G., Klein, M. H., Wang, C. C., & Austin, S. B. (2011). Congruence/genuineness. In J. C. Norcross (Ed.), *Psychotherapy relationships that work: Evidence-based responsiveness* (2nd ed., pp.187–202). New York, NY: Oxford University Press.

Koocher, G. (1998). *The science and politics of recovered memories: A special issue of* Ethics and Behavior. New York, NY: Erlbaum.

Kopp, R. (1995). *Metaphor therapy: Using client-generated metaphors in psychotherapy.* New York, NY: Brunner-Routledge.

Kottler, J. A. (1993). *On being a therapist.* San Francisco, CA: Jossey-Bass, Social and Behavioral Science Series.

Krauss, H. H. (2006). Protoscientific master metaphor for framing violence. *Annals of New York Academy of Sciences, 1087,* 4–21.

Kroger, W. S., & Fezler, W. D. (1976). *Hypnosis and behavior modification: Imagery conditioning.* Philadelphia, PA: Lippincott.

Kübler-Ross, E. (1969). *On death and dying.* New York, NY: Macmillan.

Kübler-Ross, E. (1975). *Death: The final stage of growth.* New York, NY: Macmillan.

Kübler-Ross, E. (1981). *Living with death and dying.* New York, NY: Macmillan.

Lambert, M. J. (1992). Psychotherapy outcome research: Implications for integrative and eclectic therapists. In. J. C. Norcross & M. R. Goldfried (Eds.), *Handbook of psychotherapy integration* (pp. 9–129). New York, NY: Basic Books.

Lambert, M. J., & Barley, D. E. (2002). Research summary on the therapeutic relationship and psychotherapy outcomes. In J. C. Norcross (Ed.), *Psychotherapy relationships that work: Therapist contributions and responsiveness to patient needs.* New York, NY: Oxford University Press.

Lambert, M. J., & Ogles, B. (2002). The efficacy and effectiveness of psychotherapy. In M. J. Lambert (Ed.), *Handbook of psychotherapy and behavior change* (5th ed.). New York, NY: Wiley.

Lambert, M. J., & Shimokawa, K. (2011). In J. C. Norcross (Ed.), *Psychotherapy relationships that work: Evidence-based responsiveness* (2nd ed., pp. 203–223). New York, NY: Oxford University Press.

Lave, J. (1988). *Cognition in practice: Mind, mathematics, and culture in everyday life.* Cambridge, England: Cambridge University Press.

Lave, J., & Wenger, E. (1991). *Situated learning: Legitimate peripheral participation.* Cambridge, England: Cambridge University Press.

Lazarus, A. A., & Zur, O. (Eds.). (2002). *Dual relationships and psychotherapy.* New York, NY: Springer.

Lazarus, R., & Lazarus, N. (1994). *Passion and reason: Making sense of our emotions.* New York, NY: Oxford University Press.

Lederer, W. J., & Jackson, D. D. (1968). *The mirages of marriage.* New York, NY: Norton.

LeDoux, J. (1998). *The emotional brain: The mysterious underpinnings of emotional life.* New York, NY: Touchstone.

Leonard, G. (1992). *Mastery: The keys to success and long-term fulfillment.* New York, NY: Plume.

Leven, J. (Dir.). (1995). *Don Juan DeMarco.* San Francisco, CA: American Zoetrope.

Lewin, K. (1935). *The dynamic theory of personality.* New York, NY: McGraw-Hill.

Lewin, K. (1938). The conceptual representation and measurement of psychological forces. *Contributions to Psychological Theory, 1*(4).

Linehan, M. M. (1993). *Skills Training Manual for Treating Borderline Personality Disorder.* New York, NY: Guilford Press.

Linehan, M. M., & Dimeff, L. (2001). Dialectical Behavior Therapy in a nutshell. *The California Psychologist, 34,* 10–13.

Lipsey, M. W., & Wilson, D. B. (1993). The efficacy of psychological, educational, and behavioral treatment: Confirmation from meta-analysis. *American Psychologist, 48,* 1181–1209.

Lynch, T. R., Chapman, A. L., Rosenthal, M. Z., Kuo, J. R., & Linehan, M. M. (2006). Mechanisms of change in Dialectical Behavior Therapy: Theoretical and empirical observations. *Journal of Clinical Psychology, 62*(4), 459–480.

Ma, S. H., & Teasdale, J. D. (2004). Mindfulness-based cognitive therapy for depression: Replication and exploration of differential relapse prevention effects. *Journal of Consulting and Clinical Psychology, 72*(1), 31–40.

Manicavasgar, V., Parker, G., & Perich, T. (2011). Mindfulness-based cognitive therapy vs. cognitive behaviour therapy as a treatment for non-melancholic depression. *Journal of Affective Disorders, 130*(1–2), 138–144.

Marci, C. C., Ham, J., Moran, E., & Orr, S. P. (2007). Physiologic correlates of perceived therapist empathy and social-emotional process during psychotherapy. *Journal of Nervous & Mental Disease, 195,* 103–111.

Martin, D. J., Garske, M. P., & Davis, M. K. (2000). Relation of the therapeutic alliance with outcome and other variables: A meta-analytic review. *Journal of Consulting and Clinical Psychology, 68,* 438–450.

Martin, J., Slemon, A. G., Hiebart, B., Hallberg, E. T., & Cummings, A. L. (1989). Conceptualizations of novice and experienced counselors. *Journal of Counseling Psychology, 36,* 395–400.

Matthews, W. J., & Langdell, S. (1989). What do clients think about the metaphors they receive? An initial inquiry. *American Journal of Clinical Hypnosis, 31,* 242–251.

Mayer, J. D., & Stevens, A. (1993). *An emerging understanding of the reflective (meta) experience of mood* (Unpublished manuscript).

McAdams, D. P., & Pals, J. L. (2006). A new big five: Fundamental principles for an integrative science of personality. *American Psychologist, 45*, 204–217.

McGoldrick, M., Gerson, R., & Shellenberger, S. (2008). *Genograms: Assessment and intervention* (3rd ed.). New York, NY: Norton.

Mehrabian, A., & Ferris, S. R. (1967). Inference and attitudes from nonverbal communication in two channels. *Journal of Consulting Psychology, 31*, 248–252.

Merikangas, K. R., Ames, M., Cui, L., Stang, P. E., Ustun, T. B., Von Korff, M., & Kessler, R. C. (2007). The impact of comorbidity of mental and physical conditions on role disability in the US adult household population. *Archives of General Psychiatry, 64*(10), 1180–1188.

Merriam-Webster. (2006). "Valence." In *Merriam-Webster's collegiate dictionary* (11th ed., rev. ed.). New York, NY: Author.

Messer, S. B., & Warren, C. S. (1995). *Models of brief psychodynamic therapy: A comparative approach.* New York, NY: Guilford Press.

Miller, S. D. (2004). Losing faith: Arguing for a new way to think about therapy. *Psychotherapy in Australia, 10*(2), 44–51.

Miller, S. D., Duncan, B. L., & Hubble, M. A. (1997). *Escape from Babel.* New York, NY: Norton.

Miller, S. D., Duncan, B. L., & Hubble, M. A. (2004). Beyond integration: The triumph of outcome over process in clinical practice. *Psychotherapy in Australia, 10*(2), 2–19.

Miller, S. D., Hubble, M. A., Duncan, B. L., & Wampold, B. E. (2010). Delivering what works. In B. L. Duncan, S. D. Miller, B. E. Wampold, & M. A. Hubble (Eds.), *The heart and soul of change: Delivering what works in therapy* (2nd ed., pp. 421–429). Washington, DC: American Psychological Association.

Miller, S. D., Mee-Lee, D., Plum, B., & Hubble, M. A. (2005). Making treatment count: Client-directed, outcome-informed clinical work with problem drinkers. *Psychotherapy in Australia, 11*(4), 42–56.

Miller, W. R., Benefield, R. G., & Tonigan, J. S. (1993). Enhancing motivation for change in problem drinking: A controlled comparison of two therapist styles. *Journal of Consulting and Clinical Psychology, 61*, 455–461.

Miller, W. R., & Moyers, T. B. (2004). Motivational interviewing. In G. Koocher, J. C. Norcross, & C. E. Hill (Eds.), *Psychologists' desk reference* (2nd ed., pp. 57–62). New York, NY: Oxford University Press.

Miller, W. R., & Rollnick, S. (1991). *Motivational interviewing: Preparing people to change addictive behavior.* New York, NY: Guilford Press.

Miller, W. R., & Rollnick, S. (2002). *Motivational interviewing: Preparing people for change* (2nd ed.). New York, NY: Guilford Press.

Miller, W. R., & Rollnick, S. (2012). *Motivational interviewing: Preparing people for change* (3rd ed.). New York, NY: Guilford Press.

Miller, W. R., Taylor, C. A., & West, J. C. (1980). Focused versus broad-spectrum behavior therapy for problem drinkers. *Journal of Consulting and Clinical Psychology, 48*, 590–601.

Millon, T. (1996). *Disorders of personality:* DSM-IV *and beyond* (2nd ed.). New York, NY: Wiley.

Minami, T., Wampold, B. E., Serlin, R. C., Hamilton, E. G., Brown, G. S., & Kircher, J. C. (2008). Benchmarking the effectiveness of psychotherapy treatment for adult depression in a managed care environment: A preliminary study. *Journal of Consulting and Clinical Psychology, 76*(1), 116–124.

Mineka, S., & Zinbarg, R. (2006). A contemporary learning theory perspective on the etiology of anxiety disorders. *American Psychologist, 61*, 10–26.

Mosak, H., & DiPietro, R. (2006). *Early recollections: Interpretive method and applications.* New York, NY: Brunner-Routledge.

Mosak, H., & Dreikurs, R. (1975). Adlerian psychotherapy. In R. Corsini (Ed.), *Current psychotherapies.* Belmont, CA: Wadsworth.

Mosak, H., & Gushurst, R. (1971). What patients say and what they mean. *American Journal of Psychotherapy, 25*, 428–436.

Mosak, H., & Shulman, B. (1967). Various purposes of symptoms. *Journal of Individual Psychology, 23*, 79–87.

Mozdzierz, G. J. (2011). Adlerian family therapy: An elusive and controversial challenge. *Journal of Individual Psychology, 67*(3), 186–204.

Mozdzierz, G. J., & Greenblatt, R. (1994). Technique in psychotherapy: Cautions and concerns. *Individual Psychology: The Journal of Adlerian Theory, Research and Practice, 50*, 232–249.

Mozdzierz, G. J., Greenblatt, R. L., & Thatcher, A. A. (1985). The kinship and relevance of the double bind to Adlerian theory and practice. *Individual Psychology: The Journal of Adlerian Theory, Research and Practice, 41*(4), 453–460.

Mozdzierz G. J., Murphy T. J., & Greenblatt R. L. (1986). Private logic and the strategy of psychotherapy. *Individual Psychology, 42*(3), 339–349.

Mozdzierz, G. J., Peluso, P. R., & Lisiecki, J. (2009). *Principles of counseling and psychotherapy: Learning the essential domains and nonlinear thinking of master practitioners.* New York, NY: Routledge.

Mumford, E., Schlesinger, H. J., Glass, G. V., & Patrick, C. (1998). A new look at evidence about reduced cost of medical utilization following mental health treatment. *Journal of Psychotherapy Practice & Research, 7*(1), 68–86.

Myers, D. G. (2007). *Psychology* (8th ed.). New York, NY: Worth.

Myers, D. G., & Diener, E. (1995). Who is happy? *Psychological Science, 6*, 10–19.

Napier, A. Y., & Wittaker, C. (1978). *The family crucible.* New York, NY: Harper & Row.

Nathanson, D. L. (1996). *Knowing feeling: Affect, script, and psychotherapy.* New York, NY: Norton.

Ng, K., Peluso, P. R., & Smith, S. D. (2010). Marital satisfaction, intimacy, *enqing,* and relationship stressors among Asians. In J. Carlson & L. Sperry (Eds.), *Recovering intimacy in love relationships: A clinician's guide* (pp. 331–352). New York, NY: Routledge.

Nietzsche, F. (1968). *The will to power.* New York, NY: Vintage.

Nohlen, H. U. ,van Harreveld, F., Rotteveel M., Lelieveld, G. J. & Crone, E. A. (2013). Evaluating ambivalence: Social-cognitive and affective brain regions associated with ambivalent decision-making. *Social Cognitive Affective Neuroscience* doi: 10.1093/scan/nst074.

Nolan, C. (Dir.). (2000). *Memento.* Beverly Hills, CA: Newmarket Capital Group.

Norcross, J. C. (1997). Emerging breakthroughs in psychotherapy integration: Three predictions and one fantasy. *Psychotherapy, 34,* 86–90.

Norcross, J. C. (2002). *Psychotherapy relationships that work: Therapist contributions and responsiveness to patient needs.* New York, NY: Oxford University Press.

Norcross, J. C. (2011). *Psychotherapy relationships that work: Evidence-based responsiveness* (2nd ed.). New York, NY: Oxford University Press.

Norcross, J. C., Beutler, L. E., & Levant, R. F. (2005). *Evidence-based practice in mental health: Debated and dialogue on the fundamental questions.* Washington, DC: American Psychological Association.

Norcross, J. C., Koocher, G., & Garofalo, A. (2006). Discredited psychological treatments and tests: A Delphi poll. *Professional Psychology: Research and Practice, 37*(5), 515–522.

Norcross, J. C., Krebs, P. M., & Prochaska, J. O. (2011). Stages of change. In J. C. Norcross (Ed.), *Psychotherapy relationships that work: Evidence-based responsiveness* (2nd ed., pp. 279–300). New York, NY: Oxford University Press.

Norcross, J. C., & Lambert, M. J. (2011). Evidence-based therapy relationships. In J. C. Norcross (Ed.), *Psychotherapy relationships that work: Evidence-based responsiveness* (2nd ed., pp. 1–17). New York, NY: Oxford University Press.

Norcross, J. C., & Wampold, B. E. (2011). Evidence-based therapy relationships: Research conclusions and clinical practices. In J. C. Norcross (Ed.), *Psychotherapy relationships that work: Evidence-based responsiveness* (2nd ed., pp. 423–430). New York, NY: Oxford University Press.

Novotney, A. (2013). The therapist effect: A group of psychotherapy experts is working to delineate the characteristics that make some psychologists more effective than others. *Monitor on Psychology, 44*(2), 48.

Nystul, M. (2006). *Introduction to counseling: An art and science perspective* (3rd ed.). New York, NY: Allyn & Bacon.

Ogles, B. M., Anderson, T., & Lunnen, K. M. (1999). The contribution of models and techniques to therapeutic efficacy: Contradictions between professional trends and clinical research. In M. A. Hubble, B. L. Duncan, & S. D. Miller (Eds.), *The heart and soul of change: What works in therapy* (pp. 201–225). Washington, DC: American Psychological Association.

Olfson, M., & Marcus, S. C. (2010). National trends in outpatient psychotherapy. *The American Journal of Psychiatry, 167*(12), 1456–1463.

Orlinsky, D. E. (2010). Foreword. In B. L. Duncan, S. D. Miller, B. E. Wampold, & M. A. Hubble (Eds.), *The heart and soul of change: Delivering what works in therapy* (2nd ed., pp. i–xxii). Washington, DC: American Psychological Association.

Orlinsky, D. E., Grave, K., & Parks, B. K. (1994). Process and outcome in psychotherapy—Noch einmal. In A. E. Bergin & S. L. Garfield (Eds.), *Handbook of psychotherapy and behavior change* (pp. 257–310). New York, NY: Wiley.

Orlinsky, D. E., & Howard, K. I. (1977). The therapist's experience of psychotherapy. In A. S. Gurman & A. M. Razin (Eds.), *Effective psychotherapy: A handbook of research* (pp. 566–590). Oxford, England: Pergamon Press.

Othmer, E., & Othmer, S. C. (1989). *The clinical interview using DSM-III-R.* Washington, DC: American Psychiatric Press.

Othmer, E., & Othmer, S. C. (1994). *The clinical interview using DSM-IV: Fundamentals.* Washington, DC: American Psychiatric Press.

Patterson, G. R., & Forgatch, M. S. (1985). Therapist behavior as a determinant for client noncompliance: A paradox for the behavior modifier. *Journal of Consulting and Clinical Psychology, 53,* 846–851.

Paul, G. L. (1967). Strategy of outcome research in psychotherapy. *Journal of Consulting Psychology, 31,* 109–118.

Peck, M. S. (1978). *The road less travelled.* New York, NY: Touchstone.

Peck, M. S. (1983). *People of the lie.* New York, NY: Touchstone.

Peluso, P. R. (2006). The style of life. In S. Slavik & J. Carlson (Eds.), *Readings in the theory of individual psychology* (pp. 294–304). New York, NY: Routledge.

Peluso, P. R. (2007). The ethical and professional practice of couples and family counseling. In L. Sperry (Ed.), *The ethical and professional practice of counseling and psychotherapy* (pp. 285–351). Boston, MA: Allyn & Bacon.

Peluso, P. R., Miranda, A. O., Firpo-Jimenez, M., & Pham, M. (2010). Attachment dynamics and Latin cultures: Areas of convergence and divergence. In P. Erdman, K. Ng, & Metzger (Eds.), *Cross-cultural perspectives of attachment: Theory, research, and clinical implications* (pp. 281–296). New York, NY: Routledge.

Persons, J. B. (1989). *Cognitive therapy in practice: A case formulation approach.* New York, NY: Norton.

Piercy, F. P., Lipchik, E., & Kiser, D. (2000). Miller and de Shazer's article on "Emotions in solution-focused therapy." *Family Process, 39*(1), 25–28.

Pinker, S. (1999). *How the mind works.* New York, NY: Norton.

Pinker, S. (2007). *The stuff of thought: Language as a window into human nature.* New York, NY: Viking.

Pirsig, R. (1974). *Zen and the art of motorcycle maintenance.* New York, NY: Harper Collins.

Plutchik, R. (2000). *Emotions in the practice of psychotherapy: Clinical implications of affect theories.* Washington, DC: American Psychological Association.

Polster, E., & Polster, M. (1974). Gestalt theory integrated: Contours of theory and practice. New York: Vintage.

Poon, P., Mozdzierz, G. J., Douglas, S., & Walthers, R. (2007). *Confronting patient-initiated boundary crossings: An ethical framework for clinicians* (Unpublished manuscript). Western Springs, IL.

Pope, K. S., & Vasquez, M. A. (1998). *Ethics in psychotherapy and counseling: A practical guide* (2nd ed.). San Francisco, CA: Jossey-Bass.

Prochaska, J. O. (1999). How do people change, and how can we change to help many more people? In M. A. Hubble, B. L. Duncan, & S. D. Miller (Eds.), *The heart and soul of change: What works in therapy* (pp. 227–255). Washington, DC: American Psychological Association.

Prochaska, J. O., & DiClemente, C. C. (1982). Transtheoretical therapy: Toward a more integrative model of change. *Psychotherapy: Theory, Research and Practice, 20,* 161–173.

Prochaska, J. O., & DiClemente, C. C. (1984). *The transtheoretical approach: Crossing traditional boundaries of change.* Homewood, IL: Dorsey.

Prochaska, J. O., & DiClemente, C. C. (2005). The transtheoretical approach. In J. C. Norcross & M. R. Goldfried (Eds.), *Handbook of psychotherapy integration. Oxford series in clinical psychology* (2nd ed., pp. 147–171). New York, NY: Oxford University Press.

Prochaska, J. O., DiClemente, C. C., & Norcross, J. C. (1992). In search of how people change: Applications to addictive behaviors. *American Psychologist, 47,* 1102–1114.

Psychopathology Committee of the Group for the Advancement of Psychiatry. (2001). Reexamination of therapist self disclosure. *Psychiatric Services, 52,* 1489–1493.

Psychotherapy.net. (2006). The legacy of unresolved loss: A family systems approach [motion picture]. Available from Alexandria, VA: Alexander Street Press.

Rasmussen, P. R., & Dover, G. J. (2006). Purposefulness of anxiety and depression. *Journal of Individual Psychology, 62,* 366–396.

Reis, H. T. (1984). Social interaction and well-being. In S. W. Duck (Ed.), *Personal relationships: Repairing personal relationships* (Vol. 5, pp. 21–46). London, England: Academic Press.

Rizzolatti, G., & Sinigaglia, S. (2008). *Mirrors in the brain: How our minds share actions, emotions, and experience.* New York, NY: Oxford University Press.

Rogers, Carl R., E. T. Gendlin, D. J. Kiesler, and C. B. Truax, eds. (1967). *The Therapeutic Relationship and Its Impact: A Study of Psychotherapy with Schizophrenics.* Madison, WI: University of Wisconsin Press.

Rogers, C. R. (1951). *Client centered therapy.* Boston, MA: Houghton Mifflin.

Rogers, C. R. (1957). The necessary and sufficient conditions of therapeutic personality change. *Journal of Consulting Psychology, 22,* 95–103.

Rogers, R., & Reinhardt, V. R. (1998). Conceptualization and assessment of secondary gain. In G. Koocher, J. C. Norcross, & C. E. Hill (Eds.), *Psychologists' desk reference* (pp. 57–62). New York, NY: Oxford University Press.

Ronnestad, M. H., & Skovholt, T. M. (1993). Supervision of beginning and advanced graduate students of counseling and psychotherapy. *Journal of Counseling & Development, 71,* 396–405.

Rosch, E. (2007). More than mindfulness: When you have a tiger by the tail, let it eat you. *Psychological Inquiry: An International Journal for the Advancement of Psychological Theory 18*(4), 258–264.

Rosenweig, S. (1936). Some implicit common factors in diverse methods in psychotherapy. *Journal of Orthopsychiatry, 6,* 412–415.

Rossi, E. L., & Rossi, K. L. (2007). The neuroscience of observing consciousness and mirror neurons in therapeutic hypnosis. *American Journal of Clinical Hypnosis, 48,* 263–278.

Safran, J. D., & Muran, J. C. (2000). *Negotiating the therapeutic alliance: A relational treatment guide.* New York, NY: Guilford Press.

Safran, J. D., Muran, J. C., Samstag, L. W., & Stevens, C. (2002). Repairing alliance ruptures. In J. C. Norcross (Ed.), *Psychotherapy relationships that work: Therapist contributions and responsiveness to patient needs.* New York, NY: Oxford University Press.

Satir, V. (1964). *Conjoint family therapy.* Palo Alto, CA: Science and Behavior Books.

Schneider, S. L. (2001). In search of realistic optimism: Meaning, knowledge, and warm fuzziness. *The American psychologist, 56,* 250–263.

Schwartz, R. C., & Johnson, S. M. (2000). Commentary: Does couple and family therapy have emotional intelligence? *Family Process, 39,* 29–33.

Segal, P. (Dir.). (2004). *50 first dates.* Culver City, CA: Columbia Pictures.

Seipp, B. (1991). Anxiety and academic performance: A meta-analysis. *Anxiety, Stress and Coping, 4,* 27–41.

Seligman, M. (1990). *Learned optimism.* New York, NY: Knopf.

Shacter, D. L. (1996). *Searching for memory.* New York, NY: Basic Books.

Shaver, P., Schwartz, J., Kirson, D., & O'Connor, C. (1987). Emotion knowledge: Further exploration of a prototype approach. *Journal of Personality and Social Psychology, 52,* 1061–1086.

Shepris, C. J., & Shepris, S. F. (2002). *The Matrix* as a bridge to systems thinking. *Family Journal: Counseling and Therapy for Families and Couples, 10*(3), 308–314.

Shilcock, R., & Monighan, P. (2003). *An anatomical perspective on sublexical units: The influence of the split fovea.* Retrieved from http://www.westminster.edu/staff/nak/courses/documents/WordsAnatomy.pdf.

Shulman, B. (1973). *Contributions to individual psychology.* Chicago, IL: Alfred Adler Institute.

Situated Learning. (n.d.). Retrieved from http://tip.psychology.org/lave.html.

Skovholt, T. M., & Jennings, L. (2004). *Master therapists: Exploring expertise in therapy and counseling.* Boston, MA: Allyn & Bacon.

Skovholt, T. M., & Rivers, D. (2004). *Skills and strategies for the helping professions.* Denver, CO: Love.

Smith, M., Glass, G., & Miller, T. (1980). *The benefit of psychotherapy.* Baltimore, MD: Johns Hopkins University Press.

Smith, T. B., Bartz, J., & Richards, P. S. (2007). Outcomes of religious and spiritual adaptations to psychotherapy: A meta-analytic review. *Psychotherapy Research, 17,* 643–655.

Snowden, L. R. (2012). Health and mental health policies' role in better understanding and closing African American-White American disparities in treatment access and quality of care. *American Psychologist, 67*(7), 524–531.

Snyder, D. K., & Schneider, W. J. (2002). Affective reconstruction: A pluralistic, developmental approach. In A. Gurman & N. Jacobson (Eds.), *Handbook of couples therapy.* New York, NY: Guilford Press.

Sommers-Flanagan, R., Elliott, D., & Sommers-Flanagan, J. (1998). Exploring the edges: Boundaries and breaks. *Ethics & Behavior, 8*(1), 37–48.

Sperry, L., Carlson, J., & Peluso, P. R. (2006). *Couples therapy: Integrating theory, research, and practice* (2nd ed.). Denver, CO: Love.

Sperry, L., & Sperry, J. J. (2012). *Case conceptualization: Mastering this competency with ease and confidence.* New York, NY: Routledge.

Spunt, R. P., & Lieberman, M. D. (2013). The busy social brain: Evidence for automaticity and control in the neural systems supporting social cognition and action understanding. *Psychological Science, 24*(1), 80–86.

Sroufe, L. A., & Waters, E. (1977). Attachment as an organizational construct. *Child Development, 48*(4), 1184–1199.

Stiles, W. B., Barkham, M., Mellor-Clark, J., & Connell, J. (2008). Effectiveness of cognitive-behavioral, person-centered, and psychodynamic therapies in UK primary-care routine practice: Replication in a larger sample. *Psychological Medicine, 38*, 677–688.

Stoltenberg, C. D. (1993). Supervising consultants in training: An application of a model of supervision. *Journal of Counseling and Development, 72*, 131–138.

Stoltenberg, C. D. (1997). The integrated developmental model of supervision: Supervision across levels. *Psychotherapy in Private Practice, 16*(2), 59–69.

Stoltenberg, C. D., & Delworth, U. (1987). *Supervising counselors and therapists: A developmental approach.* San Francisco, CA: Jossey-Bass.

Stoltenberg, C. D., McNeill, B., & Delworth, U. (1998). *IDM supervision: An integrated developmental model for supervising counselors and therapists.* San Francisco, CA: Jossey-Bass.

Sue, D. W., Arrendondo, P., & McDavis, R. J. (1992). Multicultural counseling competencies and standards: A call to the profession. *Journal of Counseling and Development, 70*, 477–486.

Sue, D. W., Bernier, Y., Durran, A., Feinberg, L., Pederson, P. B., Smith, E. J., & Vasquez-Nuttall, E. (1982). Cross-cultural counseling competencies. *The Counseling Psychologist, 10*, 45–52.

Sue, D. W., Carter, R. T., Casas, J. M., Fouad, N. A., Ivey, A. E., Jensen, M., . . . Vasquez-Nuttall, E. (1998). *Multicultural counseling competencies: Individual and organizational development.* Thousand Oaks, CA: Sage.

Swift, J. K., Callahan, J. L., & Vollmer, B. M. (2011). Preferences. In J. C. Norcross (Ed.), *Psychotherapy relationships that work: Evidence-based responsiveness* (2nd ed., pp. 301–315). New York, NY: Oxford University Press.

Tallman, K., & Bohart, A. C. (1999). The client as a common factor: Clients as self-healers. In M. A. Hubble, B. L. Duncan, & S. D. Miller (Eds.), *The heart and soul of change: What works in therapy* (pp. 91–131). Washington, DC: American Psychological Association.

Tashiro, T., & Mortensen, L. (2006). Translational research: How social psychology can improve psychotherapy. *American Psychologist, 61*, 959–966.

Tavris, C. (1989). *Anger: The misunderstood emotion.* New York, NY: Simon and Schuster, Touchstone Books.

Teasdale, J. D. (1999). Metacognition, mindfulness and the modification of mood disorders. *Clinical Psychology & Psychotherapy, 6*(4), 146–155.

Tolson, J. (2006). Special report: Is there room for the soul? New challenges to our most cherished beliefs about self and the human spirit. *U.S. News & World Report, 141*(15), 57–63.

Tomm, C. (2002). The ethics of dual relationships. In A. A. Lazarus & O. Zur (Eds.), *Dual relationships and psychotherapy* (pp. 44–54). New York, NY: Springer.

Truax, C. B., & Carkhuff, R. R. (1967). *Toward effective counseling and psychotherapy.* Chicago, IL: Aldine.

Tyron, G. S., & Winograd, G. (2001). Goal consensus and collaboration. *Psychotherapy, 38*(4), 386–389.

Tyron, G. S., & Winograd, G. (2011). Goal consensus and collaboration. In J. C. Norcross (Ed.), *Psychotherapy relationships that work: Evidence-based responsiveness* (2nd ed., pp. 153–167). New York, NY: Oxford University Press.

U.S. Department of Health and Human Services. (2000). *Mental health: A report of the surgeon general.* Washington, DC: Author. Retrieved from http://www.surgeongeneral.gov/library/mentalhealth/toc.html.

Valle, S. K. (1981). Interpersonal functioning of alcoholism counselors and treatment outcome. *Journal of Studies on Alcohol, 42*, 783–790.

Van Sant, G. (Dir.). (1997). *Good Will Hunting.* Los Angeles, CA: Be Gentlemen Limited Partnership.

VanWagoner, S. L., Gelso, S. J., Hayes, J. A., & Diemer, R. (1991). Countertransference and the reputedly excellent therapist. *Psychotherapy: Theory, Research, and Practice, 28*, 411–421.

Vollmer, B., Grote, J., Lange, R., & Walker, C. (2009). A therapy preferences interview: Empowering clients by offering choices. *Psychotherapy Bulletin, 44*, 33–37.

Walt, J. (2005). An interview with Scott Miller. *The Milton H. Erickson Foundation Newsletter, 25*, 1–20.

Walter, J., & Pellar, J. (1992). *Becoming solution-focused in brief therapy.* New York, NY: Brunner/Mazel.

Wampold, B. E. (2001). *The great psychotherapy debate: Models, methods and findings.* Mahwah, NJ: Erlbaum.

Wampold, B. E. (2005). What should be validated? The psychotherapist. In J. C. Norcross, L. E. Beutler, & R. F. Levant (Eds.), *Evidence-based practices in mental health: Debate and dialogue on the fundamental questions* (pp. 200–208, 236–238). Washington, DC: American Psychological Association.

Wampold, B. E. (2010). The research evidence for common factors models: A historically situated perspective. In B. L. Duncan, S. D. Miller, B. E. Wampold, & M. A. Hubble (Eds.), *The heart and soul of change: Delivering what works in therapy* (2nd ed., pp. 49–81). Washington, DC: American Psychological Association.

Wampold, B. E., & Brown, G. S. (2005). Estimating variability in outcomes attributable to therapists: A naturalistic study of outcomes in managed care. *Journal of Consulting and Clinical Psychology, 73*(5), 914–923.

Watkins, C. W. (1992). Adlerian-oriented early memory research: What does it tell us? *Journal of Personality Assessment, 59*, 248–263.

Watson, G. (1940). Areas of agreement is psychotherapy. *American Journal of Orthopsychiatry, 10*, 698–709.

Watzlawick, P. (1978). *The language of change: Elements of therapeutic communication.* New York, NY: Basic Books.

Watzlawick, P., & Beavin, J. (1977). Some formal aspects of communication. In P. Watzlawick & J. H. Weakland (Eds.), *The interactional view: Studies at the Mental Research Institute Palo Alto, 1965–1974*. New York, NY: Norton. (Reprinted from *American Behavioral Scientist, 10*[48], 1967.)

Watzlawick, P., Weakland, J., & Fisch, R. (1974). *Change: Principles of problem formulation and problem resolution*. New York, NY: Norton.

Whipple, J. L., Lambert, M. J., Vermeersch, D. A., Smart, D. W., Nielsen, S. L., & Hawkins, E. J. (2003). Improving the effects of psychotherapy: The use of early identification of treatment and problem-solving strategies in routine practice. *Journal of Counseling Psychology, 50*(1), 59–68.

White, M., & Epston, D. (1990). *Narrative means to therapeutic ends*. New York, NY: Norton.

White, M., & Epston, D. (1992). *Experience, contradiction, narrative & imagination: Selected papers of David Epston & Michael White 1989–1991*. Dulwich Centre Publications.

Whitehead, A. N., & Russell, B. (1910–1913). *Principia mathematica*. Ann Arbor, MI: University of Michigan.

Winerman, L. (2006). The culture-cognition connection. *APA Monitor on Psychology, 37*, 64.

Worden, J. W. (1982). *Grief counseling and grief therapy*. New York, NY: Springer.

Worthington, E. L., Jr., Hook, J. N., Davis, D. E., & McDaniel, M. A. (2011). Religion and spirituality. In J. C. Norcross (Ed.), *Psychotherapy relationships that work: Evidence-based responsiveness* (2nd ed., pp. 402–419). New York, NY: Oxford University Press.

Yalom, I. (1995). *The theory and practice of group psychotherapy*. New York, NY: Basic Books.

Young, J. E. (1990). *Cognitive therapy for personality disorders: A schema-focused approach* (Practitioner's Resource Series). Sarasota, FL: Professional Resource Exchange.

Young, J. E. (1999). *Cognitive therapy for personality disorders: A schema-focused approach* (Practitioner's Resource Series, 3rd ed.). Sarasota, FL: Professional Resource Exchange.

Young, J. E., Beck, A. T., & Weinberger, A. (1993). Depression. In D. H. Barlow (Ed.), *Clinical handbook of psychological disorders: A step-by-step treatment manual* (2nd ed., pp. 240–277). New York, NY: Guilford Press.

Young, J. E., Klosko, J. S., & Weishaar, M. E. (2003). *Schema therapy: A practitioner's guide*. New York, NY: Guilford Press.

Young, J. E., Zangwill, W. M., & Behary, W. E. (2002). Combining EMDR and schema-focused therapy: The whole may be greater than the sum of the parts. In F. Shapiro (Ed.), *EMDR as an integrative psychotherapy approach: Experts of diverse orientations explore the paradigm prism* (pp. 181–208). Washington, DC: American Psychological Association.

Zaltman, G. (2003). *How customers think: Essential insights into the mind of the market*. Boston, MA: Harvard Business School Press.

Index

Page references in **bold** refer to tables. Page references in *italics* refer to information boxes.